# Textile manufactures
# in early modern England

*by the same author*

The Farmers of Old England

Agrarian Problems in
the Sixteenth Century and After

The Agricultural Revolution

# Textile manufactures
# in early modern England

ERIC KERRIDGE

Manchester
University Press

This study was undertaken with the
kind assistance of the *British Academy*
and this book published with the help
of a generous grant from the late
Miss *Isobel Thornley's Bequest* to the
University of London and with the
assistance of the Marc Fitch Fund.

Copyright © Eric Kerridge 1985
Published by Manchester University Press
Oxford Road, Manchester M13 9PL, UK
*and* 51 Washington Street, Dover,
New Hampshire 03820, USA

*British Library cataloguing in publication data*

Kerridge, Eric
 Textile manufactures in early modern England.
 1. Textile industry—England—History
 I. Title
 338.4'7677'00942        HD9861.5

 ISBN 0-7190-1767-X

*Library of Congress cataloging in publication data*

Kerridge, Eric
 Textile manufactures in early modern England.
 Bibliography: p. 357.
 Includes indexes.
 1. Textile industry—England—History   I.  Title.
 TS1357.K47   1985        338.4'7677'00942        85-4945

 ISBN 0-7190-1767-X

Phototypeset in Great Britain by
Wilmaset, Birkenhead, Merseyside

Printed in Great Britain
by Unwin Brothers, Old Woking

# CONTENTS

# FIGURES

# PREFACE

A dozen and more years ago I was trying to write something about the social structure of early modern England and found I had to touch on the textile and allied industries. Having studied the secondary authorities and such stray items from primary sources as came my way, I still felt rather unclear on certain points and decided to spend a year or two looking into them. As usual, it soon became apparent that very little was what it seemed. So my scope of study steadily widened and at long last this book resulted.

I have found it generally unhelpful to follow dictionary definitions of terms of art. Lexicographers are apt to classify fibres and fabrics as 'fine' or 'coarse' and to define cloths according to the supposed nature of the fibres they are made of, irrespective of the way their yarns have been spun and woven. For example, as the author of what I regard as the best introduction to hand-loom weaving rightly observes, 'The name satin is generally misunderstood. It is usually taken to signify some kind of silk material. This is no doubt owing to the fact that this tie is for the most part restricted to silk in the case of plain materials. The term, however, has no reference to the yarn employed in the web, but only to the manner of weaving it.'[1] Similarly, 'The name diaper is now usually understood to signify any small design which is repeated geometrically over the surface which it decorates. The term diaper-weaving, however, does not really refer so much to the kind of pattern woven as to the method of weaving it.'[2]

Modern English historians, I find, have a strange tendency to credit immigrants with having made most of the technical innovations that preceded the so- called 'Industrial Revolution', and especially with the introduction of the 'new draperies', which is in fact a term that was hardly ever used outside fiscal circles.[3] However, as we shall see, there is little truth in the confident assertion that 'The English manufacturing districts were now turning out materials for which we had previously depended on imports from the Low Countries ... They were bays, says, and perpetuanas ... Their manufacture had come in gradually from the Continent.'[4] Such statements are all the more persuasive in that they are buttressed by some primary authorities, notably the record of the findings of a royal commission in 1592 to the effect that it was the Flemings who introduced baize-making into England and that Englishmen only took it up about 1578.[5] This report was likely based on a misconception; if not, then its

meaning has certainly been mistaken. Modern writers could have profited more
from the work of John James. He wrote more than a hundred years ago, but had
read everything available to him and weighed it in his mind. It cannot be
insignificant that he ended up disbelieving some of the claims made for the
Flemings. James singled out and reprinted in full the chief piece of evidence
cited in support of the theory that the inventions were of foreign origin, viz.
Elizabeth's letters patent to the aliens. They were all couched in words similar to
the ones for the Norwich strangers. These allowed them the 'exercisinge of the
faculties of makynge bayes, arras, sayes, tapstrye, mockadoes, stamens, carsay,
and suche other outlandysshe commodities as hath not bene used to be made
wythin this our realme of Englande'.[6] James almost immediately observes,[7]

> It is obvious, from the preceding pages, that the allegation that 'says' and 'stamens'
> were 'outlandish commodities', and had not been accustomed to be made in England,
> is quite incorrect; and this seems also to be the case as regards bays. Worsted fabrics
> termed 'says' were, of old, manufactured in England. They are even mentioned, with
> stamens, as articles made at Norwich in the twelfth year of Henry VII, and in the
> fourteenth year of Henry VIII, as part of the manufactures of Yarmouth. Stamens
> were, like says, undoubtedly produced and long before now well-known in England;
> at least in the days of Henry VII, for they are then enumerated among the articles
> made at Norwich. Added to this, it would appear, from the wording of the act of
> parliament, 'touching worsted weavers of Yarmouth and Lynn', made in the
> fourteenth year of Henry VIII, that these manufactures had been produced so early as
> the time of Edward IV, for it is therein recited, 'that since the seventh Edward IV, the
> making of worsteds, saies, and stammins, had greatly increased in the city of Norwich
> and county of Norfolk, and was then practised more busily than in times past at
> Yarmouth and Lynn. If we believe the old distich supposed to have been written in
> 1546, bays (that is baize) of fabric partly worsted and partly woollen, had been
> introduced here in the time of Henry VIII.

> 'Hops, reformation, bays, and beer
> Came into England all in one year.'

> Wheeler also in his History of the Merchant Adventurers, mentions that in 1564, bays
> were made in England and exported to the Low Countries. As another instance of the
> incorrectness of the above mentioned record, kerseys ... may be specified, as they
> were made in England in the time of Henry VIII, being set out in the provisions of an
> act of parliament passed in the 34th–35th year of his reign, chap. 26 ... It is difficult
> to determine whether Arras ... and tapestry were altogether new fabrics in England.
> Sufficient has however been advanced to establish the fact, that the averments in these
> Letters Patent are not to be implicitly relied upon.

James was obviously right about stamins, says, worsteds and kerseys, but he
failed to prove his case in regard to baize, even though he strained some of his
evidence to breaking point. The distich he quotes is ambiguous hearsay.
Another and seemingly more authentic version of it mentions turkeys, carp,
hops and beer, but omits 'bays'.[8] Wheeler does say baize was being made in

England in 1564 and even exported to the Low Countries, pointing quite rightly to the Duchess of Parma's proclamation prohibiting imports of baize from England; but by this time the Sandwich Flemings were already exporting it, so we still cannot tell whether or not Wheeler had English-made baize in mind.[9]

In continuing along the path James first set his feet on, I have incurred great debts to other historians. English carded woollens have been studied to excellent effect by Herbert Heaton, Dr G. D. Ramsay and Miss J. de L. Mann.[10] Continental textile history may be followed in magnificent books by Espinas and Pirenne, H.-E. De Sagher, N. W. Posthumus, J. G. Van Dillen, M. Vanhaeck, M. Emile Coornaert, and many others.[11] Hessels, Moens, Cross and the Minets, to mention but a few, have made the study of immigration into England delightfully rewarding.[12] I owe a great deal, too, to some of the unpublished theses consulted.[13] Lastly, I cannot but express my deep gratitude to Mrs Ursula Priestley and Miss Penelope Marsh, who have been exceedingly generous with their time and their expert knowledge and have saved me from some of the many pitfalls strewn in my path. For the blunders that remain I can only ask forgiveness.

One or two points require explanation. Dates are given in their modern form, except in the critical apparatus, where the original style has been retained for reference purposes. My own preference is for the English forms of foreign place names, and even for the older ones such as Bridges for Bruges, Flowers for Florence and Towers for Tours; but I have conformed to present-day usage. For the convenience of English readers, I have used the French names for some Flemish towns, as Bruges for Brugge, Ypres for Ieper, and Bailleul for Belle. Definitions of terms of art are to be found in their context and are indicated in the glossarial index of subjects by means of asterisks. Where other trades are touched on, it is only with a view to the exposition of the history of the strictly textile ones.

Figure 1 is based on that in my *Farmers of Old England*, by courtesy of the publishers, Messrs George Allen and Unwin. I am grateful to Miss Julia de Lacy Mann for her help and encouragement; to Professor F. J. Fisher and my colleagues for their generous aid; and to my wife and family for their constant support.

E.K.

# TO
# JOHN ULRIC NEF

# NOTE ON
# ABBREVIATIONS

| | |
|---|---|
| Acc | *Accession* |
| APC | *Acts of the Privy Council* |
| Colc. | *Colchester* |
| Cons. | *Consistory* |
| CPR | *Calendar of Patent Rolls* |
| Dep. | *Deposition* |
| F(M) | *Fitzwilliam(Milton)* |
| Hug. | *Huguenot* |
| I(L) | *Isham(Lamport)* |
| KR | *King's Remembrancer* |
| Lans. | *Lansdowne* |
| M.,m. | *Membrane* |
| Mun. | *Muniment* |
| O.W. | *Original Will(s)* |
| P.&M. | *Philip and Mary* |
| PCR | *Privy Council Register* |
| Pec. | *Peculiar* |
| R. | *Roll* |
| Req. | *Court of Requests Proceedings* |
| RO | *Record (Archives) Office* |
| Rot. | *Rotulet* |
| SP | *State Papers* |
| SPD | *State Papers Domestic* |
| W.&M. | *William and Mary* |

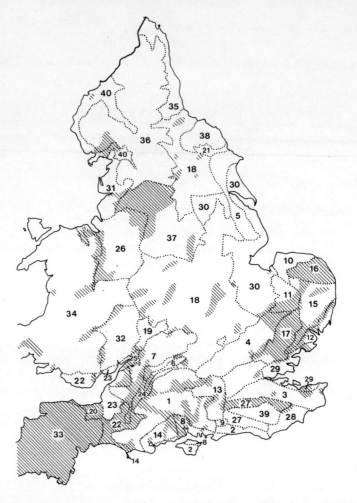

Fig. 1 The farming countries of early modern England, with the textile regions superimposed (shaded).

<table>
<tr><td>1 Chalk Country</td><td>15 High Suffolk</td><td>29 Saltings Country</td></tr>
<tr><td>2 Southdown Country</td><td>16 East Norfolk</td><td>30 Fen Country</td></tr>
<tr><td>3 Northdown Country</td><td>17 Woodland</td><td>31 Lancashire Plain</td></tr>
<tr><td>4 Chiltern Country</td><td>18 Midland Plain</td><td>32 Vales of Hereford</td></tr>
<tr><td>5 Northwold Country</td><td>19 Vale of Evesham</td><td>33 West Country</td></tr>
<tr><td>6 Oxford Heights Country</td><td>20 Vale of Taunton Deane</td><td>34 Wales</td></tr>
<tr><td>7 Cotswold Country</td><td>21 Vale of Pickering</td><td>35 North-eastern Lowlands</td></tr>
<tr><td>8 South Seacoast Country</td><td>22 Butter Country</td><td>36 North Country</td></tr>
<tr><td>9 Petworth District</td><td>23 Western Waterlands</td><td>37 Peak-Forest Country</td></tr>
<tr><td>10 Norfolk Heathlands</td><td>24 Cheese Country</td><td>38 Blackmoors</td></tr>
<tr><td>11 Breckland</td><td>25 Vale of Berkeley</td><td>39 High Weald</td></tr>
<tr><td>12 Sandlings Country</td><td>26 Cheshire Cheese Country</td><td>40 North-western Lowlands</td></tr>
<tr><td>13 Blackheath Country</td><td>27 Wealden Vales</td><td>41 Vale of London</td></tr>
<tr><td>14 Poor Soils Country</td><td>28 Romney Marsh</td><td></td></tr>
</table>

# 1

# THE RISE OF THE WOOLLEN
# MANUFACTURES

Ancient Rome had the textile expertise of the world at her command, yet her woollens were poor. To judge from surviving parchments, which show the holes through which the fleece originally grew, the sheep of those times bore fleeces of undifferentiated and uncrimped hair fit only for crude cloths. Even the flocks in Asia Minor and in eastern and north-eastern Italy gave wool that could be classed as fine by ancient standards only, meaning that it was somewhat less hairy and was white rather than red or brown.[1] In the absence of crimpy wool, no good woollen cloth as we understand the term could possibly have been made. Nor was there any long wool for making into worsted yarn.[2]

It was the peculiar use made of sheep by cultivators in north-western Europe that first gave rise to differentiated wools suited to spinning and weaving into fine cloths. Folding flocks on fallow fields eventually produced fallow sheep with short, crimpy wool for carding in preparation for spinning into yarns for woollen cloth in the narrower sense of the term, and feeding sheep in rich permanent grasslands created pasture sheep with long wool that was combed to make it ready for spinning into worsted and jersey yarns. The Mediterranean world had developed its own system of permanent cultivation, but sheep played a negligible part in it. Neither fallow nor pasture breeds evolved. Even today they have emerged in none but a few scattered places. Generally speaking, sheep were kept as much for milking as anything else. They were neither folded on the tillage nor fattened on grass. Consequently they gave wools fit only for felting, stuffing mattresses, making rugs and carpets, knitting coarse stockings or weaving rough cloths.[3] It was not until the merino breed originated at the turn of the thirteenth and fourteenth centuries that other possibilities became open. The increase of transhumant flocks of merinos in Spain (and to a lesser extent in Portugal and Italy), the organisation of the Mesta, and finally the spur given to them by Ferdinand and Isabella, all combined to throw on to the market in the fifteenth century large quantities of a new type of carding wool from which a new class of woollen cloths could be made.[4]

Otherwise, England became the great source of good wool. The draining of the polders and saltmarshes along the coast from Flanders to Pomerania led to pasture sheep being displaced by dairy cows, so that the Flemings and Hollanders came to rely on importing combing wool from the English.[5] The Netherlanders, too, developed market-gardening to a fine art, but more and more abandoned agriculture in favour of buying Baltic grain, and so gave up producing fallow wool. Instead, we are told, 'The Flemmish sheep have a soft and curled haire'.[6] Eventually, by the seventeenth century, northern France had begun to develop permanent tillage in common fields, and by the eighteenth was taking to folding on the arable the flocks that fed on the expanding sheepwalks. Before then little or no good carding or combing wool was to be looked for here.[7] England was different. Between about 686 and 1000 AD the newly invented system of permanent cultivation for temperate climes, with permanent tillage and permanent grassland, spread wherever in the lowlands the soil was strong enough to stand it. As this system matured, wool of carding quality appeared. Meanwhile the early drainage works in Romney Marsh and the Fen Country enabled large flocks of pasture sheep to be built up, and the later conversion of much Midland tillage to permanent grass further swelled the output of combing wool.[8]

Eight main breeds of arable sheep evolved in England and all gave carding wool. Of these the most widely diffused, in the Chiltern and Northdown countries, the Vale of London, the Midland Plain and elsewhere, as well as in its native haunts, was the Chalk Country breed. This bore about two pounds of middling quality wool, but had short, silvery hair on the underparts. The Southdown and Oxford Heights countries had similar breeds, only not cursed with hair. In the Norfolk Heathlands and the Breckland the fleeces weighed between one and two and a half pounds, and those of the Sandlings Country were similar, but of superior quality. In the Northwold Country the sheep gave about two and a half pounds of good wool, in the Cotswold Country three pounds of an excellent grade. The Dorset horn breed, which stemmed from parts of the Butter Country but was stocked also in the South Sea-coast Country, the Petworth District, and the Vale of London, grew fleeces of medium weight and quality. March wool, from the Kerry Hill, Clun Forest and Wenlock district just to the south of the Cheshire Cheese Country, was much esteemed, but the best carding wool of all came from the Ryeland sheep in the Vales of Hereford. Their fleeces often weighed only one pound and seldom as much as two, but were peerless in quality. Turning now to the pasture sheep, we find five closely allied breeds, two of which, the Teeswaters and the Warwicks (or Old Leicesters), were natives of the Midland Plain and remarkably similar. Both gave great weights of good combing wool, the fleeces from wethers being between four and seven pounds. Romney Marsh sheep, too, bore heavy fleeces of very long, semi-lustrous wool. Fen Country wool was no more than mediocre, but the fleeces weighed up to about twelve pounds. Then these four breeds were joined by the Mugs of the Northeastern Lowlands, which came into their own only in the latter half of the sixteenth century. Finally, there remained the various breeds of hill sheep. They grew wool that would have been recognisable to the Romans, ranging as it did between rank hair and hairy wool. In the north country, the Blackfaces gave three-pound fleeces of coarse, wavy, shaggy and hairy wool, unsuited to either carding or combing, and with many discoloured fibres. In later times some of it was used in carpets and coarse knitwear, but formerly it mostly went to make hairy cloths for frizzing and cottoning. The wool of the Cheviot sheep, however, could be incorporated in tweeds, and that of the Herdwick breed in rough Kendal cloths. In all the North Country, only the Lank sheep of the Craven district gave wool that could be carded to include in ordinary cloth. In Wales the sheep grew one-pound fleeces of short, hairy wool, fit only for coarse cloth. Peak-Forest Country wool was hardly better. In the West Country, the Dartmoor and Exmoor sheep grew mainly hair, but in more fertile parts like the South Hams the wool could be used to make cloth, and there was a marked tendency in the sixteenth century for the spread of tillage and the consequent improvement in feed to be reflected in an amelioration of much of the wool.[9]

The use of pasture and fallow wools entailed the devising of new techniques and instruments. People in ancient times combed all their wool. They had neither woolcards nor wool to card.[10] But their combs were not like those used for long wool in later times; theirs were great combs, similar to the coarse ones employed in the first scutching of flax. In Flanders in the twelfth and thirteenth centuries and in Brabant a little later, as well as in Italy, this old combing process continued. Woolcards, with wire teeth set in leather on boards with handles, were not invented until the thirteenth century and not legalised in Valenciennes until the fourteenth, and then only for certain types of cloth. Carding was girls' and womens' work, as combing had been.[11] The new comb invented in the thirteenth century was akin to the fine comb used in the second scutching of flax and was wielded by male woolcombers. It was usually armed with twenty-one teeth, three thumbs long and disposed in three rows. The woolcomber heated his comb in a furnace and then drew it through the pasture wool to align the longer fibres, called 'tops', *hoep* or *la houppe*, and separate them from the short 'noils', 'pinnions', 'comblings', *cammelinghen*, *peignons* or *entredeus* caught between the teeth. This was regarded as man's work; long toil amidst heat and fumes called for great stamina.[12] So it came about that the division between permanent tillage and permanent grass was reflected in fourteenth-century Flanders in a split between *draperie* and *saietrie*, between the carding of short wools and the combing of long ones, between carded and combed woollens.[13] The new comb and the woolcard now largely replaced the great comb. Two kinds of land, two kinds of sheep, two kinds of wool, two kinds of woollens dominated the scene.

Yet the great comb was superseded only slowly and gradually. It lingered on wherever hairy fibres went on being used. It was found in the Peak-Forest Country in the seventeenth century,[14] in Bruges, Armentières, Mechlin and

Leiden in the sixteenth, and in the Netherlands and in Florence in the fourteenth and fifteenth.[15] Carding was indispensable to the exploitation of the novel crimpiness of English fallow wools. The carder brushed a sliver of wool from one to the other of her cards alternately until all the several strands were inextricably entangled into a whole, so that short fibres could be spun into a strong yarn from which a soft-faced cloth could be woven. Although simple plain weaves, these new carded cloths were a great novelty and at first were given the distinctive name of 'pukes', 'pewkes', *puuc* or *puiklakenen*. They steadily stole the stage from burels, which were made on upright looms,[16] from camlins,[17] and from other hairy cloths, as well as from unions of hairy warps and carded wefts, amongst which may possibly be included some of the twilled stamfords or *estainforts*.[18] One of the old-fashioned cloths, however, went on almost without end. This was the wadmal, a rough fabric used for saddlecloths, horsecollar linings, draught-proof curtains, heat-resistant undercloths, cupboard cloths, and such items of working garb as mittens, stockings and waistcoats.[19]

Fig. 2 Draft for a common kind of plain weave (warp black).

Pukes were soft to the touch. Rowing them with teasels easily raised a nap that could then be shorn to leave the cloth smooth and even. One excellent type of puke was the *scharlaken*, *escarlate*, *scarlatto* or scarlet, which was cloth dyed scarlet in grain, with kermes, with or without the addition of other dyestuffs such as woad.[20] Another and much more everyday type was the 'blanket', a name that came to be applied to cloths designed for maximum insulation, in disregard of the loss of resistance to wind and rain.[21]

Kersey was an important innovation. Kersey cloth originated in England and derived its name, by way of kersey yarn, from the Woodland town credited with its invention. The manufacture of kersey cloth is recorded in Andover, in the Chalk Country, in 1262, when steps were taken to see that no Spanish wool was put into it. Before long, kerseys were being exported oversea and various corruptions of their name spread far and wide. The fact that most of these versions follow the ancient spelling of the town's name, which was 'Carsey' or something similar, serves only to confirm what we know of the early history of the yarn and the cloth.[22] Kersey yarns were spun in large guages from inferior grades of carded wool, right down to odds and ends like flocks and noils. Being so big, kersey yarns made for thick cloths, and were used in dornicks and some types of blankets and linsey-woolseys,[23] but the greatest part of them went into the cloths that shared their name. Kerseys were 'made so thick by great spinning'.[24] They were warp-backed cloths woven in twill order on kersey looms with four treadles and a special kersey sley, and usually contained up to twice as many of ends as of picks. As a rule, half the relatively small, numerous and closely set warp ends were struck with a big kersey weft in a two-and-two, unbalanced and highly prominent twill. The rest of the ends were simul-taneously struck in a one-and-three twill, so they appeared mainly on the back of the cloth, while the back-warp stitches on the face of the cloth were concealed among the face-warp threads. One of the secrets of weaving a good kersey lay in combining the adequate stitching of the weft by the back warp with the concealment of the back-warp stitches. After fulling, the back of the cloth was napped and shorn, and since this nap was raised mainly from parallel warp ends, it handled extremely smoothly lengthways.[25] The skill and pains involved in kersey manufacture[26] were fully repaid, for their structure put the fabrics in great request for tailored stockings and other garments that needed to be warm, comfortable, easy to slip on, and in some degree self-supporting.[27]

The new wools also entailed innovations in spinning. Formerly it had been usual to spin anti-clockwise in an S-twist on a rock or spindle in conjunction with a distaff. This system well suited hairy wools, whose redeeming feature was strength. The advent of the spinning-wheel in northwestern Europe in the thirteenth century was associated with the much wider adoption of the clockwise or Z-twist needed to strengthen the relatively weak yarns spun from crimpy wools.[28] The wheel abridged labour, but was not primarily a labour-saving device, for it could save only the labour performed by womenfolk as they went about their domestic activities, while incurring the extra cost of their concentration on what could be combined with nothing more profitable than singing or gossiping.[29] The wheel's arrival in Abbeville was signalled by its prohibition in 1288. In Spires at about this time it was allowed for weft yarns only. Thereafter the new device spread widely, but in all the Flemish woollen towns, in the Flemish textile colony in Florence, and seemingly in Artois, Picardy and the Rhineland, the general rule long remained that warps were rockspun and only wefts wheelspun.[30] Not until the fifteenth century did both come generally to be spun on the wheel, and even then the change was still incomplete. As late as 1537 the Leiden authorities repeated their prohibition of spinning warp on the wheel, and the rock continued in use in England long after this.[31] It held its ground in the spinning of flax and pasture wool. Wheelspun tops suited many purposes, but the wheel could never spin as tightly and finely as the rock, which was sometimes preferred on that account alone.[32]

Fig. 3 Draft for a common kind of kersey (face warp grey, back warp black).

One fabric made in tops was the say. This was a distinct two-and-two twill with a single weft and a warp twisted from two or three threads. Florence and Strasbourg persisted far longer than most places in weaving says in linen. Large numbers, too, were made wholly or partly of silk and called silk says or sagathies. Most of the later Continental says, however, were composed of wheelspun tops. Not being fulled, only scoured, their individual threads remained visible to the naked eye.[33] Says of this general kind were being made in Flanders from the twelfth century, originally from local wool, *laine nostrée*, *hierlandsche wol*. These and similar manufactures spread throughout Flanders, to St Omer, Douai, Mouy, Amiens and eventually Abbeville and Caen, to Mechlin and elsewhere in Brabant, and to Florence.[34] The *sayette* or jersey they were made of was 'wasshed out of his oile and spun cleane' or dry, on the small wheel, not the great wheel used for carded wool. This jersey might then be doubled and twisted on little twisting mills. In addition, there was a special sort of jersey, *fil ras*, that was not only degreased after combing but also soured after spinning, and then used for the warps of a variety of say called Arras, *ras, rasch, arrazi* or rash.[35] St Omer says differed in that both warps and wefts were rockspun.[36] Hondschoote says, the invention and speciality of that town, had a rockspun weft on a slackly twisted wheelspun warp, which made them extraordinarily tractile.[37] Bruges, Armentières, Lille, Arras, St Omer, Mechlin, Liège and other towns produced also *saies drappées* with carded wefts and raised and shorn naps.[38] Continental says were much bought by the English, who gave them such names as Houndscot or Ascot, St Thomas, and Amens.

Fig. 4 Draft for a two-and-two twill (warp black).

While a say's warp was made bold by doubling and twisting, a serge's was single and inconspicuous. Otherwise there was no difference between the two. The Flemings, indeed, tended to call them both says.[39] Silk serges were not uncommon. Genuine Tours and Padua ones were wholly silk, but some Florentine ones had silk warps and woollen wefts. Yet another type of serge combined a woollen weft with a linen warp. Then came the all-jersey serge.[40] From the thirteenth century onwards the jersey serge and say manufactures were pursued more or less side by side and often in the same workshops.[41] Linen-warp serge went on being made, however, in Strasbourg[42] and elsewhere, not least in Norwich and East Norfolk.[43]

Even in the Netherlands the words *hierland* and *hierlandsche*, in one or

another of their various spellings, became corrupted on occasion by the loss of
their initial letters, and were then all too easily mistaken for *Ierland* and
*Ierlandsche*. Foreigners were even more likely to fall into these errors. Thus we
find Italians writing *saja d'Irlanda*[44] and Englishmen using such words and
phrases as 'Irlonde' wool, 'cloth of Ireland', 'Irlondewever' and even 'Irlonder'.
All this strongly suggests that Flemings were directly or indirectly instrumental
in starting this kind of textile work in Norwich and East Norfolk, especially
since all these curious English terms stemmed solely from there. Later on the
names 'wurstedman' and 'worsted' or 'worsted' weaver were brought in, first as
alternatives and then as substitutes for 'Irlondewever', in a way that shows
worsted manufactures sprang from a previous industry using local or
*hierlandsche* wool.[45]

The 'Irlondewevers', some of them, became worsted weavers. They still
worked in the same or similar kind of wool, but now they took their name and
style not from the wool but from the special type of yarn they had taken to using.
Worsted originated in the East Norfolk village now called Worstead. Worsted
was primarily the name not of a cloth but of a type of yarn. It was rockspun from
tops and 'called worsted yarne ... bicause that manner of spynning was first
practised in Worsted in the countie of Norfolk'.[46] Worsted was spun 'in his oile'
from the tops of pasture wool. The rock made tops yarns of peerless quality, quite
unmatched by any spun on the wheel, the jenny or the spinning-frame. This is
why the rock so long defied competition. In some parts of England, the name
'worsted' or 'woolsted' was later applied to tops, to wheelspun tops yarns and to
cloths woven from them, but these were all misnomers. In East Anglia 'worsted'
and 'rockspun yarn' were synonymous, but then the tops and the oil were always
assumed. Worsted was thus a special type of yarn, although spun in various
grades, e.g. small woof, middle woof, warp, mantle ('mentil') warp, and headle,
heddle or 'hevel' yarn. This last was not woven up, but merely used to tie together
the laths in the headles of the loom. Perhaps mantle warp was extra strong.[47]
Some of the distinctive qualities of the tops used in spinning worsted probably
came from the way the wool was combed, for the comber could vary considerably
the lengths and qualities of tops and noils. But the nature of the wool itself was
more decisive. The worstedweavers never tired of insisting worsted was made
solely from the wools grown in Norfolk. Generally speaking, this was true; they
came from the Marshland, which lay all within the county, and was the part of the
Fen Country earliest and best drained. Only later on were supplies drawn from
the more distant parts of that country and from the Midland Plain.[48] Midland
combing wool, however, and that subsequently brought from Ireland, mostly
went to make not worsted but jersey.[49]

Worsted was used for a number of purposes, including knitting, stitching
hats, and twisting loosely into a thick, rounded twine called crewel, which was
employed in embroidery;[50] but only worsted textiles became world famous and
most by far of all worsted went into cloths.

So far no record of worsted cloth has been found before 1301, but it is significant that as early as 1329 worstedweavers were found in Lynn and throughout the greater part of East Norfolk: in Norwich, which was also the centre for finishing and marketing, in Sloley, Dilham, North Walsham, Honing, Scottow, Tunstead, Worstead, Catton and elsewhere.[51] In the course of the next hundred years or so the industry spread to Great Yarmouth and to all the rest of East Norfolk, excepting only East Dereham and district, which specialised instead in combing wool and spinning worsted.[52]

It so happens that worsted cloths were not the first ones to be made of pasture wool in this part of the world. What the earlier 'Irlondewevers' produced we have no means of knowing, but according to the worstedweavers, 'First wer made at Norwich (of the selfsame Norffolk wooll) ... cloth called Norwich whightes, then wurstedes'.[53] These whites were still being made in the middle of the fifteenth century, when they were being sold in Holland and Zealand, and, under the name of *witte Nordwiksche*, in Königsberg.[54] As this was long after the appearance of the worstedweavers, we are tempted to believe they made both types side by side. However that may be, we insist the worstedweavers were so called because they wove up worsted yarns, not because they wove worsted cloths known by that name.[55] One of the first, if not the very first, of these cloths woven in worsted was called *pannus de worsted*, cloth of worsted, or just worsted. From this same worsted yarn were later made other and different cloths, each with its own peculiar name, though commonly qualified by the preface 'worsted', and all made by the worstedweavers.

The original worsted cloth was a two-and-two twill, with three threads in each reed dent and with even proportions of warp and weft threads. By 1393 new types had appeared with double or half again as many weft threads. The three kinds were then distinguished by being called single, double and half double worsted, *worsted simplex*, *worsted duplex* and *worsted de dimidia duplice*. Single worsteds were about two yards broad and six long, doubles and half doubles both five quarters wide and respectively ten and six yards long. In addition, rolls of single worsted were woven half a yard wide and thirty yards long. To these we must add the broad mantles, the worsted rays and the worsted motleys. The rays were probably made by warping in different and varied colours and making the warp full enough to obscure the weft. Then, when a shed was opened by raising the odd and depressing the even threads, only the selected colour showed on the surface; and when the even were raised and the odd depressed, only the other colour. Thus the vertically striped warp gave rise to a horizontally striped cloth. Motleys were mottled by the criss-crossing of variously coloured yarns. By 1410 worsted chequers, worsted palls and worsted flowers had arrived on the scene. The flowers seem to have been brocaded by means of a secondary woof. Like rays, the motleys and the chequers were plain weaves. Chequers seem to have had two or more adjacent warp and weft threads woven one after another as though they were single ones, the former all being raised at the same time and the latter all struck in the same shed, and both in colours. Now the worsted range included '*les worsteds appellez mantelles, motles, paules, checkeres, raies, flores, playnes*'.[56]

Meanwhile, before 1334, the worstedweavers had taken to making worsted says, monks cloths and canons cloths. The says had their warp threads doubled and twisted. In the words of some of the later worstedweavers, 'Thear ys no dyfference betwen sayes made of worsted yarne and sayes made of Flanders sorte, but the one of whelespoone yarne and the other of rocksponne'. Monks and canons cloths had four threads in a reed dent instead of three as in the old worsteds. Monk cloths were singles, a dozen yards long and five quarters broad; canons might also be demi-doubles or doubles, two yards wide and six long or seven quarters wide and five long.[57] Like most worsted cloths, these were all wet-rolled in calenders to give them a smooth finish. Lastly, the worstedweavers in this period also made beds, i.e. fabrics intended for bed curtains and hangings, and woven from two and a half to four yards wide, in lengths of ten, a dozen or two dozen yards. These were extra-broad, loosely woven worsted says.[58] As the worstedweavers explained,[59]

> A cloath denomynated the worsteed and the cloath called the bedd, for the fashion and working, were all one, beinge both of the same drawght in the hevill and both alike wrought with fower treadles, yet the one was a fyne and a thick cloath and the other a course and thynn ... The saye ... maie also be affirmed to be that anncient cloathe called a bedd, the difference onely consisting in the breadth and fynes ... To make the bedd (which, being course, served for hangings and the like) a saye (which served for apparrell) was to make the same much narrower and fyner.

Not all beds, however, were made in worsted by the worstedweavers. From the early fifteenth century Norwich had a separate company of specialist bedweavers who made serge beds with a linen warp. In 1468 a city regulation speaks of 'lynen warp, the which is byhoveable to bedweverscrafte'. Some of these beds were also embroidered, probably with worsted crewel. Similar linen-union beds were made in Winchester also.[60]

Another linen-union cloth went by the name of linsey-woolsey, indicating a linen warp and a woollen weft, or *tiretaine* in French, *tiertein* or *tartein* in Netherlands, *tiretey* or some such in German, *thirumtej* in Danish, and similarly in other languages. This Continental name was anglicised as 'turtein', 'turtain', 'tarten' or 'tartan', in which form it has persisted to the present day. Hemp was occasionally mingled in the warp yarns; the wefts were almost invariably fell, lambs' or other inferior wool; and what resulted was a strong, warm, cheap cloth, suited to hats, shirts, waistcoats, petticoats, shifts and all sorts of working clothes.[61] Tartans were widely made in early times in Flanders and Artois, and the manufacture spread to Cologne, in 1562 to Haarlem and Leiden, and over the next hundred years to most parts of France.[62] It was no less common in England.

Baize, another and similar union cloth, was much more rarely made. Indeed,

Béthune is the only town for which there is clear evidence of its manufacture. In a fifteenth-century copy of a *ban échevinal* made sometime between 1334 and 1402, we read, '*Et que nulz ne tisse bayes en mains de xiii^c et s'aient gaunes lisières*'.[63] No one was to make baize of lower count than 1300 and then only if it had yellow lists. Another reference to baize is found in a Lille order in 1396: '*Et est assavoir que les draps qui se nomment bugle, baze, frize irlande, says d'Engleterre et samblables draps se venderont comme a usé et accoustumé*'.[64] A parallel order made a little later at Bergues-Saint-Winoc reads: '*Es te weitene dat men wel copen ende vercopen mach hier bin der stade ende bute halen vriesdouc, beukelslaken ende baye . . .*'[65] *Bugle* or *beukelslaken* is no longer understood,[66] but it is clear that baize, like frieze made from local wools, was not a hall cloth and could be traded in quite freely, and unlikely that baize was made in either of these two towns. One gains the impression that baize was not much made. However, no reason exists to doubt that this baize was much like its modern successor, being a plain weave, with a woollen weft that was about four times as heavy as the warp and crammed enough to hide it.[67] The warp was probably linen, as in some later Continental baizes.[68]

Important advances were made in the design of looms. Vertical looms were made obsolete for most purposes by the invention of horizontal ones with treadles for working the headles. The next step forward came with the horizontal broad loom. This 'tomennesette' loom reduced costs. By passing the shuttle from one to another right through the shed, a weaver and an apprentice could make as much cloth as could two fully qualified weavers on two narrow, 'omannessete' or 'osset' looms. Moreover, a broad cloth needed no more list than did a narrow. While the narrow loom made strait cloth five quarters wide or less, the broad one wove up to two yards or so wide. Small wonder the broad loom brought a new wave of prosperity first, about 1250, to the Flemish textile towns, and then, in the 1330s and 1340s, to the English. Before long, special bed and blanket looms were developed to weave four yards or more wide. In such a loom the weave was double-width: in a form of double cloth, the warp was divided into two series of ends, each series being struck in turn, and in opposite directions, by the same weft, and joined at one list or selvage only. Nevertheless, despite these new inventions, narrow looms went on being widely used, one reason being that while broad ones were excellent for plain and simple weaves, they were less suited to more intricate ones.[69]

Says, worsteds and other cloths made from tops were not fulled; the weave was generally left bold. Carded woollens were fulled, to shrink the web and felt its threads together, by being beaten when immersed in a mixture of water and fuller's earth, which is a soluble substance composed of a hydrated silicate of aluminium with an admixture of ferric hydroxide and of magnesium and calcium silicates. Fuller's earth was distinct from fuller's clay, which was for scouring, not fulling or thicking properly so called, because insoluble. Both substances were found chiefly at the foot of the escarps of the chalk hills that radiate out from Salisbury Plain. Fuller's earth became an important item of trade, but it was heavy and transported economically for long distances only by water. Consequently the beds most exploited were those at Boxley, Leeds and Detling near Maidstone. The earth was shipped down the Medway via Millhall and New Hithe to east-coast and other ports.[70] Fulling could be carried out in one of three ways: by tilt-hammers, with clubs, or by treading or walking with bare feet, which meant in practice being naked almost up to the waist. Fulling by hand or foot was much lighter than the hammering given in a fulling or tucking-mill. Cloths that were to go through the mill had therefore to be more strongly and heavily woven, lest they break, and they came out of the mill all the more highly felted. Foot-fulling was preferred for delicate cloths and for knitted caps and bonnets,[71] but was from two to twelve times as costly as milling.[72]

Water-powered fulling-mills were introduced in the twelfth century and generally adopted in England in the thirteenth,[73] but in the Netherlands and in Amiens, even in the early sixteenth century, cloths were mostly fulled by foot or, to a lesser extent, by hand.[74] An important reason for this was, 'The clothiers in Flanders, by the flatnesse of their rivers, cannot make walkmilles for their clothes, but are forced to thicken and dresse all their clothes by the foot or by the labour of men, whereby all their clothes are raised to an higher price.'[75] It was long axiomatic that English clothiers used the mill, but not the Flemings.[76] However, fulling-mills had been set up in several towns in Flanders and Brabant in the twelfth and thirteenth centuries, and some went on being used in the fourteenth century and later, more particularly in the Leie or Lys valley. Despite this, there was a marked contrast between Flanders and Brabant, where the mill was little used, and Artois, Liège and Verviers, where it was much in evidence.[77] And this was not entirely due to the flatness of Flemish rivers, but partly to the violent opposition of the foot-fullers and the coercion their sheer weight of numbers enabled them to practise, and partly to the drapers making cloths largely unsuited to milling. These three circumstances combined to form a vicious circle, but probably the ability of the foot-fullers to compel municipal authorities to deface mills was the prime mover. Much the same happened in Florence. The walkers forced the city to prohibit fulling-mills precisely because milling was so successful. Fortunately, landowners set up, on the Arno and other Tuscan rivers, mills the drapers could send their cloths to.[78] In Flanders and Brabant this Luddism without the name was all too successful. It was not until the early sixteenth century, when the Netherlands woollen manufactures were being overwhelmed by the English and it was too late to do much good, that a second great effort was made to introduce mills. Despite the opposition of the foot-fullers, expressed in strikes and other acts of coercion, the drapers in nearly all the clothing towns in Flanders and Brabant got their own way and took to sending at least some of their cloths to be fulled in water or windmills, even if it meant moving their businesses out into the country where the mills had been built.[79] Holland was even slower off the mark. Only in the 1580s and

1590s were mills eventually brought into use, once again in the teeth of opposition by the foot-fullers. Here windmills were the kind usually chosen.[80] England was then a happier land. Technical difficulties hardly ever stood in the way of watermills, and the common law disallowed restraints of trade and punished conspiracies to restrain it. Of the English clothing towns, only York was badly off, in that her mills were at some distance from the city. Bristol, Reading, Hereford, Leicester, Exeter and Salisbury had fulling-mills within five minutes of their walls. Coventry had ten or a dozen within its precincts. Thanks to the fast-flowing Itchen and its new cut, Winchester had mills within and without the walls.[81] Nevertheless, the escarpments and steep slopes of hills like the Cotswolds and the Pennines were the best places for watermills. The streams flowing from the Cotswolds into the Vale of Berkeley, for instance, were scarcely affected by winter floods or summer droughts and kept up that swift, even motion the wheels needed. Apart from the bournes in the chalk hills, English rivers never dried up, and they hardly ever froze. In this respect the Low Countries were at a decided disadvantage.[82]

In earlier times Flanders was, in a manner of speaking, clothier to the whole of Christendom. By the fourteenth century, English carded woollens were threatening Flemish superiority. In 1359 the Flemings protected their industry by banning imports from England. But the combined effect of lower production, transport and trading costs, and of customs duties, subsidy, tonnage, poundage and the Calais penny, amounting in all to a twenty-five per cent export tax on English wool, was that English white cloth could be sold in the Netherlands at a lower price than would have been paid there for the wool out of which it was made.[83] By the 1480s English cloth was pouring into the Netherlands for distribution throughout the world. Its flow was likened to a great inundation of the sea, 'inundacioni maris immensi'.[84]

# 2

## ENGLISH TEXTILE MANUFACTURES

Originally textile manufactures had been dispersed throughout the length and breadth of the kingdom. Even in the sixteenth century the geographical division of labour was incomplete. Alongside enterprises whose products sold all over the world, there were workers who served solely local consumers. Homespun wool was entrusted to a local weaver, then to a fuller and a shearman, and finally to a tailor. Woollen cloths could be worn undyed, in their natural beige or, if from black sheep, in 'sheep's russet', which was more brown than black.[1] Flax and hemp were similarly made into linen and canvas clothing or into sacks, ropes and other articles. These activities all had their place in the scheme of things, but by 1500 wide, deep, mass markets had developed. Some special trades, for instance, the weaving of horse and ox-hair into sieve-bottoms and hair cloths for drying malt,[2] and the making of coverlets from list yarns, thrums and other odds and ends,[3] were scattered indifferently; but generally the various textile manufacturers had their origins and seats in and about particular farming countries,[4] according to their peculiar endowments and characteristics. Our account of English textiles at the start of our period is therefore conducted country by country, with due allowance made for imperfect coincidence between agricultural and textile regions.

One great textile region was dispersed in the Cheese, Oxford Heights, and Butter countries, the Vale of Berkeley and thence north to Ell Brook, the easterly half of the Bristol District, the combes and valleys of the Cotswold Country where it abutted on that district and on the vale, and the Culm valley and Tiverton district of the West Country. The manufacture of West-of-England woollen cloth flourished in these parts from the fourteenth right up until the latter part of the sixteenth century, and it lingered on into the early eighteenth.[5] Western or West-of-England cloths were medium-quality, plain-weave fabrics. They were for mass consumption and their production had early been reduced to a set of relatively simple routines. They were mostly woven broad and sold 'white', i.e. undressed and undyed, and in this form they were largely exported. Their wools were carded and spun on the wheel, and their webs were heavily milled. The range of varieties included some finer cloths with plain lists, some better ones with stop-lists, and both narrow-listed and broad-listed cloths. The narrow-lists had fewer picks in their wefts and also fewer ends in their warps, between 700 and 1,200 as compared with between 800 and 1,400.[6] Yet although these Western 'whites' were the chief products of this region, certain parts of it made their own special cloths. Castle Combe made fine and expensive ones that were well known on the Continent. They were usually dyed red.[7] The Stroudwater district, which extended north to Painswick, east to Bisley, south-east to Cherington, south to Horsley, and west to Bridgend in Stonehouse, sold piece-dyed, blood-red Stroudwaters. Both the narrow-list and broad-list varieties were distinguished by their black lists of Irish or other hairy wool.[8] According to John Aubrey, who appears to have been well informed on such matters, it was running through deposits of iron that made the Stroudwater so good for dyeing red, scarlet and black, and it was certainly suitably soft for piece-dying.[9] Bristol, Chew, Cirencester, Westbury, Bruton and Chard produced coarse blue cloths, i.e. their wool was dyed before spinning in various shades of blue, mostly light sky-colour (sky-blue or plunket) or azure. As the wools for these cloths were not well sorted, carding could not make them uniform, and consequently their yarns could not be spun to a consistent standard of hardness. This was why these cloths were best dyed in the wool; but they might also be dyed a second time in the piece. Shepton Mallet cloths were much superior; they were made of Isle of Wight wool.[10] Bristol, Chard, Sturminster Newton and several towns in the south of the Butter Country made coarse whites for linings, and sold them either plain or cottoned.[11] Bristol and Chew also produced narrow cloths or 'ossets'.[12] In addition, Bristol both wove and frizzed what were called 'Welsh' and 'Irish' cloths, so signifying that their wools at least came from those parts.[13] Finally, a good deal of locally grown flax was woven up in the Butter Country into cheesecloth, butter-muslin and other linens. There was plenty of buttermilk here for the fermentation stages of the bleaching process.[14]

A second textile region was made up of the Chalk, Poor Soils, Blackheath, South Seacoast and Northdown countries and the Petworth District, and had its main seats in Reading, Wokingham, Newbury, Devizes, Haslemere, Guildford, Godalming, Wonersh, Farnham, Alton, Andover, Basingstoke, Winchester, Salisbury, Romsey, Southampton, Newport, Havant and Dorchester. This region generally made medley broadcloths under such names as 'Readings' and 'Guildfords'. The clothiers dyed their wools in various colours, rolled, teased, carded and scribbled them into delicate blends, and spun and wove them into medleys, which they then had fulled, rowed, shorn and fully finished.[15] In addition, Basingstoke and Wonersh produced dyed-in-the-wool blue cloths;[16] Salisbury, Wilton, Guildford and Newbury white ones; and Salisbury and Winchester rays, ossets and plains, the last of which were usually cottoned and served for linings.[17] From Salisbury, too, came woollen Florences or Florentines. These were woven as combination twills, with either the warp or the weft predominant, so giving rise to the highly smooth face required in superior linings.[18] Canterbury and Sandwich made a few sheep's russets,[19] and

Canterbury and Maidstone linsey-woolseys.[20] Winchester, Guildford, Alresford, Bishops Sutton and Bishops Waltham wove 'chalons', which were tapestry
coverlets originally devised in Châlons-sur-Marne. Double chalons were woven
broad, doubled over, and quilted.[21] Then there were the stockbridges, which
were narrow dozens that originated in Stockbridge and cost no more than a
quarter the price of a kersey.[22] But generally kerseys were next to medley
broadcloths in importance. These were the famous 'Reading', 'Winton' or
'Hampshire' kerseys. Clothiers in all parts of the region made them alongside
their broadcloths, and of similar Chalk Country wools. Most kerseys were
likewise medleys, but Reading, Newbury and Salisbury also made white ones.
Many blue or watchet ones were produced too,[23] especially in Basingstoke,
Wonersh, Guildford and above all Godalming, whose kerseys were reputed to
be unequalled for colour and were in much demand in the Canaries.[24]

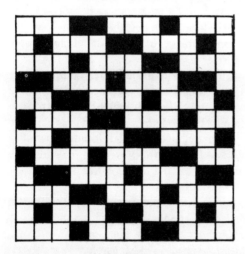

Fig. 5 Draft for one kind of
Florentine weave (weft black).

Maidstone and Canterbury kerseys were out of the general run in that they were
dozens instead of the more usual sixteen to eighteen yards.[25] The poorer
'Hampshire' kerseys often shrank badly, partly due to having been over-
stretched in tentering, partly because they incorporated fell wool, 'leaveings'
and hairy fibres from the undersides of Chalk Country sheep, and generally 'for
the manyfolde difference of sundrie spynnyngs of the same', so that the yarns
lacked uniformity.[26] At the other end of the scale, the best sorting kerseys sold
well in Antwerp and were in great request in Italy. Winchcombe kerseys, as
made by John Smalwoode alias Winchcombe the elder, the legendary Jack of

Newbury who died in 1519 or 1520, were the most famous brand.[27] Lastly, it should be mentioned that Maidstone, Canterbury, Salisbury, Hungerford, Great and Little Bedwyn and other towns also produced linens.[28]

Another textile region was sited in the Vale of Kent, the more northerly of the Wealden Vales, and in the uplands on the fringes of Romney Marsh.[29] 'Kentish' cloth, the chief product, was a rather coarse, heavy, woollen broadcloth, well dyed in the wool by the clothiers themselves and sold by them ready dressed, finished and dyed or double-dyed in almost every conceivable colour or medley of colours. In later times a few kerseys were made.[30]

The Woodland manufacturing district extended to the very limits of the country's marches with High Suffolk and the Breckland, down the Gipping valley to Ipswich, down the Stour Valley to Dedham, and down the Colne valley to Colchester. Ipswich was the chief local mart and port and an important centre for second dressing and finishing, but was little concerned with weaving; her 'clothiers' were mostly in the nature of shearmen and clothworkers.[31] The principal product in these parts was broad 'Suffolk' cloth, the wool for which was drawn mainly from the Norfolk Heathlands and the Chiltern Country. As the clothiers themselves said, this was very coarse wool and not worth the charge involved in meticulous spinning and workmanship. As for their carders and spinners, 'Some of them carde uppon newe cards and some uppon olde cards, and some spynne harde yarne and some softe, so as some parte of the clothe where the harde yarne is and whiche is carded uppon olde cards shall holde oute the breadthe a greate deale more than that which is carded uppon newe cards and soft spun.'[32] 'Suffolk' cloths were true blue, dyed in the wool. The clothiers used woad or, from about 1580, a mixture of woad and indigo, to give their wools a range of shades called, in descending order of darkness, sad blue, blue, azure, watchet, plunket and huling. Azures were twice as dark as plunkets, and blues twice as dark as azures. About one cloth in four was double-dyed, in the piece, to give a wide range of colours, before being sold by the clothiers. Some 'Suffolk' cloths were made as two-dozens and some to a greater length, but all were relatively weighty, heavily fulled, and then given at least a first dressing by the makers.[33] Only East Bergholt, it seems, and then only until 1566, sold blue cloth undressed.[34] Other and inferior blue cloths, both broad and narrow, were made in Dedham and Boxted. These were called 'vesses' or 'set cloths', signifying that they were either sad or light blue and that they were set in woad; but they were occasionally second dyed and were sold red as well as blue. They were made of the coarsest wool and used for the outer clothing of poor people in Muscovy, the Baltic countries and Barbary, and were notoriously prone to shrink.[35] Another branch of textile manufactures concerned itself with cloths whose wefts incorporated noils obtained from the woolcombers who worked for the rock-spinners and worstedweavers. Colchester greys were fabrics of this kind.[36] The broad and narrow dozen 'rawback' blankets made in Bury St Edmunds, Bildeston and elsewhere had wefts composed mostly of noils and flocks.[37] In Bury, Bildeston,

Lavenham and Denston some general clothiers and not a few specialists cottoned coarse woollens, some of which were made locally and others imported for the purpose from the Peak-Forest Country. The Woodland plains had wefts made largely of noils, and some woolcombers were encouraged to consume their own noils in weaving them on their own 'cotton looms'.[38] The sailing cloths and other linsey-woolseys made in Denston, Stratford, Cavendish, Bildeston and elsewhere, and denoted by their crumple-lists, often had noils in their wefts too.[39] Kerseys were likewise made, particularly in Coggeshall, Witham, Colchester, Halstead, Bildeston, Needham Market and Bury. Needham kerseys were the most noted, and they were mostly made as two-dozens.[40] Most of these Woodland kerseys had wefts of 'the yarns called dornix or carsey yarn', which was composed mostly of noils and waste locks of wool.[41] Lastly, Colchester produced tilt-cloths, which were the predecessors of tarpaulins as covers to throw over the tilts of wagons and barges. Some kinds were woven of coarse wool and left unscoured in order to increase their resistance to rain; others were made of canvas.[42]

The Breckland was deeply involved in the textile trades, though least of all in weaving and fulling. However, housewives' and grey and white cloths were made in the townships along the road from Bury to Mildenhall. The worst of the whites were linings, many of which were cottoned. Coarse cloths here generally had wefts made largely of noils and reconstituted thrums, or even almost wholly of noils. At the other end of the scale, however, fine, white sorting cloths were woven in carefully selected fallow wools. Mildenhall also made linsey-woolseys. All these cloths were usually woven broad and in lengths of two dozen yards.[43]

Adverting now to the Vale of Taunton Deane, we find Taunton, Bridgwater, Dunster, Minehead and other towns making broad dozens and narrow two-dozens of low-priced, light-weight woollens suitable for linings. Bridgwaters were all ossets or demi-ossets, i.e. narrow dozens. Both Dunsters and Bridgwaters were sometimes dyed red by the makers. The Taunton and Bridgwater clothiers finished a few of their cloths as friezes and many more as cottons, which sold well in France, where they served for the garments themselves rather than for their linings, Lastly, Bridgwater and some other towns in the vale made white and plunket kerseys, often in the form of dozens.[44]

The West Country was a source of plains for frizzing and cottoning and also of finished cottons. Pilton cottons, especially, were so loosely and skimpily woven as to give rise to the saying, 'Woe unto you Piltonians, that make cloth without wool'.[45] However, these plains, friezes and cottons were the country's best products. Tavistocks or 'Cornish' dozens were made of 'Cornish hair', i.e. the hair and hairy wool from the general run of West Country sheep. These cloths were woven in and about Tavistock, Bear Alston, Okehampton, Lifton, Lamerton and Lidford, and some were finished in Taunton. They were of slight value. To make them more presentable the clothiers usually rubbed flocks of wool into the webs and held them there by means of adhesives. But then even ordinary wear would cause the cloth to pill.[46]

The better grades of wool grown in Wales were woven up and fulled in the western extremities of the Cheshire Cheese Country and in the Englishry districts away to the south-west. But even the best grades were unfit for ordinary woollens. Webs made from them had to be frizzed or cottoned. A cotton or *frize sèche* had a soft, fluffy nap raised on it by half or dry-frizzing on a cottoning board by means of a metal rubber or rowing card. This nap was then shorn just enough to leave it uniform and even. Plains had been cottoned in this way for centuries.[47] They served for petticoats, waistcoats and cloak and coat linings.[48] Such narrow plains or linings, often called 'Welsh' webs or cloths on account of their wool, were woven and fulled in and near Shrewsbury, Wrexham, Denbigh, Oswestry, Chirk and other towns in the Cheshire Cheese Country. Many of them were fulled, and most of them sold, in Oswestry, and by the Oswestry ell. Here they were bought by the Shrewsbury drapers or, to a much lesser extent, by those of Oswestry, Whitchurch, Coventry and Warwick. The drapers took the cloths home, had them cottoned and shorn, and then sold them as 'Shrewsbury' or 'Welsh' cottons, largely to London and partly for eventual export to France and the Mediterranean.[49] Many other plains were finished as high friezes in Shrewsbury, Oswestry, Chester, Ruthin and elsewhere and sold as 'Shrewsbury' or 'Welsh' friezes.[50] Similar webs were frizzed, or occasionally cottoned, in Haverfordwest, Carmarthen, Tenby and Brecon.[51] High frizzing was likewise an ancient process. It involved the raising, on one side of the cloth only, of a high, irregular, tufty, curly nap, by scrubbing the surface of the wet fabric with iron rubbers and with a circular motion, so that the upper fibres formed into small curls or beads. Friezes had a hard, rough feel. They were best suited to winter gowns and rough overcoating, but were also used for doublets and jerkins. The burgesses of Haverfordwest said friezes were 'then the winter coat liveries of this nation', and Edmund Spenser depicted 'winter cloathed all in frize'.[52] Lastly, in addition to her cottons and friezes, Shrewsbury made rolls of coarse cloth, fit for floor-cloths, mops and such like, and also some penistones, ossets, dozens and kerseys.[53]

The greatest concentration of poor, coarse woollen manufactures was in the Peak-Forest Country. So hairy were the wools, the great comb had to be used in preparing them for warp yarns, and only the weft wools were carded. Leeds and Wakefield made some broad cloths, but the common products were narrow 'Northern' dozens, two-dozens and longs. These took the palm for the coarseness of their wools, for the careless and perfunctory way in which they were sorted, for fraudulent processes, and for sheer lack of skill in manufacture. It was here more than anywhere else that clothiers mixed reconstituted thrums with their wools, stretched and strained their cloths on the tenters, and rubbed flocks into their webs and glued them down with an obnoxious sullage of pig's dung and other vile substances, giving rise to the notoriously characteristic 'scent of these Northern dozens'.[54] John Leake was only telling the truth when he described England north of the Trent as a region 'wher no true clothes are made'.[55] Nor were the broad, dyed-in-the-wool 'Yorkshire' cloths superior to the others; they were 'of all the coulored clothes the worst of all'.[56] Best of a bad bunch were the penistones, which stemmed from Penistone and district, Wakefield and Barnsley. Ordinary penistones, otherwise 'forest whites', were heavily milled broadcloths, mostly dozens. The best penistones had carefully sorted wools and were good enough to be frizzed into frizadoes, for which purpose they were counterfeited in Shrewsbury and elsewhere.[57] Side by side with Northern cloths were made the equally malodorous Northern kerseys, which also had flocks stuck in them. Some were dyed watchet in the wool, but the majority were white dozens or double-dozens. More than elsewhere they were made in Halifax, Huddersfield, Bradford, Bingley, Keighley, Colne, Burnley, Padiham and Blackburn.[58] Although some of the plains made in the east of the country were cottoned there (and in such places as Bury St Edmunds and London),[59] it was on the western side that most of the cottons were produced. The looms in Manchester, Kearsley, Bolton, Blackburn, Rossendale and thereabouts wove largely white and grey plains (kennets) and checks. For the most part these were subsequently cottoned, chiefly in Manchester, and, usually being sold there, they entered commerce, and sold as far afield as France, Italy and Spain, under the name of Manchester cottons.[60] This same district also frizzed plains into 'Rochdale friezes' or 'Manchester ruggs otherwise named frices' and kerseys into kersey frizes.[61] A fiscal document drawn up in 1592 lists: 'English ruggs – None are made in England but Irish ruggs of divers sorts, from 10s. to (none shipped over) 3li.'[62] Ireland did make plains intended for high, wet frizzing, and converted some into friezes or rugs, often in the form of mantles, and some of these fabrics were from time to time brought over.[63] Yet rugs were undoubtedly being produced in Salford in 1598 and in other towns hereabouts at much the same time. It appears that Manchester and Salford rugs were made of hairy Irish wool and for some purposes could properly be classified as Irish rugs.[64]

The southern part of the Northwestern Lowlands and of the Lake District in the North Country had long manufactured cogware, which was a narrow dozen cloth usually left in its natural sheep's colour. It had the reputation of being made from the worst wool in the kingdom and was handled not by the ordinary cloth merchants, but by special cogmen, and none of it was considered worthy of alnage, search and seal, or statutory regulation. In later times the best known types were Cartmel and Kendal cloths. They were woven and fulled chiefly in and about Broughton-in-Furness and Hawkshead, and finished, dyed and marketed in Cartmel and Kendal, and Kendal greens were well known. They had formerly been used for outer clothing, and still served for light summer coats, but now were mostly employed as linings, especially hose linings. They were often cottoned and sometimes converted into friezes.[65]

Of all the carding wools the undoubted best was the 'Leominster ore' that came from the Ryeland sheep in the Vales of Hereford, and the second best was perhaps March wool. Nearly all the former and some of the latter went into the high-quality woollens made in the cities of Hereford, Worcester, Coventry and Gloucester, and the boroughs of Ludlow and Leominster. The output of these last two places was never very great and that of Hereford soon declined. Worcester made more of these cloths than did any of the other towns and they were all known in the trade by the generic name of Worcesters. They were fine broadcloths, superior in weight and quality to West-of-Englands, seven quarters wide within the lists, and made as dozens, shortcloths and above all longcloths of between twenty-nine and thirty-three yards, and between seventy-eight and eighty-four pounds weight. Two or three grades were produced, the best sorting cloth being distinguished by a blue list. For this the wool was most carefully sorted and selected, but coarse wool, noils and flocks were excluded from all yarns whatsoever. To ensure good workmanship in all the processes, they were all carried out within the cities and boroughs and under strict guild search and seal. The makers of fine cloth in Worcester and the minor centres sold most of their wares undyed, but Coventry dressed and dyed most of hers and many of those from Worcester and elsewhere also.[66] One peculiarity of best Worcester cloth as made in Worcester was that it was fulled by foot. This is shown by the frequency with which the occupations of walker, clothworker and clothier were combined in the same man; by the regular storing of fuller's earth in the same city premises where the other processes were carried out; and by the abnormally high ratio of walkers to weaver-clothiers. The scarcity of fulling mills in and near Gloucester and the deliberate destruction of some built on the Wye near Hereford, suggest the same for those two cities.[67] Worcesters were in great request on the Continent.[68] Top-quality ones were probably the best of their kind on earth. The claim by a Worcester clothier named Richard Maie in 1576, that he had given Queen Elizabeth 'the finest cloth in the worlde' was by no means far fetched.[69]

Worcesters were not the only cloths made in the towns of the Midland Plain. In Worcester herself many of the clothiers also made coarser cloths that were often dyed red or blue in the wool, and some wove bedding blankets.[70] Coventry made linsey-woolseys and kerseys and converted plains into cottons.[71] The city was also noted on both sides of the Channel for her blue thread, which, by skilful dyeing, defied all foreign competition.[72] Burford, Witney, Abingdon, and Northampton made good white cloths, though nothing to compare with Worcesters; but the products of Stafford, Newcastle-under-Lyme, Burton-on-Trent, Tamworth, Nuneaton and Ripon were inferior again in both quality and quantity.[73] Droitwich, Bromsgrove, Kidderminster and probably Stourbridge and Bridgnorth, as well as Mansfield, Mansfield Woodhouse and Sutton-in-Ashfield, all made dyed-in-the-wool blues and here and there a few medleys.[74] Linsey-woolseys were also produced in various places, and Knaresborough specialised in sameron, which was a linen-hemp mixture used for bedsheets.[75] York made chalons and Warwick frizzed and cottoned 'Welsh' plains.[76]

East Norfolk went on weaving its worsted yarns, but its worsted cloth was in a decline especially marked in the export trade,[77] for the simple reason that this branch of manufacture was becoming established in the Westkwartier of Flanders.[78] Since its diffusion in England was infinitesimal, being confined to a shortlived attempt in Glastonbury in 1551 and an isolated instance in Bristol, one could almost say worsted cloth went abroad to die.[79] Worsted motleys were no longer heard of in Norwich and East Norfolk after 1468 and worsted rays were discontinued over here after they had been taken up in Lille.[80] Such worsteds as went on being made in East Norfolk were for the most part either broadcloths only six yards long, or rolls, eighteen inches broad and thirty yards long, or half-doubles five quarters wide and a mere six yards in length, or double worsteds five quarters by ten yards and known as 'tenyards'.[81] This was but the fag-end of the fabric's life; it was outmoded and survived barely longer or better on the Continent. Over here the gap was filled by the expansion of the manufacture of worsted says, especially of monks cloths[82] and the invention of that of worsted stamins. Continental stamins are encountered as early as the thirteenth century and were made either of silk or of silk-wool union yarns.[83] Worsted was an excellent substitute for either of these and from the 1490s, possibly before, worstedweavers in Norwich, Yarmouth and elsewhere in East Norfolk, and also in Lynn, started to make stamins wholly in worsted.[84] This proved a highly successful business; it flourished for over two hundred years.[85] Yet the innovation was simple enough, for 'to make of this worsteed a stamin was but to make yt narrower and thynner in the slay'.[86] The warp threads being fewer and more closely set, the cloth was not quite so wide. Worsted was much cheaper than silk and worsted stamins were good value for money for the making of gowns, coats and petticoats.[87] The latter part of the fifteenth century also saw the rise in Norwich of the weaving of small-woof worsted on lace-looms into fringes, garters, swathe-bands, reins, bridles, stirrup straps and other narrow wares. This business was earlier forbidden to the worstedweavers and they usually left it to others.[88]

While worsted products thus changed and multiplied, a new textile industry established itself in Norwich. Dornick, which had originated in Doornijk (Tournai), was a union fabric, not altogether unlike kersey, and suitable for coverlets, beds, hangings, curtains, cupboard cloths, furniture carpets, petticoats, aproning and church vestments.[89] Continental dornicks imported from Doornijk, Russel (Lille), and elsewhere, were some of them of linen thread, some of caddis, which was not unlike worsted crewel, some of silk, some of wool, some of mixed linen and wool.[90] Ralph Horne, 'dornyx wever', who was flourishing in 1493, was probably not the first of his kind in Norwich, for coverlets were being made there from 1327 onwards by the company of bedweavers and from 1453 by that of the coverletweavers.[91] By 1548 the city boasted fifteen dornicksweavers and on this scale the business went on there for the best part of two hundred years. The merger of the bed, coverlet and dornicksweavers' companies in 1544 reflects the fact that Norwich dornicks were largely coverlets. Their range included coverlets for both single and double beds and larger, medium and narrow pieces. Nearly all were 'thread dornicks', made of about one part by weight of linen thread to two of dornicks or kersey yarn, which was composed chiefly of noils. Nearly all, too, were woven in colours on the loom. They were probably cross-rib cloths in which a heavy kersey weft was covered by a closely set warp of fine linen threads. Using much the same yarns, dornicksweavers often made linsey-woolseys also.[92]

In utilising noils, the dornicksweavers were exploiting a by-product of worsted manufacture. The Norwich and East Norfolk makers of rawback blankets also used noils,[93] and so did many of the thickwoollen weavers in Norwich, Martham and other East Norfolk towns. Their fabrics seem to have been mostly kerseys and the heavy overcoating cloths later called 'bearskins', 'fearnothings', 'fearnoughts' and 'dreadnoughts', all of which had noils in the wefts.[94] Moreover, Norwich was by no means the sole town in East Norfolk to make linsey-woolseys, which commonly incorporated noils.[95] Indeed, linen-union cloths were a significant part of the textile scene here. So were pure linens. Aylsham and some other towns made plenty of them, and Norwich herself specialised in bewpers, a variety invented in Beaupreau and used for flags and pennants.[96]

The few small woollen manufacturers in High Suffolk and the Sandlings Country restricted themselves to kersey dozens and rawback blankets.[97] Linsey-woolseys were rather more important,[98] but even they were overshadowed by linen and hempen cloths. Linen cloths were produced in Ipswich, and in the Waveney valley, in and near Diss, Beccles and Bungay. This latter district was the source of the cloths known to the Venetians as *loesti* and imported by them by way of Lowestoft for resale in Syria and elsewhere. However, most High Suffolk linens were open weaves used locally for such things as cheesecloth and butter-muslin.[99] Some flax was grown hereabouts, but the industry relied largely on imports from the Continent, and had the advantage of ready access to the Haarlem bleacheries. Buttermilk for sours was abundant.[100] A good deal of hemp was grown, especially in the Dove and Waveney valleys, and Ipswich canvas had a wide sale.[101] Woodbridge, Saxmundham, Parham, Wenhaston and many other towns near the ports and highways, busied themselves making sackcloth for corn and coal bags. In this same district, in Ipswich, Waldringfield, Eyke, Parham, Hacheston, Earl Soham and elsewhere, twillweavers were at work producing mixed linen and hempen twills, which were used for mattress covers and for working clothes like smocks.[102] Finally, Pulham specialised in making its unique 'Pulham worke coveringe' or coverlets, which were considerably more expensive than dornick ones.[103]

The easterly parts and margins of the Lancashire Plain also had linen manufactures. Locally grown flax[104] was supplemented by imports from Ireland through Chester, Liverpool and Preston, and from the Eastland via York and Hull (which, incidentally, itself made sailcloth).[105] Many of the Lancashire linens were probably cheesecloths and other simple types, but not all, and in 1576 it was claimed that 'Kentishe clothes', meaning those made after the fashion of Ghent, were being produced in Preston.[106]

In London and the suburbs, the majority of textile workers seem to have been Flemings by origin or recent descent. These London 'Dutch' and London 'French' lived in Spitalfields and other parts of Stepney, in Aldgate, Bishopsgate, Cripplegate, Shoreditch, Tower Hamlets, Southwark and other places in and about the suburbs. They mostly earned their living as silkworkers,[107] engaging, as 'narrow-weavers' or otherwise, in the manufacture of 'narrow' wares, i.e. those made and sold in penny-widths up to six pennies wide, such as tapes, ribbons, garters, fringes, tassels, galloons, girdles, inkles, cauls, trimmings, gimps, hatbands, braids and livery and other laces. This trade was often called parchmentry and its products parchment laces, due to the anglicising of *passement* and *passementerie*. Many of these loom-laces were made of ferret silk, and so sometimes called ferrets and their makers ferret-weavers, owing to yet another comic anglicisation, this time of *fioretto* or *fiorette*, which now goes by the names of floretta, floret or schappe. It is the perforated, weak, rough silk waste broken off in unwinding cocoons, further torn and broken up on purpose, and then carded like so much wool and spun on a wheel. Many different kinds of ribbon were woven, including Towers and Cullen, which were in the fashion of Tours and Cologne.[108] This industry was well suited to the metropolis, for the Vale of London had few sites for watermills and even fewer available for fulling, the port was apt to receive both silk and immigrants, and London, Westminster and Southwark provided the greatest concentration of likely customers. A few London Dutch and others wove linens, particularly towels[109] but, narrow work apart, London's main textile interests were in clothworking and finishing, shearing, pressing, frizzing, cottoning, dyeing and packing.[110]

The English wove some flax, hemp and waste silk, but had no broad silk or cotton-wool textile manufactures, and in return for their immense exports of woollens, imported from the Continent vast quantities of linen, hempen and silken yarns and cloths and of fustians and other fabrics incorporating cotton wool.

# 3

## CARDED WOOLLENS

The sixteenth and seventeenth centuries saw the old English carded woollen manufactures migrate centrifugally to remoter parts of the kingdom and to countries oversea.

As trade opened up with eastern and southern Europe, the Levant, Asia, Africa and America, and as the western style of dress spread, so kersey sales grew, and in the middle part of the sixteenth century they enjoyed a boom.[1] The West Country had started making 'Devonshire' kerseys about 1505, utilising the best of the newly improved West Country wools from east of the Allen and Fowey rivers. These kerseys were well spun, woven and fulled. How much finer the spinning was may be judged from the fact that spinners earned up to three times as much for a pound of Devonshire as of Reading kersey. Tiverton and Cullompton became noted for their kersey cloths and stockings respectively, and Crediton kerseys were famed for being exceptionally finely spun, giving rise to the saying, 'as fine as Kirton spinning.' First introduced about 1529, 'Devon' or 'Cornish' dozens became the most usual type. They were made in counts of from six to twelve hundred ends in the sley, and with a correspondingly high number of picks. Both warps and abbs were spun 'with a crosse stringe', i.e. a Z-twist, and the wool for them was often dyed.[2] These dozens were 'accompted generallie beyond the seas the truest made clothe within this realme'.[3] In later years another sort of kersey was introduced. When first mentioned in 1592, it was defined as 'rudge washe kersey, that is to saye, being made of fleece woole wasshed only on the sheepes backes'.[4]

Kersey making spread also to the Wealden Vales. It was recorded at Goudhurst in 1637, at Pembury in 1695 and at Biddenden in 1696, but never came to much in this country.[5] It was taken up in a small way in several widely scattered places, Pensford near Bristol, Prestwold in the Midland Plain. Ilminster and Beaminster in the Butter Country, Kendal and distant parts of Wales.[6] Meanwhile the Peak-Forest Country extended its range of kerseys. About 1580 the Keighley White was introduced in that town, in nearby Bingley, Cottingley and Allerton, and later in Halifax and Bradford. The use of grades of Northwold wool beneath the consideration of 'south countrymen' and, it seems, of much Lank wool, made the Keighley White so superior to most of its fellows that it could even be dyed in the piece.[7] A similar development occurred in

Rossendale, which had previously made little beyond sham kerseys, being mere twills cut, dressed and dyed to deceive.[8] Now a considerable manufacture of genuine kerseys grew up.[9] We first hear of these 'Lankaster newe devised carseyes' about 1594–5, when they first made their mark in the export trade. They were probably made of much the same wools as were the Keighley Whites.[10] By 1606 another new type of kersey had been introduced in this country, vis. the 'washer', 'wash-white', or 'half-thick' and 'quarter-thick'. It was lighter and thinner than the old Northern kersey and was fulled only a quarter or half as much, so that, being made about eighteen yards long, it could be hot-pressed and then passed off as 'Devonshire'.[11] Finally the 1590s saw the rise of the fleetingly successful broadlist kerseys. An extra-broad list was substituted for wearable cloth, so that there was under a yard between the lists at fulling, after which the cloth was widened by excessive stretching and straining on the tenters. It was very likely such broadlists that Lionel Cranfield palmed off on his Netherlands and German customers. His own factor described them as 'vile stuff'. He was cursed to his face by those who bought them. 'It is a pity', he lamented, 'that such villains as we have in England should live to spoil the drapery of our land in such sort.' From 1613 onwards, as all buyers were undeceived in their turn, sales of broadlists died away;[12] but the new and better kerseys continued to make progress and by 1638 their manufacture was well established in the Peak-Forest Country.[13]

The great centrifugal diffusion of kersey making proceeded east and south as well as west and north. From 1500 onwards the old Flemish drapery was in full decline and kerseys formed an important part of the *'nieuwe alsook lichte draperie'* that took its place. Town by town and almost from year to year, the manufacture spread throughout West Flanders.[14] In the 1560s the Flemings took their kersey manufactures to Holland.[15] Flemish and English kerseys were not exactly the same, but many of them were almost indistinguishable, so that English ones could be exported to the Continent white, dyed there, re-folded differently, printed with Flemish stamps and sold as Flemish kerseys, which was often helpful when trading with the Spanish dominions.[16] Kersey making spread to other parts of Europe too. By 1614 the Italians were weaving their own varieties from local wools, and before long the Silesians were using their own wool for kerseys that undercut English ones.[17] As their manufacture spread thus from England to the Continent, English people soon started to buy imported kerseys. Already in 1549 it is observed that 'straungers ... make and die carsies ... beyond the seaze and bringe them hether to be sold againe'.[18]

The same centrifuge that drove kersey making itself further and further afield also dispersed what had become the peculiarly English way of making kerseys. That type of kersey yarn that was composed mostly of noils, like kersey yarn itself, was an East Anglian invention, and likewise its use spread to other parts of England, especially in the south. It was adopted, for example, in the Vale of Taunton Deane, the only difference being that noils were called 'pinnions' there. By 1670 pinnions were being employed by kersey makers in the vale and 'pinnon yearne' provided their wefts.[19] In 1688 a Southampton clothier is found making kerseys with similar pinnion wefts.[20] This, it seems, is what the Flemings came to regard as the specifically English way of making kerseys. Ever since 1563 they had being trying to lure Englishmen over to teach them kersey making 'selon proprement la fachon d'Angleterre'.[21] It was the one kersey process they coveted above all, and it was one that could be combined with their stammet warp yarns to produce a kersey without any Spanish wool in it. This was a great advantage, for noils were much cheaper than any non-combing wool. Eventually the Netherlanders succeeded in their quest. In 1614 Leiden made her first provisional ordinance on the manufacture of 'stametten op de Engelsche wijze ... volghen de Engelsche maniere, so in 't wercken als in de stoffen'. The set of workers who wanted to undertake this new business were unfortunately impeded by an old rule that forbade them to use or even possess any cammeling or noils. This order was now dispensed with, on the strict condition that the cammeling was used solely in stammets in the English fashion.[22] In 1653 the Leiden manufacturers were making 'karsaaien ... op de Engelsche wijze ... op de maniere van de Engelsche goederen ... op de Engelsche maniere'.[23] By 1647 Bruges was producing 'carseyes (fabrication à la mode anglaise)'.[24] In 1676 Hondschoote was turning out 'carisees anglaises'.[25]

Even as kersey making progressed and spread, it was all the time being slowly and surely undermined by the knitters who produced nether stocks or stockings, socks and other hose without the intervention of the tailor.[26] What with knitting and foreign competition, it is a marvel English kersey making kept up as well as it did.

At much the same time that the manufacture of kerseys was started in the West Country, so too was that of the two new types of narrow cloth. We first come across them in 1513 and then under the generic name of 'straits'. They became the speciality of the Totnes and South Hams district and were designed mainly for export as lining material to the Netherlands and as dress cloth to Brittany and the Atlantic Islands. 'White straits' were made at first fifteen yards long and four-and-a-half quarters wide, later twelve yards by one and weighing eleven pounds. 'White pinned' or 'pinned white' straits, however, were by 1552 only eleven yards by three-quarters and eight pounds weight. Both types were developments from the old Tavistock cloths and like them were made of hairy wool and incorporated lambs' wool and flocks. They were likewise of small value, six and later eight of them equalling one shortcloth for customs purposes.[27] 'Pinned whites' or 'pinwhites', penwits or pennewits in Netherlands, took their name from Penwith, which is the southwesternmost hundred of Cornwall and would then have been pronounced provincially as 'Penwit'. This leads us to infer that early penwiths were made of wool grown in that part.[28] By 1584 the yarn used in these straits had become smaller and finer than before, while the cloths themselves were being made longer, up to fourteen yards, and correspondingly heavier.[29] This improvement in the yarn was possibly connected with the changeover about 1570 to Dorset Horn wool from the Butter Country.[30]

The same Dorset Horn wool that went into the later penwiths was used also in 'Dorset dozens'. It was reckoned unfit for either West-of-England cloth or Reading or Hampshire kerseys and warranted little expenditure on carding, spinning and weaving, which consequently were all of correspondingly poor quality. Both warp and weft were spun 'with an open stringe', meaning an S-twist. The warps had counts of 300 or 400 ends mostly, and none of above 500, whereas the minimum for a Devon dozen was 600, and the weft was struck 'but with one small stroke'. These Dorset dozens were so slight they could hardly be sold anywhere but abroad and for the most part solely to Normandy and Lower Brittany, where the common people were too poor to buy decent cloth and yet needed woollens in the winter instead of their usual linens and canvases. One of the first makers, if not the inventor, of Dorset dozens, about 1570, was Richard Blacheford of Dorchester. The seats of their manufacture were all in the south of the Butter Country, at Dorchester, Lyme Regis, Winsham, Broad Windsor, Combe St Nicholas, Axminster and Ilminster, and the cloths were often called Ilminster dozens.[31]

The Peak-Forest Country made even more important advances in other cloths than in kerseys. Side by side with the newly devised kerseys there had arisen by 1588 the 'New Draperies of broad woollen cloth'. Hitherto the cloths made here had nearly all been narrow. Now broad looms were increasingly used, especially in and about Leeds. In 1616 this town had become important enough to be added to the list of wool staples. When incorporated in 1626, Leeds was already the finishing, dyeing and commercial centre of a district given over to the manufacture of superior, unstrained, dyed-in-the-wool coloured and medley broadcloths such as had not in former times been made north of the Trent. At first these were counterfeits of Reading cloths and were passed off as such, but they were made of fallow wools and were not much inferior to the genuine articles. By 1647 the distinctive name of 'Leeds cloth' had been acquired. In 1662 it was said with truth, 'The nature of cloth is much changed in these late yeares and ... the New Drapery is now most in use' in this district. By 1720 these new broadcloths were making an impression in Levantine markets and their production went on rising.[32] Meanwhile a new type of cotton was started in Rossendale shortly before 1610. This was smaller spun than most and so justified its name of 'minikin', but it was carefully finished to resemble a frizado made from minikin baize and sometimes passed off as that.[33]

The centrifugal diffusion of kersey manufactures was thus paralleled in other woollen cloths. The medley trade moved from the Chalk Country and thereabouts to the Peak-Forest Country, while the manufactures of coarse, hairy cloths went further afield still. In the West Country, Tavistocks gave way to better straits and then these passed away in their turn. Even the improved penwiths were little heard of after about 1670 and had vanished without trace by the end of the century. The old friezes and cottons and the plains they were wrought upon went the same way in the end. They are hardly heard of after 1700, except that frizzing and cottoning were adopted as temporary expedients to prolong the lives of manufactures to which they had not previously been applied.[34]

Friezes and cottons were replaced by frizadoes, which were cloths made of proper carding wool and then frizzed by what was apparently a slightly new process. By 1570 the Norwich Flemings had set up the manufacture of Flanders frizadoes and in 1578 some frizadoes were being made in England from Worcester cloths and many from penistones.[35] In addition, a certain John Hastings, one of the queen's servants, promoted the transfer to Christchurch of the dying Holland frizado industry. He apparently intended to use Chalk Country broadcloths, but the patent he obtained in 1569 seems to have been little exploited for the purpose for which it was drawn up.[36]

The textile manufactures England was discarding as unprofitable were taken up elsewhere by others. Shoddy cloth manufacture was adopted with joy in La Vesdre. Such work was forbidden in the principality of Liège, leaving Walloon Limburg, especially Dison, free to concentrate on the utilisation of thrums and flocks, *queues et pennes*, imported from the rest of the world.[37] Broadlist kerseys were not as good as the cloth made in Germany and the merchants there switched to domestic suppliers. Silesian and Hungarian cloths were now 'so good cheap as that the common man desires no better'.[38] A similar fate awaited even better cloths. The writing had been on the wall for the West-of-England whites for some time and in the period 1591–1614 this branch of manufacture was successfully transplanted in Pomerania.[39] The Rhenish Palatinate and other west German principalities developed coloured cloths modelled on the Kentish ones, leaving the Wealden Vale woollen industry to a protracted decline and eventual extinction.[40] Suffolk cloths went the same way and at much the same time. Exports were in decline by 1614, and although stretching cloths for the Eastland and Barbary markets gave a temporary reprieve, this manufacture had almost withered away in the Woodland by 1685.[41] It had gone to the Continent, particularly to the Palatinate. By 1638 its diffusion, if report be believed, had reached as far as Salonika. While the very name of Suffolk cloth was forgotten over here, its type and style lived on abroad.[42] The Chalk Country medley industry likewise passed its peak in the first half of the seventeenth century. It went to the Peak-Forest Country mainly, but not all Continental towns were as unsuccessful as Bergues-Saint-Winoc in their attempts at setting up '*une draperie de draps mêlés à la façon d'Angleterre*'.[43] Even fine cloth was not exempt from the general tendency for the old manufactures to decline in the places of their birth. First the Gloucester, then the Coventry, and finally the Worcester firms succumbed.[44]

From 1608 onwards Suffolk, West-of-England and other cloths were stretched and strained until they needed special selvages to reinforce their weakened edges. It was to little avail. During the depression about 1620 these trades ailed all the more. The Clothing Committee of the Privy Council blamed chiefly 'the makinge of cloth and other draperies in forreigne parts in more aboundance then in former tymes'.[45] A report made on behalf of Bristol pointed a finger at 'the cloth made in Spayne, Portugall, France and the Low Countryes more then was wont formerly'.[46] An observer remarked that, fine ones excepted, other countries were starting to make cloths more cheaply than England.[47] It was alleged by the restored Merchant Adventurers and repeated in the House, that Germany and still more Holland had taken to producing their own cloth at the time of the disastrous Cockayne scheme promoted by King James and his ministers.[48] Hull's cloth exports were reported 'decayed by the great store of cloth now made in Danzig and other places of Prussia and kerseys made in Silesia, which doth serve the markets where our cloths were formerly vented in Poland'.[49] Thus English manufacturers were now starting to give way in the face of foreign competition.[50]

Just as with kerseys, so with other cloths, the Europeans realised the best way to imitate English textiles was to secure the services of English workers. Netherlanders had for long tried hard to get Englishmen to go over and teach woollen manufactures *'naar Engelse trant'*, *'selon proprement la fachon d'Angleterre'*. In 1450 the lord of Comene (Comines) offered special privileges to strangers *'in onse ... steide van Comene zyn commen wonen ... omme to makene Inghelsche lakenen, nieuwe draperie en andere'*.[51] By the 1560s the best hope was that English Roman Catholic textile workers might be persuaded to migrate, but these were by now few and far between, and it was a great stroke of luck for the Italian merchant Fortuni when he was able to bring a handful to Antwerp in January 1564.[52] Some Flemings re-migrated from Halstead, Colchester and Norwich to Leiden in 1577, and in later years others followed from these towns and from Sandwich. Between 1575 and 1619 Leiden received 126 immigrants from England but, while many of them were engaged in textiles, few are likely to have been experienced in the English ways of making carded woollens.[53] The chief influence on the textile manufactures of Holland was that exerted by immigrants from the southern Netherlands.[54]

With the decline of the old woollen manufactures, the situation was radically changed. Emigration from the West-of-England region started relatively early. In 1591 the Privy Council ordered bonds to be taken from the sureties for Giles Field,[55]

> That he do not give any instructions or advize for anie maner of wollen clothe to be made out of Her Majesties domynyons, neither helpe, further, councell or procure any of Her Majesties subjectes to depart this realme for or about the makinge of wollen cloth in any contry or place out of Her Majesties domynyons; and that forthwith and from henceforth he doe and shall use all his best indevours to procure those two English weavers and all other Englishmen that are now in Pomerland and have anie skill in clothe makinge to retorne home againe into Englande with all covenyent speede.

Clothing was on the increase in Holland and some English weavers went there. In 1639 the Merchant Adventurers reminded the Privy Council 'howe many families are removed out of that county [Suffolk] into Holland'.[56] One party of workers in Kentish cloth migrated to the Palatinate in 1616 and another to Holland in 1640. Other woollen workers followed to the Palatinate.[57] It was said that 140 families of clothiers and similar tradesmen deserted Norfolk and Suffolk for Holland in 1635 and 1636, and that two or three thousand had settled in the Palatinate.[58] In 1640 the Root-and-Branch Petition spoke of 'multitudes, both clothiers, merchants, and others, who, being deprived of their ministers and overburthened with these pressures, have departed this kingdom to Holland and other parts, and have drawn with them a great manufacture of cloth and trading out of the land into other places where they reside'. In the words of the Grand Remonstrance, religious vexations and oppressions,[59]

lighting upon the meaner sort of tradesmen and artificers did impoverish many thousands and so afflict and trouble others, that great numbers to avoid their miseries departed out of the kingdom, some into New England and other parts of America, others into Holland, where they have transported their manufactures of cloth ... endangering the loss of that particular trade of clothing which hath been a plentiful fountain of wealth and honour to this nation.

It is difficult to say to what extent emigration was caused by religious oppression. Bishop Wren, who by no means confined his persecutions to the Norwich Flemings, was impeached for hounding out of his diocese three thousand nonconformists, many of them textile workers; but his defence was that they had been driven out by low wages and had gone to Holland to improve themselves.[60] What is beyond doubt is that, particularly in the Woodland and especially during the Eleven Years' Tyranny, many woollen workers of one sort and another drew up their stakes and made off for Holland, the Palatinate, New England and other states of Calvinistic or sectarian complexion.[61]

Wars also speeded up the migration of industries and of workers. While trade to Silesia and Poland was interrupted by the Thirty Years' War and other conflicts, the natives of those parts got English artificers to show them how to make cloth from locally grown wools. The resultant Sleazies had coarse and loosely spun and woven yarns, but they served. When the Civil War cut them off from supplies of West-of-England whites, the Merchant Adventurers took English wool to Rotterdam and had it spun and woven up there.[62] Once the Civil War was over, England counted her losses. In 1649 'the greate number of clotheworkers, weavers, dyers, cottoners and pressers repayring from England' to Holland, Hamburg, Altona and other parts of Europe excited comment. In 1650 Thomas Violet told the Committee of the Mint, 'Our golden fleece, which is our Indies, was devoured by the rapine of the soldiers, and great quantities of the remainder transported to our industrious neighbours the Netherlanders ... Our clothiers and workmen were by continual losses discouraged, and many of them forced to take up arms, or to forsake their dwellings, and even their native country, and set up their trade in foreign parts.' The City of London Committee on Trade reported to the Council of Trade in 1651, 'Our workmen are enticed or enforced beyond seas to become teachers or servants to strangers in the art of clothing'.[63] Bradshaw knew what he was talking about when he informed Thurloe about the situation in 1651 and 1655. Holland's cloth output had grown. She 'hath drawn from us considerable numbers of weavers, dyers, and clothworkers, now settled in Leyden and other towns ... by whose help they have considerably improved their skill in cloth' made in the English fashion with Spanish, Polish, Pomeranian and 'Lyckland' (Liège) wool with the necessary admixture of English. In Franstadt (Wschowa) and Lissa (Leszno), south-soutwest of Posen, 'prodigious' industry was producing 220,000 ordinary cloths and 150,000 rashes a year. Holland and Silesia between them now made most of the coarse and soldiers' cloths used there and in Brandenburg. The truth of this was confirmed by Downing, writing from the Hague in 1660, and the rise of the Leiden coarse woollen industry has been revealed by modern research.[64] The Restoration brought no respite, rather the reverse. More workers emigrated and 'set up the manufacture elsewhere'. In 1669 the Eastland Company complained, 'Great hath been the industry of strangers in Poland and Prussia in late years to advance their manufactures of cloth by procuring English workemen and stealing fullers' earth into those parts'.[65] Emigrants to New England started the production of linsey-woolseys, kerseys and coarse cloths.[66] In 1691 the decay of the old woollen industries in England was still attributed to the growth of German manufactures, which the Venetians now sold to Turkey, but also to increasing competition from our neighbours, who used English wool, and to the French prohibition on imports of our woollens.[67] Indeed, thanks to the development of permanent cultivation and the consequent improvement of fleeces in the Paris basin as far south as Berry, to the wider adoption of the fulling mill, to assiduous imitation of English and Dutch techniques, to a few immigrants from England and more from Holland, and to protectionist policies, the French no longer made their old 'dog's hair' cloths, but also *draps de Londres*.[68] Later on, workers from Leiden helped to spread these woollen manufactures to Denmark and Spain as well. In the early eighteenth century, too, John Coward of Frome introduced into Piedmont the making of cloth *'al vero uso inglese'*.[69] In such ways the art was diffused throughout the western world.

Significantly, it was not only from England that the diffusion took place. Holland was the first recipient of these techniques, but she could not retain them long. By 1647 she was being hit by competition from towns in Brabant, Limburg and other parts of the United Provinces, and also from Berg, Jülich, Verviers, Liège, Eupen, and Hodimont, where labour and fuel were cheaper.[70] No less noteworthy is that this dispersion was confined to the coarser of the English woollens; fine clothing, as Culpepper noted, remained 'a riches peculiar to this nation'.[71] The manufacture of the fine Worcester cloths died away only between the 1690s and the 1750s, and then in the face of competition from other fine textiles.[72] What was happening earlier was that the coarser manufactures were being driven out of southern England by newly invented, superior and more profitable ones.

The first of these innovations was that of the new Stroudwaters. About 1605 Thomas Webb and other Stroudwater clothiers started to make their cloths of more finely spun yarns, to give them a better dressing, and finally to dye them stammel or scarlet in a new way that made the colour faster. Having been dressed white, these new Stroudwaters were then boiled in 'hot likoures' and shrunk to the uttermost in the dye itself, with the result that although they had been woven fully broad, they finished only six quarters wide. Dressing was in two stages. Before dyeing and shrinking, the naps were raised by means of the newly invented mosing mills. Unlike the much censured gigmill, which was a powered metal rubber, the mosing mill raised the nap gently by working the cloth with 'millfulls' or sets of 'staffs' or batteries of small teasels, which were younger and less barbed than the king teasels usually employed in dressing cloth. After shearing, dyeing and shrinking, the cloths were then dressed a second time, with king teasels and a more perfect shearing. When first invented, the new Stroudwaters were sold mainly at local fairs, and not until about 1615 were they regularly sent up to the London market. Their sales were still rising when those of white cloths and the old Stroudwaters were on the decline.[73]

Another new carded woollen was the shag, duffel, blanketing or trucking cloth. Duffel was a heavy, closely woven two-and-two twill, heavily milled, and with the nap raised high and left shaggy; it was a 'broadcloth with its shag unshorn'. This kind of cloth was first invented in Duffel, in Brabant, and so called *duffels*. The manufacture was brought over the Dutch strangers and pursued by them for a while, especially in Colchester, whence it spread to Braintree, before finally finding (by 1663) a permanent home in Witney. By 1633 duffel of English making was already on sale on the Continent. Witney duffels were made seven quarters wide. At first they were intended mainly for trucking with the Red Indians and usually dyed red or blue for this purpose. But duffel also sold well in eastern Europe and was much worn by mariners and others who needed heavy outer clothing. Children's winter coats and caps were often made of it. Fine duffels were composed of fleece wool, but inferior ones had wefts of fell wools, noils and even coarse locks. Although Witney remained the chief centre, the industry was also found in Norwich, East Dereham, Romsey, Downton, Devizes, Totnes, Holford and elsewhere.[74].

Clothiers in Witney (and Coggs, Hailey, Curbridge and Finstock) also perfected the art of using fell wool wefts in kersey and other coarse blankets.[75]

Say-dyed cloth was a new invention. Christopher Potticary of Stockton, in the Wylye valley, seems to have been the chief innovator, around 1614. Although it started in the Chalk Country, say-dyeing was taken up far less there than in the

Cheese Country, in the Frome valley. Potticary's example was first followed here by William Brewer of Lullington, Christopher Brewer of Beckington, Robert Parker of Woolverton, Richard Pyat of Rode Mill, Thomas Horner of Clifford Mill and Richard Harbury of Freshford. Their claim, that 'the new manufacture of say-dyed cloth is by all approved to be a commendable invention', is borne out by an impartial report to the Privy Council saying, 'The cloth died in the say is both commodious and useful. The dye haveing endured the scowring and cleanseinge of the fulling mill continues the colour much better than that dyed after it is fulled and thickned.'[76]

Of much greater moment was the invention of Spanish cloth. The *nieuw draperie*, with wefts of Spanish wool and warps of *hierlands*, *inlands* or homegrown, started in Flanders somewhat before 1500 and soon spread to other parts of the Netherlands, largely because of savings in cost. Spanish wool on the quayside in Bruges was now not much more than half the price of English wool at Antwerp. So it was a good move to substitute Spanish in the wefts and *hierlands*, East Country and Pomeranian in the warps. As yet no way had been found of making Spanish warps and English wool was too dear for ordinary cloths. West Germany, France and Italy copied Flanders and took to making similar Spanish cloths.[77]

Possibly some of the 'cloths after the Flanders fashion' made by the Norwich Flemings, and even by the Sandwich, Canterbury and Maidstone ones, were really *Spaansche lakens* of this kind; but in any event few were ever produced.[78] That nothing came of the Southampton Walloons' request in 1567 for permission to make '*draps d'Armentière*'[79] was perhaps due to the setting afoot the very next year of a scheme to transplant this business to Coventry. Armentières, and Haubourdin later, made both '*oultrefines à platte lyste*' and '*oultrefines à crombe liste*', all being dyed in the wool in mingled colours to produce medleys. English documents speak of '*oultrefines*' and 'cromblistes', but intend *platte* and *crombe* list *oultrefines* respectively. In Armentières the former were composed of two thirds Spanish wool to one of English, mainly that from Chalk Country, Cotswold, Northwold and March sheep. These wools may have been blended in union yarns for both warp and weft. Since a crumpled list was generally taken to signify a union cloth with diversely composed warps and wefts, the *crombe listes* possibly had pure English warps and pure Spanish wefts. It seems to have been the intention to use Chalk Country and Northwold wools for the warps in Coventry, but no mention is made of Spanish wool, and we can only hazard the guess that the wefts were to be of Ryeland wool, the 'Leominster ore' the local clothiers habitually used. In Armentières the *oultrefines* were 'not thickned by myllis but by laboure of mens fete', and there were still plenty of foot-fullers in Coventry. Nevertheless, at least some of those made over here appear to have been milled. In 1569 nine Coventry clothiers were licensed to undertake *oultrefine* manufactures; in 1584 a further licence was granted to one man; and in 1601 two others obtained a grant for fifteen years. By

1571 'ulterfine Coventries' were being exported, mainly from London and largely to Danzig. They were charged with a lower rate of customs than other cloths, because they were a yard and half shorter, and not, it seems, because they were thought to contain some Spanish wool. This manufacture of flat-list ultrafines, with the accompanying wool-dyeing and cloth-dressing, took some hold in Coventry, but appears to have declined about the turn of the sixteenth and seventeenth centuries.[80]

The Norwich Flemings introduced the manufacture of *Spaansche dekens, couvertures d'Espaigne*, or 'Spanish rugs or blankets'. These had previously been made in the Netherlands and may have originated in Duffel.[81] The old Norwich blankets had noils and flocks in their wefts, these new ones, Spanish wool.[82] Norwich, however, appears not to have pursued this trade for long. When we meet these fabrics next, it is as Spanish rugs 'made in Inglond', 'of Englishe makinge',[83] and actually emanating from Witney. This we know from a cryptic reference, in an Exchequer account drawn up in 1578, to 'Oxon blanckettes alias Spannyssche rugges', of which the output was reckoned to be about 5,200 a year of pieces in breadths of from two to two-and-a-half yards and in lengths of between two and three.[84] Witney was undoubtedly the Oxfordshire town alluded to. Here Spanish blankets rapidly became an important part of the blanket industry that dominated the town and all the countryside within twenty miles' radius. Fine Witney blankets were made in three widths: from ten to twelve quarters for double beds, from seven to nine for single ones, and six for cots and such like. It is difficult to say how much Ryeland wool and how much Spanish went into the wefts of Witney Spanish blankets. The former was almost as soft and fluffy as the latter and served well enough. Bearing in mind that the warps were English, it seems likely these blankets were Spanish in structure rather than in composition.[85] Thanks largely to the waters of the Windrush, Witney blankets had an excellent whiteness, broken only by the familiar coloured stripes, usually blue or red, woven into each end in order to indicate dimensions.[86] The great secret of making Witney blankets lay in a special kind of hollow spinning.[87]

From Witney we turn to Taunton. In and after 1580 a merchant of this town by name of William Leonard was importing, by way of Bridgwater, Barnstaple, Topsham and Lyme Regis, and chiefly from Lisbon and San Sebastian, such commodities as woad, madder, Spanish taffetas and Spanish wool. Many of his various domestic dealings were with clothiers, feltmakers and dyers in Taunton, Wells, Trowbridge and other western towns. Some of his Spanish wool he sold to feltmakers and some to clothiers.[88] In particular, he made one or two sales of Spanish wool to Taunton clothiers in and about 1582.[89] As far as we know, however, the clothiers of the Vale of Taunton Deane rarely made any considerable amount of cloth either wholly or partly of Spanish wool. One exception to this rule was Leonard himself, or so it seems, for he apparently bought no wool other than Spanish, yet he sold some broadcloths described as being 'of my makinge'.[90] Nevertheless he was rather less interested in making cloths than in buying them. He dealt in sorted ware cloths from Taunton, sorted Bridgwaters, fine Readings,[91] caffas and stamins,[92] presumably from Norwich, and also in blue abbs and completed blue cloths such as sad blues, light skies, sad skies, light vesses, sad vesses and azures. These we know, and Leonard's dealings with clothiers in Edwardstone and Stoke-by-Nayland confirm it, were the speciality of the Woodland.[93] Amongst the notable purchases he made in the Woodland were the following: in 1580, from John Browne of 'Ederstone' (Edwardstone), Suffolk, clothier, twenty 'hole clothes Spanishe sorts'; and in the same year or within one or two after, '29 hole clothes and $\frac{1}{2}$ Spanishe sorts-Suffolks', and '15 hole clothes whereof 11 weare Spanish sorts Suffolks' and were, incidentally, exported from Lyme to Lisbon.[94] It also appears that Leonard supplied John Browne and John Winterflooode of 'Edderstone' and George Manle and Mr Cardinall of 'Stoke Nayland' with both woad and Spanish wool.[95] Cardinall and the others dyed the Spanish wool and made it into woofs for Spanish-sort Suffolks; but they also sold some of these dyed-in-the-wool Spanish abb yarns, in the form of ready-made abbs, back to Leonard, from whom they had bought the wool to make them. Leonard purchased from them abbs of sad blue, sad sky, light vesse, light sky and green seawater.[96] What he did with these is made clear by his description of eight whole broadcloths 'of my makinge': two sad blues, one red, one 'light vesse', two 'assures' and two 'sadde vesses' awaited shipment from Topsham.[97] The Woodland clothiers bought Leonard's Spanish wool and made Spanish-sort Suffolks, while Leonard for his part bought not only some of their Spanish-sort Suffolks but also their Suffolk-made Spanish abbs, which he wove into his own broadcloths. One swallow does not make a summer, but perhaps the most extraordinary thing about Leonard's transactions was that they were confided to paper in accounts that have survived the ages. Likely he was not the only merchant in those parts at that time to bring in Spanish wool, for in the early 1580s 'good quantities ... of Spanish woolles' were imported into the west. And Leonard was not alone there in taking to these new manufactures, for in 1583 and 1584 he himself sold substantial amounts of Spanish wool to a Thomas Flitte or Fleete of Sherborne, a town that became noted for its Spanish cloth.[98]

Adverting now to the Woodland and taking up the threads of the story there, we take heed that one of the Stoke-by-Nayland clothiers who bought Spanish wool from Leonard was Mr Cardinall. He was the only man in the accounts who 'had the master put upon him', as the saying went, and this suggests he was in a large way of business. Perhaps he was the Mr Cardinal of East Bergholt who was having fine short and long coloured Suffolk cloths sold in Antwerp in 1568.[99] In any event, the only 'fine' Suffolks one can conceive of would have been Spanish sorts. We guess Cardinal was the man who invented and gave his name to Spanish-sort Suffolks of the kind he, Browne, Manle, Winterfloode and probably many others in due course, made in Edwardstone, Stoke-by-Nayland

and elsewhere in the Stour valley. We guess his cloths were called Cardinals just as Benedict Webb's were known as Webbs and Jack of Newbury's as Winchcombes. No cloth by the name of Cardinal appears in any of the statutory regulations; but this can be explained by assuming it was subsumed under the general category of fine short Suffolks. Cardinals made their appearance under their own name in books of customs rates and similar lists just about 1570, when many were being exported, but little or nothing is heard of them after 1701. It may be thought an obstacle to accepting that Cardinals were a variety of Spanish-sort Suffolks that for customs purposes it took no fewer than six of them to reach the equivalent of one short cloth.[100] But this fact, so far from weakening our supposition, serves only to lend weight to it. Leonard bought no 'hole clothes' from Cardinal, none, that is, as long as double dozens.[101] From this we infer that Cardinals were dozens. Let us also suppose they contained, as many Spanish cloths did, two parts of Spanish wool to one of English, the latter being the warp and the former the weft. Then it would have taken six Cardinals to have made up the amount of English wool in a standard short, double dozen cloth. But the custom on cloth was only to compensate the Crown for the loss of customs on the English wool incorporated in it. As for the Spanish wool, customs had already been paid on it at the port of entry. What little we know about cloth prices is wholly consistent with our argument. In 1568 short fine Suffolks fetched from £10 to £12 10s. in Antwerp. In 1580 Leonard was paying £7 10s. each for 'hole clothes Spanishe sorts', and he was buying direct from the clothier in Suffolk.[102] It remains to explain the disappearance of Cardinals after 1701, and this could plausibly be done by saying that by then vastly improved Spanish cloths had appeared on the market, making Cardinals obsolete, so that they shared the fate of ordinary Suffolk cloths.

Just at the time when Leonard was engaged in the transactions we have described, in the years 1580–4, Benedict Webb was also in Taunton, and he was the inventor of Spanish medley cloth. According to his own, apparently accurate, account, about 1583, when he was not long out of his apprenticeship and living in Taunton, he invented two new fabrics, of which[103]

The second sort was a sort of medly cloth which Sir William Stone, a mercer in Chepside, delt with mee for, and cald them Spanish clothes, which are now knowne thorow the kingdume and in forraine parts by the name of Webbs cloth, and by that name are entred in the custom houses, which sort of cloth hath bin and is the most usefull of any other (in the jeneral). The immytation wherof hath added more perfection to the draperey of mixed culer cloth then all the statuts made sithence Edward the 3 time. And finding that the cullers then in use in this kingdum wear verry unfiting for the nobelity and gentrey of the kingdum, as alsoe of forrain parts, I devised divers and sundrey cullers, which at this daye is made common to all, and by which more cloth hath bin worne then in former ages, and with much more plesuer and content; which manner of drapperey is now exseedingly incresed in many parts of the kingdum and in which I contenew to this daye.

Webb's claim to have been the first to make these medley cloths is upheld by John Aubrey;[104] and his statement that he was engaged in making them in Kingswood, whither he had removed in 1593 or before, is corroborated by the testimony of his neighbours and countrymen in 1618, that 'suche hath bin his industry and singular discerninge in all poyntes concerninge the mistery of drapery of wollen cloth that we have not knowen hym equalled by any', and by the report in 1630 of 'the medlie clothiers dwellinge at Kingeswood ... and thereabouts'.[105]

Webb and his imitators followed the practice of striking an abb of Spanish or Ryeland wool, or a mixture of the two, on a warp of home-grown, chiefly Ryeland, March, Southdown and Chalk Country. Spanish wool, being short and soft, had to be carded more and with a new and much finer kind of cards. It was then spun into yarns of very fine gauge that had to be woven all the more closely, resulting in a light-weight cloth with a finer, smoother, softer weft that almost obscured the coarser and stronger warp. Spanish medleys were dyed in the wool in various colours. After carding, these wools were blended and scribbled by specialist scribblers. The end products were attractively coloured medleys with distinctive narrow lists.[106]

According to Aubrey, Mr John Ashe was the second man to make Spanish medleys, in the 1620s, in Freshford, where he had chosen to settle for this very purpose. But Aubrey seems to have mistaken his informant. Webb said as early as 1618 that his cloth had already been widely copied. What is true, and what Aubrey ought to have written, is that Ashe was the second innovator in Spanish medleys and started the second generation of them in England. By the middle of this century Netherlands clothiers had overcome the difficulties in making Spanish warps and had perfected a wholly Spanish cloth. About 1650 John Ashe brought 'Dutch' technicians over to Freshford to teach these new methods. It was some time after this that his younger brother Samuel told Aubrey a pound of wool now made twice as much cloth as before the Civil Wars, which would have been no more than the solemn truth if the comparison intended had been with the time before the introduction of Spanish cloth. Ashe's invention, though not original, was important, and gave a correspondingly handsome profit. In Aubrey's words, Ashe 'gott a great estate by it *tempora Caroli primi* ... He was the greatest cloathier in his time.'[107] John Ashe was followed by Paul Methwin (Methuen) of Bradford, who married his daughter and inherited his business, and by William Brewer, who had been making say-dyed cloth in Lullington since at least 1634 and had removed thence to Trowbridge some time before 1651. Methuen brought over a 'Dutch' yarnmaker to improve his spinning and likewise earned the name of 'the greatest clothier of his time'. Brewer followed suit and in 1674 took on thirty-two 'Dutch' clothing workers, mostly refugees from the Franco-Dutch war, to teach the art of making and dressing Spanish cloth in the Netherlands fashion and more particularly the use of 'Dutch' cards and their methods of spinning. He was highly successful too and drove 'the greatest trade for medleys of any cloathier in England'.[108]

Spanish medley clothing in the Cheese Country thus developed as an offshoot of the same industry in the Vale of Berkeley and the north of the Butter Country. It took root in the Frome valley and thereabouts, in the congenial soil created by the say-dyed cloth manufacturers.[109] Say-dyeing was not in itself an innovation with great potential, but it did foster the dyeing and dressing skills needed in making Spanish medleys.[110] Spanish cloth seems to have been made in Sherborne ever since the 1580s, when Leonard was selling his Spanish wool there. From here the manufacture apparently spread to Shepton Mallet. According to Richard Watts, who published his poem in 1641, Shepton's glory lay in its manufacture of cloths, 'some of our English, some of Spanish wooll', and Spanish medleys were indeed made in Shepton, Batcombe and district.[111] Medley clothiers from here appear to have migrated north to the Frome valley and beyond. By the 1650s they had reached Bromham.[112] Spanish medleys thus became the chief sort of carded woollens made in the region roughly bounded by Sherborne, Castle Cary, Shepton Mallet, Frome, Freshford, Bradford-on-Avon, Chippenham, Netherstreet, Melksham, Warminster, Wincanton and Shaftesbury. Bradford, Frome and Trowbridge, in particular, grew apace as centres of the new industry.[113] From the selfsame point of origin, the manufacture of narrow-list, coloured Spanish medleys had spread, by 1636, to the Culm valley in the West Country, to Tiverton, Cullompton, Kentisbeare, Broadhembury, Plymtree, Uffculme, Culmstock and district.[114] Meanwhile, in the Vale of Berkeley, from its point of growth in Kingswood, the new medley manufacture had been diffused by 1663 or before at least as far as North Bradley and Wotton-under-Edge, and by the end of the century southwards as far as Uley and right into the east of the Bristol District.[115] Thus by far the greater part of the old West-of-England region had turned over from English whites to Spanish medleys. In addition, by 1627, Spanish medley making had been taken up in Cranbrook, though not, it seems, with any great or lasting success,[116] and it certainly failed to spread to the rest of the textile district of the Wealden Vales. Spanish medleys thus remained almost exclusively the business of the Cheese and Butter countries, the Vale of Berkeley, the Culm valley and the Bristol District. The work of Leonard, Webb, Ashe, Methuen and Brewer bore fruit in the grand revival of the West-of-England woollen manufacturing region.

Spanish medleys were a huge success. By 1633 men had seen them 'consume' Kentish cloths and Chalk Country medleys.[117] By 1639 the new cloth had 'so farre improved and gained such repute with the stranger' that it had 'now become one of the best and most requested manufactures of cloth in this kingdome'. Soon it had 'become the greatest of all the draperies'.[118] By 1640 it was selling for not far short of twice the price of West-of-England broadcloth, and this despite Spanish wool being cheaper than English. Yet cloth for cloth it paid less duty on being exported, because it contained less English wool.[119] Spanish medleys were in great request in all the markets, in the Eastland, in Spain and Portugal, in the Levant and even in the Netherlands, which had nothing quite the same of their own making. During the period when the Dutch had mastered the art of spinning Spanish warp and the English had not, fine Dutch Spanish cloths sold well in England; but this was no more than a temporary setback. Home demand for our Spanish medleys recovered and absorbed most of the output.[120] The manufacture continued to flourish until the middle of the eighteenth century, after which it began to be replaced by that of the 'cassimere', which was quite a different kind of Spanish cloth. Cassimeres were invented by Francis Yerbury of Bradford-on-Avon and patented by him in 1766. They were thin, narrow cloths, and made in two varieties. Both were twilled, but one had a flat wale and the other a round. Further variations were achieved by the use of different twills and yarns.[121]

Instead of going over to medleys, the Stroudwater district developed its own characteristic Spanish cloths. By 1677 the new Stroudwaters had been transformed again by the use of Spanish wool. The Spanish Stroudwaters had both warps and wefts of Spanish wool mainly, but mixed with a little English, some Leominster often being put into the abbs. Eventually, by about 1750, English wool was excluded from all but the lists of the cloth, and even there was mostly noils. Otherwise the Spanish Stroudwaters were much the same as the former English ones, and were dyed and coloured in the same way.[122] By 1682 some Worcester clothiers had likewise switched to Spanish wool for their fine cloths. These Spanish Worcesters were cloths of the finest quality, with warps and wefts composed exclusively of the best Spanish wool. They were mostly sold undyed and undressed, immediately after fulling, in the traditional Worcester way.[123] By 1684, too, a few Norwich clothiers were making some all-Spanish cloth.[124] Some Salisbury and Wilton ones took a similar course at this time or not long after.[125] It even looks as though some Kidderminster clothiers were making Spanish cloths in the 1710s.[126]

There was thus no single variety of Spanish cloth, even in England and before the eighteenth century: there were Spanish blankets, Spanish Suffolks, Spanish medleys, Spanish Stroudwaters, Spanish Worcesters, Spanish Salisburys, Norwich Spanish cloths and perhaps a few other minor varieties. It was the competition of many Spanish cloths that drove the making of English ones out of all the oldest and best manufacturing districts. As a result, English wool, with the minor exception of a little Leominster and Southdown, was virtually excluded from all the better carded woollens. Already by about 1640 they only exaggerated slightly who said that anyone who wore a cloak, coat or suit made from woollen cloth as sold at Blackwell Hall, consumed thereby not one dram of English wool.[127] But as we have seen already, much of the wool formerly clothed in the more southerly parts of the kingdom was now sent north of the Trent, and especially to the Peak-Forest Country, whither the manufacture of inferior carded woollens now largely migrated.

One use found for inferior wools no longer in request for dress cloths was in the making of rugs and carpets. In the earlier part of our period few homes had floor carpets and then usually foreign imports. Neither tapestry carpets nor the hand-knotted 'Turkey work' pile carpets, such as were being made in Windsor in 1553, in Norwich in 1583, in York in 1595 and in Bradford in 1639, nor even the carpets woven in Wilton about 1675, were suitable for floors; they were for cushion covers, chair seats, upholstery and covers for chests, hutches, tables and similar items of furniture. Some extraordinarily large hand-knotted Turkey work carpets were used for floor-coverings, but the labour costs involved were usually excessive, for each knot had to be formed separately by laying a thrum across two warp ends, folding it back under and inwards, and drawing its two ends up between the two warp ends.[128] Other coarse wools were utilised by specialist rugmakers or rugweavers for coach, bed, cradle and other similar rugs. They were woven in manifold twists, often six-ply. Rugweavers were at work in Salisbury by 1625, in Norwich by 1660, in Berkeley and Kingswood by 1663, in Colchester by 1670, in Reading by 1676 and in Calne by 1726.[129]

# 4

## WORSTEDS

The East Norfolk worstedweavers now made hardly any of their old-fashioned worsted cloths. As early as 1541 we find them well aware that 'straungers not being borne under the kinges dominion doe make and weave sayes, russelles, worsteds' and other cloths for sale in England. Worsted, we are told in 1554, 'ys nowe at this presente almost wholly decayed and brought out of estimacion and very little worne either within this realme or in any other forreine realmes'.[1] In 1564 worsted cloths 'nowe and were owte of estimation and vente'.[2] By 1580 the very wearing of them was 'now out of use'.[3] In 1618 it was regarded as remarkable 'that a fewe worsteeds have byne laytlye made' by a couple of manufacturers. In 1711 output was no higher.[4] Demand was slight and largely supplied by Continental rockspun counterfeits, especially by St Omer and Béthune ones.[5] As for the worstedweavers, they went on turning to ever newer and more profitable ways of weaving worsted, to fresh fabrics that were 'but branches of the same tree'.[6]

Well before 1503 and right up until 1581 or later, worstedweavers were making both broad and narrow bustians.[7] These were not wholly unlike the old worsted cloths and served much the same purposes. According to the worstedweavers themselves, 'A worsteed was wrought with fower treadles. To make thereof a bustian is to weave with three of the same treadles.'[8] Weaving with three treadles means a three-shaft weave and implies a two-and-one twill.

The next invention was the worsted camlet. This was a very old weave and camlets had been a regular article of commerce in western Europe ever since the thirteenth century or beyond.[9] Some were of wool, some of goat's hair, some of silk, some with linen warps or wefts, some dyed in the yarn and some in the piece. Many were hot-pressed, and some were watered (camleted) to produce a moire or wavy finish, being sprinkled with water before pressing, so that their pronounced threads were permanently bent and deformed into discrete waves. Similar effects could be achieved by inserting iron moulds into the presses along with the cloths. Some camlets, too, were figured by a patterned interchanging of warp and weft on the face of the cloth. Nevertheless, all camlets were fundamentally the same. They were all plain weaves, with their warps, and often also their wefts, composed of crewel or some other thick, rounded twist.[10] In their enigmatic way, the worstedweavers explained how camlets were woven:

'A worsteed was wrought with fower treadles ... To make the same a double chamblet is to use the two right foote treadles. To make yt single is to use the two left foote treadles.'[11] We assume that for worsted cloths and worsted says the old English hand-loom was fitted with four headles worked by four treadles; that the warp was entered in regular order; that the tie-up was that ordinarily used for two-and-two twills, with headles 1 and 2 tied to treadle 1, headles 2 and 3 to treadle 2, headles 3 and 4 to treadle 3, and headles 4 and 1 to treadle 4; and that the treadles were depressed in the usual order, first the outside right, second the outside left, third the inside right, and fourth the inside left. In weaving camlets, either the two right foot or the two left foot treadles were used. Either way a plain weave resulted. But what the worstedweavers purposely refrained from disclosing was that different weft yarns were used according to whether one proposed to work with the left foot or with the right foot treadles. The essential distinction between single and double camlets was that the single had a thick, rotund twist in the warp only, while the double had it in both weft and warp. In a single camlet the weft was dwarfed by the warp, but not so in the double.

Fig. 6 Draft for a two-and-one twill (warp black).

Worsted or Norwich camlets[12] were being made by the city worstedweavers in 1530 or before.[13] By 1547 they were on sale in Antwerp.[14] This same manufacture of broad and narrow, single and double camlets continued to flourish in Norwich throughout and beyond our period,[15] and by the early eighteenth century had spread to many other towns in East Norfolk.[16] We cannot always clearly distinguish worsted from jersey camlets; but on the other hand there is some reason to believe a few worsted camlets were sold under the name of grograins;[17] and the great success of worsted camlets is beyond all doubt.

From their original single and double camlets the worstedweavers developed a number of varieties with new and distinctive names. These inventions are best described by the weavers themselves:[18]

> A buffyn, a cattalowne, and the pearle of bewty ar all one cloathe; a peropus and paragon all one ... The paragon, peropus and philiselles may be affirmed to be double chamblet, the difference beinge onely the one was double in the warpe and the other in the uff. Buffyn, cattalowne, and pearl of bewty etc. may be affirmed single chamblet, differing onely in the breadth ... A worsteed was wrought with fower treadles ... To make the same a double chamblet is to use the two right foote treadles. To make yt single is to use the two left foote treadles. To make this a philiselle, a peropus, a paragon or a buffyn is but to alter the breadth and to make them double, treble or single in the striken; and to make this buffyn a cattalowne is to twister a thrid of one coullor with a thrid of another and strike yt with another coullor. To make the same a pearl of bewty is to make yt stript by coullours in the warpe and tufted in the striken.

A buffen or bovine, then, as its name implied, was a single camlet of the old kind, only narrower. The worsted buffins the worstedweavers started to make in 1587 were modelled on the jersey ones previously invented by the Norwich Flemings and followed their dimensions, being thirteen or fourteen yards long and half an ell wide.[19] In their competition against jersey ones,[20] worsted buffins enjoyed a large measure of success. Both kinds, however, went out of fashion in the 1620s.[21]

Worsted cattaloons were buffins with yarns of two different colours doubled and twisted in the warp and with a weft of a third hue. Some were changeable cloths, i.e. their coloration varied according to the direction and angle of view. Worsted cattaloons made their first appearance in 1606 and went on being woven in Norwich until some time in the eighteenth century.[22]

The pearl of beauty (or pearl and beauty) was like a cattaloon except that it was 'tufted in the striken', i.e. a secondary and looped weft was introduced at intervals, and the loops cut to form rows of tufts. Also, being striped in the warp, as some of the cattaloons were, and struck with a third colour, the pearl of beauty had a variegated horizontal stripe. When worsted pearls of beauty were invented is not exactly known, but it was no later than September 1617, for on the last day of that month the effects of a recently deceased worstedweaver named Paul Geyton included, along with the more commonplace buffins, nine pieces 'called Pearles' and four 'called Pearles of one other sorte'. The appraisers, it will be noticed, used a form of words suggesting they were dealing with unfamiliar fabrics.[23] The very next year the Norwich Walloons brought out their own kinds of pearl of beauty to compete with the worsted ones,[24] but none of these cloths continued in production for much over half a dozen years.

Barracans, probably made of goat's hair, were still being imported into Leghorn from North Africa in the mid-sixteenth century.[25] When some of the Norwich worstedweavers started making a somewhat similar cloth in worsted, they also changed the old name slightly to 'paragon', which was a better one to sell under. Paragons were double camlets with four warp threads in each reed dent and wefts of either double or triple twists, on account of which they were classed as either two or three-thread paragons. To render them more attractive to the eye, some had their wefts in two or three colours, and some were stitched, i.e. a secondary weft appeared somewhat briefly and infrequently on the face of the cloth. To make them even more showerproof, they could first be boiled in water and then mangled, so leaving them compacter and smoother. Made in these ways, in various colours, paragons were as resplendent as useful. Their manufacture, which worstedweavers had commenced by about 1618 or earlier, persisted still in the first half of the eighteenth century.[26]

A peropus was in most respects similar to or 'all one' with the three-thread paragon, only it could have quadruple twists in the weft. Peropus was first heard of in Norwich in 1613. Two years later worsted peropus manufacture was regulated. The broadest sort was to be twenty-four yards long and one wide, with 620 warp threads; the second sort three-quarters of a yard wide; and the narrowest half-a-yard and one-and-a-half nails. From 1615 in the city and from 1617 in Worstead, the manufacture of white, coloured and changeable worsted peropus prospered.[27]

When the filoselle was first invented by the Norwich Dutch in 1607, it was so called because its weft was composed of filoselle crewel. The worstedweavers copied it almost at once, in worsted and with worsted instead of floss silk crewel, and made it in Norwich and Worstead. Filoselle was a species of double camlet, with twofold wefts of crewel. All pieces were made twenty-four yards long. Their breadths were at first regulated in Flemish ells, but in 1613 English equivalents were used. One type was three-and-a-half quarters wanting half-an-inch broad, and the other three-quarters plus one inch. At their first invention, broad filoselles had 1,920 ends and narrow ones 1,760, but almost immediately a reduction was made to 1,680 and 1,084 respectively.[28]

By 1668 Canterbury had become the only other part to make worsted camlets.[29] But worsted camlets were far from being the only ones on the market. Many Continental ones, especially silk and tinselled varieties, continued to be imported,[30] and Norwich and several other English towns made camlets of materials other than worsted. Camlets as a class enjoyed an enormous vogue for centuries. They were used for bodices, breeches, drawers, cloaks, gowns and jackets. Lined with silk they made excellent bed-curtains and hangings. Paragons were especially good for petticoats, bodices and such like, for upholstery, curtains, valances and other soft furnishings, and above all for cassocks, undergraduates' gowns, cloaks, coats, suits, surtouts and any garment the better for being showerproof; peropuses for cassocks and cloaks; buffins for petticoats and gowns; cattaloons for women's and children's clothes; and filoselles for petticoats. Worsted versions of these varieties seem to have served all those purposes, and worsted paragons, peropuses and simple camlets were highly regarded for riding cloaks and hoods.[31]

Worsted satin was the next great invention. Amongst the Continental manufactures that by 1540 had most helped to oust the old worsted cloths, were the satins and reverse satins made in Lille and district and perhaps elsewhere but after the fashion of Lille. The worstedweavers and the Norwich citizens were additionally disturbed by the knowledge that these fabrics contained combing wool, which they took, largely mistakenly it would seem, to be the Norfolk wool from the Marshland to which they laid exclusive claim. Thereupon Thomas Marsham, mayor of Norwich, joined with John Corbet esquire and with five aldermen and six citizens and merchants to bring to the city the manufacture of three fabrics from Lille. These enterprising men took the initiative 'at their greate costes and chardges, as well in bringing of certeine strangers from the partes beyonde the seas . . . as also in making of loombes and all provision for the same, and also . . . added unto them eight persons of the most discrete and worthy men of the misterye of worstedd weaving within the sayd citie.' This company 'not onely made russels sattens, satten reverses, and fustian of Naples within . . . Norwiche, of Norfolke woolles, but also . . . learned and taught other citizens and inhabitantes of the sayd citie to make the same in suche good and perfect maner that muche better russels sattens, sattens reverses and fustians of Naples and such like, and for the easier prises' were made within the city than in parts beyond the seas. *Rijssel* is the Netherlands name for Lille, which was still largely Netherlands-speaking. By the Act of 1554 incorporating the Russells Company, the cloths were to be called Norwich satins and Norwich fustians, but in practice, though reverse satins were occasionally referred to as 'satins' and some varieties of them had their own particular names, these satins and reverse satins were always generally known as 'russells'. Their manufacture in Norwich had already been well established by 1547, and had been in preparation and development for months or years before that, so it was far too late to change names.[32]

Satins are cloths in which the warp predominates over and almost completely covers the weft. Each weft thread intersects the warp once and once only in each repeat, so that the face of the cloth has an extraordinary smoothness that can be still further enhanced by pressing. There are three main types of perfect satin weave: the five, ten and thirteen-end ones; their intersections both of warp and of weft are all equidistant. But the satin weave most frequently employed is the imperfect eight-end one. This gives a good, though slightly uneven, distribution of intersections, and has the advantage that its very imperfection helps to blur the appearance of the twill upon the surface. As all satins have their warps thrown mainly on the face of the cloth, it is usual to weave them face down. In this way only one headle out of many need be lifted at any one time, instead of all but one. All satins, however, require selvages of plain weave along each side of the web in order to prevent the weft being drawn back and the edges made uneven. Two extra pairs of headle shafts are thus needed at the back of the harness, and also separate small selvage rolls or bobbins to accommodate the longer warp necessary for the plain weave of the selvages. It was such 'russell hevels' (or headles) that distinguished the special 'satten looms' that in Norwich were permitted only to members of the Russells Company.[33]

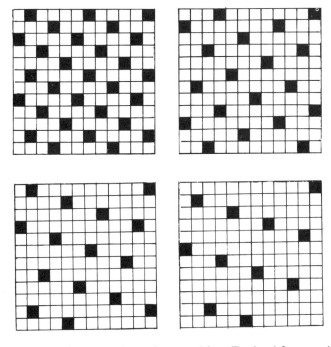

Fig. 7 Drafts for 5-end, 8-end, 10-end and 13-end satins (warp black).

Silk satins were always imported into England from various parts of the world in considerable numbers. Some of those from Italy contained a proportion of gold-and-silver tinsel threads, and some from Bruges had sham tinsel. But this city's typical product, 'satin of Bridges', ordinarily had a silk warp and a linen weft, and was therefore relatively inexpensive.[34] Rijssel, Lannoy and Armentières also made Bridges or similar linen and silk satins, but these three towns, and later perhaps also Amiens and Abbeville, turned their attention more to satins incorporating tops yarns. Armentières and Lannoy certainly came to make 'satincts wulgairement appelez demy ostades'. These so-called half-worsteds seem to have had wefts of linen and warps of tops and probably rockspun.[35] The original russells almost certainly included some with these counterfeit worsted yarns in them, but they formed a class of weave irrespective of the fibres they were made of. Russells were waled (or wealed) satins or reverse satins; they had a wale on their surface, at the intersections of warp and weft, that still showed even after calendering.[36]

Norwich russells were unique in that they were made wholly of 'rockspun yarn alias worsted yarn'.[37] This was why the worstedweavers' and russells companies had overlapping memberships and why they for long held joint inquisitions and gave joint verdicts.[38] Both broad and narrow russells were made, but then broad meant only three quarters of a yard.[39] Worsted russells were highly successful. By the late 1560s the art of making them had been diffused not only to towns in the immediate vicinity of the city but also to more distant parts of East Norfolk.[40] By 1676 worsted russells were also being made in Finningham, in the Woodland, and by early next century in Stepney.[41]

Norwich russells were by no means unchanging. Although only worsted ones were made at first, company members were free to use what fibres they liked. By 1591 some were making silk or mixed russells, with silk warps and worsted wefts, and in 1630 hair russell was invented.[42] Innovations in design were likewise made. In 1614 double russells were invented.[43] Doubled warps gave them extra weight and sheen. Perhaps by 1598, certainly by 1635, 'laced russells alias laced russell satins' had arrived. One of the earliest, if not the first, to make these was a man named Leonard Lynsey.[44]

Rijssel and other Continental towns had previously made *satins renversés* or *revêches*,[45] and the Russells Company copied these in worsted.[46] These reverses, as they were often called, were not simply satins made in reverse, with the weft predominating over the warp. This would have been pointless. In fact the word *revêche* meant 'contrary' or even 'cantankerous' rather than reverse, and reverses were figured satins, woven with two harnesses, with damask effects, which were obtained by having one harness for the design and one for the ground. Passed through the headles of both harnesses, the warp could then be raised for the ground and for the pattern simultaneously. Thus either the warp or the weft threads could be made to predominate on one side or the other. When the weaving was arranged to bring both warp and weft side by side in patterned shapes on the front of the fabric, the weft being tied down by the warp and the warp by the weft, a wide range of geometrical designs could be made. Different colours could be used for warp and weft, and these would bring out the design well, but the effect came mainly from the warp or weft threads being on one side or the other, so that they were contrary to each other and showed in contrasting lights. These cloths, then, were what were sometimes called 'foot-figured' or 'foot-damasks', because made on a pedal loom. They were a species of *satin damassé*, self-patterned satin.

In Norwich these russells satin reverses were seldom so called. Occasionally they were referred to as 'figured russells', but most usually as 'durants', 'durances', 'durables', 'durettos' or some such, on account of the permanence of their patterns, which not even bleaching would have removed. 'Durances and damasks' were regarded as forming a single class of what were known technically as 'branched cloths'. Some were made of dyed yarns and woven in colours, presumably contrasting ones, but most durances appear to have been monochromatic and piece-dyed. Several kinds of durance were made. The Norwich dyers, who were almost alone in sticking to the name 'reverse', passed judgment at various times on 'satten reverses otherwyse scallopp shells, durables and branched cloths', and on 'olyot hole and every other braunched clothe'. Francis Smalpeece, a Norwich textile wholesaler, referred to 'mountaines, mackerelles, skallopes, ollyotts, which fower goe under the name of durances'.[47] As a class, durances first appear in the records about 1580;[48] but less attention was paid to the class than to its members. Mackerel and scallop shells are still familiar patterns, but not mountains.[49] Eyelets were self-patterned cloths of a different kind. Worsted mountain is recorded in 1584 and was still being made in the seventeenth century,[50] but the other patterns were seldom made in worsted. Indeed, it emerges that members of the Russells Company never produced great numbers of the satin reverses they had introduced.

Nevertheless, all told, the company had considerable success. In the period 1558–64 it was turning out between 250 and 560 pieces of satin and reverses a year, in 1577–82 between 1,600 and 4,000. Business then declined, but recovered well in 1616–18, thanks, perhaps, to the invention of double russells.[51] Russells were used for petticoats, spring and summer coats, scholars' gowns, lawyers' bags, men's vests and waistcoats, women's boot and shoe uppers and a variety of other purposes. Their manufacture persisted into the eighteen century.

The other cloth introduced into England by the Russells Company was a kind of velours called fustian of Naples. Velours have to be woven on special looms, for they have dense piles, which more often than not are cropped level. These piles may be said to grow out of the ground webs. Warp-pile velours, which are usually called velvets and are often made in silk, have a second warp formed into loops on the surface of the cloth, so creating a pile. Weft-pile velours are similar, only their loops are formed by a second weft floating over the ground. Lucca and other Italian or Neapolitan towns, followed by Lyons, Tours and some places in Spain and the Netherlands, made velours in silk and as velvets, with which they supplied all parts of the western world.[52] But the Netherlanders made more of that was usually called *tripe de velours*, or *tripe*, *trijp* or 'tripe' for short. Tripes were genuine velours and commonly had linen grounds and jersey, silk or mingled silk and jersey piles.[53] Fustians of Naples, otherwise 'fustinapes' or 'anapes', were a kind of pile-on-pile, weft-pile velours originally devised, apparently, in the kingdom of Naples, and customarily made there in silk. Later on they were produced in the Netherlands as tripes. However composed, they were always true fustians. The ground was a two-and-two twill. Each pile pick passed successively under one end of the ground, then as a float over four ends, then under another end, and then as a float over six ends, and so on. But every single pick in turn was equally out of phase with both the preceding and the succeeding one, so that each four-end float had a six-end battened against it, and vice versa. This arrangement resulted in an unbroken succession in all directions of alternating short and long loops, the combination of which gave rise to two levels of pile, which might then be cut to give the appearance of a continuous field of almost hemispherical clusters. Such cloths, renamed Norwich fustians, were woven in worsted by members of the Russells Company in lengths of fourteen or fifteen yards and to a width of half an ell. Fustians of Naples generally sold well, being highly suited for dress and other goods, but, despite the company, claims, Norwich fustians enjoyed only a limited commercial success, and it may be that their members failed wholly to master all the techniques involved in their manufacture.[54]

No greater success attended the Russells Company's mockadoes or the worsted tufted buffins (narrow tufts),[55] but worsted carrels met a favourable response. Carrels (*carrelés*, *carletten*) were dress velours of Flemish origin. They had a ground of doubled and twisted yarn and a pile formed into squares in such a way that their pattern somewhat resembled a tiled surface; hence the name *étoffes à carreaux* or *carrelés*.[56] From 1574 onwards some russells men, and before long other weavers, copied these carrels in worsted and sold them as worsted carrels. Then, in 1633 or shortly before, more highly pitched ones were introduced. These worsted carrel paramounts had twenty-five reed dents and three ends in a dent. Carrels and paramounts were woven with a warp pile on a specially fitted velours loom.[57] To make allowance for the extra take-up for the loops, the pile warp had to be about six times as long as the ground one, and therefore needed a separate roller, or even two rollers, mounted high up above the ground-warp roller. Two harnesses were also fitted and the two warps entered upon them independently. Furthermore a special velvet breast roller was required to protect the pile from being crushed. This was a lidded outer roller with a smaller and inner roller to receive the pile. The weaver made a short length of the ground with the pile warp also woven in. Then the pile warp was raised alone and velours rods of smooth flat wire inserted into the shed, whereupon a few more ground shoots were made in order to secure the pile and the rods. Then the weaver cut the pile by drawing across his trevette, which ran along a fine groove in the velours rod. Obviously, the trevette and its blade had to be most finely and nicely adjusted; it had to be 'as right as a trevette'. The pile cut and the tufts formed, the velours rods were free to be removed and a fresh section could be woven. In making carrels, the pile warp was, at regular vertical and horizontal intervals and for short spaces, left unraised and woven into the ground, so as to create a rectangular grid of lengthwise and transverse voids in the pile. These carrels were thus a species of voided velours.

The next fabric to be converted to worsted was the flowered damask, often simply called damask. Unlike reverses, durances and other 'foot-work', these damasks were made on a drawloom. This had a monture consisting of a

comber-board, pulley box and cords, leashes weighted with lead strips called
lingoes, tail cords, a simple and a pair of guides, all of which, when operated
manually by a draw-boy, replaced the harnesses of ordinary looms and
performed tasks they could not undertake. With a drawloom, the designer could
give himself full rein. Setting up the loom was skilled work, but operating it was
not, so fine, bold patterns could readily be woven and plain, twill and satin
weaves all combined in one and the same fabric. The damasks we speak of had
satin grounds, while the extra weft threads were bound down by means of a twill
weave.

Silk damasks had long been made in Florence and other Italian cities. By the
sixteenth century, many damasks, largely linen ones, were being woven in
Flanders, and Flemish emigrants carried their arts to Amsterdam and London.
But few linen damasks, and even fewer silk ones, were even then made in either
London or the English provincial towns. England continued to rely mainly on
imports of these cloths.[58] Of all the English towns the Flemings settled in,
Norwich was the one where they established damask manufactures most firmly,
and there they produced almost exclusively union damasks with linen warps and
jersey wefts. It was from the Norwich Flemings and their union damasks that
the city and other East Norfolk worstedweavers learned to make worsted
damasks.[59] The first record of worsted damask in proceedings in the mayor's
court was in 1584, and of worsted stitched damask in 1585. In 1584, too, a
probate inventory shows damask had been made by a worstedweaver in
Pockthorpe, which was just outside the city. Assuming the art was diffused
from the city to the country, it seems not unreasonable to suppose worsted
damask was born in the first two or three years of this decade.[60] Henceforth
worsted damasks, broad and narrow, white and coloured, some stitched, and
some changeable, were numbered amongst the leading products of the
worstedweavers of Norwich,[61] and likewise of those in other East Norfolk
towns.[62] By the middle of the seventeenth century, too, this manufacture had
spread to the distant satellite town of Mildenhall, in the Breckland.[63] These
worsted flowered damasks, or damask flowers (unlike the worsted flowers,
which still went on as before), were made on drawlooms and followed the
Flemish damask flowers in having large flowery designs.[64] They were not much
less silky than silk damasks and could well be used for dress, especially for
jerkins and men's suitings, and also for hangings and curtains for beds and
windows.[65]

Next came worsted calamanco. This was woven in a broken twill or satin
weave, striped in white and various colours in the warp, with four or five threads
to a reed dent, and struck with different colours. The variegated coloration of
the warp gave rise to horizontal stripes, various parts of which then acquired
different hues and shades according to what colour of weft they were struck
with, resulting in a bright and lustrous cloth, a swatch of which looked like
nothing so much as a chestful of medal ribbons. Unless intended for men's

wear, calamanco was glossed by hot-pressing and often glazed by a coating of beeswax and perhaps by burnishing with a highly polished flint rubber. Calamancoes were used for waistcoats, jerkins, breeches, petticoats, sashes and soft furnishings. If their colours were defective, the pieces were dyed black and then often served for under-petticoats.[66] Calamancoes were first made shortly before 1594, seemingly as a riposte to printed Indian calicoes.[67] Specifically 'worsted calimankoes' were recorded in 1603. They soon won a permanent place in the range of Norwich manufactures.[68] By 1692 or 1694 flowered calamancoes had appeared, and by 1724 shaded and sprigged ones. Flowered ones were heavily brocaded, often in white, and sprigged ones were not much dissimilar. Shaded calamancoes, as their name implies, had gradual successions from darker to lighter shades of the same colour.[69] The manufacture about this time of a number of cheap mock calamancoes scarcely affected sales of the genuine article.[70]

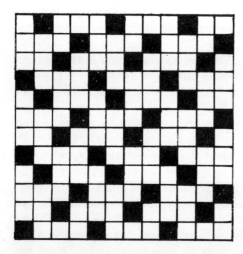

Fig. 8 Draft for one kind of broken one-and-three twill (warp black).

Philip and Cheyney was a cloth whose name has often been misunderstood. The old expression 'Philip and Cheyney' meant much the same as our 'Tom, Dick and Harry', but they err who conclude that the fabric was common, plain or coarse. *Chaine* is French for warp or chain, so to describe a cloth as 'chainies' is to imply both warp and weft are made of hardspun chain yarns.[71] Philip stands for the old French *felpe*, akin to the Italian *felpa*, meaning *peluche* in modern French, *pluche* or *pluis* in Netherlands, *Plüsch* in German, and plush in

English. *Phelpe et chaine* was thus a plush on a ground of warp yarns. In Netherlands it was *Phelp en schering*. English customs officials wrote 'phelps', but the race that made *Infanta de Castile* into Elephant and Castle christened this plush Philip and Cheyney, which suggests they had the thing itself at the hands of the Walloons rather than of the Dutch.

Plush is a type of velours with a pile longer and stiffer than usual, somewhat thinner on the ground, but regular, and all cut. The idea of making the Philip and Cheyney ground exclusively of warp yarns was to strengthen it, and for this purpose worsted could hardly be bettered. That Philip and Cheyneys had their immediate origin in a place at least partly inhabited by Walloons, as Norwich was, and that they were being made in that city as early as 1608, is beyond reasonable doubt.[72] When all-worsted ones were invented is not known, but they were certainly being made in Norwich in 1622 and after. Broad and narrow, white and coloured and, from 1640, some figured or watered, they were produced not only in the city,[73] but also in North Walsham, Hempstead, Hingham, Briston, Brinton and elsewhere in East Norfolk.[74] By 1676 manufacture had spread also to Finningham.[75] All Philip and Cheyneys were relatively expensive. Amongst other things, they went to make bed-curtains and coverings and ladies' coats.[76]

Another innovation in this period was far less successful. The appearance of the worsted element in 1608 was so fleeting that we can learn little or nothing about it.[77] Much the same may be said for the worsted delicate of 1626 and the worsted momperilla of 1627.[78]

Although there is some reason to suppose it was being made up to ten years previously, the first unequivocal record of worsted tammy manufacture in Norwich is in 1605. The gradual change of spelling undergone by this name from 'estamet' to 'tammy' had by that date proceeded as far as 'tamett'. By 1633 it had become 'tammet'. But its meaning was constant. A stammet or tammy yarn was one that had been shrunk and smoothed by scouring, and a tammy was a cloth woven thereof. This can be seen from an inventory of Isaac Morly's effects in 1661; he had just been making tammies and left a large stock of scoured yarn ready to go into them.[79] Worsted tammies were slightly better than some, but shared characteristics common to them all. They were lightweight, plain-weave fabrics with hard-spun warps and wefts, and thinly warped, with 'not above one or two thrids through the slay' (in a reed dent), so they were both strong and stringy. They were also highly glazed by hot-pressing and other means. Although sometimes made into ladies' dresses, they were peculiarly useful for light, hard- wearing, easily cleaned articles like linings, boys' caps, children's frocks and coats, clothing for West Indian slaves, curtains, roller blinds, bolting cloths and kitchen sieves and strainers. And one special form of tammy, called bunt or bunting, was sold for making flags.[80] Worsted tammies, white and coloured, broad and narrow, were made in Norwich and East Norfolk, seemingly from about 1594, certainly from 1605. At first they were woven on 'French lombs' copied from those made by the Walloons. This worsted tammy manufacture survived into the nineteenth century. It soon spread throughout East Norfolk[81] and it spilled over into Tacolneston and nearby places in High Suffolk.[82]

A mohair is a watered grograin, which in turn is a cloth made of grograin yarns, i.e. large, rounded twists. The watered effect is imparted by calendering two grograins together so that the threads of the one compress irregularly those of the other. Alternatively, a single grograin may be folded in half and then pressed. Both silk and goat's hair are well suited to making mohair cloth, but the name itself is nothing but a doublet of 'moire'. Only in modern English, specifically since 1637, has its spelling been distorted and its meaning perverted. Early sixteenth-century Continental mohairs were made in silk,[83] but worsted was adequate and less expensive. An allusion was made in 1619 to the making of mohair over here,[84] and worsted grograins had been produced in Norwich ever since about 1594. They had both their warps and their wefts twisted from at least two threads, which were usually of divers colours to give a shot effect, and they were twilled. Such grograins were well suited for conversion into mohairs, and some indeed were watered.[85] This, coupled with the fact that at least eight city master worstedweavers were making broad or narrow mohairs in 1635,[86] suggests the invention was then more than two years old. However, the first record seen of 'worsted mowheare' manufacture in Norwich is dated 1633.[87] This was all-worsted mohair; it was an offence to put wheelspun 'Suffolk yarn' in and the woof was shot with a twist of three worsted threads.[88] The mohair was then finally produced by watering and calendering in a way that even Lyons manufacturers were later pleased to copy.[89] Worsted mohairs were very successful. Their manufacture in Norwich endured for a hundred years and was conducted on a considerable scale.[90] Grograins and mohairs were dress cloths and went to the making of gowns, cloaks, coats, bodices and many other garments.[91]

A succession of minor worsted inventions followed: the formadardes or formedabilis of about 1634–8, the curl of 1637, the pinckuarina of 1638, the virginato of 1637–40, the novillian of 1641–7 and the odarato of 1644–57. None of them lasted long and only one can readily be explained.[92] The curl derived its name from the special yarn it was woven in. A Z-twisted two-ply twine was itself twisted clockwise but slackly around a fine Z-twisted yarn, and then the resulting twine itself was twisted anti-clockwise. This reversal of the twist untwisted the slack two-ply and caused it to form loops at regular intervals. If odarato was really the same as 'duretto', then it was derived from durance, perhaps being based on a broken twill.

Worsted druggets were modelled on silk drogues or drugs and were similarly plain and loosely woven. Before pressing, a drugget had a face rather like baize, but when hot-pressed it acquired a smooth and flannelly finish. A few worsted druggets were made in Norwich from the middle of the seventeenth century onwards.[93]

Another application for worsted was found in drafts, i.e. cloths woven on drawlooms in the fashion of the beds and similar pieces the dornicksweavers had been making for some time. Worsted drafts of one sort and another were being made in Antingham in 1671 and in Norwich in 1674 and 1687, but not in great numbers.[94]

Norwich also produced some worsted crapes. To *crêper*, or *cresper* in old French, is to crimp, and a crape is simply a crimped grogram. Its special characteristic is a uniform puckering or wrinkling caused by the weaving into one and the same cloth of twines or grograms twisted from yarns of different composition and torsion, one being more tightly spun or twisted than the other, or made of a different fibre, in such a way that, when wetted in the course of washing and finishing, one strand of the twist shrinks more than the other, causing the whole fabric to pucker up. One manufacturer was making 'cresp grogram' in Norwich in 1661, but probably not in worsted. By 1679, however, considerable numbers of worsted crapes were being made in the city. But this success was shortlived; very soon worsted crape was ousted by the famous Norwich mixed silk and worsted variety.[95]

Fig. 9 Drafts for some diamond twills, including bird's-eye and goose-eye twills (warp black).

Some toys were likewise made in worsted. 'Toy' apparently derives from the Netherlands *tooi*, meaning finery or attire. Silk toys were sometimes imported from the East Indies, but as early as 1587 French or Walloon ones appear to have been on sale. Toys were small-pattern point-twills, such as diamond twills, bird's-eye twills (with a spot in the centre of the diamond) and goose-eye twills (concentric bird's-eye ones). They were usually woven in contrasting dark and light colours, and were dress cloths, used for head-dresses sometimes and more commonly for skirts. Woollen toys, probably worsted ones, were being made by 1639 or before.[96] Norwich produced many toys and by 1687 most of them were in worsted.[97] By a similar act of substitution, 'Norwich' ferrandines were selling in the West End as early as 1673 at half the price of silk ones. Worsted ferrandines were made in Norwich, in Wood Norton and in the Woodland town of Finningham.[98] Their name suggests a source of supply near or through the Strait of Messina, and ferrandines had originated as silk or silk-and-hair cloths. Worsted also replaced silk and hair in tamarins, which were often striped. Norwich was making all-worsted tamarins by 1666.[99] By 1679 the city was weaving 'worsted masquerades', which were copies of the plain silk mascades or mascardoes and likewise intended for head-dresses.[100] In 1711 Norwich was also making worsted gauze.[101] By 1719 a Wood Norton manufacturer was producing a worsted version of harrateen. This was a stiff fabric, embossed in a hot-press or an engraved and heated roll in faint imitation of damask, and used for curtains and upholstery covers.[102] The early eighteenth century, too, saw a distinct vogue for worsted marvels or marbles. These were plain weaves in whose warps were alternated threads of white (or light colour) with others of one dark colour, which was exactly matched by the weft threads.[103]

For well over two hundred years the worstedweavers had busied themselves with inventions and substitutions, but not to the neglect of older products. The manufacture of 'worsted two-spoone' says, as broad, narrow and three-quarter cloths, and as white, coloured and striped beds, went on as before in Norwich and East Norfolk generally.[104] In the early seventeenth century, moreover, this branch of industry developed vigorously. In 1609 laced says came on the market, in 1615 changeable says, in 1619 chequer says, in 1624 cut says, and in 1626 branched and flowered worsted says, as well as both white and coloured worsted Carthage says.[105] To cut (as here) was to interchange the warp and weft on the face of the cloth in a set pattern. Lacing was akin to stitching, a second and contrasting weft being floated here and there and otherwise left obscured.

The best known of all the new says were the twisted or twistered ones, wheelspun varieties of which were being made by strangers as early as 1594.[106] No twistered worsted say has been found as early as that, so we guess the worstedweavers copied the idea. In 1618 the pyramid was said to have been introduced 'now lately'. It was derived from the worsted say by 'putting the same into coulours and twistering one thridd of one coulour with another colour, being made narrow, yt is now called piramides'.[107] This range of manufactures flourished for half a century and more. Cut pyramids had been invented by 1622, branched pyramids by 1625, and flowered pyramids (floramids) by 1627. Cydramids appeared at the same time and were in the same class.[108] Cameleons (chameleons) were a kind of changeable twistered say with contrasting colours in both warp and woof. The weft was doubled, but not twisted, in two different colours. Worsted cameleons are first recorded in 1630 and both narrow and broad ones were still being made in the second half of the century. Their manufacture was often combined with that of mohairs, both having similar twists and colorations, and by 1652 had spread from Norwich to Mildenhall.[109] It was largely to supply their manufacturers that the new specialist occupation of twisterers arose in East Norfolk.[110]

From these worsted says developed the worsted prunella. The prunella was like other says except for its two-and-one twill. It was often used to make gowns for barristers, clergymen and graduates, and for ladies' boot and shoe uppers. Worsted prunellas were being made in Norwich in 1662 and 1671 and in Finningham in 1676. Many of them were woven in colours on the loom and some were twistered in colours.[111]

Fig. 10 Draft for a three-and-three twill (warp black).

The worstedweavers also made serges. They substituted worsted for jersey and silk in the Walloon *serge de bois*, which was woven on a six-shaft loom, implying a three-and-three twill or possibly some more intricate twill weave, and was used for gowns. Worsted serge de bois, three quarters broad, appeared in 1616.[112] From this was derived jollyboys. Worsted jollyboys arrived on the scene in 1623 and disappeared after 1633. They were made in singles and doubles, broad and narrow.[113] Worsted jollymothers, some of them flowered, followed in 1625, but predeceased jollyboys.[114] The worsted serge of Athens first recorded in 1623 was made broad and narrow, i.e. half a yard,[115] but remains almost as much an unknown quantity as the worsted serge paramount of 1631[116] and the worsted serge debaragon (deboracon) of 1639 and after.[117] Another worsted product, princes serge or princella, otherwise princilato, otherwise princellian, otherwise presilian, otherwise presile, may have derived from the weave used in Ghentish linen *presilla*. It had a two-and-one twill and was thus the counterpart in serge of the worsted prunella. Princilatoes were made both broad and narrow, and some of them were laced.[118]

All told, worsted weaving expanded enormously. By the early sixteenth century it had already spread over the whole of East Norfolk, though least of all in East Dereham and district, which was preoccupied in combing and spinning. Outside East Norfolk worsted weaving was established only in Lynn.[119] Now it took hold in and about East Dereham[120] and carried beyond the old bounds. It brimmed over into the valleys and foothills of the Cromer Ridge along the southern limits of the Norfolk Heathlands[121] and it trickled into the High Suffolk and Woodland towns on the roads south from Norwich.[122] It was drawn westwards to the Breckland towns, especially to those where yarnmasters had long supplied worsted yarns to the weavers of Norwich and East Norfolk.[123] It had reached Thetford by 1623,[124] Bury St Edmunds (with Fornham, Icklingham and Lackford) by 1637, [125] and Mildenhall by 1652.[126] Worsted-weavers had appeared in High Suffolk, at Tacolneston, by 1669; in the Woodland, at Finningham in 1676, at Sudbury and Stowmarket by 1687, at Lavenham by 1696, and at Neednam Market by 1722.[127] The same wave of prosperity revived the industry in that old satellite King's Lynn.[128] And even although the term 'worstedweaver' had lost much of its meaning by the second half of the seventeenth century and company members included all kinds and conditions of men from farmers to hosiers to linenweavers and licensed victuallers,[129] still, that textile manufacturers in these towns styled themselves 'worstedweavers' when they wove in other yarns also, is indicative of the centrifugal diffusion of the textile industry of Norwich and East Norfolk.

Of other and independent centres of worsted weaving in England there were only three: Stepney, Canterbury and the Woodland. The Woodland clothiers had long used rockspun tops yarns for the warps of some of their cloths and now some of them started to use these 'handwarp' yarns for both the warp and the woof of fabrics variously called 'mallicas', 'mollecas', 'malakies', 'maliques', 'molickers' and 'molokers', this last form being the one ultimately settled on. Their name derived, however confusedly, from the Moluccas and Malacca, which were very much in the public eye in the 1640s when the Hollanders dispossessed the English of the islands. The French and Netherlands names *Moliques* and *Molukken* seem to have had some influence on English spelling, but the cloths themselves were made only in the Woodland and only, it seems, from the 1640s to the 1670s. The makers were interested mainly in jersey says and their molokers were in the nature of a sideline. Only five such makers can be named: William Mascoll of Cavendish, John Salter of Sudbury, Thomas Hawse of Bury St Edmunds, William Ross of Nayland, and Solomon Prockter of Bildeston. But their probate inventories alone suffice to show molokers were made of handwarp yarns, which were virtually worsted.[130] Molokers were probably hot-pressed and polished with flint rubbers to resemble silk. The shiny silk hats called molokers perpetuate the name and indicate the nature of the cloth.

The Canterbury Walloons worked a little in what they called worsted yarns. At first they were imported from St Omer especially for St Omer says. Later, worsted yarns were spun in Canterbury and district and were used also for worsted grograins and camlets.[131] Although composed of a slightly different type of wool, these yarns were almost exactly the same as genuine worsted.

Some genuine and original worsted was imported into Stepney and Whitechapel, mainly for incorporation in mixed cloths.[132] Later a few worsted fabrics were woven. About 1700 an invention was made of what the English called 'worsted plush' and the Huguenots '*plush delaine*', though how it differed from worsted Philip and Cheyney is not clear.[133] At much the same time some worsted russells were produced here.[134]

Nowhere other than these four places has ever woven in worsted in England,[135] and of these four only one, comprising Norwich, East Norfolk and their satellites, worked in worsted on a large scale.

# 5

# JERSEYS

There had been a marked division of labour between England and the Continent in the spinning and weaving of wool tops: they had not been rockspun much there and hardly ever wheelspun here. This gave the Flemish immigrants a good opportunity; they were adept in spinning and weaving jersey, and this trade, unlike most, was open to them because it was new to the towns in which they settled.

Considering how small and cheap lace-looms were and how easy they were to transport and set up, it is hardly surprising that 'say' or jersey lace was amongst the very first fabrics woven by the strangers when they arrived in an English town.[1]

Soon after they had settled in Sandwich in 1563, in Colchester and Norwich in 1566, in Southampton in 1567 and in Canterbury in 1574, the Flemings set up manufactures of their own kinds of says.[2] These were nearly all partly, and most of them wholly jersey.

In Norwich the strangers made many Hondschoote says, no doubt decorated with suitable replicas of Hondschoote seals. Worsted for the wefts was bought locally.[3] But most of the Flemish says were all-jersey. According to the general orders for the *saieterie* in 1575, all says were to be woven of dry yarn 'and not saymed', i.e. not in oil, not 'in sayme'. All, both 'of syngle and dowble warpin', were to be after the fashion either of Amiens, Mouy and other places in France or of Flanders and the Low Country, but this difference between Amiens and Lille says was not great. 'Sayes of dry cruell after the fashion of Lile, Ameens and Mouij' had to have a count of at least 2,200 ends; broad says of no less than 1,600, more if made in the manner of Lille; and narrows of no less than 900.[4] All these says, be it noted, could have either single or double warps. In other words, the Flemings employed the one word 'say' to mean both says and serges, which makes it difficult for us to distinguish one from the other. By 1581 members of the Norwich *saieterie* were also making tammy says from scoured jersey, and by 1613 broad white 'wale sayes', which were waled in the twill.[5] As early as 1567 some Norwich weavers had started to learn from the strangers their way of making says,[6] so that these types of say and serge, which prevailed still in 1639, were then being produced by both Flemish and English manufacturers.[7] As early as 1594 members of the *saieterie* had started making twistered jersey says,[8] but the quadramids they presented for the first time in 1618 were merely a response, albeit an extremely rapid one, to the worstedweavers' pyramids. Quadramids had coloured jersey threads doubled and twistered in both warp and weft. They followed English dimensions, being $27\frac{1}{2}$ yards long, one yard and half a nail broad and with 900 ends. But they had little success.[9]

The strangers, mainly Walloons, who came to Southampton, asked to bring servants with them, saying, 'We only want them for manufactures unknown in this country, as sayes . . . etc., in which unskilful workmen would do damage'.[10] Nevertheless they made few pure jersey says. The Canterbury Walloons did, and for a hundred years or so. We find amongst their effects and products jersey say, 'Dutch say', *fillets de saiette*, dry crewel, jersey yarns and wheels and all the requisites of the trade.[11] In addition, they made some Hondschoote says with worsted wefts.[12] All these says were curried by specialists and then fulled by foot.[13] Not until 1651 has evidence been found of says being sent to a Sturry fuller to 'fulle and thicke' in his mill.[14] The Sandwich Dutch also made jersey says in considerable numbers, but we learn little or nothing of the manner of their making, save that it was under much the same orders as in Norwich and Colchester.[15]

Colchester Dutch says were sold in four qualities: the *volzeghelt* (fully sealed), the *ventloote* (merchantable), the *prente* (with printed declaration of faults), and the *stuck* or piece of a cloth. For long these says were thicked only 'by the foote' in the 'foot stocke'.[16] Not until about 1585 did the Dutch start to mill any says, and they still walked the better ones. As late as 1619 only broad says of English making were usually milled, and they were jersey unions, not pure jerseys, and were excused the provisions for fulling in the Dutch regulations that remained in force until after 1656.[17] As to the original Colchester Dutch says, the only type mentioned by name was the Hondschoote, for whose wefts handwarp yarns were available locally.[18] We assume, however, that, as in Norwich, more were made of the commoner Flemish types.

Sudbury says seem to have been the sole English jersey ones before 1650. They were being made there between 1595 and 1626. The tammy says woven in the town in 1681 and the jersey dress says called borsleys, which came somewhat later, were very likely of Flemish origin, and the Hondschoote ones certainly were.[19] The jersey prunella being made in Sudbury in 1677 probably derived immediately from its worsted counterpart.[20] Englishmen invented very few fabrics in jersey, though we may admit the remote possibility that the dimity found in Soham in 1670 and in Lavenham in 1696 was one of the few. If so, it was probably a dimity only in the sense of being laced with an additional and secondary warp, not in the sense of having alternating weaves with the one the mirror image of the other.[21]

Some jersey serges seem to have owed their introduction to French Huguenots. *Serge de Nîmes*, eventually anglicised as denim, had single-thread jersey warps and wefts, both very tightly and finely spun, and woven in a three-

and-two twill.[22] Jersey denims were being made in Norwich by 1682. Alton also took up this trade.[23] Serge duroys, which were piece-dyed diamond twills, including bird's and goose-eyes, may have been brought in by Huguenots. They were being produced in Norwich in 1675 and perhaps in Colchester a little later.[24] The Huguenot *sargetiers* or *sergeurs* who settled in Bristol from 1681 onwards appear to have made jersey serges, possibly duroys.[25]

Fig. 11. Draft for a three-and-two twill (warp black).

Jersey camlets had been made in Lille, Arras, Tournai, Amiens and Valenciennes.[26] The flight of this industry from Flanders was blamed on 'les cruautés du duc d'Albe, qui firent passent en Angleterre, d'où nous tirions les laines les plus fines, plusieurs de nos fabriquants, qui y portèrent leur industrie; les Anglais, possesseurs de nos fabriques, nous privèrent de leurs laines et ne cherchèrent plus nos étoffes'.[27] These Lille or 'Lyles' camlets included a type known as grograin-camlets, *camelots dits a gros grains*, which the Norwich strangers simply called grograins.[28] It was common knowledge that some fabrics 'had names given to them because the strangers which did devise them weare forbidden to make the old, and therfor they gave them a nue name only, albeit in substaunce they weare the old stuffs'.[29] This is what made 'the new stuffe called grogryn all one with the stuffe heretofore called chamlett'.[30] These grograin-camlets were apparently all single-thread ones. In view of their big, round twists, their name was not unreasonable, but left the problem of what to call derivatives with double or treble threads. As these were slightly narrower, the strangers hit on the idea of referring to them as *bovines* or buffins. In the half-century round about 1600 the Norwich settlers made many of these broad and narrow buffins, including three-thread and changeable ones.[31] By 1614, too, the strangers had started to make jersey peropus in imitation of the recent worsted invention. The jersey one was slightly narrower, half an inch under a yard, with 620 ends.[32] Jersey camlet manufactures long continued in Norwich and later spread to Stepney, to Alton, where they included plain and figured paragons, and to Bristol, where the cattaloons largely had their ends simply in whole colours.[33]

Confusingly, the strangers also made grograins properly so called, many of which were in jersey, particularly the narrow grograins called buffins (*sic*), the Norwich 'dry' grograins, those the Maidstone settlers made in their early years, some of the Canterbury ones, and above all the great numbers produced by the Sandwich Dutch.[34]

The Flemings also introduced the jersey tammy. They were making it in Norwich in the 1570s.[35] But only a fraction of the Canterbury tammies were jersey,[36] and Maidstone produced few of any description.[37] Jersey tammy manufacture went on in Norwich,[38] but by the middle of the seventeenth century its chief seat had become the Woodland. Lavenham, Stowmarket and Langham (by Bury), for example, were all engaged in it.[39] Jersey bunting was a variety of tammy very suitable for flags because its wool was opaque even in the strongest light. Stowmarket was making it in 1675 and Sudbury (with Ballingdon), Glemsford and Cavendish clung to this trade in the eighteenth and nineteenth centuries.[40]

In Norwich the Flemings introduced 'fustians of Naples made of pure saietries, and of cowler upon the lome and alltogether playne'. These jerseys had greater success than the worsted Norwich fustians made by the Russells Company.[41] Another species of velours, the mockado, owed its introduction entirely to the Norwich Walloons. They fabricated several varieties both as singles and as doubles. Of these single mockadoes, one sort was 'of woollen yarne', i.e. it was all jersey.[42] Philip and Cheyney was invented by the Norwich Walloons shortly before 1608 and by 1623 the Canterbury Walloons had taken it up. Many or most of these plushes were mixed, but some appear to have been pure jersey, and those being made in Sudbury in 1705 clearly were.[43]

The calamancoes invented by the worstedweavers were later copied in jersey, much of it of Irish origin, in Norwich, Canterbury and the Woodland. Those being made in Langham (by Bury) in 1711 and in Bildeston in 1737 were pure jersey,[44] as probably were most of those for so long made in Lavenham.[45]

Jersey was also used to make shalloons, which were says woven from fine yarns. They were often glazed and hot-pressed to a smooth finish for the linings of suits, coats and other garments.[46] The shalloon's original name was *serge de Châlons*, suggesting it was the second notable textile invention to emanate from Châlons-sur-Marne; but it was never serge except in the exotic sense of a twill with a linen warp. Shalloons of English making are first referred to about 1640. They appear to have been made for a short time at Redcotts near Wimborne Minster and then, from 1643, at Romsey.[47] Although they came into common use in the third quarter of the century,[48] it is not until 1698 that we find an inventory showing their manufacture, and then at Alton in the Chalk Country. The industry sent down deep roots in these parts and continued in Newport, Ringwood, Romsey, Alton, Andover, Whitchurch, Basingstoke, Christchurch, Newbury and Reading throughout most of the eighteenth century.[49] The Woodland also took up this trade. In 1681 and 1682 Sudbury saymakers were weaving shalloons. Soon they became a regular manufacturing line both here and in Lavenham. Later Coggeshall and Norwich joined in. So, for a few years, did Bristol.[50]

By 1684 both crape and plush were being woven in jersey in Reading.[51] By 1705 Sudbury had turned her hand to jersey crape. Other Woodland towns made the same move.[52] Meanwhile, in the second half of the seventeenth century, Lavenham clothiers had developed something of a speciality in jersey surplice cloths.[53]

Several towns in the Midland Plain took to making jersey cloths, even if only on a small scale. Amongst the minor participants may be mentioned Banbury and Cambridge. The major ones were Kettering, Coventry and Kidderminster. In the 1660s John Jordan started the jersey shalloon industry in Kettering. By 1712 a thousand pieces a week were being sent up to London. Meanwhile jersey tammy manufacture has been embarked on, and before long jersey calamancoes and jersey everlastings had been added to the range. These everlastings, which were relatively new inventions, were finely woven, close set satins or broken twills with double or treble warps and single wefts, and were often figured or brocaded, those with bold flowers being known as Amens, signifying manufacture in the fashion of Amiens. Everlastings of one kind or another were used to make gaiters, shoe tops and liveries for sergeants and catchpoles. Within half a century of its foundation this textile district had expanded to include Rothwell, Weldon, Broughton, Desborough, Braybrooke and Little Bowden, and before long offshoots sprang up in Uppingham and Northampton.[54] Coventry 'worstedweavers' were already making jersey cloths of some sort in 1672.[55] Before the end of the century the city was producing jersey plush and jersey camlets.[56] Moreover, jersey tammies were already being made here before Samuel Smith, 'woolsteadweaver', introduced the art of weaving striped and mixed-colour ones in 1696. Smith himself concentrated on making tammies right up until his death in 1722. Other weavers, however, had meanwhile started making jersey calamancoes and shalloons, and soon the suburbs of Foleshill and Keresley were drawn into the same trades.[57] In 1717 the manufacture of jersey prunellas and striped jersey tammies was commenced in Kidderminster. Within a few years jersey camlets and jersey Philip and Cheyneys had been added to the array, and not long after jersey harrateens. The town thus moved out of Kidderminster stuffs into jerseys.[58] The next move was into floor carpets. The first wholly woven English floor carpets were the pileless jersey ones whose manufacture was started here in 1735. They were plain-weave double cloths, i.e. two cloths were interwoven one on another, having their threads interchanged in various patterns according to the desired design, but always in such a way as to bind the two together face to face to form a fully reversible floor-covering. Obviously such carpets were less durable than the Brussels and Wilton ones that ousted them, but they had a measure of success.[59]

By 1679 Tewkesbury had taken to making jersey serges and so, at much the same time, had Chester.[60] By 1698 Mansfield and Sutton-in-Ashfield were spinning jersey and weaving and dyeing a few tammies.[61] Some Goudhurst clothiers started making jersey calamancoes and camlets,[62] but generally the Wealden Vales failed to change over from carded to combed woollens. Much greater success was achieved in the Cheese, Butter and West countries, the Vale of Taunton Deane and thereabouts. Cirencester, which was a great source of jersey yarns, took little part in weaving them up, but made a few jersey Philip and Cheyneys and harrateens.[63] By 1716 Chippenham, by 1718 Melksham and by 1735 Devizes, were all making duroys.[64] By 1731 Lyme Regis was making duroys, shalloons and perhaps other jersey serges. Broadway took up duroys a little later.[65] By 1714 Taunton was weaving duroys and by about 1757 shalloons.[66] Jersey serge making started in Tiverton and district about 1690. Dunsford tells us,

> About this time the manufacture of mixed and shaded worsted serges was first introduced to Tiverton, and became, in course of twenty years, the principal source of employ, not only of the inhabitants of Tiverton, but of all the adjoining towns and villages within the compass of ten or twelve miles round ... This manufacture was at first very profitable; the kersey manufacture gradually sunk before it, and was in a few years finally expelled by it. I cannot find that kerseys were manufactured in Tiverton later than the year 1710 ... John Salter is said to have made the first piece of mixed serge for the Dutch market.[67]

By 1728 Barnstaple had built up a range of jersey products that included duroys, shalloons, tammies, plush[68] and beavers. These last were a species of velours in which the pile threads were alternately looped and unlooped, but set out of phase, so that the loops (and consequently the tufts) were arranged alternately (instead of in line), causing the foundation cloth to be more uniformly covered. As for the foundation, it could be a twill, a five-end satin or a four-end broken twill. Heavy shrinking reduced the fabric to between half and two thirds of its woven size, making the loops into a dense mass that, when cut, resembled beaver fur. Topcoats were made in this cloth.[69] By about 1720 Tiverton had introduced chain druggets (drapeens), by 1749 duroys and jersey calamancoes, by 1752 figured druggets and jersey camlets, including plain and figured paragons.[70] By 1757 Exeter was weaving jersey plush,[71] while South and North Molton took to making duroys.[72]

In the eighteenth century Colne, Halifax, Wakefield, Rossendale and other parts of the Peak-Forest Country started to make jersey serges. In the period 1710–50 Halifax, Keighley, Bradford, Bingley, Leeds, Beeston, Wakefield, Colne, Haslingden, Rochdale, Marsden and other towns set about weaving, first, shalloons and tammies and sometimes harrateens, and then calamancoes and camlets. By 1754 tammy, camlet and calamanco manufactures had spread to Knutsford. By 1732 Kendal, and by 1754 Ulverston, were weaving Irish jersey into serges, camlets and grograins. By now Stirling and Edinburgh were making jersey serges.[73] Diffusion had run its course.

# 6

## STUFFS

The diffusion of textile arts from the Netherlands to England and vice versa was no novelty in itself, but the transference that took place in the 1560s and after was on an unprecedented scale, spanned an unusually wide range of fabrics, was overwhelmingly in one direction, and was abnormally compressed into a short space of time.

The Walloons, especially, were expert in making mixed stuffs of silk, linen and jersey. As one report says, 'Jarsey is often used for uffe to silke warpe bicause it matcheth best with silke both for fines and softnes'. In Norwich the strangers made in particular narrow says, often changeable ones, with jersey wefts and with warps either wholly silk or else doubled and twisted from silk and jersey.[1] The Canterbury Walloons produced 'better' and 'worser' mingled 'silk says' with wefts of jersey and warps either of silk or of linen and silk union yarns.[2] Jersey-silk union serges were introduced, and also others with linen as well. Probably the serges of the French sort produced in Norwich had linen warps,[3] but the silk *serge de bois*, the broad 'jollyboyse', and the fine and coarse serges of Athens, which had been introduced by 1611, 1613 and 1636 respectively, all seem to have combined silk and jersey. The same is likely true of 'serdge de boise of cruell', though we cannot be sure whether the crewel was of jersey or of silk.[4] In Canterbury the Walloons made 'silk rashes', in which the warp was twisted from silk and linen, from silk and scoured stammet jersey or, in the best ones, entirely from silk, while the wefts were all of carded wool.[5] The Norwich Flemings brought with them their manufacture of stamins with silk warps and jersey wefts, and taught it to at least two of the city's woollen weavers.[6]

Many of the strangers, especially the Walloons, had a proclivity to the incorporation of linen in their tripes and in their *cangeants* or *changeants*, which had colours as changeable as those in a mallard's neck. It was this use of linen that brought the occupations of *triperie* and *cangeantrie* into such close association.[7] The introduction into Norwich by the strangers of their 'white warp' linen yarn and the increased use of flax in textiles there,[8] was nevertheless accompanied by their adoption of worsted, which the worstedweavers generously permitted, for it was only 'with the assente of the worstedweavers of the sayde citye that the stranngers (beinge workemen) might buye to converte into clothe suche worsted yarne' as they wanted.[9]

For some time England continued to import the linen, jersey and silk *mochades* made in Arras, Tournai and other Low Country towns, but a supply of home-made plain and tufted mockadoes now became available,[10] thanks to a number of the Norwich Walloons. By 1571 they had established this industry over here and by 1576 were apparently exporting part of its output.[11]

Norwich Walloon mockadoes fell into two main classes: the plain or solid ones and the tufted mockadoes or 'tufts'. The latter were voided to form a pile with discrete and distinct tufts, while the former had an unbroken and even one. Plain mockadoes might be either single or double, and the double ones either changeable or not. Tufts might be single, or double, or double and changeable. Single tufts all had the same ground as did fustian of Naples, i.e. a two-and-two twill. Double tufts were on a doubled linen ground. Double and changeable ones were on a ground of alternating doubled linen and doubled jersey yarns. Of the plain mockadoes, the single ones were either entirely jersey or had a linen ground, which was usual in mockadoes of mixed composition, and the grounds were commonly two-and-two twills. Some single mockadoes were woven in white yarns, some in coloured. Most of the doubles, and all the changeables, were dyed in the yarn and made in colours on the loom. As for the piles, they were usually jersey, but sometimes silk or partly silk, and then the cloth was called silk mockado. The piles were warp ones; those in tufted mockadoes had at least 400 threads. Plain or tufted, both, could be sold either uncut or 'cut and uncut', i.e. figured by partial cutting or 'alltogether drawne and cutt'. Partial cutting was done with a long-handled knife; otherwise shears were used. The ground for changeable mockadoes had 'fower threedes in everie slae, that is to weete, twoo of the threedes to be of flaxe and twoo other of the threedes to be of saye yerne'. No double tufts on a linen ground were to have fewer than 1,100 threads 'upon the playne mockado slae'; nor any single tufts 'upon the grownde of fustyan of Naples, that is to saye with fower [t]r[e]addels for the grownde', fewer than 1,200 threads 'beinge compassed upon the mockado slae'; nor any white tufts of any other fashion 'compassed upon the mockado slae', nor any single tufts in colours 'compassed upon the carrell slae', fewer than 1,000 ends.[12] Various qualities of the main types are known to have been made, but not all are documented. On one occasion the makers were ordered 'that they do loke that the midle sort of mockadoes be better made than they of late have made them'. At another time there was 'comaundement given to the wardens of the Wallon mockadoe makers to make good tuftes'. Careful orders were laid down, and search and seal rigorously enforced.[13] Plain mockadoes were usually fourteen yards long and half a yard wide, or, what was hardly more, half an ell less ten nails. Tufted mockadoes were mostly one yard wide. From 1588, too, smaller types of mockadoes, 'otherwyse called small bovynes', came into production.[14] Mockadoes only went to the calendrers[15] to be dyed black when their colours were bad.[16]

Norwich's output of mockadoes dwarfed that of all other English towns.[17] In 1571 some of the King's Lynn Flemings were weaving mockadoes, but had to send them to Norwich to be searched and sealed.[18] This manufacture never came to much in the London suburbs, in spite of being of very early origin; in 1583 there was living in Whitechapel one Cornelis Plaise, a mockado weaver and native of Flanders who had been in England twenty-four years and now employed a manservant in the business.[19] The Canterbury Walloons were licensed to produce both 'mouquades' and 'tofe mouquades', and one of them, Jeromye de Loye, actually made silk mockado on a ground of linen; but production here was always slight.[20] The Maidstone strangers took little advantage of their permit to weave mockadoes.[21] When requesting permission in 1576 to settle in Halstead, the Dutch asked to be allowed to make mockadoes there, but in the event produced few or none.[22] That same year the mayor of Chester confidently claimed to have persuaded a young man skilled in making 'tufte mucardo' to set up there, and the city agreed to give him his freedom 'to use the said trade'; but it was all promise and no performance.[23]

Amongst the articles fashioned in mockado were doublets, capes, cassocks, kirtles, dressing gowns, night gowns, curtains, cushion covers, upholstery and carpets.[24] If made heavily enough, mockado would have served admirably as floor carpet, and for all we know it may occasionally have done so. Pile carpets are mostly velours, and Wilton as we know it started out as a 'carpeting commonly called French carpeting or moccadoes and in Tournai and France *moucades* or *moquets*'.[25]

As we have seen, some of the Norwich Flemings made fustians of Naples composed wholly of jersey yarns. They or their compatriots also produced such fustians with grounds of linen yarn and jersey piles. These were one yard wide, either white or made in colours on the loom, and both either uncut or all cut or cut and uncut, i.e. partially cut, or cut and figured, which meant they were cut at various heights to create 'pile upon pile'.[26] By 1608, too, some Norwich Flemings were making 'Sparta velvet or velours'. It is difficult to say for certain how this was made. We know it was a 'fustian of Naples wrought *vocatur* Sparta velvet' and in those days to say a cloth was wrought usually signfied it had been rowed and shorn. The allusion to Sparta was presumably intended to suggest frugality rather than fearlessness. On the whole, then, we are inclined to the opinion that Sparta velvet was not a true velours, was without any pile, either of warp or weft, and was simply rowed or brushed to give the semblance of a pile, in short, that it was akin to what was called elsewhere rowed fustian.[27] There was nothing spurious, however, about what the strangers called, without further qualification, velours, 'valures' or 'velures'. They had 'the grownde of fustyan of Naples' woven in a two-and-two twill 'with fower treddells' and were composed variously of linen or of jersey or of linen mingled with either jersey or worsted. The 400 threads of their warp piles might be either jersey, worsted or silk, and the loops either uncut, all cut, cut and uncut, or cut and figured. These fabrics were likewise woven either white or in colours.[28] The fustinadoes the Walloons claimed as one of their products in 1612[29] may have been similar to the 'cutt fustyns alias cut uppon taffitie' of 1615 and the novatoes of the same years. These last two were made to the same dimensions as the undifferentiated velours and like them had 400 pile threads, but these were of silk.[30] Cut fustians alias cut upon taffetas were presumably reversible, cut, double cloths, with fustian and plain weaves, the face and the back weaves being regularly interchanged and cut one on another.[31] A taffeta is a thin, plain weave stiffened with extra weft threads. In Norwich, for this purpose, it was probably made in linen.

Soon after the arrival of their main party the Norwich Walloons commenced manufacturing carrels with silk or jersey piles on linen grounds half a yard wide and fourteen yards long, with 1,000 ends if the pile threads were single, 900 if they were double. Like most other velours, they could be woven white or in colours and uncut, all cut, cut and uncut, or cut and figured (pile upon pile).[32]

All told, then, Norwich became a great source of velours,[33] but not for long was she the sole English one. In 1571 a 'Dutchman' was making fustians of Naples in St Botolph's in Bishopsgate ward, and he had been in England for three years. Southwark had one alien velours weaver in 1618 and three in 1635. Two of these were from Tournai, emphasising once again that town's close association with *tripes de velours*.[34]

In 1571 a weaver of carrels and sackcloth had already dwelt three years in Tower ward, London, and now had four servant weavers. One and all were natives of Tournai.[35] Perhaps the Sandwich Dutch also made a few carrels.[36] But we do not believe either London or Sandwich carrels were velours; their squares were probably formed by means of diaper weaves in large patterns. This likelihood is suggested by the combination of carrel and sackcloth production. Exiles from Tournai figured prominently amongst those of the London Dutch who introduced the weaving of dress sackcloth, and some of these men also made carrels, diaper or striped dress canvas. Their sackcloths, too, were sometimes striped and always composed, it seems, of mixed flax and silk.[37] Similar sackcloths were woven by some of the Norwich, Sandwich, Colchester and Maidstone strangers.[38]

Caffa was another fabric introduced by the strangers. This was a figured satin with a ferret silk warp and a linen weft. A variety of satin of Bridges, it was originally called *satin caphart*, *satin caffard*, or simply *caffard*. Over here the Flemings used the forms *caffa* and *capha*.[39] To the Russells Company, however, it was a figured russell, so, although the strangers were not debarred from making it in yarns other than worsted, they had to conform to the company's specifications. In the Norwich mayor's court in December 1578, 'upon complaynte of dyverse russell-weavers that a certayne clothe called of the stranngers a capha, whiche the sayde stranggers have practized to make, being here wrought befor their comynge and named fygured russells', was being made by non-members, it was ordered that all broad ones be fifteen yards and a half long and half an English ell and one nail broad, and all narrow ones the same length and half an English yard and one inch broad. Broad cloths were to have a minimum pitch of 1,400 ends, and narrow ones of 1,100.[40] These caffas had silk or mingled silk and jersey warps and linen wefts. We first hear of them being made in Norwich in 1577. When Queen Elizabeth visited the city two years later, the strangers' pageant included a tableau or float demonstrating caffa-making. In the early 1580s caffas made up about a third of the city's output of figured russells.[41] The Canterbury Walloon *caffatiers* started a similar manufacture at much the same time as their Norwich countrymen,[42] and the London suburban Flemings boasted some *caffatiers* by 1605 or before.[43] Thus what the Russells Company feared, and what led them to oppose the Maidstone Flemings so strongly when they wanted russells included in their patent, almost came to pass. The company feared a situation in which 'forsomuche as by reason the stranngers make yt, yt is practised in all partes of the countrye, to thende to be made comon'.[44]

About 1580 the Norwich Walloons started to make plain satins with what seem to have been silk warps and jersey wefts. These likewise conformed to established English dimensions, which were nearly the same as for figured russells.[45] Then, about 1594 and again in 1603 and 1607, mention is made of their 'Spanish' satins, 'whereof the greatest parte ys sylke sayettes', i.e. union yarns of blended silk and jersey. In 1607 the specifications were fixed at 1,200 ends in a width of three quarters of a Flemish ell less one inch. By 1609 double Spanish satins were being made half a yard plus one nail wide.[46]

We have already seen members of the Russells Company making *satins damassés* and other durances modelled on Flemish ones. By 1577 or before the Norwich Walloons were weaving their own kinds of ollyets and scallop shells, with linen warps and jersey or silk-jersey wefts. Their narrow scallops had a pitch of 1,200 if white and 1,100 if made in colours. Large ones had the same count as the narrow whites and at one ell and one inch were hardly any broader.[47] The *oeillets* or 'ollyetholes' were much the same as those produced in Lille town and *chatellenie* ever since 1496. Eyelets were twills of doubled warps and doubled wefts woven in such a way as to leave a perforation or eyelet at the crossing points of warp and weft. Norwich ones were three and a half quarters wide and enjoyed considerable success.[48] The Walloon plumbets, plumettes or plommets were similar to scallops, only with a pattern of plumes. Both singles and doubles were woven half a yard wide.[49]

It was apparently about 1590 that the Norwich and Canterbury Walloons introduced the manufacture of tobines, otherwise tabines, tabies or tabbies. (The second of these forms is etymologically more correct, but in the latter part of the eighteenth century 'tabby' acquired a distorted meaning, leaving 'tobine' to distinguish the genuine article.) The first mention of tobine in Norwich is about 1594 and in Canterbury in the years 1616–18. Tobines are cloths embellished with lines and diamonds or rectangles formed by warp threads alternately floating over and dipping under two or more weft shoots. This was achieved by adding a second or tobine warp, appropriately spaced out on its own separate rollers and entered on its own headle. The same work could be, and later was, done on a drawloom; but Norwich and Canterbury earlier made mostly foot-tobines. Canterbury tobines included both silk-worsted and silk-hair mixtures, Norwich ones mainly the former. In both cities the manufacture was long continued.[50] In 1638 the man who was 'new clothed after the English fashion' had for his coloured clothes 'a tabie dublett, cloth breches, and the clooke lind with the same tabbie of the dublett'.[51]

The Walloons also brought with them their own way of weaving damasks on drawlooms with linen warps and jersey or mingled jersey and silk wefts. These union damasks had been invented in Flanders about 1520, apparently, and were being made in Lannoy in 1529. Civil strife and the Spanish conquest destroyed this industry, but some Walloon refugees succeeded in restarting it over here.[52] In 1578–9 the Norwich Walloons were making their damasks not less than three and a half quarters broad, with linen warps and jersey wefts mostly, as 'damaske flowers greate and lyttle (being beanes)'. White ones had a pitch of 1,200, those woven in colours, of 1,100.[53] The Walloons taught flowered damask-making to some of the worstedweavers and to many of the city and country laceweavers.[54] Union damasks were highly successful in England. The combination of yarns used brought the design out well and made good curtain and upholstery material. All told, Norwich and the rest of East Norfolk produced a large volume of damasks over a period of some two and a half centuries.[55] Walloon immigrants brought damask-making to Canterbury as well. Here they wove their damasks in worsted and silk and in pure silk mostly. These were more expensive than Norwich ones and sold in smaller numbers. By 1720 similar damasks were being made in Spitalfields, and by 1695 crape-warp damasks, with highly twisted silk warp yarns, were emanating from Norwich.[56]

Besides their jersey camlets, the Norwich Flemings introduced others with linen warps and jersey wefts and likewise called grograins or grograin-camlets.[57] They then went on to develop several new fabrics. In 1607 the Dutch invented the filoselle, with its weft of floss silk crewel.[58] In 1618 the Walloons introduced a newly devised pearl of beauty to compete with that made by the worstedweavers. This new invention had a linen warp and a jersey weft. It was woven half a yard and one and a half inches wide, with two warp threads in each of the 420 reed dents and with tufts of two or more colours made up of no fewer than four threads. But it was no more successful than its rival.[59] By no means confining themselves to jersey or linen and jersey buffins, cattaloons and other camlets, the Norwich Flemings also employed silk and worsted, and some of the Walloons made all-silk buffins and cattaloons.[60] Developments in Canterbury were similar. From 1623 or earlier the Walloons here were making peropuses with quadruple wefts of silk or of assorted silk, jersey and linen yarns and sometimes wholly linen warps.[61] Mixed filoselles, some with coloured stripes, were also made from 1616 onwards.[62] By 1637, too, or perhaps ten years earlier, Canterbury weavers were imitating the original Levantine camlets by making turkey paragons in hair and mixed turkey ones in hair and jersey.[63] In the third quarter of this century hair camlets made in Canterbury or London were commonly worn.[64] By 1719, it seems, London and the suburbs were producing a range of mixed jersey, hair and silk camlets.[65]

True grograins, with both warp and woof doubled and twisted, had long been made in silk in Italy and France; as unions of silk warps and jersey wefts they had been woven in the west of Flanders for a good time before the emigrants carried this industry to Sandwich, Norwich and Canterbury.[66] In Norwich we can rarely be sure in any particular instance whether grograins or grograin-camlets are being referred to,[67] but it is known that the Flemings here made 'Lyle' or 'Lyall' grograins that seem to have been the same as the original ones.[68] The settlers in Sandwich and Canterbury produced similar fabrics.[69] From about 1635 Canterbury, especially, was consuming increasing quantities of turkey yarn, by which was meant yarn spun from the hair of the Angora goat and imported from the Turkish empire. This hair had no felting properties; its virtues were in its length (between four and ten inches) and in its lustre.[70] In 1631 the Canterbury Walloons regarded themselves as practitioners in the 'weavinge of silke, jersey and worsterd,'[71] but six years later the mayor and commonalty voiced their anxieties about the consequences to local spinners of the 'late abundant ymportacion of mohaire or turkey yarne' and, a little later, of the 'great importacions of late yeares from Turkie of yarnes made of camells haire'.[72] The city's worthies were thus amongst the first to misuse the word 'mohair', and it may be doubted if they had much knowledge of camels. The only instance we know of in this period of the use of camel's hair is by a Leicester haberdasher of hats. Supposed camel's hair and yarn spun of it were imported, but under their own names.[73] The turkey yarn employed in Canterbury and elsewhere was spun from goat's hair. In the later 1630s some Canterbury grograins were made of worsted warps and turkey wefts; others of twists of silk and flax yarns, or of flax and turkey yarns; and yet others had warps of alternating doubled hair and doubled worsted twists.[74] In this business Canterbury was rivalled only by Leiden.[75]

The Norwich Walloons persisted with mixed silk and jersey grograin yarns. One of their early inventions was the crossbillet or crosset of silk. An order in 1571–2 says it is to be warped on at least 400 reed dents, 'and the chayne owght to be of dowble lynen yarne twystered, and the shootinge of saietrye dowle',[76] meaning a twist of mingled silk and jersey, of 'silk and saiet'.[77] The weave appears to have been a two-and-two twill. In 1637 John Le Blan alias White was making a similar mixed crossbillet in Canterbury.[78] Meanwhile, in 1618, the Norwich Walloons had invented 'a crossbillet derived from the said cloth called the Birds Ey', which latter was two-and-two twill, spotted in colours by having alternately three dark and three light warp ends upon which were woven alternately two or three dark picks and one light one. The new cloth, christened 'cheverato', was thus a similarly spotted chevron twill. It was woven nineteen-and-a-half inches wide with three ends in each of its 300 reed dents.[79]

Fig. 12 Draft for a two-and-two chevron twill (warp black).

Bombasine manufacture was introduced by immigrants from West Flanders in the late 1560s or early 1570s. Possibly a start had been made by some of the Walloons before they left Sandwich for Canterbury in 1575,[80] but the first record of this manufacture over here relates to Canterbury. A party of Walloons staying in Winchelsea sought leave to settle in the city and listed 'bombasin' making among the skills they wished to practise. Their petition is undated, but they arrived in Canterbury in 1574.[81] It would have taken them some few weeks to have set up the special looms required for bombasines and other *bourats*[82] and to have arranged supplies of materials, so manufacture can hardly have commenced immediately on arrival. In fact, we have seen no evidence of bombasine manufacture in Canterbury earlier than May 1588, when John Delahaye left 'one loome for to make bombasine', value £1, and £6 'in wooll, silkes and saie'. As he had no other fibre, yarn or fabric, we infer he made his warps of silk and his wefts of jersey. This silk would have been bourat (bourette), which was spun from the carded noils of combed waste silk.[83] Other inventories listing bombasine in this period add little to our knowledge of how it was made;[84] but in 1663 James Sedt left some pieces of white bombasine, worsted yarn and raw silk. Incidentally, he was a silkweaver, which in

Canterbury meant someone who made mixed stuffs with some silk in them.[85] All this fits in well with some later descriptions of bombasine: the warp was bourat silk, the weft jersey or worsted, and the weave a twill with markedly high relief, the weft yarn being the larger, unlike *plat of effen bourat*, which was similarly composed, but smooth and flat.[86]

Yet this Canterbury silk bombasine was by no means the only variety known and may not have been the first to have been made in England. The Norwich records report as follows certain proceedings on 20 November 1575:

> Commethe the Duche elders in courte, presentinge a newe worke, callinge it bombasins, which they saye at their charge is practized; and praiethe to have the searche and seale therof to their use (withoute the Wallowns); which is graunted to them by assente of the whole courte. Whereupon the Wallowns hearing that, by their byll presented alwdeth the Duche ought nott to have it, for that all white worke and whatsoever workes be made of woollen and lynnen yerne of right apperteynethe to them onelye ... The courte, consideringe to encourage all practizers that fordewarde the comon welthe to be most worthye of the benefyte, doth assente that the Duche, fyrste practizinge yt, is worthieste therof, and graunteth them the benefyt therof, wythoute the Wallowns, and ratifiethe the ordenances, as after doth ensewe.

These 'ordenances for bumbasynes', based on orders presented by the Dutch, reveal many features of their manufacture. They were 'eyther of woolle or of cotton', 21½ Flemish ells long and 'of the breadthe of three Duche quarters'. The best were sealed with a double lion, seconds with a single one, in each case with the name 'Norwich' underneath, and thirds simply with a sword. The rest were rejects; they were rent into four pieces and their makers fined.[87] Probably the wool referred to was in the form of worsted, for strangers who wove 'bayes, sayes, vellures and bombasies' were on one occasion especially exempted from the summer vacation from worsted working.[88] The reference to wool or cotton relates only to the woofs. Both woollen and cotton bombasines had linen warps, for it was on this basis, accepted by both parties and by the court, that the Walloons claimed search and seal. Moreover, both these cloths answered to the description of 'bombasines alias rash with the ground of lynen'. As far as we know, the Norwich Dutch, or one or more of their number, were the very first inventors of these types of bombasine and so also the first to weave cotton in England. Their products enjoyed great success for over a decade.[89]

The next invention came in 1605, when the Norwich Walloons brought out their own bombasine. On 3 May, says the record, 'The strangers of the Wallon congregacion doe this daye present a cloth of new device called satten cotten or bumbazie, made parte of sylke and parte of cotton woll'. This had much the same dimensions as its Dutch rival and its warp contained no fewer than 1,500 threads.[90] Both name and pitch suggest a satin silk warp and a cotton weft.

Furthermore, from 1585 and possibly earlier, some of the Norwich strangers were weaving both silk and jersey and silk and worsted bombasines along the lines of the Canterbury ones.[91] In this bombasine business the East Anglian city surpassed the Kentish; she invented three and produced all five types. The industry flourished here as almost nowhere else, and longer than anywhere else, right into the second half of the nineteenth century.[92] Bombasines were relatively expensive cloths, used for men's doublets, jackets, vests, waistcoats and suits, for bodices and ladies' dresses, and also for curtains and soft furnishings.[93]

The same looms served equally well for bombasines and for *bourats*, boratoes or boratins, as they were variously called. These were similar but balanced, and some purled with small uncut loops on the surface.[94] Boratoes were being made in Norwich or Canterbury or both by 1578, but no details are known.[95] In the first half of the seventeenth century, and possibly ever since about 1578, Norwich Walloons were making plain, striped and purled boratoes, seemingly with silk warps and jersey wefts.[96] *Bourassiers* had been at work in Canterbury ever since 1576, yet it is not until 1639 that any clear reference is made to boratin manufacture there. By 1676 the manufacture had commenced of 'hair boratins', which had hair warps, and of mixed ones, some of which apparently had warps of union yarns that included hair.[97]

By 1606 some Canterbury Walloons were weaving tuftaffeta, which was a velours with tufts of silk or of yarn in which silk was mingled. The kind made here was mixed or 'half thrid tuftafete': the ground was of linen, and the other half of silk or of a mingling or union of silk and jersey or of silk and linen.[98]

The original curl, as imported from Cyprus and elsewhere, was all silk.[99] That being made in Norwich in 1608 was probably a union of silk and jersey. Much of the curl produced in Canterbury in the 1610s was certainly such a union, for it sold at 16*d* a yard when 'silke curle all silk' was at 3*s* 4*d*,[100] and worsted curl only came later.

Figurato was invented amongst the Norwich Walloons in 1609. On 19 September they presented 'a cloath of new devise called figurato, made parte of sylke and parte of white spunne yarne', meaning linen. Figurato was woven to the same dimensions as narrow Spanish satin and in that slight width of half a yard and half a nail included no less than 1,725 ends of doubled silk, which effectively obscured the linen wefts. It was thus a figured double satin, or more likely a satinet, i.e. a four or six-end broken twill. From at least 1616 similar figuratos were being made by many of the Canterbury Walloons. Their probate inventories show these fabrics being woven in colours on the loom, which was probably the practice in Norwich also. Figurato was still being made in 1668, by which time some of it included copper threads, but after this less and less is heard of the cloth.[101] Perhaps it was partially superseded by what was described in 1638 as the 'new invention of mixtures of figured stuffs being made with course turky yarne, softe jarsey yarne, and hard wosted' that had 'not yett come to perfeccion'.[102]

Messolinas were first introduced into Norwich, probably by Walloons and certainly by Flemings, in 1594 or slightly earlier, at a time when they were still being imported. The Norwich fabrics were the same as the Italian *mezzelane* or miscellanies, as made in Mantua and later in Ghent and Lille. They had linen warps and jersey wefts and were finished by brushing. Tailors used them for coats and other men's wear.[103] Abrosite was an invention of the Norwich Walloons briefly recorded in 1608. Its name suggests it was boiled, perhaps in the dye.[104]

Brocatelle, yet another Norwich stuff attributable to the Walloons, made its first appearance there about 1590. It was one member of a class of fabrics woven on drawlooms and known as tissues. All tissues had a second warp to act as a twill binder. Most varieties of tissue, unlike brocatelle, had the warp of the satin ground heavily weighted on the roller and so woven extremely flat and even, while the binder warp was usually lightly weighted. Then on this satin warp was shot a second weft of loosely twisted tram yarn, from which the figure was formed. This second weft was then tied down. Most tissues thus had weft figures on a satin ground. The figure weft was usually varicoloured and always in hues differing from the ones used in the ground warp and weft. Frequently, too, the figure weft included gold-and-silver threads. Three or more shuttles were usually needed to weave a tissue; each colour or tinsel shoot for the figure required its own. Also, the binder had to be lifted out of the way while the satin ground was being woven. The outstanding feature of the brocatelle was its rich, raised satin figure, which was formed from a loosely floating satin warp on the background of a second and special weft that was woven as a loose float (whence the allusion to brocade) and then tightly stitched or bound down by a separate binder warp. In tying up the design (as distinct from the ground or foundation), it was the background that was tied up, not the figure. The brocatelle's ground was a plain satin weave with a white silk warp and an undyed linen weft. The background portion of the silk satin warp being raised again by means of the simple cords, a second and silken weft was loosely shot across to form a background and leave the satin figure standing out in relief. This second weft had then to be tied down securely by the separate binder warp. The first shoot, or linen thread, was made with the binder warp all lifted and the necessary part of the main warp also lifted. Then the second shoot, of silken thread, was made with the figure part of the binder warp down but with all the background part of it lifted in twill order. After this initial line of the pattern, the next and succeeding shoots followed in regular sequence and proper order, first the linen and then the silk. The two separate warps required two separate rollers. What gave the satin figure of the brocatelle its peculiar characteristic and marked this tissue off from others, was that the main satin warp roller was weighted only lightly and the binder warp roller heavily, so that the background was held hard down while the figure was left loose and elevated; and the two, being made in different colours, contrasted all the more sharply one with another. This was a luxurious and expensive cloth and used mainly for dress material.[105]

In Canterbury, by 1635, some Walloons had taken to making turkey and mixed turkey mohairs, using imported turkey goat's hair yarns, either by themselves or in twists with jersey, worsted, linen or silk. The 'silke mohaire' being woven before the end of the decade probably had silk yarn as one of its four twisted strands.[106] The throwing of hair was now a fast growing industry in the Middlesex suburbs and outskirts of London, and 'mochaire' weavers from Lille, Hainault and Artois were coming in and settling near this new source of yarn.[107] It was at this time, too, that the weaving of mohair in hair brought about the confusion of the two words.

The Canterbury Walloons also took up the manufacture of silk-jersey calamanco about 1640, and with long-lasting success.[108] From 1637 at the latest they were also making piccadillies or picotillas in mixed turkey and jersey yarns. As their name, a diminutive of *picote*, implied, they were spotted or pockmarked, which made them readily distinguishable from other druggets. In addition 'silk' druggets and piccadillies were made here from mixtures of silk and jersey.[109] Possibly the Norwich Walloons used hair in their formedabilis and princellian of 1636 and their unfathomable 'trepodelis' of 1655,[110] but a smaller proportion of hair was consumed here than in Canterbury.

Ferrandine appeared almost simultaneously in Rouen, Amiens and Canterbury, and at a time when rising numbers of Huguenots were joining the Walloon congregations in England. Bearing in mind, too, that on both sides of the Channel ferrandine was most frequently made of mixed silk and hair, we suppose the Huguenots introduced it over here.[111] Although Mrs Pepys was in fleeting possession early in 1664 of a ferrandine waistcoat whose stuff may have been woven in Canterbury, the first proof of manufacture here is dated 1668. Margaret Le Keux, who had been continuing her late husband's business, had been making mixed silk and hair ferrandines. All Canterbury ferrandines seem to have been made this way.[112]

John Agace, a Canterbury silkweaver who died in 1676, made mixed silk and hair paduasoys as well as ferrandines. Paduasoy (more correctly *poule de soie* or '*pou de soye*') was a strong, corded, flowered dress cloth woven with more ends than picks in such a way as to give a pronounced cross rib. It had been made in silk and hair in Lille since 1603.[113] Mrs Le Keux also wove tamarins from some combination of worsted, silk and hair. This kind of cloth continued in production for fifty years and more.[114]

By 1676, then, the Canterbury Walloons had many notable textile achievements to their credit. They now made a wide range of stuffs and wove in 'gold and silver or other wire or plate, hayre, jersey, worsted, wollen, cotten, linnen yarne thredd or mixtures of any of them'.[115]

About 1582 some Flemings, many of them hailing from Tournai, commenced in London the manufacture of silk plush, which had a silk pile on a linen ground. This industry was still flourishing in the 1660s.[116] Later on, Huguenots in Stepney started making hair plush, in which a hair pile grew out of a worsted ground.[117] Somewhat similar were the mixed linen and silk shag of the early seventeenth century and the Spitalfields worsted and hair shag of the early eighteenth. Shag had a longer pile than plush, but much more open and less closely woven. Men's waistcoats and breeches were often made of it. In the early part of the eighteenth century, too, mixed jersey and hair shag was made in Abingdon, Banbury, Shipston-on-Stour and Knutsford.[118]

Loom-laces woven from various combinations of linen, jersey, worsted, silk and hair were the most widely introduced and diffused of all the Flemish textile manufactures.[119] When the immigrants brought their *passementerie* to Canterbury,[120] Sandwich,[121] Maidstone,[122] Colchester and Southampton,[123] they established entirely new narrow-ware industries. In London they swelled the already large number of laceweavers.[124] In Norwich they set up alongside the existing worsted lacemakers and produced both their old 'say lace', with its mingled silk and linen warp and its jersey woof, and other laces with linen warps and small-woof worsted wefts.[125] In 1565, so it was written, as by a chronicler,[126]

> Note that nowe began lasemakinge amongst the stranngers of all handes to be so comon (for that their prises of other comodityes beganne to falle) and that manye unskyllfull persons were sett on worke, by which reason bothe muche stuffe was spoyled and the evel wrowghte lase solde so cheape as the lasemakers of the citye could have no geyne by their woorkes ... the stranngers do sett so manye on worke in makinge of lase and other sylke woorke.

From these seven centres parchmentry weaving spread out far and wide. By the 1580s it was found in several East Norfolk country towns[127] and in Chester; by the 1590s in Manchester; by the 1630s in Sherborne, York, Ashton-under-Lyne, Goudhurst and King's Lynn; by the 1660s in Reading, Bristol, Plaistow (Vale of London), Shipston-on-Stour and probably Knutsford; by the opening years of the next century in Bishops Cannings (Chalk Country), Warwick, Coventry and district, Abingdon, Derby, Hilperton (Cheese Country) and in all the Flash, that is to say the district of the Peak-Forest Country that embraces Stockport, Macclesfield, Congleton, Leek and Buxton.[128]

One line of textile development was quite separate and distinct. Tapestry has a plain weave and a 'low warp', i.e. the warp is covered by the weft. The colour of the weft is often changed several times in the course of a single pick, the weft being turned back on itself, so giving rise to solid patches of colour. Tapestry is thus akin to embroidery. The type generally made in western Europe stemmed in the first place from Arras and was called after that town. It had a linen or canvas warp and weft threads of wool, silk or other fibres, and was used for coverlets, cushion covers and wall hangings. Although the industry continued to be seated mainly in Flanders and Brabant, considerable offshoots took root in England.[129] Some hangings, table carpets, coverlets and cushion covers had previously been made in London and other towns,[130] but tapestry weaving was developed much further by Flemish immigrants in and after the 1560s. By 1561 arras cushions, meaning the covers, were the 'fyrste woorke of the strangers' in Sandwich, and similar ones were soon being made in Norwich, York and

London.[131] Cushion weaving required only a small 'quishing' loom, not very much broader than a lace one, and was light enough work to provide women with another suitable alternative to spinning and knitting, so it spread readily and by the turn of the century had reached Halifax, Bradford, Bromsgrove and elsewhere.[132] Tapestry wall hangings were a different matter. Their manufacture was introduced by William Sheldon, esquire, of Beoley. He sent a Mr Richard Hicks to Flanders to learn the art and bring back weavers, and then set up the business in Barcheston, near Shipston-on-Stour. Sheldon initiated the scheme and supplied both capital and premises, but freely acknowledged Hicks was 'the onely auter and begynner of this arte within this realm'. When exactly the tapestry looms were first erected in Barcheston we cannot say, but it was at some time between 1561 and 1568. By 1571 a branch business had been opened at Bordesley Clinton, near Beoley. Sheldon's works were now sufficiently well known for the Earl of Leicester to be able to remark to the burgesses of Warwick who sought his help, 'I marvaile you do not devise some ways amongst you to have some speciall trade to kepe your poore on woorke as such as Sheldon of Beolye'. By 1588 this same trade had spread to Shipston-on-Stour, by 1604 to Bromsgrove, and by 1618 to Abbots Morton, near Alcester. So the Sheldon school of tapestry was created. Sheldon's own business went on until 1647, being carried on after his death in 1570 by his son Ralph. The school lasted a little longer. Its special characteristic was a fondness for rural designs and for depicting flowers and fruits in the borders. In 1611 the Barcheston works completed the 'Seasons' tapestries for Hatfield House, and from the same looms came a series of maps after Christopher Saxton's. Sheldon tapestries were warped with seventeen or eighteen ends of coloured linen thread to the inch, and their wefts were mostly coloured jersey crewel.[133] Early tapestries had all been woven on vertical 'high' looms, but the sixteenth century saw the Flemish invention of tapestry weaving on horizontal 'low' looms. In this way less artistic weavers could speed up output and make reproductions of tapestries originally designed for high looms and individual customers. In and soon after 1619 King James brought in fifty Flemish tapestry weavers who worked on both high and low looms in Mortlake. Permission was granted in 1622 for the London Dutch ministers to hold divine service in Mortlake church for divers of the 'Dutch nation . . . imployed in the making of tapistries'. Many Mortlake tapestries were made on low looms and most had linen warps and mixed wefts of Naples silk, gold-and-silver thread, jersey, worsted and crewel. The industry survived here until 1703, by which time weaving tapestry hangings had become commonplace in and about London, Southwark and Westminster.[134] Huguenots later introduced the Gobelin type of tapestry weaving in Paddington, then in Fulham and finally in Exeter.[135]

By the convergence of the hitherto parallel endeavours of the worsted, dornicks, russell, Walloon, Dutch and French weavers, there eventually emerged a great new industry of fabricating mixed stuffs. Ever since about

1575, as the jersey manufacture stagnated and the baize one approached its zenith, the Norwich and Canterbury strangers, especially the Walloons, concentrated increasingly on stuffmaking. At much the same time, too, in Norwich, worstedweavers and others were following the example of the dornicks and russells men and learning to make cloths in the Flemish style. Already in 1578, for example, an Englishman who had learned the art while a servant to a Fleming, set up as a tuft mockado maker.[136] At this stage, however, worstedweavers were chiefly concerned to adopt new methods of weaving in worsted. Two of the lines of development had become closer, but they remained separate. In the next stage they merged. With the passage of time, the Dutch and Walloons, especially those of the second and third generations, started to integrate with the native English. They gradually took to going to their parish churches, preferred the English language, anglicised their Christian names and often their surnames as well, and strove by all means to be English. This movement was facilitated by the rise of religious nonconformity amongst the English and the growth of the Low Church trend in the Church of England and, conversely, hindered by the High Church reaction and Laud's persecutions, but its occurrence became almost inevitable once the Flemings had abandoned hope of returning to their homeland. Integration was relatively easy; it was natural: both branches came from the same root, from the same original race, and both were Christian, white and western European. In Norwich, especially, they intermarried and became one. Having become English, the former aliens were then entitled to buy real estate, take the oath of allegiance, become citizens of Norwich, apprentice their sons and join the Worstedweavers' Company. At the same time, erstwhile worstedweavers started to weave cloths in jersey, silk, linen and hair as well as in worsted. The company accommodated them by searching and sealing these 'mixed' or 'worsted mixed' stuffs, or simply passed them as 'worsted stuff'.[137] We can thus trace the steps by which manufacturers who were nominally worstedweavers became really stuffmakers.

Whether the cheveratoes being sealed by the company from 1618 onwards were mixed stuffs or not is not clear.[138] Thenceforth little room remains for doubt. In 1625 mixed peropus appeared for the first time;[139] in 1628 mixed says;[140] in 1634 mixed paragons[141] and mixed Carthage says;[142] in 1639 mixed damask,[143] hair cameleon, 'virginato, part of yt mixt with haire'[144] and crossbillet, which was always mixed;[145] in 1641 'worstead mixed novillian',[146] mixed pyramids[147] and, probably, mixed filoselles.[148] In the worsted rashes being made from 1634, worsted was substituted for silk in the warp, and in the mixed rash that appeared in 1642 it may be that a twist of silk and worsted was used instead.[149] The 'Spanish mowhers' in 1651 probably had a union yarn of mingled silk and worsted.[150] All these preceding dates are those of the first company inquisitions that gave rise to records about a particular fabric, not those of the commencement of manufacture, and the lag between the two is unknown and must have varied considerably, but probably rarely exceeded a handful of years. In 1613 the city assembly passed 'A Law for makinge of Norwich stuffes' that kept them quite distinct from the products of the worstedweavers, dornicksweavers and Russells Company;[151] but by 1619 the worstedweavers themselves conceded in the mayor's court that defects in 'Norwich stuffes' were insufficiently checked by their wardens, so acknowledging that they were being made by company members;[152] and in 1624 the merchants who dealt in Norwich stuffs conferred with the Worstedweavers' Company to devise new regulations for their range of stuffs in preparation for a Bill to be preferred in Parliament for the reconstitution of the company to take account of its changed character.[153] This change seems, then, to have taken place between 1613 and 1619, or at latest 1624. In the end the variety of worsted, jersey, linen and mixed cloths and stuffs made by members of what was still called the Worstedweavers' Company became so great that technical regulation and supervision were no longer humanly possible. By 1654 they had been abandoned for ever. Juries of worstedweavers, so called, were still sworn in, and inquisitions probably held, but search and seal were no longer conducted as before and verdicts seldom given on individual pieces of stuff.[154] At much the same time the Dutch and Walloons ceased to frequent their search halls; they were no longer needed.[155] 'Suffolk' and other jersey yarns were now so much used, and so much jersey drawn and spun in Norwich and other East Norfolk towns, that the Worstedweavers' Company was forced to abandon as inappropriate its old strict search and seal of yarns. Members could no longer pretend to use none but 'Norfolk' wool; many of their supplies now came from far afield, even from Ireland.[156] The company felt obliged to admit 'Suffolk' yarn and to appoint a sale hall for 'foreign' wools and yarns.[157] The fact was, many of its members now worked only partially in worsted, and some not at all. Their inventories show such a conglomeration of worsted, jersey, silk, linen and hair that it is extremely difficult to divine what yarns went into what stuffs and in what proportions and forms.[158] The worstedweavers had become general textile manufacturers. In 1661, for example, Isaac Morly, worstedweaver, was making not only a range of mixed silk and worsted stuffs, but also 'rite ups', 'rite up dimants' and 'windmell sailes'. His fellow member Thomas Barker was running a similar business and producing, amongst other things, 'right upps', 'dymonds' and a 'royall rigg'. Start-ups were boots that came up to the ankle, so right-ups were high ones or, more exactly, in this instance, the material for their uppers, much of which was woven in a diamond twill. Both these uppers and the windmill and royal (or top-topgallant) sails were made of 'whitework' linen yarn.[159]

The Russells Company contributed much to the rise of Norwich stuffs. Its members always used a great deal of worsted, but as early as 1591 some of them had taken to weaving silk russells, which were half silk and half worsted.[160] Then, in 1630, came 'a new stuff called hair russell or russell italiano', in which hair was substituted for silk.[161] By 1655 similar mixed russells were being made in Stepney.[162] By this time the demarcations between the makers of russells and of other satins were breaking down. Isaac Morly and other freemen of the Worstedweavers' Company were making mixed silk-worsted or silk-jersey satins like the ones called 'castillianoes'.[163] Henceforth, for two hundred years, the sole generalisation one can make about Norwich and East Norfolk satins and reverses is that they were various and indeterminate mixtures, unions, minglings and blends of worsted, jersey, linen, silk and hair.[164] In short, they were Norwich stuffs.

The dornicksweavers also played an important part in the development of stuff manufactures. In 1593 or before they started to use drawlooms to weave 'drafts' in their coloured linen and kersey yarns. They made draft beds or coverlets in two sizes and also draft pieces. Large draft beds were ell-wide and three yards long, small ones four-and-a-half inches narrower and nine shorter. Pieces could be in either width. Each broad draft had to have twenty-nine portees in its warp, each narrow one twenty-six. As each portee had to contain at least thirty-eight threads, the minimum pitches were respectively 1,102 and 1,008.[165] In and after the second half of the seventeenth century, the old divisions broke down somewhat and drafts came to be made in a variety of mixtures of silk, worsted and jersey, including tammy yarns.[166]

Out of this melting pot of techniques and fibres came a series of novel stuffs. The very first of these had appeared by 1578 or earlier. Worsted warps and silk wefts were combined in 'Norwich lace' and 'Norwich gartering', which, despite their names, were made in several East Norfolk townships.[167] The 'silk chequarettes' (1657) and 'silk odaratoes' (1653–4) were versions in worsted and silk of what had previously been all worsted.[168] Formerly the worstedweavers had practised the substitution of worsted for silk; now they tended to reverse the process. From 1655 onwards Norwich manufacturers were combining worsted warps and silk wefts in silk piccadillies and druggets similar to the Canterbury mixed jersey and hair ones.[169] Prunellas and princes serges underwent analogous development. After 1668 and right up into the nineteenth century, fewer of the worsted prunellas were made than of the mixed ones with silk warps and worsted wefts introduced in 1655 or shortly before.[170] Originally the strangers had woven jersey tammies and the worstedweavers worsted ones. Later the Canterbury Walloons progressed to hair tammies. Norwich took a different line and by 1662 'worstedweavers' and others were making a range of mixed or so-called silk tammies containing varying proportions of worsted and silk and possibly also of hair.[171] A new type of 'silk say' was likewise invented, having worsted warps and silk wefts. This was being produced in 1679, and probably, in the form of mixed 'monks cloth', as early as 1663.[172] About 1660, too, Norwich started to make camlets in which silk and worsted were mixed. These were highly successful and were still being made in the nineteenth century.[173] By 1674 Norwich weavers were producing 'silk' jollyboys[174] and ferrandines,[175] and soon after 'silk' grograins[176] and diamond says,[177] all composed of mixed silk and worsted, just as were, it seems, the plain and striped silk gauzes of 1682.[178]

Shortly after the strangers arrived in Norwich, two city woollen weavers were appointed to accompany the Flemish wardens on their searches 'to the entente to larne the makyng of ... stamyns.' Through this and other means the art became widespread and eventually much improved. By the middle of the seventeenth century members of the Worstedweavers' Company who specialised in mixed silk and worsted stamins were making various kinds designated as 'silk', 'rash', 'flowered' (brocaded), 'speckled', and 'glos tamins' or 'glossamines', which last were heavily pressed and glossed.[179] By 1645 there had appeared all-hair calamanco ('callemanco in heare'); by 1675 silk calamanco, with silk warp and worsted weft; by 1695 flowered calamanco similarly composed.[180] Meanwhile, from the old curls, the city stuffmakers had developed, by 1674, curlderoys, in which the fine threads were silk and the thick worsted.[181] Worsted toys, too, were soon complemented by silk-worsted ones. Between them, these two kinds were immensely successful. Previously, 'Taunton serges were much worn by women, but in a short time Norwich toys took place for that sex and became their wear.' Toys had a long run and were still going strong in Norwich in 1822. They were also made in Canterbury.[182]

One of the most famous of these new stuffs was Norwich crape. Amongst the cloths recently made by our old acquaintance Isaac Morly in 1661 was one 'cresp grograin'. In 1679 Thomas Dewing, worstedweaver, left twenty-seven worsted crapes, ten mixed crapes, and eight silk crapes, six of which were striped. Although their exact dimensions remain unknown, the three main types differed little in value and it is difficult to believe that the silk crapes were all silk. Indeed, if they had been, that fact would in all probability have been specially noted. Besides, the so-called silk crapes had slightly lower valuations than either the worsted or the mixed ones.[183] Now, crapes were used for various purposes. They were commonly dyed black for mourning attire, especially veils, and so called mourning crapes, and also for funeral clothes, and then called burying crapes. A highly crimped crape denoted deep mourning, a less crimped one light mourning. In addition, crapes were often put into bright colours for feminine adornment. This range of uses was matched by a gradation of qualities. Like other grograins, crapes could be made in triple as well as double twists, so that the ratio of worsted to silk could easily be set from one to five to five to one, and it was such variably mixed silk and worsted 'Norwich' crapes that were made in the city and the lesser towns of East Norfolk for a matter of two hundred years up to about 1860.[184] Worsted and silk were excellent for mixing in crapes, because they looked alike and shrank differently. It is therefore no wonder that some Canterbury silkweavers copied their opposite numbers in Norwich as early as 1678 and that by the opening of the next century some Stepney silkweavers had done the same.[185]

Antherine was invented in Norwich about the same time as crape, being first recorded in 1663. It was a kind of poplin, combining, in a plain weave, a fine, close silk warp and a worsted weft, so as to form a slight cross rib. Both singles and doubles were made. Antherine was presumably a bright and flowery stuff and was used chiefly for lining petticoats.[186] By 1715 the same stuff was being made in Stepney.[187] Poplins, and so called, were being made in Stepney by 1714 and in Canterbury by 1719. They, too, had silk warps and worsted wefts. By 1716 similar Venetian and Spanish poplins were being woven in Norwich. The Spanish ones were multi-coloured motleys.[188]

This period in Norwich saw the invention and ephemeral life of several other silk and worsted stuffs that little is known about. Such were the 'ephegenian' or 'effigene' of 1675–9, the 'virgins beauty' of 1679, and the baronet and silk baronet of 1679–81. Virgins beauty may have been related to virginato.[189] Of somewhat greater importance were the silk-worsted satinets introduced in Spitalfields and Norwich about 1700. It is not known whether their broken twills were four or six-end.[190]

The next major innovation was the grazet, a finely figured worsted and silk union camlet used especially for gowns. In 1685 'silke grazetts' were being woven in worsted and silk, and just the same sort of manufacture was being carried on in 1711. They occasionally went by the name of grazet camlets and were often described as being 'fine' or 'rich'. They appear to have been expensive products of the drawloom.[191]

Alepines, as made in England, were fine dress materials in a four-end broken twill, akin to satinets, with a warp of silk and a weft of worsted or jersey. They were being made in 1739 in Canterbury and somewhat later in Norwich. Their name was intended to suggest Persian silk from Aleppo.[192]

By now Canterbury manufactures were on the decline. They failed to shrug off the onslaughts from calicoes and from the general economic depression. The hopes pinned on the new, slight, plain woven, striped cloths, like the satin dimities, elatehs and dunjars of 1719, were unfulfilled. Only the dunjars had any considerable success, and they were taken up by the Norwich manufacturers. The satin dimities were neither satin nor modern dimity; they were merely laced with a secondary warp. In marked contrast to Canterbury, Norwich went from success to success. There was no end to the new inventions. Dorseteens, which were single camlets woven in tops yarns save for a linen or silk white weft stitch, came from both city and country looms in the second half of the century.[193] The messinets being made in Marsham in 1763 had Messina silk secondary warps that formed figures or flowers on plain weaves of worsted or jersey.[194] The Norwich shawl was copied from the *shal* woven in Kashmir from Tibetan goat's hair, but had silk warps and worsted wefts, often embroidered with silk or worsted crewel. This was a light and supple fabric that draped well on feminine figures.[195] The nineteenth century, too, saw the advent of challis, often regarded as the neatest and most elegant of all the silk-

worsted stuffs.[196] But now we are straying well beyond our own mounds and
bounds.

Anyone wishing to avoid the labour of studying Norwich and East Norfolk
textiles may excuse himself by fastening on such remarks by wholesalers and
worstedweavers as, 'The workmen did devyse severall names for the redyer
passage and utteraunce of the same', and, 'They ar newe names for the readyer
utterance therof', or on Thomas Fuller's words when he wrote, 'Expect not that
I should reckon up their several names, because daily increasing, and many of
them binominous, as which, when they begin to tire in sale, are quickened with
a new name ... A pretty, pleasing name, complying with the buyers fancy,
much befriendeth a stuff in the sale thereof.'[197] But our worthy Fuller had little
sympathy with feminine delight in beautiful attire or with masculine partiality
for natty suitings and fancy waistcoats or with people's pleasure in tasteful soft
furnishings, and these were just the things Norwich and East Norfolk
increasingly devoted themselves to supplying. There is a trick in every trade,
but it would be wrong to dismiss the marvellous flow of new inventions as mere
'public relations exercises', in which infinitesimal 'product differentiation' was
used to gull a 'consumerised society'. When the names of fabrics were
deliberately altered, it was more likely to be for legal reasons, as when the
Flemings called their kerseys stammets and their camlets grograins. The new
inventions were manufacturing innovations and deserved new names. When the
depositions of worstedweavers and traders are read more fully their meaning
becomes patent. William Gedney, a Marsham worstedweaver put it this way:

> The foresayd severall stuffs wer called by severall names because the workemen might
> have the better utteraunce of the same stuffs and they ... dyffer onlye in the
> workemanshippe and so differ only in shewe ... The change of wormanshippe ...
> hathe ben used this threeskore yeares and more ...and theare hathe ben more
> varyetye of wormanshipp of late yeares then was in former tymes ... The stuffes ...
> have theise severall names because of their severall kyndes of workemanshipp.

A Norwich worstedweaver named James Wilson added:

> The foresaid severall stuffes before mencioned receaved their severall names by the
> devisers that thei might have the better utteraunce of their clothes when thei wer
> made, and this he ...saith himselfe hath used. Being a workman he would devise a
> new fashion and so give a new name that he might have the better uttraunce ... For
> these xx[ti] yeares and more ever since he began to be a workeman himself in the trade
> he hath seen chaunge and variety in the workmanship of these stuffes, and well neere
> everie yeare a new invencion ... And this variety of workmanship hath ben more of
> late yeares then was in former tymes.

Other witnesses were in substantial agreement on this point.[198]

From Norwich, to a lesser extent from Stepney, and perhaps in some slight
degree from Canterbury, stuffmaking spread to other parts of the kingdom.

In the sixteenth century Kidderminster had little by way of textile manufactures. Shortly before 1600, however, clothiers here started to make what were called at first 'apernes', then 'Kiddermynster lynsey-woolseys', and finally Kidderminster stuffs.[199] When we first meet these stuffs in 1614 their warps were of English linen, but later German imports were substituted. Unlike linsey-woolseys as generally understood, Kidderminster stuffs had wefts of jersey, which by 1677 was being spun mostly from Irish pasture wool. When Kidderminster linsey-woolseys were spoken of, it was to draw a distinction between them and ordinary ones to which town names were never attached. Kidderminster stuffs were really the same or almost the same as the messolinas made in Norwich and may have derived directly from them. The secret of making these stuffs was to double and treble the weft and make it predominate over the warp. They were woven in colours on the loom, in earlier times largely as striped cloths otherwise called aprons, later in more variety, and they lent themselves well to watering. Table carpets, bed hangings, curtains, valances and upholstery covers were amongst the uses to which they were widely put. Their great success was due in part to the careful regulation, search and seal to which their manufacture was subject.[200] Kidderminster had this trade to itself; the only likely competitors, Norwich and Reading, turned to other arts.[201]

Dornicks manufacture was diffused to places within easy reach of its old base. From the middle of the sixteenth century, when sales were apparently expanding, dornicksweavers moved from Norwich and set up in East Norfolk country towns like Great Melton, Westwick, East Dereham and Reepham,[202] or in Bungay and district in High Suffolk. A second centrifugal wave started about 1615 and carried dornicks and associated manufactures to King's Lynn, Thetford, Bury St Edmunds and Peterborough. Elsewhere dornicksweavers were rare. The one in Lewes in 1616 probably represented an independent offshoot from Tournai.[203]

Stuffs incorporating worsted were made mainly in the old worsted spinning and weaving district, viz. in Norwich, East Norfolk and the satellite towns and in the neighbourhood of Bury St Edmunds, but also, to a lesser extent, in Stepney and Canterbury.[204]

It was far otherwise with mixed jersey stuffs, for jersey spinning and weaving were widespread. The favourite combination was of silk and jersey, like the mixed jersey prunellas being made in Sudbury in 1677,[205] the antherines, tamarins, calamancoes and tammies in 1696,[206] and the calamancoes in Soham in 1700 and in Stepney at about that time.[207] By now Newbury and Bristol were both making silk-jersey stuffs.[208] In and around the second quarter of the eighteenth century the manufacture of Spanish poplins spread to Kidderminster. Both these and the Irish poplins made here had silk warps and jersey wefts. They were all sent to be finished in Norwich and that city eventually absorbed, or re-absorbed, the whole business.[209] In the latter part of this century Alton was making tabinets and tabyreens, which appear to have been respectively finer and coarser silk-jersey stuffs akin to taborettes inasmuch as they had marginal tobine effects. These cloths largely went for window curtains. Like the silk-jersey bombasines made here early next century, they were finished off in London.[210] By this time similar bombasines, and Norwich crapes also, were being woven in Kidderminster and Bewdley and then sent to Norwich for finishing.[211] The sagathies made in Taunton and Tiverton in the mid-eighteenth century and the brocade damasks introduced into the latter town in 1752 likewise combined silk and jersey.[212] By 1697 or not long after the Chester sieve weavers were making mixed silk and hair tammy, which was no breach of their oath 'to keep to our occupation of weaving silk and haire search bottoms only'.[213] Norwich and London now remained as the two great centres of silk-jersey stuffmaking; even Kidderminster, Bewdley and Alton depended on them for finishing and other services.

Mockado manufacture was more thoroughly transferred. Wilton was the first English-made floor carpet with a woven pile. It was made three-quarters wide, in colours on the loom, and the pile was cut. The Earl of Pembroke started this business in 1740 by bringing over Walloon or Huguenot carpet workers. It was doubtless thanks to his efforts, too, that a patent was granted in 1741 to Ignatius Couran of London and John Barford and William Moody, both of Wilton. Couran was a 'merchant' or businessman, Barford an 'upholder' or upholsterer and therefore probably with experience of mockado and carpets, and Moody a 'clothier' and perhaps a carpet maker. Their 'new invention' was of 'French carpeting or moccadoes', i.e. hardwearing mockadoes with heavy, stiff hemp and flax grounds and thick jersey piles. The loom depicted in the original patent specification had no device for cutting the loops, so this process was either kept secret or done in the old way, by hand with a long knife. The great success of Wilton carpets prompted the innovation of handknotted carpets in Axminster, Exeter and Frome, and of Brussels carpets in Kidderminster. Wilton pile carpets drove the flat Kidderminster ones from the markets and the Midland town was saved only by the lone efforts of John Broom, who in 1749 found out the secrets of making Brussels uncut carpet. In 1755–6 Thomas Whitty of Axminster started weaving turkey carpets, but the knots were still made by hand. What the new Wilton and Kidderminster floor carpets had in common was that they were entirely woven and had several pile warps of different colours that could be looped alternately or in patterns so as to form a design on the face of the cloth, yet both kinds had a shedding movement so complicated as to preclude the possibility of long repeats and wide cloths.[214]

Finally, almost all these mixed stuffs had one thing in common: because of the difficulty in getting uniform hues on unlike fibres and of the opportunity they presented for making contrasts, they were rarely dyed in the piece, unless in black, and nearly always woven in colours on the loom.

# 7

## TOPS AND CARDED WOOL UNION
## CLOTHS

### Baizes

One of the first cloths made as a union of tops warp and carded wool weft
was baize. As we have seen, baize of some sort, perhaps with linen warps, was
on sale in the fourteenth century. Béthune may have been the only town
making hall baize subject to search and seal and intended for wider markets,
but we have no reason to suppose inferior types were not produced more
generally.

When we come to the sixteenth century we find towns in Flanders and
Brabant importing baize from what appears an outside source. In 1519 '*baeyen
oft voerlaken*' were expected to come in up the Scheldt, as though from foreign
parts.[1] In the middle of the century, the men of Hondshoote censured those of
Poperinghe, who had an exclusive privilege of weaving such fabrics, because
'par leur faulte la province est obligée de se servir de draps et bayes étrangers',
which carries the same suggestion.[2] This leaves England as the most likely
source, especially as we were importing no baize at this time.

Not to beat any further about the bush, it has been well known to scholars for
half a century that baize was exported from England to various parts of the
Continent long before 1560. In 1530 and 1535 Frans De Pape, an Antwerp cloth
merchant, was paying to have imported '*baaise*' dyed.[3] In 1538, at the
Koudemarkt in Bergen-op-Zoom, Andreas Ligsalz (Lixhals), a '*Duitsh*'
merchant in Antwerp, bought from George Cruys of London one hundred
'*baeylakenen*'.[4] Next year, at the same fair, Frans De Pape purchased of
Rowland Hill two packs and a half of '*baaise*'. In 1540 he bought two white
'*baaise*' from Humphrey Packington and five from Thomas Ly, who was Hill's
servant. In 1542 the same De Pape bought a pack of white '*baaise*' from Hill.[5] In
1544 Leonard Duppengiesser (Lenaert Doppegieter), an Antwerp merchant
born in Aachen, acquired a '*baeyslaken*' from Thomas Petrus of 'Sarum'
(Salisbury).[6] That same year a Swiss merchant from Herzogenbuschsee bought
in Antwerp five pieces of English cloth called '*bayeschelaken*'. Two years later a
Nuremberg merchant named Wilhelm Tramer bought from Thomas Loge

(Lodge), merchant of London, four pieces of English cloth described as *'bayssche laken'*. In 1546 Anton Waryn, a sworn woollen cloth meter in Antwerp, measured nine English cloths called *'bayssche laken'* and found them wanting. In that year, too, Hans Knaep of Lucerne contracted to buy from Jacob Van Gansenspoel *'xxviii packen baeyssch ingelsche lakenen'*.[7] In 1549, again in Antwerp, Cornelis Janszoen of Dordrecht purchased from Robert Lucs of London *'twintich baeyssche laekenen'*. Next year he had the ill luck to give good money to Martin Calthorp of London for *'vijf slechte laekenen genaempt baeyssche'*. From another English merchant named Jan Vode (John Wood) he took *'thien baysche lakenen'*. In 1550, too, Cornelis Corneliszoen, also of Dordrecht, bought from Richard Pyp *'een halff pack baysche witten'* that were as defective as the English greys, Castle Combes and worsteds he acquired. That same year again Jan Thomaszoen, a Dordrecht merchant tailor, purchased from a London merchant called John Rivers *'een pack baysche lakenen'*.[8] This evidence could be much expanded and even then would represent only a small part of the trade in baize, because it relates only to faulty white *'baaise'* and because many of the other faulty *'witte'* recorded may also have been baizes although not so described. Nor were the above mentioned years exceptional as far as on the baize trade was concerned.[9]

England was then the chief source of *baaise* or baize of hallmark quality, to wit, of a variety known in this country as 'handwarp'. Obviously it could not be sold under that name on the Continent, especially as it went in largely through a port we often called 'Andwarpe'.[10] This baize had a rockspun warp of pasture wool, which in East Norfolk would have been called worsted but was known in the Woodland as handwarp. Although it was common knowledge in the textile trade and therefore passed without comment, there was at least one occasion on which outsiders were successful in extracting the information that 'The worsted yarne is otherwise called handwarpe'.[11]

The seat of the handwarp baize industry was in the Woodland. Parliament gave special consideration in 1523 to the broad white woollen cloths made in Coggeshall, Bocking, Braintree and Glemsford. The object in view was the exemption of these cloths from the general prohibition on sale to alien merchants. Members of the Merchant Adventurers' Company were getting the export of white carded woollens into their hands, but the sole sale of worsted and half-worsted fabrics was not to be confided to them, and the woollens made in these four towns were regarded as union cloths. In 1551 these cloths were referred to under the heading of 'all whites' made in Suffolk, Norfolk and Essex or elsewhere 'as Coxsall whites, Glaynesfordes and other beinge handwarpes' and 'colored clothe and clothes ... made within the saide shires ... of lyke sortes commonlye called handywarpes'. Still another Statute, in 1557, explains how these handwarps differed from other broad white or coloured woollen cloths. 'Forasmuch as many persones doo counterfeit the making of Cocksall, Bocking and Braintree clothes commonly called handywarpes', it was forbidden to affix to counterfeits any deceitful lists that would make it easier to pass them off. No one was to put handwarp lists on any cloth 'excepte the warpe thereof be spunne upon the rocke or distaff'.[12] As Coggeshall men put it, 'Bayes are made altogither by handewarpe'. And handwarps were variously described as 'bayes of fyne fleece wull' and 'in waight, length and breadth equall to short Suffolk clothes saving they are afted and cottoned lyke unto a baie'.[13] Handwarps were in fact Suffolk white cloths or a superior kind of Suffolk coloured ones. Thus customs lists included 'white Suffolks called handiwarps'.[14] Handwarps of one sort and another, but all broad, weighty, full-bodied cloths, were made in Coggeshall, Bocking, Braintree, Glemsford, Witham, Clare, Cavendish and Pentlow. They were mostly made white and commonly called Glemsfords, Suffolk whites or Coggeshall whites. It was under this last name that they were best known perhaps, but to the weavers they were handwarps and to overseas merchants baizes.[15]

As to the wefts of these handwarps, they were spun from good, fine carding wool, much of it of local origin. John Norden observed in Essex in 1594, 'Ther are no great flockes of sheepe in this shire. Yet are ther sundrie places that yealde verie fine woull, but not in the depe countries: the most barren and heathye groundes yelde best woull, and especiallie Kingeswood heath, Lexden heath, Misley heath, about Ardeley, Alresforde, Thurrington, Empsted, and Typtree heath.'[16] The Sandlings Country, with all its heathy sheepwalks in Mistley, Elmstead, Thorrington, Ardleigh, Dedham, Foxhall, Rushmere, Martlesham, Danbury, Weeley, Sutton, Southwold and elsewhere, gave wool 'next to Leominster ... in fynes', and it was this that allowed Norden to describe Coggeshall whites as the best in England, for it was this wool that went into the wefts of 'all the fyne Coxall clothe'.[17]

All this agrees with evidence in depositions taken in Colchester in 1618 from a number of English and Dutch clothiers and weavers in a case brought by John Fitzwilliam and John Wither against members of the Dutch congregation there. The dispute was as to whether the Dutch made handwarps or, as they maintained, bluelist baizes, and whether their stammets were kerseys and old draperies, as the two men alleged, or new draperies, as the Dutch were bound to assert, since they were not allowed to make the old. These terms, old and new draperies, are purely fiscal and irrelevant to our present argument. Fortunately, the matter that concerns us was common ground to both parties and their evidence about it is all the more reliable.[18] Richard Johnson, a Colchester fuller aged seventy deposed as follows:[19]

> Eight and fifty yeares agoe the broad handwarpe clothes were usually made in Cogshall and longe before ... the clothes called minikins were first made at Cogshall betweene thirty and fourty yeares since and they were made ... before the Duch came to inhabite in the town of Colchester; and ... the blew list bayes and country bayes are not of the same nature and condicion with the said handwarps clothes and

minikins, for the warpe of the handwarpe clothes was spunn with the rocke and the
warpe of the blew list bayes is spun with the wheele and is of a smaller thred, and also
the uffe of the handwarpe is a fyne Lymester woll and the uffe of the blew list bayes and
country bayes is commonly made of comblinges, noyles, skynn woll and locks; and . . .
the said blew listes and country bayes do much differ from the said minikins and the
spyninge of the blew listes and country bayes is a smaller thred then the minikins were.

Other witnesses concurred. From their depositions we can build up a description
of handwarp baize. The woof was of the finest wool and 'the warpe . . . of kembed
woll', not very fine, but strongly spun in a Z-twist. The warp consisted of seventy
portees, each with thirty-eight threads, giving a pitch of 2,600 ends in a cloth up
to fourteen quarters broad. The wefts were full and the fuller the better. For every
five strokes in the coarsest grade of handwarp cloth, the medium sort had nine and
the finest eleven. With wefts like these, spun in Leominster or other fine wool and
teased and shorn like fine cloth, handwarp baize combined the strength of
worsted with the soft face of Worcesters.[20] The finest handwarps were thus top
quality dress cloths. And then, over and above the range of ordinary handwarps,
there were the minikins, which were a Coggeshall speciality. These were similar
to the other handwarps in most respects, but their yarns were somewhat smaller
and they were woven to greater lengths.[21] Minikins were sold by their makers
'nether died not cottened . . . to be freesadowes but . . . left whyte to bee wroughte
to suche use as the drapers please, either for blancketts, carpetts or otherwise as
other whyte cloathes are'. That they were sometimes called 'mynikens or
frizadose' was solely because they were so frequently frizzed; any minikin was
'like to be a friseadowe'.[22]

'Al manner of woollen broade clothes being white may bee wroughte into
freesadowes'.[23] Some frizadoes were made in England, largely from Worcesters
and penistones, and even more were imported, especially from Holland.[24] Unlike
most other Netherlands woollen towns, Leiden, Haarlem, Gouda, Rotterdam
and Amsterdam had not taken to Spanish cloth. Instead, they made frizadoes
from home-made and English cloths. About 1548–9 the English fell wool used by
their weavers became unusually scarce and it took considerable goodwill and
effort on the part of the Merchants of the Staple to keep the Hollanders supplied.
After the Flemish migrations of the 1560s, 'the great clothinge in England' so
enhanced the prices of woolfells and fell wool as to threaten the very existence of
the frizado industry in Holland; it stayed in business only by importing ready-
made English cloth and baize. Previously, it seems, the Leideners and others had
frizzed largely their own baizes, like the *oude Leidsche baaien*, which incorporated
fell wool. They would have preferred to have gone on in this way and as late as
1578 were still seeking fell wool 'to worcke the said frizadowes, bayes and
suchlyke comodities withall'. This proving fruitless, they were forced to rely on
imported cloths, a few of which were ratines but the overwhelming majority
baizes. Frizadoes of baize were always their commonest and latterly their
favoured product.[25] And the best type of baize for this purpose was the minikin.

As a document penned in 1594 explains, 'whereas a great quantitie of our white clothes which were transported into the Lowe Countries were there bought by the Duch and converted into frizedowes, now these minikins do serve for the same use and better lyked of'.[26] It was the same in England: handwarps, particularly minikins, were preferred, for the simple reason that they were substantial enough to be wrought on both sides,[27] and were good dress baizes into the bargain. And this was why they sold so well in Dordrecht and Antwerp in the 1540s and 1550s.

Ordinary handwarps went on being manufactured right up into the 1620s and minikins a great deal longer.[28] Between them they covered a great span of time. In 1618 old men could remember minikins being made in Coggeshall forty years before and other handwarps, both there and in Bocking and Halstead, even earlier.[29] The statutes show that handwarps, or crumple-list bastards, which we take to be the same, were made at Coggeshall, Bocking, Braintree, Glemsford and elsewhere in 1557, 1551 and 1523. In a lawsuit in 1575, Coggeshall baizemakers won their case after testifying 'that this maner of bayes now used in Essex was usually made in that countrye above thirtye yeares before the date of his letters patentes', meaning the grant to John Hastings in 1569.[30] John Johnson·said in 1573, 'It is not forty yeares past that Antony Bonvis, an Italian merchant, brought into England the practise of fyne clothing at Coxsall etc'.[31] Perhaps John Leake was echoing him in 1577 when he wrote 'About the 20. of H.8 began the first spinning on the distaffe and making of Coxall clothes ... Theis Coxall clothes weare first taught by one Bonvise, an Italian.'[32] Howes said the same, but, then, he merely copied Leake.[33] Johnson and Leake were not alluding to minikin baizes, for these had only just been invented. In 1618 Thomas Laurence, a sixty year old Coggeshall clothier, related how 'the broad handwarpes called mynikins for six or seven and fortie yeres since were made at Coggeshall and were devised by Richard Enewes his then maister, an Englishman'. His father had been employed by Enewes to weave not minikins but broad kerseys, and it was only after his father's time that Enewes invented minikins, which would have been about 1572, when Thomas was just starting his apprenticeship.[34] This agrees with testimony given in 1578. To an enquiry whether 'there is a newe sorte of clothe made abowte Coxall, Braintree, Bocking or Boxstede or anye other place in Suffolk or Essex like to be a friseadowe', the answer was that such was 'comonlie knowne and begone verie latelie, not past foure or five yeres since'.[35] This accords, too, with the evidence given by Richard Johnson, the Colchester fuller, in 1618, to the effect that minikins had started thirty or forty years before.[36] Nor are Leake and Johnson likely to have had in mind, when writing in the 1570s, the very first invention of broad white Coggeshalls with tops warps, for these were certainly being made in 1523 and, indeed, by 1518 or earlier. Thomas Paycocke, the famous Coggeshall clothier, who died in 1518, employed 'kembers, carders and spynners' and was engaged in making baize or some other union of combed and of carded wool.[37] It was to this new manufacture that he probably owed his fortune. However, it is of some significance that the statutes first attached the name 'handwarp' to these union cloths only in 1551. It may well be that in Paycocke's time they had wheelspun warps. We do know that baize with jersey warps, less fine than handwarp baizes and only some ten quarters broad, was being made in some Woodland towns by 1539 and probably before, and that it was still being produced in Coggeshall and district a hundred years later.[38] Very possibly it was being made as early as 1483 and was what was intended in the statutes by the term 'bastard', which meant a mongrel or union cloth.[39] If this were so, it would justify Leake's pointed remark about spinning on the distaff. It would also leave ample room for Antonio Bonvisi to have been the leading spirit in the invention of handwarp Coggeshalls somewhere about 1529–32, as Johnson and Leake suggest, for, although Bonvisi was an Italian, he had lived in England since early childhood, perhaps all his life, was a man of great parts, had business interests in the wool and woollen trades, and had made his first fortune by 1513. He was a very old man when he died in 1558, so he may even have played a part also in the invention of the original tops warp baizes in the Woodland, or, if not, his father perhaps.[40] This would explain why a Bildeston clothmaker named John Stansby was employing twelve Italian servants in his business in 1483–4.[41] This Italian connexion would repay further study, but at least we have no reason to disbelieve what Leake and Johnson say about Bonvisi and handwarps. Furthermore, if handwarp baize had been invented only about 1530 it would help to explain why it was selling so well on the Continent in the 1540s and why it fetched such good prices.[42]

For a long time the Flemings had nothing to match handwarps. If baizes were still made in Béthune, they were not dress ones. Poperinghe produced only a limited range of baizes and none finer than 54s, which were not a patch on handwarps.[43] One is inclined to think Flemish dress baize was invented in Ypres in the 1550s. Baize manufacture there was first regulated in 1554; it was still being pursued in 1558;[44] and former inhabitants were prominent in the production of Flemish dress baize in England. Within two years of their arrival in Sandwich in 1561 the Flemings were exporting this kind of baize and it is inconceivable that they developed it from scratch over here in a town where no baize and little cloth of any description had previously been made.[45] For another thing, the baizes the Flemings made in their several settlements in England were so alike they must have had a common origin in their homeland. That there was a baize boom in Flanders in the late 1550s and early 1560s is hardly to be doubted. Town after town took up the new industry.[46] But it came in one door and went out of the other. It fled and migrated *en masse*, to England, to Frankfort-on-the-Main,[47] to Leiden, where it was already established by 1562,[48] and to Amiens, where the saymakers complained '*que les tisserands fissent nouvelle marchandise appelée baye*'.[49]

Few of these seeds fell on stony ground, but none on more fertile soil than

England's. The Ypres baizemakers were delighted with Norwich. By the end of 1566, they were well settled in there.[50] In August 1567 Jacob Muus wrote to his wife, '*in de Tegelstrate te Yperen*', 'And I doubt not God, who shall help us and nevermore forsake us. We shall get a living well enough too. You would do best spinning bay and I in my position, so with God's help we shall not want.' Next month Clement Baet sent a letter to his wife '*tot Ypre ter Berde Poorte*' saying the baize trade was good in Norwich, and going on, 'I shall look for a house as fast as I can to help us into the trade, for with that a living is well gained. I am going to have a bay loom made against your coming. Your sister lets you know Lein cannot come here and do her sort of work, for one does nothing but bay work here.' In October Chrispijn Polderman sent to Frans Van Den Kasteele, '*by het 'sGraven Wal tot Ypre*', to tell him, 'Franssen my brother is with a Willem Van Den Schoore and strikes baize and earns £2 grooten a year and gets a good living'. About the end of December a girl named Maeyken wrote to her father, Pieter De Wert, urging him to come over and bring her mother, for an ample living was to be got here and there was freedom of worship as well. Recounting further news of her sister and herself, she adds, 'We are both learning bay spinning'.[51] The knowledge that these letters were preserved only because they were seized by the authorities in Flanders to help them with their persecutions, makes them all the more moving, but they also cast light on the origins of the Dutch baize manufactures and show how many of the immigrants abandoned their former occupations and learned some branch of the new trade instead. It was the same story in Canterbury. As the Flemings there said themselves, 'beyng of sondry trades and occupacions and therto fyrst brought upp as pryntyses, then refrayned, and . . . yet do, to exersyse or use the same, and theruppon dyd bend and indevor themselves to the weavyng, workyng and makyng of bays.'[52] Their old callings were often closed to them over here, but even then it is significant how many were attracted to baizemaking. Migration facilitated rather than impeded its prosperity.

It looks as though most of the Flemish makers of dress baize emigrated. Baize workers were prominent amongst the strangers arriving in Dover.[53] Baizemaking loomed large in Sandwich and by 1566 had been set up in Colchester. Only a year before a party of fifty strangers coming there from Sandwich had included eleven baizemakers and two baize fullers. By 1573 the throng of Colchester Dutch had risen to over five hundred and a large proportion of them were involved in the baize business.[54] Another party of Flemings set up baizemaking in Canterbury in the years 1574–6.[55] Meanwhile another group had trekked to Maidstone and started the industry there by 1568.[56] By 1578 or 1579, too, Dutch settlers in Thetford had established the spinning of both warp and woof baize yarns and the warping of baize yarns.[57] In or about 1576 or 1577, moreover, some of the Colchester Dutch hived off and went to make baize in Halstead.[58] These events had been paralleled in Leiden and in 1577 a party of Flemings, including baizemakers, removed thence from Colchester and

Norwich.[59] They were joined in 1588 by some of the Halstead Dutch baize-makers.[60]

Baizemaking eventually recovered in Flanders, but only slowly and partially. At Poperinghe, after the iconoclasm of 1566, the mass emigration, the raid by a band of 'beggars' from Norwich and Sandwich in 1570, the oppressive yoke of the Ghentish *geuzenrepubliek* from 1577 to 1578, the iron heel of the Spaniards from 1585 to 1586, and the depredations of the Ostend freebooters, it is no wonder the textile industry suffered.[61] Baize was still being made there in the summer of 1578, but by this time little of it was dress baize, and by 1590 none of it hall baize. All except the coarsest was now imported from England and even in the eighteenth century Poperinghe made none of a higher pitch than 54.[62] Nieuwerke only finally re-established its baizemaking in 1583.[63] Armentières recovered as well as any town and better than most. But what was lost could never be recaptured.[64] In 1609 the Poperinghe drapers drew attention to 'la petite traicte et vente des draps et bayes de ce pays et le grand nombre qu'on apporte d'Angleterre. Lesquelles se peuvent vendre par les marchans anglois a beaucoup moindre prix que ne font celles du pays, a raison de la grande abondance et petit prix des laines qu'ils ont au dict royaume d'Angleterre, au regard des provinces de pardecha.' They explained 'la diffaillance de la dicte draperie des bayes' wholly by this plenty and cheapness.[65] There was much truth in this. Amiens had her share of Flemish emigrants who left their homeland '*pour y vivre catholiquement*', but precious little is heard of baizemaking there after the 1570s.[66]

While the Flemish baizemakers in England were riding on the crest of a wave, the original English industry was still booming. In the Woodland it spread to the limits and beyond, extending to Maldon, Witham, Stebbing, Long Melford, Cavendish, Somerton, Bury St Edmunds, Timworth, Langham, Hadleigh, Nayland, Boxted, Great Waldingfield, Dedham, St Osyth and Inworth.[67] From about 1575 baize was made in Shrewsbury;[68] from 1576 in Barnstaple;[69] from near that date in the Butter Country, especially in Sturminster Newton and Chard;[70] from 1595 in Coventry;[71] from about 1607 in Rochdale, Rawtenstall, Haslingden, Bury and Rossendale generally;[72] from 1610 or before in Bristol;[73] from 1622 or earlier in the Cheese Country;[74] from 1630 and 1631 in Torrington and Crediton;[75] from at latest 1637 in Goudhurst;[76] from 1667 certainly, from 1613 possibly, in the Vale of Taunton Deane;[77] and from 1688 near Halifax.[78] What with these towns and places and the Flemish settlements, baizemaking can be said to have spread to almost all quarters of the kingdom.

The industry grew and spread in Holland also. By 1596 a manufacture of baize had commenced in Kampen and in 1648 it rivalled that of Leiden. By 1616 Amsterdam was likewise making baize. Shortly before 1589, too, the industry was introduced into Strasbourg.[79]

It was only because their baizes differed markedly from the existing English ones that the Flemings were given permission to make them over here. Permission may have been slightly easier to get because the best-known English baize was sold under another name. This situation certainly gave rise to misap-prehensions. Thus a royal commission in 1592 solemnly came to the conclusion that Englishmen only started to make baize about 1578 and that 'bayes were not known when the last Book of Rates was made and therefore not rated', and this despite a confession from the commissioners themselves that when witnesses tried to explain technical points to them, 'no man wist what they ment'.[80]

The impression made by the few stray pieces of evidence we have is that only coarse baize of lining quality was made in Flanders before the introduction of dress baize in Ypres and its imitation in Nieuwerke, Poperinghe and other towns. Even then the best dress baize, the *oultrefine*, seems to have had no more than fifty-four portees or *ganghen*, each of fifteen *pypen* or reels, amounting in the whole to 1,620 ends. These 54s had wefts of fleece wool, whereas some inferior types used fell wool, but none was allowed to include hairy or lambs' wool or flocks and other offal. As far as can be seen, the warps were always wheelspun. There is no sign of any baize approximating to the English handwarps.[81] However, the evidence is so sparse that we dare not rule out the possibility that in Ypres and elsewhere finer baizes than 54s had recently been developed. When we look at the baizes made by the Flemings in England, this possibility grows into probability.

The first Flemings to make baize in England were the Sandwich Dutch. They were allowed to import essential supplies of Flemish 'baye yarne', which suggests their fabrics were much the same here as they had been over there.[82] Before long similar yarn was being spun by Dutch and English women and children in Sandwich, and by 1621 baize chains were also being imported from Colchester.[83] Selected 'bay wool', oiled with butter, made the wefts, and the warps were of wheelspun fleece wool. Nothing but virgin fleece wool went into the baizes. Consequently they dyed well in the piece and took crimson excellently.[84] In 1584 the manufacturers were turning out what the English incorrectly called 'singles' and 'doubles', the former being the 'lowest sorte' and the latter the 'highest sorte', namely 80s and 100s, which were finer, longer and wider than the others. These 100s appear to have been invented within the previous ten years. They weighed about a fifth more than the 80s and were the first baizes in the world to be warped with a hundred portees. Sandwich was one of the only two towns ever to make them.[85] All Sandwich Dutch baizemaking was carefully regulated and conscientiously searched and sealed. In addition to the alnager's crown seal and that of the town, a third one showed the warp count, and a fourth the quality. Best baizes were sealed with a ship, middling ones with a rose, and the others with a fleur-de-lis.[86] Originally, it may be guessed, only 54s, 60s and 68s were made; the 80s and 100s came later. As far as can be seen, no Sandwich baize was ever milled; it was all walked by foot.

About 1565 some of the Sandwich Dutch removed to Colchester. The baizemakers among them had already started making their dress baize when they were joined by newcomers, from Nieuwerke, Menin, Bailleul (Belle) and other Flemish towns, who were more interested in the manufacture of coarser types.[87] Thus two distinct baize industries were carried on side by side in one and the same town.

Their dress baize the Colchester Dutch made solely of fleece wool, that for the warps coming from the Midland Plain chiefly and that for the wefts from the heath flocks of the Sandlings Country and probably from the Vales of Hereford also.[88] The makers employed scores of 'thickers' to walk these baizes 'by the foote' in the 'footestocke',[89] and they had the naps raised with locally grown teasels set in wooden frames.[90] At the outset they made only 54s, 60s and 68s, adding 80s to the range about 1571 and broad 'hundred bayes' some ten years later. The English dubbed the 54s 'singles', the 60s 'middles' or 'half doubles', and the highly pitched ones 'doubles'.[91] Colchester 100s apparently derived from the Sandwich ones and like them were in great demand because they dyed so well in the piece.[92] All the work was carefully regulated and an elaborate system of search and seal constantly maintained. Ordinary baizes bore only the loom-mark, the fuller's seal, the crown seal, and another 'to expresse the numbers of threddes of every piece, whereby the true goodness and value thereof is discerned of every buyer'. Lacking any further distinction, they were usually known as 'crown baizes'. Best baizes were marked with a cross. Unduly short ones had a large corner cut off one end and were sold as 'cutts'. Badly made ones had their lists rent off and were so called 'rents'. Even when taken up by native Englishmen, the manufacture of dress and hall baize in Colchester was always subject to the search and seal of the Bay Hall, which was run under the privileged authority of the Dutch congregation. Coarse baizes, however, were exempt from regulation. Painful handiwork, meticulously and strictly ordered, ensured hall baizes maintained their high quality for a hundred years and more, so when baizemaking decayed in other Flemish settlements, Colchester was left, in Evelyn's words, 'the only place in England where these stuffs are made unsophisticated'.[93] Her dress baize was readily recognisable 'by the clereness and evennes of the same'.[94] It was, however, by no means unchanging. The range had previously been extended upwards to the 80s and 100s, and by 1720 a new class of superfine baizes had been started, with red lists and six seals.[95]

In addition to their hall baizes, the Colchester Dutch, especially, it may be supposed, the later arrivals from Menin and elsewhere, and their English imitators, had taken up, by 1578, the manufacture of country and bluelist baizes.[96] What the Dutch called country baizes were the Woodland ones with jersey warps and coarse wefts, which we shall see later and need no description here.[97] The bluelists, however, were a Dutch invention. They had stammet jersey warps of fleece wool and wefts spun from fell wool, lambs' wool, noils and flocks. These weft wools had to be carded with 'a sort of new deepe and large cardes as hath bin of long tyme used for the same, the price of those cards being double the value of other sorts of ordinary carde'. Bluelists were made as 60s, each portee having thirty-two threads, giving a pitch of 1,920; and they had at most three strokes in the weft for every five in the coarsest type of handwarp. Because of their scanty warps of thin yarns and their sparse wefts, bluelists could not withstand frizzing or heavy dressing. They were commonly 'thicked with the mill'.[98] Michael De Butterdrier, an old Dutch baizemaker, testified in 1618, 'The Dutch have alwaies used to thicke their hall bayes at the foote and their blewlistes ... and country bayes at the mill'. This was generally true, but about 1605 the Dutch 'restrayned the thickninge with the mill, of purpose to sett their own poore people on work'.[99] Bluelists were treated as double baizes for customs purposes, but this was only on account of their inordinate length, the customs men being forced to recoup the revenue by entering them as notional minikins, 'not having any other rate for them in theire Book of Rates'. They were really singles and although later made three-quarters broader than at first, they were never as broad as minikins.[100] However, by 1603 the Colchester Dutch were making a few stammet minikins that approximated to the handwarp variety.[101]

Many or most of the Norwich Dutch baizemakers originated in Ypres and in many respects the baize they made remained basically the same.[102] But in Norwich they took to using worsted for their warps and were specially permitted to buy it for this express purpose.[103] Good fleece wool went into the wefts. In 1571 it was strictly forbidden *'eenighe corte stoffe als cammerlinck, achtertreck oft anders en sla ofte late slaen in bay ketenen'*, which was translated at the time as 'to put into any baye cettens any short stuffe as nyles and such lyke'.[104] But *sla* means not simply to put into, but to strike the weft on to the *ketenen* or warps. To forbid putting noils, flocks and such like in warps is senseless, for no one has ever found a way of doing it. Another translation was better when it said, 'putte into any baye anye shorte stuffe as nyles and suche lyke', for this avoided the difficult word *ketenen* and the spurious 'cettens'.[105] An instruction to the governors of the craft, headed 'Naughty Wolle', is more explicit. They 'shall not lett passe anye lambes woolle nor anye other shorte woolle but ... shalle carrye it owte of the citye and within fouretene dayes after the judgemente therof to bringe certificate who have yt and what is done with yt'.[106] This abhorrent short wool included what was taken from fells. It was ordered that 'no stranger whether hee bee marchant or draper undoe or unpack any pelt woolle or other short wooll' except under the strictest supervision.[107] All strangers were bidden 'that none put amonge there wull any pulling as nyls and such other for to doo to spin'.[108] To make sure no noils, flocks, or lambs' or fell wool went into baize weft yarns, a new order was made in 1575 that, 'nobody hoe he is Duch or Walloone ... shall not presume to buy heere within the cittie or within the surbarbs of the cittie any fat bay of yarn that shall bee broght without the cittie if it sholde be that before the wull therof the sayde is spun wer warranted of the governours'.[109] In 1577, too, the strangers complained that,[110] dyverse disordered parsons have practized (oute of the seyde citye) to myxte lambes woolle, shorte woolle and other unlawfull stuffe and good woolle together and do worke and spynne yt into uffe (comonly called inslaghe of bayes) at Thetford and other places oute of the seyde citye withoute regarde what sayme the same be wrowghte wythe, and they brynge it hether to be solde and is putte into bayes, which utterlye spoylethe the worke.

Evidently the wools were neither good in themselves nor properly oiled with butter. Remedy was sought in an order[111]

that from henceforthe no uffe for baietrye (comonlye called inslaghe of bayes) wroughte owte of the seyde citye shalbe put to sale to anye straunger Duch or Wallowne within the citye of Norwiche and subburbes of the same, excepte the woolle wherof the seyde uffe is made be fyrst viewed, prepared and delyvered by the artizans of the baietrye within the seyde citye to be sponne accordinge to the orders made for the same.

So far were the Norwich Dutch from putting noils and flocks into their baizes, that they were able to sell as a by-product some seventeen tons of them a year, mainly noils, necessitating a special Noil Hall for sales to 'dyvers of our people within this city ... which in tyme paste have susteyened a lyvinge as wel in making yerne of nyles as also in convertinge the same into blanket and other course clothe'.[112] The seaming of baize woof wool was also controlled. Amplifying that of 1571, a new order was issued in 1575: 'Noynt not with oyle: ... nobodye shall greace his wull to make uffe on it with any oyle or any other naughty greace but only butter.'[113] That these baizes were fulled by foot is proved by the order 'that no fullers shall com to the stars naked without a napern from the midell downwardes uppon payne of vj d every tyme ... and the correction of the menn'.[114]

In 1571 the baizes made were 54s, 60s, and 68s. The bobbin-carriers used for warping had fourteen reels each and the regulation was that 'the bay shalbe warpen with 14 pypes in 46 windes abowt and the 60 bayes in 51 windes and half abowt and the 68 bayes in 58 windes abowte', giving counts of 1,288, 1,442, and 1,624 respectively. The 54s were seven quarters broad, the 60s seven-and-a-half, and the 68s at least two ells, with a maximum when fulled of eight-and-a-half quarters. Besides full cloths, small pieces were woven in lengths of eight Flemish ells (about six yards) or less. Each cloth was ended with red stripes and the lists were also red.[115] Most baizes were dyed in the piece and a few were converted into frizadoes.[116]

Norwich men were quick to take advantage of the introduction of baizemaking. Two woollen weavers were sent to study the art, local lads were apprenticed to alien baizemakers,[117] and a group of eight citizens who set up in the trade for themselves hired a Walloon baize expert for a year to help them over the initial difficulties.[118] As early as July 1570, so it is recorded, 'The makynge of bayes hath bene attempted and practised by dyverse of ower citezins; which bayes hath not had their full profering by reason they have not passed under searche nor the defaults corrected orderlye'. The same solution was found as in Colchester; the strangers were given full rights of search and seal over the English baizemakers,[119] and these regulations were still being enforced in the early seventeenth century.[120]

The Maidstone Dutch made baize for a period of about ten years, and were turning out between one and three hundred a year in the middle of the 1570s, but no authentic record of manufacture here is found after 1577, one reference to it in a state paper in 1594 being clearly erroneous.[121] The strangers who came from Winchelsea to Canterbury in 1574 were joined a year later by the Walloon congregation formerly residing in Sandwich. In arranging this immigration, the city had purposed to choose baizemakers, and she gave them liberty to work.[122] From this time forth, right up until about 1612, the Flemings and their English imitators continued to make baize, but after 1588 the industry stagnated and from 1597 went into full decline.[123] The Dutch community in Halstead was never large, numbering perhaps about forty, and it never enjoyed privileges as full as those granted in larger towns, chiefly because the indigenous baize industry was already flourishing here and the English demanded that the Dutch submit to the borough search and seal. This caused bad blood and much recrimination. Matters came to a head in 1588 and within the year the Dutch had departed, some returning to Colchester and others making for Leiden. The only thing we learn about the Halstead Dutch baize is that, according to those of the townspeople who regretted the exodus, Dutch ones 'sold at a better price then the bayes of ther owne makinge, by reason of the seale which the seyd Duch sett to ther bayes'.[124] Little is known about Dutch baizemaking in Thetford, save that it was regulated, searched, sealed, and brought to a special Bay Hall. We catch a glimpse of one of the congregation who had sinned 'over a baize he had dyed contrary to the regulations, incurring sentence by the wardens, wherefore he was condemned to a penalty'.[125] However, the Dutch here made no great number of baizes; they concentrated rather on producing yarns and warps for the Norwich Dutch baizemakers. In 1577 they are found making 'inslaghe of bayes' for sale in the city, and a year or so later 'the Duchemen are aggreed to paye to thuse of the towne for every warpe of yarne that shalbe made or uttered by them to sell, ob. from this daye furthe'.[126]

Finally, it is not beyond the bounds of possibility that Flemings started baizemaking in Coventry. Some had settled in the city about 1570, for in that year a Dutchman trained in Geneva was invited to take up a ministry there.[127] Moreover, in 1576 the Sandwich Dutch, whose turn it was to arrange the regular colloquium of the English Dutch Reformed Churches, wrote to the London Dutch saying they had sent invitations to Colchester, Norwich, Great Yarmouth and Thetford and asking them to inform the Maidstone Dutch of the day of the meeting, and also any other communities in King's Lynn, Ipswich, Coventry and elsewhere.[128] Lynn, Yarmouth and Ipswich had communities and the Sandwich men evidently thought Coventry was to be classed with them. Baize was certainly being made in Coventry in 1595 and the next few years, but what little evidence we have suggests it was ordinary English or 'country' sort, for we find mention of 'bay wofe', 'jarsey yarne' intended for baize warps, and 'ij bays at the mill'.[129]

Although Flemish hall baize all seems to have sprung from one source, Ypres, as we think, it developed along slightly different lines in the various foreign towns to which its manufacture migrated. Yet it retained a large measure of uniformity. That it did so was due in part to the strong links that were maintained between the scattered congregations. They were in constant touch with each other and there were frequent comings and goings between them, including marriages between members of different communities, the recruitment of intended wives and husbands from the homeland, migration and temporary movement from one congregation to another, and periodic colloquia. Not surprisingly, all Flemish hall baizes long continued to have many common basic features. They were all dress cloths. They were all, in Leiden as elsewhere, made in 54s, 60s, 68s and 80s, and in two places as 100s. Leiden attempted 'brede bayen op te Zandwiche manier' in 1596 and again in 1656–8, but with scant success. Generally the 80s had 1,920 ends, the 68s 1,632, the 60s 1,440, and the 54s 1,296, and their dimensions were much the same in all places.[130] Hall baizes were walked by foot 'at home', and were mostly woven white. Their naps were raised with king teasels, not with iron rowing-cards or other devices. Only virgin fleece wool was employed. The English clothiers of carded woollens were always complaining that the strangers used fine clothing wools for their baize wefts.[131] Lastly, the manufactures were meticulously regulated, searched and sealed. As the Colchester Dutch put it in 1584, 'Our bay and say Calling, as in other Dutch Churches, is a Government over the selfsame Drapery'.[132] Infringements of the keuren or hall orders were treated as sins in the sight of God and crimes against His elect. Fraudulent trade practice was regarded as a manifestation of papistry and an injury and reproach to the Church of God.[133]

It was quite otherwise with the other baizes the Flemings made. The Colchester Dutch are outraged when they discover some members of the London Dutch Church, 'whom we nevertheless take for detestable papists', passing off naughty country baizes as Colchester hall ones.[134] All makers of Dutch hall baize had to conform with the Flemish regulations, which were enforced by the strangers themselves under the authority of the boroughs and cities.[135] But the Dutch in Colchester also made country baizes,[136] and these were not subjected to strict scrutiny. A few strangers, too, may have made dress baize without the supervision of a Flemish hall. Those who went English and yet remained in the same privileged settlement were none the less bound to observe the strangers' orders, but some became altogether detached from their former congregations. For instance, Jan Bertolf, one of the Halstead Dutch, broke the agreement that bound them all to stay in the congregation, refused to pay the fine imposed by its elders, joined the Church of England, and stayed behind in Halstead when the rest of his countrymen left the town.[137] If he then made baize, it could only have been sealed according to one of the four qualities made there.[138] Then, again, it was perfectly open to any Englishman to make Dutch baize in a town where there were no strangers at all. Even in Colchester itself he could make Dutch bluelists without let or hindrance. In 1594 in and about Colchester, so we are told, the English 'do much observe the Duch making but their spynneing and weavinge is not so cleen nor orderly handled as the Flemings doo'.[139] In the end, too, Flemish regulation broke down because no Flemings remained to carry it on. It lasted longest in Colchester, but even here the Dutch congregation disbanded in 1728 and its few remaining members became English.[140] Thus in course of time English and Flemish baizemaking merged into one. English baizes were now made in many more varieties than before and they all went through the mill.

Barnstaple or Devonshire baize had been made for ten or more years[141] before we first hear in 1586–7 of the Barnstaple town seal for baize. A commission in 1594 reported that 'of late yeres good bayes are also made in diverse parts of Devonshire after the sorte of Duch makinge' and the very next year an official came down from Westminster to Barnstaple 'to seale the beaze and new made cloths'. A later distinction between single and coarse baize indicates that beside the 'singles' and 'doubles' derived from Flemish hall baizes, other coarse country ones were made. The 1660 Book of Rates, too, shows a Barnstaple coarse baize was much lighter and cheaper than any of the other sort. Moreover, the only extant probate inventory of a Barnstaple baizemaker, that for Thomas Pearse in 1646, lists, amongst other things, two 'bayses' appraised at £7 the lot and five at a total of £7 10s, the latter presumably being of the coarse, and the former of the fine variety. Furthermore, in the 1630s, Barnstaple and Torrington were making minikins and converting some into frizadoes. Here at least, and perhaps also in Crediton and elsewhere, both country and Dutch sorts were made side by side.[142]

In 1600 three sizes of baize were being made in Shrewsbury: 'yard bayes', 'v quarter bays', and 'brodd bayes'. Judging from what was paid for 'a stringe weavinge', i.e. per end, the third type was about seven quarters broad. All appear to have been coarse jersey baizes.[143] The same is true of Taunton baizes. In 1613 the customs officers at Lyme and Topsham had to be expressly instructed not to classify them as cottons, and the only inventory seen, of the effects of one Turke of Vellow in Stogumber parish, seems to show flocks in the abbs.[144] Possibly Bristol baize owed something to the influence of the Colchester Dutch. In 1610 the city attempted to introduce the manufacture of certain kinds of baize and say cloths, conferred the freedom gratis on some Colchester men, made them several substantial loans and other disbursements, and succeeded in setting up a manufactory in Smiths' Hall. This gave grave offence to the city weavers, as a result of which the newcomers were forbidden to make anything but baize or to retail it in Bristol. In 1613 the Colchester men were excused repaying half their loan on account of poverty. The scheme met with no more than the slightest success. Only one baizeweaver has come to light, a certain Thomas Cornock, who died in poverty in 1641 in Temple parish, where he had two looms set up in an old stable and three pieces of baize worth, it was supposed, £4 apiece.[145] So-called Manchester baize was made in and around Rossendale. Both singles and doubles were made, in widths of three quarters and one yard. Their warps were jersey and largely spun from Irish wool imported via Liverpool and Wigan. These baizes were similar to coarse Barnstaple ones in quality and price.[146]

The Woodland was the chief seat of English baize manufactures, both of the handwarp and the ordinary or coarse varieties. A passage in a state paper drawn up in 1594 runs: 'It maie be alledged by some that the trade of making of baies is of long contrievance within the realme, and I graunt it was so; but they were Sudbury baies, so verie small and course that they were lytle better than a cotton, for I have knowne them soulde for xx s and xxiv s the peace.'[147] The paper was concerned with the question whether or not the English had made baize before the Flemings came and it conceded that they had, but only Sudbury ones. As far as we can see, these baizes had been made since about 1539 and probably for some time before that, possibly even further back than 1483. They were woven about seven quarters wide and up to forty yards long. They had a right and a wrong side and could be safely frizzed on one side only, because, we are told, 'they have not substance to be wrought but of one side for that the most parte of them be made and solde but for lynyngs in England'.[148] Their warps were jersey and their wefts often contained fell wool, which came predominantly from pasture sheep. Baize woof yarns of a similar kind were being spun in Thetford in 1577 from lambs', fell and other short wool.[149] 'Short wool' embraced noils, and, as their output soared, was increasingly composed of them. In 1581 the Colchester Dutch complained to the London Dutch that some baize wholesalers among their members had counterfeited Bay Hall sealing irons and put Colchester Dutch seals on inferior English baizes, which had 300 fewer ends in their chains and used comblings in their wefts – 'tot inslach cammerlijnck ghebruucken'.[150] This hit off Woodland coarse baize, like 'Coxall baies or Essex baies,' perfectly. It was rather low in pitch and its weft consisted largely of noils. The Woodlanders were expert in the use of noils in the wefts of kerseys, blankets and coarse cloths, and they followed the same practice in their coarse baizes. Both they and the Flemings had long employed fell wool for such purposes and noils were not much different.[151] But only in the Woodland had baize woof yarns ever been made entirely from noils. The concept was simple. 'Niles are carded and spun for uffe of divers finesse ... Of the breech, taile, or other offall of the fleece of wooll is made a sorte of course warpe yarne called grasior, serving for the lowest priced baies. And of the niles of the same wooll, being carded, is made the uffe of the same bay.' So composed, a cloth could correctly be described as 'a Coxsoll baye and a kersey' or simply as kersey baize.[152] Much baize was thus made entirely of pasture wool. Some Coggeshall baizes even contained recycled shoddy. A dyer in Holland remarked, *'De Cocsaelse sijn gemeenlijk ooc van 2-derhande wolle'*.[153] But noil-weft baizes of virgin wool became the usual Woodland product. They already occupied this position by 1581. As late as 1602 they were still something of a novelty in Norwich. It was decided that 'a kynde of bayes made half of woll and half of nyles within this cittie shewed to the said eight men now present maye be lawfullye made by any Inglisheman within this cittie and here put to sale, so they beare no other seale then the alnager seale.'[154] Little noil-woof baize was made here however.[155] It belonged far more to the Woodland.

As soon as we turn to probate inventories for Woodland makers of baize, we find noil-weft baizes. In 1629 George Howe of Glemsford had been engaged in making baizes, and he still had a store of noils. In 1662 William Mascoll of Cavendish had been making baize mainly, and his 'niles' are listed as though found hard by his 'oufe' and in such a way as to make it difficult to resist the conclusion that the noils were going into the woof.[156] John Salter, a Sudbury saymaker, had been making baize as well. He had bought tops, noils and coarse wool, and was using the tops for his warps and a blend of noils and coarse wool for his 'bay uffe'.[157] Thomas Hawse, a St Edmundsbury clothier, made, amongst other things, red baize, and next to his stockcards the appraisers found not only short wool, coarse wool and 'nils', but also three packs of 'nile yarn'.[158] In 1684 an East Bergholt man left 'nilles' and 'nille yarne'.[159] Tobias Groome of Melford was a baizemaker and was making nothing but baize when he died in 1666. He left twenty-three pieces of baize, three baize chains on his looms, the woof yarns to strike them with, a coarse chain, a coarse raw baize, combing wool, baize warp, some of it coarse, equal amounts of coarse and 'fine niles', coarse and fine baize woof, and a score of pounds of forcings. He evidently bought combing wool and combed it in his own shop. He then drew two qualities of tops, which he had spun into fine and coarse baize warps, and left fine and coarse noils, which he had carded and spun into fine and coarse baize woof, except that the latter may have included some forcings, i.e. the worst and shortest fibres of all.[160] A Glemsford 'baymaker' named John Allen, who died the same year, left four baizes in the looms, 'nyles' and yarn found and valued together, and 'nyles at spinners'. His baize had noil woofs.[161] At the same time, in Melford, Richard Coe's main output was the forty-six baizes he had made or was making. His stocks included 'nyles'.[162] In 1686 Ralph Noves of Glemsford had been running a similar business. He had noils, yarns and warps in his wool chamber and wool and noils out at the spinners'.[163] In 1675 William Cox the elder, a clothier in Great Coggeshall, was making baize woofs from noils and fell and lambs' wool.[164] Thomas Keble, clothier of the same town, was putting noils into his Bocking and other baizes in 1693.[165] In 1733 Thomas Bridge of Bocking left, in the Bay Hall there, thirteen long baizes and large stores of flocks and

'niles' for baize woofs.[166] Richard Chaplain had a similar business in the same
town in 1739. In the same Bay Hall he left many baizes, and elsewhere, 'bays
warpe and woof', tops, flocks, 'bay wool sortings', forcings, head wool, noils,
'good niles and saimd wool' ready to be spun.[167] These we take to have been
Bocking baizes, which were made in Coggeshall also. A Coggeshall baizemaker
named Samuel Sparhawke notes in his account book in 1687, 'I had of Thomas
Browne 4 skor 11 lbs. of fine kniles at 6d a pond' and 'cours kniles gresy' and,
in 1690, 'I had of Thomas Browne 95 pond of kniles'. Sparhawke regularly
bought noils, lambs' wool, short wool, fine tops and both 'Norfolk' and 'Essex'
wools. He purchased tops and noils, had the tops spun on wheels for warps,
and mingled the noils, the short, the lambs' and the poor fallow wools, and
had these blends spun for the woofs.[168] As noted in 1578, 'Ther is a bey made
at Coxsall and Bockinge' seven and a half quarters wide. What distinguished
these Bocking baizes, also known as 'Baukine or Fleet hundreds', was simply
that they were 100s.[169] All these types, however, Sudbury, Bocking and
others, were varieties of the same species of Woodland baize.

This way of making baize hardly spread beyond the Woodland and its
environs. As we have seen already, Norwich accepted the Woodland method,
but put it to little use. Rossendale later made counterfeit or sham Bockings[170]
and in the middle of the seventeenth century Leiden baizemakers strove,
without much success, to develop noil-woof types.[171] This left the West Country as the Woodland's only real and serious rival in this field. In later years the
coarse Barnstaple baizes incorporated noils and the 'bay yarn' from Ireland
used in the West Country was reliably reported to have been made 'of the
dross of fine combed wool', which can only mean noils.[172]

New types of baize continued to be invented. By 1634 shag baize had
arrived. It had a loosely woven weft and a long, open, unshorn nap.[173] By
1678 swanskin baize was being made in Salisbury and district and in Sturminster Newton. This was a closely woven twill with lambs' wool wefts. It was
sometimes classified as a flannel and was suitable for inner petticoats.[174] Then
there was burying baize, which was a response to an absurd parliamentary
statute compelling the dead to be buried in woollen cloth. Abraham Slater of
Glemsford was specialising in this sort of baize when he himself died in 1707.
It was made of the cheapest and worst wools. The warps were, indeed, of tops
of some sort, but the woofs were blendings of black wool, flocks, noils and
what were called, with some contradiction of terms, fine and coarse
forcings.[175] People would no longer be seen dead in old-fashioned woollen
cloths. By 1668 quinco baize had made its appearance. It was of the worst,
only fit for wadding.[176]

Amongst the many articles made from one form of baize or another may be
mentioned cloak linings, petticoats, under-petticoats, vests, waistcoats, jerkins, fishermen's shirts, soldiers' uniforms, ponchos, monastic habits,
shrouds, bootsocks, curtains, hangings, table carpets, linings for postbags,

cases, trunks, bathchairs and coaches, coverings for card and billiard tables, doors and screens, and backings for looking-glasses.[177]

Baizemaking became an important branch of textile manufactures. In 1605 baize was 'the cheifest comoditie made within this town of Colchester'.[178] Celia Fiennes found, 'The whole town is employed in spinning, weaving, washing, drying and dressing their bayes' and 'the low grounds all about the town are used for whitening' them.[179] Tops and woof wools were put out to spinsters all along the Cambridge road as far as the western limits of the Chiltern Country.[180] The Woodland towns either wove baize, or joined Kersey in supplying baize woof yarns or, like Dunmow, were 'altogether taken up about the spinning and prepareing for the bayes'.[181] In their time Sandwich, Canterbury, Maidstone, Norwich and other towns were important centres of Flemish baize manufactures. Barnstaple had a score of baizemakers in the early seventeenth century.[182]

Such statistics as we have of the production and sale of baizes are incapable of presenting anything more accurate than an impression of the order of magnitude in the business. In the 1570s and 1580s Sandwich was making between 2,000 and 5,000 a year and the strangers alone were shipping out some 2,000.[183] In 1576 Canterbury produced 710 baizes and in 1585, 785, but the annual average in this period was only 627.[184] Norwich's output rose to peaks of over 10,000 a year in the 1570s and 11,000 and 13,000 in the early 1580s, but then declined sharply.[185] The claim that the Halstead Dutch sent 7,000 baizes a year to London was absurd,[186] but by 1689 Colchester was turning out about 38,000 a year. In 1684–5 she herself shipped out 18,537 double baizes. By this period, Woodland baize manufacture had probably passed its peak, but production is still estimated in tens of thousands.[187] Exeter alone exported over 3,000 Barnstaple baizes in 1624 and between 1,000 and 3,000 a year in the period 1636–8.[188] At the other end of the scale, however, towns like Coventry and Shrewsbury counted their annual outputs in scores rather than hundreds.[189] From 27 June 1577 to 7 June 1578 the London Bay Hall received 12,947 baizes of all sorts, excluding those from Norwich, which was exempt from hallage. Norwich Bay Hall was then sealing about 10,000 a year, so the kingdom's total output of hall and coarse baizes must have been somewhere about 25,000 a year, very likely more.[190] From Michaelmas 1594 to Michaelmas 1595 a total of 10,976 baizes were reported shipped out of England. This figure included 9,121 singles, 1,725 doubles, and sixty Sudbury baizes.[191] Between 1612 and 1622 exports from London, Colchester and Maldon amounted to some 4,000 singles, 18,000 doubles and 3,000 notional minikins a year.[192] On average from 1709 to 1711 some 42,000 baizes a year were exported, and from 1712 to 1714, 53,000.[193] For the year ending Christmas 1688 the alnage and other Crown officials estimated the total production of notional minikins at 9,600, of which 5,660 were exported; and of Colchester and double baizes at 86,000, of which 35,565 were exported. Allowing for singles and other omissions, total baize production must have been of the order of 100,000 a year.[194]

England remained pre-eminent in the manufacture of baizes. Leiden became the greatest baizemaking town on the Continent and her peak was reached in 1634 with an output of 8,323 baizes, amongst which were few if any hundred baizes. Her whole output of baizes, rolls and blankets put together, which reached a peak of 23,785 in 1633, was probably less than that of baize alone in Colchester.[195] English baizes were supreme both in range and numbers.

## Flannels

The fabric most akin to baize was flannel. It had a tight, hardspun warp and a loosely spun weft of carding wool. As in baize, the weft was made to cover the warp, but, unlike baize, flannel had its surface left as smooth and soft as possible. Patterns of flannel intended to be shown at the Naples and Salerno fairs in 1680 are preserved in Hawarden. As is to be expected, they are all dyed in the piece. Some are plain weaves, some two-and-two twills. All are closely woven from single yarns into slight, thin cloths, heavily fulled and pressed to produce smooth, soft faces on both sides. Accordingly, no nap has been raised. The wefts are composed of rather hairy and kempy yet generally crimpy carding wool. The warps, which are completely covered, are made of hardspun stammet jersey.[196] Flannels were designed to offer the least possible irritation to the skin and were widely used for undervests, underpants, drawers, trousers, chest-protectors, waistcoats, petticoats (especially inner ones), soldiers' and work-men's shirts, and cloths for ablutions. They served also as sheets employed in the pressing and drying stages of papermaking and, later, like baizes, as winding-sheets.[197]

Flannel (flannen, flaning, flanion, etc.) is unheard of before the sixteenth century. Supposed earlier references arise from mere misreadings. Nor is anything known about the derivation of the name.[198] Flannel manufacture had been introduced into England by the Flemings who came to Sandwich[199] and was referred to in 1581. Two years later flannels were on sale in Canterbury. Thereafter references to English flannel multiply. By 1600 it was being exported.[200] By 1598 the industry had spread to the western parts and environs of the Cheshire Cheese Country and the Vales of Hereford, by 1678 to the Woodland, by 1682 to parts of Ireland, and by the turn of the century to Romsey, Downton, Salisbury, Taunton, Barnstaple and, in the Butter Country, to Beaminster and Llanblethian. By the latter part of the eighteenth century it was gravitating to Rossendale and Kendal.[201] However, Rossendale flannels had cotton warps and the Flemish types linen ones, and so are not our immediate concern.[202]

English flannels mostly had tops warps and carded wool wefts.[203] Nearly all Salisbury flannels were of this kind. The manufacture of white and striped flannels is often said to have started in the city about 1680, during a depression in the Levant market for Salisbury whites. But it would be nearer the mark to say that when the market for Salisbury white flannels was depressed about 1680, the manufacture was started of white flannels with thin, bright stripes, rather like the 'four-by-two' used for cleaning rifle barrels. Salisbury whites were famous for their fineness, lightness and brightness, which Aubrey ascribed to the abstersiveness of the water there, and these were flannels. Indeed, Salisbury white became synonymous abroad with English white flannel. This manufacture long preceded 1680 and may even have started as early as 1612, for 'worsted makers' were at work in the city in that year and the tops yarns employed in the flannel warps were called 'worsted'. Later on 'Irish worsted' was bought for the purpose. It is barely possible some of these yarns were really rockspun, but almost certainly 'worsted' was always used here, in the erroneous western way, to mean 'jersey'. As to the wefts, they were of Chalk Country wool, so the cloths were highly durable.[204]

Coarse flannel came to be made chiefly on the western extremes of the Cheshire Cheese Country and of the Vales of Hereford, in and about Denbigh, Wrexham, Llangollen, Oswestry, Welshpool, Hay-on-Wye, Abergavenny and Pontypool and, with the import of Irish wool and jersey through Aberdovey and elsewhere, in Machynlleth and up the Severn valley as far as Llandidloes. The Shrewsbury drapers, who were foremost in the wholesale trade, started to buy flannels in Wrexham in 1621 and were still frequenting the market there in 1645. Later, as the industry grew in its vicinity, Welshpool became the great staple, and the Shrewsbury men had no more than fleeting success in their attempt to move the market to Montgomery, despite the lower tolls there. These flannels were sold to the drapers white, for dyeing in the piece. They were widely used for shirts for soldiers and workmen, especially for ironworkers and others who sweated profusely. Eventually the industry was mechanised in Newtown and elsewhere. It finally succumbed to the 'real Welch flannels' made in Rochdale.[205] As to the genuine articles, jersey yarns for the warps were generally bought ready made, partly from Cirencester, but mainly from Ireland, to some extent via Chester, Liverpool, Bristol and Gloucester, but very largely and uncustomed, through Milford and Aberdovey.[206] Although some March and other local wool was used in the wefts,[207] these were composed mostly of blended wools from much further afield. 'Some woolles growing in Norfolke', we are told in 1615, 'are brought three score miles or more to London, and from thence carried eight score miles and more into North Wales and there draped into cloathes, and so sent back againe and sould in London.' An elaboration and clarification of this statement explains that of the wools the staplers collected for blending from various parts of southern and eastern England, they sent 'the worst to Yorkshire, Lancashire and North Wales. 1,500 *lib*. a weeke paid in Osestrie for wolls' then draped into cloth thereabouts.[208] That these wools were used for flannel wefts is shown by the further statement that the wool merchants drove a great trade 'at Oswestree, where there dwell many clothiers that make ... flannels and use onely course sorts of wooll, and buy these sorts of wooll of the staplers ready sorted'.[209] These flannels were often called 'Welsh' and ranked with friezes, toasted cheese, and goats as fit matter for chaff and banter, and 'Welsh flannel' early acquired its secondary meaning of smooth-tongued duplicity.[210]

As far as can be seen, all the other wholly woollen flannels made in England were similar to one or other of the two types described, but some flannels continued to be made with linen warps.[211]

## Kerseys

Side by side with their handwarp baizes the Woodland clothiers made handwarp kerseys. These were woven broad and bore the name of broad kerseys. In 1618 Thomas Laurence of Coggeshall recalled 'broade' kerseys' being made there and in Halstead fifty or more years previously and long before the Dutch came to Colchester. He gave to understand that they were similar to what the Dutch now called stammets. His father had woven cloths 'called then broade carsies, nowe called by the name of stamettes by the Duch'. Stammets were all one with broad kerseys, he added, except that broad kersey warps were spun 'in the sayme' or oil and had a bigger thread, while stammets had warps of scoured yarn, which made a smaller thread. Stammets, however, were fully thicked and dressed as the broad kerseys were and were generally the same as the 'handwarpe carsey cloathes'. Michael De Butterdrier pointed out that stammets were kerseys under another name, and other deponents concurred.[212] In brief, Coggeshall and Halstead were making broad handwarp kerseys before 1565, before the Flemings came.

The Flemings had long concentrated on *'de draperie van carzeyen ende stametten'*, on *estamettes* or stammet kerseys. They were usually woven broad and thicked by foot.[213] We first hear of stammets of this general nature in Florence in 1333. The *stametti di lino* obviously had linen warps, but the *stametti alla francescha* may have been all wool. Similar stammets were being made in Milan in the sixteenth century.[214] A stammet yarn was simply one that had been scoured and made smoother and finer. Any kind of yarn could be treated in this way. Stammet baize and stammet says were occasionally made, but fine stammet yarn showed to best advantage in tammy cloths and in stammet kerseys, for in kerseys the smaller the warp ends the better the cloth and the easier the weaving: if the warp were fine, the weft could be smaller also and the whole fabric much neater; if the warp were fine, a shed could be formed more easily.[215] Otherwise stammet kerseys were basically no different from any others.[216] But the Flemish immigrants into England introduced the manufacture only of stammet jersey kerseys and it was this kind of stammet kersey that was mostly made here. Already in 1566 the Norwich Flemings were preparing to make their *stametten*, 'stamett or kersey' or 'stamet carseye'. Production was in full swing by 1567 and continued for several years, though always at a low rate.[217] The Colchester Dutch had a similarly modest success with their stammet kerseys. Whether fulled by foot as they earlier were, or in the mill, which had become common practice by 1617, they were never in great request.[218] In Sandwich the Flemings were surmisedly exporting stammet kerseys as early as 1563, but neither here nor in Maidstone, Southampton or Canterbury were large numbers ever produced.[219] Continental experience was similar.[220] Stammet kerseys, like other ones, were most apt for hose, but faced the competition not only of carded kerseys but also of broad ones with rockspun warps, which were of similar quality, and of knitted goods.[221] Nor were stammet kerseys any great novelty. They had been made in Florence and elsewhere for ages. They really were 'stametts of Florence', 'stammetts of the Flowers makinge'. They were usually just called stammets in England, but were 'bought and sould, cutt out and customed beyond the seas for stametts of Florence and not for English kerseys'.[222]

One use to which stammets of Flowers were put after 1650 was the production of ratines (rateens), which were frizzed stammets (or, loosely, stammets intended to be frizzed). The manufacturers, who were found in the Netherlands, the Rhineland, northern France, and elsewhere, raised the pitch of their stammets somewhat and then frizzed them themselves or sold them to specialist frizzers in Amsterdam, Rotterdam and other places.[223] In England, however, ratine making was hardly more than a fleeting episode in the early eighteenth century in the single town of Kidderminster.[224]

## Says

For fiscal purposes, stammets of Flowers were usually rated together with rashes. Lists and books of rates speak of 'rashe or stammett of the Flowers makinge' or such like,[225] because the two were akin in size and substance and in being Flemish introductions. Possibly many of these rashes were likewise of the Flowers making, which would have been an additional reason for lumping them with the stammets. Florence was noted for her rashes and her peculiar way of fashioning them was widely copied. Mantua was far from being the only place to produce rashes *alla foggia di Firenze*. It is highly likely some Flemish towns did the same. The woollen weavers in Florence were largely Flemings by origin and the ties between Flanders and Tuscany remained close.[226] Moreover, rashes of Flowers were made of English wools and were now most conveniently made in England. However, all we know of a certainty is that the Flemings brought to England their manufactures of Arras says, otherwise rashes, and that these had stammet jersey warps and carded woollen wefts, and were unrowed and napless.[227] The strangers, mainly Walloons, who came to Southampton in 1567, made, amongst other things, narrow and broad rashes. Narrow rashes were suitable for making into doublets, while broad ones, which were up to six quarters wide, were better for larger garments like cloaks.[228] In course of time this trade came into the hands of Englishmen, and although it died out in

Southampton about the middle of the seventeenth century, it had meanwhile spread to other towns in the South Seacoast Country, notably Dibden, Romsey, Lymington and Newport, and by 1696 it was also established in Newbury.[229] The Norwich strangers also made Arras says in the early years of their settlement.[230] Similar rashes were perhaps made by some Canterbury Walloons.[231] By 1651 they were certainly sending some of their says to be milled, which can only mean the wefts were of carded wool. In Colchester, by 1585 the Dutch, and by 1619 the English, were making milled says.[232] Few if any of these are likely to have been rashes, but they were somewhat similar unions of jersey and fallow wool.

However, it was in the Woodland in the early seventeenth century that milled or union says rose to their greatest eminence, and then they were of quite a new kind, having as they did wefts of East Anglian kersey yarn and even being occasionally called kersey-says.[233] Some of the surviving inventories give a glimpse of how the Woodland saymakers worked. In 1660 Josiah Browne of Cavendish left fourteen says, 202 lb. wool, 55 lb. 'neiles', 16 lb. locks, 41 lb. warp and roof, and '108 topps', all remaining in the same woolchamber. He combed his own wool and could conceivably have intended to sell the noils, but in all probability they were destined for say wefts.[234] William Newman of Clare, who died early the next year, seems to have worked in much the same way. He had a combshop, wool and noils in his woolchamber, and nine says ready to go to the mill.[235] The effects of Thomas Underwood the younger of Hartest were appraised the same year. He had sixteen tod of fleece wool, six score of handwarp wool, 38 lb. middle wool, 189 lb. tops, 80 lb. forcings, 20 lb. fine noils, 160 lb. 'say noyles', and twenty-nine gross of yarn. He was clearly a yarnmaster and it was evidently the sale of rockspun yarn of handwarp wool that accounted for the £43 owing to him in Norwich. What his forcings and fine noils were for, we cannot say, but his medium-quality 'say noyles' were earmarked for Woodland says.[236] Many other inventories yield circumstantial evidence of the use of noils for say wefts and also show that the best tops were not spun into jersey for say warps; handwarp wool, handwarp tops, handwarp yarns went for other uses.[237] Inventories also show noils were seamed, in oil, often in rape oil, and the 'saimed nyles' put out to be spun.[238] Noil-woof says were made in towns throughout the Woodland, but rarely anywhere else. By the end of the seventeenth century some Kidderminster clothiers were producing milled says with jersey warps and carded wefts, but they appear to have used fell wool, not noils,[239] and the says being made by a Warwick stuffmaker in 1694 are unlikely to have had noil wefts.[240] Except that they had noil woofs and were put through the mill, Woodland says were much like any others. Their warps were doubled and twisted in twisting mills. They were scoured, tentered, and pressed between parchment 'papers' in say presses, and could also be hot-pressed. Some were sold white by the makers, some in whole colours, and some in mingled hues, having been dyed in the wool or the yarn.[241] Woodland noil-woof says went on being made for a hundred years and more. They completed the range of English says by providing a very low-priced variety.[242]

## Serges

The Flemings also introduced into England the manufacture of 'serge of Florence'. It was being made in Norwich in 1601, when it was described, in Edinburgh dialect, as a 'counterfuit, sic as is maid in Deip, Southamptune and Canterberry'.[243] The Canterbury Walloons did take advantage of the permission granted them to make 'Florence serge',[244] but discontinued production in 1603. After this date neither did the city chamberlain include serges in his accounts nor did the appraisers of probate inventories make further reference to '*fil de saiette blancq a faire sarges*' or '*fillet de saiette blancq portant a la sarge*'.[245] Southampton became the chief seat of this industry in England. Serges of Florence were made here from 1573 and soon gained fame as small and broad 'Hampton serges'. The sergemakers, sergeweavers and clothiers of Southampton, and later of Romsey, Dibden, Lymington, Newport and Winchester, produced on average about ten serges to one rash, and many of them nothing but serges. 'Hampton serges', like the rashes and stammets of Flowers making, had jersey warps and carded wefts.[246] These towns also made 'Hampton broad serges' alias 'cloth serges' alias 'cloth rashes', which were occasionally regarded as counterfeit ratines. These cloths, unlike, 'Hampton small serges', were rowed and shorn.[247] One thing the Hampton serges, rashes and stammets of Flowers all had in common was that they were thicked at home by foot; except for cloth serges finished in Winchester, fulling mills were not used.[248]

As far as can be seen, serges, including noil-weft ones, were being made in Taunton from 1583 at the latest.[249] The earliest extant probate records of sergemaking in the Vale of Taunton Deane reveal weft yarns spun from noils. As in western England generally, the word 'noil' was unknown; 'pinnion', akin to the French *peignon*, was used instead. In this part of the world, too, the word 'worsted' was mistaken and used to signify both combing wool in general and tops in particular, so giving rise to such quaint expressions as 'wosterd wool' and 'wosterdcomber' and causing jersey to be called 'wosterd' or 'woolsted' yarn, even though it was artlessly admitted to have been spun on a 'catherine', 'catherne' or 'turn', meaning a wheel.[250] This understood, the evidence is unequivocal. In Taunton in 1638 Martin Meruck left £9 worth of 'pennione sarge' he had just made.[251] William Cole of North Petherton had a supply of 'penions and short wool' in 1640, but whether for pinnion serge or pinnion kersey is not clear.[252] William Baylie of Taunton was still styling himself a tailor in 1644, but was really a sergemaker with stocks of wool, jersey yarn, jersey chains, abb yarn, and other materials. He left very little by way of fabric, but his was 'pynnion sarge'.[253] In 1647 John Giles of Creech was weaving from jersey and 'pininge wooll' what was almost certainly pinnion serge.[254] A Milverton sergemaker named Butcher left serge looms, jersey, short wool and pinnions. He was making pinnion serge. So were Valentine Gardner of Fiddington, Adam Vellett and Thomas Hessom of Taunton St James, John Rice of Monksilver, Joseph Conway of East Quantoxhead, Uriah Wright of North Petherton, Jane Bond of Taunton St Mary Magdalene, Nicholas Gooding of Monksilver, Richard Chaplyn of Williton and Edward Blackmore of West Buckland.[255] Benjamin Shortt, a sergemaker of Taunton St James, had no combshop, so he must have bought his large stock of pinnions. We cannot swear that each of the 206 serges he had in stock had a pinnion weft, but many or most of them must have done.[256] The same is true for Agnes Pollard of Holford.[257] Christopher Trot specialised in combing, yarnmaking and yarndyeing in Taunton St Mary Magdalene, and he surely found amongst local sergemakers most of his customers for jersey and yarns made of 'mixture pinions' and other grades of noils.[258] John Arnold called himself a comber, but was really a complete clothier. His effects included jersey spun from 'fine mixture comb wool, and 'ob' yarns, which were composed of short wool, 'fine penions' and such like. These were what he made his serges of.[259] In 1693, similarly, John Vickary of Stogumber had stocks of 'warp yarn' and 'obb pinnions'.[260] In short, throughout the length and breadth of the Vale of Taunton Deane there arose a host of clothiers, sergemakers and sergeweavers, with their attendant woolcombers, yarnmakers and yarndyers, devoting themselves wholly or mainly to the production of noil-weft serges.[261] Dyed in the wool or the yarn, and fulled and finished in the vale, these coloured, mingled and shaded Taunton serges, as they were everywhere called, were widely sold for women's dress. They were lighter than Spanish cloths, but thicker and warmer than many of the new stuffs. They served also for bed-curtains.[262] Not many cloth serges were made, and then not before about 1680.[263] These pinion serge manufactures were long continued. Taunton was still a seat of them, and the serge market for the vale, as late as 1757, and Milverton, Wellington and Broadway were engaged in the business until the end of the century.[264]

When, about 1595, Benedict Webb removed from Taunton to Kingswood, he introduced the art of sergemaking into the Vale of Berkeley. By 1691 serge was being made in Dursley, by 1701 in Wotton-under-Edge, and by 1762 in Wheatenhurst. Very likely this industry flourished in other towns in the east of the vale, and in earlier times, but few records of it have so far been unearthed and little can be said about manufacturing techniques save that jersey warps were combined with wefts of pinnions and other coarse carded wools.[265]

Union serge manufacture had started in the West Country by 1597 and by 1621 was widely and firmly established there.[266] 'The late made stuff of serges', it was remarked in 1630, 'is now in great use and request with us, wherewith the market at Exeter is abundantly funished'.[267] Tiverton and the Culm valley towns admittedly lagged behind. In 1630 Tiverton was still noted only for kerseys; in 1633 serge manufacture here was a tender plant.[268] In a run of Uffculme probate records, sergemakers' wills and inventories come to light no earlier than 1682.[269] Nevertheless, the justices of peace were right who declared in 1639 that sergemaking was 'nowe the principale of this country'.[270] The spinning side of the industry extended southwestwards to Bodmin, Camelford, Bossiney and Tregoney, and was absent only from the Stannaries district and a relatively small number of individual towns.[271] Several varieties of union serge were made, as fine, coarse, broad, narrow and long ells, which had a width of one English or long ell, as opposed to the short Flemish one. All the warps were jersey. The wefts included a few flocks and other oddments, but consisted almost entirely of short wool, particularly pinnions, without any 'clothing wooll' such as went into the old style of woollens.[272] Cloth serge was a later modification. It was being made in Totnes in 1686, but Tiverton only took it up as late as about 1720.[273] The majority of serges were woven white. In later times, however, increasing numbers were dyed in the wool in mingled, shaded or mixed colours.[274]

The first mention of serge manufacture in the Chalk Country came in 1621, in the House of Commons, where it was said, 'Of late yeres in and about ... Winchester hath ben about three thouzand todds of wooll made into cloth, serges smale and great, and into other narrow clothes'.[275] Conceivably the Member was referring to Hampton small and broad serges, but he probably had in mind Winton serges, as made in the Winchester house of correction from 1578 or soon after.[276] Inventories for sergemakers in the Chalk Country and thereabouts show them making union serges at dates early enough to corroborate the statement made in the Commons, relating as they do to Andover in 1634, Alton in 1650, Devizes in 1660, Longparish in 1673, Inkpen before 1679, Newbury in 1683 and Reading in 1684. Moreover, by 1631 sergeweavers were dwelling in Wonston and Devizes, and by 1668 in Salisbury. Some of these serges were white and others were dyed in the wool and mingled. Their weft yarns were made in a variety of mixtures of 'pynnion', lambs', fell and local fleece wool.[277] This last was largely from the flankward buttocks of Chalk Country sheep and of no high quality.[278] Noil-weft serges were not much made, except in later times in Devizes. By 1692 some manufacturers here were employing noil yarns. Henry Painter used 'mixt woolsted yearne' and 'white woolsted yearne' for his warps and 'coulered pinion yearne' and 'white pinion yearne' for his wefts. Richard Farmer bought yarns in Tetbury, which specialised in combing and in spinning jersey and noil threads, so his serges were likely pinnion ones also.[279] Cloth serge, as elsewhere, was a later development from ordinary union serge, being first found in Downton in 1725 and in Devizes in 1735.[280]

Sergemakers and woolcombers were at work in the Cheese Country before 1640 and in the second half of the century were to be found at all hands, most of all in and about Christian Malford, Bremhill, Chippenham, Calne, Lacock,

Slaughterford and Bradford-on-Avon. In the few instances when their wefts incorporated large proportions of pinnions, the serges had linen, not jersey warps.[281] The vast majority of manufacturers had their wefts spun from the kinds of wool previously carded for West-of-England cloths. The same is true of the cloth serges introduced about 1680.[282]

From 1660 or thereabouts sergemaking was taken up in the Butter Country, more particularly in and near Cardiff, Glastonbury, Beaminster, Sherborne, Broadway, Yetminster, Crewkerne, Misterton, Martock and Ilminster. Here the wefts contained considerable quantities of noils, short wool, and flocks, and some were made wholly or almost wholly of pinnions. Many of these serges were dyed in the wool. Following the by now familiar pattern of development, cloth serges made a later appearance, by 1691 or somewhat before.[283]

What little we know about the easterly part of the Bristol District suggests it was by no means immune from the great influences that swept across the textile districts of western England in the sixteenth and seventeenth centuries. By 1680 Hanham was probably not alone in the eastern part of the district in having embarked on the manufacture of union serges.[284]

Cirencester and Tetbury had already become woolcombing and yarnmaking centres supplying the Vale of Taunton Deane, the West Country and elsewhere with jersey and with noil yarn, well before the records first become ample in 1660. And these two towns also made their own serges.[285] Some of the yarnmasters themselves wove serges, and the sheer frequency and quantity in which pinnions figure in their inventories suggest they went into the weft yarns employed.[286] As for the specialist woolcombers and yarnmakers, they nearly all had large stocks of pinnions, and if not, then of fell or short wool.[287] John Cripps of Cirencester, for instance, who styled himself clothier but was really a yarnmaster, had stores of long wool, 'small long wooll', head wool, coarse warp wool, head yarn, sorting warp, 'thorrough sort yarne' and 'pinnion abb yarne'.[288]

Pinnion serges were a great success and won much of the market from Hampton ones. As early as 1601 the Southampton Flemings were using their influence with the borough to try and effect an entry into the pinnion-serge trade, saying, 'The yearne that is made in the counties of Devon and Cornwall serveth best for the abb of some sort of the sarges and stuffs made there much better than anie yearne that is spun in the county of Southampton and that without the same they cannot make the said stuffs vendable and for use.' The Walloons appointed an agent, armed him with a testimonial from the borough, and sent him off to the West Country to buy up what yarn he could. The sergemakers there took umbrage and the Devon justices bound him over for Exeter assizes and forbade him to buy any yarn in the meantime. The Walloons then appealed to the Privy Council for permission to buy three or four score pounds a week in open markets in the two counties, 'in regard of the necessary use of that contry yearne for the makeing of the said serges and stuffs without the whiche they cannot be made so good and perfect as they ought to be, which benefitt taken from them they shall not be able to aford mayntenance for a great nomber of poore famelyes unles they may have of that contry yearne to serve their tornes for the makeing of the said stuffs.' The Council acceded to this request and a few serges with what were apparently pinnion wefts came to be made in Southampton.[289]

Woodland manufacturers found it much easier to emulate the achievements of western sergemakers. From says to serges was but a short step; it only meant having a single instead of a doubled and twisted warp yarn. The woof was of noil yarn just as before. From 1662 at the latest many or most of the saymakers, and some of the baizemakers in Sudbury, Cavendish, Clare, Lavenham, Bildeston, Nayland, Bury St Edmunds and elsewhere were adding noil-woof serges to their range of products. They were largely dyed in the wool or the yarn, just as the says were. Men who combined the manufacture of says and serges, and sometimes baizes as well, were more numerous than specialists in either of the first two. Jeffery Wever of Polstead was something of an exception in that he was making nothing but serge in 1674, and even he was still styled a saymaker.[290] This noil-woof serge manufacture went on successfully for a long time. Sudbury and Lavenham, at least, were still noted for it as late as 1757.[291]

The manufacture of inexpensive union serge largely replaced that of the old kerseys, which became increasingly unprofitable, and to make this change was relatively easy. The weft wools remained much the same.[292] Both fabrics required the same kind of four-pedal looms; indeed, they were often still called kersey looms after they had been transferred to weaving serges.[293] The biggest change needed was the introduction of jersey warps. He can thus be forgiven who said, 'Kersies were serge cloths of scribbled yarn.'[294] Men hastened to make the shift from the one trade to the other once they had seen which way the wind was blowing. In 1622 'Hampshire' kerseys were not selling, but 'Hampton' serges were.[295] Such signs could not be ignored indefinitely. In the Chalk,[296] South Seacoast,[297] Butter,[298] Cheese,[299] and West[300] countries, in the Vale of Taunton Deane[301] and in Soham too,[302] probate inventories show men switching out of kersey and into serge. Not long afterwards similar moves were commencing in the Peak-Forest Country.[303] The process can be seen clearly in the West Country. We can observe a merchant, in 1617 and after, dealing in kerseys and serges side by side, and the former gradually losing ground.[304] Crediton had made the change to serges by 1630, whereas Tiverton excelled in kerseys and clung to them longer, as most Culm valley towns did.[305]

Finally, before the end of the seventeenth century, the manufacture of pinnion serges spread to Ireland, where the growing abundance of wool from English pasture sheep attracted woolcombers, sergemakers and sergeweavers from Exeter, Tiverton, Taunton, Tetbury, Bristol, Norwich and elsewhere.[306]

**Perpetuanas**

Many serges from the West Country and some from the Vale of Taunton Deane were exported through Exeter, but this city came to handle even more perpetuanas. Their export had already started by the early years of the seventeenth century. Plymouth, Dartmouth, Bristol and London joined in the trade, but it remained an Exeter speciality. Thousands of perpetuanas went out from Topsham in every year in the 1620s, 1630s and 1640s, warfare permitting. Exports started to rise steeply in the 1670s and in the next ten years or so first surpassed and then dwarfed those of serges. It appears paradoxical that while more and more serges were made, exports of them stagnated or declined, yet while exports of perpetuanas rose hand over fist, little or no evidence can be found of their manufacture.[307] Similarly, drapers' shops in towns all over the kingdom were selling perpetuanas hardly anyone seems to have made.[308] Contemporary writers and speakers, too, made great play with what was one of the most engaging factitious names in the textile trade.[309] Not to beat any further about the bush, this seeming paradox is swiftly dispelled by the simple truth: white pinnion serge was finished as perpetuana. This was why frequent use was made of such terms as 'serges or perpetuanos' and 'perpetuanoes alias serges'.[310]

Celia Fiennes describes what happened to the serges she saw sold in Exeter. Carriers brought them on horseback, straight from the looms. Fulling was to come,

> but first they will clean and scour their rooms with them – which by the way gives noe pleasing perfume to a roome, the oyle and grease, and I think it would rather foull a roome than cleanse it, because of the oyle – but I perceive it otherwise esteemed by them, which will send to their acquaintances that are tuckers, the dayes the serges comes in, for a rowle to clean their house, this I was an eye-witness of; then they laye them soack in urine.

Thus softened, but rendered no more pleasing to a lady's nostrils, the serges were soaped and thickened in the mill, after which they were scoured clean. Then they were dried and strained on racks or tenters set so close together in rows as to leave only just room for the dresser to pass between them. These racks occupied 'huge, large fields all round the town which is to the riverside'. Once dry, the serge was taken off the tenterhooks and burled to remove any knots or unwanted particles. Next it was folded and a paper placed between each fold. The serge was then laid on the lower iron plate of a coal-fired hot-press and the upper plate screwed down tightly. When it came from the press it had been transformed into a perpetuana. This was sent off to be dyed then and there, or, more frequently, was sold white to be dyed in London or on the Continent.[311] Crediton and Sandford also pressed serges into perpetuanas and stamped them with their own town seals.[312] By 1617 Amsterdam and Leiden, by 1621 London, and by 1633 Haarlem and Delft had all set up hot-presses for converting English pinnion serges into perpetuanas.[313]

Benedict Webb, recounting his career, in about 1618 we suppose, claimed he invented perpetuanas in what would have been roughly 1583. After a long spell on the Continent, 'beeing matched in the western parts in Tanton in Somerset', he examined all his swatches, which included some procured from Italy but more collected by himself in Rouen. He says,[314]

> I resolved to macke 2 sorts of drapery as the moste fittinge for many respects for this commonwelth, bothe for ower yous in the kingdume and for transeportation, the one sort beeing thin and light I called it perpetuanis, of which sort ther hath bin sithence many thousands made yerely and exported, and it is in truth for his youses the best stufe that ever was made in this kingdum, and for this 35 years hath held his reputation, onles by the defalt of the mackers sumtimes it hath an eclipse.

This fits well. In 1613 two judges declared that 'perpetuanoes and serges were at the first an invencion of the westerne partes'.[315] The first reference to perpetuanas found in belles-lettres was made in 1599. The earliest record of them being stolen in Essex occurs in 1601.[316] We have good reason to believe Webb's claim.

Serges and perpetuanas were far from being uniform. One cannot make a cloth in a mould. Crediton ones, for instance, were lighter than Sandford.[317] And quality varied from time to time, as Webb observed. In 1613 some perpetuanas were said to have been falsely made, 'for where at first their pitch in the loome was twelve hundreth, but now brought to eight hundreth, yet keep their breadth and length'.[318] According to Misselden, writing in 1621 and 1622, 'The perpetuanoes . . . have by little and little bin made worse and worse, so that now they are become quite out of use, the trade lost, the traders ruinated.'[319] This view was unduly gloomy, but by no means groundless. A memorandum prepared for the Lord Keeper in 1628 by 'one of the first that brought to light and in request a good comoditie called perpetuano' reported that abuses and frauds had reduced the fabric's weight from over twelve to under six pounds.[320] Remedies were tried. In 1619 there was an attempt to regulate the perpetuana industry by royal charter.[321] In 1621 the Commons seemed to think false making had caused cloths 'and cheiflie perpetuanas' to 'grow out of use'. They might have legislated for good handiwork had not their own labours been brought to an abrupt end.[332] In 1624 the city of Exeter promoted a Bill for perpetuanas and the true making of serges. Renewed attempts in 1635 got a favourable reception from the king, but nothing transpired.[323]

Some bad workmanship notwithstanding, the meteoric rise of perpetuanas went on with no more than momentary checks. They were so light, smooth and inexpensive, especially overseas, since they bore such low customs duties, that competing fabrics like cloth rashes could only give way before them.[324] Hence the urgency with which Southampton manufacturers sought to get their hands on pinnion yarns.[325] Their efforts were not entirely unsuccessful. From 1613 at latest Southampton and district was converting considerable numbers of

Hampton small serges into perpetuanas. In 1647 Robert Zaines left six perpetuanas and about the same number of what may well have been pinnion serges. Winchester also finished a few perpetuanas.[326] Whether or not Benedict Webb took this trade to Kingwood with him is not clear; probably he was content to make serges.[327] The Woodland, with its noil-weft serges, was well placed to make perpetuanas, and in the middle of the seventeenth century Sudbury, Colchester and Coggeshall were selling substantial numbers.[328] Canterbury and Sandwich tried to compete by making 'perpetuana says' or 'perpetuanoes of saye', but with little success.[329] The sempiternums, broad and narrow, as made in Tetbury in 1633 and after, seem to have been well received, yet failed to achieve high sales.[330] Perpetuanas were the peculiar glory of the West Country.

## Druggets

From about 1675 most of the sergemakers in the West and Cheese countries and many of those in the Vale of Taunton Deane and the Butter Country started to follow the French fashion by adding druggets to their range of products. At the same time they often switched, fully or partly, from union serges to serge duroys. Simultaneously, too, a class of specialist druggetmakers arose.[331] Meanwhile, in the Chalk Country area, from Devizes in the west to Basingstoke in the east, clothiers were likewise passing from the manufacture of union serges to that of druggets, and frequently also to that of shalloons.[332] Cirencester, Bristol and Tewkesbury also took up druggetmaking now.[333]

These druggets were usually woven narrow. Their chains were jersey and their abbs similar to those of union serges, being composed of various proportions of pinnions and fell, lambs', offal, and inferior fallow wools, including those from the backs, ribs and flankward buttocks of Chalk Country sheep. In the West Country and the Vale of Taunton Deane, far more than elsewhere, pinnions were used very liberally, and many weft yarns were wholly composed of them. Although similar in these respects to union serges, druggets differed much in their weave and workmanship. They were made in a plain, loose weave, heavily fulled, highly felted, and hot-pressed to leave a smooth face. They were usually dyed in the wool, often by the clothier or druggetmaker himself.[334] By 1739 ribbed and corded druggets had been introduced; they were still being made in Alton at the close of the century.[335] These union druggets were all relatively coarse fabrics. Whereas silk and worsted druggets were used for such things as men's coats, waistcoats and suits, union ones went for carpet coverings and surrounds and suchlike purposes, and breeches were the most that could be made of even the strong Devizes ones.[336]

# 8

## PLANT FIBRE CLOTHS AND UNIONS

Linen manufactures made progress. In Norwich, Canterbury, Maidstone and London the Flemings introduced their own highly skilled methods of making linens. The Norwich Walloons claimed to have made velours all of linen.[1] Diaper weaving was undoubtedly introduced by the strangers; before their time it was rarely if ever practised over here. Diaper looms were equipped with two or more harnesses, each with equal numbers of headles, and their treadles were likewise divided into sets, all in such a way that each set could actuate more than one harness, so whichever set of treadles was used, all the warp could be acted upon. For instance, there might be two harnesses, each of four headles, and four treadles in each of the two sets. The second harness would be connected with the four treadles of the first set in the order needed to form a twill tie on that portion of the warp entered in this harness. To the same treadles was tied up also the first harness, and in such a way as to make a reverse twill. The second set of treadles would be tied up with the reverse twill in front and the twill tie at the back. As a result of this arrangement, if the weaving were done with the first set of treadles only, a stripe of reverse twills would be made and if with the second set of treadles only, a stripe of twill, while the alternate use of one set and the other would produce an alternation of twills and reverse twills in one and the same cloth. By the addition of more pairs of harnesses, and further pairs of treadles if needed, still more intricate designs could be made. The great advantage of this system of passing warps threads through two or more sets of headles, each with its own peculiar function in making either the background or the figure or in binding the design, was that a wide range of repeated geometrical patterns could readily be woven. Such diaper was made by the strangers and served the same purposes as nowadays.[2] Another manufacture that had grown up in Southampton by 1622 and in the Butter Country before the century was out, was that of dowlas, which was a loosely spun and woven linen.[3] A type of ticking known as branched buckram was still regarded about 1590 as being of recent introduction.[4]

Linen weaving grew up in the north of the Midland Plain, in Stockton and Darlington and in the districts of Knaresborough and Wass.[5] The Lancashire

Plain and the Vale of Warrington produced more linens than ever before. 'Manchester' ticks became well known and by the 1720s Warrington had a market in huckaback napkins and tablecloths whose familiar huckle-backed squares were formed by criss-crossing warp and weft floats.[6] In Mere Woodland, Wolverton, Bourton, Milton-on-Stour, Gillingham, Silton, Motcombe and some other Butter Country towns, there arose from 1580 onwards considerable manufactures of ticking, which was in great and growing demand for bodices, stays, gaiters, mattresses, bolsters and pillows, aprons, tents, pockets and linings. These ticks were made with warps of line and wefts of tow, in twill weaves, mostly two-and-one but some two-and-two. Patterns were formed in them by interweaving dyed, bleached, and brown, unbleached *écru* yarns. As a sideline, linen sackcloth was also made. After about 1680, as these industries continued to expand, locally produced yarns were supplemented by purchases from Hamburg, Riga, Rennes and Ireland.[7] The dornicksweavers of East Norfolk and High Suffolk also engaged in making ticks, and so did some weavers in Ringwood and Fordingbridge in the Poor Soils Country.[8]

Competition from imported foreign linens was somewhat restricted by wars and customs duties after 1650,[9] but neither the English linenweavers nor the Huguenot enterprises in Richmond-on-Thames, in Ipswich (from 1681 to about 1686) and in Edinburgh, reaped great benefit.[10] The reasons why linen making prospered in Ireland were more deeply seated. Woollen manufactures of the old kinds had never flourished here, partly because both fallow wool and fuller's earth were lacking. On the other hand, as observed in 1572 and as Thomas Wentworth pointed out in 1636, both country and people were well adapted to the growing and spinning of flax. On the small farms flax was a highly eligible crop, just as it was in Flanders. Processing, spinning and weaving developed as by-employments on the farms where flax was grown. The weaving was mostly done in winter, when there was little outdoor work to do. Wentworth himself, when Lord Deputy, obtained flax seed from Holland, found it took well, fetched workmen from France and the Low Countries, and succeeded in setting up a few looms. This small light was soon snuffed out during the ensuing troubles and it was Scots and English settlers, especially those in counties Antrim and Down, who effectively founded the linen industry. By 1657 Ulsters had already made a name for themselves in the market. Then the manufactures were greatly expanded and extended by Huguenot immigrants, by far the most important of whom was Louis Crommelin, whose name was eventually anglicised as Crumlin. Before he arrived in 1698 Crommelin had spent some years in Holland and presumably learned the new Dutch method of bleaching in the piece. He worked under contract to William III and Queen Anne, but put up £10,000 of his own. He set up a manufactory and a bleachery in Lisburn, a sailcloth works in Waterford, and cambric and damask works in Kilkenny. Five hundred Huguenot families settled in Lisburn, Lurgan, Coleraine, Antrim, Dungannon and other towns in counties Antrim, Down, Armagh and

Londonderry, and they taught their trades to all those willing to serve five years as apprentices and two as journeymen. From this firm base in Ulster, linen manufactures spread much further afield.[11]

On the mainland more linsey-woolseys than ever were made. The Flemings introduced their own types,[12] and the English now used more and more noils for their wefts. We find cloths such as this being made in Soham, Bristol, Sandwich, and Kendal and district[13] in the Vale of Taunton Deane, in Milborne Port in the Butter Country,[14] in Romsey, in Reading, in Newbury, Downton, Salisbury and Dorchester,[15] in Warminster, Chippenham, Melksham and Calne,[16] and in many towns in the Midland Plain, notably in the south-east, in the district of the Ivel and Ouse valleys.[17] In the later seventeenth and early eighteenth centuries some Cheese Country serges, West Country bastard serges and perpetuanas, and possibly some Beaminster, Kendal and Scotch serges also had linen warps.[18] Other wool and linen unions were newly introduced. The flannel the Sandwich Flemings made had a woollen weft on a linen warp, and the same sort of flannel was being woven in Romsey in 1691, in Melksham in 1718, in Salisbury in 1714, and perhaps in Downton in 1725.[19] Linen was also very suitable for drugget warps. Ordinary French *droguet* had a linen chain and Huguenots may have brought this method over here.[20] The druggets being made in Kendal in 1671 probably had linen warps. A few were made this way in High Suffolk.[21] Canvas making was given a fillip in the 1560s by immigrants from the Continent. The striped canvas made in London and Sandwich had Flemish origins and 'Hartfordes London canvas' was copied from Herford. Similar dress canvas was also produced in Southampton.[22] Manufactures of industrial canvas prospered as well. In 1547 a party of Bretons was brought over to introduce the manufacture of poldavis. This art rapidly took hold in Ipswich. John Collins of that town is said to have been the first man in England to make poldavis and medrinacks (methernix, mildernix). A Breton named Francis Owdry (Oudreyn), who had been weaving poldavis in Abingdon since 1551, obtained a grant of £100 from Queen Mary in 1558 and went off to Ipswich to produce oulderons and sailcloth for the royal navy, only to find two Gypswickians, John and Richard Collins, already well entrenched. All 'hir maiesties maker' could do was to buy supplies by contract with Collins Brothers. In 1574 they obtained a patent for the manufacture of both poldavis and medrinacks, and John was given rights of search and seal in Ipswich and Woodbridge and within twenty miles of those towns,[23] which, with Saxmundham, Kirton and the rest of this district, became the principal seat of poldavis and medrinacks production.[24] Both broad and narrow cloths were made, all woven in hemp, with warps of doubled or trebled threads and wefts of treble threads driven home close with a metal batten. This 'Ipswich cloth' was widely sold for sailmaking.[25] In the early 1680s a Huguenot by name of Bonhomme set up workshops in Ipswich to make linen medrinacks, but this business soon foundered.[26] Fimble (female hemp) was preferable to linen and was much grown in this part of England, while additional supplies could readily be obtained from the Fen Country and even from the Lancashire Plain. This circumstance and the presence of numerous ports and shipbuilding yards favoured the manufacture of canvas sailcloth,[27] which was carried on alongside that of sackcloth and twills. By 1660 seamless sacks were being woven as tubular double cloths.[28]

Hemp was also used in unions with wool. By 1560 Dorchester cottons or moultons had appeared on the scene. These had hempen warps and thickly woven wefts of inferior carding wool and were heavily fulled, often thrice milled. They went for camisoles and boys' breeches.[29] Linen and hemp found further employment in the grounds of Wilton, Kidderminster and Axminster carpets.[30]

Vegetable cotton now came to be combined with flax and more rarely with hemp in unions not hitherto made in England. Cotton wool was included in much of the carpetene, 'carpetting' or 'carpetine stuffe' made in Bristol from about 1600 to 1680. This was composed, it would appear, of linen and hempen warps and either cotton or linen and cotton union yarn wefts. The result probably resembled what was until recently sold as cotton carpet. Carpetene was woven both broad and narrow and served mostly for curtains, valances and other soft furnishings.[31]

Linen warps and cotton wefts were used to make fustians. It was about 1590 that Giles Warren started making Milan fustians in Ireland. He attracted many pupils from London and elsewhere and these men constituted the whole of the first generation of Milan fustian manufacturers in London and other parts of England.[32] At much the same time a different kind of fustian manufacture commenced in the Woodland. The first mention of it relates to 1602, but a fustian weaver died in Finchingfield in 1603 and we guess he had been working there for some few years. Amongst the other towns in the Woodland and thereabouts where fustian makers set up were Ipswich, Bury St Edmunds, Colchester, Little Hadham, and, most important of all, Haverhill. Here the industry had taken a firm hold by the 1660s, and it lasted right up until the middle of the eighteenth century. From the inventories of the effects of Samuel Browne and other manufacturers, it is clear that Woodland fustians were rowed ones; they were not made with a looped pile in a genuine fustian weave; the web was simply rowed and shorn to give a soft, fluffy face to the cloth, special rowing frames being devised for the purpose. These were, in brief, brushed fabrics.[33] This was evidently a novel English way of working, for an attempt was made to copy it in Rouen about 1610 by recruiting a Suffolk fustian maker to teach the art of fustian making *façon d'Angleterre*.[34] The manufacture of fustians of one sort or another spread widely and rapidly. It had started in Maidstone and Worcester by 1605. Three years later it was already established in Gloucester, in Hawkesbury, in Stow-on-the-Wold (in the Cotswold Country), and in Crewkerne, Misterton and Merriott in the Butter Country. By 1627 it had found its way to Sherston, in the east of the Cotswold Country,[35] and by 1623 to Uckfield in the Wealden Vales.[36] By 1657 it had reached Carlisle.[37] About two years later a 'Dutchman' named Witts had introduced it in Aldbourne in the Chalk Country. His son took over the business after him, but by 1754 all that remained was the cotton spinning done in this and nearby towns to supply the London weavers.[38] However, it was not to London but to Bolton and district that the fustian industry gravitated. Bolton had already embarked on the new venture by 1601. In the course of the succeeding half century the industry spread as far as Blackburn, Oldham, Leigh, Manchester and Preston. This region now made fustians purportedly in the fashions of Wesel, Genoa, Ulm, Augsburg, Milan and Piedmont and called 'Englishe Osborrowes', 'Vessels', 'Weazells', 'Millions', 'Holmes', 'Jeans' and so on.[39] By 1674, too, the weaving had commenced here of what were undoubtedly genuine fustians, which had then to be distinguished by such designations as 'fustian tufts' and 'velvet fustians'.[40]

Other linen-cotton unions were made alongside fustians. Haverhill, the Lancashire towns, and by 1722 Coventry also, wove dimities.[41] The Lancastrians likewise made checks, thicksets and barragons (paragons or barracans). Checks were plain weaves with warp and weft stripes intersecting to form large white squares. Thicksets were velvets voided to produce fine cords. Most of these fabrics served for beds, hangings, soft furnishings and light apparel, much as fustians did.[42] Similar linen-cotton unions were apparently being made in Southwark in 1661.[43]

The next step was to weave cloths all of cotton. The Lancashire district was already moving from unions to pure cottons at the end of the seventeenth century.[44] In 1719 Weymouth and Melcombe Regis had for several years been engaged in weaving calicoes, some of them chequered, from West Indian cotton, and in dyeing and printing them in the piece, principally in shades of blue.[45] 'Manufactored cottons' of somewhat similar kinds were also being made in Stepney and thereabouts in the 1720s.[46]

The finishing touch had been put to these linen and cotton manufactures by the introduction in the middle of the seventeenth century of the art of making chintz. Printing blocks were used to form outlines that could have a body of colour painted in. This was an old Indian art, but had been bent to English tastes.[47]

# 9

# BROAD SILKS

Broad silk cloths were not woven on broad looms with two seats; they were usually only twenty-one inches wide, occasionally twenty-seven, and were broad only in contradistinction to narrow ware or parchmentry. Unlike the latter, moreover, broad silks were made of prime thrown silk. A few cloths were woven from spun waste silk, and up to three quarters wide, but even so they were not strictly speaking broad silks.

The Italians, who were acknowledged masters of the art, brought the manufacture of broad silks to Antwerp, Lille and West Flanders, and then the great migration carried it to Norwich, Canterbury and above all the London suburb of Stepney, particularly that part of it known as Spitalfields.[1] Later on the industry was reinforced by waves of Huguenots from Tours and other French towns. Some of these people had been silkweavers and silkworkers in their motherlands; others had been engaged in woollen manufactures and changed over only after arriving here.[2]

The commencement of the industry in England roughly coincided with the initiation of imports of prime silk direct from Italy. It was about 1578 that some Canterbury Walloons started making all-silk grograins and wrought grograins, which were the same, only wrought on the face with gold-and-silver and tinsel thread.[3] By 1581 a Netherlander velvet weaver was at work in Billingsgate Ward in London and before long others appeared in Portsoken Ward. By 1635 a Tournai velvet weaver had set up in Southwark.[4] Similar all-silk velvets were being produced in Canterbury in 1623.[5] All-silk buffin camlets were made in Norwich by 1603 and in Canterbury by the 1610s.[6] 'Silke curle all silk' was being woven in the latter city in 1615.[7] Sipers, a transparent silk cloth formerly much imported from Cyprus, was being produced here in 1595 and in Bishopsgate in London in 1618. It was a usual mourning material until superseded by crape.[8] By 1618 some of the London strangers had introduced the manufacture of silk cobweb lawn, suitable for ruffs, veils and kerchiefs.[9] All-silk filoselles were coming from Canterbury looms by 1623.[10]

Tuftaffeta, which could be either all silk or half linen, had long been imported into England.[11] All-silk tuftaffeta manufacture in London was first recorded in 1594 and probably commenced about 1590. In 1601 a member of the London French congregation was engaged in it. The next decade saw many tuftaffeta makers at work in London and Southwark. They were mostly Netherlanders and largely Walloons.[12] The claim by the London tuftaffeta weavers in 1633 that they numbered 10,000 only shows they were not arithmetically minded. Nevertheless they were numerous, and included a growing proportion of Englishmen.[13] By 1623 Canterbury and Norwich were also making all-silk tuftaffetas.[14] These fabrics went into fancy jerkins, cloaks and upper hose. The London and Canterbury ones were not infrequently mingled or wrought with tinsel or with gold-and-silver thread.[15] Taffeta, which formed the ground for tuftaffeta, was a thin plain weave made by the London and Southwark strangers,[16] and later by those of the other two cities. From 1622 Canterbury was producing stitched taffeta also.[17]

Gauze fabrics are ones in which crossing ends cross from one side to the other of standard ones. These crossing ends constitute what is called the doup warp. Each doup thread is twisted round under an adjacent standard thread and over and between successive picks of the weft. This is done by allowing leashes to pass behind one or more standard warp threads before emerging to the front. When these leashes are pulled, the doup and standard warp threads twist round each other. Two picks, single or double, thus suffice to complete the weave pattern. By the use of coloured threads, gauze weaves can be made to produce stripes, checks, figures and other effects. Gauzes with a flowered pattern are known as tiffanies. In olden days they were commonly starched and used for dress trimmings and linings. The Canterbury Walloons justly claimed to have been the 'inventers' of tiffanies.[18] In 1621 they had already been making them for some little time and they went on with them for about a hundred years.[19] When Anthony Cave died in that city in 1628, he left a store of silk, £20 worth of 'tiphany' awaiting sale in London, 'tiphany' looms (with a mechanism to shift the shafts so that the doup warp was pulled from side to side), and a special fixture to starch the tiffany on. In 1676 John Agace had a piece of tiffany ready wrought on the loom and 'flowered gose or tiffeny' as yet unsold in London. In 1678, too, both single and double silk gauzes were being made.[20] Canterbury remained the chief centre for tiffany and other silk gauzes, but Stepney was producing figured gauze in 1681 and possibly tiffany had been made in this vicinity since 1648 or even earlier.[21] Lichfield was also weaving tiffanies by 1674. By this time they were being made in linen as well as in silk.[22]

Figured silk satin was being produced in England in the opening years of the seventeenth century,[23] most probably in Canterbury. Satin was certainly being woven there in 1617 and figured satin in 1638.[24] By 1615 some London Flemings were also making silk satin.[25] This manufacture, however, never throve mightily in either city.[26]

Tissues of gold-and-silver thread, commonly called cloths of gold, were rarely if ever made in England in earlier times; they were imported from Venice, Florence, Lucca, Genoa, France and Flanders. While the Venetians clung to the old way of making gold-and-silver thread by gilding vellum, cutting it into strips and winding these around silk or hempen threads, Augsburg and Nuremberg had developed, in the mid-fourteenth century, the art of drawing gold-plated silver bars into wire, which could then be flattened and wound as the vellum was. However made, such gold-and-silver threads could be interwoven with silk yarns dyed in rich colours like crimson and purple.[27] Gold-and-silver thread was woven into some cloths in England in the sixteenth century and was much used in narrow ware, especially in orris work.[28] The South German system of drawing wire had been introduced in London by the 1470s, and the art of flattening the wire was apparently started in London in 1565 by Christopher Schütz and Daniel Hochstetter. As for the winding process, one Claude Durelle, we are told, 'was not the first inventor, but the first establisher of the trade by spynninge – the first that brought in the skyll of spynninge which is nowe knowen'. He was presumably from Milan, which had become the great centre for making cloth of gold by the wire method. Indeed, Milanese immigrants for some time retained a strong hold on this trade in London, and especially on the manufacture and use of flattening mills.[29] It seems to have been Milanese people, too, who started the weaving of tissues with gold-and-silver thread in London about 1611. By 1638 this new textile manufacture was already well established there.[30]

In course of time, by means of apprenticeships, the arts of broad silk manufacture came increasingly into English hands. Howes says, 'Mr John Tyce, dwelling neere Shorditch Church' was 'the first Englishman that devised and attayned the perfection of making all manner of tufted taffeties, cloath of tissue, wrought velvets, braunched sattins, and all other kinds of curious silke stuffe'. This must have been before 1615.[31] And by 1638 the London Weavers' Company was allowed to supervise all broad silk work throughout the city and suburbs.[32]

Bazin, in the form introduced by immigrants in Canterbury, was an all-silk or silk and hair dimity, with a secondary warp lacing stripes or other patterns on the face of the cloth. Susan Le Grand alias Delespine was making bazin in 1664, and was probably not alone in this; but these cloths were never much made in England.[33] In 1676 and thereabouts Canterbury was manufacturing all-silk masquerades, as the English called *mascade, mascardo* or *mascarado* says.[34] In 1672 a Londoner named Edmund Blood had patented 'a new manufacture, a rich silk shagg, comodious for garments, made of silk wast, hetherto of little or noe use, and shagged by tezell or rowing cards like as English baize, rowed fustians or dimatyes, a sort of manufacture never before known or made in this our kingdome'.[35] What success attended this attempt to make broad cloths of waste silk is not certainly known, but the silk shag being made in London in 1664 and in Stepney in 1681 seems to have been composed of prime silk.[36]

From 1620 onwards Huguenot silkworkers had been coming over in growing numbers, and in 1681 this stream came into full flood. The immigrants contributed to the growth of manufactures in England in at least two ways.

First, they taught their skills. Secondly, their presence encouraged the imposition of import duties on French broad silks. Canterbury and Stepney were already our only two considerable seats of broad silk manufactures; it was to these places that most immigrants came and here that they and their successors helped to expand the industry.[37]

Silk plush was being made in 1630 in Florence and in Tours, and it was from Touraine that the manufacture came to London. Among the numerous Huguenots relieved by the Threadneedle Street French Church were several *faiseurs de pluche* and *ouvriers en pluche*, some of whom started up their business anew over here.[38]

It was in the field of treatments and finishes that the Huguenots made their most valuable contributions to the industry. In Tours in 1644 John Evelyn saw 'the pressing and watering of grograms and chamblets, with weights of extraordinary poise, on the rolling engines'. This process was evidently akin to the watering by calender practised in Norwich. Eight years later he 'went to see the manner of chambletting silk and grograms at one M. La Dorees in Morefields'. This appears to have been the same process and one that may have been introduced into London from Tours by a Huguenot immigrant, perhaps even by La Doree himself.[39] That which made a mohair in Norwich, produced a moire in Tours and London. But the system of watering by calender developed in England proved superior to that used in Lyons and possibly in Tours.[40] One of the uses the process was put to in London and Stepney was the production of watered or sham tobines from plain-weave silks, with the object of undercutting the genuine all-silk tobines that were already being woven there in 1681 and had probably originated twenty years before.[41]

The original lustrings (often erroneously called 'lutestrings') were broad silks woven double or treble in the weft and given a high gloss by special rolling and finishing. In 1635 two immigrant 'lutestringmakers' were at work in Westminster.[42] Four years later Peter La Doree (or Dore), perhaps the same man we have already met, was granted a patent for glossing plain and figured satins, though in what way his process constituted a technical advance is not entirely clear.[43] Before long lustrings were being made in Canterbury and Stepney. In 1676 the late John Agace, silkweaver, of St Mary Northgate near Canterbury, had recently been making many 'lutstrings'. In 1681 Richard Heath of Stepney had been weaving coloured, striped and flowered 'leutestrings'. Similar cloths, incidentally, were also being woven in Amsterdam at this time.[44] The next advance was the invention in Lyons of a soaking process by which extra lustre was lent to the chain, and perhaps to the tram also, before weaving. In this way velvets no less than satins and taffetas could be rendered lustrous. This invention was hardly out before its secret had been brought into England by a Huguenot workman named Montgeorge who came over and settled here.[45] One result of this coup was a great wave of immigrants from Tours and Touraine, for while they were not allowed to make lustrings in the fashion of Lyons as long as they remained in France, they were perfectly free to do so in England, and could at the same time escape religious persecution. Almost overnight the lustrings industry mushroomed in Spitalfields and Tours declined from its former eminence.[46] Amongst the broad silks most frequently made as lustrings were taffetas, alamodes, satins, paduasoys, velvets and ducapes, which were a form of grograin. Alamodes were soft, glossy taffetas made entirely of Italian organzine. They were often dyed black and used for mourning scarves, ladies' hoods, mantles and linings. Many of these lustrings, it must be added, were brocaded.[47] According to the London Weavers' Company, alamodes had been made by some of their members intermittingly since 1663; and they appear in probate inventories of manufacturers' effects in 1676 in Canterbury and 1701 in Spitalfields.[48] Alamode lustrings, shot in colours, were introduced in London in 1684 by Jean Larguier and Jean Quet, who had recently arrived from Nîmes.[49] A new process for 'lustrating' plain black alamodes and other cloths was patented by Pierre de Cloux (Declux) in 1688. In 1692 the Royal Lustrings Company was set up to exploit this patent and to make the general run of almodes and other lustrings. By 1698 it had 768 looms at work, ninety-eight in Ipswich and the rest in London and the suburbs. The Ipswich branch succumbed in 1720, but the London business survived for some years more.[50]

Meanwhile new broad silk fabrics were introduced. Shagreen was woven and dyed to resemble shagreen leather and used to cover storage chests and cases. It was being made in Stepney in 1714 and 1715.[51] All-silk florentines had been launched in Canterbury by 1664, but Norwich only took them up a hundred years or so later.[52] By 1714 Stepney was making all-silk russells, cheverets and taffeta sarcenets. These last were very fine, light taffetas for lining millinery and for the tippets or capes of coats. Possibly, similar sarcenets were being woven in Norwich as early as 1688. Previously such cloths had all been imported.[53] Amongst the other silks made in Canterbury, Stepney or Norwich at this time, some were designated solely by the place of origin of the raw silk or of the weave. Such were the Bengals, the Piedmonts, the Venetians,[54] the Persians, which were very fine and used for lining bonnets, pelisses, hoods and cloak-collars,[55] and the Mantuas, which served for gowns and petticoats as well as for linings.[56] Venetian weaves added one mark to each mark of a five-thread satin.

Broad silk manufactures in this period were almost entirely confined to London and the suburbs, Canterbury, and Norwich. The notion that they were found in many provincial towns results merely from confusion caused by the former use of words like 'silkweaver' to cover also not only narrow-ware makers but even framework knitters.[57] The self-same Chester freemen were called stocking weavers at one stage and framework knitters at another; and we are told 'Mr Lee found out weaveing of silk stockings'.[58]

After 1720 Canterbury weaving was stricken.[59] Her broad silk manufactures migrated to Stepney or their place was filled by compensating growth in Norwich.[60] But even as Spitalfields was getting this transfusion of blood from

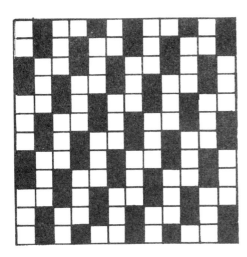

Fig. 13 Draft for one kind of Venetian weave (weft black).

Canterbury, it fell prey to a debilitating disease that was aggravated by the misguided Spitalfields Act of 1774. This raised silkweavers' wages artificially and forced employers to intensify their search for locations where their labour and other costs would be lower. Such places were readily available, and were already being taken advantage of, in the Vale of Taunton Deane, the West Country, the Woodland and elsewhere. At the end of the eighteenth century a Woodland weaver could earn more in silk than in jersey or unions and still get only two thirds of the piece-work wage fixed for Spitalfields by the justices of peace.[61] Well before 1770 silkweaving was fleeing Stepney for distant country towns, and throwing mills were going up to supply the looms in their new and dispersed locations. Broad silk manufactures were on the move to the Woodland and thereabouts, to Sudbury, Haverhill, Nayland, Glemsford, Coggeshall, Braintree, Bocking, Halstead, Hadleigh, Colchester, Earls Colne, Pebmarsh and Epping; to Tring and St Albans in the Chiltern Country; to the Chalk Country and district, to Winchester, Alton, Overton, Whitchurch, Andover, Wokingham, Odiham, Devizes and Great Ness, near Sevenoaks; to Southampton; to Bisley and to Kingswood and district in the Vale of Berkeley; to Corsley in the Cheese Country; to Ilchester, Bruton, Sherborne, Shepton Mallet and Croscombe in the Butter Country; to Taunton; to Dulverton, Bideford and Tiverton in the West Country; to Kettering, Desborough, Rothwell, Coventry and Kidderminster in the Midland Plain; to Kendal,

Lancaster and Manchester and district. Eventually Spitalfields degenerated into a centre for 'translating' or renovating old clothes. Nor was it only from Stepney that East Anglian towns gained industry. Norwich manufacturers spread their wings and set up business in the old satellite town of Mildenhall, in Great Yarmouth, Bungay and Saffron Walden. Then they went on to give work to weavers in Sible Hedingham, Bocking and Braintree. Thus the Norwich firm of Grout, Bayliss and Company vied with Courtauld and others from Stepney for the apt hands and willing fingers of the Woodlanders.[62]

# 10

## ALLIED TRADES

Knitting on two needles was already common in the fifteenth century, especially for making caps and cauls. Stockings may also have been produced in this way, but needed a seam down their whole length, which meant knitting had no advantage over weaving. Nether hose and similar garments, therefore, continued to be tailored out of kersey and other textiles. The rise of the seamless stocking and wholly knit hosiery depended on the art of knitting with four needles, an art that spread widely only in the latter part of the sixteenth century.[1] Knitting schools were now set up in town after town, in Ipswich in 1587, in York by 1590, in Lincoln and Leicester by 1591, in Norwich in 1592, in Aylsham and Reepham in 1622, in Salisbury in 1625 and so on. Girls, and sometimes boys, joined such schools at about eight years of age.[2] Many people knitted their own garments, but a big market sprang up also, and with it a whole new group of knitwear or hosiery manufactures producing socks, stockings, hose, petticoats, underwear, gloves, waistcoats, caps, scarves, cauls, coifs and other articles that needed no tailoring.[3] Sixteenth century hose comprised four main types: french hose, made very round and sometimes with canions reaching down just below the knees; gally hose, very large and ample but reaching only as far as the knees; venetians, which came down to the gartering place between the knee and the calf, where they were tied with points or laces; and netherstocks or stockings that complemented the other three and came up to or just above them. It was these netherstocks that were now knitted. By 1583, we are told, most people, and even the 'otherwise verie poor, having scarce fortie shillings of wages by the yeer', now wore stockings 'not of cloth (though never so fine) for that is thought to be base, but of jarnsey, worsted, silk, thred and such like, or else at least of the finest yarn that can be, and so curiously knit with open seam down the leg, with quirks and clocks about the ancles, and sometime (haply) interlaced with gold and silver thred'.[4] Hosiery had become knitwear and hosiers were no longer concerned with tailoring.

Linen thread hosiery was knitted in Rossendale, in Mere in the Butter Country and occasionally elsewhere; it was not generally much made.[5]

The lowest kind of woollen hosiery was called yarn or wheelspun. It was composed of inferior carded wools or of the hairy fleeces from hill farms in the North Country, Wales and the Blackmoors and, to a lesser extent, in the West and Peak-Forest countries.[6] This branch of the hosiery industry tended to develop hard by its sources of supply. It flourished best in the North Country, all the way from Richmond, Middleham and Barnards Castle in the east to Settle, Kendal and Kirkby Stephen in the west. From their headquarters in these and other towns, the hosiers conducted their business throughout the dales.[7] Similar manufactures were found in Wales and in the West Country.[8] Some poor fallow wool was put to the same use. East Anglia could draw upon the Norfolk Heathlands, the Breckland, and the Chiltern Country to supply knitters in Norwich, Great Yarmouth and East Norfolk in general,[9] Lavenham and the Woodland, and Diss and the rest of High Suffolk.[10]

Worsted crewel stockings proved acceptable and inexpensive substitutes for the Mantua silk crewel hose from which they were first copied in the early 1560s.[11] In Norwich, Aylsham, Reepham and other East Norfolk towns large numbers of stockings now came to be knitted in crewel twisted from small-woof worsted.[12] Ipswich and Lavenham knitted similar hose in rockspun handwarp wool.[13]

In the Midland Plain much of the vast and growing store of combing wool was put to good account by jersey knitters in Peterborough, Kettering, Stourbridge, Shipston-upon-Stour and many other towns.[14] Doncaster took advantage of being on the main road to the north by selling horsemen's stockings, but otherwise both this town and Rotherham specialised rather in knit waistcoats, petticoats and gloves.[15] Coventry knitted jersey caps and bonnets of various kinds, including nightcaps. All the hard caps and bonnets, which between them made up most of the output, were fulled, by foot, so as to give more protection against the wind.[16] Fulling also prepared caps and bonnets for blocking into shape like hats. Bewdley specialised in the round, flat, hard 'Monmouth' caps much favoured by seamen. These were knitted in jersey, fulled by hand or foot, blocked, shorn and then fitted with jersey tassels. These caps long continued in use by soldiers and sailors. About 1700 the manufacture of cocked caps was started here.[17] Northampton became as noted for jersey stockings as for boots and shoes and could truly be said to stand on other men's legs.[18] However, the greatest centre for jersey knitwear was in Leicester and twenty miles about. The chief products here were stockings, which were knitted on wooden needles in twists of up to five-ply.[19]

William Lee's invention of the knitting frame in 1589 gave an impetus to Midland hosiery manufactures. Framework knitting had been introduced in Market Bosworth, Catthorpe, Hinckley and other towns before 1640, but not until about 1660 did most Leicester hosiers make the change. Henry Mug, who was admitted to the borough as a 'weaver' in 1657, and Nicholas Alsop, who died in 1707, appear to have been the first to have set up frames here. Kirby Muxloe, Melton Mowbray and Loughborough went over to frames soon after,[20] and by 1680 Mansfield, by 1690 Nottingham, were knitting jersey stockings on frames.[21] Early next century frames were at work also in Towcester, Glenfield,

Barkstone, Ashby-de-la-Zouche, Whetstone, Barwell, Bedworth, Abthorpe, Chacombe, Middleton Cheney and many other towns. In particular, all the region between Rotherham, Doncaster, Peterborough, Northampton, Coventry and Derby was alive with framework knitters, framewrights, jersey combers, hosiers and hosiery workers. Mansfield, Hucknall-under-Huthwaite and Sutton-in-Ashfield had switched from dyed-in-the-wool cloths to dyed-in-the-wool stockings, but most of the Midland knitting towns were newcomers to the world of manufactures.[22] The triumph of the knitting frame nevertheless remained for long incomplete. Hand knitters were not only hostile to the frame; they were well able to compete with it in making waistcoats, gloves and even stockings, partly because these were ornamented in accordance with fashions and individual tastes, but mainly because until the invention of ribbing attachments from 1730 onwards and particularly of the Derby rib machine by Jedediah Strutt in 1758, ribs could be knitted only by hand, by an alternation of knit and purl stitches. If we add that the early frames had no more than eight needles to the inch and made relatively coarse knitwear, and that hand knitters could take their work about with them day and night, it is easy to see why the hand knitting of 'ordinary', as opposed to 'woven' or 'frame' hose, persisted so long.[23]

Other countries also took up jersey knitting. The Flemings founded what became a notable manufacture in Norwich, Great Yarmouth and East Norfolk generally.[24] Using in part fell wool from Witney, jersey hosiery took root in Tewkesbury, Cheltenham, Evesham, Pershore, Winchcombe and other parts of the Vale of Evesham,[25] and in the Butter Country, at Crewkerne, Stalbridge, Shepton Mallett, Croscombe, Wells, Glastonbury, Coleford, Bruton, Leigh-upon-Mendip, Lyme Regis and other towns north and south of the Severn.[26] It grew in Bristol and district;[27] in Kendal;[28] in Chester and Nantwich;[29] in the Woodland, at Hessett, Lavenham and elsewhere;[30] in High Suffolk, at Bungay, Beccles, Diss, Hacheston, Wickham Skeith and Wickham Market;[31] in the West Country and the Vale of Taunton Deane;[32] and, fittingly, in the birthplace of jersey, in the Channel Isles. The 'great support of the Islands' was 'in knitting and making woollen stockings'.[33] Jersey knitting also spread throughout the Chalk Country textile region, in Canterbury, Southampton, Wimborne Minster, Ringwood, Christchurch, the Isle of Purbeck[34] and Salisbury. Here, in 'the capital of the Plain', in 1625, men and women master knitters were having 'worsted wool' spun into 'worsted' yarn and knitted up by hand by women and girls, partly on the employers' premises, but mostly in their own homes.[35] In the course of the seventeenth century, too, jersey knitting on the stocking frame became firmly established in Basingstoke, Odiham, Reading, Godalming, Guildford, Farnham, Hambledon, Thursley, Farncombe, Compton and elsewhere.[36]

The silk stockings formerly favoured by the wealthy had been made to measure out of cloth or imported from Spain ready made. It was not until about 1560 that knitting silk stockings started in England. In that year Queen Elizabeth gave up silk cloth stockings in favour of knitted ones.[37] Then came the Italian invention of knitting stockings, gloves, hoods and other articles of attire in spun waste silk, and the commencement of regular English voyages by sea to and from Naples. Up until 1575 silk knitwear was mostly imported, largely from Naples; afterwards far more was made here from Neapolitan filoselle and floret refuse silks.[38] Silk stockings, cauls and sleeves had been knitted on a commercial scale in London since 1568 or before. By 1585 silk stockings were being knitted by hand in Norwich, and the same trade was later practised in Diss.[39] Output seems to have been rather limited, but it was said already in 1583 that many people had 'two or three paire of these silk neitherstocks'.[40]

In his London workshop William Lee had succeeded by 1600 in producing frames capable of knitting plain silk stockings. In partnership with George Brooke he supplied frames to the newborn framework silk knitting industry there. Lee then moved to Rouen and achieved a similar success there. He supplied the original machines, English framework knitters, and management for the *société privée* formed in 1616, while the Rouen shareholders contributed money. Lee's operation in France probably led to further improvements in frame design and manufacture, for Rouen was then a great centre for needle making and her manufacturers had much experience in knitting in silk and jersey. Meanwhile Lee, the 'first inventor of an ingene to make silke stockings', was admitted to the freedom of London in 1608 as a 'silkweaver' to knit silk stockings 'by ingyn'. In 1610 James Lee succeeded his brother as head of the English business. He had been manager in London, but now he removed to Thoroton (about halfway between Nottingham and Grantham) and developed better and more economical frames, which were set up in London. Before he had left London, James had sold off some of the old frames and in 1610 or 1611 these had been taken to Venice and installed and managed there by one Henry Mead. Incidentally, one of the men who went out to join Mead was 'Mr Joyners sonne of Cuddesdon' near Oxford. This venture had but a short success. Mead could not get replacements for the needles and returned to London with his dilapidated machines in 1621. By this time the new and improved frames were already at work in Spitalfields, St Dunstan's and other parts of Stepney, making silk stockings, purses and other articles, and it was the manufacturers here who formed the main body of the Framework Knitters' Company, which obtained incorporation in 1657.[41]

In the 1650s framework knitting in silk became established in the district of Derby, Nottingham and Sherwood Forest.[42] At much the same time as these two industrial centres developed, individual framework knitters, usually styled 'silkweavers', set up in most provincial towns to meet especially the demand for bespoke garments. Such knitters were soon found in towns as distant and diverse as Lewes, Litlington, Great Torrington, Chester, Warwick, Leek Wootton, Dishley Mill, Leicester, Oxford, Berkhamsted, Salisbury, Warminster, Gloucester, York, Christchurch, Maidstone, Godalming, Wokingham, Odiham, Guildford, and Reading.[43]

Hand knitting in silk was now eclipsed; it offered little advantage, for stockings knitted on frames in spun silk were light and elastic enough to need no ribs, and to knit so finely by hand was exceedingly tiresome. Now Spain, which had once exported hand-knit silk stockings to England, imported English framework ones.[44]

To cap all, the art of knitting cotton wool had, by 1697, reached first Gloucester and then Tewkesbury, Pershore and Evesham. In these towns the manufacturers spun their own yarn and had it knitted by hand into stockings, gloves, waistcoats, petticoats and other things.[45] About this time, too, Weymouth and Abbotsbury took to cotton stocking knitting.[46] By 1730 hand-knit cotton hosiery manufacture had spread to the region of Nottingham, Derby and Chesterfield, eventually displacing silk knitting in all but Derby and its environs. Then in 1732, a Nottingham man succeeded for the first time in knitting cotton wool on a frame. Now the industry was taken over by framework knitters and the stage was set for Jedediah Strutt.[47] In the Vale of Evesham, however, hand knitting persisted until shortly before 1750.[48]

Thus knitting became part of the English way of life and grew to be the major industry in several districts. In the early eighteenth century, it is said, Stepney and its environs had over 2,500 frames at work, Leicester more than 400, Nottingham not many fewer, Derby and Mansfield each thirty or forty, Sutton-in-Ashfield rather more, Towcester 150, Reading and district over 100, and so on, making a total, perhaps, of some 5,000 in the kingdom as a whole.[49] Needless to say, knitwear was much exported.[50]

Lee's former servants took framework knitting to Ireland, Venice and Spain, 'and so it went through the world'. In 1603 Rouen was knitting jersey stockings *façon d'Angleterre*.[51] Mead's Venetian venture collapsed, but about 1622 a certain Jones emigrated with his frames and started knitting there.[52] About 1658 some English Roman Catholic refugees took their silk stocking frames and settled in Avignon, whence the manufacture later spread to Nîmes, Lyons, Paris and elsewhere.[53] The art of knitting jersey took hold in Tricot in Beauvaisis and in 1682 Neufchâtel-en-Bray started to *tricoter*.[54] St Omer also made jersey stockings *façon d'Angleterre*, and so did Lille, where ten or a dozen frames were at work by 1725 and more like two hundred by 1738.[55] Jersey knitting spread likewise to Friesland and Holland; by 1732 the Leiden *fraamwerkers* were knitting socks, stockings and gloves in both jersey and silk.[56]

In London and many other towns wool was transformed into felt by pounding it in water by means similar to those used in fulling cloth.[57] One of felt's chief uses was in hatmaking. Felt hats seem to have been invented in Normandy in the middle of the fifteenth century, and Normans apparently introduced the art into London. Felt hats came into fashion; some feltmakers specialised in hat felts; others also made hats; and several ways were found for men to combine some or all of the processes, which were, successively, carding, basining, felting, dressing, pouncing or pounding, blocking and dyeing.[58] Makers of other kinds of hats now faced overwhelming competition. In Norwich, and perhaps in Ipswich, the existing manufacture was of Bridges thrum hats. These required considerable stitching, which in Norwich was done with middle-woof worsted.[59] Then felt hat making was brought to Lynn and Norwich by Norman or Walloon immigrants. Out of the mere sixteen 'Frenchmen' in this city in 1542, no less than half a dozen were employed by men who were foundation members of the Hatters' Company, which in 1543 claimed to 'have inventyd and begune the craft of hattes makyng within the same cyte, whiche they can now make as well and as good as ever came owte of Fraunce or Flaunders or any other realm'.[60] In course of time, felt and hat making spread throughout the kingdom. Frampton Cotterell, Westerleigh and Winterbourne, just north of Bristol, formed an important centre of the industry,[61] but it was also widely dispersed in places as far apart as Maidstone, Kendal, Denbigh and Braintree.[62] In earlier times the feltmakers used Spanish and Portuguese felting wool, later mostly Austrian (*Oesterreich*, 'Estrige', 'Ostrich'), Lithuanian ('Livland') and Polish ('Polonia', 'Polony'). With these were often mixed 'Cornish', 'Welsh' and other hairy fleeces, coney-wool, cow hair, coarse camel hair, and for the best felts even some March and Ryeland wool.[63] By 1609 beaver or castor hats had been introduced. Before the invention of 'carroting' with salts of mercury diluted in nitric acid, only beaver felt could be made both tight and supple enough to hold its shape in the wet and so to form wide and durable brims. Some hats were made wholly from beaver hair, but others had also racoon and other hair and wool in them and were known as demi-castors.[64] Then, at the end of the century, Huguenots from Caudebec near Rouen brought to Wandsworth the manufacture of Caudebec hats from soft and rainproof felt composed of a mixture of fine vicuna wool and hare and rabbit fur.[65] Finally, straw hats were the chief end product of the plaiting industry that sprang up among women and children in and about Luton, Dunstable, Toddington, Leighton Buzzard, Woburn, Hitchin, Ware, Watford and other towns in that part of the Chiltern Country.[66] Understandably, woven and knitted headgear lost ground.[67]

Before 1563 Englishwomen worked needlelace, using mainly the buttonhole stitch, and it was almost only amongst the London strangers that bonelace was made. Then came the great wave of immigrants. Bonelacemakers from Mechlin and thereabouts gravitated to Southwark, Bermondsey, Bridge Without and other London suburbs, or to Bourne End in Cranfield (in the south of the Midland Plain), where the lord of the manor befriended them. Other immigrants, from Lille and district, brought the Lille or French types of bonelace to London and the suburbs. Bonelacemarkers also set up in Honiton and Blandford.[68] Both Mechlin and Lille were varieties of bobbin, pillow or cushion lace known as great and little bonelace or wide and narrow point. They were called bonelace because the bobbins were of bone. All varieties were normally made of linen thread and ornamented with sprigs in floral or foliaged designs. Honiton and other lacemakers were able to compete successfully with those of Brabant and Flanders thanks to the novel introduction of separately made sprigs into which the loosely woven net was then worked. Bonelace was made in this fashion in the Butter Country, in and around Honiton, Sherborne, Colyton and Lyme Regis, and later at Ottery St Mary, Axminster, Ilchester, Branscombe, Beer, Seaton, Sidbury, Sidmouth, Salcombe Regis, Exmouth and Otterton. Similar lace was made in London and the suburbs; in Bradninch in the Culm valley;[69] in the Poor Soils Country at Blandford;[70] in the Chalk Country in and about Marlborough, Warminster and Salisbury;[71] in High Suffolk at Eye and Ipswich;[72] in Littledean, Norwich, Gloucester, Malmesbury, Nottingham and elsewhere.[73] But by far the greatest lacemaking region developed from its starting point at Bourne End to cover most of the south of the Midland Plain, between Banbury, Thame, Wendover, Tring, St Neots, Kettering, Spratton and Weedon Beck; and to spread also throughout a great tongue of the Chiltern Country, in Dunstable and Luton and along the London road from Tring and Wendover in the north to Amersham, High Wycombe and Marlow in the south. Men, women and children all joined in the work and gave a true ring to the saw, 'All the world and Little Billing make lace'.[74] A small amount of cheap 'tawdry lace' was made in these parts, but almost entirely bonelace of either the Mechlin or the Lille sort or some cross of the two. Mechlin predominated until about 1700 and Lille thereafter.[75] These laces were used for cuffs, ruffs, kerchiefs and similar articles,[76] and the industry flourished right up until John Heathcoat's bobbin machine of 1809 ushered in Nottingham Net. The handworkers tried to compete with the machines by lowering their standards of workmanship, but this only hastened their demise.[77]

English buttons and buttonholes, as made in Shrewsbury, had mostly been of silk. When the Flemings came, they introduced the making in Canterbury of silk, goat's hair and jersey buttons, and in Maidstone of linen thread ones. By 1625 and 1630 respectively, Ipswich and Dorchester had their buttonmakers, and in 1692 Sherborne was making silk and goat's hair buttons. London and the suburbs also engaged in this trade. But in the 1570s and after the biggest branch of this manufacture became that of coarse buttons, and this was seated in 'The Flash' in and between Buxton, Leek, Congleton, Macclesfield and Stockport. Shreds of serge, drugget, frieze, camlet or other cloth were often used to make buttonholes and were sewn onto wooden moulds for buttons, but this practice was made illegal for buttons in 1698 and for buttonholes in 1709. Another and more usual method was to cover the moulds with closely and curiously wound threads and twists of linen, silk or hair.[78] The Flash owed its success largely to the use of linen thread and the hair of horses and oxen. White horse hair was especially valuable because it could easily be dyed, but the black was also useful. From these fibres and the moulds were made numerous varieties, including many that could be sold as 'huer buttons', 'Spanische cloake buttons', 'Million titts' and such like, implying they were of

goat's hair or silk.[79] Buttons of this kind dominated the market until about
1725, when cheaper horn and metal ones from Birmingham and Sheffield
captured a large part of it.[80]

Coventry had long made her embroidery thread, but linen thread was mostly
imported in the early sixteenth century. Then the Flemings brought thread-
twisting to London and Southwark, to Norwich,[81] and above all to Maidstone.
'The trade of thridtwisting is growne to be a great trade in the towne', someone
said in 1629.[82] Long before then, indeed, it was the Maidstone twisters with
their twisting mills who drove the main trade in the borough, set the poor on
work spinning and twisting, often grew and dressed their own flax and
sometimes dyed their own thread.[83] By 1602 Chester was also making linen
thread and Knutsford followed suit.[84] About 1680 Maidstone began to feel the
competition of Axminster, Queen Camel and Combe Martin; but Queen Camel
specialised in fine 'Nuns' thread, Combe Martin in shoemakers' thread, and
Axminster in fine packthread, which also served for anglers' lines; and
Maidstone hung on to the bulk of the button thread trade for a long time yet.[85]

Rope was made in many inland towns,[86] but far more in maritime ones,
particularly in East Anglia, as at King's Lynn, Great Yarmouth, Orford and
Ipswich, where shipping and shipbuilding were much to the fore.[87] But the one
town that specialised in ropes, lines, cordage and nets was Bridport. This was
why so much male hemp (carle) was grown hereabouts and why to be 'stabbed
with a Bridport dagger' was the fate of so many felons.[88]

# 11

## FIBRES

Flax was cultivated in England, especially in the Lancashire Plain, the Cheshire Cheese and Butter countries, High Suffolk and later in Ireland and the Midland Plain.[1] Moreover, some Canterbury and Maidstone Flemings grew their own. In these places the flax was also retted, scutched and often spun. Bleaching the yarn took about six months and was frequently left to specialists, like those in Moston who at one time did a great deal of the bleaching in the Manchester district.[2] Yet much flax was imported from the Continent, chiefly from Prussia, Poland, Lithuania and Muscovy.[3] Some thread was bought from Scotland and Ireland, and more from overseas.[4] Hemp was grown and processed in many parts of England and on a substantial scale in High Suffolk and the Butter Country,[5] yet much hemp and yarn came from the Continent.[6] Cotton wool and yarn were drawn from Cyprus, Barbary and Smyrna and, by 1628 and 1634 respectively, from the East and West Indies.[7] Camel and goat's hair came from Turkey.[8] Raw silk was imported from Granada, Piedmont, Bologna ('Boloney') and elsewhere, and in later times from Turkey, Persia, Bengal, the East Indies and China. Until 1670 none of the Bengal silk was sorted and so could be used only for silk unions and hosiery. Persian silk was coarse. Italian was the best and imports of it grew rapidly from the 1570s onwards, especially when Leghorn had become a free port in 1593 and the peace with Spain in 1604 had opened Naples, Messina and Palermo to English merchants. Much Italian thrown silk was also imported. Raw silk was usually named according to where it had come from: Messina silk was from that town and from Palermo, Morea from Lepanto, Ardassa from Persia, Legis or Legge from Lahidjan, and so on.[9]

The three main classes of silk were prepared in different ways. Capiton silk was fit only for padding clothes and quilts.[10] The waste silks consisted of filoselle or floss and refuse from reels of good silk, and of floret or ferret silk, which came from inferior and insect-damaged cocoons and from miscellaneous manufacturing offal. Floret was used largely in parchmentry, filoselle in stuffs and embroidery, but both had first to be torn into pieces, carded and spun. This silk spinning was much engaged in by the London Flemings, who had probably introduced it in the first instance.[11] The preparation in London and Norwich of satin silk, i.e. spun silk shorn for use in embroidery, was the province of the silk raser, satin drawer or *satijntrekker*.[12] Prime silk, when first unwound, consists of a double thread about a thousand yards long and so fine that at least twelve strands have to be twisted together before anything else can be attempted. The resulting 'dumb singles' are then doubled and twisted into tram for wefts and organzine for warps. Tram is usually twisted between two and five turns to the inch and organzine between nine and thirty, while both are given greater strength by imparting an S-twist to the dumb singles, which themselves had a Z-twist. This whole set of twisting processes is called throwing. It was an art brought into England about 1578 by throwsters from Antwerp, Bruges, Cambrai, Paris and elsewhere who settled in Cripplegate, Whitechapel and Stepney. Their hand or pedal throwing mills consisted of a stationary outer frame and a vertically rotating inner frame. When the inner frame was rotated, it caused the reels and spindles on the outer frame to rotate also. The reels turned slowly and the spindles rapidly, the silk being twisted as it was drawn from the spindles to the reels. In 1628 the London silkthrowsters claimed to set six or seven thousand persons on work daily, and next year their company was incorporated.[13] Their skills has been widely diffused in the suburbs, but were still confined to the throwing of tram. All organzine was as yet imported from Italy, for it was impossible for hand and pedal mills to compete with the waterpowered organzine mills in Lucca and elsewhere.[14] Up until 1688 London seems to have made most of the tram used both there and in Canterbury, Norwich and other provincial towns; but in that year Macclesfield silk-throwsters were selling supplies to Spitalfields itself. The migration of throwing to the provinces had begun.[15]

In a similar way, as more and more goat's hair was imported, hairthrowsters proliferated and some men took to throwing both hair and silk.[16]

But above all the English were wool and woollen producers and in earlier times growers and manufacturers almost rubbed shoulders. Clothiers bought wool from nearby farms and made from it the kind of cloth to which it was best suited. Thus each country's system of farm management determined the basic character of the cloths woven in its vicinity.

Most Midland clothiers used locally grown fallow wools. Hereford, Leo-minster, Worcester and Coventry took most of the Ryeland wool and supplemented it with some from the March sheep and from the common flocks in the Midland Plain.[17] Clothiers in the Cheese and Butter countries, the Vale of Berkeley, the Bristol District and the Culm valley in the West Country, drew mainly from the Cotswold Country, largely through Cirencester and Tetbury, and only to a much lesser extent from the Chalk and Oxford Heights countries, the house-lamb sheep in the Butter Country, and the Midland Plain folding flocks, which last were themselves in great measure recruited from the Cotswold and Chalk countries.[18] Manufacturers in and about the Chalk Country used wool from that country's breed and also from the Southdown, Poor Soils and Blackheath countries.[19] Much the same wools, together with some from Northwold and March sheep, went into Kentish cloth.[20] Woodland and East

Anglian clothiers obtained wool from the Norfolk Heathlands and the Breckland and the Sandlings and Chiltern countries, largely through the Mattishall wool dealers, and to a lesser extent from Chalk Country, Blackheath, Southdown, Northwold, March and Ryeland flocks, this last source being reserved for the best handwarps only.[21] Plains for friezes and cottons were made in the West Country and the Vale of Taunton Deane from local wools, in the Cheshire Cheese Country and the Marches from those of Wales,[22] and in the Peak-Forest Country from Gritstone and Lank wools and even hairier ones from Scotland and Ireland. Some other cloths made in the Peak-Forest Country, like the penistones, had Midland and Northwold fallow wools in the wefts. Herdwick wool went into Kendal cloths, cogware, cottons and linsey-woolseys, and Cheviot into tweeds; otherwise the North Country had no clothing wool and therefore little by way of woollen manufactures.[23] As for the worstedweavers of East Norfolk and Lynn, all their industry depended on pasture wool from the nearer parts of the Fen Country.[24]

As country after country abandoned its own manufactures and took on new ones, the wool trade was diverted into new channels. Whereas the main supplies had formerly been of local growth, they now came from much further afield; manufacture was freed from the constraints imposed by the agriculture of its own and nearby countries. And meanwhile the agricultural revolution transformed the wool supplies of the kingdom as a whole.

As frieze making declined in the Cheshire Cheese Country and the Englishry in Wales, Milford Haven and other ports began sending mountain wool to Bristol, the Vale of Taunton Deane and the West Country for felting and other purposes.[25] Many West Country wools had meanwhile improved enough to go into kerseys. Clothiers sprang up to utilise 'wolls growen in this countrie'. As Richard Hooker went on to say, 'The woll of this countrie is verie good and carieth so longe a staple as there be no wolls doth or can so well serve for makenge of kerseys.'[26] Then, around 1570, some makers started to import Dorset Horn wool from the Butter Country for the new and improved second generation of West Country straits. This same wool was also used nearer home for the newly invented Dorset dozens.[27] From about 1588 clothiers in the Peak-Forest Country took increasingly to making proper cloths and kerseys from the inferior wools of the Norfolk Heathlands, the Northwold, Sandlings, Chiltern, Chalk and Northdown countries, and even from the worst parts of March fleeces. These new supplies compensated amply for any fall in those from the Midland Plain common fields, but had only been made available to the Peak-Forest Country by the decline of manufactures of kersey and medley cloth in the Chalk Country and thereabouts and of Suffolk cloth in the Woodland.[28] White cloth making became depressed in the West of England region and the old Cotswold wool now found destinations other than the Stroudwater towns. Meanwhile Leominster wool was in increasing request for the first generation of Spanish medleys and later for the Spanish Stroudwaters. These fabrics also provided new uses for some March, Southdown and Chalk Country wools.[29] The Stroudwater clothiers had to find a replacement for the old Cotswold wool, for the breed of sheep itself was dying out. By a lucky chance agricultural improvements were lowering the quality of Leominster wool and making it less suited to fine Worcester cloths, the output of which consequently stagnated, while at the same time, since the second generation of Spanish medleys used only Spanish wool, Leominster met less demand from that quarter, with the result that Stroudwater and other clothiers found it much cheaper and easier to obtain. Between about 1637–43 and about 1666–7 fine Leominster wool fell from 35s or 36s a stone to 20s or 22s.[30]

Earlier than this the old clothing industries of the Woodland and elsewhere had been severely hit by strong and growing demand for fallow wool from the baizemakers.[31] A Dutch 54 baize, for instance, had about twelve pounds of tops in the warp and forty of carding wool in the weft; and other baizes held to much the same proportions.[32] As the report runs, 'The Coggeshall wool whereof all the fyne Coggeshall clothes are made, being next unto Lemster wolle in fynnes, is in a manner converted wholly to the making of baies'. Southampton rashes, too, were goods into which were 'nowe converted most of the fynest wolles that were wont to be employed to the draping of fyne kerseyes and Reading clothes'.[33] Complaints were raised that 'The multitude of baies and other things made as well by Englishmen as straungers doth so wast wolls as yerelie at Christmas the most clothiers are forced to seke for woll at London at the staplers hands and into other contries farr of.'[34] Midland fallow wool, usually collected in Northampton and either woven up there or sold to Cirencester for the West of England and Taunton Deane clothiers, was now being bought up by factors for the Norwich baizemakers.[35] The old-fashioned clothiers could not compete in price with the makers of new and highly profitable fabrics and were not the last producers in such a predicament to demand public protection from the consumers, while the baizemakers, whose products the consumers favoured, were denounced for having the temerity to 'wast' wool by converting it 'into many slight and vaine comodities wherein the comon people delight'.[36] This diversion of wool supplies was felt not least by clothiers in Holland and Zealand who were cut off from the woolfells and fell wools they needed for their frizadoes, simply, as the Merchants of the Staple pointed out, because of 'the great clothinge in England' carried on by the Flemish strangers.[37]

But this new demand for carding wool was only one blade of the scissors. The other was the rise of up-and-down husbandry and the consequent proliferation of pasture sheep. The supply of fallow wool stagnated or declined, while that of combing wool increased hand over fist, forcing clothiers and converters to adapt accordingly, turn from old to new fabrics, and devise ways of making them attractive to the public. This resulted in a transformation in textiles not unlike that caused by the recent shift to man-made fibres. Already in 1610 it was reckoned the scales had been turned. Pasture sheep now preponderated over 'fielden' ones, the main stream 'being nowe all pasture sheepe', each of which bore two or three times as much wool as a fallow one.[38] The flood of pasture wool from the Midland Plain, the Western Waterlands, Romney Marsh, and the Fen, Saltings, Cotswold and Northwold countries swept all before it.[39] Pasture wool was the material cause of textile and hosiery manufactures wholly or partly composed of tops and noils.

The Vale of Taunton Deane and the West Country took to importing pasture wools from the Midland Plain, Romney Marsh and the Fen, Saltings and Cotswold countries.[40] For the warps of their flannels and baizes, manufacturers in the Cheshire Cheese Country, the Vales of Hereford, the Englishry and the Severn valley bought jersey yarns from Aberdovey, Machynlleth, Cirencester, Chester, Liverpool, Bristol and Gloucester, while relying for their wefts chiefly on purchases at Oswestry of blended wools drawn from all parts of eastern, southern and central England.[41] The yarnmakers who supplied weavers in East Norfolk, the Breckland and the Woodland continued to buy combing wool from the Marshland, but now extended their purchases into more distant parts of the Fen Country, using Stourbridge Fair, King's Lynn and the north Norfolk ports. Some wool was also bought from the Midland Plain, chiefly for jersey.[42] The Woodland clothiers went on drawing on their accustomed sources of fallow wools, but now employed huge amounts of pasture wool from the Saltings Country, Romney Marsh and the Midland Plain.[43]

Much Midland and Cotswold pasture wool went to Cirencester, Tetbury and district to be spun into jersey and noil yarns for the Midland towns as far away as Leicester, for the Cheese, Butter and West countries, for the vales of Berkeley and of Taunton Deane, and even for East Norfolk and the Peak-Forest Country. Some Midland pasture wool sold as far south as Sandwich and Canterbury, but the traffic in it was mainly to the south-west and to the east. The Woodland, the Breckland and East Norfolk were supplied from the Fen Country and the east of the Midland Plain. From farmers and graziers, directly or through factors and dealers, to clothiers, weavers, hosiers and combers, by packhorse, wagon and inland and coastal navigation, this huge easterly movement swelled from year to year.[44] The needs of the Chalk Country and thereabouts and of Southampton, Sandwich and Canterbury were met from Romney Marsh and the Saltings Country as well as from the Midland Plain. Romney Marsh wool went by sea to the West Country, via Faversham to Colchester and via Milton-next-Gravesend to London, not to speak of the cargoes destined for the Continent.[45]

A great new source of pasture wool was created in the settled parts of Ireland. Formerly the only Irish wool had been the hairy kind used in Bristol and Salford for making friezes.[46] Now English and Scots settlers stocked the new plantations in Munster and Ulster with English pasture sheep. Wool sales from these parts to the mainland were already mounting markedly by 1615, but were still overshadowed by the trade in livestock to such an extent that the settlers were tempted to 'bring their English sheep back againe into England'. It was chiefly the stopping of this livestock trade that turned the flow of wool into a flood in the 1670s.[47] Like that from the Midland Plain, this pasture wool was well suited to both jersey and noil yarns. It was used in Manchester for narrow wares, in East Norfolk for jersey calamancoes, in Rossendale and the West Country for the warps of baizes, and in the West Country and the Vale of Taunton Deane for serges.[48] The mainland also imported yarns spun in Ireland, both jersey and noil yarn, which were often called 'Irish worsted' and 'bay yarn' respectively. Noil yarn went into the wefts of baizes and serges, jersey into Norwich and Coventry calamancoes, Coventry plush, camlets and shalloons, Cheese Country and Vale of Berkeley serges, 'Manchester' baizes, Salisbury and 'Welsh' flannels, Bewdley caps, Kidderminster stuffs and the products of Bristol and district.[49] The best and probably the greatest part of this wool came from The Route, which lies between the River Bann to the west, the sea to the north, and the Antrim mountains to the south and east, and is still the greatest sheep region in Ulster. Carrickfergus and Londonderry seem to have been the ports most used. We find 'Rout wooll' in Kettering and district, in Ipswich, and throughout the Woodland, 'Rout yarn' in Norwich and East Norfolk, and 'Route' wool and yarn, including 'Rout woosted', in Kidderminster, Cirencester and Tetbury.[50] Although combing and weaving were no cheaper in Ireland than on the mainland, wool and spinning were, so western parts of England could obtain wool and yarn relatively cheaply, and Route wool especially was keenly sought by users of jersey.[51] By 1708 many West Country towns were using Irish jersey and noil yarns. About 1720 Tiverton men imported a large amount of undyed 'Irish worsted' to make piece-dyed serges, 'which was a means of manufacturing them cheaper than by dying them in wool, as they bought the materials cheaper from Ireland, on account of the lower prices of labour there, as well as for the saving one course of combing the wool'. Unfortunately this proved a false economy, the serges 'not being found equal in goodness to those made with English and Irish wool combed and spun here. It was also an unfit manufacture for the cane sleas then used.' Nevertheless, many 'Norwich stuffs' came to be made in Tiverton with Irish jersey.[52]

Originally, in 1617, the only authorised ports of entry for Irish wool and yarn were London, Bristol, Chester, Liverpool, Barnstaple, Minehead and Milford Haven. Exeter, Plymouth and Southampton were added in 1641; but the last two were removed from the list in 1688 and Exeter in 1693, for fear of facilitating illegal export to the Continent. However, Bideford and Bridgwater were included in the 1696 and 1698 lists and Lancaster and Great Yarmouth in the 1752 one. Exeter was restored next year, but to little purpose, for almost immediately the trade was thrown open to all ports.[53] These lists give some idea of the incidence of the use of Irish combing wool and yarns. The West Country was a heavy importer. By the early eighteenth century Liverpool had become the largest single authorised point of entry, followed by Minehead, Bideford,

Barnstaple, Bristol, Chester and Bridgwater, in that order. Total lawful imports now ran at about 4,200,000 lb. a year. English wool production at this time was reckoned to be some 24,000,000 lb. and Irish 5,500,000. Allowing for wool brought over in the form of yarn, these figures fit nicely enough and show the importance of Irish wool to the jersey and jersey union industries in particular.[54] From these ports, their members and creeks, the wool was widely distributed. Presumably Liverpool and Chester sent to Kendal, Rochdale, Manchester and Oswestry, Aberdovey to the upper valley of the Severn, Southampton to Salisbury, and Bristol to the lower Severn valley, Kidderminster, Coventry, Cirencester and Tetbury. Colchester, Braintree and Norwich seem to have obtained Irish yarn by sea and land from London and overland from Bristol. Through Great Yarmouth it also came via Hull from Liverpool. By the middle of the eighteenth century Norwich merchants were buying wool direct from Ireland through factors.[55]

The domestic wool trade was more complex than might appear at first sight. Wool was sold, resold, combed, sorted, blended and redistributed at all hands. First, as we have seen, the yarn trade pursued the wool trade at a higher level. Secondly, fellmongers, glovers, whittawers and parchmentmakers were important sellers of fell wool. By such hands the Witney blanketmakers obtained wool that originated in Romney Marsh, the Midland Plain or the Fen, Saltings and other countries by way of London, Southwark, Canterbury, Norwich, Colchester, Exeter, Leicester, Northampton, Huntingdon, Coventry and many other centres of mutton consumption. The same wagons that took blankets and duffels to London brought back woolfells and fell wools from all the mutton producing countries.[56] Thirdly, woolcombers, clothiers and others who bought combing wools sometimes took a little fallow or hairy wool off the same grower's hands. It could hardly be otherwise when many landowners and graziers had properties that straddled two or more farming countries or took or gave agistments for odd lots of sheep.[57] Even those manufacturers who bought nothing but pure combing wool might have noils and other fibres they could find no use for, while makers of coarse cloths might want to dispose of wool that was far too good for their own products. Such men traded amongst themselves. Thus Sandwich and Canterbury combers and converters retained the coarser carding grades that came their way and resold the finer ones to makers of carded woollens who for their part had coarse fibres to dispose of.[58] Fourthly, all fleeces other than hairy ones from hill-farm countries had to be sorted at least twice: once by the grower and once by the manufacturer. The first sorting merely enabled growers and buyers to arrive at a fair price for what would otherwise have been an unknown quality. Thus pasture wools were sorted at or before winding into such grades as fine, middle and coarse, best cleft wool, darkest cleft wool and end wool.[59] Before spinning could be contemplated a much more thorough sorting was required. At one time the Witney men were said to have sorted their fell wools as follows: head and bay wool for heavy blankets or to be sent to Kidderminster for the wefts of stuffs or to the Woodland for baize woofs or to the Vale of Evesham for yarn stockings; long wool for jersey stockings in the Vale of Taunton Deane and the Butter and West countries; middle and best tail wool for ordinary duffels, blankets, hats and rugs; and worst tail wool for horsecollars, wrappers and tilt cloths.[60] The breech, tail and the rest of the coarsest combing wool sometimes went for garters, swathe bands or bandages, fringe, and the warps of the low-priced baizes called 'grasiors'.[61] Of the Chalk Country fleeces, in earlier times the clothiers sorted the better parts into fine, middle and coarse wools for medley cloths and such like, while the worst was set aside for kersey yarn. Other fallow wools were sorted similarly.[62] Later, when superior feed had worsened Chalk Country wool, the neck, breast and bottom belly wool went for the warp and abb of carded woollens, the back and rib for drugget abb, the flank and buttock for union serges and druggets, and the tail for lists, rugs and blankets. Such second sortings were frequently followed by sales of some of the resulting sorts.[63]

In fine, what little we know of the wool and yarn trades leads us to believe the man who said, 'The places of the growing and the places of converting are as farre distant as the scope of this kingdome will give leave'. In half a century the domestic wool trade had been transformed.[64]

Yarns spun from combing wool came in from Flanders and worsted especially from Béthune. But then the wool itself had come from this side of the Channel and largely from Romney Marsh. In the early days of their settlement in Sandwich the Flemings imported 'baye yarn' through Dunkirk. This too was made of English wool. Imports of yarns from Flanders never entirely ceased, but neither were they ever very great, and little Continental wool was incorporated in them.[65] Imports from France were negligible and those from eastern Europe served only for felt. Scotch wool was rarely used.[66] Spanish and Portuguese had previously been used for felting, but with the rise of various kinds of Spanish cloth of English making, the volume of Spanish wool landed in London, and even more in western ports like Barnstaple, Bridgwater, Exeter and Lyme Regis, rose swiftly and, wars notwithstanding, almost uninterruptedly, so that every pound in 1567 had become a bag fifty years later.[67]

True sorting was the first foundation of good clothmaking, for wools ill sorted spun and shrank unevenly. Save for a few disabled men, sorting was women's work. 'The perfect and principall grounde of clothmaking', it is avowed, 'ys the true sorting of wolles, and thexperience therof consistethe only in women, as clothiers wives and their women servants.' Flemish women were renowned for their sorting.[68] It was largely 'the carefull sorteing of their wolles' that caused cloths from southern England to be so much better than those from north of the Trent. 'If the clothiers in Yorkshire', it was asserted, 'would as well severally and carefully sorte their woolles as the cloathiers in

Wiltshire doe, the same might be made as good cloathes as the cloathes in Wiltshire are ordinarily.'[69]

Insubstantial spinners and weavers, like those in the West and Peak-Forest countries in the mid-sixteenth century, were forced to buy wool weekly in pitched markets or from chapmen, but this hardly affected the general position, which was that as long as converters used wool from local breeds of sheep, they or their womenfolk could sort it relatively easily. It was otherwise once wools were drawn from new and strange sources like The Route and Spain. Then it was often better to leave the breaking, sorting and blending of the wools to the wholesalers. In this way the clothier could choose just the blend of wool or type of yarn best suited to his particular needs.[70] Woolcombers and yarnmasters already provided these services for the converters of pasture wool, but old-fashioned clothiers used to sorting their own local wools were much put out by this new way of doing business. They lost control of their accustomed supplies and could scarcely make their old kinds of cloth from new-fangled pre-sorted blends. As this radical reorganisation of wool marketing was heralded by the rise of jobbers and brokers who not only bought and stored wool as in the past, but also sold it to men who sorted, blended and resold it, complaints and lamentations rent the air in vain.[71]

The people who took over this new wool trade were the Merchants of the Staple, either members of old standing or brokers and others turned dealers who joined the company of their own volition or under orders from James I. When their export business had collapsed, the Staplers had simply switched to selling to domestic manufacturers. To a large extent this shift had been perfectly painless; it was just that Flemings who had come to England went on buying wool from their usual suppliers. This gave the Staplers entry into the home market.[72] They developed this new trade of wholesale buying, sorting, blending and selling, and recruited to their ranks upstart broggers who had taken to the same line of business. Merchants of the Staple now employed wool jobbers or drivers, brokers, breakers, sorters and blenders, and saw to the whole business.[73] The Stapler who buys wool 'of severall countryes and sortes, as northerne and westerne, pasture and fallowe, sells the same to the clothier mingled and compounded'.[74] In this way noils could easily be mixed with inferior fallow wool. The Stapler bought wool, sorted it into pasture or fallow, long or short, coarse or fine, and then each of these into four or five qualities, blended some mixtures, and then sold each where it would fetch the best price, which was where it was most needed.[75] As to the several grades of coarse carding wool, for example, they were in a class by themselves, and 'divers places, as in Yorkshire and at Oswestree, where there dwell many clothiers that make course cloth, rugs, course cottons and flannels and use only course sorts of woole, buy these sorts of woole of the Staplers ready sorted'.[76] Woolcombers in the Breckland, the Woodland and East Norfolk took to buying pasture wool from the Staplers, and so did those in Cirencester, Tetbury, Taunton and

Exeter. This was how it came about that a woolcomber and yarnmaster in the
Vale of Taunton Deane had 'fine mixture comb wool' and 'mixture pinions'
ready to be spun up. Colchester manufacturers used wool brought from London
by the regular packet service. Tiverton and other West Country kersey makers
bought wool in weekly supplies from London. Like all clothiers who sold in
London, and almost all did, they found it convenient to buy their wool there.[77]
Wool staples were appointed at London, Canterbury, Exeter, Norwich,
Worcester, Shrewsbury, Winchester, Reading, Cirencester, Sherborne,
Devizes, Taunton, Kendal, Rochdale, Richmond, Wakefield, Halifax, Coggeshall, Oswestry, Northampton, Lincoln, Woodstock, Brackley and Leicester.
Provincial staples were primarily for the sale of raw wools and the purchase of
sorted and blended ones, for which purposes market houses and weighing
machines were provided. London was far more.[78] It was increasingly on
London account that the fallow wools were bought, sorted, blended, and then
redistributed to the Peak-Forest, Cheshire Cheese, Cheese, Butter and West
countries, the Woodland, the Vale of Taunton Deane and wheresoever such
wools were converted. 'London' wool now figured in clothiers' account books
and inventories of their effects.[79] 'Thus by the indeavor of the wooll marchant
many millions of poore are sett on worke, the woolles of the severall countries
are broughte and, being sorted, are from thence [London] caried six or seven
score miles before they be used, because in those places those sortes of woolle
wilbe improved to the greatest advantage both for the king and comenwelth.'[80]
A metropolitan market in wool had been established,[81] and the slightly later
practice of clothiers buying their wool, as they did their silk, cotton wool and
linen yarn, from or through the London factors through whom they sold their
cloths, amounted to no more than a modification of existing arrangements, for
these factors were often also staplers and 'great dealers in these pinions and
niles' as well as in Spanish wool.[82]

Continental manufacturers could obtain all the carding wool they wanted
from Spain and elsewhere without recourse to England. 'Combing wool was
another matter', as Miss Mann says. Dyer expressed it like this in 'The
Fleece',[83]

> There are, who over-rate our spungy stores,
> Who deem that nature grants no clime but ours,
> To spread upon its fields the dews of heav'n,
> And feed the silky fleece; that card, nor comb
> The hairy wool of Gaul can e'er subdue,
> To form the thread, and mingle in the loom,
> Unless a third from Britain swell the heap:
> Illusion all ...
> If any wool peculiar to our isle
> Is giv'n by nature, 'tis the comber's lock,
> The soft, the snow-white, and the long-grown flake.

Hither be turn'd the public's wakeful eye,
This golden fleece to guard, with strictest watch,
From the dark hand of pilf'ring avarice,
Who, like a spectre, haunts the midnight hour ...
While the pale moon illumes the trembling tide,
Speedy to tip the canvas, bend the oar,
And waft his thefts to the perfidious foe.

No one, least of all the French, Flemings and Dutch, doubted that if England could keep her combing wool to herself, her manufactures of it would be unrivalled for price and quality.[84] This was why the worstedweavers always tried to stop the export of worsted yarns and the wools they were spun from.[85] This was why the jersey and jersey union makers did the same for their materials.[86] Some Romney Marsh and other graziers understandably preferred complete freedom of trade in wool. Their opinions found little favour.[87] Proclamations in 1614, 1622, 1630, 1632, 1639, 1656 and 1660 forbade the export to foreign parts of wools, woolfells, woollen yarn and fuller's earth, but were 'only a device for money and to blind the people' or to promote the Cockayne scheme or to overcome temporary wool shortages. Similarly, exports were prohibited in 1647 only because of an acute shortage of wool due to the destruction of sheep in the course of the Civil War.[88] It became a cornerstone of policy to prevent Irish combing wool going to the Continent,[89] and in 1641, 1643, 1648 and 1660 moves were made to prohibit the export of wool, woolfells, woollen yarn and fuller's earth from the British Isles.[90] But it was only the mounting French attempts to exclude English textile manufactures in favour of their own that provoked the prohibitions of wool exports in 1662 and after and the first consistent and earnest endeavours to enforce such laws instead of licensing the waiving of them in ordinary times for the financial advantage of the monarch.[91] Finally, the Act of Union in 1707 completed the legal edifice by stopping exports of English wool from Scotland to France.[92]

Any serious attempt to tax wool exports had always resulted in owling or nocturnal smuggling,[93] and with downright prohibition owling now assumed giant proportions, particularly from Dover, Canterbury, Sandwich, Romney Marsh and all the coast from Shell Ness to North Foreland,[94] from Southampton, under pretext of allowable shipment to the Channel Isles,[95] from Ireland, where customs officers were much laxer,[96] and later also from the east coast ports from Boston to Berwick, which had ready access to pasture wool from the Fen Country, the Midland Plain and the Northeastern Lowlands.[97] It will be understood that the draconian penalties on this owling were seldom if ever exacted. Officers seized the wool when they could, but refrained from prosecuting. 'The owlers saved their necks, the officers avoided a struggle, and the law of Parliament bowed to the unwritten code of expediency thus established.'[98] Nothing could stop sales of Romney Marsh wool to France, Flanders and Holland; its roots were too fast in the channels of commerce, and nature had its course. Over and above this, the decline of textile manufactures in Sandwich and of jersey and worsted consumption in Canterbury meant Romney Marsh wool sought other markets, and since many operatives in these towns had lost their former trades, it was on the cards that some of them would resort to less reputable means of livelihood. It was no mere accident that some of the most determined owlers were Canterbury Walloons.[99] Export prohibitions were costly to enforce and hardly succeeded in raising the price of wool overseas.[100] Home manufactures could have been better assisted, perhaps, by imposing a high export tax on wool; but then, prohibition was intended to hurt a hostile country.

In England the woolcombers, who were of vital importance to all manufactures using pasture wool, were, in numbers, ability, capital and business, a most considerable body of men.

East Norfolk had few sheep and drew its pasture wool mainly from the Fen Country. It was generally recognised in 1547 that in the worsted industry 'the most parte of the saide poore persons dwell farre of from the said bredes of the saide wooles'. Yet this distance was not great by the standards of a later age, for in that time most of the wool came from Marshland, which was in Norfolk, and so there was substance in the worstedweavers' claim that they only used wool from their own county.[101] In Norwich the types of worsted called small woof, mantle warp and headle yarn were all spun from wool taken off the fells the butchers sold to the whittawers and parchmentmakers. This wool was certainly from pasture sheep, for it yielded not only inferior tops but also noils for the wefts of blankets; and the pasture sheep consumed in Norwich were fed and fatted in Marshland.[102] Thus no worsted was spun in Norwich from any but Norfolk raw wool. Nevertheless, the claim that none but Norfolk wool was employed by worstedweavers became increasingly remote from the truth, partly because from 1467 onwards more and more wool was drawn from districts of the Fen Country in counties other than Norfolk,[103] and mostly because worstedweavers relied chiefly on buying worsted from the East Dereham district and from towns in and near the Breckland like Thetford, Bury St Edmunds, Mildenhall and Soham.[104] Apart from the East Dereham district, East Norfolk had few woolcombers in the middle of the sixteenth century, and most of these were small fry who worked on fell wool in Norwich.[105] Combing grew in the city after 1565, but in the Flemish manner, with imported combs. A few of the immigrant combers came from Hainault, Artois and Brabant, and one from Cologne, but most of them were Flemings. By 1568 no fewer than eighteen Walloon and a hundred and fifty Dutch combers had settled in the city. But many of these were women, who could have done no more than work on hairy wools with great combs and were not woolcombers in the ordinary sense of the word. Nevertheless, some of the strangers combed pasture wool with small combs and disposed annually of many tons of noils. In 1624 there were over thirty strangers who were woolcombers and between them employed many journeymen in the city.[106] Those of the later Norwich woolcombers who were also yarnmasters still made a little small-woof worsted from fell wool, but mainly various gauges of jersey, and all their yarns were largely intended for knitting. Many of these yarnmasters, indeed, were themselves hosiers.[107] The Great Yarmouth woolcombers and yarnmasters conducted much the same kind of business,[108] and so did some of the King's Lynn ones, though more worsted was made here and part of it sold in Norwich.[109] In the 1580s and later, woolcombers set up in many towns along the northern bounds of East Norfolk, just below the Cromer Ridge, and in Wells-next-the-Sea and elsewhere in the Norfolk Heathlands. Through Wells St Peter and other ports, 'Lincolnshire' wool was imported from the more northerly parts of the Fen Country. From the tops of this the jersey-drawers produced jersey for Norwich.[110] In addition, by 1681 Cirencester was selling some wool and jersey to Norwich and to Thetford for Norwich,[111] and by Defoe's time jersey was coming to the city from Ireland, through Bristol and then overland, and even from the Peak-Forest Country.[112]

In the extreme west of East Norfolk, many towns on the roads to Downham Market, King's Lynn, the Marshland and beyond, had their woolcombers and yarnmakers, but the greatest concentration was in East Dereham, Weston Longville, Mattishall, Mattishall Burgh and nearby places like Great Fransham, Hoe, Wendling, Swanton Morley and East Tuddenham.[113] They supplied the worstedweavers with worsted and the dornicksweavers with noil kersey.[114] Thetford was another centre of these trades, and had in addition a colony of 'Dutchmen' who made baize yarns.[115] Worsted from these places naturally ranked as 'Norfolk', but then so did the similar 'Norwich' yarn from Bury St Edmunds, Mildenhall, Brandon Ferry and thereabouts.[116] What the worsted-weavers dubbed 'Suffolk' or 'Cambridgeshire' yarn was the jersey made in Mildenhall, Soham, Isleham and elsewhere.[117] However, the special importance of Breckland and district lay in becoming the greatest single source of worsted. Some Bury clothiers combed for themselves and more and more of them took to specialising in combing and yarnmaking. Some retained the style of 'clothier', but were really no different from the other woolcombers and yarnmasters.[118] Unlike the worstedweavers, who were far too busy with their weaves to bother with much else, the Woodland clothiers made relatively simple fabrics and were left with the time, energy and resources to see to much of their own combing. As befitted her position, Bury had some clothiers of the Woodland type, but the yarnmasters overtook them. When the comber John Willsone died in 1663 he left among his other effects several pounds' worth of 'Norwiche yarne', more yarn in Norwich awaiting sale, and a good deal of 'nyle' yarn also.[119] John Cutting, the 'clothier' who died in 1687, was really a yarnmaster supplying worsted to the Norwich market.[120] In 1729 Edward Cheaveley, 'cloathier', left 188 lb. of tops in the spinners' hands, 142 lb. of noils, and forty-seven gross of yarn in Norwich.[121] Bury acquired a growing reputation for her 'Norwich' worsted.[122] She became the head and heart of a combing and spinning region more than a dozen miles in radius and extending into the Woodland and the Chiltern and Fen countries as well as over the greater part of the Breckland. It stretched to Mildenhall, Isleham and Soham in the north-west, Kentford and Newmarket in the west, Ashley in the south-west, Wickhambrook, Stansfield and Stanstead in the south, Felsham and Battlesden in the south-east, Woolpit and Wetherden in the east, Finningham, Walsham-le-Willows and Ixworth in the north-east, and Thetford and Brandon in the north. Most towns within this compass came to stand largely by combing wool and spinning yarns,[123] and their woolcombers and yarnmasters conducted their businesses in much the same way as the Bury ones did. Robert Fitch of Brockley Green, Thomas Underwood the younger of Hartest, Benjamin Danaby 'clothier' of Ixworth, Samuel Owers of Tostock and Albert Costen of Ashley all sold in Norwich batches worth scores and hundreds of pounds of the worsted they had spun from the wools they combed.[124] For the most part Mildenhall and Barton Mills drove a similar trade. Robert Crannis carried on business just as other yarnmasters did; he deposited yarns for sale in his hutch in Norwich yarn market.[125] The Soham men, too, worked for Norwich in much the same way.[126] It was thus with good reason that the worstedweavers had their rights of search and seal for worsted extended to Suffolk, Cambridgeshire and Essex.[127] But the noil yarns from this Breckland region were mostly sold to Woodland clothiers.[128] Thomas Underwood, for example, disposed of his to saymakers in Cavendish and elsewhere.[129]

Much of the pasture wool used in the Woodland came from the Midland Plain. It was combed for the baize, say and serge manufacturers by their journeymen,[130] or by independent woolcombers,[131] some of whom did no more than comb and draw at task.[132] Combers who prospered branched out into yarnmaking,[133] and then, perhaps, into clothing or hosiery. Some yarnmasters sold their jersey in both the Woodland and East Norfolk.[134] Glemsford, Lavenham, Needham Market, Sible Hedingham, Stanstead and Finningham were amongst the chief suppliers of this 'Suffolk' yarn in the Norwich market.[135] In later times some yarnmasters in Lavenham and elsewhere sold jersey to London. In 1740, for instance, William Deekes of Hadleigh had nearly £40 'due at London for yarn'.[136] This shift of direction was largely the result of the migration to Spitalfields of jersey weaving from Canterbury and of jersey knitting from Norwich.[137] Previously only towns on the southernmost bounds, like Billericay, and those, like Colchester, with excellent communications with London and the Kent ports, had sold jersey yarns and chains to Spitalfields and to Reading, Newbury, Andover, Whitchurch, Sandwich and Canterbury.[138] Woolcombing and yarnmaking in the Woodland were thus much as described by Reyce in 1618:[139]

> At this day there is another kind of this trade, nott long since found outt ... commonly called kembing. The artificers hereof doe furnish themselves with great store of wool, every one so far as his ability will extend. This wool they sort unto many

severall purposes; being washed, scoured, kembed and trimmed, they putt it outt to spinning, of which they make a fine thred according to the sort of wool . . . Now when their wooll is made into yarne, they weekely carry it to London, Norwich and other such places where it is ever readily sold to those who make thereof all sortes of fringes, stuffes and many other things.

Woolcombers sprang up in High Suffolk also, at Bungay, Palgrave, Yaxley, Hacheston, Wortham, Framlingham and elsewhere, and in Ipswich. The yarns some of them made were intended mainly for the knitters in those parts, and some combers were also hosiers. The noils remaining seem to have gone mainly to the wefts of the local linsey-woolseys.[140]

As we have just seen, Reading and the northeasterly Chalk Country towns drew jersey yarns from Billericay and the southern Woodland, but wool was combed and jersey spun in Salisbury, Newbury and other towns, especially in the district of Marlborough, Devizes and Urchfont,[141] and supplies were to be had also in Southampton and Romsey. In these two towns, and in Dibden and Lymington too, some of the sergemakers and clothiers had their own combshops.[142] The skills introduced by the Hampton Walloons had soon been passed on.

The Sandwich Dutch included many woolcombers; a score and more were listed in 1582. One of them, Andrew Van Howle, who died at the end of the century, was also a yarnmaster and appears to have sold his wares in London and oversea as well as in his own town.[143] The Walloons brought woolcombing to Canterbury and long continued to dominate the craft there. They gave rise to yarnmasters who employed combers on task work and specialised in making jersey yarns and chains for manufacturers in Flanders and Holland as well as in their adopted city.[144] As the Canterbury converters shifted more and more from jersey and worsted to silk and hair, they came to consume, it was said, no more than one part in forty of the wool combed there, and the woolcombers and yarnmasters were forced to rely almost wholly on sales oversea to places like Middelburg and Rotterdam.[145] Canterbury combers also processed fell wool,[146] which, like the fleeces they and the Sandwich men bought, came partly from the Saltings Country and mainly from Romney Marsh.[147] This great source of pasture wool gave rise to other woolcombing centres in Dover, Hythe and elsewhere, and the wool shipped from these and other ports, notably Rye, to England and the Continent, was largely ready combed, often ready spun, and sometimes even ready warped.[148]

As befitted so vast a store of pasture wool, the Midland Plain likewise had its woolcombers. In Coventry and district some of them also made jersey yarns for such of the city's tammy makers as did not undertake their own combing.[149] Specialist woolcombers set up in Brigstock, Wellingborough, Uppingham and other nearby towns, mainly to serve the sergemakers in Kettering and district.[150] Jersey combers in Leicester, Hinckley, Market Bosworth, Gilmorton, Northampton, Nottingham, Derby, Abingdon, Oxford, Cambridge,

Mansfield and Darlington supplied chiefly the local hosiers and knitters.[151] It was much the same in the Fen Country: Peterborough, Haddenham, and Brandon Ferry had woolcombers and jersey drawers who worked mainly for the local hosiers.[152]

Much of the new New Cotswold and Midland Plain pasture wool flowed to the south and west. Tewkesbury and Gloucester combed some of it, but far more went to the woolcombing district formed by Malmesbury, Colerne, Midsomer Norton, Marshfield, Cricklade and above all Tetbury and Cirencester.[153] These two great wool marts now turned their attention to the new fibres.[154] Cirencester became a bustling town of woolcombers and yarnmasters. In the 1660s and 1670s these trades were often combined in the same person, but a further division of labour was already leading to the emergence of specialist yarnmakers. Twice a week the greatest wool market in England was held here, and one of the biggest yarn markets also.[155] Tetbury had a similar business, though on a rather smaller scale and with less specialisation between combers and yarnmakers. By 1779 some hundred and fifty woolcombers were at work here.[156] The other towns were less important, but, despite minor differences, business was conducted in essentially the same way throughout the district. Defoe's description is accurate as far as it goes. From the Cotswold Country and from all parts of the Midland Plain, including the vales of York and of Stockton and Darlington came a never ending stream of pasture fleeces, to be joined by a large flow of fell wool. Jersey and noil yarns were sold to manufacturers as far afield as Frome, Warminster and Taunton, and thus the West Country was furnished.[157] So far from exaggerating, Defoe understated the scope of this yarn trade. In 1663 Edward Meeke, a Cirencester 'woosted coomer', had £65 of 'debts dew in the west'. In 1686 Robert Peake of the same town had debts for yarn 'to be received at Exetor'. This was precisely the trade the Cirencester men claimed in a petition to Parliament in 1708. But it was not only the west they served. Peake also had debts to be received at Norwich. In 1682 Edmund Betterton of Cirencester was owed for his yarn at Fairford £15, at Witney £4, at Thetford 8s 6d, and at Norwich three separate sums of £68, £11 10s, and £9, not to speak of two lots of yarn awaiting sale in the city, one in George Kemble's hands worth £16 and another lying at the Black Swan valued at over £5. In the next century Tetbury was selling combed wool and yarns to Coventry, Kidderminster and Leicester.[158]

The Devizes woolcombing district seems to have developed as an offshoot of the Tetbury and Cirencester one. The two were only twenty to thirty miles apart and the Devizes men sold some of their yarn in Tetbury. However, Devizes, Urchfont, Potterne, Marston, Calne and Marlborough made up a district that was concerned mainly with supplying yarns to the Cheese Country and the westerly parts of the Chalk Country. The first 'sergekeymer' mentioned in Devizes in 1631 had only just attained his majority and cannot have been at work there very long. The first known recorded death of a 'woollstead comber' in Devizes happened in 1660, in Marston in 1662, and in Urchfont in 1667, but all three men appear to have been combing in these places for a considerable time. In all likelihood several woolcombers set up in the district about 1630. These master combers were for the most part also yarnmasters,[159] but many serge and druggetmakers hereabouts and in the Cheese Country took up combing for themselves, and some Devizes woolcombers were also sergemakers. The gulf between the two trades was not wide.[160]

Woolcombing and yarnmaking developed in the Butter Country, at Shepton Mallet, Beaminster, Lyme Regis, Crewkerne, Cardiff and in the district of Leigh-upon-Mendip and Coleford. Much of the jersey went to local hosiers.[161] Woolcombers appeared, too, in the Vale of Berkeley, at Dursley and Horsley,[162] and in the Bristol District, where they largely worked on Irish wool.[163] In the Vale of Taunton Deane, wools and yarns were obtained from Cirencester, Tetbury and district, but many of the sergemakers combed for themselves, and woolcomber-yarnmasters, some of whom also engaged in sergemaking, were found in Taunton, Creech, Charlinch, Fiddington, Wellington, Minehead and elsewhere. Woolcombing and yarnmaking were stimulated by the import of Irish wool through Watchet, Minehead and Bridgwater. This helps to explain the rise of the Dunster yarnmasters, who served the vale as far south as Wiveliscombe.[164] Few West Country clothiers undertook their own combing, so the influx of Irish wool encouraged woolcomber-yarnmasters in Barnstaple, Exeter, Tiverton, Crediton and other towns.[165] The small body of woolcombers and yarnmakers in Chester after 1673 relied on Irish wool.[166] Rossendale baizemakers used mainly Irish yarns for their warps until, towards the close of the seventeenth century, woolcombers started work here, largely on Irish wool.[167] At much the same time woolcombers, and later woolcomber-yarnmasters, set up in Marsden, Skipton, Leeds and possibly Halifax and other towns in the east of the country. By 1695 Kendal also had woolcombers.[168] London commenced woolcombing in the middle of the sixteenth century. Combers, many of them Flemings, settled in Stepney, Shoreditch, Bermondsey, Cripplegate and Colman Street, and the spinning of jersey, and perhaps of worsted, sprang up in Spitalfields and other parts of Stepney, which was where most of the weavers lived. Nevertheless London and the suburbs imported most of their tops yarns from the Woodland, Sandwich, Ireland and elsewhere.[169] Woolcombing made rapid progress in Ireland. By the middle of the eighteenth century many great yarnmasters here sold their wares to Bristol, the West Country and other parts of the mainland.[170]

The art of woolcombing needs little explanation. One required a pair of combs, a post with a pad to fix one of them on, an iron stove combpot for heating their teeth, and oil for the wool. Waste butter could be used, or olive oil, but rape oil was often preferred. Boston and Wisbech had been making this since 1554 or before, and on the other side of the kingdom Caerleon started to do the same about 1600. A heated comb was fastened to the pad with its teeth horizontal and a mass of oiled wool was transfixed on them and raked with the second comb, the process being repeated until all the fibres were straight and parallel. The longer fibres or tops were then gently drawn off by hand, while the shorter ones or noils were left to be plucked off the teeth. Strictly speaking, this drawing of the longer fibres was a separate and distinct process, and was often performed by another operative, called a drawer, who might be the comber's mate; but at other times and places it fell to one of the combers.[171] In earlier times combpots were always heated with charcoal. The first record of the use of coal for this purpose in the Breckland comes from Tostock in 1780, when Samual Owers had 'two seacoal combpots'.[172] Coal gave off sulphurous fumes damaging to the wool and required special pots. Whatever the fuel, combing was hot and unpleasant work; but it was not highly skilled and necessitated no long apprenticeship.

The proportions of tops drawn off and of noils remaining could be varied at will. Sometimes as much as a sixth or a quarter or more of the wool was left as noils.[173] In 1622 Norwich manufacturers complained, 'Nowe the comers doe buy their wooll and doe drawe forth the same so farre as that they make almost no nyle at all; and so the yarne made naught and unprofitable'.[174] The fewer, longer and better the tops, the more, the longer and better the noils; and how the wool was drawn depended on the requirements of the woolcomber's customers. It then remained for the master comber to sort and blend the fibres into uniform batches suited to particular kinds and grades of yarn.[175]

Next to the sorting of the wool, it was spinning that did most to decide the quality of the woven cloth. Evenness was of the first importance. If some of the yarn had been spun too hard and some too soft, the cloth itself would be uneven in breadth and other respects.[176] Fineness was often essential. The acknowledged superiority of the Crediton kerseys was due to fine spinning. Westcote avers 'that 140 threads of woollen yarn spun in that town were drawn together through the eye of a tailor's needle'. This is credible, for wool can be spun into a pound of yarn scores of miles long.[177] And the Southampton manufacturers avowed one kind of West Country yarn the 'best for the abb of some sort of the sarges and stuffes made there muche better than anie yearne that is spun in the county of Southampton'.[178] There is no doubt the art of spinning was much improved in the sixteenth and seventeenth centuries. In 1585, we are told, the 'yarne wherewith the...clothes called plaine white straighte and pinned white straightes' are made 'is growen smaller and finer'.[179] It was partly due to better spinning that Woodland cloths had shed some of their weight by 1601.[180] John Aubrey said spinning in his part of the world had so improved in the last forty years that a pound of wool now made twice as much cloth as it did before the Civil Wars, though he was reliably informed the Dutch and French still spun finer than the English.[181]

The different methods of spinning were explained as follows:[182]

Spinnings of wooll are of three sorts, viz. either upon the greate wheele, which is called woollen yarne, whereof there are divers sorts (warp, and abb or wofe, and list yearn); or upon the small wheele, which is called garnesey or jarsey yarne, bicause that manner of spynning was first practised in the Isle of Garnesey or Jarnesey, whereof also there be divers sorts; or upon the rock, which is called worsted yarne by 1 E.6 c.6 bicause that manner of spynning was first practised in Worsted in the countie of Norfolk, whereof also there be divers sorts, whereof one called middle uffe yarne is specially mencioned in 1 E.6 c.6. Jarsey and worsted yarnes be made of combed wooll and woollen yarne is made of carded wooll ... Worsted is spun in his oile. Jarsey is wasshed out of his oilie and spun cleane. Niles are carded and spun for uffe of divers finesse. Of the breech, taile, and other offall of the fleece of wooll is made a sort of course warpe yarne called grasior, serving for the lowest priced baies. And of the niles of the same wooll, being carded, is made the uffe of the same bay. The worsted yarne is otherwise called handwarpe. Jarsey yarne maketh warpe for the finest stuffe. It is often used for uffe to silke warpe, bicause it matcheth best with silke both for fines and softnes. One fleece of wooll may be divided into four or five sorts of several fines, and every of these sortes of wooll may be converted into yarnes of several fines at the pleasure of the workeman. Of the coursest combed wooll are made garters, swath bands, baies called grasiors, and fringe in greate quantitie. The longest staple wooll is fittest to be combed.

The yarnmasters and baize, say, serge and drugget makers, and clothiers, all put out their noils to be spun on the great wheel,[183] and their tops either on the small wheel or on the distaff and rock. But the spinning of wool on the rock was confined to eastern England and concentrated in East Anglia. Celia Fiennes was struck by the way East Anglian people habitually spun out in the streets and lanes, some with the wheel and 'some with the rock and fusoe'. When he was in High Suffolk, Thomas Baskerville saw 'the women in this country spinning up and down the way ... with rock and distaff in their hands'. John Dyer sang the same tune:[184]

> ... and many yet adhere
> To th'ancient distaff, at the bosom fix'd,
> Casting the whirling spindle as they walk;
> At home, or in the sheepfold, or the mart,
> Alike the work proceeds. This method still
> Norvicum favours, and the Icenian towns:
> It yields their airy stuffs an apter thread.

Rock spinners abounded in Ipswich,[185] but flax was still spun on the rock and in High Suffolk much more was produced of linen than of worsted yarn. Some handwarp yarn was spun in the Woodland and some worsted in Canterbury and district, but otherwise the production of rockspun tops yarns belonged to Breckland and district and parts of East Norfolk.[186] In the remainder of the kingdom all wool was spun on great or little wheels or 'turns'.

Largely and increasingly the spinsters worked directly for clothiers and yarnmasters. One of the most striking features of this business was the multiplicity of spinning houses from which wools were put out. In 1695, for example, a Billericay woolcomber had 'topps at all the spining houses employed'.[187] Branch depots were often set up some distance away from the main seat of manufacture. Taunton Deane clothiers and Cirencester yarn-masters often had two or more such branch spinning houses. In 1721 Robert Pittman of Cirencester had one in Minety and another in Winchcombe, about eight and twenty-four miles away respectively.[188] In 1538 a Burford clothier was said to be sending every week one cartload of wool to be carded and spun in Abingdon and a second one to Stroudwater, which were twenty-three and twenty-eight miles away. Witney blanketmakers put their spinning out up to thirty miles off.[189] In 1725 Samuel Capell of Stroud had one of his spinning houses in Prestbury, just north of Cheltenham and some fifteen miles from his headquarters. Some Worcester manufacturers fetched yarn in from Tewkes-bury, seventeen miles away. In 1625 a Winchester man was sending wool to his spinning house in Salisbury, whence it was put out both in the city and in the nearby country towns.[190] In the eighteenth century some clothiers in the Peak-Forest Country put spinning out up to thirty or forty miles away, while Cerne Abbas spun yarn for the West Country, which lay at no less a distance.[191] Canterbury woolcombers and manufacturers had jersey and worsted spun for them up to seven or eight miles from the city in places like Faversham, Whitstable, Herne, Chislet, Littlebourne and Nackington.[192] In 1666 a St Edmundsbury clothier had 'wooll at the three spinning houses' apparently situated in Fornham, Lackford and Icklingham, between two and eight miles out on the Mildenhall road. In 1685 a Lavenham clothier had tops being spun for him 'at Stanton spinhouse' and 'at Eselum spinhouse'. Stanton lay halfway between Bury and Diss, and Isleham was right out in the Fen Country, respectively twenty and twenty-nine miles from Lavenham. Other clothiers here also employed spinsters in Isleham and Soham.[193] In 1680 a Diss hosier was sending wool ten miles to be carded and spun in Debenham.[194] A clothier in Ballingdon, by Sudbury, had his yarns spun in a score of towns within twelve miles' radius.[195] Woodland manufacturers set spinsters on work in Bishops Stortford and in Great Dunmow, which Celia Fiennes found 'altogether taken up about the spinning and preparenge for the bayes'.[196] Colchester men put their spinning out up to 40 miles away, at Belchamp Walter, Helions Bumpstead, Ashdon, Hinxton, Abington, and Stoke Bridge, Ipswich.[197]

Whereas the spinning and marketing of tops yarns were largely in the hands of substantial yarnmasters, no comparable class of persons dominated the carding wool side. The fundamental cause of this difference between the two branches was that woolcombing was whole-time occupation for a man, while carding was one for women and children who often devoted only a part of their time to it. Clothiers making carded woollens usually obtained their yarns either by putting wool out to people on their spinning-books or by buying in pitched markets supplied by spinsters working on their own accounts or by yarnmen or badgers who made the round of independent domestic spinners, supplying them with wool and buying their yarns.[198] Similar yarnmen provided like services for flax spinners in the Lancashire Plain and High Suffolk.[199]

As an exception to the general rule, the rise of Spanish cloth was accompanied by that of 'market spinners' who were roughly the counterparts of the combing yarnmasters. 'The markett spinners', we are told, 'vent much of theyr yarne to those that make the dyed and drest clothes', i.e. Spanish medleys.[200] A howl of complaint and abuse from the makers of obsolescent white cloth about 1630 heralded the triumph of the market spinners and the Spanish medley clothiers. The white clothiers failed to beat back their rivals despite using every trickery up to and including a Bill in Parliament ostensibly to safeguard the welfare of spinsters.[201] It was impossible to stem so strong a growth. Although market spinners appeared on the scene hardly earlier than 1590, by 1615 they were already 'soe many in number that it is supposed by men of judgement that more than half the cloathes that is made in Wiltshire, Gloucester and Somersettshire is made by the means of theise yarnemakers'. It was estimated in 1630 that they made two thirds of all the yarn used.[202] The market spinners carried on their business alongside the woolcombers and yarnmasters in Devizes, Urchfont, Potterne, Bishops Cannings and thereabouts and in towns along the road from here to Tetbury and Cirencester. They bought supplies of wool, carefully distinguished between abb Spanish and warp English, had it carded, spun and dyed, and sold warp, abb and list yarns. Some scribbling, carding and spinning, especially of Spanish wool, the market spinners had done on their own premises, but English wool was more often put out. James and William Filkes of Devizes regularly had between £100 and £200 worth of wool and yarn at home and out at the spinners'. Their fellow townsman Robert Palmer had an outhouse workshop equipped with six spinning wheels and eight pairs of woolcards. Richard Farmer, 'clothier', had at least two spinning houses stocked with sorted warp and abb wools and two dozen woolcards on the premises. John Andrewes ran a similar business. Market spinners did a little dyeing, especially of list yarns, but mostly put this work out. Some yarn went straight to clothiers in the Cheese Country and some was sent to Tetbury for sale to the Vale of Berkeley and more distant places. Farmer and Andrewes, for example, left large stocks of yarn as yet unsold in Tetbury. Perhaps not all, but most of these yarns went to 'coloured' clothiers who made Spanish medleys.[203] The close connection between the market spinners and these clothiers can also be seen in the manner of the formers' demise. As the arts of scribbling, carding and spinning Spanish wool became more widely diffused, the market spinners' functions were gradually taken over by the increasingly able and wealthy Spanish clothiers.[204]

Hardly a town was without spinners of one sort or another. Flax was spun in High Suffolk and East Norfolk for the linen and sailcloth weavers and the makers of Norwich stuffs;[205] in Coventry, Maidstone, Barnstaple and their vicinities for the threadmakers and twisters; and in Kidderminster for the clothiers.[206] Norwich, Gloucester, Weymouth, Abbotsbury, Aldbourne, Bolton, Manchester and other towns saw the advent of cotton spinners.[207] In Bridport and elsewhere hemp was spun for ropes, cordage and nets, and in other places for canvas and other cloths.[208] Ipswich and Norwich had scores of women and children spinning flax, wool, jersey and worsted.[209] Spinners abounded in and about the Breckland, in the East Dereham district, in the Woodland, High Suffolk and the Chiltern Country.[210] Leicester, Coventry, Northampton, Peterborough and many other Midland towns acquired more and more jersey spinners. Worcester long retained her cards and wheels.[211] The West Country as far south-west as Bodmin, Camelford, Bossiney and Tregoney was full of spinners on the great wheel and the small.[212] Southampton and all the towns in the Chalk Country and thereabouts had work aplenty for carders and spinners.[213] London and the suburbs spun fibres of all sorts. By somewhat earlier than 1769 Kendal was receiving waste silk from London, boiling it in soapy water, carding it, spinning it, dressing it and sending it back again.[214] The textile, hosiery and allied trades and their suppliers of yarn covered between them nearly the whole kingdom.

# 12

## DYES

The English dyers' forte had always been in colouring wool and yarn. In the Woodland,[1] in the Wealden Vales,[2] in Reading, Basingstoke, Salisbury and other towns in and about the Chalk Country,[3] in the Vale of Taunton Deane and Culm valley, and wherever kerseys, medleys, serges, druggets and other cloths were dyed in the wool,[4] it was usual for the clothier to have his own dye-house and not unknown for him to prepare his own woad in his own woad house; only novices and incomplete clothiers relied on outside dyers. It was much the same with dyeing yarns. Spanish medley clothiers, Taunton Deane yarnmasters and Maidstone twisters are all found on occasion dyeing their own.[5] This dyeing in the wool or the yarn, or 'dry drapery' as it was sometimes called on account of the wool having to have its natural oil removed before dyeing, was especially suited to mixed wools and hard waters, both of which made it difficult to achieve a uniform shade when dyeing in the piece. Many clothiers in the Vale of Taunton Deane, the Woodland, Kidderminster and elsewhere did at least some of their own dyeing in the piece,[6] but only the Stroudwater ones had a fixed policy of dyeing all their own cloths.[7]

Even in countries where most of the dyeing was done in the wool or in the yarn, there were always some clothiers who were unable to dye, so scope remained for specialist dyers even in the Wealden Vales, in the Chalk Country and in Reading, Basingstoke and Maidstone.[8] Then there were countless clothiers who sold their products white or blue and left them to be dyed or re-dyed to the order of the merchant or retailer. Although some dyeing was done in Exeter, Rochdale and elsewhere, West and Peak-Forest country fabrics were largely sold to the merchant undyed,[9] and so were Worcester cloths,[10] not to mention the old West-of England whites. The Canterbury[11] and Norwich weavers were preoccupied with their inventions and left dyeing to specialists. Norwich was well served by dyers and woadsetters, and in addition the calendrers were allowed to blacken worsted fabrics that had already been woaded by the setters. Despite some opposition, Flemish dyers were also permitted to ply their trades.[12] Some hosiers undertook their own dyeing, but the majority put this work out, and the dyeing of wool was usually left to specialists.[13]

Dyeing centres sprang up in various places. Ipswich and Colchester dyed white cloths and re-dyed blue ones. Knaresborough dyed cloths, yarns and stockings, Shrewsbury cottons and flannels, Exeter and Tiverton serges.[14] Only two provincial towns, however, developed large dyeing industries: Coventry and Norwich.[15] Coventry dyed her own cloth and thread and became the dressing and dyeing centre for a much wider area. By 1608 her dyers and woadsetters were colouring 'Gloucestershire' West-of-England cloths. Later on, the strongest selling points of Coventry tammies were their finish and dyes.[16] But the greatest place in England for piece-dyeing was London. Here were dipped not only many of the West-of-England and Worcester whites, numerous cottons and friezes and most of the West Country serges,[17] but also her own laces and broad silks.[18] The hair weavers were almost alone in having their own dyehouses and undertaking their own work;[19] otherwise the city dyers were specialists of both English and Flemish descent who excelled in dyeing silken fabrics, but were less expert in woollens.[20] 'London-dye' cottons were no less regarded by drapers than 'Flanders-dye' kerseys,[21] but the Netherlanders were generally better at dyeing in the piece.[22] Coloured English woollen exports were mostly dyed in the wool, the yarn or the say.

The average blue clothier or woadsetter only needed one copper vat. He varied the strength of the dye and produced finely graded shades of blue by adding more woad for successive batches of work.[23] This batch system was equally applicable to all wool and yarn dyeing. After a run of batches of different colours and shades, a medley cloth could be made.[24] The one difficulty was with scarlet. This needed a vat to itself, and preferably a pewter one. With two vats, then, almost any work could be undertaken, piece-dyeing included, and only the largest dyers had more.[25] Even in the biggest textile centres, batch work sufficed, for they afforded a number of common or public dyers, each of whom confined himself to one or two colours, allowing the manufacturer to go from one to another. Thus Norwich had specialist blue, black and green dyers.[26]

London, Norwich, Exeter and many other towns already had, or were engaged in, acquiring or extending works by which water was piped to individual streets or houses.[27] All dyers had pumps, but some of this water came from underground sources and, like well water generally, was only suitable for reds or for dyeing cloths made wholly or largely of cotton wool. River water was essential for clear blue, yellow or green wools and woollens. Most clothiers had their workshops within easy reach of a stream. A bourne that dried up in summer was no good. Only a river could give them all the water needed for scouring, washing, rinsing and fulling, as well as for dyeing. As long as it came from a river, it mattered little how the water was conveyed to the dye-house, but proximity had every advantage. Many London dye-houses were hard by the Thames.[28]

Whether over separate furnaces or over a range,[29] dye-vats were widely heated with wood fuel, which in the larger towns often took the form of charcoal. Wood and charcoal were burned by coloured clothiers and dyers in the

Vale of Taunton Deane and the Cheese Country right up until the middle of the eighteenth century.[30] Reading medley clothiers also used wood. And this was despite ready access to coal from across the Bristol Channel, up the Thames, and from the pits in Kingswood, Mangotsfield and Midsomer Norton.[31] Mansfield dyers, who had coalmines almost at their doorsteps, always heated their vats with wood.[32] Furthermore, clothiers in the Woodland and the Wealden Vales burned wood almost to a man,[33] even though in the latter country wood was so dear as almost to drive the clothiers out of business and coal was easy to obtain via Maidstone or Newenden,[34] and, as the Woodlanders themselves pointed out, wood fuel was becoming so scarce that for want of it all sorts and qualities of men burned seaborne coal in their dwellings to such an extent that a shortage of wood-ash hindered the clothing business.[35] The scarcity or abundance of wood was evidently immaterial to the question of whether or not it was to be burned in dye-furnaces. The crucial factor common to all these places and manufactures was that the cloths were dyed in the wool. Although this was never made explicit, spongy wool absorbed coal fumes and was spoiled by them. Some London dyers claimed 'this wool of these several colours' could be dyed as well or better using coal, but this was easier said than done.[36]

Vats for piece-dyeing could easily be fired by coal. By 1553 dyers in Flanders were using 'none other fuell then coles that are dygged out of the ground'.[37] By 1578 London dyers, like the hatters, had 'long sithens altered their furnaces and fierie places and turned the same to the use and burninge of sea coals'. In 1637 they were dyeing 'wooll cloathes, silkes and other stuffs with sea coales'.[38] By the end of the century coal-fired dye-vats were in use in Exeter, Coventry, Warminster and other towns where cloths were dyed in the piece.[39] Coal could also be used to burn the lime added to woad to assist its fermentation,[40] but not in heating when dyeing in the wool.

An additional advantage in burning wood for dyeing wool was that wood-ash or potash was used to degrease the wool in readiness for dyeing, and, together with urine, to promote fermentation in the woad.[41] Greasy wool would take no colour properly, but the grease once removed and the wool immersed in boiling water before going into the dye-vat, any colour would take, and blue from woad or indigo would hold fast without the addition of any mordant. The Woodland clothiers rightly claimed they could not dye their wool without wood-ash and complained in 1636 when it came into short supply, which was partly because the ash-burners who usually served them were tending to sell further afield and to soapmakers, saltpetre men and linen bleachers.[42] Wool dyers, like window-glass makers, used ash from their own furnaces and could get more from Wealden ironmasters and from farmers who burned wood in their dairies; but the bulk came from professional ash-burners in High Suffolk, the Woodland, Reading and elsewhere. These men burned both wood and straw.[43]

In contrast to substantive ones like woad and indigo, most dyes were merely adjective and required to be used with a mordant. Alum was the supreme fixative, but gall-nuts and sumach were also used for blacks, and bran-liquor (one part of bran boiled in five of river water) with mealy dyestuffs like madder. Alum had the added advantage that it brightened colours. Argol, which was a crude tartar from the crust formed on the sides of wine vessels, was mainly a brightener, dyed articles being back-boiled in it, but it also helped fixation.[44]

Woad was the greatest dyestuff.[45] It was employed in varying strengths for blue, azure, watchet, plunket and huling, was the only dye for blue cloth before indigo was introduced, and went on being used, either strengthened with indigo or as a ground for it, or as a 'setting', in all kinds of woollens, for a wide range of fast colours far removed from blue itself and even including black, claret, tawny, violet, purple, green, puke, mustard, grey, murrey and brown-blue.[46] Black was obtained by repeated tinctures of woad, madder or indigo or of some combination of these, and various mixtures of these stuffs gave rise to a number of differing hues.[47] 'Oaded wooles', say Wealden clothiers, 'is the ground of all true coullors'. According to May, 'The ground of good colours is substantial woading, without which divers colors cannot be perfectly made, as blacks, russets, tawneyes, purples, greenes and such like.' Blith writes, 'Woad is the staple and chief of the dyers trade, layeth a foundation for all holding colours.' In 1727 a trade description of a cloth ends up, 'It's a very fashionable colour and what will wear very well, it being woaded'.[48] This was why woaded quince, tawny and black cloths were considered superior to unwoaded ones and why it was laid down in 1549 that no dyer should make any woollen cloth brown, blue, puke, tawny, mustard, grey or marble, unless already perfectly grounded with woad.[49]

Between a fifth and a seventh of the cost of a woollen cloth was attributable to dyeing, and a large part of this to the dyestuff itself. In the 1570s much woad was still being imported, some from enemy lands, and there was great concern to bring down 'the high price of forreine woad (which devoureth yeerely great treasure)'. The answer was to substitute blue indigo (anile), but first English dyers had to be taught its use by an expert sent over by the king of Portugal in 1577. The next concern was to find a second source of indigo, so as to avoid being at the mercy of a single supplier who from 1580 was effactually our arch-enemy Spain.[50] Anile was already in use in England in 1579. It had ten times the tinctorial power of woad, but was expensive and usually employed only as an additive, at the approximate rate of one part of anile to forty of woad. This practice was approved for making a ground on which to madder for black, and in Basingstoke, the Woodland and elsewhere it was used for blue.[51]

Another substitute for woad was found in logwood, also called block, violet, peach or campeachy wood. This was cheap and yielded a splendid, but fugitive, purplish blue. Only by boiling the stuff in alum solution before dyeing could the colour be made fast. For this reason the use of logwood by itself was justifiably stigmatised as fraudulent, until the invention in 1605 of a process that produced a true and fast colour by treating and 'raising' the logwood with gall-nuts.[52] After this, logwood was widely used, both for black and for blue, almost invariably in a lawful way in conjunction with alum, gall-nuts or sumach or some combination of them.[53]

Next to woad the commonest dyestuff was madder; in Norwich it warranted a marketplace to itself. After treatment with alum, or used with bran-liquor, madder gave fast reds, violets and purples; mixed with weld it produced orange and ginger; and incorporated in medleys it helped to form sky-colour. Things once set with woad and indigo could then be maddered to make black, and even if unset could be blackened provided galls or sumach were mixed with the madder.[54] Kermes was now too costly for ordinary purposes and madder was substituted in forming scarlets.[55] Then, not long after 1560, cochineal (vermilion) started coming in. This had ten times the colouring power of kermes and was used especially for scarlet and stammel. Mixed with lemon juice, it also gave incarnadine.[56] Gum-lac imparted scarlet or crimson to silk and made it glassy, stiff and heavy.[57] Increasing use was made of the various redwoods (guinea woods), mainly sandalwood (saunders, Pernambuco wood) and brazil (braziletto, Jamaica wood). These were not for silks, but woollens were boiled in a solution of the finely ground wood, which itself had been boiled with galls. Saunders gave a brick red, and brazil claret, pink and carnation. Brazil was properly used with alum. If vinegar or lemon juice were then added, a canary-sack colour resulted; if vitriol, purplish violet; if potash, a true purple. But all brazil colours were prone to rapid fading.[58] Safflower was inferior to redwood in woollens, but suited silk, especially when the red was brightened by back-boiling in argol.[59]

Weld (dyer's weed) was the chief source of fast yellows in deep lemon or broom-flower shades. It was used with urine or alum, and with both for woollens.[60] Yellow dye-woods came into wider use. 'Young' or 'new' fustic ('zante' or Venetian sumach) gave yellows from which fawn, cinnamon and orange could be derived. 'Old' fustic was introduced only later, in the second half of the seventeenth century. Mixed with slaked lime, it gave a fast yellowish hair colour.[61] Saffron was rarely if ever used. Perhaps it went into the linen sold as 'crocus', which may well have been dyed deep yellow.[62] Verdigris was limited to linens, to which it lent yellowish and greenish colours.[63] Green-weed (grassing-wood or wood-wax) was used for some coarse cloths,[64] but no single dyestuff gave a good, fast green, only a mixture of woad and weld.[65] This was a difficult branch of dyeing. Norwich looked on a Fleming who could make 'perfect greenes' as a great catch.[66] Once the redwoods had been introduced, orchil (archil, orchilla, 'jarecork' or simply 'cork') was less frequently used. It was made from sea-rock lichens and mixed with wine and lime to give fugitive reds and violets. It also served to blacken kerseys that had been set with woad.[67]

Common or Flanders blacks were really ultra-black blues and purples. True or Spanish black could only be made with copperas mixed with galls,[68] and, optionally, and especially for silk, with steel filings or slip also. This last was the steel powder recovered from the refuse troughs of grindstones and blade-mills. It was much used in dyeing silk and silk cloths and stockings, and selling silk by weight encouraged dyers to add slip in excessive quantities. Sometimes, too, silk weights were fraudulently increased by loading the dye with antimony and litharge (lead calx).[69]

In 1640 the famous scarlet Bow-dyes were invented. The cochineal was worked in pewter vats and kettles with an addition of aquafortis into which powdered pewter had been mixed. The effect of this combination of pewter and saltpetre was to turn red-rose crimson into flame colour.[70]

All these dyestuffs allowed the production of a wide range of colours. In 1572 the London dyers used woad and madder for blacks, brown-blues, violets, purples, blues, azures, watchets, russets, murreys, and tawnies; madder and brazil for reds and carnations, and, with weld, for orange; woad and cochineal (or kermes) for violet, murrey, purple, russet, and ash-colour; weld for yellow and gold; and woad and weld for grass, popinjay and other greens.[71] In 1622 the Norwich dyers employed woad for blacks, russets and purples; woad and madder for oranges, tawnies and 'deroys'; woad and indigo for blues; woad and weld for primrose, french and other greens; weld and madder for golden yellow and 'gingerlynes'; madder or kermes or cochineal for red and carnation; and cochineal and dye-woods for ash, silver, peach, dove-colour, 'gredelines', crimsons, murreys and buffs.[72]

Drysalters in London and the provinces[73] supplied the dyers. Up until 1635, when the works started in the Blackmoors in the early years of the century finally achieved high and stable sales of a good quality, much or most of the alum used came from the Papal States, with smaller amounts from Spain, Alum Bay in the Isle of Wight, the coast from Boscombe to Canford and Branksea or Brownsea Island, a short-lived workhouse in London, and such tiny sources as the alum springs at Oakengates.[74] Woad had been grown in England ever since ancient times, but it was only after 1560 that greater acreages and the use of indigo led to the falling off of imports of weaker sorts of the stuff from Provence.[75] Weld, madder and saffron were all cultivated in England, but supplies were also imported, and the greater part of the madder used came from Flanders and Zealand.[76] Copperas was brought in, too, although increasing amounts came from works on the Isle of Sheppey, between Queenborough and Whitstable, Canford and, later, Branksea Island.[77] Nearly everything else was wholly imported. Orchil came from Spain and the Canaries; gall-nuts from Venice and Leghorn or direct from Sicily and Turkey; argol from Leghorn, Venice and Genoa; 'young' fustic from Venice; lac from India; cochineal from Latin America; indigo, dyewoods and fustic from the West and East Indies, Central and South America, Virginia, South Carolina and, later, Florida also.[78]

# 13

## MACHINES

Textile manufactures depended on increasingly complicated machines, more and more of which came to be moved by horse or water power.

The rock and distaff admitted of little or no improvement, but spinning wheels did. Jersey wheels, which were also used for flax and waste silk were considerably improved. Saxony wheels, as adopted in England from 1555, were equipped with flyers and bobbins for winding the yarn and with a pedal that left the spinster with both hands free for manipulating the fibres, thereby allowing output to be increased. Double wheels with two spools were an even greater advance; they also pointed the way to future progress.[1]

From double wheels there evolved the spinning engines vulgarly called 'injuns' or 'jennies'. As far as can be seen, the first inventor of the spinning jenny was Nicholas Doughty of Norwich, who in 1644 claimed to have 'contrived an ingen for the more speedy spininge of yarn', which the city permitted him to use 'for his best benefitt'.[2] A further development came in 1568, when Israel Reynolds and Henry Geange claimed to

> have attained to the art of makeing an engine for the cleansing and miling of all such silke as is the wastes and spoyles of the silke throsters, by which engine the said silke is reduced from trash of no vallew into merchantable and vendable condition. And also one other engine to spine the same so wrought by the former, att which engine many women and children may worke att once drawing out the threeds with both theire hands, one boy or girle turning with one hand for 20 or 30 of them, at which said engine children of 9 or 10 yeeres of age may be brought to worke and to get them good wages in a very short tyme.

This second engine was clearly bold in design.[3] In 1678 Richard Dereham and Richard Haines (of Sullington) obtained a patent[4] for a

> spinning machine whereby from six to one hundred spinners and upwards may be employed by the strength of one or two persons to spin linen and worsted thread with such ease and advantage that a child three or four years of age may do as much as a child of seven or eight years old, and others as much in two days as without this invention they can in three days.

By the early years of the eighteenth century the spinning jenny was in ordinary use in Norwich.[5] It was invented a hundred years before blinkered devotees of the theory of 'The Industrial Revolution' will hear of its existence.[6] Nevertheless, since early jennies were restricted mainly to spinning jersey, linen and waste silk, it is not utterly inconceivable that it was really left to James Hargreaves to invent, at some time between 1764 and 1767, an engine better suited to the spinning of weft yarns from carded wool and cotton. It may seem strange and unlikely for such an invention to have been even contemplated at so late a date and when spinning frames had so nearly been perfected, but these frames were much better for warp than for weft yarns.[7]

The next great development in mechanical spinning was certainly the invention of the spinning frame, 'a most curious machine' says Dyer[8], 'invented by Mr Paul. It is at present contrived to spin cotton; but it may be made to spin fine carded wool.' It was

> A circular machine of new design
> In conic shape: it draws and spins a thread
> Without the tedious toil of needless hands.
> A wheel, invisible beneath the floor,
> To ev'ry member of th' harmonious frame
> Gives necessary motion. One, intent,
> O'erlooks the work: the carded wool ...
> Is smoothly lapp'd around those cylinders,
> Which, gently turning, yield it to yon cirque
> Of upright spindles, which, with rapid whirl,
> Spin out, in long extent, an even twine.

The essential idea was to use drafting rollers. According to the patent, 'As the prepared mass, rope, thread or sliver passes regularly through or betwixt the rowlers, cillinders or cones, a succession of other rowlers, cillinders or cones, moving proportionately faster than the first, draws the rope, thread or sliver in any degree of fineness which may be required.' Similar rollers had long been used in twisting and jersey mills, and even earlier than 1714 a water-powered twisting mill with eighty bobbins had been set up near Leeds. The problems associated with differential speeds were solved in 1730 by Lewis Paul, the son of a Birmingham physician. Then John Wyatt overcame the technical difficulties involved in drawing out the roving and proceeded to set up a working model in Sutton Coldfield in 1733. Paul patented the frame in 1738 and he and Wyatt built their first mill in Birmingham in 1741. Wyatt superintended the machinery, which was driven by two asses, and cotton yarn was successfully spun, even though the business failed to prosper. In 1742–3 a man named Edward Cave set up under licence in Northampton a larger water-powered frame to supply cotton yarn to the local hosiers. This mill was not a great commercial success, but it stayed open for a considerable time and in 1764 was sold intact with the original machinery and to all appearances as a going concern. Meanwhile another similar frame for roller drafting had been erected in Leominster about 1744–8 by Daniel Bourn. It worked until 1754, when it was destroyed by fire. Finally, in 1758, Paul patented the improved machines that set the pattern for future developments. The mill soon after set up in Rochdale for spinning jersey, 'being upon the plan and in the nature of a silk mill or engine', probably owed something to Paul's designs, and the water-frame patented by Richard Arkwright in 1769 was based on them.[9]

Both Arkwright and Hargreaves were concerned in making cotton yarn for hosiery and therefore moved their businesses to the vicinity of Nottingham, which was the centre for cotton hosiery.[10] Similarly it was silk hosiery that attracted mills for throwing organzine silk to Derby. Water-powered throwing mills had been at work in Lucca and northern Italy since the fourteenth century, but it was not until 1704 or just after that a man by the name of Crotchett started a small mill of this kind in Derby. Crotchett was bankrupted in 1713 and his mill leased to a friend of his, one John Lombe, the son of a Norwich worstedweaver. It was John's brother Thomas, the owner of a London mercery business, who in 1717 commenced the construction on an island in the River Derwent of similar but larger and improved mills, which, when finally completed in or about 1730, employed some 300 women.[11] Meanwhile, however, throwing mills modelled on the earlier Derby one had been set up at Sewardstone near Waltham Abbey and at Little Hallingbury in Bishops Stortford.[12] After 1730 throwing mills spread rapidly, in 1732 to Stockport, in 1740 to Sherborne, in 1743 to Macclesfield, in 1752 to Congleton, in 1758 to Sheffield, and later to Taunton, Lancaster, Pebmarsh, Tring, St Albans, Glemsford, Sudbury and whithersoever silkweaving went.[13]

In weaving the greatest advances came with the introduction from Flanders in the middle part of the sixteenth century of the velours loom and the drawloom. This latter was of particular importance. As Hooper justly declares,[14]

> There can be no doubt that this invention is the most important in the whole history of textile development. All the finest pattern-weaving of the Eastern, as well as the Western world, ancient and modern, has been done on the drawloom principle, and even the invention of the Jacquard machine, which is often supposed to have superseded it, did not alter the essential principle of drawloom weaving in the least. Jacquard's invention only rendered the tedious process of tying up the design on the cords of the loom itself unnecessary. Jacquard substituted for the tie-up, an endless band of cards, on which the pattern to be woven was punched line by line. The design for the tie-up of the cords of the drawloom was worked out, or draughted, on paper, ruled out in squares, in exactly the same way as is requisite for the punching of the cards used in the Jacquard machine. In some of the early accounts of its introduction into this country, Jacquard's invention is called 'the new drawloom engine.'

As Celia Fiennes so succinctly put it, 'Its a very ingenious art to fix the warps and chaine in their loomes to cast their work into such figures and flowers, there stands a boy by every loome and pulls up and down threads which are fastened to the weaving and so pulls the chaine to the exact form for the shuttle to work through.' Drawlooms paved the way to powered weaving. They were complicated machines and cost at least twice as much as pedal looms. But even before the draw-loom was generally introduced, the scope of pattern weaving had been widened by the use of the two-harness method, where a figure harness forms the design in large, while another harness deals with the detailed weaving. In particular, it was possible to weave point designs, i.e. figures with a centre line, both halves alike, only pointing in opposite directions, as though reflecting each other.[15]

Little improvement was made to the ordinary treadle broad loom before John Kay invented his fly-shuttle in 1733. At first it could be used only when the weft was in a single colour; but this was no obstacle to its adoption in Colchester. Reporting on the baize manufactures there, Postlethwayt said in 1757, 'About these there are 600 looms, and upwards, employed, each managed by one hand, since the engines invented by Solomon Smith; and there are not 20 in the whole town managed by two hands'. Smith was the Colchester baizemaker who was Kay's chief partner and the first man to make his device workable and put it into operation. The third partner, William Carter of Ballingdon, apparently introduced the fly-shuttle in baizemaking in Sudbury and district. In 1735 Kay himself implanted his innovation in the Rossendale baize industry. Thus the fly-shuttle was for long employed almost solely in weaving baize. Only after the invention about 1760, by John's son Robert, of a drop shuttle box that allowed two or more fly-shuttles to be used for the same weft, did they pass into general practice; and they were adopted in Witney and the Cheese Country only about 1814, when good weavers' servants had become scarce there.[16]

Mechanisation progressed much fast in narrow weaving. The old narrower looms wove only one lace or ribbon at a time. They were light, compact, table-top instruments, easily worked by one woman, old man or child. The big, new Dutch engine-loom wove many lengths of parchmentry simultaneously, had mechanically propelled shuttles, and could be minded by one man. Our first evidence of this machine comes from Leiden in 1604, when some of the *saaipassementwerkers* protested against '*der eerste uitgevonden passementlint-molens*', specifically, three '*saeypassementlintmolens*', and demanded their pro-hibition. The say-lace mill was evidently the '*nieuw uitgevonden werktuig*' patented in the town that very year by Gabriel Hanedous and Pieter Bodijn. By the time it was introduced in London in 1610, it had already undergone further development. Some engine-looms now had one or two dozen shuttles each, and as many warp beams, one for each ribbon being woven. By 1636 a hundred such looms were said to be at work in London and the suburbs, and were accused of having taken away the work of 1,200 or 2,000 'natyve borne subjects'. King Charles prohibited the Dutch loom in 1638, and some operators were harassed and prosecuted; but neither in England nor the United Provinces was it possible to kill off so beneficial an innovation. Even if it displaced some women and children, it gave work to many skilled men. The people most likely to have suffered were those who went on trying to run workshops with handlooms, and they were probably the ones who organised the protests and outcries, and the riot in 1675. By then engine-looms had come down in price and were taking over all the work in plain weaves. In Spitalfields they wove silk ribbon and in Manchester inkle.[17] Eventually these looms were made automatic, having their pedals controlled by tappets. John Kay patented his way of doing this in 1745.[18]

The use of the old gig-mills was bad practice, for their wire teeth were much harsher than the hooked bracts on the fruiting heads of two-year-old king teasels. As a contemporary observer explains, 'The heart of the thread is fretted and almost dissolved by the gig-mill, which maketh the cloth wear ill and quickly wear out'. Furthermore, unscrupulous men used their gig-mills to strain and stretch the cloth. A man and a boy with a gig-mill could replace up to ten men rowers, but the work was spoiled rather than abridged. These machines were prohibited by penal statute, not to preserve needless jobs, but to protect the consumer, and so to safeguard trade and industry. The mosing mill, first introduced by the makers of Stroudwater reds, was quite a different kettle of fish. It had a battery of small, first year's teasel heads fixed to its roller, and raised the nap gently in preparation for a second and final rowing with king teasels by handworkers. The mosing mill was likewise managed by a man and a boy, and it saved the work of eight hand-rowers without in any way damaging the cloth.[19]

Completed cloths were usually pressed between papers in cold, iron-screw packing presses.[20] Worsted cloths in all varieties of weave also went though an earlier pressing process: they were first immersed in hot water and then calendered to make them smooth. The calender was a kind of mangle in which a large and heavily weighted box, up to ten tons, was, by means of a horse or man-powered treadmill, drawn across the two or more cylindrical rollers that pressed the cloth down on to a flat table. Some linens and fustians were also given this treatment.[21] In or before 1549 hot-presses were introduced in England. They were heavily built screw presses with two iron or steel plates, the lower of which formed the top of a rectangular furnace, while the upper one was sometimes double and filled with hot charcoal. Hot-pressing gave a finish to rashes, grograins, tammies, bombasines, milled says, shalloons, coarse kerseys and worsted and jersey hose, and it converted noil-weft serges into perpetuanas. It flattened the wet threads, filled out the cloth, pressed the folds, and gave a lustrous, glossy finish.[22] Sometimes hot-presses were also used for watering. This process, commonly applied to camlets and later extended to grograins, tammies, Philip and Cheyneys, and other fabrics, was more usually performed by means of calenders or rollers than of presses. Moreens and harrateens, however, had metal shapes pressed or rolled into them. Later special watering rolls were devised for this purpose. The earliest one so far discovered was already at work in Kidderminster in 1716. It was made of brass; the cast-brass rollers were cut and engraved to impart a particular pattern to the cloth. Machines of this kind were relatively expensive; when a hot-press cost £8 or £10, a brass watering roll cost £20.[23] Glossing rolls, like those used in Norwich to put a sheen on cloths that had already been hot-pressed and so, for example, to convert camlets into camletees, were considerably cheaper.[24] Yet another machine for imparting a finish to cloth was the *friseermolen* or frizzing mill invented in Leiden about 1697 by Jan Van Eyck and adopted in Amsterdam, Rotterdam, Halifax and Rochdale by the middle of the next century.[25]

Whether the 'engine for the cleansing and miling' of waste silk devised by Reynolds and Geange in 1658 also included a carding device, is not clear. Probably no true carding machine was invented until much later. In 1748 Lewis Paul patented two mechanical carders, the second of which had cards mounted on a cylinder that rotated against a concave shell covered with cards. Earlier in the same year Daniel Bourn of Leominster patented a rotary machine with four cylinders mounted with cards. None of these machines was an unqualified success for all purposes; the most any of them could do properly was to card wool for feltmaking.[26]

Most of the machines in the textile and allied trades had wooden frames and parts, with metal components, fittings and facings. Looms were fashioned from oak, beech or ash, and only rarely and in part from soft wood. They were fitted with elm or iron screws, nuts and bolts, cane sleys and metal plates and gears. Shuttles and spools were carved out of solid wood. The turner's lathe and the graver's knife were much in evidence.[27] We find a 'turnour or maker of loomes'[28] and hear the complain that 'our trade of makeing of stockins hath at severall times been much hindred for want of a sufficient and careful turner'.[29] Spinning-wheels demanded both turners and wheelwrights.[30] Turners came over with the Flemish immigrants, and the Canterbury weavers always had 'a turner for framying of ther lomes', as well as carpenters, joiners and locksmiths.[31] Metalworkers, too, were busy about the making of machines and tools. The knitting frame had up to 360 needles, always metal and usually steel, and scores of other metal parts.[32] In London in 1635 a hundred or more needlemakers were at work. Most of them were members of the Blacksmiths' Company, not the Needlemakers', so it may be inferred that they largely made iron or steel needles.[33] It was perhaps the increased demand for knitting needles that encouraged some of the London strangers to invent, in or shortly before 1624, a powered grindstone for pointing needles. Unfortunately, the stone was prone to disintegrate at high speed, and on representations from the Needlemakers' Company that it was dangerous to men's limbs, took away many livelihoods, and conduced to the use of bad materials, the engine was prohibited.[34] Much of the knitting frame being iron or steel and the needlemakers being in the nature of specialist blacksmiths, the framesmiths still often styled themselves blacksmiths, and so are now not easily to be distinguished.[35] It is nevertheless certain that framemaking rose to importance. 'Many frames are made for exportation', we are told in 1657, a batch of thirty or forty being bespoken by one Italian merchant alone.[36] But, then, the frame was an English invention; there was no comparable export of looms.

Inventors and pioneers had either to make their own looms and frames or have them made to specification by specialist craftsmen. Even in established trades it was not unknown for the master weaver to make his own looms. Some East Norfolk weavers constructed their own loom-frames and then fitted them out with parts that seem to have been bought ready made.[37] When the Flemish baizemakers first came to Norwich, they had looms specially made for them there. One of the earlier arrivals writes home, 'I am going to have a baize loom made against your coming'.[38] Some of the Flemish drapers in Canterbury long continued to have their own turner's shops, equipped with lathes for making spindles and bobbin blanks, and this despite a general liberty to all the Walloons here to have their own carpenters, turners, joiners and others for making their machines.[39] We have seen how the Lee brothers and their associates made their own knitting frames, and many of the early framework knitters did the same. When Thomas Selby of Nottingham died in 1659, he left a 'silk stocking frame . . . which frame was of my owne makeing'. The English Roman Catholic framework knitters who settled in Avignon about 1658, built their own frames and had the metal parts made to order by local clockmakers and locksmiths.[40] Inventors everywhere went about things in much the same way, but in the deepest secrecy. Nicholas Alsop, who introduced knitting frames in Leicester, had to work hidden in his cellar. When John Broom was constructing his own Brussels carpet loom in Kidderminster about 1749, he had to work in just as much secrecy.[41]

Nevertheless, machine and tool making became very widespread. Looms were made in Exeter, Colchester, Canterbury, London, Norwich and Necton (Norfolk Heathlands) amongst other places;[42] knitting frames in London, Nottingham, Shelford and Castle Donington;[43] wooden knitting needles in Leicester; spinning wheels and spindles in Wymondham, Great Bardfield, Tewkesbury, Norwich and Leicester;[44] shuttles, bobbins and spools in Canterbury, Southampton, Winchester, Reading and London;[45] sleys in Norwich, Kidderminster, Leicester, London and Wotton-under-Edge;[46] combs in Norwich, Coggeshall and London;[47] and cards almost everywhere.[48] Colchester specialised in renovating cards disposed of by the baizemakers. The wools for their wefts could not 'be well broken, opened and cleered but with such a sort of new deepe and large cardes as hath bin of long tyme used for the same, the price of those cardes being double the value of other sorts of ordinary carde'. But worn ones refurbished still served for normal purposes.[49] In the early part of our period, combs were imported from Rouen and Tourcoign, shuttles, bobbins and spools from Flanders and cards from Rouen; and this trade was long continued.[50]

When one considers fulling, mosing, watering and glossing mills, velours, draw and engine looms, knitting and spinning frames, jennies and hot-presses, one realises the mechanisation of the textile and allied trades had made great progress by the end of our period. But industrial structures were not greatly altered by it, and then only by the reinforcement of the existing tendency towards the rise of the independent industrial master.

# 14

## MASTERS AND SERVANTS

Hitherto most writers on the textile and allied trades have tended to view them in a social rather than a technical light, as when they contrast merchant employers in the west of England with independent masters in the West Riding. George Unwin went much further and saw textile developments largely as a protracted struggle between commercial and industrial capital.[1] We prefer to emphasise the strong links between industrial organisation and technique.

Wool from hill sheep was worthy only of rough weaving, such as could readily be done by part-time farmers and other relatively unskilled operatives, who seldom had either the technical or the financial ability to undertake the finishing processes. Moreover, in no single town or hamlet was enough cloth woven to support the services of a skilled fuller or clothworker. The whole business was therefore typically divided between, on the one hand, spinners and weavers in widely scattered hill-farms, hamlets and towns, and, on the other, merchant clothiers who were established in a few big collecting and finishing centres.

The Peak-Forest Country was full of little weaver-clothiers who bought their wool, prepared it, spun part of it, and finally sold their handiwork straight from the loom. There were a few weavers who owned no loom, but some of these hired a loom along with their cottage, and were clothiers of a sort. About half the weaver-clothiers had but one loom apiece. To own four or five loom seats was a rarity; three was as many as most men could aspire to. But, then, they were commonly also part-time farmers with house-cows, lean stock, and sometimes even a little tillage or a packhorse.[2] One description[3] of such men tells us they

> altogether doe lyve by clothemaking, and the greate parte of them neither getteth corne nor hable to kepe a horse to carry woolles, nor yet to buy muche wooll at once; but hathe ever used onely to repayre to the towne of Halyfaxe and some other nigh theronto and ther to buy upon the woolldriver some a stone, some twoo, and some three or foure, according to their habilitee, and to carye the same to their houses, some iij, iiij, v and vj myles of, upon their headdes and backes.

They sold their webs upon the bare thread, in Rochdale, Halifax, Colne, Bradford, Wakefield, Huddersfield, Newcastle-under-Lyme, Leeds, Bolton, Salford, Manchester and the Derwent valley towns, to merchants who put them out to specialists to be fulled, frizzed, finished and perhaps dyed. It was milling above all that made the raw web into a merchantable commodity, and the fullers in these towns showed a marked proclivity to turn merchant.[4]

On the western extremes of the Cheshire Cheese Country and in the south-western Englishry, plains for cottons and friezes were largely produced by little associations consisting typically of three men: a weaver and a fuller, both part-time farmers, and an 'owner', i.e. a farmer or small proprietor who had had his own wool spun into yarn for the making of a single cloth. (The chief exception to this rule was that Oswestry had several specialist fullers.) When the cloth had been fulled, the partners would often go to market together and split the proceeds on the spot. They lived so near the cloth markets, the transaction was simply effected. 'Many of them', we are told, 'carieng their cloth upon their backs, they can all come together and make their market and buy their vitailes and goe home in one daie.' They usually sold in Oswestry, Wrexham, Ruthin, Denbigh, Chester, Welshpool, Montgomery, Tenby, Carmarthen or Haverfordwest, to the clothworkers or merchant drapers of those towns or of Shrewsbury, Whitchurch, Warwick or Coventry. The Shrewsbury drapers were far and away the most successful in this business; they dominated the Oswestry market, which was much the largest. The drapers had to pay cash on the nail for the plains and then put them out to clothworkers and shearmen for conversion into cottons or friezes. Shrewsbury specialised in cottons. She had much the largest body of the necessary craftsmen, achieved the greatest expedition in the finishing processes, plains bought on Monday being cottoned and on the road to London by Wednesday, and gained the quickest sales and returns, so ensuring a supply of coin for further purchases.[5]

The Cartmel and Kendal cloth trades were similarly organised. Both the weavers and the fullers were part-time farmers of little financial or technical ability. In 1577 the weaver-clothiers were described as 'cotegers whose habylytye wyll not stretch to buy anye substance of wolles to mayntayne any worke or labor, nor yet to fetch the wooll'.[6] Undressed cloths were sold to merchant drapers, more especially the leading lights of the Kendal shearmen's company, and they saw to the frizzing and shearing, and sometimes the dyeing also, and then marketed the finished products.[7] Bristol, too, imported, frizzed, cottoned and finished rough Irish cloths.[8]

A similar business structure in the most part of the West Country was little changed by the successive rises of the kersey and union cloth manufactures. Hooker[9] in 1599 described it thus:

First the merchant or clothier buyeth the weaver his cloth and payeth present money, the weaver buyeth the yarn of the spinster and payeth present money, the clothier he sendeth his clothes to the tucker or fuller and he when his work is finished hath likewise his money, and then the merchant or clothier doth dye them in colors . . . or send them to London or elsewhere to his best advantage.

We need only elaborate slightly and say the weavers bought yarns not only from the actual spinsters but later also from yarnmasters. The weavers were frequently part-time farmers. About half of them had only one loom, a fifth two looms, and a quarter three, four or five. These were largely narrow looms, but journeymen weavers were employed in some shops. Weaving was seldom put out, unless by fullers or woolcombers who did a little clothing as a sideline.[10] Usually cloths were sold straight from the loom to merchants in Tiverton, Exeter, Barnstaple, or, more rarely, Okehampton, Bridport, Dunster or Taunton. The merchants saw to the fulling and then carried out all the finishing processes, including hot-pressing and sometimes dyeing, by their own workmen and largely on their own premises. They could thus justly be called merchant clothiers or drapers.[11] In Exeter, after 1642, this business was increasingly dominated by wealthy merchants who were also fullers or dyers or both. From the ranks of these merchant fullers and merchant dyers there arose a group of rich businessmen who were at once drapers, mill-owners and export merchants.[12]

In the Peak-Forest Country, however, the introduction of new fabrics led to organisational changes. The 'new drapery' of dyed-in-the-wool broadcloth in Leeds and district was produced by complete clothiers who undertook all the processes from dyeing to shearing, putting out only the fulling and some of the spinning. It was from such men that some merchant employers were eventually to spring.[13] There were similar but much swifter developments in the jersey and jersey union manufactures in this country. Woolcombers could easily become yarnmasters, and yarnmsters sergemakers or baizemakers, but the latter for long continued to rely on the Rochdale merchant drapers who bought the baizes and had them fulled and dressed rather as they had previously dealt with the plains.[14] In the fustian trade, too, something of the old system of organisation persisted for a time. The weavers bought their own cotton wool and linen yarn, often from the same merchant to whom they sold their cloths. But in the middle part of the seventeenth century there arose merchant drapers who had their own yarns warped and their own cotton wool spun and wound, put these out to be woven by specialist weavers, then either saw to the calendering, perching, cutting and dyeing themselves in their own workshops or put these processes out, and finally sold the finished products.[15]

The introduction of flannel making in the western extremities of the Cheshire Cheese Country and of the Vales of Hereford and in the Severn and Dovey valleys in Wales, brought with it some new forms of organisation. Although the finishing processes were changed, the drapers' functions remained much what they had been Although the Shrewsbury drapers bought in Wrexham and Welshpool instead of in Oswestry, they dominated this trade as surely as that in cottons. But the wools and yarns for flannels were purchased by petty owners or clothiers who put their work out to the weavers and the fullers. Flannel clothiers were thus mean and miniature merchant employers.[16]

The Shrewsbury drapers likewise attended to the finishing and marketing of the penistones, kerseys and baizes made in the borough by specialist master weavers who had up to two broad looms and one narrow one apiece, took apprentices, and employed journeymen.[17] This was the usual form of organisation where textile manufacture involved a relatively high level of expertise and required close supervision by a qualified master. In Kendal and Ulverston the linsey-woolsey and jersey manufactures were started by independent craftsmen from whose ranks emerged a number of large master weaver-clothiers.[18] In addition to her merchant drapers and to her small band of clothiers who cottoned, dressed and dyed the plains they had had woven for them on the putting-out system,[19] Bristol had some masters who made baize, linsey-woolsey, drugget and other stuff,[20] and a few carpetene manufacturers, some of whom were large masters with from three to five looms, some being broad ones.[21]

According to Unwin, the merchant employer and small master of the 'domestic system' had replaced the master craftsman of the guild system in Coventry. He holds up as proofs the acknowledged facts that journeymen weavers were at one time being paid a third of what their masters earned for weaving each piece, that every cottager or journeyman was permitted to become a master on payment of twenty shillings, and that far more drapers than weavers held municipal office. He also says the drapers ousted the dyers from the cloth trade and ensured their control of it by an agreement with the queen in 1568. This assertion is unsupported by the state paper cited in sole evidence and is as absurd as a similar one about the Norwich Russells Company.[22] Nor does the by-law of 1524, laying down at what rates the clothiers were to pay the weavers and fullers, afford him any help.[23] None of the facts he adduces, nor any combination of them, proves his point. Were Unwin right, the Coventry weavers would be small masters. But he himself displays evidence that some of them employed journeymen, and that men outnumbered masters is implied by the Weavers' Company ordinance forbidding any member to keep more than two broad looms and two narrow or four narrow ones only.[24] In fact the Coventry weavers were very far from being small masters. In 1550, for example, a weaver named John Bond had three broad looms, one kersey loom, four spinning wheels and four pairs of cards, all in his own workhouse. We infer he employed about four journeymen weavers, had one or two apprentices, and put four women on work. He was a large master, like many of the other city weavers. We find one with three looms apparently broad, one with one broad loom and three bastard looms for linsey-woolseys, one with three broad looms, one with one broad and one narrow, three with two broad and one narrow, one with one broad and three narrow, three with two broad ones, one with two looms of which one was certainly broad, one with one broad loom, and another with one loom of unknown size. There is no sign that Bond or any of the others normally put any weaving out. We therefore guess most successful and established weavers had between two and six assistant weavers, either servants or apprentices near the end of their terms. On this assumption, we might hope to find a large number of weavers without looms of their own, but not in the probate records, for they would largely have been young men. Besides, by no means were all the men without looms either journeymen or servants. To be a Coventry 'clothier' meant one paid less attention to the weaving side of the business and concentrated more on buying wool, preparing yarn, and finishing and selling cloths. In the seventeenth century some men used the style 'weaver and clothier' to signify they were weavers who had extended their activities to all the processes up to and including fulling. But those who called themselves simply 'clothiers' either had no loom or only one and put out all or most of their chains and yarns to mere weavers. None of these clothiers operated on a large scale, however, and taken altogether they put out only a small proportion of the weaving done in the city. Nathaniel Cheese is about the sole clothier found who put all his weaving out, and he only had one cloth at the weaver's and one at the fuller's. There was seldom much advantage in putting one's weaving out if one could do it oneself, and in 1544 clothiers were expressly permitted to weave their own cloths as long as they paid subscriptions to the Weavers' Company. As the city drapers rather unkindly pointed out, these were not clothiers in the fullest sense.[25] Indeed, the putting-out system was much stronger amongst the few baizemakers; they merely prepared the yarns and warps and put the rest of the work out to weavers, fullers and clothworkers.[26] In short, the domestic system of merchant employer and small master was scarcely known in Coventry clothmaking. The passage Unwin cites about journeymen being paid a third of the price of the weaving, really comes from an act by which the city government fixed what wages master weavers were to pay their servants.[27]

Drapers were amongst the wealthiest men in Coventry. Their business was to buy fulled cloths, have them dressed and dyed, either by their own servants or by putting them out, and then sell them. Earlier on some dyers had taken up draping, but in Coventry there was hardly any demarcation between drapers and dyers. Drapers were allowed to dye or have dyed. Indeed, in 1529 it was ordered that all inhabitants of the city could lawfully occupy the craft of woadsetting.[28] It was because they only entered the production cycle after fulling that the drapers could so conveniently handle other Worcester cloths, plains for cottoning or frizzing, and later also West-of-England whites, to which they largely switched when the old Coventry cloth manufactures died away.[29]

Although they traded in jerseys, the Coventry drapers had no part to play in their weaving or finishing; the new industry was in the hands of manufacturers who undertook all the processes between spinning and dyeing. They were essentially weavers and predominantly large masters with several looms at work on their own premises. Samuel Smith, who had introduced striped and mixed tammy manufacture in 1696, continued in business until his death in 1722 and styled himself 'weaver' to the very end. He then had three looms in his weaving shop and employed his own warpers, weavers and others, besides running a sale-shop. His fellow tammy makers ran similar businesses on much the same scale and shared his style of life.[30] Not the faintest hint is found of a merchant employer.

Likewise in Worcester, weavers who were successful in business were large masters. The Act of 1534 that legalised the control by the Clothiers' Company of clothmaking within the city, says its members 'sett aworke' the wool breakers and sorters, the carders, spinners, weavers, fullers, shearmen and dyers. This may well have been literally true, but then 'set awork' has to be taken in a general sense, as when a car manufacturer sets awork a tyre firm. The clothiers set the weavers and others awork by buying their products and services. Obsessed by Marxist hallucinations about 'social class' and 'class legislation'. Unwin misconstrues this Act. All it intended was the prohibition of woollen manufacturing by farmers and graziers in the 'hamletts, throps and villages adjoyning to the seid citie, borowes and townes' of Worcester, Kidderminster, Bromsgrove, Evesham and Droitwich. It was a constant source of irritation to boroughs and cities that men who set up business in suburbs and liberties just outside their boundaries took advantage of municipal and company facilities without paying a penny piece towards them and without conforming to the relevant rules and by-laws. This was why the London companies sought authority in the suburbs and liberties. All the Act did was to make town industries coincide with municipal jurisdictions. It was thus of a piece with the city ordinance of 1558 that prohibited the employment by citizens and inhabitants of spinners who lived without the city bounds and yet within twelve miles of its centre. In Worcester the master weavers employed assistant weavers and the clothiers set weavers and others on work, but merchant employers and small masters in no way came into the matter. Any master weaver could become a clothier simply by putting some yarn out to be spun and some cloth to be fulled.[31]

In Worcester the weavers shaded into the clothiers. Some men, indeed, used the style of 'weaver clothyer' or 'walker clothier', and thus reflected the smooth passage possible from one occupation to the other. For a clothier to own two or three looms, or, more rarely, four or five, was to be among the chief of the occupation. The typical clothier's career reached its peak with the ownership of three broad looms with a cloth being woven on each, three cloths out at the fuller's, and three awaiting sale. Bearing in mind the likely number of grown-up sons, it is improbable that the average clothier with three looms had fewer than three servants or journeymen to weave for him, and perhaps three apprentices, one or two of whom might be his own sons. In addition, many clothiers had most of their spinning done in their own spinning chambers. Usually, too, they saw to the marketing of their own cloths, and sometimes also those made by their lesser brethren. They rarely dyed their cloths, but when they did, it was

often by their own servants. Most of their weaving was done on their own looms
in their own weaving shops, but some was put out to master weavers. Putting
out was the best way to lop temporary peaks of production and avoid the
extravagance of a new shop. The majority of clothiers rose from the ranks of the
weavers, but a few fullers became clothiers by putting out some wool and yarn,
thus lending point to the mention of Worcester men among the 'many good
clothiers' who in 1554 protested against the Act of 1551 making it unlawful to
weave or put to weaving or making broadcloth unless one had been apprenticed
to weaving for seven years, and explains why the city was exempted from the
provisions of the replacing Act in 1554, for it was unnecessary there to have
served in the clothing trade in order to set up as a clothier. Generally speaking,
and leaving aside some youngsters and a few downright failures, all weavers,
clothiers and dyers were independent industrial masters. To cap all, Worcester
was a fully fledged textile town and half the members of the city government of
twenty-four were drawn from the clothing industry. As for merchant
employers, they were conspicuous only by their absence.[32]

Similar again was the industrial structure that came to prevail in Kidderminster. Before stuff manufacturing started here, textiles played only a minor
part in the life of the town. Some of the early clothiers had held land in the
town's common fields and had been part-time farmers. Once the new industry
took hold, however, these sidelines were laid down. As Richard Baxter said,
stuff weaving found work for all. The suburb of Franche remained partly
agricultural, but Kidderminster itself stood upon clothing.[33] Textile manufactures here had many vicissitudes and experienced many developments, changes
and innovations, yet all without commercial capital achieving any dominance
over industrial capital or vice versa, and without any hint of conflict between the
two.

The manufacture of Kidderminster stuffs was likewise dominated by large
masters. Weaving was put out only occasionally and in small volumes. A sample
of probate inventories shows two journeymen or servant weavers with no loom
of their own, six weavers with one loom apiece, two of these being narrow ones,
one 'weaver clothier' who seems to have had one loom, one man with one broad
loom and two narrow ones who was also a clothier in the sense that he wove up
his own yarns, one clothier with one broad loom and one narrow, three each
with one broad and two narrow, two with at least two looms each, six with three
apiece and in one instance certainly all broad ones, and one with five looms of
which one was certainly and the others probably broad. All these looms stood in
their owners' own workshops. There was also a fuller who undertook some
weaving. To find one single clothier in a substantial way of business and yet
without a loom of his own, we have to wait until 1710. There were thus four
weavers with only one loom, while seven had four or more loom-seats, and four
of these men appear to have had six seats apiece. What we glimpse is a trade
dominated by large masters with between two and six assistant weavers in their

shops. The first rung of the ladder was occupied by weavers working for wages in other men's shops. As the next step one got one's own loom and set up on one's own account, buying wool and putting it out to be spun and perhaps the yarn to be dyed. This made one a weaver-clothier, like Mr Edward Woodward. Climbing to the next rung made one a complete clothier with one's own weavers, shearman and dyer, and a spinning house of one's own where spinsters could be set on work at at piece-rates and supervised by the master. Some clothiers, however, preferred to put their dyeing out, probably because they could not get the knack of this work themselves.[34] There was thus some scope for specialist dyers.[35] A few clothiers, although doing all their own sorting, washing, dyeing, carding, warping, tentering, rowing, shearing, finishing and pressing, put their spinning and weaving out.[36] Everyone put his webs out to be fulled in suburban mills like the one at Heathy Hill.[37] This analysis is perfectly consistent with the statistics compiled in 1677. Then there were 417 looms at work, 157 master weavers, 187 journeymen, and 115 apprentices. Most masters had two or three looms each; only one had as many as seven. Since all those who had two apprentices were under orders to employ two journeymen[38] (no distinction any longer being made between journeymen and servants), it would seem that apprentices and journeymen were about equal numerically, as dictated by the broad loom itself, for it took one qualified man and one assistant to work it. This in turn implies that those who had recently graduated from their seven years of apprenticeship went on to serve an average of seven years as journeymen, though it goes without saying that some never set up for themselves, while others made haste to do so. Assuming an average of three loom-seats per master, 157 of them would have had about 300 assistants between them. However, some weavers had one loom only, so the average master weaver is likely to have had two journeymen and two apprentices. Whatever one makes of the statistics, it is plain that the putting-out system never came to much in Kidderminster and that the manufacture of stuffs was the business of substantial master weavers and clothiers.

This conclusion matches Richard Baxter's description of life in the town he had made his own:[39]

> My people were not rich. There were among them very few beggers, because their common trade of stuff weaving would find work for all, men, women, and children, that were able; and there were none of the tradesmen very rich, seeing their trade was poor, that would but find them food and raiment. The magistrates of the town were few of them worth 40*l* per annum, and most not half so much. Three or four of the richest thriving masters of the trade got about 500*l* or 600*l* in twenty years, and it may be lose 100*l* of it at once by an ill debtor. The generality of the master workmen lived but a little better than their journeymen, (from hand to mouth), but only that they laboured not altogether so hard.

When the town moved out of Kidderminster stuffs, by way of friezes, into says, Philip and Cheyneys, tammies and harrateens, industrial structure stayed essentially the same. In these trades we find, for example, three weavers with one loom apiece, two with two, five with three, one with four, four with five, one with six, and three with more than one but the exact number not known. Disregarding this last group for the moment, except insofar as corroboration is lent to the general conclusion, it would appear that weavers in a small way of business, with only one or two looms, constituted no more than about a third of the whole. These were the young men coming up or those lacking the skill or character needed for greater success. Two thirds of all the weavers had three or more looms and about one third had five looms or more. In other words, most of the looms were in central workshops run by large masters. But this is far from all. The styles 'weaver' and 'clothier' were by now being used somewhat indiscriminately, but still the men with only one loom were usually mere weavers, while those with several looms were more often than not complete clothiers who prepared their own wool, put it out to be combed and spun, dyed their own yarn, warped it, wove it on their own looms, and dressed and pressed the fabric in their own shops. The only exceptions were a few men who could not dye or had no hot-press of their own, and those who lopped peaks of business by putting some of their weaving out. Edmund Read, for example, had five looms with tammies on them and other tammies being woven by four 'out-workers' on their own looms. In his lodging-chambers he had no less than seven beds for indwelling servants. Judging from this, it seems likely two thirds of the masters had five or more assistant weavers each. Certainly large masters predominated; hardly a trace is found of merchant employers or of small, dependent masters.[40]

For the period when clothing still flourished in Gloucester, the probate inventories are unavailable, and in the period for which they are available, the clothing industry there was all but extinct. Its structure appears to have resembled that of Coventry and Worcester, which is understandable, considering that they all made cloth of high quality. In September 1602 the master weavers of Gloucester, organised in the Fraternity of St Anne, allowed the journeymen weavers of the city and suburbs to meet regularly and in working hours for the purpose of running their own mutual benefit society and of electing their own stewards to attend to its day to day business. The journeymen were described as 'servants of the said trade of weaving' and the relationship was clearly one of masters and servants. It is significant that Unwin deals so briefly and cavalierly with a record that bluntly contradicts his theory that such yeomanry organisations were composed of small masters who were struggling against merchant employers. Gloucester clothmaking was dominated by large masters.[41]

It was much the same in Witney and district. There were many large master clothiers with up to four blanket or broad looms at work on their own premises. Half the clothiers had two looms, one fifth three or four, and a third one loom only. Some of the larger men put part of their weaving out to specialist weavers with one or two looms, but such weavers were also essentially independent industrial masters, and the clothiers themselves commonly employed servant weavers, it would seem up to half a dozen in number. Generally speaking, neither weavers nor clothiers had any considerable agricultural interest.[42] The Tewkesbury weaver-hosiers, who produced hose, serge and drugget and often attended to their own combing, were independent masters, not a few of them in a large way of business.[43] So were the Banbury jersey weavers, the Stourbridge clothiers and the Knaresborough sameron makers.[44] In Leicester, Bromsgrove, Mansfield, Tamworth, Stourbridge and other Midland towns, too, there were not a few coverlet, linsey-woolsey, linen damask, kersey, and custom weavers with up to half a dozen looms who were independent masters and frequently also part-time farmers.[45]

The initial Dutch settlement in Sandwich is said to have had 406 men, women and children, 'whereof ther be masters in the facultie of makyng of bayes and says but only viij, and all the rest be servants unto them, savyng the minister only'. Relevant probate inventories are scanty, but they suffice to show that this master and servant relationship continued to the end. We find men with one broad loom, two broad looms, two narrow looms and ten lace ones, two broad and six narrow, and lace looms only.[46]

In Canterbury, too, large masters predominated. The only baizemaker we know much about had four looms.[47] Among the say and silk weavers we find six without looms, but three of these were widows who understandably preferred to put their weaving out. Wives often worked beside their husbands in silkweaving, but women could not easily manage the work by themselves and would hardly want to oversee a workshop full of weavers. Thus Susan Le Grand alias Delespine, who died in 1664, made damasks, druggets, figuratoes, rashes and other fabrics by putting out chains and weft yarns to no fewer than nine different specialist weavers.[48] Another of these six loom-less persons was a woolcomber who had branched out into clothing and put his weaving out, we suppose, because he had little understanding of that side of the business.[49] The remaining two made up their own warps and attended to everything except the weaving itself, which they put out, for reasons we cannot guess at.[50] Apart from these six, all the manufacturers we know of had their own looms on their own premises. One sixth of them had one loom only and the rest two or more, the exact number not always being recorded. As far as we can see, however, one tenth of the manufacturers had three looms, one seventh four, one sixteenth five, and one twelfth six or more, up to ten.[51] It is not possible to compare these estimates with the records of the tax taken from aliens for their looms, for these fail to distinguish accurately between lace-looms and what were called here 'great looms'.[52] However, in 1665 there were at least 126 master weavers and in 1694 perhaps nearly 1,000 looms of all kinds; and we learn that 334 of the great looms at work in the city in 1719 were in the hands of fifty-eight master weavers. Finally, we have Celia Fiennes's word that she saw twenty drawlooms working in the house of one single silkweaver.[53] Assuming each master weaver's own family included three people who took a hand in the business, all these observations and sets of figures are roughly consistent with each other. Masters and servants or journeymen were about equal in numbers, but most of the production came from the looms owned by large masters who employed journeymen to do a great deal of the weaving. In 1643 the Canterbury journeymen weavers were clearly a considerable body of men and distinct enough from the master weavers for the city to be called upon to arbitrate between the two.[54] The final stage in the complete silkweaver's business was the sale of his products to the merchants of London and elsewhere. All told, silkweaving was a highly skilled occupation and the rewards were commensurate. We find seven estates of between £1,000 and £1,700 odd, eight others of over £500, four over £300, four over £200, eight over £100, and eighteen smaller.[55]

The weavers of broad silk cloths and unions in Stepney and district were much like their Canterbury counterparts. Although alien masters were often accused, with apparent justification, of employing young lads in their looms, in lieu of apprentices probably, there is no reason to suppose they had fewer qualified journeymen than did the English masters, who were only removed from them by a descent or two. Even when limited by order to three looms in a house, some of the strangers owned and worked six, eight and twelve. In 1685 an alien named Peter Marishall was employing seven journeymen, four of them English. Natives or immigrants, denizens or citizens, it made no difference: large masters prevailed. On the bottom rung were the numerous journeymen who worked other men's looms; above them, the weavers with one or two looms who wove other men's yarns; and at the head, the complete silkweavers or manufacturers. A handful of men, and not extraordinarily wealthy ones, had few or no looms of their own, and, for what appear to be purely personal reasons, put out all or most of their weaving. Few manufacturers did any throwing; they mostly bought thrown silks from the silkmen, twisted them perhaps, warped them on their own warping mills, and wove them up. Dyeing was usually put out to specialists. Warping and weaving were at the heart of the silkweaver's business. Anyone who put out his warping and his weaving, and his dyeing as well, was in the nature of a merchant employer, and some men of this type made their appearance in course of time.[56] By the early eighteenth century some wealthy merchant employers had emerged, amongst whom the biggest half dozen, like Thomas Eades, and Lekeux and Son, claimed to have employed two hundred or more looms in good times and thirty fully and sixty partially in bad ones. It is significant, however, that these merchant employers produced only the simpler fabrics. Eades, for instance, made almost entirely camlets and calamancoes.[57] All the tissue and other fine weaving Spitalfields became famous for, was done on drawlooms, many of them with compound montures. Although the drawloom reduced the striking of the weft to a routine operation calling for little skill or judgment, the designing and draughting of the pattern for these distinctive and often individual fabrics, and the tying up of the loom were all highly skilled operations to be performed only by artistic or clever and experienced weavers or persons working under their immediate direction. Therefore this sort of production remained the preserve of the large industrial master.[58] As for the Stepney hair and plush weavers, they were not much unlike the silk ones. They commonly had about four looms in their shops, bought the hair ready thrown, prepared their own warps and attended to the rest of the business themselves. Indeed, they went one step further in this than did the silkweavers, for they also dyed their own yarns and pieces, since they alone understood the fibres well enough.[59] Finally, the cotton cloth and union manufacturers were likewise mostly large masters.[60]

In Norwich, East Norfolk, King's Lynn and other places, the worsted-weavers had a generally uniform way of arranging their businesses, save that there were proportionately more loom owners in the city than elsewhere. On the whole roughly half the owners had one or two looms and half from three to ten. Of the lesser masters, about half had only one loom and half two; of the superior ones, half had more than three looms. The overwhelming majority of these looms were found in the owners' workshops; very few were placed in journeymen's houses. Outside Norwich, weavers rarely had over six looms, but, then, they often possessed house-cows, which city men seldom did, and sometimes farms that demanded attention.[61] Occasional self-denying ordinances failed to curb the accumulation of looms. One Worstedweavers' Company order, that none in Norwich keep above four broad looms and one narrow, and in other towns no more than three looms broad or narrow, though not long enforced, serves at least to indicate scales of production. In 1583 some weavers were fined for having too many apprentices, some five, some six, some seven. It is not wholly unrealistic to assume these weavers had, by and large, roughly as many apprentices as journeymen, and, in fact, one of the men fined had seven of each.[62] The stamp of the large master is unmistakable. As single worsteds, worsted beds and bustians went out, broad looms were less and less in evidence.[63] Even so, journeymen weavers were clearly numerous and not all were successful in becoming their own masters. At least half the men with single looms were purely and simply specialist weavers who took warps from others and were paid for striking a weft on them. Some masters with from two to five looms were also weavers pure and simple, or, if they wove their own yarns, did so only on little lace-looms, which are not at present under consideration. Nevertheless, some of these mere weavers were, or were on the way to becoming, large masters.[64] These worstedweavers who did nothing but weave had their work from complete worstedweavers who lopped peaks in their workloads by putting some weaving out[65] or from others who contracted it all out. All these types of entrepreneur were found both within and and without the city, but masters who put out weaving were much more numerous, and on average a good deal wealthier, in Norwich than elsewhere. However, even the bigger men amongst these putters out[66] by no means exceeded in wealth the richer of the men who either did all their own weaving or put only part of it out. They too lived in some affluence and left estates running into thousands of pounds.[67] As to the worstedweavers without looms, who included those who had retired and young men who had not yet gained a footing, they were more numerous in the smaller towns[68] than in Norwich,[69] in total possibly twice as numerous. The full significance of this is not entirely clear. Perhaps retired worstedweavers were inclined to remove from the city to their native country towns. However, one reason loom-less weavers obviously had for preferring small towns was that in Norwich none of them could afford so much as a house-cow, whereas in East Norfolk country places they more often than not had part-time farms with up to three or four cows and two or three acres of corn.[70]

Worstedweavers in other towns made many of the same fabrics as did their Norwich brethren, but often with some lag in time, for most of the new inventions originated in the city. It must be added, however, first, that no single town other than Norwich had anywhere near as extensive a range of products; secondly, that toys, pearls of beauty, cattaloons, pyramids, princilatoes, bombasines, mockadoes, tufted buffins, mohairs, grograins, cameleons, crapes, calamancoes, baronets, tammies, grazets, gauzes, stamins, druggets, rashes, poplins, marvels, prunellas, and generally all fabrics incorporating silk, were rarely made in East Norfolk towns other than Norwich; and, thirdly, that flowered damask was mostly produced in these smaller towns.[71] It was woven on a drawloom, which was difficult to set up in the first instance but correspondingly simple to work thereafter. Long, unbroken runs of the same pattern of flowered damask were thus suitable undertakings for mediocre weavers. As for silkweaving, it was in this period always confined to a restricted number of cities and straitly circumscribed towns in order to safeguard valuable materials and economise on scarce skills by facilitating the swift and convenient interchange of services.

Many of the lesser worstedweavers, especially those working for wages, supplemented their incomes by making lace,[72] and when this was taken over by the engine-loom, by twisting yarns.[73] Twistering mills and lace-looms were cheap to buy and easily worked by the womenfolk and children.

In respect of industrial structure the Norwich Flemings seem to have differed little from the native English. According to their own custom, the goods and chattels left by deceased strangers were not appraised but simply sold off by the executors. Even when wills were proved, few inventories were filed; and there were seldom compelling reasons for proving a will, for strangers were not allowed to own freehold estates here. Nevertheless, some probate evidence is available. For obvious reasons, many of the strangers were very poor,[74] and often had only tenuous or indeterminate connections with the textile trades;[75]

but we find one market spinner and warper of jersey,[76] three men with one loom each, two with two, one with three, two with four, one with six, one with seven, two with fourteen each, and one with nineteen. One of the men with fourteen looms had half of them in his own two workshops and half in other men's houses; but all the other masters had all their looms in their own weaving shops. In addition, one substantial stuff manufacturer seems to have put all his weaving out.[77] Although the looms were mainly narrow, we derive an impression of a body of independent industrial masters among whom large employers were both numerous and pre-eminent. This impression is strengthened by returns made of Dutch and Walloon church membership in 1568 and of all aliens in 1622. These show fifty-seven and 105 weavers respectively, one in three of them a journeyman.[78]

The dornicksweavers were industrial masters employing up to ten or a dozen journeymen in their workshops, not to speak of draw-boys. An earlier company by-law limited each weaver to six looms on his own premises, but later some had nine looms in their shops. There is no sign that any weaving was ever put out.[79] It was much the same with the bedweavers,[80] with the manufacturers of such things as tiltcloths and bewpers, and with the weavers of blankets and carded woollen broad cloths,[81] save for a solitary Spanish clothier who put his weaving out.[82]

When we look closely at the other manufacturers who wove nothing for themselves, we realise even more clearly that textile production in this district was the province of the large industrial master. All told, fourteen men, other than the Spanish clothier, appear to have put all their weaving out. Of these, six were in a relatively small way of business; they hardly correspond to anyone's notion of what a merchant employer was. Two or three of the others seem to have had subsidiary interests in retail or wholesale trade. Special circumstances, now unknown, may well have obtained in most or all of the businesses instanced, for in none was there any obvious reason for a preference for putting out. It was left to the eighteenth century to see the gradual emergence of firms that specialised in putting out the weaving of the simpler fabrics such as camlets, calamancoes and prunellas.[83] Certainly much work was always put out; few manufacturers had their own scouring shops,[84] and none dyed or calendered.[85] But weavers rarely put spinning out; they were content to buy their yarns. Weaving was put out from time to time, and later on a more regular basis; but, then, it was put out to specialist weavers with up to five looms in their own workshops. In short, large industrial masters dominated production.

The linen, twill and sackcloth weavers in East Norfolk, High Suffolk and the Sandlings Country were mostly independent craftsmen. Some three fifths of the masters had merely one loom apiece, and the rest rarely more than three narrow ones. To a great extent the firm was the family and the size of one the size of the other. Few journeymen were employed, and fewer remained long in that station. The weavers usually bought their yarns and, unless they bleached their own linen ones, had nothing to do but weave them up, except that when they also made linsey-woolsey, they often sheared and finished it for themselves. Many weavers were also part-time dairy farmers, and some clearly devoted most of their time and energy to agriculture.[86] The canvas, poldavis and medrinacks weavers in the west of the Sandlings Country and the east of High Suffolk were a class apart. They had unusual skills and worked as large masters, with up to nine looms each and a dozen journeymen weavers, all brought together in central workshops where an eye could be kept on them.[87] The linenweavers of Mere, Gillingham and other parts of the Butter Country were likewise independent masters. We find, for example, seven who had no loom, six with one apiece, eight with two looms, two with three, and one with four. Whether they bought flax and had it dressed and spun, or purchased brown or white thread, the manufacturers had their yarns bleached or dyed when necessary and then usually wove them up in their own workshops, with the help of apprentices and journeymen or servants, weaving being only occasionally put out.[88] Linenweavers in the Lancashire Plain were likewise independent masters. They bleached their own yarn or bought it white from yarnmasters, who frequently availed themselves of the services of the Moston whitsters, and then wove and sold their own cloths. It was only in the eighteenth century that it became common for the merchants to have finished pieces bleached.[89] In Ireland weaving was much more of a winter by-employment on farms where flax was grown, dressed, spun and bleached. Once the landowner or other undertaker had set up the industry in a particular locality, the farmer-weavers were left to carry on as independent producers in full charge of all the processes, until, in later times, the merchants took to having linens bleached in the piece.[90] The bleaching of yarn added up to a third on to its value, but took about six months, occupied a not entirely inconsiderable amount of land, and tied up a good deal of capital, but was within the means and capabilities of most complete linenweavers. On the other hand, the 'Dutch' system of bleaching in the piece, as applied to fine linen in the Netherlands, and later in Southwark, Manchester, Prestwich and several places in Ireland, with its repeated bucking and crofting, was only economic when conducted on a large scale and as a continuous process.[91] Whichever method was used, throughout the whole of our period, in the vast majority of places where linen manufacturing was undertaken, linenweavers remained in every sense their own masters.

The Kettering textile district was one of a number where putting out was of greater importance, principally because manufactures were limited to a small range of inexpensive, simple, mass produced fabrics whose weaving was readily reduced to a routine task requiring little or no supervision by the clothier. Kettering specialised in making jersey cloths of simple structure in plain weaves, chiefly shalloons and tammies. Many of the 'sergeweavers', as they were called, were really complete clothiers who bought, sorted and combed their wools, put them out to spin, made their own warps, had them woven on their own looms, tentered and finished them on their own premises, and then sold them. These men usually had between three to six looms in their shops and employed no fewer workmen than looms. Masters like this left estates of between £70 and £200 odd and lived in some affluence. Then there were other men who were purely and simply weavers, owning one, two or three looms and living modestly or even meanly, buoyed up perhaps by their prospects of rising in the world and becoming clothiers. Lastly, there were some sergemakers or sergeweavers who put their warps and weft yarns out to mere weavers but in all other respects were complete clothiers, and left estates of between £60 and £300 odd, except in a few instances where they had a draper's sale-shop or some other second source of income. All three groups of entrepreneurs were roughly equal in size. As for the specialist hot-pressers, they had their own presses and shops and were masters in their own right. None of these people, incidentally, took any interest in agriculture; at the most they had a house-cow, a pig or two, and perhaps a hive of bees.[92] In this district all the mere weaver had to do was to strike the warps supplied to him. Such work could well be put out, either in Kettering itself or in one of the smaller towns in the neighbourhood; since the clothier had no need to see the work on the loom, the weaver could live at some distance from him. But putting out made little difference to social structure, for the mere weavers were independent masters (if not servants or journeymen) and were often themselves employers of labour. The fact that some weaving was contracted out, in no way meant that small masters were being employed by merchants.

In the Chalk Country and district the ways in which the textile industries were organised were neither uniform nor constant, and least of all in the old carded woollen trades. In Basingstoke we find one weaver with three looms, one kersey clothier with three narrow ones, a general clothier with one broad loom and three narrow ones, one clothier with a single loom, and two men who were clothiers in some vague sense, but in a small way and without looms. It seems to have been not unusual for clothiers to have several looms in their weaving shops and also their own woad and dye houses, and occasionally they did their own shearing and finishing as well. They clearly employed servants or journeymen in some numbers. In addition a few of them combined clothing with running farms with up to two plough-teams and forty acres in corn, or with participation in the malt and meal trades. The clothiers normally put their spinning out, but rarely any weaving.[93] In Godalming, Guildford, Fetcham and Bramley the clothiers operated in much the same way.[94] Weaving was more frequently put out in Salisbury than it was in Wilton and Stockton, but then the parties were weaver-clothiers and mere weavers. A sample shows five weavers without looms, two men with one broad loom each, two with two broad looms, one with two narrow ones, one with two broad and one narrow, one with one broad and two narrow, and one with three broad and two narrow. Irrespective of whether they called themselves weavers or clothiers, most of the owners of looms were in fact clothiers, and among them large masters were prominent.[95] The kersey clothiers of Wimborne Minster had from two to ten narrow looms each and employed up to four or so servant or journeymen weavers, besides apprentices and others.[96] In his *Pleasant History of John Winchcombe* (1633) Thomas Deloney tells us 'Jack of Newbury' had 200 looms and 200 men who 'wrought in these loomes all in a row', the authenticity of which may be judged from the fact that this John Winchcombe the elder expired a hundred years and more before Deloney put pen to paper, that our poet says he was a broadweaver when he was really a kersey clothier, and that no building in the world could have accommodated such a long row of looms. Ignoring justifiable poetic licence, the clothiers of kerseys and carded woollens in Newbury, Speen, Alton, Reading, Havant, Southampton, Romsey, Lymington, Carisbrooke, Newport, Christchurch, Wareham, Dorchester, Devizes, Bere Regis, Mere, Edington and elsewhere, though they usually dyed and dressed, and sometimes fulled, on their own premises, seem to have put most of their weaving out,[97] and generally to have availed themselves of the services of master weavers. We cannot always be sure which looms were narrow and which broad, but about half these weavers had three or fewer loom seats and half four or more, while a quarter had as many as eight. Many of the master weavers obviously employed considerable numbers of servants or journeymen. A few master weavers branched out and became clothiers, but most fulfilled their ambitions by being large master weavers, with perhaps a part-time farm into the bargain.[98] Once again, what appears to have decided whether or not weaving was to be kept under the clothier's eye was the nature of the work itself. Fine kerseys, medley cloths and florentines required close oversight; other kinds of cloth could well be left to specialist weavers.[99]

The introduction of new fabrics and techniques enhanced the larger master's role. Southampton and district sergeweavers who acquired a broad loom could easily blossom out as clothiers. We find mere weavers with no loom of their own, others with one, and yet others with one broad and one narrow; and also clothiers with one or two broad looms, or one broad and one narrow, or two broad and one narrow. In addition there were a few clothiers who put their weaving out and some who did their own combing or dyeing.[100] Flannel making hardly changed industrial organisation in Salisbury,[101] but a bare handful of large masters made the early Wilton carpets and a partnership of three the later ones.[102] The Reading serge, drugget, crape and plush makers were large masters with up to eighteen looms in their weaving shops.[103] In Alton the sergemakers had their own dyehouses and hot and cold presses and up to six looms apiece.[104] In Andover and Middleton we find three sergeweavers with two looms each, two weavers with three broad ones, and one with four all apparently broad. Several men had part-time farms, but the flockbeds on their premises seem to have been for textile servants.[105] It was much the same in Devizes and Little Cheverell, except that here the masters often did their own combing as well.[106] In Newbury, too, the drugget and serge clothiers wove on their own premises as a rule; in 1730 one of them had no less than three separate loom shops.[107]

In all the carded wool manufactures in the Woodland and the Breckland, the clothiers sorted, carded and often blued their wool and then put all the rest of the work out, except that some men ran their own shearing shops. A few rawback blanket makers provided the exception to prove the rule that ordinary clothiers rarely wove; when they kept a loom it was more for the instruction of apprentices than anything else. The wools used were so coarse they were not worthy of expensive spinning or weaving, and it was only by the most skilful preparation that they could be made fit to spin at all. The crucial processes were sorting, blending, carding and dyeing, so the clothiers kept these in their own hands.[108] Those who changed over to making baize carried on in much the same way; they bought either wool, to put out for combing, or else tops and noils, and did their own dyeing, sorting, and carding, and often their own warping.[109] Disregarding those who were really no more than shearmen or clothworkers,[110] and bearing in mind that some men also ran farms and now and then had their own plough-teams,[111] we see these clothiers forming a gradation from those of slender means to others who left goods and chattels worth up to £900 and more. A few of the most successful attained to riches. Thomas Spring of Lavenham was not alone. The single town of Coggeshall gave rise to the Guyons as well as the Paycockes. Matthew Guyon was a notably rich clothier, and 'Thomas Guyon the Great Clothier', who died in 1664, was credited 'with near £100,000 which he raised by the bay trade'.[112] The clothiers were complemented by a large number of master weavers, the majority owning only one broad loom, but a substantial minority two, three or four, some of which stood in other men's houses. Masters with two or more looms would seem to have had as many servants or journeymen and an apprentice or two. They often owned or hired a house-cow, but had no agricultural interests to speak of,[113] in which respect they stood in marked contrast to the clothworkers and shearmen, who often had part-time farms.[114]

The newer fabrics would seem to have been introduced by new men who styled themselves 'saymaker', 'fustian maker', 'woolcomber' or even 'goodman'. When our evidence starts, we still find many such masters with from two to four looms and some with up to as many as nine, which might be in their own shops or in the houses of their servants or journeymen. They wove their own says, serges, shalloons, tammies and calamancoes, or fustians and dimities, and often did their own combing. They left effects of up to £500 or more.[115] By 1660, however, the weaving of jerseys and jersey union cloths had been reduced to a repetitive and routine operation that could safely be left to specialist weavers. Amongst these 'sayweavers' and 'fustian weavers', the ones without a loom, those with one narrow loom, those with two, with three, and with four, existed in even proportions, indicating an industrial ladder climbed by successively higher age and ability groups: apprentices, journeymen and servants, and masters who laid loom to loom. They left a wide range of estates up to £150 or so.[116] Thanks to their specialist services, there had grown up a class of 'saymakers' or 'clothiers' who put all their weaving out, conducted business on an enlarged scale, and accumulated estates of up to £1,200.[117] Above these, too, stood a few men, usually styled 'clothier', who engaged in the mass production of a small number of the simpler types of jersey, carded, and union fabrics, such as says, serges, tammies, linsey-woolseys, baizes, blankets and lining cloths. These manufacturers bought much of their yarn, put nearly all their manual work out, and concentrated on general management. They could thus amass estates of up to and over £2,000.[118] Hedgthorn of Coggeshall, for example, made mainly serges and shalloons. At the time of his death, he was still employing six woolcombers, some or all of whom paid their own mates to work alongside them, sixty weavers with one loom each, and six with two apiece. Four of the weavers with but a single loom were admittedly old men, well past their best, and possibly turned out on average no more than one piece in two months; another was a schoolmaster who wove somewhat less than full time; and some others were truly slow or lazy; but Hedgthorn also had seventeen occasional weavers who only worked at odd times and often took a long time to complete a piece. Some of the constant weavers took 'pretty many' chains, the irregular ones only one at a time. The clothier gave out his chains and weft yarns, and all the weaver had to do was to wind on the warp and strike the weft. Supervision was superfluous and distance no object. One weaver lived in Stoke-by-Nayland, one at Audley, one at Stanway, one at Lexden, several at the Hythe just outside Colchester, and many in Magdalene Street inside the town.[119] Between richer clothiers and the poorer master weavers stretched a wide gap, and this was often broadened further by the saymakers and clothiers having a sideline in farming, which mere weavers hardly ever had.

Of the Colchester weavers and clothiers,[120] who by 1573 had been swamped by the many 'Dutch' and the few 'French' Flemings,[121] we know little. Nor have we much detailed knowledge of the strangers, for their goods and chattels were perhaps not much listed, and any way few probate inventories survive from this archdeaconry. When Thomas Roose died in 1568 he had three broad looms and two narrow. In 1609 John Soones left thirty-two pieces of says small and great worth just over £40, wool and yarn in various places, six pairs of shears, a say press and seven looms.[122] Our belief that these two large masters were typical of the first generation of Colchester say and baize makers appears at first sight to be gainsaid by the return on Dutch strangers in 1622, for this shows sixty-eight such makers and only 104 weavers.[123] But the strangers had never been licensed to set up as mere weavers, for weaving was a trade already practised by the English. Immigrants were permitted to weave, but only in their capacity as baize and say makers, as weaver-clothiers on their own looms. If strangers wanted to employ weavers, they might only take on English ones.[124] It was only an exaggeration when a Dutch baizemaker claimed in 1633 to set on work 200 households of spinners, fifty-two of weavers, and thirty-three of other workpeople. Not only did he put out much of his weaving, he also let out looms on weekly terms to some of his weavers.[125] As usual, the growth of putting out by clothiers was matched by the rise of large master weavers. During a recession of trade in 1602 specialist weavers were forbidden to have more than four looms working in their own houses, and when this rule was relaxed in 1608 the warden of the Weavers' Company reserved the right to call upon those with more than four looms in their shops to stop one or more of them, in order to allow poor weavers with only one loom to keep their heads above water when trade was bad. In 1612, too, no weaver was to be permitted a combination of narrow or broad looms that would result in him employing more than five 'weavinge persons'.[126] This division of labour between master weavers and clothiers went on opening up. By the 1680s baize and say makers who put out all their weaving were leaving estates of up to about £3,500.[127] Meanwhile, Colchester and the Woodland had, industrially speaking, fully merged the one with the other. As early as 1590 the town's weavers are found complaining that some clothiers 'put there cloths to wevinge in the contrye, whereby the pore wevers here are destitute of work'. The clothiers, for their part, blamed the Colchester weavers' poor workmanship. The upshot was a commission of three clothiers and three weavers who were to draw up, agree, and enforce orders for true weaving, which was then to be confined to the town. Thus oil was poured on troubled waters; but the tide was not turned. Conversely, as we have seen, clothiers in Coggeshall and elsewhere took to employing weavers in Colchester.[128]

In the West of England textile district successful woollen clothiers waxed wealthy. They commonly had proprietary rights in their own fulling mills and employed two or three workmen to do their scouring, fulling and tentering. The Stroudwater clothiers, however, rarely had their own fulling mills; but they had their own mosing mills and did their own dyeing, so their involvement in manufacturing was no less close. In later days, too, most medley clothiers dyed their own yarns. Clothiers of all kinds often had one or two looms on their premises, and perhaps a servant weaver, for the instruction of apprentices, the making of exemplars, and other occasional uses. They also had spinning wheels to occupy their womenfolk. In addition, many clothiers were fully fledged farmers with servants in husbandry and dairymaids, while others were landed proprietors and even lords of manors. The clothier's own riders and other servants gave out the wool to spinners and carders and the warps and weft yarns to weavers, and received and brought back the finished articles. His own servants, too, usually did the warping,[129] so the weaving contracted out amounted to no more than striking with a shoot in a plain weave, requiring some dexterity and judgment, but nothing that could not easily be picked up in the course of a very short apprenticeship. The average weaver was in a small way of business, either owning one broad loom or working as a journeyman on someone else's and doing a little weaving on his own account on a narrow loom. An experienced weaver and a young lad between them could comfortably work a broad loom. Some men came to own two, three or even four looms, which were operated with the help of sons, journeymen and apprentices. In addition weavers frequently owned a house-cow or two, and some developed an interest in agriculture. Ambitious men then had at least two avenues open to them: they could move over into dairy farming and rise into the ranks of the family farmers,[130] or they could take extra warps to give out on sub-contract to fellow weavers, start to make a few cloths for themselves, and in one way or another become petty clothiers in their own right.[131] Entry into the weaving trade was easy and into the clothing business by no means impossible, but one had a long and hard way to go to become a complete clothier with one's own fulling mill as headquarters.[132] To this general picture only two important exceptions are to be made. Market spinners grew up to supply white and coloured yarns to the early Spanish medley clothiers, facilitating their nascent industry by relieving them of this care, and then died away as the manufacturers took over all the processes and developed into complete clothiers.[133] And in Stroudwater and district the fullers were their own masters.[134]

Weaving chambers with three or four looms in them were not uncommon, but central workshops much bigger than these were very rare. The more exaggerated accounts of William Stumpe's establishment at Malmesbury Abbey are hardly justified by the original description of it by John Leland.[135] All he says is,

> Ther was a litle chirch joining to the south side of the *transeptum* of the abby chirch ... Wevers hath now lomes in this litle chirch ... This Stumpe was the chef causer and contributer to have thabbay chirch made a paroch chirch. At this present tyme every corner of the vaste houses of office that belongid to thabbay be fulle of lumbes to weve cloath yn, and this Stumpe entendith to make a stret or 2 for clothiers in the bak vacant ground of the abbay that is withyn the tounes walles. There be made now every yere in the toune a 3,000 clothes.

Even what were vast for houses of office, i.e. necessary houses or privies, can hardly have been huge edifices by other standards. Neither they nor the little church or chapel can have housed very many broad looms. Nor is it stated that the looms standing in the houses of office were being worked; possibly they were stored there pending delivery to weavers. The clothiers intended to be attracted to the new street or streets could hardly have been envisaged as men in a big way of business. Nowhere is it ever suggested the abbey itself was converted into a weaving shop. Stumpe himself appears neither as a clothier nor as a weaver, but as the leading light of the town who saw to it that Malmesbury, like Tewkesbury, Christchurch and other places, took over the abbey church, and also as an energetic town developer. In fact, it was only with the much later invention of cassimeres that weaving began to be concentrated in large workshops in Devizes and Trowbridge.[136] This was possible because the looms were narrow and necessary because the weaves were new and intricate.

The serge and drugget manufactures developed independently. Serge and drugget makers worked on their own account and largely did their own weaving. Some, indeed, still styled themselves 'sergeweavers' and had evidently risen from their ranks. Still others, notably in Cirencester and Tetbury, betrayed their origins by being called 'worsted combers'; they were woolcombers who had branched out. Amongst all these manufacturers we find some with only one loom, some with two or three, or with three narrow and one broad, and so on up to a maximum of seven. Large masters were not at all uncommon. From their ranks emerged a group of masters who put much of their weaving out. Abraham Selfe of Cirencester, for example, who died in 1698, had three looms in his long loft and four in his weaving chamber, yet still put some weaving out. In 1748 Robert Rogers of Atford had his own dye-house, wool loft, workshops with cards and combs, four druggets out at the mill for fulling, a weaving shop with two narrow looms, and two druggets put out to weavers in their own homes and on their own looms. All told, perhaps as many as half the serge and drugget makers came to be men without looms who put all their weaving out and were yet not markedly wealthier than their colleagues who did all their own weaving. The division between these groups apparently arose for purely technical reasons; some thought their weaving would be done better on contract.[137] Correspondingly, in addition to the sergeweavers without looms who were servants and journeymen, others sprang up with one, two or three looms of their own.[138]

In the Vale of Taunton Deane the introduction of new fabrics made little change in industrial organisation, excepting only the arrival on the scene of woolcombers and yarnmasters. Although the hurdle between them was a low one, the weavers and the clothiers formed two quite distinct occupations. The master weavers were about equally divided between those with one, two and three looms, but a few people had four, and servants and journeymen were numerous. Weaving was a relatively simple business when in the hands of trained experts, for no intricate fabrics were made here. The weaver's wealth tended to grow with the number of his looms, while the clothier's or sergemaker's increased in inverse proportion to his. Clothiers and sergemakers with two looms left on average about £110, those with one loom £150, and those with no loom £190, although we have to make an exception for a few wealthy men who let looms out to weavers in their homes. The more a manufacturer prospered, the more he put his weaving out and concentrated on buying and selling and on combing and dyeing wool and dressing and pressing cloths. He had his spinning, weaving and fulling done on contract, but aimed at seeing to everything else himself on his own premises by his own workmen. Ordinary weavers were generally much less well off than clothiers and sergemakers, and all the more so since some men in these latter classes, like some fullers also, had their own farms. In all this, little difference is seen between Taunton and the other towns in the vale. Some of the meanest weavers lived in Taunton and some of the richest manufacturers in places like Fiddington, Holford, North Petherton and Bridgwater.[139]

The same sharp division between mere weavers and clothiers existed in the

Culm valley district of the West Country. The clothiers carded and dyed for themselves, but gave all their spinning, weaving and fulling out. They often gained considerable wealth and some left estates of not much under £2,000.[140]

The manufacture of 'Kentish' and other carded and union cloths in the Wealden Vales (and in Maidstone and Canterbury) was organised by clothiers who dyed their own wools, often worked one loom, occasionally ran a fulling mill or a shearman's shop, but put the bulk of their work out, to weavers with from one to three looms, to master fullers and clothworkers, and to a multitude of spinsters. Weavers rarely had agricultural interests, for they were far too busy in their looms, but the clothiers did, and often occupied capital farms.[141]

Some textile and allied trades were conducted in much the same way almost everywhere. Tapestry hangings, for instance, were always woven in big workshops by large masters and their servants,[142] and so were floor carpets,[143] whereas rug and coverlet weavers worked on their own.[144]

Narrow weavers in London and the suburbs owned anything up to half a dozen or more little table-top looms and so gave work to their own families and to others.[145] Little strength was needed to work these looms, which thus provided a lifeline for all and sundry. 'Many poore children', it is said, were 'sett on worke by the same, and old men likewise have gott theire liveings by workeinge upon the said single loomes and kepte themselves and their families from begginge and ydlenes.'[146] Similar narrow weavers sprang up also in Bristol, Manchester, Knutsford, Chester, Devizes, Leicester and other towns.[147] A few appeared in Norwich and East Norfolk,[148] but more laces and garters were made by master worstedweavers as a sideline, and by journeymen wanting to supplement their wages.[149] Various mixtures of similar arrangements obtained in Maidstone and Goudhurst,[150] Sandwich,[151] and Canterbury.[152] Then came the engine loom. Not long after 1662 large masters appeared in Stepney with from three to ten 'indian loomes' in their workshops and many persons in their employ. The 'Dutch' looms set up in Manchester and in Middlewich and district from 1670 onwards were run by 'gentlemen weavers' with up to a dozen such machines in their workshops.[153]

Apart from a few walkers in the original sense, the majority of fullers were either clothiers or worked as master millers. Either way, fulling mills could not be run without employing a few workmen and most fullers approximated to large masters.[154] So did calendrers.[155] Shearmen and other clothworkers, however, were mostly either servants to clothiers or merchants or else worked in a small way as their own masters. The London Clothworkers' Company resulted from the amalgamation in 1528 of the fullers' and shearmen's guilds, but in reality the bulk of the manual workers were small master shearmen and packers, while the leading members were wholesale cloth merchants, rather like the merchant fullers of Exeter and the merchant shearmen of Kendal.[156]

Adverting now to the allied trades, bonelace making was from the outset conducted on the putting out system. Lacemen supplied thread to be worked up at piece rates by womenfolk and children in cottages, farmhouses, and lace schools.[157] In the making of buttons and button-holes, the needlework and many other tasks also fell to women and children. Men were hardly employed except for fashioning moulds. This business was of the first importance to cottagers and small farmers in the Flash. 'Flashmen' from Macclesfield, Leek, Congleton and Stockport went the rounds of the hill farms selling not only spices and haberdashery but also horse and ox hair, linen thread, moulds and dyestuffs, and buying up completed buttons and holes. But where these were worked in silk and goat's hair, as in Sherborne, the manufacture was carried on by large masters in their workshops, presumably because both materials and products were too valuable to be entrusted to a large number of widely scattered outworkers.[158] (This explanation would seem far fetched to Antwerp merchants putting out diamonds for working and polishing by peasants in Herenthals, but other days, other ways, and the better gem diamonds are not so disposed.) The Maidstone threadtwisters were independent masters using mainly family labour, but some flax was put out to be spun and some yarn to be dyed. Coventry threadmakers worked in much the same way.[159] But ropers needed workmen in their ropewalks.[160] Cappers were usually miniature clothiers who put all their spinning, knitting and fulling out.[161] Most hatters and feltmakers were their own masters. In London the merchant haberdashers of hats co-ordinated the relatively poor trades of cappers, trimmers, feltmakers, hatters, band-makers, feather dressers and so on; but the master feltmakers and hatters were independent and often large masters employing many journeymen and pickers and carders of wool.[162] Likewise the master feltmakers and hatters in Frampton Cotterell and district commonly owned both the hats and the materials they were made of, often employed workmen in their shops, and sometimes ran part-time farms, all of which gave them the status of large masters able to deal on equal terms with the Bristol haberdashers of hats. Similar situations prevailed in Norwich, Worcester and other provincial towns.[163]

North Country knitwear was simply bought up by merchants from knitters who obtained their own wool.[164] Elsewhere hand-knitting was mostly organised by hosiers who put yarns out to women in their own homes, and the knitwear trade was much favoured by widows possessed of the necessary capital. In the late 1650s no fewer than ten of the Leicester stockingers were women and at least two of them were certainly widows.[165] Nevertheless the majority of hosiers were men, because hosiery was usually combined with woolcombing or another man's occupation. East Anglian hosiers were often also combers, dyers, haberdashers, shopkeepers or farmers. Thus we find a large farmer who was at the same time a hosier and a dyer. Some hosiers hereabouts ran extensive businesses. A Bury St Edmunds man put knitting out in his own town, in Mildenhall and in Newmarket; and a Diss hosier had work done for him in Debenham. Hosiers' fortunes obviously varied greatly, largely in accordance with their range of activities. In 1682 a merchant of Great Yarmouth left £613 raised mostly from hosiery and haberdashery. In 1662 a hosier and farmer in Aylsham left just over £900.[166] Knitwear manufacture was organised in a similar way in the district of Coleford, Leigh-upon-Mendip and Shepton Mallet, and hosiers' effects were valued at sums up to about £800.[167] Even in Leicester hosiery was often combined with woolcombing by equally well-to-do men.[168] Elsewhere, too, although they prepared and twisted their own yarns, and did other things besides, all such hosiers had something of the merchant employer about them.[169]

The knitting frame brought great changes. Hosiers now gave out yarns, and ultimately often lent frames, to a relatively small number of master framework knitters, some of whom, especially in the latter half of the seventeenth century, expanded their businesses and developed into large masters with shops housing several frames worked by journeymen. In and around Leicester, Nottingham and Derby, knitters appeared with up to six of their own frames in their own workshops. They took the hosiers' yarns and returned them their knitwear, but were large masters in their own right; and the jersey knitters among them also had their own cows and sheep and up to ten acres of land in the common fields.[170] In Stepney, large masters with sometimes as many as ten frames of their own emerged from the ranks of the silk stocking knitters.[171]

The more successful and affluent of the specialist dyers employed some highly skilled and well paid servants, but only calico printers ran large workshops or factories.[172] Although theirs was a much lowlier occupation, the independent hot-pressers who set up in Exeter, Bristol, Worcester, Kidderminster, Alton and other towns, not least in London, and even alongside the calendrers in Norwich, were master craftsmen of some substance. Their hot-presses alone cost £5 or more each, and they often had cold-presses as well.[173]

Few silk or hair weavers threw any of their own fibres. Organzine silk was all imported throughout most of the period, but specialist throwsters produced tram silk in England and threw nearly all the hair, though some hair yarn was also imported. Throwsters bought silk and hair and had it thrown on their own mills, doubling wheels and bobbins in their own workshops, mainly by female labour. Close supervision was needed both for technical reasons and because silk and hair were expensive relative to their volume and weight and petty larceny was always a danger to be reckoned with. It was a modest workhouse that contained no more than six mills, and since each mill needed one operator, throwsters were in the nature of large masters employing often as many as a dozen or more assistants.[174] Water power, when it came, greatly enlarged the throwster's scale of production.

That journeymen and servant woolcombers were numerous wherever their trade flourished is testified not only by direct references to them but also by the combs, stocks and pots in shops owned by combers, yarnmasters, hosiers, clothiers and other converters who were themselves obviously of too high a

station in life to comb with their own hands.[175] Yet it is unlikely that most of
these journeymen and servants remained employees all their working lives, for
the industry was expanding rapidly, wages were relatively high, and to set up as
a small master was not prohibitively expensive.[176] In some places, notably
Norwich, journeymen and small master combers were roughly equal numerically,[177] reflecting the fact each of the latter needed one of the former as a
workmate.[178] Many such small masters, who undertook nothing beyond the
combing and drawing, were to be found where there were large woolcombers
and yarnmasters with much combing to put out, especially in and about East
Dereham, Bury St Edmunds, Cirencester and Tetbury, and Devizes and
Urchfont;[179] and also in the Woodland, where wealthier clothiers like
Hedgthorn of Coggeshall availed themselves of similar services.[180] Some small
combers made their lives more comfortable, secure and, in view of the nature of
their work, more healthy, by keeping their own house-cows, growing their own
vegetables, fruit, and corn, or buying a birding piece and doing a little
shooting.[181] A few even changed over and made farming their main
occupation.[182] Yet others put money into sale-shops and dealt in such articles as
lace, cloth, hats, linen, hosiery and haberdashery, while still going on
combing.[183] Alternatively, one could buy a little wool, comb it and draw it on
one's own account, have it spun up, by one's own family perhaps, and sell the
yarn. If one could get this yarn twisted or warped before sale, so much the
better.[184] The next step up might be to start in a small way as a dyer of wool or
yarn,[185] or as a serge or baize maker,[186] or as a hosier,[187] simply by putting yarn
out for weaving or knitting. But the most obvious course, and the one that often
brought the greatest rewards, was to buy and comb more and more wool, put it
out to be spun and perhaps twisted and dyed, and sell yarn to manufacturers
and converters, in short, to become a gentleman woolcomber, a woolcomber
and yarnmaster and eventually, it might be, simply a yarnmaster.

Woolcomber-yarnmasters abounded in the Breckland and its environs, in
East Dereham and district, and later in other parts of East Norfolk. Reyce was
not exaggerating when he recounted the great gains to be made from this trade.
In the seventeenth century such men left goods and chattels up to £600 and
more. John Cutting of Bury St Edmunds left £1,591 in 1687 and Samuel Owers
of Tostock £1,332 in 1780.[188] Gentlemen woolcombers and yarnmasters
attained to similar wealth in the Woodland. Nicholas Wells of Lavenham left
£1,659 odd in 1667.[189] Joseph Fishpoole's business at Billericay in 1695–6 was
remarkably large. He ran his own farm, kept his own coach and horses, and left
goods and chattels valued at over £5,000.[190] Thomas Benne, a Colchester man
of Dutch descent who sold baize chains to Sandwich, was, amongst other
things, a brewer, a maltster, and a farmer with lands worth £100 a year.[191] Some
High Suffolk towns, and Ipswich too, had substantial woolcombers and
yarnmen who worked chiefly for the local hosiers.[192] Newbury, Devizes,
Canterbury, Sandwich, and some towns in the Vale of Taunton Deane also had

their yarnmasters.[193] But only one district, that in the south-east of the Cotswold Country, in and around Cirencester and Tetbury, rivalled the Breckland one. Tetbury had some big businesses. Thomas Hill, for instance, left an estate of over £428 in 1697. Cirencester woolcombers and yarnmen frequently left as much or more, not uncommonly between £900 and £1,700. Here, too, the division of labour between woolcombers and yarnmakers became clearly marked,[194] and the concentration of effort patently intense. Unlike their opposite numbers elsewhere, the Cirencester men rarely had money, time or energy to spare for such things as farming, weaving, the grain trade, innkeeping or the purchase of parts in ships.[195]

The market spinners of Devizes, Urchfont and district were akin to yarnmasters, but on a smaller scale. They bought the wool, carded and scribbled it on their own premises, and then had it spun either in their own workhouses or by putting it out. James and William Filkes of Devizes regularly held between £100 and £200 worth of wool and yarn at home or at the spinners', but inventories seldom totalled in excess of £250. However, market spinners were more inclined than were woolcomber-yarnmasters to employ labour on their own premises. Robert Palmer of Devizes had an outhouse equipped with six spinning wheels and eight pairs of cards.[196]

Lastly we come to one of the most important but least recorded group of workpeople: the spinners. A certain amount of spinning was done by children, especially girls. Spinning schools were set up in many towns. Norwich had some by 1570, Aylsham and Reepham by 1622. In 1597 Ipswich appointed 'a good teacher to spyne all kynd of woole'. In 1623 King's Lynn started a worsted spinning school. Ten years later Shrewsbury had a 'jersey schoole'. The usual practice in these schools was probably that followed in Lynn and, incidentally, in modern typing schools: scholars who had received a grounding in the subject were paid fit wages for their work until such time as they became fully proficient. These wages, we venture to guess, were commonly handed over to the parents, just as if the children had been working at home.[197]

Some of the adult spinsters really were self-employed; they worked 'at their own hands'.[198] But the majority were indwelling servants and other womenfolk in the households of farmers and others, or else the wives and daughters of their outdwelling servants, journeymen or day-labourers. It was customary for dairy and house maids to sit down and spin when they had no other work to do. 'Here in England', remarks Yarranton, 'one woman or good housewife hath, it may be, six or eight spinners belonging to her, and at some odd times she spins, and also her children and servants'.[199] In the Chalk Country the wives, daughters and maidservants of family farmers and rural craftsmen undertook some of this work, but most of the carding and spinning was done either by the womenfolk of cottagers and of part-time farmers who went out to work on farms, or by the servants of market spinners or of capital farmers.[200] It was much the same in the Chiltern Country, where yarns were spun for Bury St Edmunds, Reading,

Spitalfields and elsewhere.[201] In High Suffolk[202] and the Woodland[203] much if not most of the wheel spinning was put out to capital farmers. The clothiers were at pains to point out that it was their practice 'to carry our wooll oute to carding and spyning and put it to diverse and sundry spynners who have in their houses diverse and sundry children and servauntes'.[204] In 1622 the complaint was made that 'yeomans and farmers wives of good ability' were procuring for themselves, their children and servants the greater part of the spinning work given out from the packhouses, 'whereby the poor are being deprived of it'.[205] In the Midland Plain, though a little spinning was done on family farms and much more on part-time ones and in graziers' households, by about 1650 spinners outnumbering all the others put together were provided by maid-servants to capital farmers, as can be seen by the inventories of garrets and servants' quarters. Gentlemen and working farmers owned the majority of the spindles at work, and in addition their labourers' womenfolk supplemented family incomes by spinning.[206] Most of the spinners in the Cheese[207] and Butter[208] countries lived on the part-time and poorer family farms, for dairy work pre-occupied other farm households; but then carding and spinning were not much engaged in here, for the yarn used came largely from the Chalk and Cotswold countries. The West Country also imported a good deal of yarn, especially from the Cirencester and Tetbury district, but, with little dairying to do, spinning was the almost universal sideline of the female inhabitants, all, from mistress to maid, being engaged in making yarn for the market.[209] Thus, while most of the spinning and carding in England was done on the putting out system, it was put out less to small masters and people of similar social standing than to capital farmers, who were themselves in the nature of large masters. This situation was somewhat altered from 1658 onwards by the introduction of the jenny for spinning jersey, linen and waste silk, these engines being operated largely by master spinners; but this was a slow and partial change.[210]

In fine, putting out reigned supreme only in such processes as carding, spinning and knitting by hand, which were naturally domestic industries; but it was important also in combing and weaving. Woolcombing was not a highly skilled occupation, and it is difficult to imagine how anyone in those times would have set about building a large shop to house a great number of combpots each with its own flue and chimney. Where weaving was much put out on contract, it was either in order to lop peaks of output or because the work itself was simple enough for the clothier to be content to leave the weavers to their own devices. Although the form of industrial organisation depended to some extent on topographical conditions, as when in hilly countries the early processes were scattered and the later ones concentrated, this form varied principally according to the relative height of the technology employed, always considering the exact time and place. This proposition can hardly be stood on its head by saying that the technology was chosen to suit the locality, for baize weaving was put out in Coventry and calendering in Norwich even though both cities were strongholds of the manufacturing weaver, because striking baize warps was simple and worstedweaving was intricate enough to absorb all the abilities of the worstedweavers. Nor can it be contended that the scale of production determined the form of organisation. The Hartlebury fuller who put his wool out to spinners and his yarn to weavers, and the Bromsgrove clothier who had his spinning, weaving and fulling done on contract, adopted these courses not because they produced on a large scale but because they made coarse cloth.[211] The crucial question was always how rare or widespread the skills were, and this depended mainly on how long they had had to be taught and diffused. It was for this reason that in all 'new manufacture, all sorts of these people are masters in their trade and work for themselves. They buy and sell their materials that they work upon, so that by their merchandise and honest labour they live very well'.[212] In short, everything we learn reinforces and confirms Miss J. de L. Mann's perception: what mattered was whether or not the work had to be done under the master's eye.[213] And even when and where certain processes were put out on contract, it was not to poor, dependent persons so much as to capital farmers and large masters. The exploitation of small masters by merchant employers, the conflict between industrial and commercial capital, and the class struggle, all these exist only in fevered imaginations. There was no 'class division', no classes, only the division of labour, the pursuit of careers open to the talents, and individuals, with all their strengths, weaknesses and peculiarities. Nevertheless, it remains as true as ever it was that in our period, in Unwin's very words, 'The new capital built up was not employed primarily in trading, but in bringing together a greater number of workmen, belonging sometimes to different branches of manufacture, and thus organising industry upon a larger scale.' At the same time, too, 'small masters, whether employed by the large master or the trader' were 'still very numerous', it being 'a fairly easy alternative to the discontented or ambitious journeyman' to set up as his own master. We have actually met the full range of industrial types enumerated by Unwin: the merchant employer, who was both trader and employer; the large master, who was at once employer and foreman; the small master, who combined in himself the functions of foreman and manual worker; and the journeyman or servant. These types personified specialisations arising from the division of labour both within and without particular industries.[214]

Those best suited to being servants, journeymen or small masters received no less benefit from the social division of labour than did anyone else. Working conditions were neither hard nor harsh. Other than Sundays, holidays were few and far between, but people were by no means confined to their workshops throughout the year. All textile and similar work ceased during harvest time, and most textile workers went out to help in gathering in the crops. Whether these were growing on their own land or, more usually, on that belonging to others, harvesting was a gainful occupation. More important, it provided that change that is as good as a rest and the fresh air, sunshine and bodily exercise that promote physical and mental health. In the meantime, large masters had an opportunity to organise any changes in their products or methods of production they might have in mind, and to prepare everything against the time when they could get weaving again. In Norwich a by-law of long standing ordered all worstedweavers to leave off work for a month or so, and the East Norfolk country weavers always had at least five weeks off, by order. But the exact length of this 'leaving weaving', as it was called, depended on how long it took to get the harvests in. On 14 September 1610, harvesting not yet being finished and the spinners not back at work, the worstedweavers decided not to resume before the 20th. In 1553 weaving was forbidden for eight weeks from 14 August.[215] In 1631 the dornicksweavers fixed their leaving weaving for the six weeks from 8 August to 18 September. To make sure the looms were duly silenced, all the headles and warps were fastened with lead seals.[216] The city imposed similar regulation on the Flemings here, and those in Colchester also had compulsory vacations.[217] Something of the kind was universally practised.

Terms of service were advantageous to servants. No woollen weaver, fuller, clothworker, shearman or dyer might be taken into service for a term of less than one whole year, and undue departures and dismissals were liable to penalty.[218] Furthermore, justices of peace usually interpreted the statute to mean masters were bound to keep on full pay until the end of the year all servants who became sick or disabled, other than by insanity, while in their service. If the worst came to the worst, the justices would see to it that the sick and disabled were relieved.[219] Servants might change masters in mid-term, provided they left no cloth unfinished at the old master's and the new master undertook to compensate the old for any financial loss entailed.[220] Although woolcombers and other textile workers not specifically mentioned in it were not protected by this Statute of Artificers in 1563, they were all formally brought under it in 1603.[221]

Of journeymen's terms of employment we know little. Amongst the rules for woolcombers provisionally approved in Canterbury in 1599 was one forbidding the employment of men dismissed for drunkenness or evil living, and another stipulating that a fortnight's notice of termination of engagement be given by either side.[222] But this single item of information is not much to go on.

We assume journeymen's and servants' total real earnings were roughly equal. Since day-labourers in husbandry may well have lost more days than textile journeymen, it signifies little that in Devon in 1654 weavers' wage rates were assessed at 8d a day and labourers' at 11d.[223] But no such difficulty arises with respect to servants. One need not accept the belief that assessed rates bore a close relation to actual rates of pay (though not to real earnings), in order to be able to agree that the relative assessments for textile and agricultural servants reflected their relative positions in the labour markets. Thus it can hardly be entirely insignificant that the lowest category of carter or servant in husbandry in Wiltshire and Essex (and so in the West of England and Woodland districts) was assessed at from £2 to £4 a year when common weavers and other textile workmen were only allowed from 26s 8d to 38s. It would seem that wages were higher in agriculture than in textiles.[224] In the Wealden Vales, however, these positions were reversed,[225] and in the West Riding in 1647 there was nothing between them.[226] It is thus perhaps no mere coincidence that textile manufactures grew in the other districts, but not in the Wealden Vales. Beyond these tentative conclusions it would be foolhardy to venture far. Until 1603 the rates assessed were maxima and rarely took full account of payments in kind. Yet the impression that farm wages were higher than textile ones in the agriculturally propserous parts of England as a whole is somewhat strengthened by other observations. According to the Venetian ambassador in 1557, many Englishmen ate five or six times a day, and more of flesh than anything else. Farm workers may not have been so fortunate, but they usually ate well.[227] However, the old saws that the herring was the 'Yarmouth capon' and sprats 'the weavers beef of Colchester' faintly suggest poor textile workers sometimes fared less well than the general run of people.[228] And when John Aubrey said, 'Our cloathiers . . . keep their spinners but just alive', he may have had in mind other textile workers as well. Then there is Blome's remark, 'Only in the clothing-woodlands many are brought to poverty'.[229] This probably alludes to the partial dependence of textile workers on overseas markets liable to disruption by wars. During such stands in trade, clothing workers had little or nothing to fall back on; few saved for a rainy day and most had hardly any land and had to buy their own food.

We are on slightly firmer ground when we assert English textile workers were generally better off than Continental ones. Aubrey thought the Dutch and French worked more cheaply. Munn found the French workers' standard of living a third lower than the English. Defoe roundly declared, 'The working manufacturing people of England eat the fat, and drink the sweet, live better and fare better than the working poor of any nation in Europe. They make better wages of their work, and spend more of the money upon their backs and bellies than in any other country.' English textile manufacturers, he goes on, 'not only employ more people, but those people gain the most money, that is to say, have the best wages for their work of any people in the world.' Elsewhere he enlarges on this topic, one of his favourites, saying of textile workmen in England,[230]

> They eat well, and they drink well; for their eating, (viz.) of flesh meat, such as beef, mutton, bacon, etc. and in proportion to their circumstances, 'tis to a fault, nay, even to profusion; as to their drink, 'tis generally stout strong beer, not to take notice of the quantity, which is sometimes a little too much, or good table beer for their ordinary diet; for the rest we see their houses and lodgings tolerably furnished, at least stuff'd well with useful and necessary household goods: even those we call poor people, journey-men, working and pains-taking people, do thus; they lye warm, live in plenty, work hard, and (need) know no want.

Even if Defoe were carried away by his enthusiasm, he would have lost all credit had he been grossly inaccurate about a matter of common observation. Extraordinary interruptions and stands of trade apart, we believe his description substantially correct.

Of all these workpeople, the woolcombers seem to have been the best off. Their services were usually in great demand. If a shortage of jobs developed in one town, there were always fresh fields to be opened up. Thus the first sergemakers in Kettering and district attracted woolcombers from Coggeshall and Halstead, from Cirencester and Colerne, from Taunton and North Petherton, from Romsey, and from Chulmleigh away in the West Country.[231] In 1662 in Coggeshall a servant comber, over twenty-four years of age, combing and drawing daily five pounds of warp wool, had his wages assessed at £5 a year, plus 10s livery, the same as for a best weaver of fine cloth or best servant clothier, and only 10s less than for a second-class hind, carter or servant in husbandry.[232] In 1630 in the Breckland and the north of the Woodland, woolcombers' servants had their wages assessed at £2 a year, with livery extra, which came to 10s more than weavers' servants were allowed. Journeymen woolcombers working at piece-rates were assessed at 1d a lb. if single, 2d if married. This meant their earnings approximated to those of servants.[233]

Journeymen and servants were not the only people to work for wages; many small masters also did so. Wiltshire wage assessments distinguish between servants or workmen serving by the year and weavers and others working by the piece, Essex ones between weavers and combers paid by the year and 'householders kembing or drawing by task' or householder weavers working by the piece. Weavers' rates were sometimes assessed by the number of portees or ends in the warp and of strikes or picks in the weft; but in practice the weight and size of the threads were of no less importance, so such assessed rates could hardly be enforced, and the Essex justices sensibly set the rate at what the weaver and clothier could agree upon.[234]

When trade came to a standstill, the covenant servant was much better placed than the journeyman or small master. Journeymen might be laid off work at short notice and any master might learn of a complete failure of orders and be left with nothing but the payments due for work in hand. When the Woodland clothiers returned from seeing the Duke of Suffolk in 1525 to tell the people they could provide no work, covenant servants were not immediately affected.[235] When two or three hundred women made suit to the Duke of Norfolk in 1529 'to have the clothiers to set them, their husbandes and chylderne on work', it was day and piece work they mostly had in mind.[236] In 1586 it was the poorer sort wont to live by spinning, carding and working wool at piece and daily rates who were left without employment.[237] When, about 1620, clothiers were commanded to keep on work people they had summarily dismissed, these cannot have been yearly servants. Required to maintain employment for one month, the clothiers could only see their way clear to do so for a fortnight.[238] In the West of England district some of the greatest distress was felt by weavers who lacked work for their own looms.[239] Much the same situation obtained in the Woodland and elsewhere.[240] No mention is made of servants under contract; unemployment was not rife among them. Similar misfortunes beset the Woodland and the Chalk Country and environs during the hard times of 1629–31,[241] and the West Country in 1639.[242] In the depression from 1711 to 1749 the loudest complaints in Colchester and the West of England district came from weavers working at piece-rates; they were short of orders and the rates were lowered on what work they could get.[243]

In periods of dearth, too, covenant servants suffered least. When we are told in 1595, 'Sondrie workefolkes with their famelies with sondrie poor artificers (depending uppon the clothiers) are like to be verie much distressed by reason the clothiers in this time of dearth do not anie thing increase their wages', we are inclined to believe these unfortunates either worked by the day or the piece, or, possibly, were yearly servants dwelling out and not in receipt of livery.[244] Indwelling servants may have been on short commons during dearths, but then most people were. Such servants had no complaint and no expectation of any variation in their wages. Nor had outdwelling servants if supplied with meat and drink. Not many were, however, and most could only pass unscathed through a dearth if they had saved part of their salaries. Even then, a prolonged dearth effectually lowered their real wages. Nevertheless, those who suffered most were probably true journeymen and piece-workers, living as they did from hand to mouth and 'their humour being such that they will not provide for a hard time, but just work so much, and no more, as may maintain them in that mean condition to which they have been accustomed'. This seems a rather sweeping generalisation; there was probably a minority of thrifty poor then as now. The fact remains that when corn was cheap, clothiers found labour dear, bad and hardly to be come by. It was in the dear years for corn that work was best and cheapest done.[245]

When dearth coincided with a standstill in trade, small masters and journeymen, working at their own hands as they did, found themselves in dire straits. In the years 1629–31 Colchester and Woodland weavers were said either to have been paid 7d or 8d less for weaving a baize or compelled to weave longer baizes for the same money. In Coggeshall the poorer ones were on the verge of starvation. In Bocking they could neither pay their rents nor lay in a stock of wood for the winter. In many towns people were forced to sell not only their beds but also their wheels and other tools of trade, 'many hundreds of them havinge no bedds to lye in, nor foode but from hand to mouth'. Had they not been paid weekly or even daily, many would have perished.[246] Such things were not seen in Defoe's day.

In hard times like these, in 1586, in the 1620s, and in 1629–31, the Privy Council took to intervening and compelling the clothiers to keep their outworkers on at the due and accustomed wages;[247] and those who were not kept on constituted the greater part of the burden on the poor rates.[248] Such situations were likewise unknown to Defoe.[249]

It would thus appear that Defoe's glowing descriptions of the standards of living of English workmen are not fully applicable to outworkers or to times other than his own. The abatement of dearths and commercial standstills was undoubtedly one of the principal means by which the lives of the poor were made more secure and comfortable.

In at least one respect, however, workers by the day and the piece continued to be at a disadvantage: they lived under the threat of being paid in truck. Wherever and whenever textile, hosiery, lace and other trades had such wage rates determined outside the individual firm, either by collective bargaining between associated employers and employees or by guild, municipal or parliamentary regulation, firms struggling to exist had recourse to paying small masters and others in truck; and in bad trading times many clothiers with large unsold surpluses took refuge in this expedient. No amount of legislation or law enforcement ever eradicated this evil, for driving the payer of truck out of business only worsened the financial positions of the payees and made them all the more agreeable to being paid in truck by someone else. Amongst the recipients of truck we find at various times Southampton spinners and Colchester baize weavers; but by the very nature of things it is unlikely that more than a small fraction of such occurrences ever came to light.[250]

In some ways, then, small masters were worse off than servants. Just what life was like for the small master and his family is difficult to reconstruct, but some idea can be gained from an admittedly later but first-hand description of the home life of a Spitalfields broad silk weaver. The children were given no schooling. As soon as they could talk they were taught to wind quills, and as soon as they were big enough to sit in a loom they were set to weaving. As their mother also wove, meals normally consisted of bread and perhaps a red herring or a bit of cheese, except for the cooked dinner on Sunday. When the children started weaving, their father gave it up. He kept the loom in repair, supervised the work, and took the finished goods to the warehouse. But most of the time, according to the children, 'he was out talking with other men'. One child relates, 'Sometimes I used to get fidgety and want to get up and move about. To prevent this father used to tie me down to the loom in the morning, before he went out, and dare me to leave it till he came back. I have often been tied to the loom all day and eaten my meals as I sat there.' When the chance came to work in a factory, the children felt themselves much better off: 'In the factory we had regular wages, which made us feel very proud.'[251] It would be absurd to suppose all small masters' families were treated thus; for one thing, women and children could only weave light materials like silk, bunting, or narrow ware. Still, it is well known that children of ten years of age, and sometimes of five or six years, were put to work by their parents at such light tasks as spinning, winding, burling, knitting, and weaving lace.[252]

Spinners were in a special position. Those who put wool out to be spun often had to deal largely not with poor spinsters but with working or gentlemen farmers or others who were their equals or betters. Nor do independent spinsters seem to have been in an inferior bargaining position. We read of plenty of spinsters getting a living at their own hands.[253] On one extraordinary occasion we hear the clothiers of Godalming, Farnham and Wanborough complaining they 'can get no spinners in the summer time when they should do most good in their trade' because woadmen are competing for their services and 'the spinsters are occupied in and about the said oade, wherewith they seem to be better pleased then with spinning'.[254] The point is, spinsters had a wide range of other possible employments such as harvesting, picking fruit, gardening, knitting and lacemaking, and were far from being at the mercy of the clothier, the market spinner or the yarnman. The impression gained is that people who wanted spinning done had perforce to compete for spinsters' services and often to seek far afield for them. There had once been a time when East Anglian woolcomber-yarnmasters had been unable to expand fast enough to give work to all who wanted to spin for them, but this was a passing phase[255] and in 1629 spinners employed by the yarnmen supplying Norwich had the whip hand to such an extent that none dared reproach them for bad work or short measure. Then the weavers deplore that the yarnmen 'take advantage of the spinners fraud by their owne neclect out of supposed streight of tyme which themselves may inlarge and their diligence by tymely search easily prevent'. But an impartial report says the yarnmasters[256]

> themselves, in regards of the multitude they sett on worke, and there spinners repayring unto them at one instant of tyme to bringe home there worke, in regarde of there carrying of them to there markitt at Norwich, are impossibilited to search and looke into ther severall worke before the sale of them; as alsoe that there threatning them to putt them out of there worke little or nothing prevailed with them, they usually answering that yf they worke not for them they may for others.

It was more or less the same everywhere. In the West of England in 1639, 'The clothyers confess that the spinners that nowe spinne to them doe abuse them in sophistcating theire yarne'.[257]

Giving short measure was the commonest fraud. When yarns were sold by weight, borough yarn beams and yarn weighers often afforded the customer some protection.[258] But the chief difficulty was met by yarnmasters and clothiers who put wool out for spinning. Where pasture wool was spun, the reel staff was often the metewand, and this was the occasion of some serious disputes between yarnmasters and worstedweavers. In large towns where spinners and converters were in close contact, the solution to such problems was usually found in introducing the clock-reel. This clocked up the number of turns made by the reel as the yarn was wound on to it. Clock-reels were already in use in Norwich in 1584.[259] and in Coventry in 1599.[260] The worstedweavers tended to favour the clock-reel and the yarnmasters sale by weight. In the end, after a meeting in Bury St Edmunds at which both sides were represented by learned counsel, and after a hearing by the Privy Council, it was agreed in 1630 that yarnmasters should continue selling by the reel staff of one yard about, each staff having on it a dozen of worsted, i.e. fourteen leas of eighty yards, each lea having forty threads. This method had the advantage of simplicity. Any country spinner could provide himself with a reel staff, which was just a length of wood with two iron pins driven in half a yard apart, so that each wind about came to one yard.[261] In 1633 Ireland, and in 1671 Kidderminster, adopted similar courses for their linen yarns.[262] Sad to relate, however, nothing ever put a stop to spinners cheating by reeling short.[263] Being paid a penny for each six or seven double knot or knotch of yarn on the yard reel,[264] they were tempted to shorten down the distance between the pins. Conversely, when trade was bad in 1631, some yarnmasters and clothiers increased the distance by a sixth or even a fifth, whereupon the spinners called for a re-assessment of their rates of pay, to which the Cambridgeshire justices responded by raising them by slightly more than a sixth, to a penny for six double knots, while their opposite numbers in Suffolk and Essex signified their willingness to conform, provided only that everyone else did and that everyone used the same length of reel.[265]

Disputes may have been fewer where yarn was weighed, but rates of pay were no less complicated, varying as they did from one type of yarn to another. At one time, for example, spinsters were paid 4$d$ a lb. for yarn for 'Reading' kerseys and from 6$d$ to 1$s$ for that for 'Devonshire' ones.[266] In parts of the West of England district, in the period 1602–5, spinners had assessed rates of 2$d$ a lb. for warp and 1½$d$ for abb yarn for cloths pitched at 700, 2½$d$ and 1½$d$ respectively when for cloths of 800 but less than 900, 2¾$d$ and 1¾$d$ for 900s, 3½$d$ and 2$d$ for 1,000s, and 4$d$ and 2½$d$ for 1,100s or higher. A similar scale, with a top rate of 3$d$, seems to have been in operation in 1593.[267] In 1588 and again in 1676 West Riding spinsters earned from 1½$d$ to 2¼$d$ a lb. according to the type of yarn.[268]

Scores of widely differing kinds and grades of yarn were spun in various places[269] and rates of pay were calculated one way and another, so even if we knew how much spinning was done by particular individuals it would still be impossible to work out average earnings at any one time or period. West Riding spinsters seem to have earned from 2$d$ to 4$d$ a day. In 1636 it was said to be possible to get up to 4$s$ a week spinning for the Canterbury weavers. According to Defoe, Woodland spinsters could make 9$s$ a week when their services were in great demand.[270] If the Canterbury figure seems rather low, this is probably because by that date the influx of Turkey hair yarns had spoiled matters for the worsted and jersey spinners there.[271] Rough spinning for coarse cloth would seem to have brought in about 3$d$ a day when fine spinning brought in about 9$d$. But even half a noble a week, a mark a month, was a comfortable living for a single person, living alone and paying for a cottage. In practice, by no means all spinsters were in this situation; many lived in families. It must be remembered, however, that only a minority of women took up spinning as a wholetime occupation, and that many spinsters worked for masters or mistresses as yearly servants and received no extra payment for spinning. In the end, the only safe generalisation that can be made is that spinning was profitable.

Immigrant workpeople were generally worse off than the English. Colchester people said the strangers paid insufficient wages. English weavers in London accused them of 'frugalitye and cheape liveing', and so of unfair competition.[272] Certainly, they 'pestered' houses in London and Stepney by living one family to a room, and things were similar in Canterbury.[273] Indeed, they could hardly have been otherwise. The English only accepted the immigrants on the understanding they were Christian refugees from papal oppression, and considered this acceptance an act of generosity. The Flemish immigrants were aliens and treated as such. They were not allowed to enter into formal apprenticeships, nor to employ more than two alien servants apiece.[274] They might not follow any trade nor do any job that any native had previously engaged in locally, except only to provide baking, tailoring and a few other services of their own traditional kinds to their own fellows. No alien might become a burgess or citizen. None might be a retailer, nor sell wholesale any but his own products, and then only to fellow strangers, or in other boroughs or cities, or overseas.[275] Strangers were permitted to settle only in certain specified boroughs, cities and liberties, and then only when some of their number introduced new inventions. They received no protection from statutes governing apprenticeship, terms of employment or rates of pay. No agreement they made among themselves concerning such matters was enforcable by law.[276] They were allowed no relief from the poor rate; yet they had to contribute to all church and poor rates in the parishes they dwelt in, and at the same time were held responsible for relieving their own poor and for maintaining their own ministers. In addition to paying all the usual borough or city rates for watch and ward, for walls, gates and other works, and for special contributions for wars and other emergencies, they were liable to pay 'foreign' fines to the municipalities. In Canterbury their looms were taxed, and everywhere their cloths.[277] For customs purposes they received the same treatment as all other aliens and paid heavier duties on both imports and exports. When the Silk Office was set up, they paid heavier taxes to that. In 1622 they were compelled to pay a special tax, equivalent to half the customs outward, on all their inland trade. In that year, too, unapprenticed stranger dyers were subjected to an extra tax.[278] It may be that these later exactions were intended to fall mainly on newly arrived Huguenot immigrants, but no kind of alien was expressly exempted from them. All strangers, too, were assessed at higher rates for subsidies, shipping money, musters money and other extraordinary contributions to the Crown.[279] Immigrants, then, paid roughly twice as much as the English by way of local and state taxes. It should not be thought the English people were, in general, unkind to the strangers. Buildings were put at their disposal for sale halls and church houses and dwellings were found for them. Queen Elizabeth gave alms from her privy purse to relieve the Dutch and Walloon poor. The city of Norwich also gave generously to the same cause.[280] In later times, the Huguenots were assisted no less amply.[281] Nevertheless, the English people regarded England as their own country, just as the Dutch and Walloons thought of the Netherlands as theirs, as they showed by donations for the relief of their fellow countrymen remaining there and for the upkeep of the fighting forces they hoped would liberate their homeland and make possible their return to it.[282] All things considered, it must be concluded that the immigrants generally tended to live less well than Englishmen in the same station in life. Their opportunities were fewer and their outgoings heavier. In 1589 many of the Norwich strangers could not afford to indulge in 'leaving weaving', and some were again exempted for the same reason in 1616. In Colchester, too, although the Dutch Bay Hall ordered vacations in the usual way, they were not always enforced as strictly as they might have been. Indeed, in 1715, their piece-rates having been lowered, the baize weavers demanded the cancellation of the whole of the August vacation.[283]

Finally, let us remember that in those days people were free to live their own lives. Even the humblest workman, weaver or spinner was at liberty to choose for whom to work.[284] Anyone could become a clothier if he had the abilities. 'He might commence operations at any point in the multiple business of clothmaking.'[285] Peter Blundell was a poor Tiverton lad who earned a living running errands for carriers, looking after their horses and doing them various little services. He saved up, bought a single kersey, found a carrier who owed him a good turn, and got him to carry it up to London for him gratis and to pay him what it fetched. After having thus for some time exchanged services with the carrier, Blundell at length bought a horseload of kerseys and took them to London himself. Then he started to perform this service for local clothiers until he was able to set up in manufacturing for himself. Honesty, industry and enterprise carried him from poverty to riches and enabled him to found Blundell's School and to leave £100 to the poor of Tiverton, £5 each to the two men who wove kerseys for him continually, and £50 to the carrier who took his packs to London.[286] It was this freedom to rise that made the lot of the small master worth enduring. His life was far from easy, but he was sustained by independence and responsibility and by the hope of rising in the world. Weavers, clothworkers, overseers and servants, all saw opportunity beckoning. Weavers saved money, added loom to loom, bought houses, and either set themselves up as clothiers or saw their sons do so. It was harder to rise during slumps and easier during booms, but sooner or later opportunity would present itself and perchance be seized.[287]

# 15

## SALES

The main provincial cloth markets were centres for the fulling and finishing trades. Wholesalers like the Norwich grocers,[1] the Tiverton and Exeter fullers,[2] the Shrewsbury drapers,[3] the Kendal shearmen, and cloth merchants of Rochdale, Manchester, Leeds, and other towns,[4] bought semi-finished goods and sold them wholly or nearly finished. In addition, some of these and other towns served as entrepôts for textile wares destined for more distant markets. Thus Maidstone had a kersey market, and Ipswich, Sudbury and Bury St Edmunds were cloth marts for the smaller towns roundabout them.[5]

Cross-country and coastal trade was extensively engaged in. Exeter sent many cloths to ports on the south coast. Okehampton manufacturers made some sales in Bridport, and Culmstock ones in Bridgwater and Taunton.[6] From the Butter Country cloths went to Weymouth and Lyme Regis, from the Cheese Country to Bristol, Salisbury, Blandford and Dorchester, from the Chalk Country to Southampton.[7] Some Kidderminster stuff went straight to Worcester, and from here textiles were sent down the Severn to Bristol.[8] Stroudwater cloths occasionally went by direct sale to Ireland.[9] It was not unknown for Woodland clothiers to sell their cloths to a merchant in Taunton.[10] Provincial fairs attracted a great deal of trade. Maidstone had a 'shew of brodeclothes' at her Candlemas, May and St Faith's fairs.[11] The Tombland Fair that opened in Norwich every Good Friday attracted buyers from as far away as Ripon and Newcastle-on-Tyne. Stourbridge Fair, held at Casterton near Cambridge in September, lasted three weeks and in part resembled a makeshift Blackwell Hall, where cloths from all parts of the kingdom were bought and sold wholesale. An Ipswich merchant by name of Henry Blois came here and bought Needham kerseys and some perpetuanas, which he dispatched by road to London for sale.[12] Selling at fairs seems to have been a good way for outsiders to get a first foothold in the market. Stroudwater cloths of the improved kind were on sale at country fairs for some ten years before the London merchants took them up.[13] Yet another type of cross-country trade was practised by travelling salesmen. The 'Manchester men' not only sold direct to such places as Chester, Liverpool and Hull; some became, 'saving their wealth, a kind of pedlars', as Defoe calls them. They carried their goods to country shopkeepers' 'Manchester houses' everywhere. In 1590 John Cocke of Cocke Bank in Hartshead in

Ashton-under-Lyne was astride his mare and leading his nine packhorses loaded with friezes to Bury St Edmunds, Dereham, Norwich, Spalding, Walsingham, Wymondham and down Watling Street as far south as Dunstable. Edward Ellor of Manchester made the rounds of Kendal, Wigan, Heptonstall, Worcester, Gloucester, Bristol, Sherborne and Salisbury. Kendal packhorse men took cloth to sell in Chester and all along the road to Southampton, and brought back figs, raisins of the sun, madder, woad, alum and canvas, the round trip taking about a month. Some West Riding men adopted similar practices.[14] In somewhat the same way, alien dealers in Canterbury, Norwich and Sandwich wares supplied sale-shops in London and Westminster simply by going from door to door.[15]

Nevertheless, the main stream of trade was through the normal wholesale channels to London. Clothiers in a small way of business were especially inclined to sell in places like Sudbury and Maidstone, but all the more substantial manufacturers and dealers in the Woodland and Wealden towns sold most of their wares straight to London.[16] After the middle of the sixteenth century, when the Venetian, Genoese and Spanish merchants had deserted Southampton, clothiers and serge and drugget makers throughout the Chalk Country,[17] like similar manufacturers in the Cheese and Butter countries and the Vale of Berkeley,[18] made the great majority of their sales in London. Weavers and merchants in Canterbury and Sandwich sent fabrics to London by common carriers on land and sea.[19] The greater part of the cloths made in the Peak-Forest Country and the Kendal district found their way to the City.[20] So did Witney blankets,[21] Taunton serges and Culm valley Spanish cloths.[22] Many, perhaps most, of the kerseys and perpetuana-serges marketed in Tiverton and Exeter were subsequently sold in London.[23] It was to the metropolis that Worcester, Bromsgrove, Kidderminster, Coventry and Shrewsbury dispatched the bulk of their goods.[24] Thither went the greatest part of Norwich and East Norfolk textile and hosiery wares.[25] Honiton sent weekly consignments of bonelace up to Town, and Shepton Mallet and district stockings and other knitwear.[26] Provincial manufacturers and London merchants sought out each other. By 1518, for example, some Londoners were making annual excursions to the various provincial towns to place their orders.[27]

Although London had the densest concentration of consumers in the British Isles, she became the great centre for commerce in textiles, hosiery and allied products primarily by virtue of distributing them within and without the kingdom. Having reviewed the various textile regions of England, Defoe goes on to say,

> All these send the gross of their quantity to London, and receive each other's sorts in retail for their own use again. Norwich buys Exeter serges, Exeter buys Norwich stuffs, all at London. Yorkshire buys fine cloths, and Gloucester coarse, still at London; and the like of a vast variety of our manufactures.

He by no means exaggerated, Norwich purchased Kentish broadcloths, Devon dozens, Hampshire, Newbury and northern kerseys, Bridgwaters, Manchester cottons, Welsh friezes and much besides. Other textile towns drove similar trades.[28] Textiles, knitwear and the like streamed in and out of London by packhorse, cart, wagon, ship, barge, lighter and all known means of transport. Some fabrics went by sea, as in the packet boats that carried baizes, says, serges and perpetuanas from Wivenhoe to London; some by river, as along the Yare and the Severn; and most of them by road, and largely by regular carrier services to and from London.[29] In an economic sense, each commodity had one single nationwide market. Irrespective of whether they passed through London or were transported cross-country, all goods sold at London prices, give or take the cost of carriage; and London was the head and heart of a congeries of all these metropolitan markets.

In London, cloths were sold at Bartholomew's Fair in West Smithfield.[30] Otherwise the stipulated place of sale for carded woollens was Blackwell Hall in Basinghall Street. It was open for sales from Thursday noon until Saturday morning. In the hall, clothiers and dealers could trade directly with members of the clothworkers', drapers', mercers' and other companies, and with merchants who adventured capital in overseas traffic. After several annexes failed to suffice, the hall was entirely rebuilt in 1588, only to be soon outgrown, so Leadenhall was also brought into use, unofficially in 1622, officially in 1638. In 1631, too, and again after the Restoration, Blackwell Hall itself was extended.[31] Even so, the halls were now dealing with such huge numbers of cloths that a wholly pitched market was out of the question. As it happened, it was also undesirable. By 1518 cloths were usually bought either 'in the contre and the skantlyns takyn or sealed by the byer', or beforehand by indenture on terms 'agreed for accordyng to skantlyns or samples by the same parties to be consented and agreed', or on sheer trust and without any earnest payment, or by the merchant and his supplier covenanting for future deliveries. Cloths bought in any of these ways might be delivered straight to the merchant's warehouse without going near the halls. If, however, the merchant refused to accept cloths on grounds of quality, then these rejects had to go to the hall. Thus most cloths were not pitched in the halls, only warehoused, and were not searched in open hall by officials, but by the merchant's servants in private, or not at all, trust being placed in a swatch or scantling and the clothier's word, with the right reserved to return or exchange faulty goods. Christ's Hospital, which was the ultimate recipient of the hall fees, acknowledged these business practices, saying,[32] the parties

> doe make contracts for the said clothes etc. in the countery and bring them afterwards to London unto innes and warehouses and other places, to bee there sould, or to be transported into forraigne parts, or retayled in the Citty, without bringing the same to the publique marketts to be searched and viewed, upon pretence that the same were not brought to London to be sould.

To take one specific instance, there was an agreement between a Cranbrook clothier and a London merchant by which the latter paid £40 at the sealing of the contract for four coloured cloths to be delivered unless the clothier repaid the money on a certain date 'at or within the shopp of John Rolfe scrivenor' on the Cornhill.[33] The next stage in market development replaced sales to merchants by sales through factors. Clothiers simply committed wares to factors to sell on their behalf. Some members of the Clothworkers' Company were first off the mark; they could easily set up as factors, since they prepared cloths for sale and had all the right contacts. Moreover, with the triumph of Spanish cloths, which came to London ready dressed, there was little other than factoring for substantial clothworkers to turn their hands to.[34] Yet it was not mainly from clothworkers that the factors emerged, but from the clerks, porters and other minor hall functionaries. They simply took to working on the side, storing goods for future sale, complying with the regulations by having the necessary entries made in the hall books, seeing to the paperwork, cutting through the red tape, and generally fixing things for the clothiers, and finally selling for them.[35]

Similar developments occurred in all branches of the textile trade. Norwich (and thereby Lynn and all East Norfolk) worsteds and stuffs had always been excused hallage in London. They were searched and sealed in Norwich and that was the end of the matter. Fabrics of all kinds were bought up by Norwich merchants, put out to be shorn, calendered and dyed as required, and then stored for sale by them 'in there innes, in close chambers and corners'. The Norwich merchants sold some cloths through factors overseas, in Amsterdam for example, but far more to London factors and merchants who usually ordered by post from patterns. Later, in the early seventeenth century, some worstedweavers took to selling through London factors.[36] Although directed to sell in Leadenhall, Colchester baize and say manufacturers were temped to take a leaf out of the Norwich book and often sold privately to merchants or through factors and consigned the goods to warehouses and inns in London. The Bell Inn in Gracechurch Street seems to have been a favourite store for baizes.[37] Canterbury and Sandwich goods, and later Bolton and district fustians, were handled in much the same way. The London weaver could justly complain in 1595 that the 'Canterbury and Sandwich brokers have put his nose (as the proverbe is) quite out of joynte'.[38] Specialist hosiery factors also sprang up.[39]

Hall factors were already conspicuous by 1607; by 1671 they handled nearly all the sales. By 1615 their ways had become common knowledge. They sold for the manufacturers and supplied them with dyestuffs and other materials, including wool (especially Spanish and blended wools), linen yarn, silk, cotton wool and hair. Clothiers had always given 'day' or credit to the merchants, allowing them a fortnight or so's credit and receiving payment on account of previous deliveries when making new ones. These were mostly book credits; specialities were not usually entered into. Now, when dealing through factors, the clothiers had to await payment, but the sums owing to them were partly cancelled out by the price of the goods the factors supplied them with. In the normal course of events the balance was in the clothier's favour, allowing him to draw on the factor by bill of exchange.[40] Another result of the rise of the factors was that wholesale drapers in Shrewsbury, Manchester and elsewhere no longer needed to keep a partner in London.[41]

The rise of the warehouseman and the factor was part and parcel of a general abandonment of pitched for sample markets and of halls in favour of inns and warehouses. Kerseys were no longer brought to the market hall under the sessions house in Maidstone in 1610, 'but sold in innes and other howses'. In Exeter most serges came to be warehoused and sold privately.[42] In fine, provincial manufacturers gradually stopped selling their goods in London and so escaped all regulation of sales there. Either the goods went to London only after having been sold to a merchant, or they were indeed sold in London, but by a factor, not by the makers.

As the Blackwell Hall factors acknowledged in 1674, textiles were exported not only from London, but also from ports near the seats of manufacture.[43] Canterbury and Sandwich merchants exported says, baizes and other local fabrics to France and the Low Countries. Rye also sent out baizes, cottons and kerseys.[44] Colchester[45] and Ipswich[46] exported Suffolk cloths, baizes, says, serges and shalloons mostly. King's Lynn and Great Yarmouth handled some of these and also a few worsteds and Norwich stuffs.[47] Southampton shipped plains, cottons, kerseys, medleys, baizes, says and serges;[48] Lyme Regis and Weymouth cottons, baizes, and 'Dorset' dozens;[49] Hull northern kerseys, 'Yorkshire' cloths and Rochdale baizes;[50] Chester and Bristol cottons;[51] Exeter, Plymouth, Dartmouth and Bridport kerseys, serges, perpetuanas and Spanish cloths.[52] Not all these exports were made by merchants belonging to the ports they went out of. An Ipswich merchant exported baize from Plymouth and a Taunton man stamins from Topsham.[53] Despite all, the port of London was paramount. Early in the sixteenth century getting on for half of English woollen exports went out from there, in the 1540s perhaps as much as three quarters, and in the 1660s probably no less.[54]

The main overseas markets for different fabrics can just be made out through the mist. West-of-England whites were ultimately bound mainly for Germany and Central Europe, to a smaller extent for the Low Countries. Kentish cloths went to the Low Countries, Germany, Italy and Spain; Suffolks, Stroudwaters and other coloured cloths to the Eastland, Russia, and Mediterranean countries and the Levant; cottons and friezes to France and the Mediterranean chiefly, but also to Germany, the Low Countries and New England; Hampshire and northern kerseys to Poland, Germany, Hungary, Italy, the Levant and beyond, as well as to France and the Netherlands; the best Devon dozens to Spain and the Indies, the middle sort to the Low Countries, and a few of the worst to France; Godalming kerseys to the Canaries; and Dorset dozens, penwiths and similar cheap cloths to Brittany, Lower Normandy, Madeira, the Canaries and the Azores.[55] After 1620 West-of-England whites, often dyed and finished in Coventry, went to the Levant and to India, where they were occasionally used for vests, cloaks and mantles, but more frequently for floor coverings, soft furnishings, elephant blankets, prayer mats and the like.[56] 'Leeds' woollens of the 'new drapery' found markets in the Levant and the Eastland.[57] In earlier times Spanish cloth generally sold well in Holland, but by 1664 the best markets were being reached through Hamburg and Ostend, and by 1685 France was probably the biggest buyer.[58] More particularly, Spanish medleys sold well in Mediterranean and Levantine countries, in the Netherlands and in the Eastland.[59] Baizes went to the Low Countries, Germany, Italy, Spain, Portugal, North Africa, South America, the West and East Indies, in a word, to all the world.[60] Along with Norwich and Canterbury stuffs, says, serges, shalloons, flannels, knit stockings and Spanish cloth, they found their way to Holland, Zealand, Brabant, Flanders, Naples, Rome, Venice, Leghorn, Florence, Spain, Portugal, Scandinavia, the Baltic countries and Virginia.[61] Perpetuanas went everywhere, including India, but especially to the Mediterranean lands, Latin America and Africa.[62] Druggets sold best in Flanders, Brabant, Germany, Italy, Spain, Portugal, the Americas and the Indies.[63] What broad silks were exported went mainly to Germany, Portugal, the West Indies and the American colonies.[64]

The new inventions transformed England's overseas exports. By 1593 serges and other new fabrics made up the larger part of Southampton exports.[65] Whereas the old Eastland trade had been in Suffolks and other cloths made of English carding wool, by 1697–99 Spanish and other broadcloths constituted two-fifths of this trade, kerseys, dozens and perpetuanas about three-tenths, and baizes, says, stuffs and cottons another three. Even under these ill classified headings, the victory of the new fabrics can be discerned.[66] The Merchant Adventurers had formerly exported mainly white cloths; but by 1674 they sent out more dyed than undyed ones and turned a deaf ear to the plaintiff cries of the few remaining white clothiers. According to one report, company members dispatched about 50,000 broadcloths of one kind and another, 1,000 pieces of baize and 20,000 of stuff. In 1693 they were expected to export 15,000 broadcloths and 250,000 pieces of 'new drapery', i.e. mainly jersey and jersey unions.[67] In the year 1668–9 French textile and hosiery imports shown in the London custom-house books amounted to some £63,000, of which about £26,000 was in Norwich stuffs, serges, perpetuanas, rashes, baizes, flannels and wrought silks, £5,300 in worsted or jersey hose, and over £12,400 in Spanish cloths.[68] In 1618 three-tenths by value of Holland's textile imports from England consisted of baizes, says, serges and perpetuanas. Some of the remainder were probably Spanish cloths and tops-warp kerseys, and new fabrics made up about a third of the combined textile and hosiery total.[69] Well over half the value of the total exports to all parts of textiles other than silks and linens in 1697 consisted of baizes, rashes, says, serges, perpetuanas, flannels and stuffs.

By 1715 the proportion had risen to two-thirds. Allowing for Spanish cloths, broad silks and other fabrics, it may be guessed that the old kinds of cloth accounted for about a third of the exports in the earlier year and a quarter in the later one.[70] Other records and estimates confirm James's conclusion that by the middle of the eighteenth century the new had quite outgrown the old.[71]

Contemporaries estimated between a quarter and a half the production of English woollens went oversea in the later seventeenth century, but much less in time of war than of peace.[72] But, of course, the peacetime figure was so high precisely because the wartime one was so low; exports did not flow out smoothly and continuously, but intermittingly. The alnagers reported that in the relatively peaceful year ending Christmas 1688 over two thirds of the says, serges, perpetuanas and stuffs (other than Norwich ones) went oversea, nearly three fifths of the minikin baizes, two fifths of the Colchester double baizes, one third of the other baizes and of the kerseys, dozens, penistones and Spanish cloths, three fifths of the English long cloths and one-fifth of the short, and all told just under a half of all these fabrics. As for the Norwich stuffs, it was generally supposed only about one quarter was exported. It would have suited the alnagers' book to have exaggerated home consumption, but we have no evidence they did.[73] All in all, we should probably not be far out if we concluded about a third of England's textile production in this period was exported.

At this time textiles made up about four-fifths of total exports.[74] It is easy to see over half the exports were composed of fabrics of relatively recent origin, but difficult to discover what proportions of fallow and pasture wool were embodied in the textile and hosiery exports as a whole. The only worthwhile statistical study of early sixteenth century exports is not much help for this purpose because it assumes that only worsted beds and worsted cloths in the original sense were made of worsted and that no others contained combing wool.[75] However, we need no statistics to tell us English textiles then used much more fallow than pasture wool. We have excellently prepared statistics of exports in the period 1697–1715,[76] but even when we know how many cloths of which kind and of what value were exported, we are a long way from ascertaining what fraction was pasture and what fallow wool. We have to make allowance for the noils in the wefts of baizes, says, serges, perpetuanas, druggets and kerseys, and for the tops in many union cloths and yarns the exact composition of which is often in doubt. The fallow wool put into some union cloths and yarns is unlikely to have been precisely counterbalanced by the noils in kerseys and other cloths. All we can say with any degree of assurance is that English fallow wool was no more than a small fraction of all the wool incorporated in English textiles sold abroad.

English textile and allied manufactures faced fierce competition in both domestic and foreign markets. Many of the requisite techniques were widespread throughout the civilised world. Even within the relatively short early modern period we are concerned with, the Flemings and French Huguenots diffused their skills not merely to England but also to the northern Netherlands, Picardy, Artois, Normandy, the Rhineland, northern Germany and other places; and the currents of technical knowledge ran in numerous and labyrinthine courses in a multitude of other directions.

Linens of all kinds were extensively woven in Prussia and the Eastland, the Netherlands, Germany, Brittany and Switzerland;[77] canvases and sailcloths in the Netherlands, Artois, Brittany, Normandy, Prussia and Spain;[78] linen-cotton and pure cotton fustians and other cloths in northern Italy, Switzerland, south Germany, Westphalia, the Rhineland, Hamburg and all the Netherlands;[79] and innumerable kinds of silk and silk union fabrics in China, Persia, India, the East Indies, the Levant, Italy, Spain, Lyons, Tours, Rouen, Lille, Bruges, Ghent, Antwerp, St Omer, Amsterdam, Rotterdam, Utrecht, Haarlem and elsewhere.[80] Dornicksweavers were at work in Lille as well as Tournai.[81] Bonelace was a Flemish[82] and loomlace a Hollander speciality.[83] Tapestry came largely from the southern Netherlands, but also from Delft, Amsterdam, Strasbourg, Otterberg and Paris.[84] Ghent, Audenarde and Wervik were noted for their carpets.[85] Linsey-woolsey manufactures became almost ubiquitous in northwestern Europe.[86] Kerseys came to be made in Lille, Armentières, Poperinghe, Haubourdin, Mechlin, Leiden, Breda, Delft, Haarlem, Amersfoort, Amsterdam, Châlons, Beauvais, Vitry-le-François, Florence, Milan, Venice and other towns, as well as in Silesia.[87] Holland and the Palatinate took to making Suffolk and Kentish cloths.[88] Spanish cloth manufacture spread from Flanders to Holland, France and elsewhere. *Spaansche dekens*, rugs or blankets were made in Leiden by refugees from Duffel, and also, it appears, in Kampen. Later on, and before 1617, Poperinghe had recovered sufficiently to be able to contemplate the revival of the same industry.[89] The manufacture of fine Spanish cloth never entirely died out in the southern Netherlands, but migrated largely to Leiden, Verviers and other places. From 1620 onwards many French towns took it up, especially Abbeville, Caen, Elboeuf and others in Normandy. Como and other Italian towns did the same. Even Spain stirred herself and joined in to a small extent.[90] From Ancona, Roubaix, Lannoy, Bruges, Arras, Amiens, Lille, Brussels, Valenciennes, Rouen, Abbeville, Douai, Poitiers, Le Mans, Tours, Leiden, Haarlem, Delft, Utrecht, Amsterdam, Altona, Piedmont, the Levant and Morocco came an astonishingly rich and wide variety of camlets.[91] Stamins were made in Florence, Lille, Lannoy, Leiden, Amiens, Rheims, Poitiers, Châlons, Amboise, Le Mans and other towns.[92] Satins and reverses were woven in Bologna, Lucca, Bruges, Abbeville, Amiens, Valenciennes, Lille, Lannoy, Tournai, Armentières, Leiden, Haarlem and Amsterdam.[93] Tripes and velours like mockadoes, carrels and fustians of Naples came from Italy, Lyons, Tours, St Omer, Bruges, Arras, Tournai, Abbeville, Lille, Lannoy, Roubaix, Tourcoign, Ghent, Toufflers, Valenciennes, Armentières, Amiens, Antwerp, Cologne, Haarlem, Delft, Amsterdam, Utrecht, Kampen, Leiden, Aanbreng in Friesland

and elsewhere.[94] Leiden and some French towns made bunting.[95] Tammies and similar cloths were woven in Lille, Linselles, Bruges, Haubourdin, Poperinghe, Ypres, Houplines, Nieuwkerke, Armentières, Leiden, Aachen, Eupen, Verviers, Beauvais, Caen, Abbeville, Châlons, Metz, Valence, Montelimar and several other places.[96] From Ancona, Venice, Lille and Leiden came mohairs;[97] from Florence, Abbeville, Amiens, Valenciennes, Lille, Lannoy, Amsterdam and Rotterdam, plush;[98] from Rouen, Amiens and Venice, ferrandines;[99] from Bruges, plumbets;[100] from Leiden, crossets, curls and beavers;[101] from Beauvais, Amiens and the Limousin, flannels;[102] from Ghent, Wervik, and Leiden, carpetene;[103] from Arras, Amiens and St Omer, sagathy.[104] Venice, Florence, Mantua, Amiens, Abbeville, Amsterdam, and Holland and Flanders generally, made rashes of one kind and another.[105] Damasks, silken, woollen or union, were at various times produced in Italy, Lyons, Tours, Tourcoign, Roubaix, Lille, Lannoy, Leiden and Amsterdam.[106] Druggets originated in France and were much made in Rouen, Rheims, Châlons, Amboise and Touraine, Orleans, Amiens, Abbeville and elsewhere in Picardy, Lille and other Flemish towns, Leiden, and also Uzès and Piedmont.[107] Almost every kind of grograin could be obtained from the Levant, Tours, Leiden, Frankfort-on-the-Main, Kampen, Delft, Amsterdam, Valenciennes, Lille, Roubaix, Poperinghe, Ypres, Hondschoote or Ancona.[108] Bombasines were made in Wesel, Bruges, Augsburg, Leiden, Hondschoote, Kampen, Amsterdam, Leeuwarden, Harlingen, Bolsward, Amersfoort, Twenty, Osnabrück, Hamburg, Bremen, Haarlem, Delft, Poperinghe, Tournai, Lille, Amiens, and parts of Holstein;[109] boratoes in Leiden, Amsterdam, Lille, Roubaix, Tourcoign, Tournai, Beauvais and Castres;[110] calamancoes in Amsterdam, Harlingen, Leiden, Altona, Lille, Bruges, Valenciennes, Roubaix, Lannoy, Châlons, Abbeville, Rheims, Rouen, Poitiers and elsewhere in Artois, as well as in the Limousin.[111] The manufacture of messolinas continued in Mantua and was taken up in Ghent, Bruges, Lille, Leiden and other towns. The Abbeville bélinges, too, were similar.[112] Crape was made in Hondschoote for a time, and later in Zurich, Lille, Haarlem and other towns.[113] Lille, Ghent, Rouen and Venice produced tissues and brocatelles.[114] Lille, Rouen and several other French towns made poplin.[115] Grazets were supplied by Lille and other towns, including some in Languedoc.[116]

Says had long been made in Mantua, Florence, Amiens and Mouy, as well as in many towns in Flanders and Brabant. Now their manufacture spread to Leiden, Middelburg, Breda, Flushing, Leeuwarden, The Hague, Gouda, Kampen, Delft, Haarlem, Amsterdam, Liège, Frankental, Calw, Strasbourg and Piedmont. Hondschoote says were produced not only in England, but also in Florence, Bruges, Delft and Leiden.[117] Serges of all kinds, including shalloons and denims, were supplied by numberless towns. Flanders and Brabant contributed large numbers. Many others were made in France, in and about Amiens, Dieppe, Rouen, Rheims, Chartres, Orleans, Beauvais, St Omer,

Abbeville, Crèvecoeur, Aumale, Tricot, Montreuil, Châlons, and Nîmes. On top of these were heaped the serges of Mantua, Florence, Liège, Leiden, Altona and Strasbourg.[118] Various types of baize were woven at one time and another in Poperinghe, Ypres, Ghent, Nieuwkerke, Menin, Bailleul, Nipkerke, Godeswaersvelde, Mesen, Bruges, Armentières, Hondschoote, Beauvais, Leiden, Kemmel, Kampen, Amsterdam, Sneek, Frankfort-on-the-Main, Liège, Limburg, Strasbourg, Amiens, Castres, Nîmes, Montpellier, Palencia, Barcelona, Portalegre and Covilhã, and also in Silesia.[119] Duffel manufacture spread to Amsterdam, Kampen, Elburg and other places.[120]

Then there were the fabrics never or rarely made in England. Monks cloths, for instance, were hardly ever produced here any longer. They were succeeded by the *frocs* of Walloon Flanders, Orleans, Lisieux, Caen, Bolbec, Gruchet, Bernay, and all the Pays de Caux from Fécamp to Dieppe and Aumale. The Canterbury Walloons claimed to be skilled in this manufacture, but seem never to have practised it. In England the word 'frock' was acquiring the meaning of an article of feminine attire instead of the cloth it was made of.[121] A few bazins were woven in Canterbury, but they came chiefly from Piedmont, Lyons, Roubaix and Amiens.[122] A little caddis lace came to be made over here, but no broad caddis. This was imported from Amiens, Beauvais, Chartres, and places in Languedoc and the Auvergne.[123] Ligatures were made in Lille, Hesdin, Bruges, Leiden and Haarlem, and later in Ghent, but not in England. They were a kind of linen paragon, about eighteen inches broad, with floral and bird designs embroidered or stitched in jersey or silk twists, and were intended for making bodices. Later versions had cotton wefts.[124]

This already intense competition in textile markets was further sharpened by a great rise in imports from Asia, particularly from the East Indies and India. Calicoes were on sale in England by the 1550s, and by the 1640s chintz (or pintado, as it was sometimes called in earlier times), was already being used here for quilts, curtains, hangings and other soft furnishings;[125] but it was not until the 1650s, when the East India Company substituted white backgrounds for the red ones of the original types, that shopkeepers took to stocking the full range of painted and printed calicoes.[126] Then the company sent out to India patterns for dress cloths in floral designs in 1662 and for hangings and coverlets in branched designs in 1669. These appealed to English tastes. By 1683 the finest ladies were wearing calico. This was the year, too, when the company first organised the manufacture of ready cut waistcoats and of ready made chintz counterpanes, bed-hanging, curtains, valances and other soft furnishings. With the Dutch East India Company taking similar steps, the markets were overwhelmed.[127] Moreover, direct imports of silk cloths from Bengal, Persia and China had already started. The first large consignment of cheap wrought silks from China apparently arrived in England in 1639.[128] These silks and calicoes took the ground from under the feet of the Canterbury and Stepney silkweavers and somewhat harmed the worstedweavers. The air was filled with lamentations from the silkweavers.[129] They mostly liked to believe they were outsold solely because the Indians worked for a penny a day,[130] but a better explanation runs along these lines: when the weavers have made lustrings for the spring dress trade, they find themselves outsold by East India Company damasks and satins, 'which makes the mode for that spring', so they are 'constrained, with vast costs and charges, to alter their fashion for the next year, when in comes more East Indian ships with goods of quite another form, and all the weavers are in the dirt again. Thus for several years have the London and Canterbury weavers been disappointed.[131] The East India Company was highly successful in setting fashions, the Indians were past masters in the arts of dyeing cotton in fast colours and of ensuring an even distribution of the insolubly coloured lake, and a combination of the two sets of people was irresistible. From 1669 drapers in Stepney, Mile End New Town, Mitcham, Wandsworth and Bristol started to organise the printing of calicoes and linens in branched patterns for hangings. These held their own in the market for a brief while, but the East India Company overcame them by arranging the immediate manufacture of similar goods in India, and it took English calico printers forty years or so to arrive at a clear technical superiority.[132] Canterbury manufacturers also strove to compete. In 1719 Peter Le Keux showed the Commissioners of Trade a batch of new fabrics, some of wool, some of silk and wool, some of silk and linen, 'which pleased them very much to see we could make stuffs so much cheaper than callicoes'.[133] For the most part, however, the silkweavers abandoned all ideas of competing and sought the protection of the state. Thanks largely to their Huguenot origins and connexions and to the current hostilities with France, their efforts were crowned with success. In 1701 the import of Asian coloured calicoes and wrought silks was prohibited, and in 1720, with effect from 1722, the use of all calicoes other than all-blue ones. These were hollow victories however. Smuggling defeated the import prohibitions, and stopping the printing of calico only encouraged people to print linen-cotton unions instead.[134]

In such competitive markets it is not surprising that English manufacturers suffered some reverses or that our textile exports were not always successful in sweeping all before them. Towards the end of the seventeenth century French competition began to make itself felt in Italy; by the middle of the next century it had driven the English out of all but the more expensive sectors of the Levant market.[135] Light fabrics like perpetuanas were hardly suitable for cold winters in Anatolia and Persia, and the decline of the old English carded woollens, and especially of Suffolk cloths, which had formerly sold well in this part of the world, left little to compete with the heavier French products.[136] But had we not relinquished old-fashioned cloths, we could hardly have succeeded in making and selling new and more profitable ones.

Neither the French nor the Dutch nor the Venetians could withstand the unfettered competition of the newer English woollens, unions and stuffs.[137] The new cloths inundated the markets just as the old ones had done a hundred years before. In 1657 it was rightly claimed,[138] 'We cloath half of Europe by our English cloth ... and our worsted stockins are in great request all Europe over, espetially in France and Flanders, so that, almost, whole man is not only covered and thatched, but is even fine and neate in our cloth, stockins and shooes'. In the 1720s and 1730s English textiles were worn throughout the world: in France, which strove so hard to keep them out, in the Turkish Empire, by Persian nobles, by Armenian and Georgian merchants, by the people of Spain and Portugal and their empires, and by Europeans in all their stations and factories from Mocha on the Red Sea to Goa in India and Macao in China. Italy, Spain, Portugal and Turkey took our baizes; these, with Germany and Holland, our broadcloths; Flanders, Russia and Spain, our stuffs; Portugal and Germany, our druggets; France and Flanders, our flannels; Flanders and Russia, our serges; and Norway, Denmark and Russia, our coarser woollens. English cloths, from camlets to druggets, were the general wear throughout Europe as far as Muscovy, Poland, Sweden, Budapest, Belgrade, Venice, Rome, Lisbon and Seville. Even the monks and nuns wore English baizes, says, serges and perpetuanas.[139] In short, in those times, an Englishman could say,[140] without much exaggeration,

> Nothing can answer all the ends of dress but good English broad cloth, fine camlets, druggets, serges and such like; these they must have, and with these none but England can supply them; be their country hot or cold, torrid or frigid, 'tis the same thing, near the equinox or near the pole, the English woollen manufacture clothes them all; here it covers them warm from the freezing breath of the Northern Bear, and there it shades them and keeps them cool from the scorching beams of a perpendicular sun. Let no man wonder, that the woollen manufacture of England is arriv'd to such a magnitude, when in a word it may be said to cloathe the world.

# 16

## THE PATHS OF PROGRESS

England was blessed with the peace and the rights of property that gave free play to the instinctive industry and ingenuity of her inhabitants. Nowhere was the rule of law so secure or the freedom of ownership more jealously guarded. Freedom of trade, which is the hallmark of property, was cherished: the grand object of customs administration was revenue, not so-called 'protection of industry'; and the common law disallowed restraints of trade. Whatever the faults of various English monarchs and their governments, at least they had no national economic policy; every man and every family and other voluntary association was left free to pursue his or their economic aims.

English people generally tolerated Christians of most denominations. It was, for instance, a presumably Roman Catholic Duke of Norfolk who was instrumental in securing for Norwich a large party of Flemish Calvinst immigrants whom the Church of England helped and assisted.[1] Queen Mary drove out many English and foreign protestants; Charles I, with Archbishop Laud and Bishop Wren, harried nonconformists; and James II would have repatriated the French Huguenot refugees;[2] but only against the Anabaptists did the Crown consistently take stern and drastic action. Even the Corporation Act of 1661, reactionary as it was, gave no more than minor inconvenience to the nonconformist manufacturer.[3] England thus served as a refuge for the reformed churches in their hours of need.

But it was not always solely for religion's sake that immigrants came in. Artificers and artisans were mobile and similar forces drew men from Coggeshall, Cirencester and Taunton to Kettering, from Tetbury to Ireland,[4] or from the Netherlands to England. Flemings made venturesome emigrants and they had been coming over here for hundreds of years. Of the 1,674 strangers in London and the suburbs who had entered the country in the first five years of Elizabeth's reign, only 712 were found to 'professe relligion'; the rest had 'not come for cause of relligion'.[5] A further enquiry in 1571 showed that 2,561 of the 7,143 London strangers had, by their own confession, come merely to seek work. 2,663 neither belonged to the Dutch, French or Italian reformed church nor attended Church of England services. 889 claimed to be Church of England, but some of these in fact went to no legally recognised place of worship. These last two categories probably included some Anabaptists who were not keen to be burned at the stake. Approximately 2,650 aliens (less than two-fifths of them) could claim to have come for religious reasons.[6] But it is not always exactly clear what precisely constituted a religious reason. Men gave answer that they had come 'for feare of the Duke of Alba', 'for the troubles that were in Fraunce', 'because his countrey was distroyed with enemies', 'for safeguard of there lyves', 'for kyllinge of a soldiore', and so on and so forth.[7] Many of these people appear to have been religious refugees only in the sense that they had fled out of the path of the wars of religion. An immigrant's motives were often mixed, sometimes frankly so. There was the Antwerp merchant, a native of Jülich, who 'came into England for religion and trade of merchandize together'; the Augsburg man whose 'comminge was for religion, and to lerne the Englishe tongue, and also to use the trade of merchaundize'; the butcher from Cleves who had come 'to see the countrye, and now remayneth here for religions sake'; and the Antwerp goldsmith who 'came hether to seeke worck, and also for religion'.[8] Only a small minority gave answers that make them appear religious refugees pure and simple, being couched in such terms as 'for conscience sake', 'for the worde of God', 'for the Gospell', or 'for the persecutions sake in France'.[9] A large proportion of the immigrants came for ordinary, everyday reasons. One after another responds that he has come 'to learne his occupacion', 'for to encrease his knowledge in that arte', 'to learne languages', 'to learne the English tongue', 'to se the cuntrye', 'to see the realme', 'to seke adventures', 'for killinge of a man', 'to see fasshions', 'to seeke his father and mother', 'to see a syster of hers', 'to se a cosyn of hers', 'to see her children', 'to see his frindes'. There is the grieving widow who 'tarieth here for her husband'; the 'carver in stone sent for over hither when the King did byuld Nonesutch'; the man left here 'by pyrattes who took him goinge into Spaine'; the one who came 'when Calais was lost'; and the one who returned from Boulogne 'as a soldier' to enjoy his pension here. England was a pleasant place and some people 'came over myndinge to dwell heare'. Also London had many skilled craftsmen and many Flemings and others thought it worth their while to come there to learn how to make buttons or to be a blacksmith or a goldsmith or some such.[10]

Perhaps we should not pay such close attention to the responses made by the London strangers. It would have been excusable if they had unduly feared the purpose of the enquiries or mistaken the drift of the questions. Furthermore, to ask an immigrant why he had come to England was really to put two distinct questions to him: why he had emigrated from his native land, and why he had immigrated here. A Calvinist bowyer flees from his native Zutphen to Wesel, 'but his handiwork not being much required' there, he removes to Emden, 'but his craft not enabling him to continue there, he is going elsewhere', either back to Holland or across to England.[11] If he goes to England, it will only be in order to get his livelihood, for he feels safe in either Wesel or Emden, both of which have reformed churches with services in the Netherlands tongue. A man might well emigrate 'for religion' and immigrate 'to get a living'. When asked why he

had come, he could as well give the one answer as the other. All we really know
is that some of the strangers' motives were religious, some mundane and some
mixed.

The English had a good notion of what the position was. The first party of the
Colchester Dutch were regarded as having been 'banished for Goddes worde'. A
second party seems to have been believed when they said they were 'of late
driven out of Flanders, for that their consciences were offended with the masse,
and for fear of the tyranny of the Duke of Alva, to save their lives and keep their
consciences'.[12] But the Canterbury burghmote, when imposing restrictions on
further immigration in 1583, pointed to 'so many as are alreadie here abyding
that are not come for theire consciences as protestants for defence of theire faith
and the worde of God and whom the Elders of the Congregacion will not allow
of and answeare for'. In 1641 it was taken for granted that some immigrants
would not be admitted into the Walloon congregation, for not all were religious
refugees, still less Calvinists.[13] The London Weavers' Company usually gave a
cordial welcome to Protestant religious refugees, so it can hardly be insignificant
that they at one time accused certain members of the French congregation of
'coming hither (as they say) for the Gospells sake' and yet being 'without any
Christian regard for the native borne of our country'.[14] The scepticism implied
in the words 'as they say' is on a par with the London weavers' suggestion that
now the wars and persecutions, from which the strangers had fled, had come to
an end, the immigrants should be compulsorily repatriated.[15]

That most of the French Huguenots who fled their country did so on account
of religious persecution, appears obvious. This persecution came from two
distinct but connected quarters: the king and the Roman Catholic Church, and
fellow guildsmen and business colleagues. From this latter quarter it came, for
the most part, only after 1661,[16] when the French linen and silkweaving
industries were depressed[17] by, amongst other things, war, excessive taxation, *le
socialisme d'état*, and English, Dutch and Flemish competition.[18] Many
Huguenots engaged in these industries emigrated to the United Provinces,
England and elsewhere. But the French woollen and knitting industries
remained prosperous,[19] and the Huguenots occupied in them largely preferred
to escape persecution not by emigration but by outward conformity. The crucial
question, when deciding whether to flee the country or to conform outwardly,
was the state of business.[20] Moreover, the Huguenot entrepreneurs in depressed
businesses who migrated attracted followers from amongst Roman Catholic
workpeople,[21] for whom the state of trade was no less important. Furthermore,
there is no reason to suppose that the Huguenots, both presbyters and laymen,
who stayed behind in France, conforming outwardly and worshipping in secret,
were one whit less religious or sincere than those who went abroad, saving and
excepting those who left home to serve in the forces of William of Orange. It
would seem that business prosperity helped to strengthen the will to survive
underground, whereas the Huguenot linen and silk workers were better off in

England, where they were protected from their strongest competitors as well as from their cruel oppressors.

Even if, for the sake of argument, we grant that all emigration from the Netherlands, France and elsewhere had essentially religious causes, still England was by no means the only land for the emigrants to go to, nor in most respects the most eligible. Calvinist reformed churches were not allowed in England in the ordinary way. It was just that a limited number of alien congregations of restricted size were suffered in certain towns, by special privilege, under the tutelage of the Crown and the Church, provided they refrained from proselytism amongst the English, and on condition that their members paid extra taxes, took no trade from the English, and taught their new inventions to the natives. This was far short of the full religious freedom and equality that Calvinists were accorded in Geneva, Lausanne and many towns in Holland, Zealand, Germany and Scotland. At no time before 1688 did Protestant nonconformists in England enjoy complete, unquestionable and permanent religious freedom. Nor, after the sixteenth century, were any special privileges granted to new alien congregations. Yet England was throughout one of the havens preferred by Calvinist refugees, many or most of whom chose to shelter under the wings of the Church of England and submit to the Magistracy of the ungodly rather than to join their brethren and co-religionists in the places where they were all-powerful.

It is no less remarkable that so many Dutch and French speakers should have preferred England, where the people made little or no effort to understand 'double Dutch' and usually belittled and ridiculed foreign languages, to places like Geneva and Holland where their native tongues were always spoken.

No less noteworthy is that hundreds and thousands of land-lubbers made the often unpleasant and occasionally dangerous sea voyage to England rather than go overland to some other refuge. But this was probably because they felt they would be safer over here: dykes are good, but the Channel is better.

One reason why many Flemings preferred England was that their forbears had come over to engage in weaving, beer brewing, wood carving, glass staining and other pursuits, and had proved that England was a good place to get a living in.[22] It still was. The general tenor of letters written by Dutch people in Norwich to their families and friends in Ypres is unmistakable: 'We shall get a living well enough. . . . we shall not want. . . . here is great trade. . . . it is not hard to get a living. . . . my brother . . . gets a good living. . . . I earn a good living. . . . we are having a good time and gain from everything.'[23] England was the best place for the textile and allied industries, especially for their woollen branches, and this is what brought in many of the immigrants. 'The religious refugees had other countries open to them; they did not hurry over without looking where they were going. England offered them safety . . . and it gave them privileges; but it also offered better opportunities for profit.'[24] As far as we are concerned here, the whole issue resolves itself into the simple question, Why was England so apt for woollen and wool union manufactures?

The first reason is that England still grew much carding wool and yet had become almost the sole producer of combing wool, and this of unmatched quality. Given freedom of trade, and uninterrupted commerce, it may have been economical to convert Romney Marsh wool on the Continent, but not Midland pasture wool, nor that from the Fen Country. And trade between England and Flanders was being disrupted and unlikely to be restored for a very long time. Continental manufacturers, therefore, had every incentive to shift their operations to as close as possible to their sources of raw material.

The most important immediate cause of English industrial success in general was an ample and unimpeded supply of inexpensive food and drink stuff. The low cost of living was much appreciated by the Flemings who came to England. As one of them wrote in a letter home in 1567, 'More can be bought at Norwich for a stiver than, as I hear, for three in Ypres'.[25] It was the general opinion that it would take an earthquake to drive the strangers away, because they could not hope to live 'anything near so well at home'.[26] Food, drink, fuel and housing were all relatively cheap here.[27] Consequently the standards of living were high and the costs of labour low. As Hakluyt put it, 'The people of this realme, by the great and blessed abundance of victuall, are cheaply fed, and therefore may afoorde their labour cheape.'[28] Thurloe was informed that manufacturers in England could undersell those in the United Provinces 'by reason of their high rates of houses and victuals, to which all labourers wages are proportioned'.[29] Josiah Child thought manufacturing costs were lower here than in Holland and ascribed this to our lower fuel and food prices.[30] In 1654 voices were raised in Rossendale and Manchester, saying, 'Unlesse cotton woolle be brought downe to a much lower rate then nowe sould at, the manufacture of fustians will revert to Hamburrough, from whence, by our cheaper making then they, we gained it.' And it is some measure of the lowness of English labour costs that cotton wool prices here had risen to three times the German ones before this protest was evoked.[31] Defoe felt sure English textile workers had the best wages in the world for their work. 'And yet', he says, 'which is peculiar to England, the English manufactures are, allowing for their goodness, the cheapest at market of any in the world.'[32]

A further reason for the competitiveness of English textile and similar wares was that, in the woollen and wool union trades at least, the productivity of labour was higher than elsewhere, which is merely another way of saying that manufacturing profits were usually higher pound for pound. But in a free, competitive society such as then obtained, manufacturing profits have their sole source in successful innovation and a prolonged run of profits is sustained only by an endless stream of innovations. English labour productivity was high because Englishmen possessed the virtues of industry and ingenuity, to which good government gave free play. Although wages were relatively high, labour costs were relatively low.[33] This permitted the textile masters to select what fabrics to manufacture with scant regard for wage costs. Thus, although labour made up about half the cost of West-of-England white cloths, five-sixths of that of jersey cloths, and nine-tenths of that of Norwich stuffs,[34] England encountered little difficulty in discarding the old manufactures and expanding the new, for while she had a general advantage over many countries in respect of working costs, her particular comparative advantage was always that she was far and away the greatest producer of the main raw materials, in earlier times fallow wools and in later times pasture wools.

In the early sixteenth century English carded woollens could be sold in the Netherlands at less than the price there of as much wool as they were made of.[35] A hundred years later we could undersell the Hollanders in the common fabrics then in vogue.[36] In 1663 members of the *warpnering* in Leiden reported, 'Eight or nine years past, some members of our occupation began to make serges of the same kind as the English, of very good fashion and in brisk demand as well; but as soon as the misunderstandings between Holland and England were obviated and English goods began to flood in again here, our infant industry was nipped in the bud'; for the simple reason that 'the English article was sold here better cheap than we ourselves could make it.' Not only that, 'English serges were quite ... driving out our messolinas and druggets and greatly hindering the growth of our cloth druggets.' And English says stole the market from Leiden linsey-woolseys.[37] The French common people could afford to wear woollens now, thanks to cheap English imports their own manufacturers had no hope of competing with.[38] Despite French proximity to the source of wool supplies and the unrivalled experience and expertise of the Netherlanders, England's Spanish cloth succeeded in both underselling and outselling that from any other part of the world. Significantly enough, English exports of serge and Spanish cloth were but momentarily checked by the doubling of the French import duties in 1667 and continued right up until 1687 to surmount what had been designed to be an impassable tariff barrier.[39] In the seventeenth century English cloths completely undersold those made by the Venetians in their established markets in the Levant and elsewhere. It was not until the last quarter of the century that the French started to whittle away English sales in Mediterranean lands, and then partly because their cloths were softer and brighter but chiefly due to their readier access to raw materials and markets. Even then the English retained the top end of the market until the middle of the next century.[40] Fortunately for them the North American market was now growing rapidly. Pennsylvania, Maryland and Massachusetts, like New Hampshire before them, were taking to weaving coarse housewives cloth, the peasants employing their own labour on their own wool in slack seasons. But American cloth cost more to make and market than the price fetched there by a superior English product. English carded cloths, druggets, serges and stuffs flooded in.[41]

England as a whole had no need to entice textile workers in, but several municipal authorities made special grants for the development of manufactures intended to set the poor on work. The inducement most frequently given was the bestowal of the freedom of the city or borough. When Robert Taylor and Francis Barton were persuaded in 1675 to remove from Norwich to Chester 'to sett upp a manufacture for imploying of the poore', what they first demanded and received was 'an assurance of their beeing made freemen'.[42] The 'yonge man who had good skill in making of jersey hose and tufte mucado that had promised to repaire to this citie to dwell' was given his freedom 'to use the said trade of jersey hose and tufte mucadow.' Similar grants were made to the weavers who came from Shrewsbury to introduce the manufactures in which that town excelled.[43] In 1681 the borough of Ipswich set on foot no less than four separate schemes to attract textile manufactures. First, they assisted some Norwich stuff weavers to come and settle and sent a ship to remove their furniture free of charge. Secondly, they persuaded a Suffolk clothier by name of Firmin to set up a woollen weaving business in the town. Thirdly, they offered some Huguenot linenweavers freedom from all borough taxes and poor rates and a stock of money sufficient for twenty or thirty looms. Fourthly, they helped some London adventurers to start Huguenots patronised by the French Church in Threadneedle Street in the manufacture of medrinacks. All these schemes failed. Even the broad silk weaving business conducted in Ipswich by the Royal Lustrings Company collapsed in 1720 after a comparatively short life.[44] The borough of Leicester tried to get its paupers to make kerseys, then sent away for teachers, in 1584 of spinning, weaving, fulling and baizemaking, in 1589 of jersey knitting and cap making, all in vain, for knitting sprang up spontaneously and weaving never came to much.[45] In 1610 Bristol corporation managed to attract a few workers from Colchester and started a tiny, poverty-stricken baize manufacture.[46] Preston's attempts in 1689 to encourage a man from Ireland to make serges failed miserably.[47] Robert Cecil arranged for fifty paupers in his borough of Hatfield to be instructed in the arts of knitting and making cloths and fustians. He generously supplied a suitable house and paid the undertaker £100 a year, but little or nothing came of it all. To have achieved much success the scheme would have needed to have enlisted the support of the local landowners and farmers, but they kept aloof, fearing it 'would prove like the trade of those alchymists which to multiplie vj d to xij d are occasioned to spend ten tymes the value thereof'.[48] Quite undeterred, the undertaker, William Morrell, turned projector and promoted a scheme for the manufacture of bonelace, linsey-woolsey and drafts not only in Hatfield but throughout Hertfordshire. Seven years later, in 1625, failure was undeniable, and the lord lieutenant explained how it had come to pass. From the outset the local landed gentry had obstinately refused to put up the capital required. For two successive years, in no fewer than eight towns, capital stocks had been provided out of the poor rates, but were then liquidated, 'the profit of the work not finding support for the workmen'. It was impossible for him, he added, to call on the county to pay the projector's costs, for the project itself was a burden they wished to free themselves of.[49] In the 1650s Lymington made strenuous attempts to put its poor to work, and so wipe out begging, by providing an assisted clothing manufacture. Sir John Oglander, Mr Tichbourne and other gentlemen burgesses living outside the precincts were to be approached for the necessary financial help. Whether or not they were foolish enough to waste their money, the scheme was attended with little or no success.[50] When the Earl of Leicester and 'the gentlemen of the countrye' placed at Beverley's disposal from year to year for six years a stock of £2,000 in money or wool, to put the poor on work, nothing came of it.[51]

In 1577 the city of Chester received a charitable bequest of two hundred marks for relief of the poor. Three shearmen were supplied with a stock of wool and a convenient workhouse, the old, half timbered market building in Northgate Street being moved and re-erected just outside North Gate. Having undertaken to make Shrewsbury cottons, friezes, baizes, coarse russet cloths and such like, and finding a 'want of citizens of this city to supply the same', the three men procured some Shrewsbury weavers to come and work for them. But the Chester weavers 'so managed the saide suche foren weavers for theire suche repaire to this citie as enforced them to departe hence'. The city assembly was nevertheless persuaded to order that the foreigners be given their freedom and be allowed to make their cloths, provided they worked in 'everie their owne dwellinge howses or shoppes and not ellswheare'. In the end, very little was achieved and the poor benefited hardly at all,[52] and the parallel attempt to gain the cotton and frieze market from Shrewsbury was a complete failure.[53] The young man who was given his freedom in 1576 was probably successful in jersey combing and knitting, and the two men who came from Norwich in 1675 may have had some slight fortune in their venture in sergemaking; but in any event these were strictly private enterprises.[54] It is interesting, too, that the Chester weavers seem to have had no strong objection to weavers coming in from Shrewsbury, as long as they confined themselves to working privately in their own trades, and not in a workhouse for the poor.

York had similar but worse experiences. Two weaving establishments were set up for the unemployed in 1567 and 1569, but their products proved unsaleable. In 1574 handicapped persons were put to spinning hemp and flax. In 1579 the city spent £400 on wool for the poor to work on.[55] In 1597 the corporation contracted with a man from Hartlepool to introduce the making of fustians in order to give work to the poor. He was granted a rent-free house, an interest-free loan, a patent for ten years, and the freedom of the city gratis, all to no good purpose. Next, in 1619, the city council induced a Norwich worstedweaver named Edmund Whalley to come and employ the poor in making Norwich stuffs. He too was given his freedom, a house and a loan. It took just a year for this scheme to fail, and then the city wrote off the £280 they had sunk in it. In the 1630s a more modest project was started, a master being paid £20 a year to teach the poor jersey spinning. At much the same time an attempt was made to introduce the making of Kendal cloth in the hospital or workhouse for paupers. Neither effort was fruitful. In 1655 the 'Jersey House', as it was still called, was converted into a workhouse for two woollen weavers who had been brought to the city to provide the poor with spinning, carding and other work. The weavers were to supply instructors in these tasks at their own charge, and in return they received the freedom of the city, a gift of £50, an interest-free loan of £100 for seven years, the use of Jersey House and the adjoining land for a nominal rent, and as many spinning wheels and cards as they needed in the first year. It was all money down the drain, but the corporation never hesitated to throw good money after bad. In 1698 it was the turn of a supposed sergemaker to be invited in from Masham, because the poor were increasing daily 'for want of employment and of some publicke manufacture whereupon to sett them to worke'. As always, failure followed.[56]

Ireland had similar experiences. Strafford brought linen workers from France and the Low Countries and imported Dutch flax seed and Continental spinning wheels and looms, but is said to have lost £30,000 of his own money when the project foundered. After the Restoration, Ormonde also brought Netherlanders and Dutch wheels to his colonies at Chapelizod and Carrick-on-Suir, but without success. As has been pointed out, 'In the parts of the country to which his efforts ... were chiefly directed, the linen trade never flourished. On the other hand, it grew unexpectedly and without special encouragement in the North.'[57]

No amount of orders, regulations, subsidies and instructions could implant textile manufactures in unsuitable places and no clothier worth his salt would have undertaken such a task. Without gifted entrepreneurs, no considerable industry could be established; with them, no extraordinary assistance was needed.[58] When the Earl of Leicester marvelled that the burgesses of Warwick did not devise some special trade to keep their poor on work as Sheldon of Beoley had done,[59] he was more likely, considering his remembrance of the episode at Beverley and his knowledge of Sheldon's work, to have been suggesting the encouragement of private enterprise, rather than the municipal employment of work-shy paupers. Municipalities were fit for giving the poor relief, entrepreneurs for giving them work.

There was no shortage of men of enterprise; they came from divers walks of life. The Earl of Pembroke was the leading spirit in the introduction of Wilton piled floor-carpets, in association with a 'merchant', a clothier, and an 'upholder' or upholsterer, 'merchant' then being a general style rather like our 'businessman' or 'company director' and covering such occupations as banking and underwriting as well as wholesale trade.[60] William Sheldon, who brought tapestry making to Barcheston, was a wealthy landowner. He sent a man to Flanders to study the art, fetched weavers from there, supplied the capital, and saw to the setting up of the whole business.[61] 'Divers honest cityzens' of Norwich instituted the craft of making felt hats. One man was a capper, but the other seventeen came from a wide variety of occupations. They brought over and employed six or seven 'Frenchmen' who were skilled in the work. Later some of these citizen hatters were amongst the group of entrepreneurs who invented the making of russells. 'By the cost, charge and good diligence of certen of the merchauntes of the city of Norwich, the fyrst practising of the said russells etc. within the same citie was first invented by the said merchauntes', who included Thomas Marsham, the then mayor, six aldermen, six other citizens who put up most of the money, seven worstedweavers, and Robert Hendry and Richard Tompson, two of the original hatters. Hendry and Tompson, with John Sutton and John Cooke, were the governing partners, and the company of twenty-one finally formed had two other hatters in it also. Workmen were brought over from Flanders, but all the individual businesses and the company that regulated them were run by Norwich men.[62] When the main body of strangers was invited into the city in 1565, the first and key groups were brought over by a small number of Flemish entrepreneurs who then provided employment to later immigrants.[63] It was much the same in other Flemish settlements; the masters brought their servants and workmen with them.[64]

Everything and everybody depended on a few talented individuals. Richard Enewes invented minikin baize in Coggeshall.[65] John Jordan introduced the manufacture of shalloons in Kettering and John Salter that of mixed serge into Tiverton.[66] Richard Blacheford, 'merchant', was one of the first makers, if not the original inventor, of 'Dorset' dozens. Giles Warren, gentleman, introduced the manufacture of Milan fustians.[67] Samuel Smith, who started striped and mixed tammy making in Coventry in 1696, was still styled 'weaver' when he died in 1722, experimenting and innovating to the very end. He had gone on with tammies, but had also introduced the manufacture of camlets and of linen-cotton dimities. And all the time, justifying his alternative style of 'mercer', he went on running a sale-shop for mercery, drapery and grocery wares.[68] Benedict Webb was reared in the clothing trade and then apprenticed, at the age of sixteen, to a London 'French' merchant and wholesale linen draper, who sent him to Rouen as his factor. After some years in France, Webb returned with a large collection of swatches and settled in Taunton, where he devised and invented both perpetuanas and Spanish medleys. After moving to Kingswood, he went on making serge and Spanish cloth, cultivated rape, crushed the seed for oil, and still found time to go on an important trade mission to France.[69] The long succession of innovations in Spanish cloths was then continued by other outstanding men like Ashe, Methuen, Brewer, and Yerbury. The early machine inventors were no less remarkable.[70]

Inventors frequently needed financial and commercial backers to see them started, and we catch some glimpses of these enterprising men also. Such were the Norwich merchants who supported the russells venture, the Mr Greaves of London who sponsored the manufacture of striped tammies and prunellas in Kidderminster, Lionel and Jeffrey Ducket and others who promoted the making of Armentières cloth in Coventry, John Hawkins the London goldsmith who pushed the invention of Milan fustians, and Sir William Stone the Cheapside mercer who encouraged Webb to go ahead with his Spanish medleys.[71]

Successful innovators were well rewarded for their pains. We may be wrong in guessing Thomas Paycocke made his fortune by an innovation in baize manufacture,[72] but no doubt remains about the Spanish clothiers. Webb had his financial ups and downs, but at one time he was able to dispend £2,000 of his profits on research and development,[73] and John Ashe of Freshford 'gott a great estate' by his invention of Spanish warps.[74] Even minor innovations brought their rewards.[75]

A continuous flow of profits depended on an unbroken succession of inventions and innovations. No one appreciated this with greater nicety than the worstedweavers. 'Our trade', they said, 'is most benefited by our newe inventions and varyinge of our stuffes.'[76] This attitude was reflected in the parliamentary statutes they promoted and in their allusion elsewhere to the succession of 'Norwich whights, then wursteds, then monkes clothes, after them russells, after them sayes, bustyns, chamletts, and sutche other lyke comodities, all which grew in tyme owt of request'.[77] This had always been the position. As the worstedweavers said, 'There was as much invention and alteracion of stuffes from the first making of worsteeds till 7 Edward 4 as have bynn synce.'[78] The worsted trade was thus a living model of the economy as a whole.[79] Generally, the innovations needed to create profits came from the ranks of the worstedweavers themselves, but nothing guaranteed that the spark of invention would always come exactly when it was most wanted, so at certain junctures the weavers found themselves compelled to look about elsewhere for an innovation to adopt at second hand. Hence the Russells Company and the invitation to refugee Flemish drapers.[80] Sometimes an imitator rather than a pioneer, East Norfolk was none the less remarkable for the constancy of its stream of inventions. Canterbury, too, though starting later and stopping earlier, gave rise to a similar and no less notable flow.

Canterbury and Norwich, with the rest of East Norfolk, largely lived by twirling the whirligig of fashion, so many of their fabrics enjoyed a brief period of roaring trade followed by a long spell of slow but steady turnover. So fickle was fashion that it was plausibly argued that any restriction of the weight of wagons would be prejudicial to the Norwich trades, which had to bring their goods to London weekly, 'there being such great alterations in the fashion of their stuffs'.[81] Stepney textiles, too, were mostly oriented to the world of fashion, and so were East Indian ones. But no manufacturer was entirely immune from such influence and no business could remain profitable unless, at the very least, it kept abreast of current innovations. To take the clearest examples, this was why the Vale of Taunton Deane turned successively to serges, duroys and shalloons; Coventry to Armentières cloths, tammies, camlets, plush, calamancoes and shalloons; the West Country to baizes, serges and perpetuanas, druggets, duroys, tammies, shalloons, calamancoes and camlets; the Peak-Forest Country to its new draperies, newly devised kerseys, fustians, baizes, shalloons and tammies; Kidderminster to its stuffs, tammies, Philip and Cheyneys, prunellas, poplins and floor carpets; the Chalk Country district to serges, shalloons, druggets and crapes; the Woodland to handwarps, baizes, broad kerseys, Spanish Suffolks, fustians, says, serges, tammies, prunellas, shalloons, calamancoes, antherines and crapes; and the West of England to Spanish medleys, serges, new Stroudwaters, Spanish-warp medleys, Spanish Stroudwaters, druggets, duroys and cassimeres.

Patents of invention were usually pointless. The fashion might have passed by the time a grant had been made, and the secret of success was to be first in the market and make hay while the sun was still shining. It was open to anyone to pick a new fabric apart to see how it was made, and any employee who had mastered the art was free to leave and work for another or to set up on his own. If the inventor gave higher wages to induce his workmen to stay with him, they could all the sooner save up what they needed to hive off and start their own businesses. It is much easier to copy than to invent and once the path had been smoothed for them, other manufacturers could readily adjust to the new situation created by an innovation. In the Woodland it was not long before 'many clothiers ... altered theire making of broad clothes into making of bayes'.[82]

New fabrics rarely if ever came in to fill vacancies left by the demise of old ones. When the Kidderminster men wanted a stop-gap to tide over the failure of their stuff trade, they turned to frizzing, which could speedily be set up just because it was an old art.[83] There is nothing to say the Woodland clothiers who took to making baize did so because their old products were not selling well; rather it was the new that drove out the old.[84] When it was said in Canterbury in 1639, 'The manufacture of silke rashes and sayes ... being decayed, then the makeing of Phillip and Cheney came into use ... Now of late alsoe the makeing of Phillip and Cheney decaying as the aforesaid other manufactures have donne, then came in this new invention of mixtures of figured stuff,' this seems to have been a parochial way of looking at the events.[85] What really happened was that the Canterbury men were copying new inventions that were already driving their existing products out of the market, whereas in earlier times their baizes had been ousted by their own novelties of silk rashes and says. Philip and Cheyney had probably been introduced in Norwich before Canterbury manufacturers took it up, and it may have been invented on the Contingent originally.[86] This is not to deny that innovations were ever made in depressed industrial districts, only that depressed industrialists often attempted innovations and that they were likely to succeed if they did.

A strong inducement to clothiers to move on to new products was the hope of greater profit. As someone observed, 'Dyvers clothers thentofore making broad clothes have changed ther loomes and spynnynges to the making of new inventions, because it is traded with lesse stock, the retournes being quicker and the gaynes greater comparing weight to weight.'[87]

Innovations pushed up wool prices to heights that made the production of many older fabrics uneconomic. In 1560 it was lamented that, 'In tymes past moche rockespon yarne have ben spente by wevyng of russelles, chamblettes, bustians, sattens and in souche other like devyses, to the great decaye of worstedes.'[88] Before long it was being said that, 'The multitude of baies and other things made as well by Englishmen as straungers doth so wast wolls . . . the most clothiers are forced to seke for woll . . . which ys the chief cause of the great prices of woll, to the greate decay of clothiers.'[89] Some of the best wools were diverted from fine cloths and kerseys to baizes and rashes.[90] Instead of being put to what was regarded as proper use, they were converted 'into many slight and vaine comodities wherein the comon people delight'.[91]

Having bought up their competitors' wools from under their noses, the innovators then attracted away their spinners. In the course of observations on the spinning of combing wool, an East Anglian remarked, 'Of these spinners, (for that the gaine of this worke is so advantageable and cleanly, in respect of the clothing spinning, which is so uncleane, so laboursome, and with so small earnings), they have more which offer themselves than there can at all times worke be provided for.'[92] Thus the baizemakers 'drawe the most spinners unto them, wherby the clothiers are forced eyther to leave their manner of clothinge or ells to seeke further for spinners then easie or commodious for them, and therby clothinge greatly decaied and those baies dailye increased.'[93] Similarly, the Spanish medley clothiers, and the market spinners who supplied them, were known to 'give greater prizes then the white men doe' for spinsters' work.[94] It helped not at all that spinsters for the white clothiers tried to achieve parity of earnings by spinning more and worse yarn; this only hastened the fall of the white cloth industry.[95] In vain, too, did the Merchant Adventures and the white clothiers scheme against the market spinners and promote Bills designed to cripple their operations.[96] The new fabrics ousted the old because they were more profitable to all concerned in their manufacture. Much the same sort of situation arose when broad silks replaced jerseys and jersey unions in the Woodland and in Taunton. The silk manufacturers paid higher wages than the woollen clothiers could afford.[97]

In the end it was no use the old-fashioned clothiers trying to restore their dwindling profits by lowering the quality of their work or by stretching and straining their cloths. Stretched cloths might be tolerated by revised regulations,[98] but not by the majority of consumers. This was revealed in March 1622, when over three thousand 'tolerated' Suffolk cloths remained unsold in Blackwell Hall but hardly any fine ones.[99]

In these and other ways the new products drove out the old. Thus did the old Suffolk cloths go down before baizes, says and serges. Thus when the making of mixed serges was started in Tiverton, 'the kersey manufacture gradually sunk before it and was in a few years finally expelled by it'.[100] When the Kent and Chalk Country coloured and medley cloths of the old kinds went down, their makers acknowledged it was 'through the growth of an excellent sorte of clothe, which is made cheifely in the counties where white cloth is made, called Spanish cloth; and this if it consume the other clothing in that manner it hath' would entirely extinguish it.[101]

Driven out of their former strongholds by innovations, the old products (and some of their producers) took refuge in remote parts, where no innovation was afoot and costs were lower: the centrifugal diffusion of cast-off technology had commenced. The old coloured cloth industries of the Woodland, the Wealden Vales and the Chalk Country district took flight to backward countries, to central and eastern Europe and to the Peak-Forest Country.[102]

Meanwhile the innovators came into their own. By 1615 we are being told, 'There is more people supposed to be employed in this new manufacture than by all the clothiers of the kingdom', meaning all the old-fashioned clothiers.[103] In 1616 the 'new drapery' was said to be consuming at least a third of the kingdom's growth of wools.[104] In 1621 the Commons were told that 'the new drapery of perpetuanas [and] stuffs' was 'the only means for the turning of wools'. One member asserted, 'The new drapery doth imploy three times as many men and hath three times as much gaine' as the older woollen manufactures.[105] In 1622 it was claimed, 'The trade of bays of late time is equall to the trade of white cloths.'[106] In 1639 it was recognised that serge manufactures were 'nowe the principale of this [West] Country'.[107] By this time, too, the makers of baizes, says and serges were much the most important converters of wool in the Woodland.[108]

New inventions engendered prosperity. 'As for an example, what money one worstead maker bringes into the towne ... and how manye have theire livinges under him, and what wealthe he bringes to the town wheare he dwelles, Norwiche may sufficientlie declare, which by a fewe worstede makers ... hathe growen to greate wealthe and riches'.[109] To a greater or lesser extent it was true of all the worsted, jersey, silk and union cloth manufactures that they were more laborious than the ones they displaced. Worstedweavers said, 'The value of the stuffes ariseth from the labour and industrie of them', and reckoned raw materials amounted to no more than 'the tenth parte of their price ordinarely, and in some not the twentithe'.[110] It was said in the Commons in 1621, 'More men [are] requisite to the makeing of new draperies then old, and therfor must needs be disproporcion in the price and they dearer.'[111] Contemporaries estimated it took twenty-five workers of all kinds one week to make a Suffolk cloth and from thirty to forty for a Kentish one, while an equal weight of pasture wool required three times as many to convert it to knit stockings, between three and five times as many to make it into ordinary stuff, and up to ten times as many for the finest fabrics. And silk textiles were thought to employ comparable numbers.[112] It may be cautiously accepted that weight for weight pasture wool gave work to three times as many people as did fallow wool. But each pasture sheep gave on average twice as much wool as a fallow one, and when fallow sheep were replaced it was by roughly four times as many pasture ones, with a resultant increase in the production of wool of about eightfold.[113] We may thus hazard a guess that the domestic growth of wool multiplied about fourfold. Most of this growth eventually came from pasture sheep, so pasture wool may have come to employ about ten times as many people as fallow wool once had done. If one then makes allowance for the Spanish wool and for the flax, hemp, cotton, silk and hair utilised, one is left with a rough idea of the extent to which textile and hosiery manufacturers expanded in this period.

Various estimates were made by contemporaries of the numbers employed in the different textile centres and districts, but they must be treated with caution. To believe in statistics is to share in one of the great superstitions of the present age. Early modern people were inclined to the medieval habit of using large round numbers to express unimaginably great magnitudes. They were often rather like schoolboys with their 'millions' of marbles.[114] Yet a few of these estimates are worthy of mention. Possibly 8,000 persons were engaged in the woollen trades in Tiverton and district in 1612, and Defoe may not have been far out when he guessed about 120,000 busied themselves in the various trades that contributed to the production of Norwich stuffs, but then including the whole of East Norfolk, all the satellite towns, and the combing and spinning region in the Breckland and thereabouts, and always providing the figures are taken to relate to part-time workers also.[115]

Other estimates derived the number of workers from that of the looms in operation. It is not altogether incredible that the West of England region had 1,222 looms in 1620, that each loom gave work, in normal times, either part or whole-time, to sixteen persons, and that a total of 19,552 men, women and children found employment in one or another of the textile trades.[116] It is not entirely beyond the realms of possibility that Canterbury had 1,400 weavers in 1665 and Colchester from 1,500 to 1,600 in the period 1707–15. In 1677 Kidderminster seems to have had 459 weavers and perhaps 3,000 spinners.[117]

Yet another kind of estimate starts with the total number of sheep, calculates the amount of wool they would have produced, and then arrives at the number of persons required to work it up, all, unfortunately, without any means of ascertaining the number of sheep.[118]

We are thus left with two groups of statistics: plausible ones for a few localities and bogus ones on a national scale. All we really know is that a large and rapidly growing part of the population of the kingdom was directly or indirectly engaged in the textile and hosiery trades.

Yet Continental manufactures remained strong. Those of the southern Netherlands and France became more widely dispersed, but not only to England. Once the great troubles had run their course, the southern Netherlands took to specialising in fine linens, but at the same time woollen and wool union manufactures staged a partial recovery.[119] By this time, too, woollen and linen working had spread eastwards across Europe. Textile markets were expanding and also becoming more crowded.

Meanwhile the textile manufactures in which England had achieved preeminence were already starting to spread beyond our shores. To a certain extent this diffusion was precipitated by a coincidence of falling profit rates and excessive labour costs. In some places agricultural prosperity helped to push textile wages up. Although there were occasions when East Anglian milkmaids left to earn more spinning at their own hands, in the highly crucial matter of weavers' wages it seems that clothiers were often at a disadvantage. One reason why the manufacture of bunting outlived that of most other jersey textiles in the Woodland was that women and girls could do the weaving, this being relatively light work.[120] That female labour participated in silkweaving helps to explain the ease with which this industry replaced woollen manufactures in rich agricultural countries where men's wages were high. This argument has an especial force when applied to the Woodland, the Vale of Taunton Deane, the Chalk Country and other arable districts where there was little demand for milkmaids and correspondingly less for female labour in general. But such arguments should not be pressed far, for agricultural systems had little or no influence on the distribution of manufactures. It was simply that large manufacturing populations could only be maintained by profitable manufactures. Although it had been said, 'Clothing in the ... wylde of Kent is the nursse of the people', because 'where clothing is comonly used is so populous that the soyle therof is not able by any encrease therof to maynten and fynde the one half of the inhabitauntes except clothing be maynteyned',[121] in fact, a hundred years later, it had largely been replaced by other and apparently more remunerative occupations in which were seen 'the insolence and carelessnesse of servaunts requiring more wages and doing lesse worke heare then any countrey of England'.[122] Agriculture was one of these growing occupations, the tillage area having been greatly extended,[123] but it was only one of several, and the rising cost of wood fuel probably impeded woollen manufactures as much as did high wage rates.[124]

Nevertheless, a big disparity in costs conduced to the migration of industry from one place to another, and some woollen workers left the Wealden Vales for the Rhenish Palatinate and elsewhere. In pursuit of lower costs the fustian, baize, serge and shalloon manufactures of the Woodland and the Chalk Country eventually found their way to the Peak-Forest Country,[125] and West Country serge making was starting to remove to Ireland before it was stopped in its tracks by the Woollen Act of 1699.[126]

Continental manufacturers had to exert themselves to imitate English fabrics if they hoped to compete with them, but the French in particular had their path smoothed for them by low wages and by protective tariffs and regulations. Wages in such places as Amiens, St Omer, Abbeville, Lille, Roubaix, Lannoy and Tourcoign were now so much lower than in most English textile towns that they were an almost irresistible attraction against which prohibitions of the export of wool and machinery and of the emigration of skilled workers eventually proved powerless.[127] Holland was different; there the manufacturers had to rely far more on their skill.

Although unsuccessful with their hundred baizes 'opte Zandwiche manier', Leiden drapers were by 1653 turning out a range of 'baaien ... op de Engelsche wijze verwaardigd', 'op de maniere van de Engelsche goederen gevrocht', and these made up a large part of 'de nieuwe gepractiseerde Engelsche goederen' that 'op de Engelsche maniere binnen dese stadt werdende gemaect ende gedrapiert'.[128] By 1667 Beauvais was making baize à la façon d'Angleterre.[129] By 1682 Colchester baizemakers were even trying to set up in Portugal.[130] By 1647 Bruges had finally managed to produce 'carseyes (fabrication à la mode anglaise)'. By about 1720 Piedmont was making 'kersì, che pure si fabbrica in Inghilterra'.[131] Serges 'façon de Londres', 'de Londres', 'façon d'Angleterre' were being made in Lille by about 1640, and from 1665 in St Omer, Abbeville and several other French towns.[132] About 1652 some Leiden men began to make 'sergiën van deselve nature als de Engelse', but had to stop when peace returned.[133] As for converting serges into perpetuanas, this had been started in Leiden by 1617, in Amsterdam by 1618, in Haarlem and Delft by 1633, and in Harlingen by 1654.[134] Before long perpetuanas alias serges impériales were being produced in Beauvais, Nîmes, Montpellier, Castres and other French towns, and eventually in Nieuwkerke.[135] By the end of the eighteenth century Leiden, Roubaix, Amiens, Châlons, Joinville, Chaumont and other Continental towns were making everlastings under such names as éverlestines and eversines.[136] By 1718 Lille included in her range of camlets, some of which were woven an English ell wide, 'polimis de laine façon d'Angleterre', which were akin to our cattaloons, and by 1732 'les camelots rayés à la façon d'Angleterre'. About 1750 Lille became alarmed when Roubaix sought permission to make 'camelots et polimits façon d'Angleterre'.[137] Now Abbeville, too, was producing English-style paragons, and perhaps Piedmont was also.[138] In 1667 Beauvais was manufacturing 'revêches à l'anglaises'.[139] When, early in the seventeenth century, Lille, Lannoy, Roubaix and Tourcoign reintroduced the making of union damasks, they were described as 'satincts damassés tant unis que à fleurs, de nouveau inventés et travaillés ... à la fachon d'Angleterre ... par les esprits inventifs residans au dit lieu de Roubaix'.[140] Early in the eighteenth century the French took to making shalloons façon d'Angleterre.[141] Calmandes, callemandes, calaminken or kalemanken were imitations of English calamancoes. This trade, first introduced in Roubaix in the seventeenth century and in 1696 still regarded there as a 'manufacture estrangère', was later taken up in Lille, in various towns in the Limousin, in northern France, Holland and Friesland and in Altona.[142] Beauvais and Amiens copied their jersey-warp flanelles from England, and Brive later made flannels and other 'étoffes anglaises'.[143] Crape made of jersey and silk was a manufacture introduced into Zurich about 1675 by Huguenot refugees, but that of '*les crepons en soie facon d'Angleterre*' was first started in Lille, by 1680 or 1681, by refugees from stricken Hondschoote.[144] Later on Amiens, Angers and Alençon also made '*crêpe d'Angleterre*' in imitation of Norwich crape.[145] Efforts were made to bring to Rouen the Woodland way of producing rowed fustians.[146] The manufacture of grazets established in Lille and Roubaix by 1694 and in parts of Languedoc not long afterwards, appears to have been taken from Norwich.[147] Woollen druggets in imitation of Wessex ones came to be made in Amiens, Rouen, Châlons, St Omer, Abbeville, Amboise, Parthenay, Niort, Chaumont and other towns in Picardy, Normandy, Touraine and Poitou, and also in Leiden and Piedmont.[148] In 1692 a man from Valenciennes was given the exclusive privilege of manufacturing in Amiens '*peluches façon d'Angleterre*', which appear to have been the same as the woollen plushes of Lille, Lannoy and Abbeville.[149] And the prunellas being made of English wool in Lille in the 1730s probably derived from English ones.[150]

As a result of this wider diffusion of techniques, England lost much of her woollen and wool-union export trade. Norwich, Sandwich and Canterbury had long since abandoned baizemaking, and now, in the latter part of the eighteenth century, Colchester and the Woodland, and Barnstaple and the West Country also let it go.[151] After 1750 the West Country serge industry was afflicted; by 1782 it was all but dead.[152] By this time, too, milling, malting, hop-growing and market gardening, with silkweaving and other trades, had almost entirely supplanted woollen and wool-union manufactures in Reading, Basingstoke, Canterbury and all the towns in and about the Chalk Country.[153]

The time had come for England to start a fresh round of innovations.

# NOTES

## Preface

[1] L. Hooper, *Handloom Weaving*, 1920, p. 180

[2] Ibid. 199.

[3] P. Ramsey, *Tu. Econ. Probs*, 1963, p. 76.

[4] G. N. Clark, *Wealth Engld*, 1946, p. 50; cf. J. Clapham, *Concise Econ. Hist. Brit.*, Cam. 1949, p. 241; G. Unwin, *Studs in Econ. Hist.*, 1958, p. 291; J. E. Pilgrim, 'Rise "N.Draperies" in Ess.', *Univ. Birm. Hist. Jnl*, 1959–60, vii, 59.

[5] BL, Lans. 71, no. 51, fo. 108 (107) v.

[6] Ibid. 7, no. 81, fos. 194 v. sqq.; J. H. Hessels, *Ecclesiae Londino-Batavae Archivum*, Cam. 3 vols. 1887–97 iii, 41–3; *CPR*, Eliz. ii, 336; iii, 209–10; *APC*, xiii, 370; Kent RO, Sandwich Boro. Recs, Ltrs Pat. f. Strangers 3 Eliz.; W. Boys, *Colls Hist. Sandwich*, Cant. 2 vols. 1842, pp. 740–1; Cant. Cath. Lib. Wall. Recs. Misc. Docs portf. 1 nos. 2–5; Cty Recs. Chamb's Accts 1602–1, fo. 68; Nfk RO, Cty Recs. Du. & Wall. Strangers Bk fo. 17; J. James, *Hist. Worsted Manuf. in Engld*, 1857, pp. 107–9.

[7] Ibid. 109–10.

[8] J. Stow, *Annales*, (contd & augm. E. Howes), 1615, p. 948.

[9] J. Wheeler, *Treatise Comm.*, 1601, p. 39; H. J. Smit, *Bronnen tot de Geschiedenis van den Handel met Engeland, Schotland en Ierland*, Hague, 2 vols in 4 pts, 1928–50, vol. ii, 854, 856; *Cal. Ltrs & S. P. rel. to Engl. Aff. presvd prin. in Archives of Simancas*, 4 vols., 1892–9, i, 356; *Cal. SP For.*, 1563, p. 608; BL, Add. 48011, fos. 1, 3, 4.

[10] H. Heaton, *Yks. Woollen & Worsted Inds.*, Oxf. 1965; G. D. Ramsay, *Wilts. Woollen Ind. in 16th & 17th cents*, 1965; J. de L. Mann, *Cl. Ind. In W. of Engld fr. 1640 to 1880*, Oxf. 1971; *Docs Illus. Wilts. Text. Trades in 18th cent.*, Wilts. Rec. S. 1963, xix.

[11] G. Espinas & H. Pirenne, *Recueil de Documents relatifs à l'Histoire de l'Industrie drapière en Flandre. 1e partie*, Brux. 4 vols. 1906–24; H.E. De Sagher, idem *2e partie*, Brux. 3 vols. 1951–66; N. W. Posthumus, *De Oosterse Handel te Amsterdam*, Leyd. 1953; *Bronnen tot de Geschiedenis van de Leidsche Textielnijverheid*, Hague 6 vols. 1910–22; *De Geschiedenis van de Leidsche Lakenindustrie*, Hague 3 vols. 1908–39; J. G. Van Dillen, *Amsterdam in 1585*, Amst. 1941; *Bronnen tot de Geschiedenis van het Bedrijfsleven en het Gildewezen van Amsterdam*, Hague 3 vols. 1929–74; T. Leuridan, 'Précis de l'histoire de Lannoy' in *Mémoires de la Société Impériale des Sciences et de l'Agriculture et des Arts de Lille*, 3e série, 1868 iv; 'Histoire de Linselles', *Bulletin de la Commission Historique du Départment du Nord*, 1883 xvi; *Histoire de la Fabrique de Roubaix* (pt iv of *Histoire de Roubaix*), Roubaix, Paris & Lille (1863) 1864; M. Vanhaeck, *Histoire de la Sayetterie à Lille*, Lille 2 vols. 1910; E. Coornaert, *Un Centre Industriel d'autrefois: la draperie-sayetterie d'Hondschoote (XIVe–XVIIIe siècles)*, Paris 1930; *Une Industrie Urbaine du XIVe au XVIIe s.: l'industrie de la laine à Bergues-Saint-Winoc*, Paris 1930.

[12] J. H. Hessels, op. cit.; *Archives Lond.-Du. Ch.*, Lond. & Amst. 1892; F. W. Cross, *Hist. Wall. & Hug. Ch. at Cant.*, Pubs H.S.L. 1898 xv; W. & S. Minet, *Registres des Eglises de la Savoye, de Spring Gardens et des Grecs 1684–1900*, id. 1922 xxvi; *Livre des Tesmoignages de l'Eglise de*

*Threadneedle St 1669–1789*, id. 1909 xxi; *Livre des Conversions et des Reconnoissances faites a l'Eglise Francoise de la Savoye 1684–1702*, id. 1914 xxii; *Regs of Ch. of Le Carré et de Berwick St 1690–1788*, id. 1921 xxv; W. Minet & W. C. Waller, *Regs. Ch. known as L Patente in Spittlefields fr. 1689 to 1785*, id. 1898 xi; W. J. C. Moens, *Reg. Bapts in Du Ch. at Colc. fr. 1645 to 1728*, id. 1905 xii; *Walls & their Ch. at Norwich: their hist. & regs 1565–1832*, id. 2 pts 1887–8 i.

[13] K. J. Allison, 'Wl Sup. & Worsted Cl. Ind. in Nfk in 16th and 17th cents.', ts. thes. PhD, Leeds Univ. 1955; K. H. Burley, 'Econ. Devpt Ess. in later 17th & early 18th cents.', ts. thes. PhD, Lond. Univ. 1957; J. K. Edwards, 'Econ. Devpt Norwich 1750–1850', ts. thes. PhD, Leeds Univ. 1963; A. M. Millard, 'Imp. Trade Lond. 1600–40', ts. thes. PhD, Lond. Univ. 1956; J. E. Pilgrim, 'Cl. Ind. in Ess. & Sfk 1558–1640', ts. thes. MA, Lond. Univ. 1939.

## Chapter 1

[1] M. L. Ryder & S. K. Stephenson, *Wl Growth*, Lond. & NY 1968, pp. 18 sqq., 23, 345, 411; K. D. White, *Rom. Fmg*, 1970, pp. 71, 301–3 306.

[2] J. P. Wild, *Text. Manuf. in N. Rom. Provs*, Cam. 1970, pp. 24–5 et pass.; 'Prehist. & Rom. Texts.' in J. G. Jenkisn, *Wl Text. Ind. in GB*, Lond. & Boston 1972, p. 6.

[3] R. Davidsohn, *Geschichte von Florenz*, vol. iv, pt. ii Berl. 1925, pp. 56–7, 66; E. Staley, *Guilds Flor.* 1906, pp. 155–6; I. L. Mason, *Sheep Breeds Med.*, s.l. 1967, pp. 4, 8, 10, 129–30, 155–6 et pass.; E. Topsell, *Historie of Foure-footed Beastes*, 1607, pp. 598–60; R. De Roover, *Bus., Bkg & Econ. Thought*, Chic. & Lond. 1976, pp. 87, 113; I. Origo, *Merch. Prato*, 1957, pp. 55, 69; J. Klein, *Mesta*, Cam. Mass., 1920, pp. 3, 6, 7.

[4] Ibid. 3 sqq., 27–8, 30–2, 37, 46, 325–6; R. Dallington, *Svy Gt Du.'s State of Tuscany in . . . 1596*, 1605, pp. 30, 39; J. V. Vives, *Econ. Hist. Sp.*, Princeton 1969, pp. 251–2, 256, 299, 302–3; J. H. A. Munro, *Wl, Cl. & Gold*, Brux. & Tor. 1972, p. 4; J. Heers, *L'occident aux XIVe et XVe s.*, Paris 1963, p. 118.

[5] J. Munn, *Obs. on Brit. Wl & Manuf.*, 1739, p. 3; W.C. *Engld's Int. by Trade Asserted*, 1671, p. 3; J. Smith, *Chronicon Rusticum-Commerciale or Mems Wl*, 2 vols. 1747 ii, 12, 18, 19, 210, 213–14, 319, 417–18; G. De Poerck, *La Draperie Médiévale en Flandre et en Artois*, Bruges 3 vols. 1951 i, 10, 13, 218; Coornaert, *Hondschoote*, map I; Posthumus, *Geschiedenis*, ii, 257, 296, 298–9; W. Brulez, *De Firma Della Faille en de Internationale Handel van Vlaamse Firma's in de 16e eeuw*, Brux. 1959, pp. 46, 51; R. Sprandel, 'Zur Geschichte der Wollproduktion in Nordwestdeutschland' in M. Spallanzani, *La Lana come Materia Prima*, Flor. 1974, pp. 97, 99, 103, 105–6; A. E. Verhulst, 'La Laine indigène dans les anciens Pays-Bas entre le XII et le XVIIe s.', ibid. 17, 25, 27.

[6] Ibid. 27; Topsell 599; J. De Vries, *Du. Rural Econ. in Golden Age 1500–1700*, New Haven & Lond. 1974, pp. 71–2, 169 sqq., 241–2; R. Dumont, *Types Rural Econ.*, 1957, pp. 370–1; G. Lefebvre, *Les Paysans du Nord pendant la Révolution Française*, Bari 1959, pp. 196–8, 204–5, 747–8.

[7] A. J. Bourde, *Influence Engld on Fr. Agronomes 1750–1789*, Cam. 1953, pp. 131, 135 sqq., 142, 209–12; J. Jacquart, 'Fr. Ag. in 17th cent.' in P. Earle, *Essays in Eur. Econ. Hist. 1500–1800*, Oxf. 1974, pp. 170–1, 173; Smith, *Mems Wl*, i, 239, 251; ii, 135, 208, 419; pace G. Duby, 'La Révolution Agricole Médiévale', *Revue de Géographie de Lyon*, 1954 xxix, 361–2.

[8] H. C. Darby, *Med. Fenld*, Cam. 1940, pp. 147 sqq., 155 sqq., 163–4, 177 sqq.; my *Ag. Rev.*, 1967, pp. 42 sqq., 109 sqq., 141–2; J. H. A. Munro, 'Wl-Pr. Scheds & Qlties Engl. Wls in later M.A.', *Text. Hist.*, 1978 ix, 1476, 154.

[9] Ibid. 121, 147, 154, 158; my *Ag. Rev.*, 311 sqq.

[10] Wild, *Text. Manuf.*, 24; M. Hoffman, *Warp-weighted Loom*, Universitetsforlaget (Norw.) 1964, pp. 284–7.

[11] Ibid. 284–5; De Poerck i, 7 sqq., 55 sqq.; De Roover, *Bus.* 95–6; Staley 149–50; W. Endrei, *L'Evolution des Techniques du Filage et du Tissage*, Paris & Hague 1968, pp. 15, 16, 50–1.

[12] Ibid. 51; Espinas & Pirenne i, 23–4; ii, 476, 648, 676–7, 711; iii, 78, 248, 336, 407, 461; De Sagher i, 104; Posthumus, *Bronnen*, i, 157–8; De Poerck i, 48–51.

[13] Ibid. i, 300.

[14] *Miscellanea*, Thoresby S. 1895 iv, 163–6; HMC, *14th Rep*, App. pt iv, 572; N. Lowe, *Lancs. Text. Ind. in 16th cent*, Chetham S. 3rd ser. 1972 xx, 34–6, 41–2, 105–6; inf. 19.

[15] *Manners & Hsehld Exs in 13th & 15th cents*. Roxburghe Club 1841, p. 533; Verhulst 11 sqq.; Endrei, *L'Evolution*, 51; Davidsohn vol. iv pt. ii, 54; G. Willemsen, 'La Technique et L'Organisation de la Draperie à Bruges, à Gand & à Malines au milieu du XVe s.', *Annales de l'Académie Royale d'Archéologie de Belgique*, 6e série 1920–1 viii, ix (lviii–ix), viii, 21–2; De Sagher i, pp. xviii, 104, 523; ii, 29–31; iii, 533; R. H. Tawney & E. Power, *Tu. Econ. Docs*, 3 vols. 1935–7, iii, 201; G. Espinas, *La Vie Urbaine de Douai au Moyen Age*, Paris 3 vols. 1913, ii, 748–9; Origo 350; Posthumus, *Geschiedenis* i, 56; Bronnen i, pp. xviii, 10, 20–1, 46–9, 53, 59, 74–5, 77, 79, 80, 158, 204, 302; ii, 650, 665–6; Espinas & Pirenne i, 23–4, 265–6, 294–7; ii, 474, 476; iii, 336, 407, 461.

[16] Ibid. i, 139; iii, 467; J. Strutt, *Compl. View Dress & Habits People Engld*, 2 vols. 1842, ii, 14; Smith, *Mems Wl*, ii, 448; C. W. Cole, *Colbert & Cent. Fr. Mercantilism*, 2 vols. 1964, ii, 384, 574, 579; J. S. Furley, *Cty Govt Winch.*, Oxf. 1923, p. 81; A. Woodger, 'Ecli. Burel Weaver', *Text. Hist.*, 1981 xii, 60–1, 65, 69, 73–4; C. Gross, *Gild Merch.*, Oxf. 2 vols. 1890, ii, 204; T. Smith, *Engl. Gilds*, EETS 1870 xl, 350; De Poerck i, 207–8, 299, 300; iii, 27.

[17] Ibid. i, 48, 51, 55–7, 210, 236, 276–7, 280–1, 286; ii, 33, 67, 146; F. Keutgen, *Urkunden zur Staedtischen Verfassungsgeschichte*, Berl. 1901, pp. 372–3, 380; Hoffman 286–7; R. Ehrenberg, *Hamburg u. England im Zeitalter der Koenigin Elisabeth*, Jena 1896, p. 287; S. Tymms, *Wills & Invs fr. Regs Commy Bury St Edm's & Arch.* Sudbury, Camd. S. 1850 xlix, 2–4; H. Laurent, *Un Grand Commerce d'Exportation au Moyen Age*, Paris 1935, pp. 70, 76, 153, 161–2, 172–3; H. Amman, 'Deutschland u. die Tuchindustrie Nordwesteuropas im Mittelalter', *Hansische Geschichtsblaetter*, 1954 lxxii, 31; Espinas & Pirenne i, 129, 183; ii, 81; iii, 272, 456, 497.

[18] Ibid. i, 184, 224, 236, 446–7, 611; iii, 254–5, 286, 444, 455, 457, 466, 569, 587, 810, 812–13, 821; Davidsohn vol. iv pt. ii, 67; Strutt ii, 9; De Poerck i, 64, 214–16, 238–9, 275, 299, 300; iii, 147, 180–1; cf. A. Doren, *Studien aus der Florentiner Wirtschaftsgeschichte*, Stuttgart 2 vols. 1901–8, i, 45–7, 49; De Sagher iii, 406–7; P. Racine, 'A Propos d'une Matière Première de l'Industrie textile placentine: La Carzatura' in Spallanzani, *La Lana*, 178–81; Laurent 65, 71, 76–7, 107; *Cal. SP Ven.*, i, 2; N. Bonds, 'Some Ind. Pr. Mvts in Med. Genoa' in D. Herlihy, R. S. Lopez & V. Slessarev, *Econ., Soc. & Govt in Med. It.*, Kent, O. 1969, pp. 127–8; F. B. Pegolotti, *La Practica della Mercatura*, Cam., Mass. 1936, p. 426; cf. E. M. Carus-Wilson, 'Haberget: med. text. conundrum', *Med. Archaeol.*, 1969 xiii, 148 sqq.

[19] A. Friis, *Ald. Cockayne's Proj. & Cl. Trade*, Copenhagen & Lond. 1927, p. 440; R. Plot, *Nat. Hist. Oxon.*, Oxf. 1677, p. 279; A. Plummer & R. E. Early, *Blanket Mkrs 1669–1969*, 1969, p. 22; W. de G. Birch, *Hist. Chars & Const. Docs Cty Lond.*, 1887, p. 259; T. S. Willan, *Tu. Bk Rates*, Man. 1962, p. 65; N. S. B. Gras, *E. E. Customs Syst.*, Cam., Mass. 1918, pp. 291, 293, 298; *Rates Marchandizes*, s.v. wadmell; E. A. Lewis, *W.Pt Bks 1550–1603*, H. S. C. Rec. Ser. 1927 xii, 23, 40; Tawney & Power iii, 200; P. McGrath, *Merchs & Merchandise in 17th cent. Brist.*, B.R.S. 1955 xix, 73; D. Defoe, *Plan Engl. Comm.*, 1728, p. 182; Burley, thes. 409; *Rates Marchandizes*, 1642, pp. 41, 54; K. Bahr, *Handel u. Verkehr der Deutschen Hanse in Flanderen waehrend des 14. Jahrhunderts*, Leip. 1911, p. 136; A. Clark, *Story Mon.*, vol. i. Llandybie 1962, p. 140; J. G. Jenkins, *W. Woollen Ind.*, Cardiff 1969, p. 111; E. M. Carus-Wilson, 'Icel.Trade' in E. Power & M. M. Postan, *Studs in Engl. Trade in 15th cent.*, 1933, p. 175; J. G. Nichols, *Unton Invs rel. to Wadley & Faringdon*, Berks. Ashmolean S. 1841, pp. 19, 29; PRO, SPD Eliz. 250/34; Stat. 12 Chas 2 c.4; Brist. RO, Cons. Ct inv. 1624/72; Kent RO, Cons. Ct Cant. Reg. Accts & Invs 6 fo. 372v.; Inv. Regs 14 fo. 248; 15 fo. 304; Hoffman 51, 194–5, 198 sqq., 420.

[20] J. H. Munro, 'Med. Scarlet & Econ. Sartorial Splendour' in N. B. Harte & K. G. Ponting, *Cl. & Clo. in Med. Eur.*, 1983, pp. 13 sqq.; & v. Hoffman 265–8; D. Sella, 'Rise & Fall Ven. Woollen Ind.' in D. Pullan, *Crisis & Chg. in Ven. Econ. in 16th & 17th cents*, 1968, p. 111; De Poerck i, 213; iii, 125; Keutgen 327; T. Twiss, *Blk Bk Adm.*, 4 vols. 1871–6, ii pt ii, 196–7; Bahr 149–50; Amman 36–7; Posthumus, *Bronnen*, v, 637; C. Verlinden, 'Draps des Pays-Bas & du Nord de la France en Espagne au XIVe s.', *Moyen Age*, 1937, xlvii, 33–4; C. Mollwo, *Das Handlungsbuch*

*von Hermann u. Johann Wittenborg*, Leip. 1901, p. 46; J. A. Goris, *Etude s. les Colonies Marchandes Méridionales . . . à Anvers de 1488 à 1587*, Louvain 1925, p. 252; L. Guicciardini, *Descrittione di Tutti Paesi Bassi*, Antwerp 1567, pp. 119–20; Gras 109, 120, 266–7, 274 sqq., 284–7, 289–91, 302, 309–11, 455 sqq., 588; Tawney & Power iii, 201; *Rates Marchandizes*, s.v. skarlet cl.; E. Coke, *Insts Laws Engld*, pts ii–iv 1642–4, iv, 29, 30; N. E. Bang (& K. Korst), *Tabeller over Skibsfart og Varetransport gennem Øresund 1497–1660*, Copenhagen & Leip. 2 vols. 1906–33 ii pt A, pp. 281, 486; G. Schanz, *Englische Handelspolitik gegen Ende des Mittelalters*, Leip. 2 vols. 1881, ii, 106; T. S. Willan, *Early Hist. Ru. Co.*, Man. 1956, p. 53; Espinas & Pirenne i, 140; ii, 386, 418, 539–40, 588; iii, 247, 278, 286, 291–3, 296, 498.

[21] Ibid. i, 325–7; W. Horman, *Vulgaria*, 1519, p. 167; Gras 283, 285, 361, 527, 544–5; J. Ruinen, *De Oudste Handelsbetrekkingen van Holland en Zeeland met Engeland*, Amst. 1919, p. 103; De Poerck i, 246; ii, 20; Coornaert, *Hondschoote*, 208; C. L. Kingsford, *Stonor Ltrs & Papers 1290–1483*, Camd. 3rd ser. 1919 xxix, xxx, vol. i, 153; Ess. RO, Arch. Ct Colc., Reg. Wills 1514–35 fo. 16v.; W. Sfk RO, Ep. Commy Ct Bury inv. 1667/38.

[22] W. Brulez, 'Engels Laken in Vlaanderen in de 14e en 15e eeuw', *Handelingen van de Genootschap voor Geschiedenis te Brugge*, 1972 cviii, 6; B. McClenaghan, *Springs of Lavenham*, Ips. 1924, p. 4; Gross ii, 4; J. Hamilton & N. Beldiceanu, 'Recherches autours de Qars, nom d'une étoffe de poil', *Bull. S.O.A.S.*, 1968, xxxi, 330–1, 333, 341 sqq.; L. J. Wilhelmsen, *Engl. Text. Nom.*, Bergen 1943, p. 40.

[23] T. S. Willan, *Inld Trade*, Man. 1976, p. 109; Plummer & Early 46; A. Plummer, *Witney Blanket Ind.*, 1934, p. 182; J. A. Giles, *Hist. Witney*, 1852, pp. 49, 52; F. G. Emmison, *Eliz. Life: Home, Wk & Ld*, Chelmsford 1976, p. 15; Hants. RO, Cons. Ct. O.W. & Invs 1630 Sam. Hoopper/Soton; Nfk RO, Cons. Ct invs 1602/239; 1615/52; 1639/98; Arch. Ct inv. 1706–7/30; Cty Recs. Bks Mayor's Ct 16 fos. 425, 471; 20 fos. 9v.–10, 44v.; Devon RO, Fortescue Coll. FC. 21.

[24] *Reply Cardmakers & Engl. Wooll Clothiers to Objns Sp. Wooll Clothiers*, s.l.n.d.; BL, Lans. 114 no. 24 fos. 92v.–3.

[25] Ibid.; Ehrenberg 269; Emmison, *Home, Wk & Ld*, 76; M. Dunsford, *Hist. Mems Tiverton*, Exeter 1790, p. 36; *Rates Marchandizes*, s.v. stockings; Stats 1 H.4 c.19; 4 E.4 c.1; 17 E.4 c.5; 1 R.3 c.8; 27 H.8 c.12; 33 H.8 c.18; 3 & 4 E.6 c.2; 5 & 6 E.6 c.6; 4 & 5 P. & M. c.5; 14 Eliz. c.10; 3 Jas c.16; Soms. RO, Cons. Ct Bath & Well. inv. N–O 18; Nfk RO, Cons. Ct inv. 1584/42; Wilts. RO, Arch. Ct Wilts. inv. Jn Beere 1684 Lacock; ex Dioc. Reg. Sarum. invs Ric. Kendall 1600 Mere; Hy Noble 1601 Edington; Lichfield Jt RO, Cons. Ct O.W., Jn Bond 1550 Cov.

[26] R. Hakluyt, *Orig. Writings & Corr. 2 Ric. Hakluyts*, Hak. S. 2nd ser. 1935 lxxvi–vii, 183, 191–2.

[27] R. Hakluyt, *Prin. Navs, Voyages, Traffiques & Discoveries Engl. Nation*, Glas. 12 vols. 1903–5, iii, 270; *Discourse Com. Weal this Realm Engld*, ed. E. Lamond, Cam. 1929, p. 82; *Rates Marchandizes*, s.v. stockings; McGrath, *Merchs*, 283; W. Harrison, *Descron Engld*, ed. G. Edelen, Ithaca 1968, p. 148; Kingsford i, 153–4; PRO, Exch. KR, Bills & Ans (Glos.) bdl. 16 no. 178; SPD Eliz. 251/2; Nfk RO, Cons. Ct inv. 1584/42; Soms. RO, Arch. Taunton inv. 1668/65; E. Sfk RO, Blois Fam. Archives, Hy Blois's Acct Led. fo. 41.

[28] Endrei, *L'Evolution*, 17–19, 52–3, 85, 105–6, 172; Doren i, 46–7. Twists are called S or Z acc. to dir. ltr's centre stroke.

[29] HMC, *13th Rep.*, App. pt ii, vol. ii (1893), p. 266; cf. Endrei, *L'Evolution*, 85.

[30] L. White, *Med. Tech. & Soc. Chg*, Oxf. 1962, pp. 119, 173; De Sagher i, 521; A. Thierry, *Recueil de Monuments Inédits de l'Histoire du Tiers Etat:* 1e série, Région du Nord vol. iv Paris 1870, p. 53; Keutgen 372–3; Davidsohn vol. iv pt ii, 54; De Poerck i, 60–3.

[31] Ibid. 62–3; Laurent 189–90, 197–9; Posthumus, *Bronnen*, ii, 404; Bodl. Aubrey 2 fo. 64.

[32] De Poerck i, 63, 67.

[33] Ibid. 7, 217 sqq.; ii, 182–3; iii, 121–2; Coornaert, *Hondschoote*, 201–2; Doren i, 97; Davidsohn vol. iv pt ii, 69.

[34] Ibid.; P. Deyon & A. Lottin, 'Evolution de la Production textile à Lille aux XVIe et

XVIIe s.', *Revue du Nord*, 1967 xlix, 23; Posthumus, *Bronnen*, i, 311, 503, 515; ii, 695; iii, 103–4; Verhulst 24; J. R. Verellen, 'Lakennijverheid en Lakenhandel van Herentals in de 14e, 15e en 16e eeuw', *Taxandria*, nieuwe reeks 1955 xxvii, 164; E. Ashtor, 'Obs. on Ven. Trade in Lev. in 14th cent.', *Jnl Eur. Econ. Hist.*, 1976 v, 584; Ammann 1–3, 8, 16, 36–7, 47; Thierry 359; Goris 278, 292, 297, 308–9, 311–12, 316; A. Derville, 'Les Draperies Flamandes et Artésiennes vers 1250– 1350', *Revue du Nord*, 1972 liv, 365–7, 369; G. Willemsen, 'La Grève des Foulons et des Tisserands en 1524–5 et le Règlement Général de la Draperie Malinoise de 1544', *Bulletin du Cercle Archéologique de Malines*, 1910 xx, 134, 159, 168, 173, 184; 'La Technique', 19, 44, 124; J. Denucé, *Koopmansleerboeken van de XVIe en XVIIe eeuwen in Handschrift*, Antwerp, Brux., Ghent & Louvain 1941, pp. 38–9; Bahr 149; H. A. Enno van Gelder, *Gegevens Betreffende Roerend en Onroerend Bezit in de Nederlanden in de 16e eeuw*, Hague 2 vols. 1972–3, ii, 12, 15, 16; Laurent 71–2, 77–8; *Algemene Geschiedenis der Nederlanden*, vol. iv Utrecht, Antwerp, Brux., Ghent & Louvain 1952, pp. 206–7; A. Mahlik, 'Wl of M.A.' in Spallanzani, *La Lana*, 373–4; *Cal. SP For.*, 1578–9 p. 43; De Poerck i, 18, 217–18, 227 sqq., 251, 256, 270, 279–82, 289; Bonds 128, 130; Vanhaeck i, 1 sqq., 12, 13, 17, 20, 135; ii, 1 sqq.; E. Maugis, 'La saieterie à Amiens', *Vierteljahrschrift fuer Sozial-u. Wirtschaftsgeschichte*, 1907 v, 1, 2; De Sagher i, 201 sqq., 514–16, 530–3, 537, 540–1, 543, 552 sqq., 636–8; ii, 90, 118, 223, 388 sqq., 658; iii, 593–5; Coornaert, *Hondschoote*, 14, 15, 24–7 et pass.; *Bergues*, 44, 52 sqq.; Espinas & Pirenne i, 9, 139, 161, 194 sqq., 236, 347 sqq., 359 sqq., 371 sqq., 377, 380–2, 396, 419, 443, 449, 454, 459, 476 sqq., 489, 499, 512, 516, 529 sqq., 613; ii, 342–3, 649 sqq., 705; iii, 68, 71, 73, 236–8, 240, 246, 251, 255, 259, 267, 471–2, 634; iv, 2 sqq., 51–2.

[35] Ibid. i, 161, 533–4; Maugis 14; PRO, SPD Eliz. Add. 33/71; Exch. KR, Deps by Commn 44 & 45 Eliz. Mich. 1 m. 7r.; De Sagher ii, 90, 347 sqq., 362 sqq., 388–90, 423; Coornaert, *Bergues* 27; *Hondschoote*, 14, 190, 193–5, 199 sqq., 208–9, 214–15; Vanhaeck i, 148, 150–2, 227–30, 238–9; P. Deyon, *Amiens – capitale provinciale*, Paris & Hague 1967, pp. 180 sqq., 193–4; De Poerck i, 42, 51, 67, 216 sqq., 251–3, 300; ii, 104–5, 182; iii, 121.

[36] Ibid. i, 226–9, 231; Espinas & Pirenne i, 373, 377, 380–2, 419, 454, 459, 476, 516, 533; iii, 236–8, 246, 251, 255, 259, 267.

[37] De Poerck i, 220, 225 sqq., 231; De Sagher ii, 343, 347 sqq., 378 sqq., 387 sqq., 413–15, 435 sqq.; Deyon 181; Vanhaeck i, 227, 230; ii, 144; Coornaert, *Hondschoote*, 189–90, 199 sqq., 215.

[38] Ibid. 214, 223; Espinas & Pirenne i, 139, 348 sqq., 371, 396, 449, 459; Willemsen, 'La Grève', 134; Vanhaeck i, 228–9, 231–3; ii, 141–2, 146, 212; De Sagher i, 201, 204, 297; De Poerck i, 228–31, 251–2, 256; ii, 182.

[39] Ibid. i, 217, 224–5; ii, 186; iii, 123.

[40] Ibid. i, 217–18; Davidsohn vol. iv, pt ii, 69; Posthumus, *Geschiedenis*, ii, 329; *Bronnen*, vi, 88, 523; Ruinen, 81, 83; G. Schmoller, *Die Strassburger Tucher-u. Weberzunft*, Strasbourg 1879, pp. 157–8, 587; Brulez, *Della Faille*, 229; C. Weiss, *Histoire des Réfugiés Protestants de France depuis la Révocation de l'Edit de Nantes*, Paris 2 vols. 1853, i, 42; Goris 262–3.

[41] Ibid. 242–3, 292, 297; Ashtor 572; De Poerck i, 217; Coornaert, *Hondschoote*, 24–5; *Bergues*, 58; Espinas & Pirenne i, 44, 127, 307; ii, 594–5; iii, 495, 817; De Sagher i, 194–5, 197; iii, 225, 465; Laurent 97.

[42] Schmoller 157–8, 522, 542, 572, 579; Keutgen 399.

[43] L. F. Salzman *Engl. Inds. M.A.*, Oxf. 1923, p. 229; N. J. M. Kerling, *Comm. Rels Holl. & Zeeland w. Engld fr. late 13th cent. to Close M.A.*, Leyd. 1954, p. 74; W. Hudson & J. C. Tingey, *Recs. Cty Norwich*, Norwich & Lond. 2 vols. 1906–10, ii, 406; Ruinen 81, 83, 103; *Cal. SP Ven.*, i, 14, 15, 62, 87, 151, 305; ii, 352, 357, 361; Gras 334, 454 sqq., 461, 463–5, 474, 477–8, 480, 485 sqq., 494, 497, 646; W. S. Unger, *Bronnen tot de Geschiedenis van Middelburg in den Landsheerlijken Tijd*, Hague 3 vols. 1923–31, ii, 50.

[44] Verhulst 24; cf. Ashtor 584; Davidsohn vol. iv pt ii, 69; Posthumus, *Bronnen*, i, 311, 503, 515; ii, 695; Coornaert, *Bergues*, 44; De Poerck i, 218, 251; Derville 365; Willemsen, 'La Technique', 19; 'La grève', 159.

[45] Nfk RO, Cty Recs. O. Free Bk & Memo. 1317 to 1549 fos. 63(58)–66(61), 81(76)v.; Acct R.

1420–1 acct ald. Gild St Geo.; W. Hudson, *Leet Jurisd. in Cty Norwich during XIIIth & XIVth cents.*, Selden S. 1892 v, 75; Hudson & Tingey ii, pp. lxiv, lxv, lxvii; Stat. 6 H.8 c.12.

[46] PRO, SPD Eliz. Add. 33/71.

[47] Ibid.; Nfk RO, Cty Recs. Bks Mayor's Ct 16 fos. 296v., 322v.; Ass. Bks 2 fos. 38(57), 39(58)v., 147(167)v., 149(169)v.; 3 fo. 82; 2nd Bk Worstedweavers fos. 7v.–8; Cons. Ct invs 1584/88; 1593/29; 1603/160; 1605/47; 1634/74; 1642/92; 1675/62; J. F. Pound, *Norwich Cs Poor 1570*, Nfk Rec. S. 1971 xl, 99; Edwards pp. x, 177–8; Hudson & Tingey ii, 119; *APC*, 1616–17 p. 49; BL, Add. MS 12504 fo. 88v.

[48] Smith, *Mems Wl*, i, 84; Stat. 33 H.8 c.16; my *Ag. Rev.*, 140, 228, 313–14; inf. 145.

[49] Smith, *Mems Wl*, ii, 26; T. S. Willan, *Engl. Coasting Trade*, Man. 1938, pp. 93–4.

[50] Inf. 77.

[51] Hudson & Tingey i, 74, 302; ii, pp. xxvi, lxiv–v; 34–5, 40; *CPR*, E.2 ii, 344.

[52] Stats 14 & 15 H.8 c.3; 21 H.8 c.21; 26 H.8 c.16; *Cal. Freemen Gt Yarmouth 1429–1800*, Nfk & Norwich Archaeol. S. 1910, pp. 9, 19–21, 23–4; *Cal. Freemen Lynn 1292–1836*, idem 1913, p. 85; Nfk RO, Cty Recs. 1st Bk Worstedweavers fos. 2, 4, 5, 6v.–9, 13, 14, 16v., 17, 19, 20, 85; 2nd ditto fos. 9v., 13v., 15, 19v., 29v., 32, 56v., 58; Bk Mayor's Ct 5, p. 8; Cons. Ct inv. 1635/103; Q. Sess. Bk 1562–7; inf. 153.

[53] Nfk RO, Cty Recs. Misc. Docs con. Trade & Comm., Controversy resp. Rts Cits Norwich: Touching the allegacion that the Queenes Majestie doth lose her custume; Hudson & Tingey ii, p. lxix; PRO, Exch. KR, Deps by Commn 44 & 45 Eliz. Mich. 1 m.3d.

[54] Posthumus, *Bronnen*, i, 356; Kerling, *Comm. Rels*, 84.

[55] BL, Add. 12504 fo. 82v.

[56] Ibid. no. 63 & fo. 82; N. H. Nicolas, *Privy Purse Exs Eliz. York & Wardrobe Accts Ed. IV*, 1830, pp. 117, 129, 132, 135; PRO, Exch. KR, Deps by Commn 44 & 45 Eliz. Mich. 1 m.7r.; Req. 157/134 fos. 72, 77(2); Stats 17 R.2 c.3; 20 H.6 c.10; 23 H.6 c.3; 7 E.4 c.1; 11 H.7 c.11; 12 H.7 c.1; 19 H.7 c.17; 5 H.8 c.4; 6 H.8 c.12; 14 & 15 H.8 c.3; 21 H.8 c.21; 25 H.8 c.5; 26 H.8 c.16; 33 H.8 c.16; 1 E.6 c.6; 5 & 6 E.6 c.7; Hudson & Tingey ii, 150–1; Gras 691–2; Nfk RO, Cty Recs. 1st & 2nd Bks Worstedweavers; *Rot. Parl.* iii, 637.

[57] Ibid.; Stats 20 H.6 c.10; 23 H.6 c.3; 7 E.4 c.1; PRO, Exch. KR, Deps by Commn 44 & 45 Eliz. Mich. 1 mm.7r., 8d.; Req. 157/134 fos. 72, 95(3); De Poerck ii, 230; Espinas & Pirenne iii, 20; Gras 527, 547; Posthumus, *Bronnen*, i, 27; Brulez, 'Engels Laken', 6; Hudson & Tingey ii, 150–1.

[58] Ibid. 150–1, 406; Gras 691–2; *Rot. Parl.* iii, 637; Stats 20 H.6 c.10; 23 H.6 c.3; 7 E.4 c.1; Nicolas 129; E. M. Carus-Wilson & O. Coleman, *Engld's Exp. Trade 1275–1547*, Oxf. 1963, p. 199; J. James 69, 81–2; Nfk RO, Cty Recs. 1st Bk Worstedweavers fos. 13, 75–6, 85v.; 2nd ditto fos. 2, 3v., 6, 7, 14v., 51, 88v.; PRO, Req. 157/134 fo. 72; BL, Add. 12504 no. 63 & fos. 82v, 87.

[59] Ibid. fo. 82.

[60] Gras 121, 454 sqq., 463–5, 473, 477–8, 485, 487, 497; Hudson & Tingey ii, 99, 230, 406; Nfk RO, Cty Recs, O. Free Bk & Memo. fos. 81(76)v.–82(77).

[61] Kent RO, Cons. Ct Cant. Regs. Accts & Invs 2 fos. 225v.–6, 364; 3 fos. 34v.–6; Inv. Papers 12/31; M. F. Mazzaoui, *It. Cotton Ind. in later M.A. 1100–1600*, Cam. 1981, p. 167; F. W. Weaver, *Soms. Med. Wills 2nd ser. 1501–30*, Soms. Rec. S. 1903 xix, 321–2, 324, 340; Strutt ii, 12; De Poerck i, 30, 37, 231–2, 272, 274, 290; ii, 199; iii, 158; De Sagher iii, 303; Espinas ii, 736, 797–8; Espinas & Pirenne ii, 170.

[62] Ibid. i, 183, 326; ii, 23, 26–8, 32–3, 62, 65, 81, 83, 86, 90, 95, 170, 203, 284, 589; iii, 284; J. Craeybeckx, 'Les Industries d'Exportation dans les villes flamandes au XVIIe s.' in *Studi in Onore de Amintore Fanfani*, vol. iv Milan 1962, pp. 438, 451; De Sagher iii, 303; Espinas ii, 736, 797–8; Ammann 24; Verlinden 28; Cole ii, 385, 577, 579; F. Irsigler, 'Ind. Prod., Internat. Trade & Pub. Fins in Cologne', *Jnl Eur. Econ. Hist.*, 1977, vi, 283, 285; Posthumus, *Geschiedenis*, ii, 321; *Bronnen*, ii, 609, 613, 694; iii, 4, 20, 60, 500; v. 371–2, 377; Smith, *Mems Wl*, ii, 436, 443–4, 446–7, 453; J. Sion, *Les Paysans de la Normandie Orientale*, Paris 1909, pp. 169–70; De Poerck i, 30, 37, 232, 272, 274, 276.

[63] Espinas & Pirenne i, 325–6; De Poerck i, 246; ii, 18.

[64] Ibid. 230.

[65] De Sagher i, 519; cf. Coornaert, *Bergues*, 35.

[66] De Poerck iii, 26.

[67] Posthumus, *Bronnen*, v, 458.

[68] Ibid. ii, 696.

[69] Endrei, *L'Evolution*, 34, 82–4; Heaton 126; Twiss ii, 196–7; Woodger 61, 64–7, 71–4.

[70] Smith, *Mems Wl*, i, 174–5; *APC*, 1623–5, pp. 105, 135, 285, 366; 1628–9, p. 375; PRO, PCR 1639, pp. 520–1 (fos. 255v.–6); SPD Jas 129/42; 130/56; Chas 425/40; 428/44–5; 457/14; 482/26, 79; Worcs. RO, Cons. Ct inv. 1648/126; Hakluyt, *Orig. Writings* 189; Willan, *Coasting Trade*, 120–1, 124, 134, 136–7, 139; B. Holloway, 'Acct Pits Fuller's Earth in Beds.', *Phil. Trans. R.S. Lond.* 18 vols 1809, vi, 674–5; Ramsay, *Wilts*,. 2; C. W. Chalklin, *17th cent. Kent*, 1965, pp. 178–9; D. C. Coleman, 'Econ. Kent under Later Stuarts', ts. thes. PhD Lond. Univ. 1951, pp. 163, 165; Burley, thes. 303–5; T. Fuller, *Hist. Worthies Engld*, 3 vols. 1840, i, 165; iii, 199; BL, Harl. 6288 fo. 62v.

[71] De Poerck i, 14; De Sagher ii, 437; iii, 190; Stats 22 E.4 c.5; 7 E.6 c.8; 8 Eliz.c.11; M. D. Harris, *Cov. Leet Bk 1420–1555*, EETS 4 pts 1907–13, cxxxiv–v, cxxxviii, cxlvi, pp. 640, 659, 672–3.

[72] *APC*, 1616–17, p. 90; Deyon 187; R. Van Uytven, 'Fulling Mill', *Acta Historiae Neerlandica*, 1971 v, 10.

[73] E. M Carus-Wilson, 'Ind. Rev. 13th cent.' in *Essays in Econ. Hist.*, ed. by her 1954, pp. 41 sqq.; Keutgen 373.

[74] Posthumus, *Bronnen*, i, 658–9; iii, 545; iv, 86, 94, 100–2, 106–8, 124–5, 165, 177, 179, 314; v, 162, 170, 175, 181, 184, 414, 642, 683; vi, 63–6, 70–1, 84 sqq., 107–8, 275; *Geschiedenis*, iii, 660–1; De Poerck i, 100–2; De Sagher i, 299, 300; ii, 437, 617; Espinas ii, 779; Willemsen, 'La grève', 118–19; Deyon 186–7; Coornaert, *Hondschoote*, 204–5; J. Demey, 'De "mislukte" Aanpassingen van de Nieuwe Draperie, de Saainijverheid en de Lichte Draperie te Ieper', *Tijdschrift voor Geschiedenis*, 1950 lxxxiii, 228, 231–2; V. Derode, 'Quelques Documents pour servir à l'Histoire de l'industrie à Lille', *Mémoires de la Société Impériale des Sciences & de l'Agriculture & des Arts de Lille*, 3e série 1868 (1867) iv, 411.

[75] Hakluyt, *Orig. Writings*, 189.

[76] PRO, SPD Eliz. 46/41.

[77] Posthumus, *Geschiedenis*, i, 62; Espinas & Pirenne ii, 689; Van Uytven, 'Mill', 2 sqq.

[78] Ibid. 4, 5; Doren i, 389; Davidsohn vol. iv pt ii, 53.

[79] *Algemene Geschiedenis der Nederlanden*, iv, 204; Demey 228, 231–2; Willemsen, 'La grève', 118–20; W. Van Waesberghe, 'De Invoering van de Belse Draperie te Brugge tijdens het Calvinistische Bewind, en verdere Evolutie', *Handelingen van de Genootschap voor Geschiedenis te Brugge*, 1972 cix, 35–7, 48; PRO, SPD Eliz. 46/41; De Sagher i, 322–3, 350, 353, 356–7, 508–9; ii, 54–6, 77–80, 82–4, 304, 324–5, 606, 608, 617; iii, 190–3, 202 sqq., 410–11; Van Uytven 'Mill', 8, 9.

[80] Ibid. 12; Posthumus, *Geschiedenis*, i, 61–2; iii, 661; *Bronnen*, iii, p. x; iv, pp. x, 272, 277, 281–2, 285–6, 289–91, 364, 417–8, 427, 440, 457–8, 466–7; v, 162, 414, 416, 452, 487, 527, 539, 561; vi, 280, 340–1; E. Rijpma, *De Ontwikkelingsgang van Kampen tot omstreeks 1600*, Groningen & Hague 1924, pp. 88, 104; De Vries 241; E. Baasch, *Hollaendische Wirtschaftsgeschichte*, Jena 1927, pp. 90, 96.

[81] Carus-Wilson, 'Ind. Rev. 13th cent.', 46 sqq., 58; J. Youing, *Tuckers Hall Exeter*, Exeter 1968, pp. 70–1, 74–5; W. B. Stephens, *17th cent. Exeter*, Exeter 1958, pp. 137–9; Stat. 2 & 3 P.&M. c.14; *VCH Leics.*, iv, 87; C. Phythian-Adams, *Desolation Cty*, Cam. 1979, p. 49; Cov. RO, Weavers' & Clothiers' Co. Recs., Misc. Papers re dispute bet. clothiers & drapers: petn to PC; PRO, Exch. Augm. Off., Parl. Svys (War.) 11, fo. 6; cf. B. B. Woodward, *Hist. & Descron Winch.*, Winch. n.d., p. 293; T. Atkinson, *Eliz. Winch.*, 1963, pp. 199, 200.

[82] J. Smyth, *Descron Hund. Berkeley*, Glouc. 1885, p. 4; Carus-Wilson, 'Ind. Rev. 13th cent.', 51, 59; Hakluyt, *Orig. Writings*, 189; Heaton 54–5.

[83] O. De Smedt, *De Engelse Natie te Antwerpen in de 16e eeuw*, Antwerp 2 vols. 1950–4, i, 46–7; E. E. Rich, *Ord. Bk Merchs Staple*, Cam. 1937, p. 14.

[84] Ibid. 13; Munro, *Wl, Cl. & Gold*, 182–3; R. Davis, 'Rise Antwerp & its Engl. Conn.' in D. C. Coleman & A. H. John, *Trade, Govt & Econ. in Pre-Ind. Engld*, 1976, p. 4.

## CHAPTER 2

[1] W. Smith & W. Webb, *Vale-Royall Engld*, 1656, p. 18.

[2] B. H. Cunnington, *Recs. Co. Wilts.*, Devizes 1932, p. 157; R.E.G. & E. F. Kirk, *Rets Aliens dwg in Cty & Subs Lond. fr. reign Hy VIII to Jas*, Pubs H.S.L. x, 3 pts 1900–7 ii, 101, 291; J. F. Pound, 'Soc. & Trade Structure Norwich 1525–75', *Past & Pres.*, 1966 no xxxiv, 65, 67; *Cs Poor*, 97; M. G. Davies, *Enforcemt Engl. Apprshp*, Cam. Mass. 1956, pp. 133–4; Emmison, *Home, Wk & Ld*, 195; Chester RO, Guild Recs. Weavers' Co. Bk 1697–1817; Nfk RO, Cty Recs. Bk Mayor's Ct 13, p. 181; Leics. RO, Arch. inv. 1709/80.

[3] *Cal. Freemen Lynn*, 25, 37, 39, 41, 45, 47–8, 53, 55–7, 62–3, 65, 68, 73; Tymms 4; W. G. Benham, *Oath Bk or Red Parch. Bk Colc.*, Colc., 1907, p. 175; J. Smyth, *Names & Surnames all Able & Sufficient Men ... within Co. Glouc. in 1608*, 1902, pp. 41, 71, 74–5; Schanz, *Handelspolitik*, ii, 107; Heaton 18, 55–8; Gras 120, 469, 527, 535–6, 539, 542–4, 546, 551, 553; M. A. Havinden, *Hsehld & Fm Invs in Oxon. 1550–90*, 1965, pp. 153, 304; C. Worthy, *Devon Wills*, 1896, p. 58; M. Cash, *Devon Invs 16th & 17th cents.*, Devon & Corn. Rec. S.n.s. 1966 xi, 44, 130–1; H. Fishwick, *Hist. Par. Rochdale*, Rochdale & Lond. 1889, p. 51; D. M. Woodward, *Trade Eliz. Chester*, Hull 1970, pp. 9, 10; Lowe 113; E. A. Lewis 165–6, 253–4; *VCH Soms.* iv, 57, 227; *Suss.* ii, 257; Stat. 34 & 35 H.8 c.10; PRO, SPD Eliz. 252/2; PCC wills Alenger 18; parch. invs p.1660 no 329; Kent RO, Arch.Ct Cant. Inv.Reg.5 fo. 19v; Maidstone Recs. Burghmote Bk 4 fos. 14v., 83v.; Worcs. RO, Cons. Ct inv. 1609/124; Wilts. RO, Pec. Ct Dean Sarum. invs Ed. May 1615, Th. Tiszer 1626 both Sherborne; Leics. RO, Arch. inv. 1614/205; Bodl. Arch. Ct Berks. O.W. etc. 222/45.

[4] My *Ag. Rev.*, 41 sqq.

[5] J. Leland, *Itin.*, 5 vols. 1906–10, i, 131–2, 135–6, 142–3, 145, 149, 152, 240; ii, 24; v, 83–4, 97–8, 100–1, 103; Smyth, *Names*, 26–7, 31–3, 35–6, 41, 54–5, 58–60, 62–3, 69 sqq., 146–7, 149 sqq., 179 sqq., 192 sqq., 215–7, 224 sqq., 230 sqq., 236 sqq., 274 sqq.; *VCH Wilts.*, iv, 116, 128, 139–40; R. Perry, 'Glos. Woollen Ind. 1100–1690', *Trs Brist. & Glos. Archaeol. S.*, 1947 (1945), lxvi, 75; R. Blome, *Brit.* 1673, pp. 104, 198; Ramsay, *Wilts.* 1 sqq.; 'Distr. Cl. Ind. in 1561–2', *Engl. Hist. Rev.* 1942 lvii, 362, sqq.; E. S. Lindley, *Wotton-under-Edge*, 1962, pp. 152–4; Glos. RO, Cons. Ct invs 1662/3; 1663/4, 91, 98, 104, 158, 164, 167, 196, 279; 1664/40; 1684/40, 82, 89, 100, 148; 1691/116; Brist. RO, Cons. Ct invs 1636 Ric. Dyer/Olveston; 1663/73; Soms. RO, Arch. Taunton inv. 1640/90; PRO, PCC parch. invs p. 1660 nos 363, 3935; Wilts. RO, Preb. Ct Uffculme invs bdl. 1 no. 23A; bdl. 2 no. 21; ex Dioc. Reg. Sarum. invs Jn Turner 1564 Gt Knoyle; Th. Mallard 1605 Gt Sherston; Th. Pytman 1620 Mere; Thomazine Gwyer 1633 Mere Zeals; Th. Graye 1642 Tisbury; Mary Piddle 1666 Ryme; Pec. Ct Prec. or Chantor bdl. 1 nos. 35, 37; 4 nos. 1, 21; 14 no. 57; 15 no. 45; Pec. Ct Treas. box 1 no 14; bdl. 11 Jn Franklin 1630; bdl. 11 Jn Laurence 1688; Preb. Ct Chardstock bdl. 2 nos. 6, 9; acc. 122: Chittoe Ct Bk, 1616 prob. Wm Rashwood/Studley; Cons. Ct Sarum. Th. Bourne 1625 Semley; Ric. Banstone als Macy 1702 Cutteridge in N. Bradley.

[6] Ibid. Jn Barsdale 1606 Seendhead; Wm Chiver 1614 Bromham; acc. 122: Stanley Ct Bk, 1618 prob. And. Wilcocks (Wilcox); 1626 prob. Jn Scott; Ramsay, *Wilts.* 4, 18, 19; Mann, *Cl. Ind.* 8; Friis 439, 453–6; Stats 5 & 6 E.6 c.6; 4 & 5 P.&M.c.5; 18 Eliz.c.16; 27 Eliz.c.17; 4 Jas c.2; PRO, SPD Eliz. 244/129; HMC, *Var. Colls* i, 162, 167–8; *Sackville MSS*, ii, 41, 211; Cunnington, *Recs Co. Wilts.* 2–4, 15; *VCH Wilts.* iv, 116.

[7] Ibid. 130–2; G. D. Ramsay, *Jn Isham, Mercer & Merch. Adven.*, Northants. Rec. S. 1962 xxi, 160; De Smedt ii, 331, 341, 361; J. Strieder, *Aus Antwerpener Notariatsarchiven*, Stuttgart, Berl. & Leip. 1930, pp. 141, 199, 200, 218, 220; W. Notestein, F. H. Relf, & H. Simpson, *Commons Debates 1621*, New Haven 7 vols 1935, ii, 325; E. M. Carus-Wilson, 'Evids Ind. on some 15th- Manors', *Econ. Hist. Rev*, 2nd ser. 1959 xii, 190, 197 sqq.; HMC, *Sackville MSS*, ii, 20, 37, 76, 117, 123, 130, 151.

[8] Ibid. 190 sqq.; Smyth, *Berkeley*, 26; *Names*, 274 sqq., 286 sqq., 297 sqq.; Ramsay, 'Distr.', 362, 365 sqq.; 'Rep. R. Commn clo. ind. 1640', *Engl. Hist. Rev.*, 1942 lvii, 486, 489; D. Defoe, *Tour thr. E. & W.*, 2 vols. 1928, ii, 43; PRO, PCR 1633–4 pp. 107, 372–3, 384 (fos. 50, 193v.–4); SPD Chas 287/77; PCC parch. invs p. 1660 nos 361, 368, 3422, 3892, 4502; paper invs 1661–1725 no. 28; invs 1718–82 bdl. 18 nos. 109, 237; 21 no. 9; 24 no. 100; 25 no. 67; Stat. 5 & 6 E.6 c.6; Glos. RO, Cons. Ct invs. 1663/83, 86, 148, 202, 230; 1664/30, 40; 1667/108; 1684/44, 48, 99; I. S. Leadam, *Sel. Cs in Ct Req.*, S.S. 1898 xii, 205.

[9] Bodl. Aubrey 2 fo. 141; Hearne's Diaries 158 p. 32; Mann, *Cl. Ind.* 10.

[10] Ramsay, *Wilts.* 24. 'Distr.', 362, 364, 366–7; PRO, PCC invs ser. i no. 97; *APC*, 1617–19 pp. 194, 202; Stats 5 & 6 E.6 c.6; 2 & 3 P. & M. c.12; 35 Eliz. c.9; 4 Jas c.2; J. Vanes, *Led. Jn Smythe 1538–50*, HMC, JP xix, 1974 (Brist. Rec. S. 1975 xx) 32, 49, 71, 81, 85, 91, 100, 144, 227, 258; M. G. Davies 111; Tawney & Power iii, 204.

[11] Soms. RO, DD/X/GB Combe Svy Bk 1704 fo. 155; Stat. 2 & 3 P. & M. c.12; PRO, PCC parch. invs p. 1660 no. 9326; Exch. KR, Deps by Commn 6 Jas East. 30; SPD Jas 75/4; Eliz. 111/38 ('Charge' erron., 'Charde' recte).

[12] W. S. Unger, *De Tol van Iersekeroord*, Hague 1939, p. 94; Heaton 5, 6, 287, 294; Strieder 104; Goris 630; Posthumus, *Geschiedenis*, ii, 326; *Bronnen*, iii, 14, 38, 463, 473–4, 479, 481, 492; v, 18; *Fs. Anc. Bk Weavers' Co.*, n.d., fo. 19; De Smedt i, 50, 300; ii, 386, 417.

[13] Ibid. ii, 335; Vanes, *Led.*, 148, 178; Bodl. Rawlinson A478 fo. 99v.; McGrath, *Merchs*, 78; D. Jones & H. W. King, 'Ed. Grey, last feud, bn Powys', *Montgoms. Colls*, 1885 xviii, 353; Hakluyt, *Prin. Navs*, iii, 269; PRO, SPD Eliz. 15/67; Brist. RO, Cons, Ct invs 1624/72; 1635 Hugh Davis/St Mary Pt; 1636 Jn Jones/Clifton; A. H. Johnson, *Hist. Wpfl Co. Drapers Lond.*, Oxf. 5 vols 1914–22, ii, 395.

[14] Mann, *Docs.*, pp. xvi, xx, xxi, 102–3, 116, 123; my *Ag. Rev.*, 199; S. H. Higgins, *Hist. Bleaching*, 1924, pp. 10, 11; Cunnington, *Recs Co. Wilts.*, 23.

[15] Ibid. 14, 169; G. Markham, *Engl. Housewife*, 1631, pp. 170–1; Mann, *Cl. Ind.*, 284–5; R. Watts, *Y. Mans Looking-Gl.*, 1641, p. 43; C. Bailey, *Transcripts fr. Mun. Archives Winch.*, Winch. 1856, pp. 67–8, 85; J. Waylen, *Hist. Mil. & Mun. Tn Marlborough*, 1854, pp. 274, 517–8; Leland i, 111; iv, 92; v, 82; *VCH Hants.*, v, 42; *Suss.*, ii, 256; *Wilts.*, iv, 116, 128; Defoe, *Tour*, i, 145; Ramsay, *Wilts.*, frontis., 2, 19; *Isham*, 95, 115; 'Distr.', 363; 'Rep.', 491; Leconfield, *Petworth Manor in 17th cent.*, 1954, p. 117; Blome 39, 40, 110; Friis 59, 129, 250, 438, 453–6; HMC, *Var. Colls*, i, 73; *11th Rep.* App. pt vii, 224; F. J. Baigent & J. E. Millard, *Hist. Anc. Tn & Manor Basingstoke*, Basingstoke 1889, pp. 319, 355, 386; J. Aubrey, *Nat. Hist. & Ants Sy*, 5 vols. 1719; iii, 314, 346; *APC*, 1630–1, pp. 136, 187–8; M. G. Davies 262; Fuller, *Worthies*, ii, 4; Bodl. Arch. Ct Berks. O.W. etc. 80/122; Stats 15 R.2 c.10; 5 & 6 E.6 c.6; 4 Jas c.2; BL, Harl. 70, fo. 27 (26); PRO, SPD Chas 177/56, 60; 182/45; 240/22–3; Interreg. 3/13; PCC invs ser. i nos. 174, 411, 419; parch. invs p. 1660 no. 11133; Wilts. RO, Cons. Ct Sarum. Humph. Atheath 1635 Warfield; Jn Willmott 1698 Reading; Wm Crosse 1605, Wm White 1676, Jn Stokes 1699, Ed. Errwood 1714, all Devizes; ex Dioc. Reg. Sarum. Jerome Planner 6 Jan. 9 Chas, Wokingham; Arch. Ct Sub-dean Sarum. 1611/5; 1612/15; 1615/4, 12, 20; 1617/5; 1618/12; 1621/9; 1622/1; 1626/6; 1627/16; 1629/3; 1632/16; 1637/14; 1680/17; 1685/22; 1688/10; 1715/10; 1731/18; Pec. Ct Dean Sarum. 1689 Th. Kate/Bere Regis; 1691 Wm Tickner/Wokingham; Pec. Ct Treas. box 2 no. 89; Hants. RO, Pec. Ct W. Meon, Jas Andrewes 1634; Pec. Ct Meonstoke etc. Giles Tanner 1567 Soberton; Arch. Ct O.W. & Invs Ric. Carter 1563, Robt Burbridge 1645, both Basingstoke; Cons. Ct O.W. & Invs Roger Coles 1626 Alton; Jn Guy 1628 Andwell in Basingstoke; Ric. Hollis gent. 1628, Ric. Whieller 1635, both Newport (I.W.); Ric. Bowden 1637 Carisbrooke; 1650 bdl., no. 3; unclass invs D/2/A: 2/40.

[16] Ibid. O.W. & Invs, Jn Warner 1628, Jn Smythe 1638, both Basingstoke; Guildford Muniment Rm, Loseley MSS 1965; 1966/2–4.

[17] Ramsay, *Wilts.*, 20–2, 24, 109, 142; Mann, *Cl. Ind.* 9, 14, 21; C. Haskins, *Anc. Trade Guilds & Cos Salisbury*, Salisbury 1912, pp. 84–5; Stats. 7 R.2 c.9; 12 R.2 c.14; 7 H.4 c.10; 9 H.4 c.5; 11 H.4 c.6; 1 R.3 c.8; 3 & 4 E.6 c.2; 18 Eliz. c.16; *APC*, 1630–1, p. 356; Willan, *Tu. Bk Rates*,

74; *Cal. SP Ven.*, i, 80, 84; *VCH Wilts.*, iv, 116, 125, 140; Defoe, *Tour*, i, 189; R. C. Anderson, *Bk Exams & Deps 1622–44*, Soton Rec. S.4 vols. 1929–36, i, 46; PRO, SPD Eliz. 244/50, 105; Chas 285/28; PCC invs ser. i no. 174; D. F. Lamb, 'Seaborne Trade Soton in 1st half 17th cent.', ts. thes. M.Phil. Soton Univ. 2 vols. 1971, pp. 58, 136, 207, 218–19, 224, 227, 230–2, 234, 236–7, 241–2, 248–9, 253 sqq., 259, 261–2, 266–8, 271, 273–4, 284.

[18] Ibid. 278; Willan, *Tu Bk Rates*, 74; *Rates Marchandizes*; Stat. 1 R.3 c.8.

[19] Kent RO, Arch. Ct Cant. Inv. Regs 5 fos. 4, 196; 10 fos. 364–6, 392–4; Cons. Ct Cant. Regs Accts & Invs 9 fo. 263.

[20] Ibid. 2 fos. 225v.–6, 364; 3 fos. 34v.–6; 6 fo. 163; 8 fos. 357–8; 9 fo. 238; 10 fo. 184; 11 fos. 90, 274; 13 fo. 488; Inv. Reg. 14 fo. 599; Maidstone Recs. Burghmote Bk 3 fo. 5v. (p. 10); PRO, Exch. Ld Rev. Misc. Bks 215 fos. 15 sqq.; 219 fos. 10, 58.

[21] T. Smith 351–2; Salzman 200; J. S. Furley 80–1; Atkinson 199; *VCH Hants.*, v, 41, 477 sqq.; HMC, *6th Rep.*, pt i, (1877), App. p. 602; Ammann 35; Gras 121, 466–7, 473, 480.

[22] Willan, *Tu. Bk Rates*, 73; Goris 262–3, 291, 630; McGrath, *Merchs*, 283; De Smedt ii, 332, 334, 347, 443; Friis 439; Unger, *Bronnen*, iii, 119; *Rates Merchandizes*, 85; *Rates Marchandizes*.

[23] Ibid.; J.B., *The Merchants Avizo*, 1607, pp. 9, 11; A. K. Longfield, *Anglo-Ir. Trade in 16th cent.*, 1929, p. 158; *VCH Hants.*, v, 261, 424, 482 sqq.; *Suss.*, ii, 256–7; *Sy*, ii, 344–5, 347; *Wilts.*, iv, 140; vi, 127; *Soms.*, ii, 411; Bailey 67–8, 85; Ramsay, *Wilts.*, 19–21, 109; 'Distr.', 362, 364–7; L. Roberts, *Marchants Mapp Comm.*, 1638, 2nd pt 181 erron. 189 recte, 193; J. S. Davies, *Hist. Soton*, Soton 1883, p. 27; J. Coker, *Svy Dors.*, 1732, p. 5; Tawney & Power iii, 201–3, 208; Friis 439; Blome 86, 106; E. Nevill, 'Mar. Lics Sarum.', *Geneal.*, 1915 xxxi, 182; HMC, *Sackville MSS*, ii, 146; *11th Rep.*, App. pt iii, 95; M. G. Davies 262; *APC*, 1630–1 pp. 187–8; J. Childrey, *Britannia Baconica*, 1660, p. 50; C. Dale, *Wilts. Apprs & their Mrs 1710–60*, Wilts. Rec. S. 1961, xvii, 16, 34, 62, 66, 99, 107, 120, 135, 151, 173; Lamb 224, 298, 301, 312, 314–15, 319–20, 322–3; J. L. Wiggs, 'Seaborne Trade Soton in 2nd ½ 16th cent.', ts. thes. MA Soton Univ. 1955, p. 45; Stats 33 H.8 c.18; 3 & 4 E.6 c.2; 5 & 6 E.6 c.6; 4 & 5 P. & M. c.5; 14 Eliz. c.10; 18 Eliz. c.16; 3 Jas c.16; Bodl. Arch. Ct Berks. O.W. etc. 99/3; Nfk RO, Cons. Ct inv. 1591/154; Kent RO, Arch. Ct Cant. Inv. Reg. 5 fo. 53v.; PRO, SPD Eliz. 250/47; Eliz. Add. 11/113; Chas 182/45; 285/28; PCC invs ser. i nos. 174, 411; parch. invs p. 1660 nos. 4625, 11133; Wilts. RO, ex Dioc. Reg. Sarum. invs Ric. Kendall 1600 Mere; Hy Noble 1601 Edington; Arch. Ct Sub-dean Sarum, 1627/16; 1629/7; Dors. RO, Pec. Ct Wimborne Minster, ex-par. wills & invs nos. 51, 141(1); Hants. RO, Arch. Ct O.W. & Invs Jn Mathew 1641, Hy Watridge 1650, both Alton; Jn Morton 1653 Soton; Cons. Ct O.W. & Invs Jn Prior 1624 Bramley; Sam. Hoopper 1630 Soton; Hy Parr 1647 Havant; 1650/3; Robt Gover 1664 Romsey.

[24] Ibid. Jn Warner 1628, Jn Smythe 1638, & Arch. Ct, Th. West 1649, all Basingstoke; Aubrey, *Sy*, iv, 4; M. Postlethwayt, *Univ. Dict. Trade & Comm.*, 2 vols. 1757, ii, 770; R. Pococke, *Travs thr. Engld*, Camd. S.2 vols. n.s. xlii, xliv 1888–9, ii, 164.

[25] Kent RO, Cons. Ct Cant. Reg. Accts & Invs 8 fos. 357–8; Arch. Ct Cant. Inv. Reg. 7 fos. 62–3; Maidstone Recs. Burghmote Bk 3 fos. 22v., 42v., 53 (pp. 45, 85, 106).

[26] Stat. 33 H.8 c.18; PRO, PCC parch. invs p. 1660 no. 11133; Hants. RO, Cons. Ct O.W. & Invs Sam. Hoopper 1630 Soton; Arch. Ct. O.W. & Invs Th. West 1649 Basingstoke.

[27] F. Edler, 'Winchcombe Kerseys in Antwerp (1538–44)', *Econ. Hist. Rev.*, 1937 vii, 57 sqq.; 'Van Der Molen, Commn Merchs Antwerp' in J. L. Cate & E. N. Anderson, *Med. & Hist. Essays in Honor J. W. Thompson*, Chic. 1938, pp. 95–6, 104, 108; De Smedt ii, 332; T. Deloney, *Pleasant Hist. Jn Winchcombe*, 1633; Guicciardini 122; W. Money, *Hist. Anc. Tn & Boro. Newbury*, Oxf. & Lond. 1887, p. 203; *Ltrs & Papers Hy VIII*, xvi no. 625; PRO, SPD Eliz. 15/67; BL, Lans. 152 fo. 229 (240).

[28] Wilts. RO, Arch. Ct Sub-dean Sarum. 1632/9; ex Dioc. Reg. Sarum. Jn Crouche 1586 W. Combe in Gt Bedwyn; Wm Caston 1598 Hungerford; Matt. Browne 1634 L. Bedwyn; Kent RO, Maidstone Recs. Burghmote Bks 3 fos. 5v., 8v. (pp. 10, 16); 4 fos. 14, 28, 51, 116v., 120v., 165v., 173, 179, 189v., 193, 220v., 233v.; 5 fos. 6v., 8; Cons. Ct Cant. Reg. Accts & Invs 12 fo.

33; Inv. Regs I fos. 9, 115v., 116v., 117v.; 17 fo. 460; 19 fo. 472; Arch. Ct Cant. Inv. Reg. 7 fo. 63v.

[29] Ibid. 61 nos. 12, 24, 36, 127, 195; Inv. Papers 17/74; 33/172; 41/201; Cons. Ct Cant. Regs Accts & Invs 8 fos. 242–4; 10 fos. 215v.–6; 12 fo. 33; 16 fos. 391v.–2; Inv. Papers 7/80; 12/94; 16/10; 34/69; Inv. Reg. 4 fo. 3; Const. Ct Roffen. Paper Invs bdl. 7 no. 4; bdl. 9 no. 2; BL, Add. R. 19167; PRO, SPD Eliz. 106/49; PCC parch. invs p. 1660 no. 4259; invs 1718–82 bdl. 18 no. 21; D. H. Willson, *Parl. Diary Robt Bowyer 1606–7*, Minneapolis 1931, p. 82; Defoe, *Tour* i, 115; Ramsay, 'Distr.', 363 sqq.; J. L. M. Gulley, 'Wealden Landscape in early 17th cent.', ts. thes. PhD Lond. Univ. 1960, pp. 204–5; E. Melling, *Kentish Sources*, vol. iii, Maidstone 1961, pp. 108 sqq.

[30] Ibid.; id. vol. vi, 1969, pp. 43–4; Stats 5 & 6 E.6 c.6; 4 & 5 P.&M. c.5; 8 Eliz. c.6; 4 Jas c.2; Friis 58, 129, 438, 453–5; Kent RO, Cons. Ct Roffen. Paper Invs bdl. 9 no. 2; Arch. Ct Cant. Inv. Reg. 61 nos. 12, 36, 127, 195; Inv. Papers 33/172; Cons. Ct Cant. Regs Accts & Invs 8 fo. 243v.; 10 fo. 216; 16 fo. 392; Inv. Papers 7/80; 16/10; 34/69; Bodl. Top. Kent a.I fo. 26; Ramsay, 'Distr.', 362 sqq.

[31] Ibid. 362, 364 sqq.; W. R. & R. K. Serjeant, *Ind. Prob. Recs Ct Arch. Sfk 1444–1700*, Ind. Lib. B.R.S. 1979–80, xc, xci, 293, 448; G. A. Thornton, *Hist. Clare*, Cam. 1930, pp. 150–2, 160–1, 186; Unwin, *Studs*, 264–6, 269, 271 sqq., 278, 288–9; Pilgrim, thes. 227 sqq.; Blome 208–9, 211–12; M. G. Davies 45; *Manners & Hsehold Exs*, 334, 336, 339; Stats 5 & 6 E.6 c.6; 4 Jas c.2; Kerling, *Comm. Rels*, 235; J. Webb, *Gt Tooley of Ips.*, Sfk Rec. S. 1962, pp. 9, 24, 136–7; N. Bacon, *Anns Ips.*, Ips. 1884, p. 365; A. Clark, 'Ess. Woollen Manufs', *Ess. Rev.* 1908 xvii, 205–6; Twiss 196–7; W. Sfk RO, Ep. Commy Ct Bury, Reg. Bk Wills 24 fos. 40, 42v.; invs 1573–8/31, 43; 1667/170; 1680/200; Nfk RO, Cons. Ct invs 1602/330, 335; 1618/96, 206; 1628/99; E. Sfk RO, Arch. invs 2/161; 3/6, 23; 18/69; BL, Egerton 2651 fo. 24; PRO, PCC parch. invs p. 1660 nos. 572, 2887, 2913, 7798; SPD H.VIII vol. 151 fos. 128–31; Eliz. 209/102.

[32] Ibid. 106/48.

[33] Ibid.; & 132/22; 209/102; Jas 131/40; PCC parch. invs p. 1660 nos. 572, 2887, 2913, 7798; Stats 5 & 6 E.6 c.6; 8 Eliz. c.6; 4 Jas c.2; BL, Harl. 70 fos. 12(11)v. (p. 13), 27–8 (26–7); Cott. Titus B.v fo. 254(251) (244); E. Sfk RO, Arch. invs 1/120; 3/23; W. Sfk RO, Ep. Commy Ct Bury, Reg. Bk Wills 24 fos. 40–2; invs 1573–8/97; 1667/170; Webb, *Tooley*, 137; Vanes, *Led.*, 309; D. C. Coleman, *Sir Jn Banks*, Oxf. 1963, p. 26; F. G. Emmison, *Eliz. Life: Wills Ess. Gentry & Merchs pr. in PCC*, Chelmsford 1978, pp. 314–15; Ramsay, 'Distr.', 362, 364 sqq.; Blome 209; Friis 58–9, 129, 438, 453–5; J. May, *Dec. Este Clo.*, 1613, p. 30; Thornton 186; *Winthrop Papers*, Mass. Hist. S. 5 vols 1925–47, i, 302–3; G. H. Rendall, *Dedham in Hist.*, Colc. 1937, p. 44; R. Reyce, *Breviary Sfk* (1618) ed. F. Hervey 1902, p. 22; Pilgrim, thes. 10 sqq.

[34] Stat. 8 Eliz. c.16; PRO, SPD Eliz. 209/102.

[35] Ibid. 244/50, 105; Eliz. Add. 34/22; H.VIII vol. 232 fo. 17; Stats 8 E.4 c.1; 1 R.3 c.8; 3 H.7 c.11(12); 14 & 15 H.8 c.11; 27 H.8 c.12; 3 & 4 E.6 c.2; 43 Eliz. c.10; *Manners & Hsehld Exs*, 334–5; McClenaghan 25; Smit ii, 24, 131; H. Zins, *Engld & Balt. in Eliz. Era*, Man. 1972, p. 162; Unwin, *Studs*, 276–7; Schanz, *Handelspolitik*, ii, 107; Harris, *Cov. Leet Bk*, 697, 714–5; Kent RO, Arch. Ct Cant. Inv. Reg. 5 fo. 53v.; Nfk RO, Cty Recs. Ass. Bk, 3 fos. 34–5, 307v.

[36] Ibid. Bk 2 fo. 147(167)v.; PRO, PCC parch. invs p. 1660 no. 7798; Webb, *Tooley*, 43; Posthumus, *Bronnen*, i, 356; J. M. Lappenberg, *Urkundliche Geschichte des Hansischen Stahlhofes zu London*, Ham. 1851, pt. ii, 117; De Smedt ii, 350; W.Sfk RO, Ep. Commy Ct Bury invs 1647-8/15, 88; 1664/22; 1680/200.

[37] Ibid. 1664/22; 1665/97; 1667/170; Blome 211; Nfk RO, Cty Recs. Ass. Bk 2 fo. 147(167)v.; PRO, PCC invs. ser. i no. 524.

[38] Ibid. parch. invs p. 1660 no. 3941; Nfk RO, Cons. Ct inv. 1672/39; Bacon 357; W. Sfk RO, Ep. Commy Ct Bury invs 1663/96; 1665/97; 1666/50; 1667/80; 1669/101; 1670/51; 1680/200; cf. 1663/108.

[39] Ibid. 1573–8/31; 1662/115; 1667/170; Nfk RO, Cons. Ct inv. 1672/39; F. W. Steer, *Fm & Ctge Invs Mid-Ess. 1635–1749*, Chelmsford 1950, pp. 71–2, 81; Stats 1 R.3 c.8; 3 H.7 c.11(12); E. Sfk RO, Arch. inv. 3/49.

[40] Ibid. 1/120; Blois Fam. Archives, Hy Blois's Acct Led. fo. 41; Bacon 357; Gras 526–8, 536, 538, 542, 647, 689; Pilgrim, thes. 28, 126, 201; Emmison, *Home, Wk & Ld*, 76; Nfk RO, Cons. Ct inv. 1591/154.

[41] Ibid. Cty Recs. Bks Mayor's Ct 5 pp. 502–3; 16 fos. 425, 460, 471; 20 fos. 9v., 10, 44v.; PRO, Req. 157/134 fo. 96(4); PCR 1631–2 p. 269 (fo. 135); Exch. KR, Deps by Commn 44 & 45 Eliz. Mich. 1 mm. 3d., 9.

[42] Benham 179; Plot, *Oxon.*, 279; Nfk RO, Cons. Ct inv. 1606/150.

[43] Tymms 168–9; Friis 438; Ramsay, 'Distr.', 362; H. Prigg, *Icklingham Papers*, Woodbridge 1901, p. 102; Stats. 4 & 5 P.&M. c.5; 4 Jas c.2; Nfk RO, Cons. Ct inv. 1636/187; W. Sfk RO, Ep. Commy Ct Bury invs 1573–8/31, 97; 1647–8/56; 1650/55; 1652/80; 1662/55; 1663/96; 1665/97, 139; 1666/50.

[44] M. G. Davies 111; *Winthrop Papers*, iii, 150, 152; T. Gerard, *Part. Descron Co. Soms.*, Soms. Rec. S. 1900 xv, 55; Willan, *Tu. Bk Rates*, 74; *Rates Marchandizes*; McGrath, *Merchs*, 78, 282; Stephens, *Exeter*, 10, 29, 30, 67, 104; 'For. Trade Ply. & Corn. Pts in early 17th cent.', *Devon Ass.*, 1969 ci, 131; Tawney & Power iii, 200, 203–4; M. Sellers, *Acts & Ords. Eastld Co.*, Camd. 3rd ser. 1906 xi, 20; Friis 67, 377–8, 438–9, 453–5; J. J. Bourhis, 'Le Trafic du Port de Dartmouth 1599–1641', ts. thes. Dip. d'études supérieures, Univ. de Bret. Occ. 2 vols. 1972, i, 97; Stats. 5 & 6 E.6 c.6; 2 & 3 P.&M. c.12; 43 Eliz. c.10; 4 Jas c.2; Schanz, *Handelspolitik*, ii, 108; Vanes *Led.*, 310; H. C. M. Lyte, *Hist. Dunster*, pt i, 1909, pp. 297 sqq.; E. A. Lewis 4, 16, 20–1, 24, 40; *VCH Wilts.*, iv, 126; R. W. Dunning & T. D. Tremlett, *Bridgwater Boro. Archives*, vol. v, Soms. Rec. S. 1971 lxx, 21–2, 74; A. H. Powell, *Anc. Boro. Bridgwater*, Bridgwater 1907, pp. 200–1; Lichfield Jt RO, Cons. Ct, Th. Smyth 1603 Cov.; BL, Harl. 70 fo. 13 bis (p. 16); Soms. RO, Cons. Ct Bath & Well. invs Simon Aishford 1634 Dunster; Bart. Weston 1639 Stogursey; Arch. Taunton invs 1638/24; 1670/29; 1681/90; 1688 Lewis Pollard/Holford; 1690 Agnes Pollard/Holford; 1720/4; 1726–7/2 Wm Bowden/Minehead; Bpl., N. Devon Athenaeum, Bpl. Boro. Recs., Sess. Ct Recs. vol. 10: 8 Jan. 17 Chas 2; PRO, SPD Eliz. 4/6; 6/52; 239/54; Jas 75/4; PCC invs 1718–82 bdl. 21 no. 65; Leland i, 166.

[45] Ibid., 170, 172, 239, 300; T. Westcote, *View Devon in 1630*, Exeter 1845, p. 61; Dunsford 32, 41; Wilts. RO, Preb. Ct Uffculme, bdl. 5 no. 15; BL, Harl. 5827 fo. 9(7)v.

[46] Schanz, *Handelspolitik*, ii, 107, Stats 7 E.4 c.2; 1 R.3 c.8; 3 H.8 c.6; 6 H.8 c.9; 27 H.8 c.12; 5 & 6 E.6 c.6; 7 E.6 c.9; McGrath, *Merchs*, 283; Friis 439; Willan, *Tu. Bk Rates*, 73; my *Ag. Rev.*, 316; *Rates Marchandizes*; De Smedt ii, 332, 334.

[47] Ibid. 333; T. C. Mendenhall, *Shrewsbury Drapers & W. Wl Trade in XVI & XVIII cents.*, 1953, pp. 4, 21, 42; Gras 278; W.Sfk RO, Ep. Commy Ct Bury invs 1665/97; 1669/101; 1670/51; BL, Cott. Titus B.v fo. 252(242)(249); Soms. RO, Arch. Taunton inv. 1688 Lewis Pollard/Holford; Brist. RO, Cons. Ct invs 1633 Philip Towenston (endorsed Townsend) Temple par.; 1624/72; Roberts, *Marchants Mapp*, 2nd pt, 226; Stat. 6 H.8 c.9; Nfk RO, Arch. Ct. Norvic. inv. 1718–19/35; Willan, *Tu. Bk Rates*, 74; *Rates Marchandizes*; *Cal. Wynn Papers 1515–1690*, 1926, pp. 189–90, 281, 312; Kent RO, Cons. Ct Cant. Reg. Accts & Invs 16 fo. 219.

[48] Ibid. Arch. Ct Cant. Inv. Reg. 1 fo. 9; Westcote 61; Stats 6 H.8 c.9; 27 H.8 c.12; 4 & 5 P. & M. c.5; 3 Jas c.17; *APC*, 1627, p. 194; Guildhall Lib., Commy Ct Lond. (Lond. Div.) invs box 9 Chas Barnes 1702 St Matt. Fri. St; *Winthrop Papers*, iii, 152, 161.

[49] Ibid.272, 288–9; Pococke i, 232; ii, 15, 177, 180, 196; Ramsay, 'Distr.', 362–4, 366; Roberts, *Marchants Mapp*, 2nd pt, 28, 226; *APC*, xxxiii, 9, 34, 353; xxx, 606; 1619–21 pp. 56–7; R. I. Jack, 'Cl. Ind. in Med. W.', *W. Hist. Rev.*, 1981 x, 449; D. G. Hey, *Engl. Rural Commun.: Myddle under Tus & Stuarts*, Leic. 1974, pp. 154–5; J. G. Jenkins, *W. Woollen Ind.*, Cardiff 1969, pp. 105, 111–12, 114; Willan, *Coasting Trade*, 95; C. A. J. Skeel, 'W. Woollen Ind. in 16th & 17th cents.', *Arch. Camb.*, 1922 lxxvii (ii), 227, 249; Aberystwyth, Cons. Ct St Asaph, O. W., Admons & Invs 1661 Th. Price/Wrexham, Th. Edwards gent. Oswestry; 1662 Th. Wilkinson/Wrexham; 1665 Th. Glover/Oswestry; S. Leighton, 'Recs Corp. Oswestry', *Trs Salop Archaeol. S.*, 1880 iii, 136; R. Gough, *Hist. Myddle*, Sunninghill 1979, pp. 38, 47–8, 64, 78, 104, 143, 147, 149–50, 154; P. Heylyn, *Microcosmus*, Oxf. 1636, pp. 490–1; E. A. Lewis 60, 67, 76–7, 84, 110, 117, 122, 140, 168,

174, 177, 201, 204–5, 227–8; G. Owen, *Descron Penbrokshire*, H.S.C. Rec. Ser. 4 pts 1892–1936, i, 56–7; Mendenhall 4, 8, 10–12, 28–9, 32, 42, 54, 58, 211–12; T. Kemp, *Bk Jn Fisher*, Warwick n.d. 146, 155; W. Cathrall, *Hist. Oswestry*, Oswestry n.d. 51–3; W. J. Slack, *Ldshp Oswestry*, Shrewsbury 1951, p. 39; I. Watkin, *Oswestry*, Lond. & Oswestry 1920, p. 333; BL, Cott. Titus B.v fo. 252 (242)(249); Lans. 152 fo. 239; 162 fo. 197 (210); Cov. RO, Cty Recs. Leet Bk 30 Eliz.–1834, p. 20; PRO, SPD Eliz. 15/67; 157/4, 5; Jas 80/13; 133/37; Exch. Ld Rev. Misc. Bk 255 fos. 77–8, 82; Stats 6 H.8 c.9; 33 H.8 c.3; 34 & 35 H.8 c.11; 5 & 6 E.6 c.6; 4 & 5 P.&M. c.5; 8 Eliz. c.7; 3 Jas c.17; 21 Jas c.9; Shrewsbury Lib. MSS 3359 fo. 5v.; 4274, agrt Nov. 1600; Chester RO, Cty Recs. Ass. Bk 1539–1624 fo. 168 (165)v.

[50] Ibid.; Mendenhall 4, 8; De Smedt ii, 333; PRO, SPD Eliz. 157/4, 5; E. A. Lewis 255, 284; Woodward, *Trade Eliz. Chester*, 13; R. I. Jack, 'Cl. Ind. in Med. Ruthin', *Denbighs. Hist. S. Trs*, 1963 xii, 24; J. G. Jenkins, 'Woollen Ind. Montgoms.', *Montgoms. Colls*, 1963–4 lviii, 52; Watkin, loc. cit.; *APC*, xxxiii, 9, 34, 353; Stats 6 H.8 c.9; 34 & 35 H.8 c.11; 4 & 5 P.&M. c.5; 8 Eliz. c.7; 21 Jas c.9; Fuller, *Worthies*, iii, 53.

[51] Ibid. 485; Stat. 5 & 6 E.6 c.6; De Smedt ii, 332; E. A. Lewis xxxii, 11, 16, 55, 59, 60, 80, 88, 90, 110, 122–3, 141 sqq., 149, 152, 174, 185, 195, 198, 214; Vanes, *Led.*, 89; Pococke ii, 25; *C.J.*, ix, 116; Leland iv, 178; Owen pt i, 148; Jack, 'Cl. Ind. Med. W.', 449; Kent RO, Arch. Ct Cant. Inv. Reg. 5 fo. 19; Willan, *Inld Trade*, 9, 38; Tawney & Power iii, 200, 203, 205; W. Rees, *Svy Du. Lanc. Ldshps in W. 1609–13*, Cardiff 1953, p. 192; E. M. Jones, *Exch. Proc. (Eq.) con. W.: H.VIII–Eliz.*, id. 1939, p. 298; HMC, *13th Rep.*, App. pt iv, 327; Jenkins, *W. Woollen Ind.*, 111; D. R. Phillips, *Hist. V. Neath*, Swansea 1925, pp. 317, 667, 689; B. G. Charles, *Cal. Recs Boro. Haverfordwest 1539–1660*, Cardiff 1967, pp. 3, 9, 29, 97, 136, 215, 218, 233.

[52] Ibid., 97; Duhamel du Monceau, *Art de Friser ou Ratiner les Etoffes de Laine*, s.l. 1766, pp. 1, 5; Espinas & Pirenne i, 675; De Sagher i, 519; Posthumus, *Geschiedenis*, ii, 317; Hoffman 229 sqq.; De Poerck ii, 242; iii, 40; P. I. G. Bataille, *Glossario Italiano Tessile*, Biella n.d., s.v. tessuto frieze; P. S. Donaldson, 'Geo. Rainsford's *Rittrato d'Inghilterra* (1556)'; *Camd. Misc.*, xxvii Camd. 4th ser. 1979 xxii, 91; Tawney & Power iii, 200; *Discourse Com. Weal*, 82; Jones & King 353; E. Spenser, *F.Q.*, Bk vii, C. vii, st. 31; Stats 1 R.3 c.8; 6 H.8 c.9; 27 H.8 c.12; 34 & 35 H.8 c.11; 4 & 5 P.&M. c.5; 8 Eliz. c.7.

[53] W. de G. Birch 259; Chester RO, Cty Recs. Ass. Bk 1539–1624 fo. 166(163)v.; Shrewsbury Lib. MSS 3359 fo. 5v.; 4274.

[54] Leland i, 42; Heaton 68 sqq., 134–5, 205–6, 342; Ramsay, 'Distr.', 362, 364; M. G. Davies 110; Tawney & Power iii, 203; D. Defoe, *Compl. Engl. Tradesman*, Edin. 1839, p. 77; R. Boyson, *Ashworth Cotton Enterprise*, Oxf. 1970, p. 1; Lowe 26–8, 30, 34–6, 41–2; G. H. Tupling, *Econ. Hist. Rossendale*, Chetham S. n.s. 1927 lxxxvi, 178–9; Fishwick, *Hist. Rochdale*, 53–4; W. B. Crump & G. Ghorbal, *Hist. Huddersfield Woollen Ind.*, Huddersfield 1935, p. 32; *APC*, xx, 163; xxx, 602; 1627–8, p. 307; J. May 24–7, 33; BL, Lans. 114 no. 24 fo. 92v.; Stats 14 & 15 H.8 c.1; 5 & 6 E.6 c.6; 39 Eliz. c.20; 4 Jas c.2; Lancs. RO, Cons. Ct Cestr. invs Supra: 1632 Jas Haslame/Falinge in Spotland; 1635 Ric. Greenhalgh/Town Miln, Rochdale; Nic. Ogden/Michell Hey in Spotland; Jas Howerth/Risingbridge; 1663 Jn Holte/Lwr Clough; Oliver Ormerod/Wolfenden; 1668 Jos. Ingham/Goodshaw; 1672 Jn Brearley/Ogden; Mary Taylor/Lowerplace; Wm Buckley/Crawshawbent in Saddleworth; Grace Kershawe/Hamer Miln; 1673 Jn Pilling/Brookclough; 1674 Th. Duckworth/Redlees in Bury; Jn Butterworth/New Hey in Butterworth in Rochdale; Jn Holden/Musbury; 1676 Is. Holden/Haslingden; Robt Holden/id.; Jn Hey/Rawtenstall; Jas Tattersall/Tonge End; Nat. Hoyle/Bacup; 1679 Th. Hopwood/Digyate in Rochdale; Jas Lord/Rockcliffe; 1680 Jn Ashworth/Greenes; Hy Hargreaves/Goodshaw; Infra: 1673 Jn Whythead/Tunshill in Rochdale; 1679 Jon. Milne/Shawfield in Spotland; Robt Jenkenson/Butterworth Hall; 1685 Josh. Wardle/Scowt in Hundersfield; 1707 Sam. Scolefield/Lanehead in Saddleworth; PRO, SPD Chas 294/93; Eliz. 287/96; 239/54; 111/38.

[55] Ibid.; J. Vanes, *Docs Ill. O'seas Trade Brist.*, Brist. Rec. S. 1979 xxxi, 131; cf. Defoe, *Tour*, ii, 187.

[56] *Misc.*, Thoresby S. iv, 163–6; Defoe, *Plan*, 87, 182–3; W. de G. Birch 259; Nfk RO, Cons. Ct inv. 1709–10/152; Northants. RO, Arch. Ct Northampton Admons & Invs 1724/108; Stats 4 & 5 P.&M. c.5; 4 Jas c.2; PRO, SPD Eliz. 111/38; 252/2; *APC*, xxx, 602.

[57] Ibid.; Ramsay, 'Distr.', 362–3, 365–8; Crump & Ghorbal 32; Friis 439, 453–5; McGrath, *Merchs*, 78, 282; Willan, *Tu. Bk Rates*, 74; *Ru. Co.*, 140; De Smedt ii, 332; *Rates Marchandizes*, s.v. woollens; E. B. Schumpeter, *Engl. O'seas Trade Stat. 1697–1808*, Oxf. 1960, p. 70; PRO, SPD Eliz. 252/2; Exch. KR Deps by Commn 33 Chas 2 Mich. 33; Shrewsbury Lib. MS 3359 fo. 5 v.; W. Sfk RO, Ep. Commy Ct Bury invs 1663/108, 214; 1670/77; Stats 5 & 6 E.6 c.6; 39 Eliz. c.20; 4 Jas c.2; BL, Lans, 114 no. 24, fo. 93.

[58] Ibid. fo. 92v.; T. S. Willan, *Eliz. Man.*, Chetham S. 3rd ser. 1980 xxvii, 51; *Inld Trade*, 109; J. May 33; Heaton 179, 182–4, 206, 222, 251; W. E. Preston, *Wills pr. in Ct Man. Crosley, Bingley, Cottingley & Pudsey*, Brad. Hist. & Ant. S. Loc. Rec. Ser 1929 i, 33–4, 37, 39, 40, 48–9, 103–4; Roberts, *Marchants Mapp*, 2nd pt, 28; Ramsay, *Isham*, xxvi–vii, 160; Lowe 3–5, 7, 30–1, 36, 38; Defoe, *Tour*, ii, 187, 198; W. Bennett, *Hist. Burnley 1400–1650*, Burnley 1947, p. 86; HMC, *14th Rep.*, App. pt iv, 573; M. Prestwich, *Cranfield*, Oxf. 1966, pp. 52–3, 55–7; Stats 33 H.8 c.18; 5 & 6 E.6 c.6; *APC*, xxx, 602; xxxi, 79; 1627–8, p. 307; PRO, SPD Eliz. 111/38; 279/95; Exch. KR Deps by Commn 3 Chas Mich. 46.

[59] Stat. 7 Anne c.13; W.Sfk RO, Ep. Commy Ct Bury inv. 1667/80; Kent RO, Arch. Ct Cant. Inv. Regs 3 fo. 196; 5 fo. 19; Cons. Ct Cant. Reg. Accts & Invs 16 fo. 219; Woodward, *Trade Eliz. Chester*, 13.

[60] Ibid. 42–3; Willan, *Eliz. Man.*, 51, 53; *Inld Trade*, 109; *Ru. Co.*, 253, 260; A. P. Wadsworth & J. de L. Mann, *Cotton Trade & Ind. Lancs. 1600–1780*, Man. 1931, p. 13; W. M. Bowman, *Engld in Ashton-under-Lyne*, Ashton-under-Lyne 1960, p. 416; Tawney & Power iii, 203; A. H. Johnson ii, 395; HMC, *14th Rep.* Appt. pt iv, 572, 605–6; E. A. Lewis 240, 255; C. Fiennes, *Jours*, ed. C. Morris 1949, p. 224; Wilhelmsen 67; Stats 33 H.8 c.15; 5 & 6 E.6 c.6; 7 Anne c.13; Lowe 2, 3, 28–9, PRO, SPD Eliz. 15/67; 20/42; 33/16; 111/38; Jas 128/74; 137/10; Chas 294/93; Exch. KR Deps by Commn 3 Chas Mich. 46; 1656 Mich. 19; 33 Chas 2 Mich. 33; *Palatine Notebk*, Man. 1881 i, 126–7.

[61] Ibid. 127; Stat. 6 H.8 c.9; Bowman 557; Willan, *Eliz. Man.*, 51, 53; *Inld Trade*, 109; J. M. Bestall & D. V. Fowkes, *Chesterfield Wills & Invs 1521–1603*, Derbys. Rec. S. 1977 i, 203; J. Aikin, *Descron Country fr. 30 to 40 m. rd Man.*, 1795, p. 154.

[62] BL, Lans. 71 no. 51 fo. 107 (108).

[63] Roberts, *Marchants Mapp*, 2nd pt, 222; L. M. Cullen, *Econ. Hist. Ire. s. 1660*, 1972, pp. 23, 32–3; *Anglo-Ir. Trade 1660–1800*, Man. 1968, p. 5; Longfield 80 sqq., 214, 219–20, 223; Vanes, *Docs*, 14; E. A. Lewis 256; Smith, *Mems Wl*, ii, 22; McGrath, *Merchs*, 231–3, 283–5; E. de Fréville, *Mémoire sur le Commerce Maritime de Rouen depuis les temps les plus reculés jusqu' à la fin du XVIe s.*, Rouen & Paris 2 vols 1857, i, 298; C. Armour, 'Trade Chester & State Dee Nav. 1600–1800', ts. thes. PhD. Lond. Univ. 1956, pp. 275 sqq.; BL, Sloane 2902 fos. 136–7, 139 (134–5, 137).

[64] PRO, SPD Eliz. 111/38; Jas 128/74; Exch. KR Deps by Commn 3 Chas Mich. 46; 33 Chas 2 Mich. 33; Woodward, *Trade Eliz. Chester*, 9, 10, 13, 15; Lowe 3, 4, 14, 15, 33–4, 36, 106–7, 109–11; HMC, *14th Rep.*, App. pt iv, 605; Defoe, *Compl. Engl. Tradesman*, 79; *APC*, xxx, 602–3; Stats 5 & 6 E.6 c.6; 39 Eliz. c.20; *Pal. Notebk*, i, 127; Bowman 556–7; Tupling 169, 181, 187; F. G. Emmison, *Eliz. Life: Disorder*, Chelmsford 1970, p. 311; Nfk RO, Cons. Ct inv. 1634/195; De Smedt ii, 332.

[65] Ibid.; H. L. Gray, 'Engl. For. Trade fr. 1446 to 1482' in Power & Postan 8; Longfield 156, 161; BL, Add. 34324 fo. 14 (90) (75); Stats 13 R.2 stat. 1 c.10; 1 H.4 c.19; 9 H.4 c.2; 1 R.3 c.8; 3 H.8 c.6; 6 H.8 c.9; 27 H.8 c.12; 4 Jas c.2; 7 Jas c.16; my *Ag. Rev.*, 164, 315; Blome 235; Fiennes 191; Woodward, *Trade Eliz. Chester*, 13, 16; Postlethwayt ii, 836; Nicolas 24; Wadsworth & Mann 22; J. D. Marshall, 'Kendal in late 17th & 18th cents.', *T.C.W.A.A.S.*, n.s. 1975 lxxv, 211–12, 214–15; R. S. Ferguson, *Boke off Recorde . . . of Kirkbiekendall*, C.W.A.A.S. ex.ser. 1892 vii, 22 sqq., 31 sqq., 50 sqq., 85–6, 108, 110, 118, 138, 142, 145–6, 176–7, 258 sqq.; J. Raine, *Wills & Invs fr. Reg. Arch. Richmond*, Surtees S. 1853 xxvi, 35, 107; Willan, *Inld Trade*, 8; E. Hughes, *N. Country Life in 18th cent.*, 2 vols. 1952–65, ii, 4; *Disc. Com. Weal*, 82; C. M. L. Bouch & G. P.

Jones, *Sh. Econ. & Soc. Hist. Lake Dist. 1500–1830*, Man. 1961, p. 263; Pococke ii, 2; D. Fleming, *Descron Co. Westmoreland*, C.W.A.A.S. tract ser. 1881 i, 8; Fuller, *Worthies*, iii, 302.

[66] Ibid. 268; Leland ii, 58, 74, 91, 108; Blome 230; Smyth, *Names*, 2 sqq.; Friis 438, 453–6; Ramsay, 'Distr.', 362, 364–6; *Isham*, 160; Harris, *Cov. Leet Bk*, 262, 636, 639–40, 656 sqq., 687–9, 721–4, 727, 738, 766, 776–7, 787, 790, 796; G. F. Townsend, *Tn & Boro. Leominster*, Leominster n.d. 73, 178, 256; P. Clark, A. G. R. Smith & N. Tyacke, *Engl. Com. 1547–1640*, Leic. 1979, pp. 169–70; A. D. Dyer, *Cty Worc. in 16th cent.*, Leic. 1973, pp. 109, 114–15; 'Prob. Invs Worc. Tradesmen 1545–1614' in *Misc. ii*, Worcs. Hist. S.n.s. 1967 v, 12–15, 18–19; *Cc. Chars & Grants Tn Ludlow*, Ludlow n.d. 41; HMC, *12th Rep.*, App. pt ix, 416–7; *APC*, 1621–3, p. 265; 1626, p. 383; 1627, p. 80; 1627–8, pp. 130–1, 152–3; 1628–9, pp. 80, 399; PRO, PCR 1632–3, p. 293 (fo. 137); SPD Jas 131/80–1; Chas 105/102; 225/87; 527/97; Interreg. 3/13; PCC parch. invs p. 1660 nos. 2130, 2335, 2348, 2428, 3442, 3595, 3672, 3716, 11135; invs 1718–82 bdl. 18 no. 170; 27 no. 79; BL, Lans. 114 no. 24 fos. 92v.–3; Stats 25 H.8 c.8; 5 & 6 E.6 c.6; 1 Mary stat. 3 c.7; 2 & 3 P.&M. c.14; 4 & 5 P.&M. c.5; 4 Jas c.2; Cov. RO, Weavers' & Clothiers' Recs Weavers' Acct Bks 1523– 1634, 1646–1735; Tit. p. etc. Ord. Bk; Weavers' Min. Bk Ords 1659–1771; Misc. Papers re dispute bet. clothiers & drapers; Cty Recs. Leet Bk 30 Eliz.–1834, pp. 20, 39, 64, 68, 70, 202; Birm. Lib. MSS 257484–5; Glos. RO, Cons. Ct inv. 1648/40; Lichfield Jt RO, Cons. Ct, Jn Bond 1550, Harry Bowettre 1558, Th. Bowater 1559, Matt. Arnold 1578, Jas Brisbie 1585–6, Jn Showell 1599, Wm Cooke yr 1603, Allen Rylye 1604, Marmaduke Chambers 1604–5, Robt Baylye 1606, Th. Farnes 1607, Francis Rodes 1611, Ric. Falkner & Sam. Gilbert 1633, Jn Becke & Jn Browne 1634, Geo. Mathew 1635–6, Wm Hunt 1636, Ed. Berry 1636–7, Steven Burrow 1637, Geo. Bagott & Ed. Clifton 1641, Nat. Cheese 1647, Simon Awson 1674, Benj. Bedford 1680, Th. Bowater 1681, Jos. Smith 1729, all Cov.; R. Johnson, *Anc. Customs Cty Hereford*, 1882, pp. 121–3; Worcs. RO, Cons. Ct 1601/143; 1604/9; 1605/30, 145; 1608/104a; 1614/39; 1616/114; 1617/13; 1624/67; 1629/62; 1636/ 115; 1639/92; 1644/41, 106.

[67] Ibid. 1605/118a, 145; 1610/63b; 1629/62; 1639/92; 1643/114; 1644/25; 1645/54; 1720 Jn Fearne walker clothier; R. Johnson 122–3; R. Bigland, *Orig. Hist. Cty Glouc.*, ed. T. D. Fosbrooke 1819, p. 424.

[68] De Smedt ii, 331, 349, 361; Friis 453–6; Posthumus, *Bronnen*, iv, 450; Willemsen, 'La Grève', 148.

[69] PRO, SPD Eliz. 107/34; cf. BL, Lans. 114 no. 24 fos. 92v.–3.

[70] Worcs. RO, Cons. Ct, 1608/7; 1616/114; 1624/67; 1626/38, 121; 1629/62; 1639/127.

[71] Ibid. 1609/167d; Lichfield Jt RO, Cons. Ct, Jn Bond 1550, Th. Bowche 1592, both Cov.; Mendenhall 32; Harris, *Cov. Leet Bk*, 689; Cov. RO, Cty Recs. Leet Bk 30 Eliz.–1834, p. 20.

[72] Ibid. 7, 8, 40; Willan, *Inld Trade*, 61, 66–7; *Eliz. Man.*, 73; K. J. Smith, *War. Apprs & their Mrs 1710–60*, Dugdale S. 1975 xxix, 37, 45, 53, 80–1, 106, 120, 134, 137, 149; *Disc. Com. Weal*, 128; Gras 647; Stat. 12 Chas 2 c.4; Lichfield Jt RO, Cons. Ct, Jn Smith threadmaker 1728 Cov. St Mich.; Glos. RO, Cons. Ct inv. 1700/104; Kent RO, Cons. Ct Cant. Regs Accts & Invs 6 fo. 373; 12 fo. 4.

[73] Leland i, 82, 122; Bodl. Hearne's Diaries 158, p. 29; Cons. & Arch. Cts Oxf. 5/5/21; 52/4/9; 83/3/50; 83/4/64; 297/2/28; 299/3/25; PRO, SPD Jas 128/75; 142/44; Exch. KR Misc. Bk 41 fo. 20; Northants. RO, Arch. Ct Northampton, Admons & Invs 1724/108; R. H. Gretton, *Burford Recs.*, Oxf. 1920, pp. 655–6; Ramsay, 'Distr.', 362, 364–5, 369; N. J. Williams, 'Mar. Trade E.A.Pts 1550–90', ts. thes. D.Phil. Oxf. Univ. 1952, pp. 90, 140; Defoe, *Compl. Engl. Tradesman*, 77; J. C. Cox, *Recs. Boro. Northampton*, vol. ii, Northampton 1898, pp. 218, 288–9; Pococke i, 221; Postlethwayt ii, 763, 835, 846; Worcs. RO, Cons. Ct 1690/6.

[74] Ibid. 1560/88, 129; 1606/27; 1622/66; 1624/72; 1625/212; 1631/170; 1646/79; 1648/126; 1690/41; 1720 Jas Lacy sr clothier Bromsgrove; J. R. Burton, *Hist. Kidderminster*, 1890, pp. 171–2; Stat. 25 H.8 c.18; Leland ii, 85, 87, 95; Notts. RO, Man. Ct Mansfield, portf. 1 nos. 1, 2, 13; 9 no. 10; 16 no. 2; 46 no. 16.

[75] P. C. D. Brears, *Yks. Prob. Invs 1542–1689*, Yks. Archaeol. S. Rec. Ser. 1972 cxxxiv, 61–

2, 138; *Wills & Admons fr. Knaresborough Ct R.*, Surtees S.2 vols. civ, cx, 1902–5 i, 73, 96, 211; ii, 50.

[76] T. Kemp, *Bl. Bk Warwick*, Warwick n.d. 71 sqq.; *Bk Jn Fisher*, 146, 155; Heaton, 13, 15, 31, 36, 51, 55–8, 265; D. M. Palliser, *Tu. York*, Oxf. 1979, pp. 159, 162.

[77] Gras 120, 215, 278 sqq., 344–5, 414 sqq., 422 sqq., 431–4, 448, 450 sqq., 459, 462, 465, 467, 469–70, 473, 476–7, 480–1, 483, 485–8, 491, 495, 497–8, 527, 531, 533, 535–7, 540 sqq., 583, 589, 607, 621, 623, 657, 659–60, 681, 684; Zins 173, 175; *APC*, xii, 63; Carus-Wilson & Coleman 199, 200; H. L. Gray, 'Tabs Enr. Customs & Sub. Accts, 1399 to 1482' in Power & Postan 324–5, 359; 'Engl. For. Trade' ibid. 4, 6, 13, 36, 361, 364; M. M. Postan, 'Econ. & Pol. Rels Engld & Hanse fr. 1400 to 1475' ibid. 145; BL, Add. 12504 no. 63.

[78] Edler, 'Van Der Molen', 96, 99; PRO, Exch. KR Accts Var. bdl. 520 no. 24 fo. 4; Goris 276, 291, 298; Willan, *Tu. Bk Rates*, 65; *Rates Marchandizes*; Vanhaeck i, 90, 241, 259, 272–3, 309; ii, 58, 61, 91; De Sagher i, 337; iii, 416; Leuridan, 'Lannoy', 339; E. Coornaert, *Les Français et le Commerce International à Anvers fin du XVe et XVIe siècle*, Paris 2 vols. 1961, i, 63; *Hondschoote*, 25; BL, Cott. Galba B. x fo. 6v.; Kent RO, Arch. Ct Cant. Inv. Reg. 5 fo. 286.

[79] Ramsay, 'Distr.', 364; *APC*, iii, 415; iv, 180, 341; W. Cunningham, *Alien Immigrants to Engld*, 1897, p. 145; W. Whittingham, *Troubles abowte the Booke of Common Prayer*, s.l. 1574, p. v; PRO, SPD Ed. 6, 13/74–6; 14/3; 15/55; BL, Lans. 2 nos. 54, 68–9.

[80] Vanhaeck i, 241; ii, 57.

[81] Stats 20 H.6 c.10; 11 H.7 c.11; Nfk RO, Cty Recs. 1st Bk Worstedweavers fos. 2, 3, 5, 6v.– 9, 14, 19, 82; 2nd ditto, fos. 1 sqq., 6v., 30., 42v., 43v., 46v., 62; Ass. Bk 2 fos. 123(142)v., 132(152)v., 135(155).

[82] Ibid. 132(152)v., 135(155); Bk 3 fos. 35, 82; Misc. Docs, Ords of Worstedweavers 1511; 1st Bk Worstedweavers fos. 4, 75; 2nd ditto, fos. 6v., 11, 88v.; Cons. Ct inv. 1628–68/117; PRO, Req. 157/134 fos. 72, 77(2); Stats 11 H.7 c.11; 12 H.7 c.1; 19 H.7 c.17; 14 & 15 H.8 c.3; 22 H.8 c.1; 25 H.8 c.5; 33 H.8 c.16; 1 E.6 c.6; 5 & 6 E.6 c.7; Gras 214, 527, 547.

[83] Smith, *Mems Wl* ii, 445–7, 452, 459, 462; Posthumus, *Bronnen*, vi, 229, 239; De Poerck ii, 79; Pegoletti 425; Davidsohn vol. iv pt. ii, 69; Laurent 97; Vanhaeck i, 93–4, 293, 305; ii, 118, 211– 12; Deyon 173, 175; Cole i, 32; ii, 384, 576–8; W. C. Scoville, *Persecution Huguenots & Fr. Econ. Devpt 1680–1720*, Berkeley & L.A. 1960, pp. 176–7.

[84] H. Ellis, *Orig. Ltrs Ill. Engl. Hist.*, 3rd ser. 1846, i, 379; Stats 11 H.7 c.11; 12 H.7 c.1; 19 H.7 c.17; 6 H.8 c.12; 14 & 15 H.8 c.3; 22 H.8 c.1; 25 H.8 c.5; 1 E.6 c.6; 5 & 6 E.6 c.7; BL, Add. 12504 no. 63; no. 65 fo. 88v.; Nfk RO, Cty Recs. Liber Albus fos. 94–6; 1st Bk Worstedweavers fos. 5, 40v., 75; 2nd ditto, fos. 28, 34, 88v.; Bk Mayor's Ct 9 p. 261; Ass. Bk 2 fos. 132 (152)v., 135(155); 3 fos. 35, 82.

[85] Ibid. fo. 306v.; Cons. Ct invs 1671/47; 1718–21 (stamped) 169; Arch. Ct Norvic. invs 1703–6/ 12; 1709–10/61; PRO, PCC parch. invs p. 1660 no. 1789.

[86] BL, Add. 12504 no. 64 fo. 82.

[87] Brist. RO, Cons. Ct inv. 1662/31.

[88] Notts. RO, Man. Ct Mansfield portf. 22 no. 4; Soms. RO, Arch. Taunton inv. 1726–7/4; PRO, SPD Eliz. Add. 33/71; 34/23; Exch. KR Deps by Commn 44 & 45 Eliz. Mich. 1 m.7; BL, Add. 12504 no. 65 fo. [87]; Pound, *Cs Poor*, 97; Hudson & Tingey ii, 103; Nfk RO, Cons. Ct invs. 1592/62, 103, 138; 1595/90, 120; 1598/147; 1603/160; 1615/30; Cty Recs. Strangers Bk fo. 20; Ass. Bk 3 fos. 82, 131v.; Bks Mayor's Ct 12 fo. 326; 16 fo. 296.

[89] Ibid. 8 p. 167; 10 p. 574; Cons. Ct invs. 1602/239; 1606/66; 1615/52; 1640/81; 1646/50; Tymms 136; Jones & King 347, 352; Cash 18–19; Lichfield Jt RO, Cons. Ct, Geo. Harvey 1650 Cov.; W.Sfk RO, Reg. Bk Wills 13 fo. 585; Kent RO, Arch. Ct Cant. Inv. Reg. 5 fo. 19v.; Cons. Ct Cant. Reg. Accts & Invs 10 fo. 326; Nichols, *Unton Invs*, 4, 5, 11, 23–4, 29; *Rates Marchandizes*; B. Dietz, *Pt & Trade Early Eliz. Lond.*, Lond. Rec. S. 1972, p. 27.

[90] Ibid. 3, 9, 21, 33, 37, 48, 54, 56, 59, 61, 67, 72, 74, 83–4, 91, 93, 98, 101, 105, 113, 118, 127, 133; *Rates Marchandizes*; Gras 572, 697; Leuridan, 'Lannoy', 343; T. S. Willan, *Studs in Eliz. For. Trade*, Man, 1962, p.76; *Tu. Bk Rates*, 22–3.

[91] Hudson & Tingey i, 401; ii, 118, 230, 310–12, 406; Gras 613, 615, 619, 621, 658–60, 662–3, 672, 680; Nfk RO, Cty Recs. O. Free Bk & Memo. fos. 77(72), 81–2(76–7)v.; Bk Mayor's Ct 6 pp. 49, 256; Pound, 'Soc. & Trade Structure, 55, 65, 67.

[92] Ibid. 55, 60, 65, 67; *Cs Poor*, 54, 97; Williams, thes. 90; *Winthrop Papers*, iii, 310; Stat. 5 & 6 E.6 c.24; PRO, Req. 157/134 fos. 93(1), 96(4); Exch. KR Deps by Commn 44 & 45 Eliz. Mich. 1 mm. 3d., 9; PCR 1631–2 pp. 107, 267–9 (fos. 50, 134–5); B. Cozens-Hardy, 'Mar. Trade Pt Blakeney' in Nfk Rec. S. 1936 viii, 29, 32, 34–5; Worcs. RO. Cons. Ct 1614/45; P. Millican, *Reg. Freemen Norwich 1548–1713*, Norwich 1934, pp. 55–8; Nfk RO, Cons. Ct invs 1602/239; 1603/145A; 1606/66; 1615/52; 1625/264; 1639/98; 1640/81; 1646/50; 1674/33; Arch. Ct. Norvic. inv. 1706–7/30; Cty Recs. Misc. Docs. N. Drapery in Norwich; Ass. Bks 2 fo. 147(167)v.; 3 fo. 17v.; 4 rev. fos. 2, 6, 9–12, 15v., 23, 34, 42v., 46v., 67, 74, 76, 79, 82v., 95v., 97, 102, 103v., 115v.; 5 fo. 83(93); Bks Mayor's Ct 5 pp. 191, 215, 502–3; 10 p. 574; 11 fo. 110v., 12 pp. 780, 900, 946; 13 p. 68; 15 fos. 68, 521v.; 16 fos. 425, 460, 471; 20 fos. 9v., 10, 44v., 298, 454.

[93] Ibid. 10, p. 240; 15 fo. 418v.; Ass. Bk. 2 fos. 147–8(167–8)v.; Cons. Ct invs 1589/119; 1723/18; Arch. Ct Norvic. inv. 1720–1/43; Allison, thes. 391.

[94] P. Corfield, 'Prov. Cap. in late 17th cent.' in P. Clark & P. Slack, *Crisis & Ord. in Engl. Tns 1500–1700*, 1972, p. 280; Edwards 29; J. F. Pound, 'Govt & Soc. in Tu. & Stuart Norwich 1525–1675', ts. thes. Ph.D. Leic. Univ. 1974, p. 296; Unger, *Bronnen*, iii, 511; W.Sfk RO, Ep. Commy Ct Bury inv. 1717/43; Nfk RO, Cons. Ct invs 1592/53; 1606/150; 1724/68; Cty Recs. O. Free Bk & Memo. fos. 77, 82, 162(72, 77, 128); Bks Mayor's Ct 5 p. 255; 11 fos. 59, 244; Ass. Bk 2 fos. 38–9(57–8), 58(77)v.; Hudson & Tingey ii, 230.

[95] Ibid. lxxxii; PRO, PCC parch. invs p. 1660 no. 580; Exch. KR Deps by Commn 44 & 45 Eliz. Mich. 1 m. 3r.; Nfk RO, Cty Recs. Strangers Bk fos. 24v., 25v., 33, 38; Bks Mayor's Ct 13 p. 68; 16 fo. 471; Cons. Ct invs 1606/66; 1615/52; 1629/123; 1630/6; 1633/295; 1646/50; 1666/77; Millican, *Reg.* 95.

[96] Ibid.; M. G. Davies 131; *Manners & Hsehld Exs*, 311; *Cal. SPD 1664–5*, p. 137; J. F., *Merch's Wareho.*, 1696, p. 31; S. Kramer, *Engl. Craft Gilds: Studs in their Prog. & Decl.*, N.Y. 1927, p. 111; Allison xcvi; Nfk RO, Cty Recs. Ass. Bk 3 fo. 64v.; Misc. Docs. N. Drapery in Norwich; Cons. Ct invs 1590/108; 1593/99; 1595/106; 1621/69; 1625/218; 1629/16; 1646/50; 1672/10; Arch. Ct Norvic. inv. 1717–18/27.

[97] Nfk RO, Cons. Ct invs 1584/43; 1636/187; Pilgrim, thes. 49, 233.

[98] F. G. Davenport, *Econ. Devpt Nfk Man. 1086–1565*, Cam. 1906, pp. lxxxiii–iv; Nfk RO, Cons. Ct invs 1626/83; 1703–8/300–1; 1730/3; E. Sfk RO, Arch. invs 15/82; 18/69; 23/5; W. Sfk RO, Ep. Commy Ct Bury inv. 1662/96.

[99] Ibid. 1650/122; 1660/134; 1661/270, 293; 1662/237; 1663/16, 52; 1664/47, 111; E. Sfk RO, Arch. invs 2/45, 47, 54, 60; 3/8, 155; 6/10; 7/93; 8/64; 9/8; 12/22; 13/90; 14/70; 15/8; 26/39; 27/21, 49; 31/36; Serjeant 1, 4–6, 16, 25–6, 30, 32, 40–1, 43, 47, 50, 52, 59, 63, 69, 70, 89, 91, 100, 113, 115, 120, 123, 127, 136, 153, 155, 165, 173, 185, 188, 200, 215, 226–7, 229, 232–3, 235, 243, 245, 252, 275, 285, 290, 298, 302–4, 310, 321, 328, 337, 354, 364, 368–70, 372, 378–81, 391, 400–2, 405, 427, 431, 435, 440–1, 443–4, 450–1, 454, 462, 468, 471–2, 479, 481, 483, 487, 493 sqq., 499, 507, 511, 517, 524, 529, 533, 538, 555, 568; Nfk RO, Cons. Ct invs 1584/43; 1592/4; 1593/264; 1606–7/39, 176; 1611/69, 216; 1613/180, 191, 276; 1614/56; 1618/70, 122, 244; 1621/18, 28; 1626/83, 217; 1628/165; 1630/168, 174; 1647/60; 1663/155; 1665/72, 76; 1692–3/129; 1703–8/300, 369; 1709–10/117; 1723/28; Arch. Ct Nfk invs 1728–42/235; 1743–53/72; F. C. Lane, *Andrea Barbarigo, Merch V. 1418–49*, Balt. 1944, pp. 61, 69, 75, 105, 192; *Ven. & Hist.*, id. 1966, pp. 118–19, 122; *Cal. SP Ven.*, i, 80, 83–4, 151; N. Evans, 'Commun. S. Elmham, Sfk, 1550–1640', ts. thes. MPhil Univ. E.A. 1978, pp. 95, 202; M. G. Davies 131, 139; Postlethwayt ii, 765; H. M. Doughty, *Chrons Theberton*, 1910, p. 169; Blome 172, 207–8, 215; N. B. Harte, 'Rise Protection & Engl. Linen Trade 1690–1790' in N. B. Harte & K. G. Ponting, *Text. Hist. & Econ. Hist.*, Man. 1973, p. 103; Allison xcvi.

[100] B. Dietz 4, 5, 26, 38, 44, 46, 51, 90, 95, 101, 104, 117, 126, 130, 132, 153; De Vries 240;

Higgins 11, 12; Brulez, *Della Faille*, 249; Baasch 92–3; A. Yarranton, *Engld's Imprvt by Sea & Ld*, 1677, p. 54; my *Ag. Rev.*, 85–7.

[101] Ibid. 79, 85; Nfk RO, Cons. Ct invs 1611/69; 1613/191; 1618/70, 122, 244; 1626/217; 1630/168; 1723/28; 1730/3; Yarranton 144–5; N. Evans 78, 94–5; Kent RO, Cons. Ct Cant. Inv. Reg. 15 fo. 302v.; W.Sfk RO, Ep. Commy Ct Bury inv. 1663/27.

[102] Ibid. 1652/18; 1680/200; Blome 208, 213; Willan, *Inld Trade*, 10; J. Ogilby, *Brit.* 1675, p. 108; E. Sfk RO, Arch. invs 2/126; 12/71; BL, Lans. 108 no. 78 fo. 141(151)v.; PRO, SPD Eliz. 34/23; Serjeant 19, 41, 54, 73, 76, 84, 90, 123, 133, 136, 143, 147, 179, 190, 265, 271–2, 297, 301, 323, 339, 342, 349, 352, 376, 381, 429, 452, 454, 469, 492, 508, 513; Nfk RO, Cons. Ct inv. 1662–3/105.

[103] Ibid.1588/45; 1603/145A; 1630/174; 1709–10/117; Tymms 258; Stat. 5 & 6 E.6 c.24.

[104] G. C. Miller, *Blackburn*, Blackburn 1951, p. 328; W. Bennett, *Hist. Burnley 1650–1850*, Burnley 1948, p. 77; *Pal. Notebk*, i, 126–7; Willan, *Eliz. Man.*, 58 sqq.; Aikin 154; Pococke ii, 210; Stat. 33 H.8 c.15; Defoe, *Tour*, ii, 259–60; my *Ag. Rev.*, 145–6; Lowe 5, 15, 43–5, 58; M. G. Davies 226; Harte 103; Lancs. RO, Cons. Ct Cestr. Supra inv. Ric. Ball 1700 The Banks in N. Meols; Wadsworth & Mann 47, 59.

[105] Ibid. 11; Stat. 33 H.8 c.15; Bowman 416, 557; Longfield 88 sqq., 222; Cullen, *Econ. Hist. Ire.*, 24; L. Roberts, *Treasure of Traffike*, 1641, pp. 32–3; *Marchants Mapp*, 2nd pt, 222; Lowe 15; Woodward, *Trade Eliz. Chester*, 7–9; Leland v, 40–1; C. Gill, *Rise Ir. Linen Ind.*, Oxf. 1925, p. 6; Raine 228–9; J. M. Lambert, *2,000 Yrs Gild Life*, Hull & Lond. 1891, p. 208.

[106] Chester RO, Cty Recs. Ass. Bk 1539–1624 fo. 166(163)v.

[107] Kirk i, 202, 205–8, 213, 273 sqq., 279–80, 288 sqq., 320–2, 333, 343–4, 389–90, 392, 402 sqq., 409, 411, 423–4, 427 sqq., 442 sqq., 449–51. 453 sqq., 462 sqq., 470 sqq., 478–9; ii, pp. xi, xii, 3, 7–10, 12, 14, 16, 18 sqq., 25, 27 sqq., 37 sqq., 46, 51 sqq., 66 sqq., 72 sqq., 79 sqq., 94, 96 sqq., 218 sqq., 260 sqq., 271, 274 sqq., 289, 292, 294–5, 297–9, 301 sqq., 315 sqq., 323, 325–7, 329–30, 332–5, 338–9, 347–50, 365 sqq., 372–3, 393; iii, 138 sqq., 148, 155 sqq., 162–3, 166 sqq., 187 sqq., 198 sqq., 206, 208–9, 215–17, 219–20, 222 sqq., 381, 402–3, 408 sqq., 424 sqq.; W. Page, *Ltrs Denization & Acts Naturalization f. Aliens in Engld 1509–1603*, Pubs H.S.L. 1893 viii, pp. li, 39, 40, 57–8, 62, 74, 108, 121, 129, 193, 202, 212, 228–9; W. C. Waller, *Exts fr. Ct Bks Weavers' Co. Lond. 1610–1730*, id. 1931 xxxiii, 3–5; S. L. Thrupp, 'Aliens in & around Lond. in 15th cent.' in A. E. J. Hollaender & W. Kellaway, *Studs in Lond. Hist.*, 1969, p. 265; S. Ruytinck, C. Calandrinus & A. Van Culenbergh, *Gheschiedenis ende Handelingen die voornemelick aengan de Nederduytsche Natie ende Gemeynten wonende in Engelant*, Marnix-Vereeniging serie iii 1873, i, 299; V. B. Redstone, 'Engld during Wars Roses', *Trs R.H.S.*, n.s. 1902 xvi, 197; T. G. Wyatt, 'Pt Played by Aliens in Soc. & Econ. Life Engld during reign Hy VIII', ts. thes. MALond. Univ. 1951, pp. 102–3; PRO, SPD Jas 88/113; 99/43; 102; Hessels, *Archives*, 230; *Archivum*, ii, 910–11; iii, 1071, 1710.

[108] Ibid. 1784, 2128, 2894; Waller 4, 5; Kirk i, 279, 288 sqq., 389, 424, 428–9, 463; ii, 10, 33, 53, 67, 89, 261–2, 265–6, 268, 279, 281, 286, 291, 296, 325, 335, 337, 355–6; iii, 405, 425 sqq.; *Fs. Anc. Bk Weavers' Co.* fos. 31v.–2; Cash 164–6; M. K. Dale, 'Lond. Silkwomen in 15th cent.', *Econ. Hist. Rev.*, 1932–4 iv, 324 sqq., 331; F. Warner, *Silk Ind. U.K.*, n.d. 105–6; Minet, *Threadneedle St*, xlix, 1; T. C. Colyer-Fergusson, *Regs Fr. Ch. Threadneedle St*, vols. iii, iv Pubs H.S.L. xvi, xxiii, 1906–16, iii, 268; *Ca. Commonalty Corp. Weavers*, s.l.n.d.; BL, Lans. 26 no. 63 fo. 184(166); PRO, SPD Chas 2, 21/108; Stats 33 H.6 c.5; 3 E.4 c.3; 22 E.4 c.3; 1 R.3 c.10; 1 H.7 c.9; 19 H.7 c.21; 14 Chas 2 c.13; Guildhall Lib. Weavers' Co. Ord. & Rec. Bk 1577–1641 fos. 47–8, 302, 352; Commy Ct Lond. (Lond. Div.) invs box 1, Edm. Gibbs 1666 Acton; Ric. Fouler 1667 St Sepulchre's; 2, Wm Taylor 1667 Stepney; 4, Jn George 1725 St Botolph's W/o; 6, Wm Gass 1720 St Dunstan's, Stepney; 9, Hy Wheeler 1678 Stepney; Jas Woolfinden 1699 St Dunstan's, Stepney; Th. Baxter 1700 St Botolph's W/o; Stephen Dubarle 1701 St Giles-in-the-Fields; Cty Lond. RO, Ct Orphs invs box 1, Th. Willsonne 1665; box 2, Jn Barton 1666; box 5, Geo. Farrar 1668; box 7, Barack Justian & Jn Carter 1670; box 11, Nic. Russell 1672, Wm Richardson & Ant. Adams 1673.

[109] Guildhall Lib. Commy Ct Lond. (Lond.Div.) invs box 2, Wm Venham 1666 St Giles-in-the-Fields; Kirk ii, 55, 105, 114, 205–6; iii, 158, 403; Waller 3; *Fs. Anc. Bk Weavers' Co.*, fos. 19v., 20.

[110] Kent RO, Arch. Ct Cant. Inv. Reg. 5 fo. 19; G. Unwin, *Ind. Org. in 16th & 17th cents*, 1963, pp. 44–5, 57, 112 sqq., 142, 199, 228 sqq.

## Chapter 3

[1] M. Abrate, 'Il Memoriale di Hy Pugnet' in Fanfani 20; W. Brulez, 'Les Routes commerciales d'Angleterre en Italie au XVIe s.' ibid. 125 sqq.; *Della Faille*, 45, 279, 520; H. Van Der Wee, *Growth Antwerp Mkt & Eur. Econ.*, Hague 3 vols. 1963, ii, 186; Edler, 'Winchcombe Kerseys', 57 sqq.; *Cal. SP Ven.* i, 83, 207, 329; Zins 39, 173, 186–7; Ehrenberg 329–30.

[2] Ibid. 269, 272–3; W. Borlase, *Nat. Hist. Corn.*, 1758, p. 286; Hakluyt, *Orig. Writings*, i, 192; T. Risdon, *Chorographical Descron or Svy Co. Devon*, 1723, p. 11; R. Carew, *Svy Corn.*, 1769, fo. 23; BL, Harl. 5827 fos. 9(7)v., 10(8); Lans. 48 no. 65 fos. 154v.–5; 114 no. 24 fos. 92v.–3; Vanes, *Docs*, 121; HMC, *Sackville MSS*, ii, 146; Westcote 60–1, 121; Ramsay, 'Distr.', 362, 365–8; Mann, *Cl. Ind.*, 309; Roberts, *Marchants Mapp*, 2nd pt, 28; Stow, *Ann.* 870; Bourhis i, 97; ii, 137; Willan, *Tu. Bk Rates*, xvi; Dunsford 36, 39, 41, 43, 50, 201; Youings 68–9, 72; P. L. Hughes & J. F. Larkin, *Tu. R. Procls*, New Haven & Lond. 3 vols. 1964–9, iii, 102–4; Stephens, *Exeter*, 4, 10, 28–9, 67, 104, 135; *Donations Pet. Blundell*, Exeter 1792, pp. 7, 8; Stats 5 & 6 E.6 c.6; 4 & 5 P.&M. c.5; 35 Eliz. c.10; J. R. Chanter & T. Wainwright, *Rep. Bpl. Recs*, Bpl. 2 vols. 1900, i, 173, 176; Donaldson 92; Wilts. RO, Preb. Ct Uffculme, bdl. 5 no. 15; Devon RO, Huntsham MS PZ1; PRO, PCC parch. invs p. 1660 no. 11603; SPD Eliz. 15/67; 20/42; 22/58; 111/38; 157/3; 250/47; 251/2; Eliz. Add. 11/113; Exch. KR Accts Var. bdl. 520 no. 24 fo. 22v; no. 25 fos. 51v.–2; Deps by Commn 12 Chas East. 41; 6 Jas East. 30.

[3] Ibid.

[4] Stat. 35 Eliz. c.10; L. Mascall, *Cattell*, 1587; p. 217; W. Marshall, *Rural Econ. W. Engld*, 2 vols. 1796, i, 269.

[5] Kent RO, Cons. Ct Cant. Inv. Papers 7/80; 34/69; Cons. Ct Roffen. Paper Inv. 9/2.

[6] Ferguson 77, 118; Soms. RO, Cons. Ct Bath & Well. inv. Jn Nickles 1634 Pensford; Leics. RO, Arch. inv. 1627/21; Wilts. RO, Pec. Ct Dean Sarum. Wm Lacke er 1692 Beaminster; W. Davies, *Gen. View Ag. & Dom. Econ. N.W.*, 1810, p. 501; E.Sfk RO, Blois Fam. Archives, Hy Blois's Acct Led. fo. 86v.

[7] Heaton 197; HMC, *14th Rep.*, App. pt iv, 573; *APC*, xxx, 603; my *Ag. Rev.*, 164, 315; Stat. 39 Eliz. c.20; Preston i, 13, 33–4, 140–2; *Yks. Diaries & Autobiogs in 17th & 18th cents.*, Surtees S. 1886 lxxvii, 11, 38; Lincs. RO, Heneage of Hainton Coll. 3/2; PRO, Exch. KR Deps by Commn 14 Chas Mich. 21 mm. 2d., 5; 28 Chas 2 Mich. 29 mm. 2 sqq.

[8] W.S., *Golden Fleece*, 1656, p. 38; J. May 32–3.

[9] Tupling 169, 181; Fishwick, *Hist. Rochdale*, 58; Willan, *Inld Trade*, 109.

[10] PRO, SPD Eliz. 250/76; 253/122; Lincs. RO, Heneage of Hainton Coll. 3/2; HMC, *Sackville MSS*, ii, 5, 12 (cf. 28–9, 44, 62, 97, 130, 177, 205); J. Haynes, *View Pres. State Clo. Trade in Engld*, 1706, p. 13.

[11] J. May 32–3; Stats 4 Jas c.2; 7 Anne c.13; 11 Geo. 2 c.28; 14 Geo. 2 c.35; Defoe, *Plan*, 182; *Compl. Engl. Tradesman*, 77; *Tour*, ii, 189; E. Sfk RO, Arch. inv. 16/71; PRO, Exch. KR Deps by Commn 14 Chas Mich. 21 mm. 3, 5; 28 Chas 2 Mich. 29 mm. 2 sqq.

[12] HMC, *Sackville MSS*, ii, 5, 15, 22, 25, 34, 39, 40, 77, 130–1, 138–9, 143, 196, 203, 205, 217; Prestwich 52–3, 55–7; Heaton 197.

[13] Ibid. 198; R. G. Wilson, *Gent. Merchs*, Man. 1971, p. 12.

[14] H. Van Werveke, *Brugge en Antwerpen*, Ghent n.d. 147–8; Demey 229; Van Der Wee ii, 187; Coornaert, *Hondschoote*, 12, 26, 66; De Sagher i, 194–5, 197, 200; ii, 95, 226, 314, 560, 606, 617, 619, 655–6; iii, 66, 99, 216–18, 225, 263, 312, 416, 418, 421, 604; Vanhaeck ii, 142; De Poerck i, 224–5; Posthumus, *Bronnen*, v, 159.

[15] Ibid. iii, 517, 608; iv, 335; v, 435, 540; vi, 329, 418–9, 513–4; Van Dillen, *Bronnen*, ii, 181–2.

[16] L. de Alberti & A. B. W. Chapman, *Engl. Merchs & Sp. Inq. in Canaies*, Camd. ser. 1912 xxiii, 64–6; Unger, *Bronnen*, 559–60, 577.

[17] *VCH Hants.*, v, 485; Zins 182, 212; HMC, *Sackville MSS*, ii, 195–6, 203; R. W. K. Hinton, *Eastld Trade & Com. Weal in 17th cent.*, Cam. 1959, pp. 17, 35; W. G. Endrei, 'Engl. Kersey in E. Eur.', *Text. Hist.*, 1974 v, 96; J. Macek, 'La Posizione Sociale dei Tessitori nelle Città Cèche e Morave nei secolo XIV–XVI' in M. Spallanzani, *Produzione Commercio e Consumo dei Panni di Lana nei secoli XII–XVIII*, Flor. 1976, p. 587; M. Abrate, 'Imprenditori e Tecnici Stranieri nell' Industria Laniera Piemontese agli Inizi del XVIII secolo', ibid. 119; De Sella, *Commerci e Industrie a Venezia nel secolo XVII*, Ven. & Rome 1961, p. 60.

[18] *Disc. Com. Weal*, 63, 65.

[19] Soms. RO, Arch. Taunton inv. 1670/29; PRO, PCC invs 1718–82 bdl. 21 no. 65.

[20] Ibid. parch. invs p. 1660 no. 4625.

[21] De Smedt i, 304.

[22] Posthumus, *Bronnen*, iv, 261–3.

[23] Ibid. v, 12, 13.

[24] Craeybeckx 429.

[25] Coornaert, *Hondschoote*, 66.

[26] Inf. 133.

[27] Stephens, *Exeter*, 28–30, 67, 104; Borlase 286; Willan, *Tu. Bk Rates*, 73; Friis 439; Bourhis i, 97; M. G. Davies 110–11; *Rates Marchandizes*; BL, Lans. 26, no. 63 fo. 184 (166); Harl. 5827 fo. 9(7)v.; Stats 5 H.8 c.2; 7 E.6 c.9; 4 & 5 P.&M. c.5; 18 Eliz. c.16; 27 Eliz. c.18; Westcote 61; *APC*, xxx, 492; PRO, SPD Eliz. 15/67; 239/54; 243/114; Devon RO, Marwood Coll. T.92; De Smedt ii, 332, 334, 350.

[28] Ibid. 332; Bourhis i, 97; Borlase 286.

[29] Stat. 27 Eliz. c.18.

[30] Pococke ii, 143; PRO, SPD Eliz. 243/114; Exch. KR Deps by Commn 6 Jas East. 30.

[31] Ibid.; SPD Eliz. 33/16; 239/54; Eliz. Add. 34/23; Chas 2, 95/86; Stat. 12 Chas 2 c.4; Nfk RO, Cons. Ct inv. 1634/195; Gerard 135; Friis 439; Stephens, *Exeter*, 104; McGrath, *Merchs*, 282; J. Collinson, *Hist. & Ants Co. Soms.*, Bath 3 vols. 1791, i, 2nd pt, 2, 18; ii, 478; C. H. Mayo, *Mun. Recs Boro. Dorchester*, Exeter 1908, pp. 402, 410 sqq., 422 sqq.; Soms. RO, Cons. Ct Bath & Well. inv. Jn Slape 1589 Combe St Nic.; Arch. Taunton inv. Wm Coffin 1668 Ilminster; M. Weinstock, *Studs in Dors. Hist.*, Dorchester 1953, p. 35.

[32] PRO, SPD Eliz. 252/2; Heaton 79, 97–9, 108, 220, 229 sqq.; Stats 4 & 5 P.&M. c.5; 14 Chas c.32; 7 Anne c.13; J. P. Earwaker, *Lancs. & Ches. Wills & Invs 1572 to 1696*, Chetham S. n.s. 1893 xxviii, 18, 19; Mann, *Cl. Ind.* 37–8; 'Clothiers & Weavers in Wilts. during 18th cent.' in L. S. Pressnell, *Studs in Ind. Rev.* 1960, p. 86; HMC, *11th Rep.*, App. pt vii, 214; *14th Rep.*, App. pt iv, 573; Defoe, *Tour*, ii, 203; J. T. Rutt, *Diary Th. Burton Esq.*, 4 vols. 1828, i, 126; *C.J.*, vii, 467, 588; Wadsworth & Mann 9; HMC, *Sackville MSS*, ii, 146.

[33] PRO, Exch. KR Deps by Commn 3 Chas Mich. 46; 3 & 4 Chas Hil. 23; T. S. Willan, 'Man. Clothiers in early 17th cent.', *Text. Hist.*, 1979 x, 176; cf. Lancs. RO, Cons. Ct Cestr. Supra inv. Jn Bordeman 1628 Bolton; N. E. Bang & K. Korst, *Tabeller over Skibsfart og Varetransport gennem Øresund 1661–1783 og gennem Storebaelt 1701–48*, Anden Del: Tabeller over Varetransport, 1st Halvbind, Copenhagen & Leip. 1939, pp. 4, 12, 20, 28, 36.

[34] Burton 180; Worcs. RO, Cons. Ct O.W. etc. Ob. Spencer 1712 Kidderminster; De Smedt ii, 433; Bourhis i, 97; Woodward, *Trade Eliz. Chester*, 13, 15; W. B. Stephens, 'O'seas Trade Chester in early 17th cent.', *Trs Hist. S. Lancs. & Ches.*, 1969 lxx, 25; E. B. Schumpeter 35.

[35] Ibid. 70; Willan, *Tu. Bk Rates*, 74; Friis 453–5; BL, Harl. 1878 fo. 101 (85); Lans. 26 no. 62 fo. 181(163); no. 64 fo. 187; Nfk RO, Cty Recs. Strangers Bk fos. 26, 34v., 38; N. Drapery in Norwich; Kent RO, Arch. Ct Cant. Inv. Reg. 5 fo. 19; PRO, SPD Eliz. 250/76.

[36] Ibid. 106/47; 130/48; 250/76; Suppl. vol. 32 fos. 41, 43; Exch. KR Entry Bks Decrs & Ords ser. i vol. 6 fos. 191, 331v., 345; *CPR*, Eliz. iv, 354; BL, Lans. 26 no. 62 fo. 181(163); no. 64 fo. 187; 27 no. 66 fos. 148–9; A. H. Johnson ii, 213–14; Noy 182–3.

[37]  L. Dechesne, *Industrie Drapière de la Vesdre avant 1800*, Paris & Liège 1926, pp. 38, 41, 60, 62 sqq.; P. Lebrun, *L'Industrie de la Laine à Verviers pendant le XVIIIe & le début du XIXe s.*, Liège 1948, pp. 52–4, 82–3, 187 sqq., 221, 231.

[38]  HMC, *Sackville MSS*, ii, 195–6; Macek 587; Heaton 197–8; PRO, SPD Chas 2,379/127; Notestein & al. ii, 365; S.-E. Åström, *Fr. Cl. to Iron*, Helsinki 1963, p. 70; Prestwich 55–7, 83, 304.

[39]  Ibid.; *APC*, xxi, 301; Smith, *Mems Wl*, ii, 210; Hinton 17; A. F. W. Papillon, *Mems Th. Papillon Lond. Merch (1623–1702)*, Reading 1887, p. 63.

[40]  Fuller, *Worthies*, ii, 115; Gulley 208, 211, 280; Defoe, *Tour*, i, 115; *Rsns f. Ltd Exp. Wooll*, s.l. 1677, pp. 4, 13; Coleman, thes. 159, 161; Stephens, 'Chester', 25–6; Bodl. Top. Kent a.I fo. 26; Kent RO, Cons. Ct Cant. Inv. Papers 16/10; 34/69; PRO, PCC invs 1718–82 bdl. 18 no. 221; SPD Eliz. 15/67; 106/49.

[41]  Ibid. 132/21–2; Jas 40/25; Chas 407/97; PCR 1639, p. 197 (fo. 95); *APC*, ix, 385; Blome 208; M. Reed, 'Ips. in 17th cent.', ts. thes. PhD Leic. Univ. 1973, pp. 27–8; Pilgrim, thes. 18 sqq.; Mann, *Cl. Ind.*, 20; Åström 69, 70; J. Kirby, *Sfk Trav.*, 1764, pp. 51, 63, 207, 261, 269.

[42]  Suppa s.v. suffolk; Roberts, *Marchants Mapp*, 2nd pt, 181 erron. 189 recte; J. Child, *Essay on Wl & Woollen Manuf.*, 1693, p. 13; PRO, SPD Chas 424/100.

[43]  Coornaert, *Bergues*, 96.

[44]  W. Camden, *Brit.*, ed. Gibson 1695, p. 506; Clark, Smith & Tyacke 170–1; Bigland 424–5; HMC, *Sackville MSS*, ii, 151.

[45]  PRO, SPD Jas 40/25; 131/55; BL, Stowe 354 fo. 63(104); 554 fo. 45.

[46]  McGrath, *Merchs*, 140–3.

[47]  T. Culpepper, *Tract agst Usurie*, 1621, p. 12.

[48]  Notestein & al. ii, 76–7, 325, 365; PRO, SPD Jas 130/39.

[49]  Hinton 17; cf. HMC, *Sackville MSS*, ii, 95, 195.

[50]  PRO, SPD Jas 128/51; 131/55.

[51]  De Sagher ii, 29, 30; De Smedt i, 303–4.

[52]  Ibid.; G. D. Ramsay, *Cty Lond. in Internat. Pol. at acc. Eliz. Tu. Man.*, 1975, p. 203; PRO, SP For. Eliz. vol. 67 fos. 224(235)v.–225(236).

[53]  Posthumus, *Geschiedenis*, ii, 12, 58–9.

[54]  Ibid. 22, 24–5, 33, 44–5, 53–6, 79–81, 98–9.

[55]  *APC*, xxi, 301.

[56]  PRO, SPD Chas 224/44; 424/100; *Rsns f. Ltd Exp. Wooll*, 13.

[57]  Gulley 211; Smith, *Mems Wl*, i, 215.

[58]  Child, *Essay on Wl*, 13; PRO, SPD Chas, 2, 421/161.

[59]  S. R. Gardiner, *Const. Docs Puritan Rev. 1625–60*, Oxf. 1906, pp. 143, 214–15.

[60]  R. W. Ketton-Cremer, *Nfk in Civ. War*, 1969, pp. 73–4, 76–9; Clarendon, *Hist. Rebellion & Civ. Wars in Engld*, Oxf. 6 vols. 1878, ii, 418.

[61]  Smith, *Mems Wl*, i, 167–8, 183; ii, 37, 262–4; S. C. Powell, *Puritan Vil.*, Middletown, Conn. 1963, pp. 41, 152; N. C. P. Tyacke, 'Migration fr. E.A. to N.E. befe 1660', ts. thes. PhD Lond. Univ. 1951, p. 58, App. I pp. i, xxi, xxxix, lxi, lxxix, cix, App. III pp. iv–vi; R. Coke, *Engld's Imprvt*, 1675, pp. 13, 32–3; Ammann 60–1; PRO, SPD Interreg. 9/5; L. A. Harper, *Engl. Nav. Laws*, N.Y. 1939, p. 311.

[62]  Ibid.; R. Coke 32–3; H. Parker, *Of a Free Trade*, 1648, p. 35; Smith, *Mems Wl*, i, 183, 337; McGrath, *Merchs*, 282; Brist. RO, Cons. Ct inv. 1662/17; C. Te Lintum, *De Merchant Adventurers in de Nederlanden*, Hague 1905, pp. 177–8.

[63]  M. James, *Soc. Probs & Plcy during Puritan Rev.*, 1930, p. 60; PRO, SPD Interreg. 1/34; 15/93.

[64]  Ibid. 205/41; M. James 60–1, 161–2; R. Coke 32–3; T. Birch, *Coll. State Papers Jn Thurloe*, 7 vols. 1742 i, 200; iv, 86; vii, 848; Posthumus, *Geschiedenis*, iii, 1184–7; Åström 69–72; Bodl. Top. Kent a.I fo. 26; J. K. Fedorowicz, *Engld's Balt. Trade in early 17th cent.*, Cam. 1980, pp. 50, 94–6.

[65]  Papillon 63; R. Coke 17; PRO, SPD Chas 2, 95/20; Philanglus, *Britannia Languens*, 1680, pp. 56–7, 158–9.

[66] Smith, *Mems Wl*, ii, 157.

[67] *Linnen & Woollen Manuf. Discoursed*, 1691, pp. 7, 8.

[68] Smith, *Mems Wl*, i, 251, 265–6, 378, 388–9; ii, 109, 117, 212, 410–12, 426–9, 438–9, 442–3, 447–50, 461; Cole ii, 383, 576–7; A. C. Wood, *Hist. Lev. Co.*, 1964, pp. 141–3; *Cal. SP Ven.* xxxiv, 249; P. Benedict, *Rouen during Wars Rel.*, Cam. 1981, p. 14; Posthumus, *Bronnen*, v, 637–8; vi, pp. viii, 3, 4.

[69] Ibid.pp. vii, viii, 385, 410–12; Smith, *Mems Wl*, ii, 140–1, 210, 215, 460–2; H. E. S. Fisher, *Port. Trade*, 1971, pp. 48–9; Endrei, *L'Evolution*, 106; *Laws in Ven. f. Prohibition For. Cl.*, s.l. n.d.; Abrate, 'Industria Laniera Piemontese', 119.

[70] Ammann 60–1; Baasch 35, 82, 90–2, 99, 100; Dechesne 38 sqq., 57 sqq., 112; Lebrun 52–4, 66 sqq., 82–3, 124, 128, 130 sqq., 138, 141, 143, 150, 187 sqq., 192, 213 sqq.; Posthumus, *Bronnen*, iv, 462–3, 483; vi, pp. vii, 10, 23, 26, 29, 32, 396–7, 444 sqq.; *Geschiedenis*, i, f. p. 371; M. Barkhausen, 'Govt Contr. & Fr. Enterprise in W. Ger. & L. Countries in 18th cent.' in Earle, *Essays*, 228,253–5.

[71] Culpepper 12; Defoe, *Plan*, 182–3.

[72] Mann, *Cl. Ind.*, 41–2; Lichfield Jt RO, Cons. Ct, O.W., Benj. Bedford 1680, Th. Bowater 1681, Jos. Smith 1729, all Cov.; PRO, PCC parch. invs p. 1660 nos. 2335, 2348, 3442; invs 1718–82 bdl. 27 no. 7.

[73] Ibid.bdl. 18 nos. 109, 237; 21 no. 9; 24 no. 100; 25 no. 67; paper invs 1661–1725 no. 28; parch. invs p. 1660 nos. 361, 368, 3422, 3892, 4502, 8410, 9658; PCR 1633–4, pp. 107, 372–3, 384 (fos. 50, 193v.–4, 199v.); SPD Chas 241/1, 36; 243/73, 78; 287/77.

[74] Plummer, *Witney*, 8, 67, 128, 151, 157; Giles 48, 51; Plot, *Oxon.*, 279; Bang iiA, 410; McGrath, *Merchs*, 72; Coleman, thes. 188; Defoe, *Plan*, 182; *Compl. Engl. Tradesman*, 77; Pococke ii, 196; Posthumus, *Bronnen*, v, 463; Warner 400–1; *Winthrop Papers*, iii, 286; Jn Gay, 'Trivia' bk i, l. 47; Cash 156–7; Soms. RO, Arch. Taunton inv. Agnes Pollard 1690 Holford (cf. 1720/4 Ric. Startt mercer Porlock); Wilts. RO, Cons. Ct Sarum. Hy Painter 1692 Devizes; Jos. Chubb 1725 Downton; Hants. RO, Arch. Ct O.W. & Invs 1720 Jn Dawkins sr Romsey Infra; W.Sfk RO, Ep. Commy Ct Bury inv. 1664/22; Nfk RO, Cons. Ct invs 1634/195; 1723/18; 1724/68; PRO, PCC parch. invs p. 1660, no. 7931; Bodl. Cons. & Arch Cts Oxf. O.W. etc. 79/1/45.

[75] Ibid.60/4/27; 79/1/45; 166/2/25; 169/4/3; 170/4/9; 300/6/44; Plot, *Oxon.*, 278–9; Plummer, *Witney*, 11, 22, 67, 128, 154, 182, 278; Plummer & Early 9, 10, 18, 22, 39, 46; Giles 47–9, 51–2; *L.J.*, iv, 361; cf. Pococke i, 205; Glos. RO, Cons. Ct inv. 1682/11; E. Lisle, *Obs. in Husb.*, 1757, p. 427.

[76] Ramsay, *Wilts.*, 82, 104–6, 108–9; PRO, SPD Chas 184/65, 76; 268/5; 454/29, 84; PCR 1634–5 pp. 183–4 (fo. 83); 1639–40 pp. 373, 382–3 (fos. 182, 186v.–7); 1640 p. 549 (fo. 271).

[77] Munro, *Wl, Cl. & Gold*, 4, 5, 183; Posthumus, *Geschiedenis*, i, 206–7, 214; Rich 15, 16, 18, 32; Schanz, *Handelspolitik*, i, 68; De Smedt i, 47; De Sagher i, 102–3; Willemsen, 'La Technique', 17, 24; Unger, *Bronnen*, iii, 117, 161, 381–3, 713–5, 717–8, 829; BL, Lans. 152 fo. 229 (240); Sella, *Commerci e Industrie*, 57.

[78] Moens, *Norwich*, 265; Nfk RO, Cty Recs. Strangers Bk fos. 19, 25v.–6, 33, 34v., 37–8; Ords con. Wl 1577 fos. 10v., 16v., 17v., 18v., 21; Keure (Bk Du. Ords) fos. 10v., 17v., 18v., 19, 31; Duties on Arts Manuf. 1566–89 fos. 1, 3; *CPR*, Eliz. iv, 39, 40; Kent RO, Maidstone Recs. Burghmote Bk 1 fo. 44; Bk 3 fo. 5 (p. 9); Sandwich Recs. Ltrs Pat. f. Strangers 3 Eliz.; L. Bl. Bk fo. 192; Cant. Cath. Lib. Wall. Recs. Misc. Docs portf. 1 nos. 2–5.

[79] PRO, SPD Eliz. Add. 13/81.

[80] De Sagher i, 102 sqq., 189, 192–4, 299, 300, 307, 322–3, 344, 347, 350, 353, 356, 363, 365, 370, 435 sqq., 451, 476; ii, 309–12; Willemsen, 'La Grève', 148; G. D. Ramsay, *Pol. Tu. Merch. Adven.*, Man 1979, p. 70; Guicciardini 119; F. E. Leese, 'Cal. & Anal. w. intro. 2 Eliz. Pt Bks', ts. thes. B. Litt. Oxf. Univ. n.d. pp. 25–6, 44, 68, 84–5, 98, 102–3, 106, 109, 111, 117, 129, 136; 'N. Draperies at Cov.' (Cov. Cty Lib.) pp. 2 sqq., 11, 12; HMC, *15th Rep*. App. pt. x, 125, 149; *CPR*, Eliz. iv, 157; PRO, SPD Eliz. 46/2, 4–8, 41–2, 47, 52–3, 55 erron. 56 recte.

[81] Ibid. 250/76; Eliz. Add. 13/81; De Smedt ii, 417; Posthumus, *Bronnen*, iii, 505; Hakluyt, *Prin. Navs*, iii, 269; *N.&Q.*, 4th ser. 1871 viii, 259.

[82] Moens, *Norwich*, 265; Nfk RO, Cty Recs. Strangers Bk fos. 25v., 37, 86v.; N. Drapery in Norwich; BL, Lans. 26 no. 58 fo. 164 (151); no. 59 fos. 175v.–6 (158v.–9); no. 60 fo. 178 (160); no. 62 fo. 182 (164).

[83] Ibid. no. 64 fo. 187 (169); Harl. 1878 fo. 100 (85).

[84] Ibid.; PRO, Exch. KR Accts Var. bdl. 347 no. 19; SPD Eliz. 249/20.

[85] PRO, PCC parch. invs p. 1660 no. 7931; HMC, *De L'Isle & Dudley MSS*, i, 286, 297–8; Bodl. Cons. & Arch. Cts Oxf. 60/4/27; 300/6/44; Plummer, *Witney*, 11.

[86] Ibid. 128; Plot, *Oxon.* 25, 278; cf. Havinden 159.

[87] Bodl. Hearne's Diaries 158 p. 32; Plot, *Oxon.*, 278.

[88] BL, Harl. 70, fos. 6v.–8(5v.–7), 10(9), 10v. bis, 13 bis, 14v., 15(16), 18(17), 19(18), 20(19)v., 22(21)v., 27(26), 31(30), 39(38), 48(47) (pp. 1, 2, 4, 8, 11, 16, 19, 20, 24–6.

[89] Ibid. fos. 7(6) v., 8(7) (pp. 3, 4).

[90] Ibid. fo. 27(26).

[91] Ibid. fos. 13(12), 13 bis, 27(26) (pp. 15, 16).

[92] Ibid. fos. 11(10), 20(19)v.(p.10).

[93] Ibid. fos. 8(7)v., 18(17), 23(22), 27(26) (pp. 5, 24).

[94] Ibid. fos. 8(7)v., 11(10), 15(16) (pp. 5, 10, 20).

[95] Ibid. 8(7)v., 18(17), 23(22), 27(26), 31(30) (pp. 5, 24).

[96] Ibid. fos. 12(11)v., 28(27) (p. 15).

[97] Ibid. fo. 27(26).

[98] Ibid. fo. 13 bis (p. 16); Lans. 48, no. 64 fo. 152.

[99] Unwin, *Studs*, 275.

[100] H. Hall, *Hist. Custom-Rev. in Engld fr. earliest times to yr 1827*, 2 vols. 1885, ii, 243; De Smedt ii, 332, 334; Willan, *Tu. Bk Rates*, 73; Friis 439; McGrath, *Merchs*, 282; *C.J.*, xvii, 366; *Rates Marchandizes*; *Rates Merchandizes* 85; Stats 4 Jas c.2; 12 Chas 2 c.4; cf. Coleman, *Banks*, 27.

[101] BL, Harl. 70, fos. 8(7)v., 11(10), 12(11)v., 15(16), 27–8(26–7) (pp. 5, 10, 13, 20).

[102] Ibid. fo. 8(7)v. (p.5); Unwin, *Studs*, 275; cf. W.Sfk RO, Ep. Commy Ct Bury inv. 1573–8/97; PRO, PCC parch.invs p.1660 nos. 572, 2913.

[103] Glouc. Lib. Smyth of Nibley MSS S.Z.23.2 no. 4: The progres of the whole lif of Mr Ben. Webb written by himselfe; & v.S.Z.23.2 no. 2; E. Moir, 'Bened. Webb, Clothier', *Econ. Hist. Rev.*, 2nd ser. 1957 x, 257–8.

[104] Bodl. Aubrey 2 fo. 144.

[105] Glouc. Lib. Smyth of Nibley Papers vol. viii, pp. 28, 30, 42, 54, 57, 77, 95, 97; PRO, SPD Jas 98/81; Chas 177/53; Moir 258; Vanes, *Docs*, 111; Mann, *Cl. Ind.*, xvii.

[106] Ibid. 92; 'Wilts. Fam. Clothiers', *Econ. Hist. Rev.*, 2nd ser. 1956 ix, 242–4, 246, 248, 250–1; C. Dale 14, 65, 86, 97, 120, 172; Pococke ii, 37; W. R. Scott, *Recs Sc. Clo. Manuf. at N. Mills 1681–1703*, Sc. Hist. S. 1905 xlvi, pp. lxxxvii–viii, 55–6; *Rates Merchandizes*, 86; Watts 42–3; Lisle 427; Defoe, *Plan*, 183; Haynes, *Clo. Trade*, 14, 15; Tawney & Power iii, 102; *Dial. bet. Dick Brazenface the Cardmaker & Tim. Meanwell the Clothier*, s.l. n.d. 5; *Clothiers Ans. to Cardmakers Reply*, s.l. n.d.; J. Tann, 'Aspects Devpt Glos. Woollen Ind.', ts. thes. PhD Leic. Univ. 1964, p. 209; J. Chamberlayne, *Magna Britanniae Notitia*, 1710, p. 28; Glouc. Lib. Smyth of Nibley MSS S.Z. 23.2 no. 5: Part.of my grievances; Stat. 12 Chas 2 c.4; PRO, PCC invs 1718–82 bdl.25 no. 83; parch.invs p. 1660 no. 7657; SPD Chas 380/85; Chas 2, 372/154.

[107] Ibid. Chas 268/5; PCR 1632–3 p. 322 (fo. 149v.); 1634–5, p. 183 (fo. 83); 1636–7 p. 99 (fo. 45); Bodl. Aubrey 2 fos. 64, 144; Mann, *Cl. Ind.*, 11–14.

[108] Ibid. 11–13; Ramsay, *Wilts.*, 115; Bodl. Aubrey 2 fo. 144; W. H. Jones, *Brad.-on-Avon*, Brad.-on-Avon 1907, pp. 54, 56; cf. PRO, PCR 1639–40 pp. 382–3 (fos. 186v.–7); Scott, *Recs* lxxxviii.

[109] Et v. J. P. M. Fowle, *Wilts. Q. Sess. & Assizes, 1736*, Wilts. Rec. S. 1955 xi, 78; M. F. Davies, *Life in Engl. Vil.*, Lond. & Leip. 1909, p. 26.

[110] Ramsay, *Wilts.*, 129–30; PRO, PCR 1639 p. 323 (fo. 157); 1639–40 pp. 373, 382–3 (fos. 182, 186v.–7); Mann, *Cl. Ind.*, 8.

[111] Ibid. xvii, 8; Wilts. RO, Pec. Ct Dean Sarum. Jer. Derby 1692 Sherborne; PRO, PCC parch. invs p. 1660 no. 7657; Watts 42–4; Defoe, *Tour*, i, 217, 279; *VCH Dors.* ii, 360.

[112] Ramsay, *Wilts.*, 126–7, 135.

[113] Ibid., 103, 114; C. Dale 131; Money, *Hist. Newbury*, 308; M. F. Davies 24–7, 33; Pococke ii, 37; Defoe, *Tour*, i, 271, 281; Mann, *Cl. Ind.*, 32–3; 'Wilts. Fam.', 242 sqq.; HMC, *Var. Colls*, i, 135; Devizes Mus. Wm Gaby His Booke, pp. 5, 18; Wilts. RO, Cons. Ct Sarum. Wm Withers 1711 Boreham in Warminster; PRO, PCC invs 1718–82 bdl. 21 no. 38; 22 no. 140; 24 no. 42; 33 no. 125; parch. invs p. 1660, no. 9236.

[114] Ibid. nos. 1112, 9963; SPD Chas 380/85, 87; Bourhis i, 97; Youings 72; Stephens, *Exeter*, 28–30, 48, 51; Chanter & Wainwright ii, 72; Bpl., N. Devon Athenaeum, Bpl. Boro. Recs. vol. 14 Sess. Ct Recs 1677–1716, loose sh. bet. pp. 156–7.

[115] *C.J.*, xvi, 119; xvii, 68; xxvii, 732; Glos. RO, Cons. Ct inv. 1663/149; Marcham Coll. F26; Tann 124, 209; PRO, PCC parch. invs p. 1660 nos. 8428, 8687; SPD Chas 177/53; Mann, *Cl. Ind.*, xvii, 13; Lindley 152–4.

[116] Kent RO, Cons. Ct Cant. Inv. Reg. 18 Jn Gilles clothier Cranbrook 14 Feb. 1627.

[117] PRO, SPD Chas 240/23.

[118] PRO, PCR 1639 p. 323 (fo. 157); J. P. Cooper, 'Econ. Reg. & Cl. Ind. in 17th-cent. Engld', *Trs R.H.S.*, 5th ser. 1970 xx, 87.

[119] PRO, SPD Chas 475/64.

[120] Ibid. 240/23; 475/64; *APC*, 1630–1, p. 356; Wood 44; E. B. Schumpeter 35, 70; H. E. S. Fisher 145; Ramsay, *Wilts.*, 114, 116, 118–20, 140 sqq.; Willan, *Ru. Co.*, 260; Stephens, *Exeter*, 28–30, 67, 104; Hinton 114; W. H. Jones 62–3; Åström 73, 75; Mann, *Cl. Ind.*, 15, 18, 50.

[121] Ibid.37 sqq., 50–1; *VCH Wilts.*, iv, 160–1; W. H. Jones 67; Pococke ii, 37; H. R. Exelby, 'Ind. Rev. in Text. Inds Wilts.', ts. thes. MA Brist. Univ. 1928, p. 6; Flint. RO, Plas Teg MS 909.

[122] Mann, *Cl. Ind.*, 14; *C.J.*, xxvii, 732; A. T. Playne, *Hist. Pars Minchinhampton & Avening*, Glouc. 1915, pp. 141, 149; PRO, PCC invs 1718–82 bdl. 20 no. 267; 24 no. 100; 25 no. 85; parch. invs p. 1660 no. 3892.

[123] Ibid. no. 3715.

[124] Ibid. no. 3225.

[125] Ibid. no. 7998; invs 1718–82 bdl. 20 no. 267; C. Dale 86, 120; Smith, *Mems Wl*, ii, 120; Benson & Hatcher 579; Flint. RO, Plas Teg MS 909.

[126] Worcs. RO, Cons. Ct O.W. etc. 1710 Jn Jones clothier; 1712 Ob. Spencer; 1716 Stephen Lea er; 1717 Ed. Parrins; 1718 Wm Dearne clothier.

[127] *Ca. Manufs Grograin Yarn*, n.d.; Haynes, *Clo. Trade*, 3, 14; Smith, *Mems Wl*, ii, 43; PRO, SPD Chas 475/60.

[128] Ibid. Eliz. 252/2; Cash 18, 19; Dyer *Cty Worc.*, 119; McGrath, *Merchs*, 87, 271–4; Burton 180; Corfield, 'Prov. Cap.', 274, 305; HMC, *De L'Isle & Dudley MSS*, i, 290; Heaton 266; C. E. C. Tattersall, *Hist. Brit. Carpets*, Benfleet 1934, pp. 34–6, 38, 41–2, 45, 51 sqq., 62–3, 65 sqq., 83 sqq., pls i, ii, v–x, xii-xiv, xxv-vi; A. F. Kendrick, *Engl. Dec. Fabs 16th to 18th cents.*, Benfleet 1934, pp. 16 sqq., 33, 36 sqq., 47–8, 80–2, pls iv, vi, ix-xi, xiii, xv, xxvi; R. Davies, *Life Marmaduke Rawdon of York*, Camd. S. 1863 lxxxv, 121; J. C. Hodgson, *6 N. Country Diaries*, Surtees S. 1910 cxviii, 30.

[129] *VCH Glos.*, xi, 224; P. Slack, *Poverty in Early Stuart Salisbury*, Wilts. Rec. S. 1975 xxxi, 74; Glos. RO, Cons. Ct invs 1663/4, 207; PRO, PCC parch. invs p. 1660 nos. 329, 16139; Wilts. RO, Pec. Ct Treas. box 4 no. 32; Bodl. Arch. Ct Berks. 58/1; 98/146; 209/30; 219/115; Nfk RO, Cons. Ct inv. 1674/33.

**Chapter 4**

[1] Stats 33 H.8 c.16; 1 & 2 P.&M. c.14.

[2] Nfk RO, Cty Recs. Strangers Bk fo. 16.

[3] *APC*, xii, 63.

[4] BL, Add. 12504, no. 65 p. 3; Nfk RO, Arch. Ct Norvic. inv. 1682–3/120; Cons. Ct inv. 1710–14/150; PRO, PCC parch. invs p. 1660 no. 5543.

[5] H. Hall ii, 240; Ess. RO, Pec. Ct Abp Cant. in Pec. Deanery Bocking inv. Ric. Chaplain 1739; Ramsay, *Isham*, 159–60; Willan, *Tu. Bk Rates*, 65; Gras 572; B. Dietz 155; De Smedt ii, 416–17; *Rates Marchandizes*, s.v. yarn; *Disc. Com. Weal*, 16; Millard, vols. ii, iii; PRO, SPD Eliz. 8/31; Exch. KR Accts Var. bdl. 520 no. 24, fo. 4; BL, Lans. 8 fo. 75.

[6] BL, Add. 12504 no. 64 fo. 82.

[7] Hudston & Tingey ii, 134, 379; PRO, Exch. KR Deps by Commn 44 & 45 Eliz. Mich. 1 m.7r.; Stat. 19 H.7 c.17; Nfk RO, Cty Recs. Bks Mayor's Ct 8 p. 398; 9 pp. 155, 253; 10 p. 231; Ass. Bks 3 fos. 64v., 196v., 306v.; 4 fo. 44v.; Strangers Bk fo. 20v.; Misc. Docs. Controversy resp. Cits Norwich, Touching the Allegacion that the Queenes Majestie doth lose her custume; cf. Lancs. RO, Kenyon of Peel MSS 9 Corr. 21/47.

[8] BL, Add. 12504 no. 64 fo. 82; cf. PRO, Req. 157/134 fo. 95(3) rev.; Dunning & Tremlett 63.

[9] Laurent 97; Davidsohn vol. iv pt. ii, 69; Ehrenberg 287; Bahr 136; Edler, 'Van Der Molen', 82, 104, 119.

[10] Ibid. 82: *Rates Marchandizes*, s.v. chamlets; Willan, *Tu. Bk Rates*, 16; B. Dietz 48, 75, 83; Postlethwayt i, 438; PRO, PCR 1639 p. 44 (fo. 18v.); J. Evelyn, *Diary*, Oxf. 6 vols. 1955, i. 94; iii, 65; Nfk RO, Cons. Ct invs 1692–3/140; 1731/18; V.&A. Text. Dept., Counterpart Patts sent to Sp. & Lis. by Mr J.K. 1763; Bridewell Mus. Norwich, Patts Norwich Manufs 1769 fos. 90 sqq., 110 sqq.; & v. Patts Norwich Manufs 1794–7; Bk F. Tuthill & Fils, Norwich; ex inf. Miss P. Marsh.

[11] BL, Add. 12504 no. 64 fo. 82; (Bernard G. K. A) *Joyfull Receyving of the Queenes most excellent Majestie into hir Highnesse Citie of Norwich*, n.d.; cf. PRO, Req. 157/134 fo. 95(3) rev.

[12] Mx RO, Arch. Ct Mx invs 1673 Jn Hoptkins, 1678 Jn Meade shopkpr, both St Clem. Danes; Kent RO, Arch. Ct Cant. Inv. Reg. 11 fo. 223; Cons. Ct Cant. Inv. Paper 21/21; Nfk RO, Cty Recs. 2nd Bk Worstedweavers fo. 61v.; PRO, Exch. KR Deps by Commn 44 & 45 Eliz. Mich. 1 m. 3r.

[13] Ibid. m. 7r.; Nfk RO, loc. cit.; cf. Stat. 5 & 6 E.6 c.7.

[14] Strieder 222.

[15] G. Hill, *Hist. Engl. Dress*, vol. ii 1893, p. 205; Hudson & Tingey ii, 134; Warner 290, 658H & L; Edwards v, vi, 55, 57, 305; BL, Add. 12504 no. 63; PRO, PCC invs 1718–82 bdl. 23 no. 159; parch. invs p. 1660 nos. 1603, 1771, 3602, 4051; Nfk RO, Cty Recs. Bks Mayor's Ct 8 pp. 512, 546, 630, 674; 9 pp. 46, 144, 260, 263; Ass. Bks 3 fos. 64v., 131v., 196v., 306v.; 4 fo. 44v.; Misc. Docs, Touching the Allegacion etc. ut sup.; Cons. Ct invs 1671/47; 1674/58; 1681/66; 1692–3/65(64); 1703–8/110, 390; 1710–14/31, 396; 1716–17/169; 1788–1849/9; Arch. Ct Norvic. invs 1674–5/163, 200, 216; 1715–17/103; 1754–67/43.

[16] Ibid. 1700–2/62; 1754–67/59; Cons. Ct invs 1718–21 (stamped) 169; 1731/18.

[17] PRO, Exch. KR Deps by Commn 44 & 45 Eliz. Mich. 1 mm. 7r., 8.

[18] BL, Add. 12504 no. 64 fo. 82; Nfk RO, Cty Recs. Bk Mayor's Ct 14 fo. 252v.

[19] Ibid. 15 fo. 134v.; Ass. Bk 3 fos. 306v.–7; Strangers Bk fo. 106; Duties fos. 65, 67 sqq.; Alnage Accts 1580–1610; N. Drapery in Norwich; BL, Lans. 26 no. 57 fo. 161(149); no. 62 fo. 181(163)v.; no. 64 fo. 187; 71 no. 51 fo. 107(108); Moens, *Norwich*, 78; *Rates Marchandaizes*, s.v. grograins Lile or Norwich, buffins; *Disc, consisting of Motives f. Enlargement & Freedome of Trade*, 1654, p. 29.

[20] Ibid.; Willan, *Inld Trade*, 67; PRO, Exch. KR Deps by Commn 44 & 45 Eliz. Mich. 1 m.3; Nfk RO, Cons. Ct inv. 1591/169; Cty Recs. Bks Mayor's Ct 13 pp. 141, 459; 14 fos. 6(11), 229, 237v., 252v.

[21] Ibid. 14 fos. 7(13), 113, 140v., 166, 229, 237v., 252v., 254v.–5, 331, 361v., 410, 456v.–7; 15

fos. 73v., 101v., 103, 145, 185v., 191, 198, 202, 216v., 238, 260v., 362v., 375; Cons. Ct invs 1614/148; 1617/157; 1619/137.

[22] Ibid. 1710–14/295; Arch. Ct Norvic. 1706–7/20; Cty Recs. Bk Mayor's Ct 14 fos. 140v., 410; F. C. Recs. Wall. Ch. 5, 6; Munn 5; PRO, SPD Jas 35/27; Kent RO, Cons. Ct Cant. Inv. Reg. 9 fo. 117v.; BL, Add. 12504 no. 63; no. 64 fo. 82.

[23] Ibid.; Nfk RO, Cons. Ct inv. 1617/157.

[24] Inf. 72.

[25] F. Braudel & R. Romano, *Navires et Marchandises à l'entrée du port de Livourne (1547–1611)*, Paris 1951, p. 45; J. James 22–3; Verlinden 28.

[26] BL, Add. 12504 no. 64 fo. 82; PRO, PCC parch. invs p. 1660 no. 4051; *Disc. f. Enl. & Freedome of Trade*, 29; S. Purchas, *Microcosmus*, 1619, p. 269; Postlethwayt i, 221; Posthumus, *Bronnen*, v, 321, 345; Lancs. RO, Cavendish of Holker Coll. 1/45 fo. 2; Mx RO, Arch. Ct Mx inv. 1678 Jn Meade shopkpr St Clem. Danes; Lambeth Pal. Pecs Abp Cant. in Pec. Deaneries of the Arches etc. inv. Mich. Garey 1666 St Mary Aldermary; Munn 5; Nfk RO, Cons. Ct invs 1635/165; 1628–68/117; Cty Recs. Bks Mayor's Ct 16 fos. 155v., 162v., 170v., 186, 196v., 205, 209v., 236, 299, 399v.; 20 fos. 12, 17, 45v., 56v., 58v., 122, 179, 188, 209, 280, 285v.

[27] Ibid. 14 fo. 445v.; 15 fos. 21v., 30v., 80, 101, 103v., 107, 117v.–18, 127, 130, 134, 139v., 145, 158, 168, 179, 190v., 198, 202v., 216v., 222v.–3, 238, 260v., 271, 326v., 362v.–3, 375, 383, 388v., 393v., 417, 468, 473v.–4, 487v.–8, 510v., 518v., 521, 528v., 533v.; 16 fos. 9v., 16, 17, 20v., 34v., 48v., 93v., 116, 117v., 120, 122v., 131v., 141v., 145v.–6, 151, 196, 277, 298v.–9, 308, 318, 332v.–3, 349, 353v., 355, 369v., 371v.–2, 375, 381, 390v.–1, 403, 405v., 413v., 419v., 426, 433, 440, 442, 447, 459v.–60, 474, 476–7, 480; 19 fos. 101–2;20 fos. 12v., 23v., 54, 194, 204v., 209, 229v., 231, 238, 270, 280, 285v., 292v., 312v., 332; Strangers Bk fo. 113v.; Cons. Ct invs. 1617/115; 1634/195; 1635/163; 1639/211B; 1710–14/295; Purchas 269; BL, Add. 12504 no. 64 fo. 82.

[28] Ibid.; Purchas 269; McGrath, *Merchs*, 282; PRO, SPD Jas 35/27; PCC parch. invs p. 1660 no. 580; Nfk RO, Cty Recs. N. Drapery in Norwich; Strangers Bk fos. 110A, 111v.; Bks Mayor's Ct 14 fos. 237v., 253, 255, 307v., 410, 457; 15 fos. 9, 80, 158v., 185v., 202v., 216v.; 16 fo. 155v.; 20 fos. 340, 345 (presentmt), 358v., 398v., 422; Cons. Ct invs 1617/51, 115 (Worstead); 1628–68/117; 1647/189; F. C. Recs. Wall. Ch. 5, 6.

[29] Kent RO, Cons. Ct Cant. Inv. Paper 21/21; PRO, C.O., BoT Orig. Corr. vol. 21 no. 209 (MFQ 134) fo. 156.

[30] Gras 511, 560; Burley thes. 409; Smith, *Mems Wl*, ii, 43; De Smedt ii, 386; *Rates Marchandizes*; Roberts, *Marchants Mapp*, 2nd pt 94, 193; Wheeler 23; Willan, *Tu. Bk Rates*, 16, 30; B. Dietz 23, 48–9, 75, 83, 86–7, 93, 101, 105, 114, 118, 126, 153; Millard i, 52, 83–4, App. pp. 14, 18, 35; vols. ii, iii; PRO, SPD Eliz. 8/31; BL, Lans. 8 fo. 75.

[31] J. Taylor, *Praise of Hemp-seed*, 1620, p. 4; J. Gay, 'Trivia' bk i, l. 6; PRO, SPD Chas 149/55; Defoe, *Compl. Engl. Tradesman*, 79; Postlethwayt i, 221, 438; *Ca. Manufs. Grograin Yarn*; Worthy 148; B. E. Howells, *Cal. Ltrs rel. to N.W. 1533–c.1700*, Cardiff 1967, p. 129; U.C.N.W. Ban. Gen. Coll. 5582; Mx RO, Arch. Ct Mx inv. 1673 Jn Hoptkins/St Clem. Danes; Lambeth Pal. Pecs Abp Cant. in Pec. Deaneries of the Arches etc. inv. Mich. Garey 1666 St Mary Aldermary; Guildhall Lib. Commy Ct Lond. (Lond. Div.) invs. box 9 Eliz. Shales 1700 St Dunstan's in the West; Ess. RO, Bp Lond. Commy Ct f. Ess. & Herts. Reg. Wills, Reg. 4 fo. 101v.; Arch. Ct Colc. Reg. Wills, Reg. 6 fo. 177; Kent RO, Arch. Ct Cant. Inv. Reg. 11 fo. 223; Nfk RO, Cons. Ct inv. 1619/137; Cty Recs. Bks Mayor's Ct 15 fo. 202v.; 16 fo. 155v.

[32] Ibid. 15 fo. 92; Stats 33 H.8 c.16; 1 E.6 c.6; 1 & 2 P.&M. c.14.

[33] Hudson & Tingey ii, 410; Nfk RO, Cons. Ct inv. 1617/51; 1588/117.

[34] Stow, *Ann.* 867; Wheeler 23; Craeybeckx 425; Ramsay, *Isham*, 31, 160; Gras 572, 577–9, 703; *Rates Marchandizes*; Willan, *Tu. Bk Rates*, 52; Cash 4; De Smedt ii, 379, 386, 416; Schanz, *Handelspolitik*, ii, 256; Van Der Wee ii, 187; B. Dietz 3, 8, 9, 20, 50, 60, 67, 73–4, 83–4, 87, 93, 118, 126, 128, 133, 154; Millard i, App. p. 38; vols. ii, iii; PRO, SPD Eliz. 8/31; BL, Lans. 8 fo. 75; Hants. RO, Cons. & Arch. cts, unclass. invs D/2/A: 2/178.

[35] Thierry iv, 359–61; Vanhaeck i, 27, 47, 91, 95, 142, 240; ii, 44, 50–1; Leuridan, 'Lannoy', 339; De Sagher i, 337; Brulez, *Della Faille*, 5, 245, 267, 476, 478, 511; Maugis 15, 51, 53.

[36] S. W. Beck, *Draper's Dict.*, n.d., s.v. russell.

[37] Bernard, op. cit.; BL, Add. 12504 no. 65 p. 4; PRO, Req. 157/134 fos. 77(2), 91(2); Exch, KR Deps by Commn 44 & 45 Eliz. Mich. 1 m. 3r.; Nfk RO, Cty Recs. Ass. Bks 3 fo. 131v.; 4 fo. 44v.; 5 fo. 82.

[38] Ibid. Bks Mayor's Ct 9 fo. 139; 11 fos. 251v., 312v.; *APC*, xii, 63.

[39] Stats 33 H.8 c.16; 1 E.6 c.6; 1 & 2 P.&M. c.14; Hudson & Tingey ii, 408; BL, Lans. 26 no. 57 fo. 161(149); no. 62 fo. 181(163)v.; no. 64 fo. 187; Nfk RO, Cons. Ct invs 1617/51, 157; 1634/74; 1640/145; 1692–3/115; 1716–17/169; Arch. Ct Norvic. invs 1674–5/200, 216; Cty Recs. N. Drapery in Norwich; Bks Mayor's Ct 8 pp. 48 erron., 53, & entry 29 Jan. 6 Eliz.: 9 fos. 6, 19, 139, 165, 198, 253, 263 & entry 18 May 17 Eliz.; 11 fos. 251v., 312v.; 12 fo. 135.

[40] M. G. Davies 131.

[41] W.Sfk RO, Ep. Commy Ct Bury inv. 1676/47; Guildhall Lib. Commy Ct Lond. (Lond. Div.) invs box 8, Th. Flower 1702, Abr. Lennigni 1714, both Stepney.

[42] Inf. 82.

[43] Hudston & Tingey ii, 134, 380, 408, 410.

[44] Ibid. 412; Nfk RO, Cons. Ct inv. 1635/163; cf. B. Jons., *Everyman in his Humour*, act iv sc. 7.

[45] Deyon 173–4; Deyon & Lottin 24; Vanhaeck i, 240; ii, 44, 90; Maugis 15.

[46] Stats 1 & 2 P.&M. c.14; 9 Geo. c.9; BL, Add. 12504 no. 65 p.4; Hudson & Tingey ii, 408.

[47] Ibid. 408, 410; cf. 134, 380; Nfk RO, Cty Recs. Ass. Bk 3 fos. 280v.–1; Bks Mayor's Ct 10 pp. 86, 419, 731 bis, 782; 11 fos. 130v., 274v., 412; 12 fo. 135; 14 fo. 410; Strangers Bk fos. 94–5; Alnage Accts ad init.; PRO, Exch. KR Deps by Commn 44 & 45 Eliz. Mich. 1 mm. 1, 3r.; SPD Eliz. 287/95; Jas 35/27; Beck s.v. durants; *Rates Marchandizes*, s.v. durance; *Disc. f. Enl. & Freedome of Trade*, 29; Willan, *Inld Trade*, 67, 123–4; Emmison, *Disorder*, 312; Bang iiA, 472, 490; Munn 5; Kent RO, Cons. Ct Cant. Reg. Accts & Invs 6 fo. 371.

[48] Ibid. Arch. Ct Cant. Inv. Reg. 11 fo. 219.

[49] PRO, SPD Eliz. Add. 34/23; Req. 157/134 fo. 93(1).

[50] Ibid.; SPD Eliz. Add. 34/23; Exch. KR Deps by Commn 44 & 45 Eliz. Mich. 1 m.3r.; Nfk RO, Bk Mayor's Ct 11 fo. 412; BL, Add. 12504 no. 63.

[51] Ibid. no. 65, p. 3; Hudson & Tingey ii, 412–3.

[52] Cole ii, 192–3; Brulez, *Della Faille*, 304, 522; Goris 252, 262–3, 319; Weiss i, 42; G. Botero, *Treatise con. Causes Magnificencie & Greatnes Cities*, 1606, p. 56; R. Doehaerd & C. Kerremans, *Les Relations Commerciales entre Gènes, la Belgique et l'Outremont d'après les Archives Notariales Génoises 1400–1440*, Brux. & Rome 1952, pp. 612–13; Mollwo 19; L. Van Nierop, 'De Zijdenijverheid van Amsterdam Historisch Geschetst', *Tijdschrift voor Geschiedenis*, xlv–vi, 1930–1 xlv, 24–5, 33–4, 40, 156, 161 sqq.; Van Dillen, *Bronnen*, i, 504; ii, 363, 513; Posthumus, *Bronnen*, vi, 16; J. L. M. Eggen, *De Invloed door Zuid-Nederland op Noord-Nederland uitgeoefend op het einde der XVIe en het begin der XVIIe eeuw*, Ghent 1908, pp. 173–4; Baasch 103; Gras 372, 511–13, 560, 572, 574 sqq., 705; *Rates Marchandizes*, s.v. velvet; De Smedt ii, 416; Ramsay, *Isham*, 160; Wheeler 23; Willan, *Tu. Bk Rates*, 27; B. Dietz 3, 7–9, 21–3, 31–2, 36, 43, 50–1, 67–8, 72, 74, 83, 86–7, 92–3, 101, 112, 129, 154; Craeybeckx 425; var. Tours velours may be seen at Plessis-les-Tours.

[53] Vanhaeck i, 238–9, 241, 259, 272–3, 317; ii, 58; De Sagher iii, 416; Goris 279, 297; De Poerck ii, 211; Eggen 174, 176; Leuridan, *Roubaix*, 15, 16, 20–1, 27, 37, 51, 54, 56; 'Linselles', 214; 'Lannoy', 339–40, 343; J. A. Faber, *Drie Eeuwen Friesland*, Wageningen 2 vols. 1972, ii, 439; A. K. L. Thijs, *De Zijdenijverheid te Antwerpen in de XVIIe eeuw*, s.l. 1969, p. 54; Van Dillen, *Amst.*, p. xxxviii; *Bronnen*, i, 573; ii, 294–5, 329; iii, 53–4; Baasch 96; Deyon 175; Maugis 78, 98; A. Dietz, *Frankfurter Handelsgeschichte*, Frankfort-on-the-Main 2 vols. 1910–21, iii, 270; Posthumus, *Bronnen*, iii, 16, 17, 38, 40, 57, 133, 309, 469–70; vi, 177–9, 212; *Geschiedenis*, ii, 327; Rijpma 41, 96; Van Nierop xlv, 24; Nfk RO, Cty Recs. Strangers Bk fos. 66, 101v.

[54] Ibid. N. Drapery in Norwich; Stat. 1 & 2 P.&M. c.14; PRO, Req. 157/134 fos. 77(2), 99(1); Exch. KR Deps by Commn 44 & 45 Eliz. Mich. 1 m.3r.; BL, Add. 12504 no. 65 p. 4; Lans. 26 no. 57 fo. 161(149); no. 58 fo. 164(151); no. 59 fos. 175v.–6(158v.–9); no. 60; no. 62 fo. 181(163); no. 64 fo. 187; 71 no. 51 fo. 107(108); Hudson & Tingey ii, 409.

[55] Ibid. 412; BL, Lans. 26 no. 57 fo. 161 (149); Nfk RO, Cty Recs. Ass. Bk 3 fos. 227, 295; Bk Mayor's Ct 15 fos. 59, 202v.; Misc. Docs, Touching the Allegacion etc.

[56] Vanhaeck i, 248; Posthumus, *Bronnen*, iii, 309; E. Sabbe, *De Belgische Vlasnijverheid*, vol. i Bruges 1943, p. 195.

[57] PRO, Exch. KR Deps by Commn 44 & 45 Eliz. Mich. 1 mm. 3r., 8r.; SPD Eliz. 250/76; Req. 157/134 fo. 95(3) rev.; Nfk RO, Cty Recs. Bks Mayor's Ct 11 fos. 130v., 274v., 404; 12 fo. 304; 16 fos. 185v., 196v., 205, 440, 442v., 447v., 464; 2nd Bk Worstedweavers fo. 116v.; Cons. Ct inv. 1633/74.

[58] Ibid. 1694–6/43; Endrei, *L'Evolution*, 40, 123; Davidsohn vol. iv pt ii, 71 sqq.; Eggen 173; Van Dillen, *Bronnen*, ii, 363, 593; Kirk i, 458; iii, 138–9; W. McMurray, *Recs 2 Cty Pars*, 1925, p. 445; R. Campbell, *Lond. Tradesman*, 1747, p. 259; PRO, SPD Chas 180/70; Leics. RO, Arch. inv. Ric. Ayshefilde 1591 Leic.; Gras 512, 560, 575, 578, 697; Wheeler 23; Ramsay, *Isham*, 31, 160; Willan, *Tu. Bk Rates*, 21; Roberts, *Marchants Mapp*, 2nd pt 95, 181; *Rates Marchandizes*; C. H. Firth & R. S. Rait, *Acts & Ords Interreg.*, 3 vols. 1911, ii, 1219; Baasch 93; De Smedt ii, 379; *Fs. Anc. Bk Weavers' Co.*, fo. 20; BL, Lans, 691 fo. 43v.; Guildhall Lib. Commy Ct Lond. (Lond. (Lond. Div.) invs box 2 Hugh Jones 1665 Geo. Alley, Turnmill St, St Jas, Clerkenwell.

[59] Inf. 72.

[60] Nfk RO, Cons. Ct inv. 1584/88; Cty Recs. Bk Mayor's Ct 11 fos. 404, 412.

[61] Ibid. fos. 640v., 684v., 703v.; 12 pp. 147, 177, 303, 509; 14 fos. 6(11), 77v, 113, 133, 140, 179, 229, 252v.–3, 254v., 330v.–1, 361v., 410, 422v., 444, 457; 15 fos. 30v., 59, 80, 101, 126v., 158, 223, 260v., 388v., 510v., 518v., 521, 533v.; 16 fos. 17, 76v., 93v., 131v., 145v.–6, 156, 179, 196v., 209v., 236, 241, 299, 333, 349v., 353v., 399v., 405, 440, 477; 20 fos. 6v., 12, 17, 23, 54, 179, 194, 204v., 209, 229v., 231v., 238, 246, 270, 280, 292, 306v., 332, 350, 358v., 386, 422v., 433; Ass. Bk. 4 fo. 44v.; Duties fos. 63v., 65 sqq.; Alnage Accts; Cons. Ct invs 1591/169; 1633/56; 1635/165; 1639/211B; 1640/143; 1692–3/140; 1703–8/390; 1710–14/150, 231, 391; Arch. Ct Norvic. invs 1709–10/61; 1715–17/103; 1754–67/43; BL, Add. 12504 no. 63; Fiennes 149, 245; Munn 5; Warner 658J & L; Edwards 55.

[62] Ibid. 39; Warner 285; Munn 5; Nfk RO, Cons. Ct invs 1617/115; 1626/69; 1631/137; 1637/94; 1640/48; 1646/109; 1637–68/19; 1664/14; 1671/65; Arch. Ct Nfk Invs 1728–42/259, 350.

[63] W. Sfk RO, Ep. Commy Ct Bury inv. 1652/80.

[64] Nfk RO, Cty Recs. Bks Mayor's Ct 16 fo. 440; 19 fo. 102; 20 fos. 246v., 270, 280, 422v.

[65] Worthy 151; Fiennes 152; Kent RO, Arch. Ct Cant. Inv. Reg. 1 fo. 9; R. Keen, 'Messrs Best, Brews Chatham' in M. Roake & J. Whyman, *Essays in Kentish Hist.*, 1973, pp. 239–40.

[66] V. & A. Text. Dept Stud. Rm A.36; Norwich weaver's patt. bk 1767; Counterpart Patts sent to Sp. & Lis. by Mr J.K. 1763; Bridewell Mus. Patts Norwich Manufs 1769, fo. 61; J. James 363; Postlethwayt i, 428; Vanhaeck i, 162; Edwards 56, 204; Defoe, *Compl. Engl. Tradesman*, 78–9; F. *Engl. Chintz*, Benfleet 1935, p. 37, pl. 1; Nfk RO, Cons. Ct invs 1603/13; 1716–17/169; PRO, SPD Eliz. Add. 33/72.

[67] Ibid.; 34/23; Eliz. 250/76, 78; Req. 157/134 fo. 91(1); Wadsworth & Mann 119.

[68] *Rates Marchandizes*; Fiennes 149, 245; Warner 658I; Edwards 55, 204; Munn 5; Purchas 268; PRO, Exch. KR Deps by Commn 44 & 45 Eliz. Mich. 1 m. 3r.; PCC parch. invs p. 1660 no. 5543; BL, Add. 12504 no. 63; Lancs. RO, Cavendish of Holker Coll. 1/46 pp. 10, 12; Nfk RO, Cty Recs. Bks Mayor's Ct 14 fos. 7(13), 77v.; 15 fo. 417; invs Arch. Ct Nfk 1728–42/246; Arch. Ct Norvic 1727–8/61; Cons. Ct 1603/120; 1628–68/117; 1702/10; 1703–8/110; 1710–14/31, 150; 1716–17/169; 1723/110; Bridewell Mus. Patts Norwich Manufs 1769 fo. 61; Patts Norwich Manufs 1794–7; V. & A. Text. Dept, Norwich weaver's patt. bk 1767; Counterpart Patts sent to Sp. & Lis. by Mr J.K. 1763.

[69] Ibid.; Norwich weaver's patt. bk 1767; Bridewell Mus. Patts Norwich Manufs 1769 fo. 61; Patts Norwich Manufs 1794–7; Patt. Bk 1792; 'F. Tuthill & Fils, Norwich'; Munn 5; PRO, PCC invs 1718–82 bdl. 23 no. 159; Nfk RO, Cons. Ct invs 1692–3/140; 1694–6/43; 1709–10/214; 1710–14/31.

[70] Ibid,; 1718–21/282; PRO, PCC invs 1718–82 bdl.23 no. 159

[71] De Poerck i, 227; Espinas & Pirenne i, 509, 533; pace Wilhelmsen 110.

[72] PRO, SPD Jas 35/27.

[73] Munn 5; Nfk RO, invs Arch. Ct Norvic. 1674–5/200; Cons. Ct 1633/56; 1638/211B; Cty Recs. Bks Mayor's Ct 15 fo. 388v.; 16 fos. 141v., 146, 162v., 196, 277v., 333, 463v.; 20 fos. 34, 254v.–5, 270, 280, 285v., 292, 306, 312v.–13, 318, 331v.–2, 340, 345, 350, 358v., 386, 438.

[74] Ibid. fo. 345v.; Cons. Ct invs 1640/143; 1637–68/19; 1662/4; 1703–8/253; 1709–10/195; 1710–14/149; Arch. Ct Norvic. invs 1682–3/171; 1700–2/62; *Disc. f. Enl. & Freedome of Trade*, 29; PRO, PCC parch. invs p. 1660 no. 1603; Munn 5.

[75] W.Sfk RO, Ep. Commy Ct Bury inv. 1676/47.

[76] Ibid. 1652/80; Kent RO, Cons. Ct Cant. Inv. Paper 21/21; Inv. Regs 9 fo. 117; 15 fo. 303; Lancs. RO, Cavendish of Holker Coll. 1/46 fo. IV., pp. 9, 12, 30, 50–1.

[77] PRO, SPD Jas 35/27; Nfk RO, Cty Recs. Bk Mayor's Ct 14 fo. 174v.

[78] Ibid. 16 fos. 107v., 141v., 155v.

[79] Ibid. 14 fo. 77v.; Cons. Ct inv. 1634/74; PRO, PCC parch. invs p. 1660 no. 580; SPD Eliz. Add. 33/72.

[80] Ibid.; Beck s.v. tammy; Postlethwayt i, 508; J. James 217, 363; Munn 5; Hants. RO, Cons. Ct O.W. & Invs Jn Tomse 1667 Winch.; Guildhall Lib. Commy Ct Lond. (Lond. Div.) invs box 2 Hugh Jones 1665 Geo. Alley, Turnmill St, St Jas, Clerkenwell; BL, Add. 36666 fo. 11v.

[81] Ibid. 12504 no. 65 p. 1(fo. 86); PRO, PCC parch. invs p. 1660 no. 580; Req. 157/134 fo. 72; Nfk RO, Cty Recs. Bks Mayor's Ct 14 fos. 77v, 225; 15 fo. 488; 16 fos. 179, 186; invs Arch. Ct Norvic. 1703–6/1; 1709–10/61; Cons. Ct 1615/144; 1617/157; 1634/74; 1640/143; 1662/4; 1703–8/110; 1723/110.

[82] Ibid. 1669/84; Arch. Ct Nfk 1728–42/350.

[83] Edler, 'Van Der Molen', 82, 105; H. Clouzot, *Le Métier de la Soie en France (1466–1815)*, Paris n.d. p. 49; cf. PRO, SPD Chas 2 Entry Bk 71, p. 10.

[84] Purchas 269.

[85] Lancs. RO, Cavendish of Holker Coll. 1/46 fo. 1, pp. 5, 12, 20, 51; PRO, Req. 157/134 fo. 95(3) rev.; Hudson & Tingey ii, 412; Nfk RO, Cty Recs. Bks Mayor's Ct 13 p. 459; 14 fos. 113, 254v.; 15 fo. 118; Cons. Ct invs 1603/120; 1633/56; 1640/143; cf. Coornaert, *Hondschoote*, 218; Posthumus, *Bronnen*, iii, 118, 195, 483. 'Grogram', *Grofgrein & Grobgruin*, are errors due to mistranscription.

[86] Nfk RO, Cons. Ct invs 1633/56; 1634/195; Cty Recs. Bks Mayor's Ct 16 fos. 464v., 470, 480v.; 19 fos. 101–2; 20 fos. 16v., 33v., 46, 50v., 56, 59.

[87] Ibid. 16 fo. 447v.

[88] Ibid. 20 fos. 16v., 46, 50v.

[89] N. K. A. Rothstein, 'Silk Ind. in Lond. 1702–66', ts. thes. MA Lond. Univ. 1961, p. 141; Clouzot 41, 49, 50.

[90] Nfk RO, Cons. Ct invs 1635/163; 1639/211B; 1650/60; 1651/32; 1666/77; 1718–21 (stamped) 169; Cty Recs. Bk Mayor's Ct 20 fos. 179, 204v., 209, 229, 231v., 254v., 270, 280, 292, 306v., 312v., 332, 339v.–40, 358, 386, 398v., 422; Lancs. RO, Cavendish of Holker Coll. 1/45 fo. 2; 1/46 fo. 1v., pp. 5, 9, 11; PRO, PCC parch. invs p. 1660 no. 2336.

[91] Kent RO, Arch. Ct Cant. Inv. Reg. 7 fo. 9; G. P. Piccope, *Lancs. & Ches. Wills & Invs fr. Eccl. Ct Chester*, Chetham S. xxxiii, li, liv 1857–61, liv, 2; PRO, SPD Chas 475/60.

[92] Lancs. RO, Cavendish of Holker Coll. 1/46 fo. 2, pp. 5, 51; Nfk RO, Cty Recs. Bks Mayor's Ct 16 fo. 480v.; 20 fos. 17, 34, 50v., 179, 188v., 205, 208v.–9, 229v., 254, 280, 332v., 345, 398v., 433, 438; Cons. Ct invs 1635/165; 1639/211B; 1647/189.

[93] Ibid. 1628–68/117; 1665/52; (cf. 1694–6/43); PRO, PCC parch. invs. p. 1660 nos. 580, 2336,

5543; cf. W. Sfk RO, Ep. Commy Ct Bury inv. 1705/20; Lancs. RO, Cavendish of Holker Coll. 1/46 pp. 9, 11, 30, 32; Bridewell Mus., Patts Norwich Manufs 1769, end papers.

[94] Nfk RO, Cons. Ct invs 1602/239; 1606/66; 1671/65; 1674/58; 1687/156; Hill ii, 195.

[95] PRO, PCC parch. invs p. 1660 nos. 580, 1789; inf. 84.

[96] Millard i, App. p. 30; Harrison 145; J. James 231; Bridewell Mus., Ord. Bk 'Norwich 1791'; cf. Bang iiA, 221, 264, 332, 339–40, 348, 350, 372, 393, 403, 405–6, 408, 410, 436–7, 448, 460–2, 484, 486, 543–4.

[97] Nfk RO, Cons. Ct invs 1687/156; 1694–6/43; 1697–8/62; 1710–14/391.

[98] Ibid. 1718–21 (stamped) 169; Arch. Ct Norvic. 1674–5/200; W. Sfk RO, Ep. Commy Ct Bury invs 1676/47; 1705/20; PRO, PCC parch. invs p. 1660 no. 1603; Mx RO, Arch. Ct Mx inv. Jn Hoptkins 1673 St Clem. Danes; & v. Hants RO, unclass. invs D/2/A: 2/178.

[99] Nfk RO, invs Cons. Ct 1666/77; 1694–6/43; Arch. Ct Norvic. 1703–6/12; Aberystwyth, Ep. Cons. Ct St Asaph, O.W., Admons & Invs 1667 Th. Platt jr Wrexham; 1668 Ric. Paine mercer Oswestry; PRO, PCC parch. invs p. 1660 no. 2336.

[100] Ibid. no. 1789.

[101] Nfk RO, Cons. Ct inv. 1710–14/396.

[102] Ibid.1718–21 (stamped) 169; Munn 5; F. M. Montgomery, 'Jn Holker's Mid-18th cent. "Livre d'Echantillons"' in V. Gervers, *Studs in Text. Hist.*, Tor. 1977, pp. 221, 228; cf. *VCH War.*, ii, 256.

[103] BL, Add. 36666 fo. 6v.; Nfk RO, invs Arch. Ct Norvic. 1703–6/1; 1706–7/20; 1709–10/61; Cons. Ct 1702/10; 1703–8/390; 1710–14/31, 150, 295; 1716–17/169; 1723/110.

[104] Ibid. 1617/157; 1628–68/117; 1677/53; Cty Recs. Ass. Bk 5 fo. 4 (13); Bks Mayor's Ct 11 fo. 340v.; 14 fos. 253, 255, 307v.–8, 409v.; 15 fos. 21v., 59, 73v., 80, 101, 107, 126v., 134, 140, 145, 158v., 168, 179, 185v., 191, 198, 202, 216v., 223, 260v., 271, 363, 383v., 388v., 417, 487v., 518v.; 16 fos. 20v., 40v., 48v., 93v., 116, 120, 122v., 141, 151, 163, 171, 179, 196v., 205, 209v., 231, 277, 318, 333, 349, 399v., 413, 435v., 447v., 460; 20 fo. 38; Munn 5.

[105] Kent RO, Cons. Ct Cant. Inv. Reg. 15 fo. 303v.; Nfk RO, Cons. Ct invs 1633/56; 1634/74, 195; Cty Recs. Bks Mayor's Ct 14 fo. 253; 15 fos. 30v., 80, 271, 356v., 510v., 518v.; 16 fos. 34v., 107v., 116, 118, 131v., 146, 150v.–1, 156, 162v.–3, 170v.–1, 179, 186, 196v., 205, 209v., 231, 277, 349, 355v., 371v.–2, 381v., 399v., 413, 447v., 460, 470; 20 fos. 46, 50v.

[106] Ibid. Strangers Bk fo. 111; PRO, SPD Eliz. Add. 34/23.

[107] BL, Add. 12504 no. 64 fo. 82.

[108] Kent RO, Cons. Ct Cant. Inv. Reg. 15 fo. 303v.; Bang iiA, 437, 462; Nfk RO, Cons. Ct invs 1633/56; 1635/163, 165; 1639/211B; 1666/77; Cty Recs. Bks Mayor's Ct 15 fos. 393v., 403; 16 fos. 9v., 76v., 141v., 277, 349, 399v., 413v., 440, 447v., 474v.; 19 fo. 102; 20 fos. 231v., 238, 246v., 254v., 270., 280, 292, 306v., 332v., 339v., 350, 358v., 442v.; *Disc. f. Enl. & Freedome of Trade*, 29.

[109] Ibid.; Lancs. RO, Cavendish of Holker Coll. 1/45 fo. 2; 1/46 pp. 49, 51; W. Sfk RO, Ep. Commy Ct Bury inv. 1652/80; PRO, PCC parch. invs p. 1660 no. 2336; Nfk RO, Cons. Ct invs 1646/60; 1647/189; 1650/60; 1651/32; Cty Recs. Bks Mayor's Ct 16 fos. 294, 298v., 433, 447, 460, 464; 20 fos. 17, 246v., 254v., 270, 280, 292.

[110] Ibid. 16 fo. 303v.; Cons. Ct invs 1635/190; 1664/14; 1730/26; Arch. Ct Norvic. inv. 1707–8/17; Millican, *Reg.* 147–8.

[111] W. Sfk RO, Ep. Commy Ct Bury inv. 1676/47; Nfk RO, Cons. Ct invs 1628–68/117; 1671/47; Mx RO, Arch. Ct Mx inv. Jn Hoptkins 1673 St Clem. Danes; Smith, *Mems Wl*, ii, 43; PRO, PCC invs 1718–82 bdl. 23 no. 159; cf. Bang iiA, 563.

[112] BL, Add. 12504 no. 63; Nfk RO, Cty Recs. Bks Mayor's Ct 15 fos. 80, 223; 16 fos. 34v., 333, 349, 403.

[113] Ibid. 15 fos. 473v., 487v., 510v., 521v., 533v.; 16 fos. 20, 34v., 40v., 107v., 442v.

[114] Ibid. fos. 76v., 150v., 155v.

[115] Ibid. 15 fo. 468; 16 fos. 141v., 162v., 403; 20 fo. 50v.

[116] Ibid. 16 fo. 349.

[117] Ibid. 20 fo. 270v.; PRO, PCC parch. invs p. 1660 no. 1789.

[118] Nfk RO, Cons. Ct inv. 1635/163; Cty Recs. Bks Mayor's Ct 19 fos. 101–2; 20 fos. 45v.–6, 50v., 56, 58v.–9, 84, 179, 188v., 204v., 312v.; Lancs. RO, Cavendish of Holker Coll. 1/45 fo. 2; 1/46 pp. 5, 6, 11; Sabbe, *Vlasnijverheid*, i, 369, 416; Bridewell Mus. Ord. Bk 'Norwich 1791'.

[119] Pound, thes. 74, 80, 94, 326; sup. 90.

[120] Nfk RO, invs Arch. Ct Nfk 1728–42/361; Cons. Ct 1663/33; 1723/81; 1731/18.

[121] Ibid. 1611/152; 1677/117; 1703–8/253; 1710–14/149; Arch. Ct Norvic. invs 1682–3/46; 1674–5/194; 1692–3/155; 1700–1/62; 1706–7/23, 38; 1707–8/64.

[122] E. Sfk RO, Arch. inv. 15/27; Nfk RO, Cons. Ct invs 1630/198; 1635/103; 1662/148; 1699/11, 50; 1700–1/33; 1709–10/189; 1710–14/205; 1716–17/134; 1728/59; 1742–63/11, 160; Arch. Ct Nfk invs 1728–42/246, 259, 350.

[123] Nfk RO, Cons. Ct inv. 1697–8/11; inf. 153–4.

[124] Nfk RO, Cons. Ct inv. 1637/118; Thetford, King's Ho. Boro. Recs. vol. 4 Ass. Bk 1624-39 p. 226; vol. 9 Sess., Ct Rec. & Freemen's Reg. Bk 1610–1756 (16 Dec. 1623).

[125] Tymms 168.

[126] W. Sfk RO, Ep. Commy Ct Bury inv. 1652/80.

[127] Ibid. 1676/47; 1677/87; 1686/150; 1696/91; 1701/79; Blome 212–13; E. Sfk RO, Arch. inv. 15/69; Nfk RO, Cons. Ct inv. 1669/84.

[128] Ibid. 1709–10/254; Arch. Ct Norvic. invs 1674–5/231; 1707–8/18, 21; 1715–17/52; Cty Recs. Bk Mayor's Ct 24 p. 243; *APC*, 1621–3 p. 456; *Cal. Freemen Lynn*, 151, 170, 173, 179, 183, 185–6, 188, 191.

[129] Nfk RO, Arch Ct Norvic. invs 1707–8/59; 1717–18/27; Cons. Ct inv. 1703–8/192; Thetford, King's Ho. Boro. Recs. vol. 9, at 16 Dec. 1623.

[130] W. Sfk RO, Ep. Commy Ct Bury invs 1662/115, 210; 1665/97; 1670/132; 1676/60.

[131] Kent RO, Cons. Ct Cant. Regs. Accts & Invs 7 fos. 227, 270–1; 8 fo. 85; Inv. Papers 7/92; 9/107; 16/77; 21/21; Cant. Cath. Lib. Wall. Recs. Misc. Docs portf. 1 nos. 18, 24, 26; 4 no. 49; PRO, PCR 1637–8 pp. 82, 578 (fos. 39v., 291v.).

[132] Guildhall Lib. Commy Ct Lond. (Lond. Div.) invs box 8 Th. Flower 1702, Ann Hue wid. 1703, Jn Dollond 1715; box 9 Gaspard Pilot/Wheeler St, Geo. Thackery/St Dunstan's, both 1701; Th. Crette/St Dunstan's, Mrs Eliz. Pilot/Wheeler St, both 1702, all of Stepney; PRO, PCC parch. invs p. 1660 no. 2440.

[133] Guildhall Lib. Commy Ct Lond. (Lond. Div.) inv. box 5 And. Poupard 1714 Stepney; Nfk RO, Cons. Ct inv. 1703–8/110; R. Davies 24; Munn 5.

[134] Guildhall Lib. Commy Ct Lond. (Lond. Div.) invs box 8 Th. Flower 1702, Abr. Lennigni 1714, both Stepney.

[135] Cf. J. H. Clapham, 'Tranf. Worsted Ind. fr. Nfk to W.R.', *Econ. Jnl*, 1910, xx, 195 sqq., 207–9; Edwards, pp. x, xi.

## Chapter 5

[1] Nfk RO, Cty Recs. Strangers Bk fo. 20; PRO, Exch. KR Deps by Commn 44 & 45 Eliz. Mich. 1 m. 3r.; Cant. Cath. Lib. Wall. Recs. Misc. Docs portf. 1 nos. 2–5; inf. 79.

[2] H. M. Godfray, *Registre des Baptesmes, Mariages et Morts et Jeusnes de leglise Wallonne et des Isle de Jersey, Guernesey, Serq, Origny etc. establie a Southampton par patente du Roy Edouard Sixieme et de la Reine Elizabeth*, Pubs H.S.L. 1890 iv, 3 sqq.; Cant. Cath. Lib. Cty Recs. Burghmote Bk 1630–58 fos. 176v., 207; Chamb's Accts 1592–1602 fos. 423, 473v.; Wall. Recs. Misc. Docs portf 1 no. 8; Kent RO, Sandwich Recs, L. Bl. Bk fos. 192, 204v.; N. Red Bk fos. 110–12; Yr Bk C & D fo. 274; PRO, Req. 157/134 fo. 95(3); Nfk RO, Cty Recs. Strangers Bk fos. 19, 26, 33, 111.

[3] Ibid. 20v., 22–3, 25, 34v., 36v.–7; Bks Mayor's Ct 10 fo. 240; 12 p. 315; Alberti & Chapman 66; BL, Lans. 26 no. 57 fo. 161(149); PRO, Req. 157/134 fo. 83(9); SPD Eliz. 253/22.

[4] Ibid. 77/58; 287/95; Interreg. 101/6; Exch. KR Deps by Commn 44 & 45 Eliz. Mich. 1 m. 7r.;

Posthumus, *Bronnen*, v, 80; vi, 219; *Geschiedenis*, ii, 308, 324; Nfk RO, F. C. Recs. Wall. Ch. 5, 6; Cty Recs. Strangers Bk fos. 66–8.

[5] Ibid. Ass. Bk 5 fos. 3(12)v.–4(13).

[6] Ibid. Bk Mayor's Ct 8 p. 565.

[7] Ibid.; 12 fo. 315; Alnage Accts; Duties; F. C. Recs. Wall. Ch. 5, 6; Cons. Ct invs 1589/200; 1603/111, 157; 1634/58; BL, Add. 12504 no. 63; Lans. 26 no. 62 fo. 182(164); no. 64 fo. 187; 71 no. 51 fo. 107(108); PRO, Exch. KR Accts Var. bdl. 347 no. 19; SPD Interreg. 101/6.

[8] Ibid. Eliz. 34/23; Pilgrim, thes. 204; J. Harland, *Ho. & Fm Accts Shuttleworths of Gawthorpe Hall*, Chetham S. xxxv, xli, xliii, xlvi 1856–8, p. 225; Nfk RO, Cons. Ct inv. 1614/148; Cty Recs. Strangers Bk fo. 111.

[9] Ibid. fo. 114v.

[10] PRO, SPD Eliz. Add. 13/81; & v. no. 80.

[11] Cross 184; Kent RO, Cons. Ct Cant. Regs Accts & Invs 7 fos. 227, 270; 10 fo. 29; 12 fos. 479–80; Inv. Papers 12/45; 17/85; 18/111; 21/21; Inv. Regs 9 fo. 456; 11 fo. 652; 17 fos. 186, 208; Cant. Cath. Lib. Wall. Recs. Misc. Docs portf. 4 no. 17; Cty Recs. Chamb's Accts 1592–1602 fos. 423, 473v.; cf. BL, Lans. 26 no. 62 fo. 182(164); no. 64 fo. 187.

[12] W. Somner, *Ants Cant.*, 1640, pp. 175–6. Somner's corrections, made in 1662 f. projected 2nd edn, & found in Cant. Cath. Lib. copy of 1st edn, are incorporated in Nic. Battely's 1703 edn (App. p. 31), but terms of art remain mistranscribed. Doc. now lost.

[13] Cant. Cath. Lib. Cty Recs. Burghmote Bk 1630–58 fo. 207.

[14] R. Hovenden, *Regs Wall. or Strangers' Ch. in Cant.*, Pubs H.S.L.3 pts 1891–8 v, 752 cites Wall. Recs G1 no. 92. I could not find this doc., but Hovenden is trustworthy.

[15] HMC, *Salisbury MSS*, iv 1892, pp. 573–4; Kent RO, Arch. Ct Cant. Inv. Regs 12 fos. 14, 15; 16 fo. 339; Cons. Ct Cant. Reg. Accts & Invs 1 fo. 30v.; Inv. Papers 12/31; Inv. Reg. 16 fo. 443; Sandwich Recs. Ld & W. Treas's Accts 1620–1; Treas's Vols Accts 38 fos. 4, 55v., 90, 152, 191, 253, 279; PRO, SPD Jas 129/69.

[16] Ibid. 129/70; Chas 378/40; Hessels, *Archivum*, iii, 1085; Ess. RO, Arch. Ct Colc. O. W. bdl. 4 no. 334; 36 no. 6; 37 no. 9; 43 no. 3.

[17] PRO, SPD Jas 15/17; Chas 378/40; *APC*, 1616–17 pp. 89, 90; Friis 452; Evelyn iii, 177.

[18] Pilgrim, thes. 204, 205, 206.

[19] J. James 209; Postlethwayt ii, 765; PRO, SPD Eliz. 253/122; Chanc., Jud. Proc. (Eq. side) Chanc. Mrs' Docs., Exhib, Mr Tinney nos. 17–19, bks 12, 16, 18, 21, 25, 28; Nfk RO, Cons. Ct invs 1625/196–7; 1626/119; Munn 5; W. Sfk RO, Ep. Commy Ct Bury inv. 1682/156.

[20] Ibid. 1677/87.

[21] Ibid. 1670/77; 1696/91.

[22] Cash 164–6; Munn 5; cf. Vanhaeck i, 240, 278–9.

[23] *VCH Hants*. v. 488; Nfk RO, invs Arch Ct Norvic. 1682–3/120; Cons. Ct 1710–14/31.

[24] Ibid. 1681/85; Bridewell Mus. Patts Norwich Manufs 1769, end papers; Ord. Bk 'Norwich 1791'; PRO, PCC parch. invs p. 1660 nos. 3602, 7809; Munn 5.

[25] C. E. Lart, *Regs Fr. Chs Brist.*, *Stonehouse & Ply.*, Pubs H.S.L. 1912 xx, pp. ix, xi sqq., xx, xxv–vi, 1 sqq.; *C.J.*, xv, 312.

[26] Deyon 173–4, 176, 193; Maugis 62, 70, 98; A. Dietz ii, 268; Goris 243; Smith, *Mems Wl*, ii, 435; Cole ii, 183–5, 384, 577; Vanhaeck i, 27, 80, 93.

[27] Ibid., 80, 330–1.

[28] Ramsay, *Isham*, 160; *Disc. f. Enl. & Freedome of Trade*, 29; Hudson & Tingey ii, p. lxxxii; Munn 5; Maugis 70; Guicciardini 119; B. Dietz 86–7, 93, 105, 118; Nfk RO, Cty Recs. N. Drapery in Norwich; *Rates Marchandizes*, s.v. chamlets; BL, Add. 12504 no.63; Lans. 26 no. 60 fos. 177–8(159–60); no. 62 fo. 182(164)v.; no. 64 fo. 187; 71 no. 51 fo. 107(108); PRO, SPD Eliz. 250/76; Exch. KR Deps by Commn 44 & 45 Eliz. Mich. 1 m. 3r.; Accts Var. bdl. 347 no. 19.

[29] PRO, Req. 157/134 fo. 95(3).

[30] PRO, Exch. KR Deps by Commn 44 & 45 Eliz. Mich. 1 mm. 7r., 8.

[31] Ibid. m. 3; Moens, *Norwich*, 78; *Disc. f. Enl. & Freedome of Trade*, 29; Willan, *Inld Trade*, 67; *Rates Marchandizes*, s.v. grograins Lile or Norwich, buffins; BL, Lans. 26 no 57 fo. 161(149); no. 62 fo. 181(163)v.; no. 64 fo. 187; 71 no. 51 fo. 107(108); Nfk RO, Cons. Ct invs 1591/169; 1614/148; 1617/157; 1619/137; Cty Recs. N. Drapery in Norwich; Alnage Accts; Duties fos. 65, 67 sqq.; Ass. Bks 3 fos. 306v.–7; 5 fos. 3(12)v.–4(13); Bks Mayor's Ct 13 pp. 141, 459; 14 fos. 6(11), 7(13), 113, 140v., 166, 229, 237v., 252v., 254v.–5, 331, 361v., 410, 456v.–7; 15 fos. 73v., 101v., 103, 134v., 145, 185v., 191, 198, 202, 216v., 238, 260v., 362v., 375; Strangers Bk fo. 106.

[32] Ibid. 113v.; cf. Ass. Bk 5 fos. 3(12)v.–4(13); Cons. Ct inv. 1614/148.

[33] Ibid. 1692–3/65(64); Postlethwayt ii, 743; *VCH Hants.*, v. 488; Pococke ii, 159; J. Latimer, *Ann. Brist. in 17th cent.*, Brist. 1900, p. 485; I. Grubb, *Quakerism & Ind. befe 1800*, 1930, p. 142; A. Plummer, *Lond. Weavers' Co. 1600–1970*, 1972, p. 302; W. Curtis, *Sh. Hist. & Descron. Tn Alton*, Winch. 1896, p. 123; Frds' Ho. Lond. Jas Dix's MSS, B4B, B5B, B6B, B7B, B8B, B9B, B10B, B12B, B13B, B14B, B15B, B16B, B18B, B19B, B20B, B22B, B23B, B24B; MS Box D1/15/2; Brist. RO, Recs. Brist. & Frenchay S.F., A9/1, pp. 17, 39, 46, 51, 61, 77, 79, 80, 99, 101; A9/2, pp. 6 sqq.

[34] Nfk RO, Cty Recs. N. Drapery in Norwich; Duties fos. 46 sqq.; F. C. Recs., Wall. Ch. 5, 6; BL, Lans. 26 no. 59 fos. 175v.–6(158v.–9); no. 60 fos. 177–8(159–60); no. 62 fo. 181(163)v.; no. 64 fo. 187; 71 no. 51 fo. 107(108); Boys 747; Kent RO, Sandwich Recs. Ld & W. Treas's Accts 1620–1; Ld & W. Treas's Draft Accts 1585–6 pp. 7 sqq.; Treas's Vols Accts 38 fos. 4, 90, 152, 191, 253, 279; Maidstone Recs. Burghmote Bks 1 fos. 43v.–4; 3 fo. 5(p. 9); Cant. Cath. Lib. Wall. Recs. Misc. Docs portf. 1 no. 8; PRO, SPD Eliz. 250/76.

[35] Ibid. 77/58; BL, Lans. 26 no. 57 fo. 161(149); Nfk RO, Cty Recs. Ass. Bk 5 fos. 3(12)v.–4(13); Ords con. Wl fos. 10v., 16v., 17v., 18v.; Keure fos. 10v., 18, 19; Cons. Ct inv. 1694–6/43.

[36] PRO, PCR 1637–8 pp. 82, 578 (fos. 39v., 291v.); Kent RO, Cons. Ct Cant. Inv. Reg. 20 fos. 392–3; & v. Inv. Paper 11/114; Cross 184.

[37] Cross 183 'stamettes' recte; *CPR*, Eliz. v, 40 'stamelles' erron.; & v. PRO, SPD Eliz. 43/19, 20.

[38] Nfk RO, invs Cons. Ct 1650/60; 1694–6/43; 1709–10/25; Arch. Ct Norvic. 1703–6/12.

[39] Blome 212; Postlethwayt ii, 765; J. Ogilby, *Brit.* 1675, p. 146; B. Martin, *Nat. Hist. Engld*, 2 vols. 1759–63, ii, 53; W. Sfk RO, Ep. Commy Ct Bury invs 1668/173; 1707/93; 1711/49.

[40] C. G. Grimwood & S. Kay, *Hist. Sudbury*, Sudbury 1952, p. 92; Munn 5; Unwin, *Studs*, 301; K. H. Burley, 'Ess. Clothier 18th cent.', *Econ. Hist. Rev.*, 2nd ser. 1958 xi, 291–2, 298; PRO, Chanc., Jud. Proc. (Eq. side) Chanc. Mrs' Docs, Exhibs, Mr Tinney nos. 17–19, bks 12, 16, 18, 21, 25, 28.

[41] Nfk RO, Cty Recs. Strangers Bk fos. 25, 62, 63v., 66, 80, 101v.–2.

[42] Ibid. fos. 34v., 80v.

[43] PRO, SPD Jas 35/27; Nfk RO, Cons. Ct invs 1619/137; 1636/149; Cant. Cath. Lib. Wall. Recs. Misc. Docs portf. 1 no. 26; Kent RO, Cons. Ct Cant. Inv. Papers 6/114; 12/45; 18/111; 21/21; 26/120 (cf. 9/107); Inv. Regs 11 fo. 652; 14 fo. 256; 19 fo. 69; 20 fos. 369, 392–3, 691; W. Sfk RO, Ep. Commy Ct Bury inv. 1705/43.

[44] Ibid. 1711/49; 1735–9/10; Nfk RO, Arch. Ct Norvic. inv. 1754–67/43; Cant. Cath. Lib. Wall. Recs. Misc. Docs portf. 4 nos. 67–9; PRO, C. O., BoT Orig. Corr. vol. 21 no. 209 (MFQ 134) fos. 149, 151; J. James 243.

[45] Ibid. 277; W. Sfk RO, Ep. Commy Ct Bury inv. 1696/91.

[46] J. James 362; Munn 5; Montgomery 222; Defoe, *Tour*, i, 288; Wilts. RO, Pec. Ct Dean Sarum. Wm Pile clothier 1731 Lyme Regis; PRO, Chanc. Petty Bag: Misc. Papers, Exhibs &c. bdl. (box) 70, folder marked 'no. 49–144', nos. 49–59; Devon RO, Bedford (Russell) Coll. M.29 no. 4; PRO, SPD Chas 475/60.

[47] Ibid.; A. L. Clegg, *Hist. Wimb. Minster*, B'mouth 1960, p. 180.

[48] Mx RO, Arch. Ct Mx inv. Jn Hoptkins 1673 St Clem. Danes; Hants. RO, unclass. invs D/2/A:2/178; Guildhall Lib. Commy Ct Lond. (Lond. Div.) invs box 5 And. Poupard 1714 Stepney; box 9 Chas Barnes 1702 St Matt's, Fri. St; E. Sfk RO, Arch. inv. 16/71; W. Sfk RO, Ep. Commy Ct Bury inv. 1717/43.

[49] Munn, op. cit., pref.; Martin i, 117; *VCH Hants.*, v, 487–8; Curtis 123; Defoe, *Tour*, i, 142, 180–1, 288–9; *Compl. Engl. Tradesman*, 78; Postlethwayt i, 245, 939; J. James 231; Pococke i, 83; ii, 49; Gross ii, 349; C. Dale 59; BL, Add. 26774 fo. 49v.; Hants. RO, unclass. invs D/2/A:2/ 181; Bodl. Arch. Ct Berks. O. W. etc. 48/175; PRO, Chanc. Jud. Proc. (Equity side) Chanc. Mrs' Docs, Exhibs, Mr Unkn no. 176.

[50] Ibid. Mr Tinney nos. 17–19, bks 16, 18, 21; Postlethwayt ii, 765; Martin ii, 56; *Magna Brit. & Hib.*, sev. vols 1720–31, i, 722; HMC, *Var. Colls*, viii, 589; Nfk RO, Arch. Ct Norvic. inv. 1754–67/ 43; W. Sfk RO, Ep. Commy Ct Bury invs 1682/14, 156; 1696/91; 1701/16; Grubb 140–1; Frds' Ho. Lond. Jas Dix's MSS, B23B, B24B; Brist. RO, Recs. Brist. & Frenchay S.F., A9/2, pp. 10 sqq.

[51] PRO, PCC parch. invs p. 1660, no. 8548.

[52] PRO, Chanc. Jud. Proc. (Equity side) Chanc. Mrs' Docs, Exhibs, Mr Tinney nos. 17–19, bks 16, 18, 21; W. Sfk RO, Misc. E.3/32; Ep. Commy Ct Bury inv. 1705/43.

[53] Ibid. 1668/173; 1686/20.

[54] H. A. Randall, 'Kettering Worsted Ind. 18th cent.', *Northants. Past & Pres.*, 1970–1 iv, 313, 316–18; P. A. J. Pettit, *R. Fors Northants.*, Northants. Rec. S. 1968 xxiii, 182; J. Morton, *Nat. Hist. Northants.*, 1712, pp. 16, 26; *VCH Northants.*, ii, 333; *Ruts.*, i, 237; J. James 231, 363; Postlethwayt ii, 352; Defoe, *Compl. Engl. Tradesman*, 77; Munn, op. cit., pref.; F. M. Eden, *State Poor*, 3 vols. 1797, ii, 530; K. J. Smith 29, 105; Posthumus, *Bronnen.*, v, 79; vi, 219; *Geschiedenis*, ii, 308, 324; C. A. & D. Thurley, *Ind. Prob. Recs Ct Arch. Ely 1513–1857*, Ind. Lib., B.R.S. 1976 lxxxviii, 24, 87, 130 (cf. 44); PRO, Chanc. Petty Bag: Misc. Papers, Exhibs etc. bdl. (box) 70, folder marked 'no. 49–144', nos. 73 sqq.; Northants. RO, Lamb & Holmes Coll. 58, 60, 74–5, 278, 281, 315–17; Y.Z. Coll. 272, 4611, 9806; Arch. Ct Northampton, Admons & Invs 1697/3; 1712/38, 105, 110; 1713/70; 1714/10, 47, 168; 1715/110; 1716/99; 1717/1; 1718/118; 1719/5, 23; 1721/49; 1723/34, 127; 1724/49, 108; 1744 Jn Jordan; PRO, PCC invs 1718–82 bdl. 21 no. 108; Bodl. Pec. Ct Banbury O.W. & Admons 32/1/47; 36/2/39; 50/3/19.

[55] Cov. RO, Cty Recs. Leet Bk 30 Eliz.–1834 pp. 260, 351, 400.

[56] Ibid. 260, 400; *VCH War.*, ii, 256; viii, 168; B. Poole, *Cov.; its Hist. & Ants*, Cov. 1870, pp. 358–9; Lichfield Jt RO, Cons. Ct O.W. Sam. Smith 1722 Cov.

[57] Ibid. & Jn Baskeby 1715, Jn Barbar 1720; *VCH War.*, ii, 256; viii, 168; Poole 358; Defoe, *Tour*, ii 83; *Compl. Engl. Tradesman*, 77; J. James 217; Smith, *Mems Wl*, ii, 195; Warner 108; Eden iii, 740 bis; Postlethwayt ii, 835; A. Lynes, *Hist. Cov. Texts*, Cov. 1952, p. 11; K. J. Smith 7, 8, 11, 13, 15, 18 sqq., 27–8, 34, 36–8, 40, 46, 49, 50, 53, 55–6, 58–9, 61–2, 65, 68, 70 sqq., 77, 79, 84, 87, 91–2, 94–7, 102, 110–11, 114, 117, 119, 122, 125–6, 128–9, 134, 143, 146–7, 149, 152, 154–5; Cov. RO, Cty Recs. Leet Bk 30 Eliz.–1834 pp. 351, 360, 400.

[58] B. Gibbons, *Nn. & Sugs f. Hist. Kidderminster*, Kiddermnster 1859, p. 45; Fiennes 231; Worcs. RO, Cons. Ct O.W. etc. 1718 Wm Fereday, And. Walker; 1721 Nic. Penn; 1726 Jos. Crane, Th. Hill; 1727 Edm. Read, Jos. Nicholls, Ric. Billingsley; 1731 Jos. Reynolds – all Kidderminster; Munn 5; Burton 180.

[59] Ibid. 181–2; Pococke i, 230; ii, 7; Tattersall 109–10, 117–18, 120.

[60] T. Rath, 'Tewkesbury Hosiery Ind.', *Text. Hist.*, 1976 vii, 141; Chester RO, Guild Recs. Weavers' Co. Bk 1697–1817, rev., Whsle Sergeweavers' Oath; & v. Stephens, 'Chester', 25.

[61] Fiennes 73; Notts. RO, Man. Ct Mansfield O.W. etc. portf. 46 no. 16.

[62] Coleman, thes. 160.

[63] R. Atkyns, *N. Hist. Glos.*, ed. Rudder, Circencester 1779, p. 345.

[64] PRO, PCC invs 1718–82 bdl. 35 no. 30; Wilts. RO, Arch. Ct Wilts., Zeph. Fry 1717 Chippenham; Arch. Ct Sarum. Jas Stantiall 1718 Melksham.

[65] Ibid. Pec. Ct Dean Sarum. Wm Pike clothier 1731 Lyme Regis; G. Roberts, *Hist. & Ants Boro. Lyme Regis & Charmouth*, 1834, pp. 120, 151, 153–4, 158, 177–8; Collinson i, 2nd pt, 18.

[66] Ibid. iii, 294; Postlethwayt ii, 743; Defoe, *Compl. Engl. Tradesman*, 78; *Tour*, i, 266; Martin i, 55–6; Soms. RO, Arch. Taunton invs 1714–15 Th. Hellyer/Taunton St Jas; *cf.* 1720/4 Ric. Startt mercer Porlock.

[67] Dunsford 53, 201, 208.

[68] J. B. Gribble, *Mems Bpl.*, Bpl. 1830, p. 542; cf. Soms. RO, Arch. Taunton inv. 1720/4 Ric. Startt mercer Porlock.

[69] Posthumus, *Bronnen*, v, 297, 337, 637; *Geschiedenis*, ii, 326; A. H. Slee, 'Some Dead Inds N. Devon', *Devon Ass.*, 1938 lxx, 216; Dunsford 57.

[70] Ibid. 55, 57, 209, 230, 235–6; Pococke i, 141.

[71] S. D. Chapman, *Devon Cl. Ind. in 18th cent.*, Devon & Corn. Rec. S. n.s. 1978 xxiii, 88.

[72] Slee 215.

[73] Defoe, *Tour*, ii, 198; J. James 201, 221–2, 263–5, 311, 633, App. p. 6; Heaton 250, 264, 267 sqq., 275, 298, 387; Tupling 180, 183; Wadsworth & Mann 88, 256; Fishwick, *Hist. Rochdale*, 58; E. Baines, *Hist.*, *Dir. & Gaz. Co. Pa. Lanc.*, Liv. 2 vols 1824, i, 619–20; Eden iii, 810, 821; *C.J.*, xxvi, 355; Cullen, *Anglo-Ir. Trade*, 58; Smith, *Mems Wl*, i, 370–1; Marshall, 'Kendal', 210, 212; R. Thoresby, *Ducatus Leodiensis*, 1715, p. 83; Pococke i, 50, 52, 204–5; ii, 1, 9; Scott, *Recs*, 83.

## Chapter 6

[1] Nfk RO, F. C. Recs. Wall. Ch. 5, 6; Cty Recs. N. Drapery in Norwich; Duties fo. 67; invs Cons. Ct 1605/47; Arch. Ct Norvic. 1682–3/120; BL, Lans, 26 no. 62 fo. 182 (164); no. 64 fo. 187; PRO, SPD Eliz. Add. 33/71 (quot.); Interreg. 101/6; cf. Willan, *Tu. Bk Rates*, 55.

[2] Kent RO, Cons. Ct Cant. Reg. Accts & Invs 9 fo. 100; Inv. Papers 21/21; 26/120; Cant. Cath. Lib. Cty Recs. Burghmote Bk 1630–58 fo. 168; Wall. Recs. Misc. Docs portf. 1 no. 26; Cross 184; PRO, PCR 1639 p. 145 (fo. 69); SPD Eliz. Add. 34/23.

[3] Ibid. Eliz. 249/20; BL, Lans. 26 no. 62 fo. 182(164); no. 64 fo. 187; Nfk RO, Cty Recs. N. Draper in Norwich; Cons. Ct inv. 1636/149.

[4] Ibid.; Arch. Ct Norvic. 1674–5/200; Cty Recs. Strangers Bk fos. 66v., 67v.; Ass. Bk 5 fos. 3(12)v.–4(13); F. C. Recs. Wall. Ch. 5, 6.

[5] PRO, SPD Eliz. Add. 34/23; PCR 1639 p. 145 (fo. 69); Cant. Cath. Lib. Wall. Recs. Misc. Docs portf. 1 no. 26; Wall. Wills G1/96; Cty Recs. Chamb's Accts 1592–1602 fos. 26–7(91–2), 191; J. M. Cowper, *Cant. Mar. Lics*, 1st ser. 1568–1618, Cant. 1892, cols 336, 441; Kent RO, Cons. Ct Cant. Reg. Accts & Invs 14 fos. 312, 389; Inv. Papers 16/32, 59; 17/85; 18/111; Inv. Regs 7 fos. 265, 456; 8 fo. 78; 11 fo. 652; 12 fo. 377; 14 fo. 588; 15 fo. 303; cf. fo. 5.

[6] Hessels, *Archivum*, iii, 41–2; *CPR*, Eliz. iii, 209–10; Nfk RO, Cty Recs. Ass. Bk 3 fos. 306v.–7; Bk Mayor's Ct 8 p. 565; Strangers Bk fo. 17.

[7] Ibid. fo. 98.

[8] PRO, Exch. KR Deps by Commn 44 & 45 Eliz. Mich. 1 m. 4r.; cf. Nfk RO, Arch. Ct Norvic. inv. 1706–7/85.

[9] Nfk RO, Cty Recs. Strangers Bk fos. 21v.–3; cf. Bk Mayor's Ct 12 p. 315.

[10] Warner 30; Smith, *Mems Wl*, ii, 458; Ramsay, *Isham*, p. xxix; Willan, *Tu. Bk Rates*, 41; *Studs*, 254; *Disc. f. Enl. & Freedome of Trade*, 29; *Rates Marchandizes*; W. de G. Birch 260; B. Dietz 3, 8, 21–3, 30–1, 44, 49, 54, 56, 60–1, 69, 73–5, 78, 86–7, 92–3, 98, 104, 106, 113–15, 128, 131, 153; Millard vols. ii, iii; BL, Lans. 8 fo. 75; PRO, SPD Eliz. 8/31; Exch. KR Accts Var. bdl. 520 no. 24 fos. 3v., 24.

[11] Ibid. bdl. 347 no. 19; SPD Eliz. 20/49 (c.1575 recte); 77/58; 253/122; Interreg. 101/6; 128/103; *CPR*, Eliz. iii, 209–10; Moens, *Norwich*, 25, 36, 244–6; Bernard, op. cit.; Bang iiA, 66, 71, 76, 81, 189, 203, 282, 449, 473; Nfk RO, Cons. Ct invs 1590/130; 1603/13; F. C. Recs. Wall. Ch. 4–6; Cty Recs. Duties fos. 2v., 35 sqq., 53 sqq.; N. Drapery in Norwich; Misc. Docs, Touching the Allegacion etc.; Ass. Bk 3 fo. 227; 2nd Bk Worstedweavers, scrap no. 31; Strangers Bk fos. 24, 33, 80; Bks Mayor's Ct 8 pp. 570, 704; 9 pp. 108–9, 264, 517; 10 pp. 86, 123; 15 fo. 85; BL, Add. 12504 no. 63; Lans. 26 no. 58 fo. 164(151).

[12] Ibid. no. 57 fo. 161(149); no. 59 fos. 175v.–6(158v.–9); no. 60 fo. 178(160); no. 62 fos. 181–2(163–4); no. 64 fo. 187; Kent RO, Cons. Ct Cant. Reg. Accts & Invs 6 fo. 371; Nfk RO, Cons. Ct

invs 1590/130; 1603/13; Cty Recs. N. Drapery in Norwich; Duties fos. 35 sqq., 53 sqq.; 1st Bk Worstedweavers fo. 88 (loose, ad fin.); Strangers Bk fos. 62, 79, 80–1, 83v., 89v.; Ass. Bk 3 fo. 227; Bks Mayor's Ct 8 p. 570; 15 fo. 85.

[13] Ibid. 10 p. 123.

[14] PRO, SPD Eliz. 253/122; Exch. KR Deps by Commn 44 & 45 Eliz. Mich. 1 mm. 7r., 8; Accts Var. bdl. 347 no. 19; BL, Lans. 26 no. 57 fo. 161(149); no. 60 fo. 178(160); no. 62 fos. 181–2(163–4); no. 64 fo. 187; Nfk RO, Cty Recs. Alnage Accts; Duties fos. 68–70; Strangers Bk fo. 109v.

[15] Ibid. fo. 75v.

[16] Ibid. fo. 79.

[17] Ibid. Alnage Accts.

[18] Ibid. Strangers Bk fo. 75v.; Moens, *Norwich*, 36.

[19] Kirk ii, 373.

[20] Somner (1640) 175–6 erron. 'stoffe', recte 'toffe' or 'tofte'; Kent RO, Arch. Ct Cant. Inv. Reg. 9 fo. 294.

[21] Ibid. Maidstone Recs. Burghmote Bk 3 fo. 5 (p. 9); *CPR*, Eliz. iv, 39, 40.

[22] PRO, SPD Eliz. 120/22.

[23] Chester RO, Cty Recs. Ass Bk 1539–1624 fo. 171.

[24] Kent RO, Arch. Ct Cant. Inv. Reg. 9 fo. 73v.; Cons. Ct Cant. Reg. Accts & Invs 10 fo. 326; Nfk RO, Cons. Ct invs 1606–7/20; 1681/67; Lichfield Jt RO, Cons. Ct O.W., Th. Atherall 1637 Cov.; Cole ii, 178–9, 574, 577; Charles 3, 215, 218, 233.

[25] *VCH Wilts.*, iv, 181; Postlethwayt i, 456.

[26] Thijs 45; BL, Lans. 26 no. 57 fo. 161(149); no. 58 fo. 164(151); no. 59 fos. 175v.–6(158v.–9); no. 60 fo. 178(160); no. 62 fos. 181–2(163–4); no. 64 fo. 187; 71 no. 51 fo. 107(108); Add. 12504 no. 65 p. 4; Nfk RO, Cty Recs. N. Drapery in Norwich; Alnage Accts; Strangers Bk fos. 25, 62, 63v., 66, 79v., 101v.–2; Bk Mayor's Ct 11 fo. 403; F. C. Recs. Wall. Ch. 4; PRO, Exch. KR Deps by Commn 44 & 45 Eliz. Mich. 1 m. 3r.; SPD Eliz. 250/76; 287/95.

[27] Ibid. Jas 35/27; Stat. 12 Chas 2 c.4.

[28] PRO, Exch. KR Deps by Commn 44 & 45 Eliz. Mich. 1 m. 3r.; SPD Eliz. 77/58; 250/76; BL, Lans. 26 no. 57 fo. 161(149); no. 59 fos. 175v.–6(158v.–9); no. 60 fo. 178(160); no. 62 fos. 181–2(163–4); no. 64 fo. 187; 71 no. 51 fo. 107(108); Thijs 45; Nfk RO, Cty Recs. N. Drapery in Norwich; Alnage Accts; Duties fos. 63v., 65 sqq.; Strangers Bk fos. 24–5, 38, 63v., 79v.–81; Bks Mayor's Ct 12 p. 315; 13 p. 433; F. C. Recs. Wall. Ch. 4.

[29] Ibid. 5, 6; & v. PRO, SPD Interreg. 101/6.

[30] Purchas 269; J.Taylor 4; R.Head & F. Kirkman, *Engl. Rogue desc. in Life Meriton Latroon,* 1928, pp. vii, 332; Nfk RO, Cty Recs. Strangers Bk fos. 113v.–4.

[31] Prestwich 428.

[32] Kent RO, Cons. Ct Cant. Reg. Accts & Invs 6 fos. 371v.–2; PRO, SPD Eliz. 77/58; 250/76, 78; 287/95; Interreg. 101/6; BL, Lans. 26 no. 57 fo. 161(149); no. 58 fo. 164(151); no. 59 fos. 175v.–6(158v.–9); no.60 fo. 178(160); no. 62 fo. 181(163)v.; no. 63 fo. 184(186); no. 64 fo. 187; 71 no. 51 fo. 107(108); Add. 12504 no. 63; *Disc. f. Enl& Freedome of Trade*,29; Nfk RO, Cty Recs. Wall. Ch. 5, 6; Cty Recs. N. Drapery in Norwich; Alnage Accts ad init.; Duties fo. 35; Ass. Bk fo. 227; Strangers Bk fos. 24, 26, 37v.–8, 62, 63v., 79, 96v.; 2nd Bk Worstedweavers, scrap no. 31; Bks Mayor's Ct 9 pp. 108–9; 11 fos. 130v., 274v.; 12 p. 304.

[33] Ibid. Duties fos. 35 sqq., 53 sqq., 66–9; Alnage Accts.

[34] Kirk ii, 54; PRO, SPD Jas 99/43; Chas 302/41.

[35] Kirk i, 455.

[36] HMC, *Salisbury MSS*, iv, 573.

[37] Kirk i, 392, 405, 426–7, 431, 441, 453–5, 462, 464, 466–7, 474; ii, 56, 60, 66–7, 69, 73–5, 82, 88, 114–15, 119–20, 123, 132; B. Dietz 45, 72; Willan, *Inld Trade*, 65; *Tu. Bk Rates*, 50–1; *Rates Marchandizes.*

[38] P. Morant, *Hist. & Ants Colc.*, 1748, p. 72; *CPR*, Eliz. iv, 39, 40; Nfk RO, Cty Recs.

Strangers Bk fos. 25v., 33, 38; Kent RO, Maidstone Recs. Burghmote Bks I fos. 43v.–4; 3 fo. 5(p. 9); Chamb's Accts (Paper Bks) no. 5 fo. 3v.; no. 7; Sandwich Recs. N. Red Bk fos. 110–12.

[39] Postlethwayt i, 426, 615; Goris 278–9; Thijs 36; Van Nierop xlv, 23–4, 37–8; J. G. Nichols. 'Invs Wardrobe . . .' in Camd. Misc. iii, Camd. S. 1885 lxi, 13; A. Conyers, Wilts. Exts f. Debts, Ed. I– Eliz. I, Wilts. Rec. S. 1973 xxviii, 56; BL, Cott. Galba B. x fo. 6v.; cf. Nfk RO, F. C. Recs. Wall. Ch. 5, 6.

[40] Nfk RO, Cty Recs. Strangers Bk fos. 94v.–5.

[41] Ibid.Bks Mayor's Ct 10 pp. 727, 782; 11 fos. 1, 13; Ass. Bks 3 fos. 306v.–7; 4 fo. 44v.; Duties fos. 39, 40, 60v., 61v., 63v., 65–7; Alnage Accts; Bernard, op. cit.; Moens, Norwich, 308; BL, Add. 12504 no. 63; cf. Harl. 70 fo. 10(p. 10).

[42] Cross 192; Kent RO, Cons. Ct Cant. Inv. Reg. 9 fo. 117; Cant. Cath. Lib. Wall. Recs. Wall. Wills G.1/96.

[43] Kirk iii, 142–3, 156–8; Hessels, Archives, 8; Archivum, iii, 1158; Thijs 44–5; Ruytinck & al. 299.

[44] CPR, Eliz. iv, 39, 40; Nfk RO, Cty Recs. Strangers Bk fo. 94v.

[45] Ibid. fo. 100v.; Ass. Bks 3 fos. 306v.–7; 4 fo. 44v.; Bk Mayor's Ct 12 p. 135; Cons. Ct inv. 1605/ 47; PRO, SPD Eliz. 250/78.

[46] Ibid. Eliz. Add. 34/23; Jas 35/27; Req. 157/134 fo. 93(1); Exch. KR Deps by Commn 44 & 45 Eliz. Mich. 1 m. 3r.; Nfk RO, Cty Recs. Strangers Bk fos. 111v., 112v.; F. C. Recs. Wall. Ch. 5, 6; Rates Marchandizes, s.v. Sp. satins; Woodward, Trade Eliz. Chester, 14.

[47] Moens, Norwich, 77; BL, Lans. 26 no. 57 fo. 161(149); no. 59 fos. 175v.–6(158v.–9); no. 64 fo. 187; Nfk RO, Cty Recs. Strangers Bk fos. 93v.–4; Ass. Bk 3 fos. 280v.–1; Bk Mayor's Ct 10 pp. 86, 419, 782.

[48] Ibid. pp. 419, 731; 11 fos. 130v., 274v.; 12 p. 135; Ass. Bk 3 fos. 280v.–1, 306v.; Strangers Bk fos. 96v.–7; Duties fos. 63v., 65 sqq.; Alnage Accts; Cons. Ct inv. 1636/149; F. C. Recs. Wall. Ch. 4– 6; BL, Add. 12504 no. 63; Williams, thes. 90; Willan, Inld Trade, 67, 123–4; Vanhaeck i, 238, 243; De Smedt ii, 332; PRO, SPD Eliz. 253/122; 287/95; Interreg. 101/6; Exch. KR Deps by Commn 44 & 45 Eliz. Mich. 1 mm. 3r., 7r.

[49] Ibid. m. 8r.; Accts Var. bdl. 347 no. 19; SPD Eliz. 250/76, 78; Brulez, Della Faille, 245, 590; Van Nierop xlv, 26; BL, Lans. 26 no. 57 fo. 161(149); no. 58 fo. 164(151); no. 59 fos. 175v.– 6(158v.– 9); no. 60 fo. 178(160); no. 62 fo. 181(163)v.; no. 63 fo. 184(166); no. 64 fo. 187; 71 no. 51 fo. 107(108); Nfk RO, Cty Recs. N. Drapery in Norwich; Alnage Accts; Duties fo. 70; Kent RO, Cons. Ct Cant. Reg. Accts & Invs 6 fo. 372.

[50] Ibid. Inv. Papers 8/109; 11/114; 16/32; 17/85; 20/78; 26/120; 27/116; Inv. Reg. 9 fo. 117; Nfk RO, F. C. Recs. Wall. Ch. 4–6; PRO, Exch. KR Deps by Commn 44 & 45 Eliz. Mich. 1 m. 3r.; Req. 157/134 fos. 93(1), 95(3) rev.; SPD Eliz. 34/23; Jas 131/15; Chas 529/91; Interreg. 101/6; C. O., BoT Orig. Corr. vol. 21 no. 209 (MFQ 134) fo. 152; Edwards 58; Roberts, Marchants Mapp, 2nd pt, 27; S. A. Courtauld, 'E.A. & Hug. Text. Ind.', Proc. H.S.L., 1929 xiii, 131; Hooper 228, 318–19; cf. Lane, Ven. & Hist., 26; Sella, Commerci e Industrie, 127.

[51] R. Davies 24.

[52] Nfk RO, Cty Recs. Strangers Bk fos. 96v.–7; F. C. Recs. Wall. Ch. 4–6; Cons. Ct invs 1594/ 29; 1642/92; PRO, Exch. KR Deps by Commn 44 & 45 Eliz. Mich. 1 m. 3r.; Maugis 62; CPR, Eliz. iv, 40; Bang iiA, 27; Leuridan, 'Lannoy', 339; Roubaix, 54–5.

[53] Ibid. 54–5, 100; Nfk RO, Cty Recs. Strangers Bk fos. 94, 96v.–7; Cons. Ct invs 1594/29; 1642/ 92.

[54] Ibid. 1592/62, 138; 1593/175.

[55] Warner 285, 658J; Lancs. RO, Cavendish of Holker Coll. 1/46 fos. 1, 2, p. 6; Nfk RO, Cty Recs. Alnage Accts; Duties fos. 63v., 65 sqq.; Ass. Bks 4 fo. 44v.; 5 fos. 3(12)v.–4(13); Bks Mayor's Ct 10 pp. 727 bis, 778; 11 fos. 1, 13, 233, 274v.; 12 pp. 304, 418, 509, 882; Cons. Ct invs 1694–6/43; 1703–8/110, 390.

[56] Ibid. 1694–6/43; C. O. BoT Orig. Corr. vol. 21 no. 209 (MFQ 134) fo. 146; Kent RO, Cons. Ct Cant. Inv. Papers 7/92; 16/32; 17/85.

[57] Nfk RO, Cty Recs. Duties fos. 35 sqq., 53 sqq.; Strangers Bk fos. 25v., 79; Maugis 62; Vanhaeck i, 27, 80.

[58] PRO, SPD Jas 35/27; Nfk RO, Cty Recs. Strangers Bk fos. 110A, 111v.; Ass. Bk 5 fos. 3(12)v.– 4(13).

[59] Ibid.; Strangers Bk fo. 114v.; F. C. Recs. Wall. Ch. 5, 6.

[60] Ibid. 5, 6; Cty Recs. Ass. Bk 5 fos. 3(12)v.–4(13); Cons. Ct inv. 1619/137; PRO, SPD Jas 35/27.

[61] Kent RO, Cons. Ct Cant. Inv. Reg. 11 fo. 652; cf. 15 fos. 302–3.

[62] Ibid. 9 fo. 117; Inv. Paper 11/114.

[63] Ibid.; 12/45; Inv. Regs 15 fo. 303; 20 fo. 393; cf. Guicciardini 119; Gras 560; Goris 319; Brulez, *Della Faille*, 283, 512, 522, 588; Wheeler 23; Willan, *Tu. Bk Rates*, 30; B. Dietz 43, 86–7, 93, 101, 118.

[64] Mx RO, Arch. Ct Mx inv. Jn Hoptkins 1673 St Clem. Danes; *Ca. Manufs Grograin Yarn*; Munn 5.

[65] Plummer, *Lond. Weavers' Co.*, 302.

[66] Guicciardini 119; Posthumus, *Bronnen*, iii, 118, 195, 483; Wheeler 23; Roberts, *Marchants Mapp*, 2nd pt, 76; Willan, *Tu. Bk Rates*, 30; B. Dietz 103; *Rates Marchandizes*; De Sagher iii, 341, 349; Coornaert, *Hondschoote*, 25, 217–9; Brulez, *Della Faille*, 45, 251, 266, 326, 330, 511, 589; Denucé 89–91, 97; Barkhausen 270; Kent RO, Cons. Ct Cant. Inv. Reg. 15 fo. 303.

[67] Moens, *Norwich*, 262; Nfk RO, F. C. Recs. Wall. Ch. 5, 6; Cty Recs. Alnage Accts; Bk Mayor's Ct 8 p. 570; Ass. Bks 3 fos. 227, 306v.–7; 5 fos. 3(12)v.–4(13).

[68] Ibid.; Duties fos. 46 sqq.; Cons. Ct inv. 1592/100; *Rates Marchandizes*, s.v. grograins Lile or Norwich; PRO, SPD Eliz. 250/76.

[69] Ibid.; *APC*, viii, 345; HMC, *Salisbury MSS*, iv, 573–4; Kent RO, Cons. Ct Cant. Inv. Paper 11/114; Inv. Reg. 15 fo. 303; cf. Cant. Cath. Lib. Wall. Recs. Misc. Docs portf. 1 no. 8.

[70] *Ca. Manufs Grograin Yarn*; Roberts, *Marchants Mapp*, 2nd pt 181, 193; Vanhaeck ii, 105–6; Brulez, *Della Faille*, 589; Wood 72–3; J. Haynes, *G.B.'s Glory*, 1715, p. 10; Defoe, *Plan*, 15; Posthumus, *Geschiedenis*, ii, 275, 3˄5; Millard i, App. pp. 18, 35; vols. ii, iii.

[71] Cant. Cath. Lib. Wall. Recs. Misc. Docs portf. 1 no. 18.

[72] Ibid. no. 24; PRO, PCR 1637–8 pp. 82, 578 (fos. 39v., 291v.); & v. Kent RO, Cons. Ct Cant. Inv. Regs 17 fo. 456; 20 fos. 369, 392–3; Bodl. Rawlinson A.478 fo. 28; Millard vols. ii, iii.

[73] Ibid.; Leics. RO, Arch. inv. Jn Stringer 1670.

[74] PRO, PCR 1637–8 pp. 82, 578 (fos. 39v., 291v.); 1639 pp. 24, 144–5 (fos. 8v., 68v.–9); SPD Chas 409/39; Smith, *Mems Wl*, ii, 43; cf. Kent RO, Cons. Ct Cant. Inv. Paper 11/114.

[75] Posthumus, *Bronnen*, iii, pp. ix, 299, 340–1, 479, 481–3; iv, p. ix; v, pp. ix, 8 sqq., 236; vi, 213 sqq.; *Geschiedenis*, ii, 272–3; cf. Rates Marchandizes.

[76] Nfk RO, Cty Recs. Strangers Bk fo. 66; PRO, SPD Eliz. 287/95.

[77] Ibid. Interreg. 101/6; Nfk RO, F. C. Recs. Wall. Ch. 5, 6; cf. De Poerck ii, 182.

[78] Kent RO, Cons. Ct Cant. Inv. Reg. 20 fos. 392–3.

[79] Purchas 269; BL, Add. 12504 no. 63; Nfk RO, Bk Mayor's Ct 15 fo. 140; Strangers Bk fo. 114v.; cf. Vanhaeck i, 238; V.&A. Text. Dept, Norwich weaver's patt. bk 1767; PRO, PCC parch. invs p. 1660 no. 2336.

[80] De Smedt ii, 386, 417; Kent RO, Arch. Ct Cant. Inv. Reg. 5 fos. 41, 286; Cons. Ct Cant. Reg. Accts & Invs 1 fo. 30; Cross 183–4.

[81] Ibid.; Somner 175–6.

[82] Kent RO, Cons. Ct. Cant. Regs Accts & Invs 9 fo. 100v.; 12 fo. 497.

[83] Ibid. 9 fo. 100; cf. Mazzaoui 165–6, 199.

[84] Kent RO, Cons. Ct Cant. Regs Accts & Invs 9 fo. 307; 12 fo. 497.

[85] Ibid. Inv. Paper 16/77.

[86] Posthumus, *Bronnen*, iii, 469; *Geschiedenis*, ii, 324; J. James 364; cf. Bridewell Mus. Ord. Bk 'Norwich 1791'.

[87] Nfk RO, Cty Recs. Strangers Bk fo. 84; cf. Thijs 57.

[88] Nfk RO, Bk Mayor's Ct 12 p. 315.

[89] Ibid.; Duties fos. 68 sqq.; Cons. Ct inv. 1591/169; F. C. Recs. Wall. Ch. 5, 6; PRO, SPD Eliz. 253/122; Interreg. 101/6; BL, Add. 12504 no. 65 p. 1 (fo. 86); cf. Bang iiA, 121, 195, 216, 247, 258, 264, 282, 284, 304, 346, 348, 394, 410, 437, 462, 473.

[90] Nfk RO, Cty Recs. Strangers Bk fo. 109v.

[91] Ibid. Duties fo. 67; F. C. Recs. Wall. Ch. 5, 6; Cons. Ct invs. 1605–47; 1636/149; 1628–68/ 117; PRO, Exch. KR Deps by Commn 44 & 45 Eliz. Mich. 1 m. 3r.; SPD Eliz. 253/122; Interreg. 101/6.

[92] Moens, Norwich, 79; Warner 658H & K; Edwards 305, 403; Hill ii, 205.

[93] Ibid. 195; A. Dietz ii, 267; Mx RO, Arch. Ct Mx inv. Jn Hoptkins 1673 St Clem. Danes; Nfk RO, Cons. Ct inv. 1610/135; Ess. RO, Arch. Ct Colc. Reg. Wills 6 fo. 35; Posthumus, Bronnen, iv, 109, 111.

[94] Ibid. iii, 38, 40, 53, 57; Nfk RO, F. C. Recs. Wall. Ch. 5, 6; Rates Marchandizes; PRO, SPD Interreg. 101/6; Van Nierop xlv, 25, 159; Thijs 40; BL, Lans. 26 no. 63 fo. 184(166); Kent RO, Cons. Ct Cant. Reg. Accts & Invs 12 fo. 497.

[95] BL, Lans. 26 no. 63 fo. 184 (166); PRO, SPD Eliz. 253/122; Eliz. Add. 34/23; cf. Kent RO, Cons. Ct Cant. Regs Accts & Invs 3 fo. 146; 6 fo. 372; Inv. Paper 11/114.

[96] BL, Lans. 26 no. 63 fo. 184 (166); PRO, Exch. KR Deps by Commn 44 & 45 Eliz. Mich. 1 m. 3r.; Nfk RO, F. C. Recs. Wall. Ch. 4–6; Cons. Ct inv. 1605/47.

[97] PRO, PCR 1639 pp. 144–5 (fos. 68v.–9); R. Steele, Bibl. R. Procls Tu. & Stuart Sovs, Oxf. 2 vols. 1910, i, 216; Cant. Cath. Lib. Wall. Recs. Wills G.1 no. 96; Misc. Docs portf. 1 no. 8; Le Livre des Actes du Consistoire de l'Eglise Wallonne de Canterbery: les choses resolues et arrestees du 5 de Juillet 1576 au 24 de Juin 1578, pp. 73–5; Nfk RO, Cons. Ct inv. 1718–21/169; Kent RO, Cons. Ct Cant. Inv. Paper 26/120.

[98] Ibid. Inv. Regs 7 fos. 5, 456; 11 fo. 652; (& v. Inv. Paper 11/114); Cowper, Cant. Mar. Lics, col. 390; PRO, PCR 1639 p. 145 (fo. 69); Jn Donne satire 4 ll. 32–3.

[99] Rates Marchandizes, s.v. curles, sipers; Millard vols. ii, iii.

[100] Kent RO, Cons. Ct Cant. Inv. Regs 7 fo. 265; 9 fo. 117; PRO, SPD Jas 35/27.

[101] Ibid. 131/15; Interreg. 101/6; PCR 1639 pp. 144–5 (fos. 68v.–9); Nfk RO, Cty Recs. Strangers Bk fo. 112v.; Cons. Ct inv. 1636/149; F. C. Recs. Wall. Ch. 5, 6; Kent RO, Cons. Ct Cant. Inv. Papers 16/32, 59; 20/78; Inv. Regs 9 fos. 117, 201; 11 fo. 652; 12 fo. 247; Harland 637; Steele i, 216; Stat. 12 Chas c.4; cf. Purchas 268.

[102] Cant. Cath. Lib. Wall. Recs. Misc. Docs portf. 1 no. 26.

[103] Craybeckx 429, 434; Mazzaoui 80; Deyon & Lottin 25; A. de Maddalena, 'L'Industria tessile a Mantova nel '500 e all' inizio del '600' in Studi in Onore A. Fanfani, iv, 619, 621, 628, 652; Posthumus, Geschiedenis, ii, 320; Bronnen, v, 402–4, 407, 412, 420, 423, 428; Rates Marchandizes, s.v. misselanes; Millard vols. ii, iii; PRO, SPD Eliz. 250/78; Eliz. Add. 34/23; Jas 35/27.

[104] Ibid.

[105] Ibid.; Eliz. Add. 34/23; Evelyn iii, 531; Van Nierop xlv, 24; Hooper 285 sqq.; cf. Cole ii, 177, 179.

[106] PRO, PCR, 1637–8 pp. 82, 578 (fos. 39v., 291v.); 1639 pp. 144–5 (fos. 68v.–9); PCC parch. invs p. 1660 no. 2336; Steele i, 216; Kent RO, Cons. Ct Cant. Inv. Papers 8/109; 20/78; Inv. Reg. 19 fo. 69.

[107] PRO, SPD Chas 302/41.

[108] PRO, C. O. BoT Orig. Corr. vol. 21 no. 209 (MFQ 134) fo. 149; Kent RO, Cons. Ct Cant. Inv. Paper 8/109.

[109] Ibid. 16/32; 17/85; 18/111; Inv. Reg. 20 fo. 393; Posthumus, Bronnen, v, 441; Vanhaeck i, 80, 93; ii, 237, 264; cf. Friis 439; J. James 209.

[110] Nfk RO, Cons. Ct inv. 1636/149; PRO, SPD Interreg. 101/6.

[111] Cole ii, 384, 574, 577–8; Deyon 173; Posthumus, Bronnen, v, 79.

[112] S. Pepys, *Diary*, ed. R. Latham & W. Matthew 9 vols. 1970–6, iv, 28; Kent RO, Cons. Ct Cant. Inv. Papers 21/21; 23/42; 26/120; cf. PRO, PCC parch. invs p. 1660 no. 2440.

[113] Vanhaeck i, 243; Rothstein 276; Kent RO, Cons. Ct Inv. Paper 26/120.

[114] Ibid. 21/21; PRO, PCC parch. invs p. 1660 no. 2440; Soms. RO, Arch. Taunton inv. 1720/4 Ric. Startt mercer Porlock.

[115] Cross 246; & v. Cant. Cath. Lib. Wall. Recs. Misc. Docs portf. 1 nos. 18, 24, 26; 4 no. 49; PRO, PCR 1637–8 pp. 82, 578 (fos. 39v., 291v.).

[116] Ibid. 1639 p. 145 (fo. 69); SPD Chas 180/70; 302/41; Millard i, 51; Laurent 71, 77; Bang iiA, 405, 449, 462, 490; A. E. Christensen, *Du. Trade to Balt. ab. 1600*, Copenhagen & Hague 1941, p. 184; Guildhall Lib. Weavers' Co. Ord. & Rec. Bk 1577–1641 pp. 354, 481; Cty Lond. RO, Ct Orphs invs box 1, Th. Marriott textor 1664.

[117] Plummer, *Lond. Weavers' Co.*, 59; Guildhall Lib. Commy Ct Lond. (Lond. Div.) invs box 8 Ann Hue 1703 Stepney.

[118] Ibid. box 9 Gaspard Pilot 1701, Mrs Eliz. Pilot 1702, both Wheeler St., Spitalfields, Stepney; Rothstein 578–9; Pococke i, 9; ii, 280; Eden ii, 584; HMC, *14th Rep.*, App. pt vi, 43; Stat. 12 Chas 2 c.4; *Rates Merchandizes*, 75; Bodl. Arch. Ct Berks. O.W. etc. 184/124; Pec. Ct Banbury O.W. & Admons 53/4/57; Pec. Ct Aylesbury O.W. & Admons 27/3/17; BL, Add. 36666 fo. 36.

[119] PRO, SPD Chas 529/91; Exch. KR Deps by Commn 44 & 45 Eliz. Mich. 1 m. 3r.; Nfk RO, Cty Recs. Strangers Bk fos. 58v.–60; BL, Add. 12504 no. 65 p. 3; Cant. Cath. Lib. Wall. Recs. Misc. Docs portf. 1 nos. 2–5; Kent RO, Cons. Ct Cant. Regs Accts & Invs 6 fos. 367, 373; 7 fo. 23; 9 fo. 307; 12 fos. 3, 479; Inv. Papers 26/120; 27/116; Inv. Reg. 14 fo. 245; Arch. Ct Cant. Inv. Regs 9 fo. 294; 10 fos. 344–5.

[120] Ibid. 12 fo. 17; 19 fo. 268; Cons. Ct Cant. Regs Accts & Invs 6 fos. 367; 7 fo. 270; 8 fo. 85; 10 fo. 238; 13 fos. 250–1; Inv. Paper 26/120; Cowper, *Cant. Mar. Lics*, col. 425; Somner 175–6; Cant. Cath. Lib. Cty Recs. Chamb's Accts 1577–87 fo. 307v.; Wall. Recs. Actes du Consistoire de l'Eglise Francaise a Canterbury 1581–4 fos. 11, 39v. (pp. 17, 72); Wills G. 2/61; Misc. Docs portf. 1 nos. 2–5.

[121] Boys 747; Kent RO, Sandwich Recs. N. Red Bk fos. 41v., 110–12; Yr Bk A & B fos. 7–8; Arch. Ct Cant. Inv. Reg. 16 fo. 339; Cons. Ct Cant. Regs Accts & Invs 7 fo. 23; 12 fo. 3.

[122] Ibid. Inv. Reg. 17 fo. 442; Maidstone Recs. Burghmote Bks 4 fo. 149; 5 fo. 10v.

[123] Morant, *Colc.*, 72; PRO, SPD Eliz. 78/9; Jas 129/70; F. G. Emmison, *Wills at Chelmsford*, Ind. Lib. B.R.S. lxxviii–ix 1958–61 lxxviii, 206; A. L. Merson, *3rd Bk Remembrance Soton 1514–1602*, vol. iii Soton 1965, p. 46.

[124] Hessels, *Archives*, 11, 18; Waller 5; Plummer, *Lond. Weavers' Co.*, 57.

[125] Moens, *Norwich*, 153 sqq.; BL, Add. 12504 no. 65 p. 3; PRO, Exch. KR Deps by Commn 44 & 45 Eliz. Mich. 1 m. 3r.; Req. 157/134 fos. 72, 77(2), 95(3) rev.; Hants. RO, unclass. invs D/2/ A:2/ 178; Nfk RO, Cty Recs. N. Drapery in Norwich; Ass. Bk 3 fos. 254, 295v.; Bk Mayor's Ct 9 p. 108; 12 p. 93; Strangers Bk fos. 20, 38, 58v.–60.

[126] Ibid. fo. 20.

[127] Ibid. invs Cons. Ct 1592/282; 1593/375; 1637/94; Arch. Ct Norvic. 1703–6/12.

[128] Willan, *Eliz. Man.*, 76; Wadsworth & Mann 14; Pococke i, 210, 212; *Cal. Freemen Lynn*, 150; K. J. Smith 6, 9, 23–4, 27, 84–5, 94, 109, 116, 128, 136, 155; Bowman 420; Warner 138, 297; Fiennes 224; J. James 202; Defoe, *Tour*, i, 83; *Compl. Engl. Tradesman*, 78–9; Aikin 154; Postlethwayt ii, 835; Poole 359–60; Lynes 11; W. Stukeley, *Itinerarium Curiosum*, 2 vols. 1776, i, 58; J. H. E. Bennett, *R. Freemen Cty Chester*, Rec. S. Lancs. & Ches. li, lv 1906–8, p. 125; C. S. Davies, *Hist. Macclesfield*, Man. 1961, p. 124; Anon. *Berisfords, Ribbon People*, Lond. & York 1966, p. 15; W. B. Stephens, *Hist. Congleton*, Man. 1970, p. 139; *VCH War.*, viii, 168; S. C. Ratcliff & H. C. Johnson, *War. Co. Recs*, vol. vi Warwick 1941, p. 87; J. Prest, *Ind. Rev. in Cov.*, 1960, p. 44; Bodl. Arch. Ct Berks. O.W. etc. 204/95; Kent RO, Cons. Ct Cant. Inv. Reg. 17 fo. 320; Leics. RO, Arch. inv. 1621/86; Chester RO, Cty Recs. Ass. Bk 1539–1624 fo. 220(217)v.; Ches. RO, Cons. Ct Cestr. O.W. & Admons, Infra: Ralph Nixson 1666 O. Knutsford; Robt Booth 1667 Chester; PRO, PCC parch. invs p. 1660 no. 3373; Brist. RO, Cons. Ct invs 1636 Jas Yevans; 1640 Ric. Day; 1663/10; Soms. RO, Arch. Taunton inv.

1668/18; Wilts. RO, Pec. Ct Dean Sarum. Th. Tiszer 1626 Sherborne; Pec. Ct D. & C. Sarum. roll I no. 14; Cons. Ct Sarum. Lionel Day 1695 Abindgdon; Ed. Steevins 1729 Hilperton.

[129] De Poerck, 236–9; Eggen 176–8; Goris 303; Enno ii, 31, 33; Sabbe, *Vlasnijverheid*, i, 22, 72; Espinas & Pirenne i, 139, 223 sqq.; Horman 167; W. G. Thomson, *Hist. Tapestry*, 1930, pp. 87 sqq., 105 sqq., 126 sqq., 189 sqq.

[130] Ibid. 137, 145, 263; *Tapestry Weaving in Engld*, n.d., 7 sqq., 15–17, 28, 46–7; Gras 459, 463.

[131] Thomson, *Tapestry Weaving*, 46; D. M. Palliser 131; *CPR*, Eliz. iii, 209–10; Hessels, *Archivum*, iii, 41–2; Kirk i, 205, 209, 274–5, 357, 390; ii, 270, 284, 286, 299, 318, 325, 332, 334, 339; iii, 336, 348, 356, 379–80, 405; Kent RO, Sandwich Recs, C. Ltr to Sir Wm Cecil 1561; Nfk RO, Cons. Ct invs 1633/295; 1666/77.

[132] Worcs. RO, Cons. Ct O.W. etc. 1609/124; Heaton 265; Preston 61–3; PRO, SPD Eliz. 252/2; E. A. B. Barnard & A. J. B. Wace, 'Sheldon Tapestry Weavers & their Wk', *Archaeologia*, 1928 lxxviii, 311 sqq.

[133] Ibid. 256–8, 260–1, 266–9, 271–2, 279–80, 284, 287 sqq.; A. J. Humphreys, 'Eliz. Sheldon Tapestries', ibid. 1925 lxxiv, 182 sqq., 191 sqq.; Thomson, *Tapestry Weaving*, 45, 47 sqq.; *Hist. Tapestry*, 264 sqq.; Kendrick 53–5, pl. XVI; HMC, *Var. Colls*, i, 297; Kemp, *Bl. Bk Warwick*, 48.

[134] Hessels, *Archivum*, iii, 1296, 1885, 1944, 1974–5, 1992–3, 1995, 2025–6, 2463–4, 2498; Aubrey, *Sy*, i, 82; Blome 222; *L.J.*, viii, 344; A. Haynes, 'Mortlake Tapestry Fcty 1619–1703', *Hist. Today*, 1974 xxiv, 32 sqq.; PRO, PCC parch. invs p. 1660 no. 1071; Kendrick 55–7, 74, pls XXXIV–VI; Thomson, *Hist. Tapestry*, 277 sqq., 292–3, 359–60; *Tapestry Weaving*, 66 sqq., 90, 96, 103, 128–31, 134, 136–7, 143, 159–60.

[135] Ibid. 153–5; Weiss i, 333; J. S. Burn, *Hist. Fr., Wall., Du. & other For. Prot. Refugees settled in Engld*, 1846, pp. 130–1.

[136] Millican, *Reg.*, 147; Nfk RO, Bk Mayor's Ct 10 p. 201.

[137] Ibid. 20 fo. 306.

[138] Ibid. 15 fo. 140.

[139] Ibid. 16 fos. 41, 48v., 196v., 294, 349, 381v., 399v., 405, 419v., 447v., 460, 480; 20 fos. 54, 56, 179, 238, 270, 280.

[140] Ibid. fo. 306v.; 16 fos. 196v., 236, 435v.; Arch. Ct Norvic. inv. 1715–17/103.

[141] *Disc. f. Enl. & Freedome of Trade*, 29; PRO, PCC parch. invs p. 1660 nos. 580, 2336, 3602, 4051; Nfk RO, Cons. Ct inv. 1628–68/117; Cty Recs. Bks Mayor's Ct 16 fos. 464, 470; 20 fos. 16v., 46, 285v.

[142] Ibid. 16 fo. 470.

[143] Ibid. 20 fos. 246v., 312v., 332, 339v., 358v.; Cons. Ct invs 1702/10; 1703–8/390; 1709–10/214; 1710–14/150, 295; 1716–17/169; 1718–21 (stamped) 169, 282; Arch. Ct Norvic. invs 1703–6/1, 12; 1709–10/61; 1715–17/103; 1754–67/43, 59; Edwards 305.

[144] Tymms 168; Nfk RO, Cons. Ct invs 1639/211B; 1647/189; Cty Recs. Bk Mayor's Ct 20 fos. 205, 208v.–9, 254, 270v., 306.

[145] Ibid. fo. 306v.; Cons. Ct inv. 1639/211B.

[146] Ibid. 1647/189; Cty Recs. Bk Mayor's Ct 20 fos. 313, 340, 345.

[147] Ibid. fo. 318v.; cf. Harland 225.

[148] PRO, PCC parch. invs p. 1660 no. 580; Nfk RO, Cons. Ct inv. 1647/189; Cty Recs. Bk Mayor's Ct 20 fo. 345.

[149] Ibid. fos. 188, 194, 306, 313, 332v., 345, 422v.; 16 fo. 464; Cons. Ct invs 1640/143; 1650/60.

[150] Ibid. 1651/32.

[151] Nfk RO, Cty Recs. Ass. Bk 5 fos. 3(12)v.–4(13).

[152] Ibid. Bk Mayor's Ct 15 fos. 256v.–7.

[153] Ibid. 16 fo. 13v.

[154] Ibid. Bks 23–5.

[155] Nor are any further recs to be found.

[156] Inf. 152–3.

[157] Nfk RO, Cty Recs. Ass. Bk 5 fos. 157(167)v., 266(276)v.; Bk Mayor's Ct 16 fos. 41v., 43, 48, 58v.

[158] Nfk RO, Cons. Ct 1628–68/117; 1676/62; 1681/67; 1686–7/156; 1692–3/65(64); 1710–14/31; Arch. Ct Norvic. 1674–5/200, 216; 1682–3/120; 1703–6/12; 1708/1; 1715–17/90; Pec. Ct D. & C. 1681–6/19; PRO, PCC parch. invs p. 1660 nos. 580, 1771, 5543.

[159] Ibid. 580 (Morly); Nfk RO, Cons. Ct inv. 1628–68/117 (Barker). Royal = top-topgallant.

[160] Nfk RO, invs Cons. Ct 1591/154; 1681/66; Arch. Ct Norvic. 1674–5/200, 216; Kent RO, Arch. Ct Cant. Inv. Reg. 10 fo. 252; PRO, PCC parch. invs p. 1660 no. 1603; cf. B. Jons. *Everyman in his Humour*, act iv sc. 7.

[161] PRO, PCC parch. invs p. 1660 no. 3602; Nfk RO, Arch. Ct Norvic. inv. 1674–5/216; Hudson & Tingey ii, 412; Lamb 383; Lancs. RO, Cavendish of Holker Coll. 1/46 fos. 1, 2, pp. 6, 9, 32, 45.

[162] Ibid. p. 11; Guildhall Lib. Commy Ct Lond. (Lond. Div.) inv. box 8 Th. Flower 1702 Stepney.

[163] Lancs. RO, Cavendish of Holker Coll. 1/46 fos. 1, 2, pp. 5, 6, 9–11, 31; PRO, PCC parch. invs p. 1660 no. 580; Nfk RO, Cons. Ct invs 1681/66; 1716–77/169.

[164] Ibid. 1647/189; 1628–68/117; 1666/77; 1674/58; 1681/66; 1716–17/169; Arch. Ct Nfk 1728–42/350; Arch. Ct Norvic. 1674–5/163, 200; 1754–67/43, 59; Pec. Ct D. & C. 1681–6/19; PRO, PCC parch. invs p. 1660 nos. 580, 1603, 2336, 5543; Warner 285, 290, 658J & L; Edwards 39, 55.

[165] PRO, SPD Jas 157/34; Chas 206/64; Interreg. 22/139; PCR 1631–2 pp. 267–8 (fo. 134); Nfk RO, Cty Recs. N. Drapery in Norwich; Bks Mayor's Ct 12 p. 946; 13 p. 68; Cons. Ct invs 1593/372; 1602/239; 1606–7/66; 1633/295; 1640/81; 1646/50; 1674/33; 1692–3/115.

[166] Ibid. 1628–68/117; 1686–7/156; 1694–6/43; 1710–14/31; Arch. Ct Norvic. 1674–5/216; 1703–6/12; PRO, PCC parch. invs p. 1660 nos. 1771, 1789, 2440, 3602.

[167] PRO, SPD Chas 529/91; BL, Lans. 26 no. 63 fo. 184(166); Nfk RO, Cty Recs. N. Drapery in Norwich; Alnage Accts; Strangers Bk fo. 60; 1st Bk Worstedweavers fo. 88, loose ad fin.; Kent RO, Cons. Ct Cant. Reg. Accts & Invs 6 fo. 373; E. B. Schumpeter 35.

[168] Lancs. RO, Cavendish of Holker Coll. 1/46 fo.1, pp. 5, 49–51.

[169] Ibid. 49, 51; Defoe, *Wks*, ed. J. S. Keltie, Edin. 1869, p. 544; Nfk RO, invs Cons. Ct 1681/66; 1694–6/43; 1703–8/110, 390; 1710–14/231; 1723/110; Arch. Ct Norvic. 1674–5/162–3, 200, 216; 1682–3/120; 1703–6/12; 1706–7/20; Pec. Ct D. & C. 1687–94/30; PRO, PCC parch. invs p. 1660 nos. 580, 1603, 1789, 3602.

[170] Ibid. nos. 580, 1603, 1789, 2440, 3602; Nfk RO, invs Arch. Ct Norvic. 1674–5/216; Cons. Ct 1716–17/169; Rothstein 578, 580; Warner 285, 290, 658I; Lancs. RO, Cavendish of Holker Coll. 1/46 pp. 5, 6, 11.

[171] Ibid. fo. iv., pp. 5, 6, 10, 11, 31–2, 51; Kent RO, Cons. Ct Cant. Inv. Paper 11/114; Inv. Reg. 20 fos. 392–3; PRO, PCR 1637–8 pp. 82, 578 (fo. 39v., 291v.); PCC parch. invs p. 1660 nos. 2336, 5543; Nfk RO, invs. Arch. Ct Norvic. 1703–6/1; Cons. Ct 1694–6/43; 1628–68/117.

[172] Ibid.; Arch. Ct Norvic. 1682–3/120; Cty Recs. Misc. Docs, Touching the Allegacion etc. ; PRO, PCC parch. invs p. 1660 no. 1789; cf. Posthumus, *Bronnen*, v, 405 sqq., 412, 420; *Geschiedenis*, ii, 320.

[173] Nfk RO, Cons. Ct invs 1703–8/390; 1710–14/31; PRO, PCC invs 1718–82 bdl. 23 no. 159; parch. invs p. 1660 nos. 580, 3602.

[174] Ibid. no. 1603; Nfk RO, Arch. Ct Norvic. inv. 1674–5/216.

[175] PRO, PCC parch. invs p. 1660 nos. 1603, 4051.

[176] Nfk RO, Cons. Ct inv. 1710–14/31.

[177] Ibid. 1628–68/117; 1686–7/156.

[178] Ibid. Arch. Ct Norvic. inv. 1682–3/120.

[179] Ibid. 1674–5/163, 200, 216; 1703–6/1, 12; 1709–10/61; 1715–16/103; 1754–67/43; Cons. Ct 1681/85; 1687/156; 1702/10; 1710–14/31, 231, 396; 1716–17/169; Cty Recs. Bk Mayor's Ct 8 p. 565; Bridewell Mus. Patts Norwich Manufs 1769 fo. 64; PRO, PCC parch. invs p. 1660 nos. 1603, 1789, 1946, 3602.

[180] Ibid. nos. 1789, 3602, 5543; invs 1718–82 bdl. 23 no. 159; Roberts, *Treas.*, 42; Wadsworth & Mann 119; Warner 658I; Nfk RO, Cons. Ct invs 1694–6/43; 1703–8/390; 1710–14/31.

[181] Ibid. 1646/60; 1681/67, 85; 1682/12; 1688–9/59B; 1694–6/43; Arch. Ct Norvic. 1674–5/216; Pec. Ct D. & C. 1681–6/19; PRO, PCC parch. invs p. 1660 nos. 1603, 1789.

[182] Nfk RO, invs Cons. Ct 1702/10; 1703–8/390; 1718–2 (stamped) 282; Arch. Ct Norvic. 1703–6/1; 1709–10/61; J. James 231; Warner 658I & J; PRO, C.O., BoT Orig. Corr. vol. 21 no. 209 (MFQ 134) fo. 151.

[183] Nfk RO, Pec. Ct D. & C. invs 1681–6/49; 1687–94/30; PRO, PCC parch. invs p. 1660 nos. 580, 1789.

[184] Ibid. nos. 580, 1789; E. Sfk RO, Arch. inv. 16/71; Nfk RO, invs Cons. Ct 1681/85; 1682/ 12; 1684/80; 1687/156; 1694–6/43; 1702/10; 1703–8/110, 390, 1709–10/152; 1710–14/31, 231, 295, 396; 1716–17/169; 1718–21 (stamped) 282; Arch. Ct Norvic. 1682–3/120; 1703–6/1; 1706–7/20, 85; 1709–10/61; 1754–67/43; Pec. Ct D. & C. 1681–6/19; Warner 283, 285, 658I; Fiennes 149, 245; J. James 220–1; Munn 5; Soms. RO, Arch. Taunton inv. 1720/4 Ric. Startt mercer Porlock; Hudson & Tingey ii, p. xcii; Cole ii, 567; Smith, *Mems Wl*, ii, 42, 187; Edwards 55, 59, 305, 403.

[185] Guildhall Lib. Commy Ct Lond. (Lond. Div.) invs box 8 Th. Flower 1702 Stepney; box 9 Geo. Thackery 1701 St Dunstan's, Stepney; Kent RO, Cons. Ct Cant. Inv. Paper 27/116; cf. A. P. Hands & I. Scouloudi, *Fr. Prot. Refugees relieved thr. Threadneedle St Ch. Lond. 1681–7*, H.S.L. Qto Ser. 1971 xlix, 110.

[186] Hill ii, 195; E. Sfk RO, Arch. inv. 16/71; Mx RO, Arch. Ct Mx inv. Jn Hoptkins 1673 St Clem. Danes; Nfk RO, invs Cons. Ct 1628–68/117; 1694–6/43; Arch. Ct Norvic. 1674–5/200; 1682–3/120; PRO, PCC parch. invs p. 1660 nos. 1771, 5543; Munn 5.

[187] Guildhall Lib. Commy Ct Lond. (Lond. Div.) inv. box 8 Jn Dollond 1715 Stepney.

[188] Ibid. & Isaac Burgess 1714 St Dunstan's, Stepney; Nfk RO, Cons. Ct inv. 1716–17/169; PRO, C.O., BoT Orig. Corr. vol. 21, no. 209 (MFQ 134) fos. 154, 156; Brist. RO, Recs Brist. & Frenchay S.F., A9/1, p. 71.

[189] PRO, PCC parch. invs p. 1660 nos. 1789, 3602; Nfk RO, invs Pec. Ct D. & C. 1681–6/19; Cons. Ct 1682/12; 1687/156; 1702/10.

[190] Ibid. 1703–8/110, 390; Arch. Ct Norvic. 1709–10/61; Guildhall Lib. Commy Ct Lond. (Lond. Div.) inv. box 8 Th. Flower 1702 Stepney; Warner 285, 290, 658J; Edwards 305; cf. Munn 5.

[191] Nfk RO, Cons. Ct invs 1684/80; 1710–14/31, 396; Hill ii, 195; Vanhaeck i, 248.

[192] J. Dyer, *Poems*, 1770, 'The Fleece', bk iii, 147; Wood 76; Munn 5; Cross 204–5; Sella, *Commerci e Industrie*, 27.

[193] PRO, C.O., BoT Orig. Corr. vol. 21 no. 209 (MFQ 134) fos. 152–3; Bridewell Mus. Patts Norwich Manufs 1769 fo. 120; Ord. Bk 'Norwich 1791'; Nfk RO, Arch. Ct Norvic. inv. 1754–67/ 59.

[194] Ibid.; Rothstein 577; Montgomery 221.

[195] P. Clabburn, *Norwich Shawls*, Norwich 1975; Edwards 305, 403.

[196] Ibid. 362; Warner 285, 658K & M; Moens, *Norwich* 79; ex inf. Miss P. Marsh.

[197] Fuller, *Worthies*, ii, 488; PRO, Exch. KR Deps by Commn 44 & 45 Eliz. Mich. 1 mm. 7r., 9r.

[198] Ibid. 7r., 8r., 8d.

[199] F. J. Powicke, *Life Rev. Ric. Baxter*, 1924, p. 40; Worcs. RO, Cons. Ct O.W. etc. 1613/ 204d; 1614/169; 1622/66, 152; 1624/72; 1625/212; 1690/112.

[200] Ibid. 1614/169; 1625/212; 1631/170; 1649/27; 1670/372; 1671/6; 1690/112; 1710 Jn Jones; 1711 Ric. Callow sr; 1714 Mr Ed. Woodward; 1716 Wm Radford jr; 1718 Marg. Lea wid., And. Walker, Wm Dearne; 1727 Ric. Billingsley, Jos. Nicholls, all Kidderminster; J. F., op. cit. 26; McGrath, *Merchs*, 271–4; Defoe, *Tour*, i, 82; *Compl. Engl. Tradesman*, 77, 79; *VCH Worcs.*, ii, 293–4; Burton 174 sqq., 180; Gibbons 44; Plot, *Oxon.*, 278–9; R. Baxter, *Reliquiae Baxterianae*, ed. M. Sylvester 1696 lib. i, pt i, pp. 19. 20, 89, 94; Stat. 22 & 23 Chas 2 c.8; Yarranton 98–9, 111–12, 146; PRO, PCC parch. invs p. 1660 no. 7892; Tattersall 45; R. Davies 164.

[201] J. M. Guilding, *Reading Recs*, 4 vols. 1892–6, ii, 240, 252, 266; inf. 115, 135–6.

[202] Nfk RO, Cons. Ct inv. 1685/57; Q.Sess.Bk 1562–7 (22 May 4 Eliz.); Cty Recs. 2nd Bk Worstedweavers, scrap no. 50; Bk Mayor's Ct 6 p. 326.

[203] Ibid. 5 pp. 191, 215; 2nd Bk Worstedweavers, scrap no. 50; invs Cons. Ct 1637/194; 1703–8/ 300; Arch. Ct Norvic. 1706–7/30; *VCH Suss.*, ii, 258; *Cal. Freeman Lynn*, 142, 167; Allison 351; Serjeant 3, 18, 194; PRO, PCR 1631–2, pp. 107, 232, 265, 270, 272 (fos. 50, 116v., 133, 135v., 136v.); Thetford, King's Ho. Boro. Recs. vol. 9 (15 Mar. 1622).

[204] W.Sfk RO, Ep. Commy Ct Bury inv. 1676/47; & v. sup. 72–3, 77–8, 82–5.

[205] W. Sfk RO, Ep. Commy Ct Bury inv. 1677/87.

[206] Ibid. 1696/91; cf. Nfk RO, Cons. Ct inv. 1694–6/43.

[207] W. Sfk RO, Ep. Commy Ct Bury inv. 1700/3; Rothstein 578; Plummer, *Lond. Weavers' Co.*, 302.

[208] Grubb 142; C. Dale 33; W. Money, 'Guild & Fellowship Clothworkers Newbury', *Jnl Brit. Archaeol. Ass.*, n.s. 1896 ii, 266–7; *Rsns Humbly Offered f. Restraining Wearing Wrought Silks etc.*

[209] Worcs. RO, Cons. Ct O.W. etc. 1727 Hy Pearsall/Kidderminster; Burton 180; Gibbons 45; Waller 65; Warner 327.

[210] Ibid. 330; Curtis 123; *VCH Hants.*, v, 488; Hooper 227; cf. V. & A. Text. Dept. Norwich weaver's patt. bk 1767; Counterpart patts sent to Sp. & Lis. by Mr J.K. 1763.

[211] Burton 180–1; *VCH Worcs.*, ii, 296; Warner 327–8.

[212] Dunsford 55, 57, 235–6; Martin i, 55–6; Postlethwayt i, 816; ii, 743; Defoe, *Tour*, i, 266; *Compl. Engl. Tradesman*, 78; Smith, *Mems Wl*, ii, 323; Kent RO, Cons. Ct Cant. Inv. Reg. 15 fo. 303; cf. Munn 5; E. Sfk RO, Arch. inv. 16/71.

[213] Chester RO, Guild Recs. Weavers' Co. Bk 1697–1817 rev.

[214] *VCH Wilts.*, iv, 181; Pococke i, 230; ii, 48; Tattersall 62–3, 65 sqq., 113–15, 120; Burton 182–3; Cole ii, 178–9, 577.

**Chapter 7**

[1] Unger, *De Tol*, 85.

[2] Coornaert, *Hondschoote*, 105.

[3] De Smedt ii, 361.

[4] Strieder 362; Smit ii, 497.

[5] De Smedt ii, 343–5; cf. PRO, SPD Hy 8, vol. 236 fo. 179.

[6] Smit ii, 562; Strieder 167.

[7] Ibid. 169, 198, 201, 206.

[8] Smit ii, 709.

[9] De Smedt ii, 350–1; & v. 343–5, 361.

[10] PRO, SPD Eliz. 20/15, 42.

[11] Ibid. Eliz. Add. 33/71; cf. W. Sfk RO, Ep. Commy Ct Bury invs. 1660/189; 1686/79.

[12] Stats. 14 & 15 H.8 c.1; 5 & 6 E.6 c.6; 4 & 5 P.&M. c.5; 4 Jas c.2.

[13] PRO SPD Eliz. 106/47.

[14] Friis 438.

[15] Ibid.; Ramsay, 'Distr.', 364–5, 367; Pilgrim, thes. 48–9; K. W. Glass, *Sh. Hist. Glemsford*, Glemsford 1962, p. 28; Willan, *Tu. Bk Rates*, 74; Smit ii, 766; Strieder 302; Willemsen, 'La Grève', 148; De Smedt ii, 342 sqq., 348, 350; *Laws in Ven. f. Prohibition For. Cl.*, s.l. n.d.; W. Sfk RO, Acc. 634 p. 38; Nfk RO, Cons. Ct inv. 1629/134.

[16] J. Norden, *An Hist. & Chorographical Descron Co. Ess.*, Camd. S. 1840 (ix) p. 9.

[17] Ibid.; PRO, SPD Eliz. 250/47; my *Ag. Rev.*, 77–80; & v. BL, Lans. 26 no. 56 fo. 147.

[18] W. J. Hardy, 'For. Settlers at Colc. & Halstead', *Proc. H.S.L.*, 1889 ii, 182–3; PRO, Exch. KR Deps by Commn 15 Jas Mich. 31.

[19] Ibid. m. 2(1)r.

[20] Ibid. mm. 2(1)–5(4), 7, 8d., 10r., 12d.; BL, Lans. 114 no. 24 fos. 92v.–3.

[21] PRO, Exch. KR Deps by Commn 15 Jas Mich. 31 mm. 2(1)r., 7; BL, Harl. 1878 fo. 99(84).

[22] Ibid.; Lans. 27 no. 66 fo. 149; 71 no. 51 fo. 107(108)v.; 114 no. 24 fos. 92v.–3; W. de G. Birch 259, 264; McGrath, *Merchs*, 271–4; *Rates Marchandizes*, s.v. bayes; *Disc. f. Enl. & Freedome of Trade*, 29; PRO, SPD Eliz. 106/47; 250/47.

[23] Ibid. 106/47.

[24] *Ords Clwkrs' Co.*, 1881, pp. 33, 58; *Rates Marchandizes*, s.v. penistones, frizadoe; *Disc. Com. Weal*, 65; Willan, *Tu. Bk Rates*, 27, 74; Brulez, *Della Faille*, 33, 423; De Smedt ii, 350–1, 433; Coornaert, *Anvers*, ii, 115; Goris 276, 291, 299; B. Dietz 37, 43, 49–51, 55, 60, 67–8, 73, 86–7, 94, 127; Smit ii, 726.

[25] Ibid. 1180 sqq.; Posthumus, *Bronnen*, ii, 670, 694–6; iii, pp. ix, 60, 66, 75–6, 81 sqq., 543–5, 573–4, 634–5; iv, 258, 282–4; v, 470; vi, 516–17; *Geschiedenis*, ii, 255, 318–19; Enno i, 569; Van Dillen, *Bronnen*, ii, 467; Rich 126; *APC*, x, 322, 370; *CPR*, Eliz. iv, 354; BL, Cott. Tib. D. viii fo. 41(40); *Cal. SP For.*, 1578–9 no. 164; PRO, SPD Eliz. 130/48; 250/47; Eliz. Add. 11/113.

[26] Ibid. Eliz. 250/47; Eliz. Add. 11/113 (disregarding tentative date in cal.).

[27] Westcote 61; J. J. Alexander & W. R. Hooper, *Hist Gt Torrington*, Sutton, Sy 1948, p. 168; *Rates Marchandizes*, s.v. bayes; BL, Lans. 27 no. 66 fos. 148–9.

[28] Friis 438; J. F. Shepherd & G. M. Walton, *Shipping, Marit. Trade & Econ. Devpt Col. N. Am.*, Cam. 1972, p. 180; H. S. K. Kent, *War & Trade in North. Seas* Cam. 1973, p. 108; T.E. Hartley, *Proc. in Parls of Eliz. I*, i, 1558–81 Leic. 1981, pp. 381, 390, 401; Nfk RO, Cons. Ct inv. 1629/134.

[29] PRO, Exch. KR Deps by Commn 15 Jas Mich. 31 mm. 2(1)r., 4(3)r., 7r.

[30] Stats 14 & 15 H.8 c.1; 5 & 6 E.6 c.6; 4 & 5 P.&M. c.5; Noy 182–3; PRO, SPD Eliz. 106/47.

[31] Ibid. 88/22.

[32] Ibid. 111/38.

[33] Stow, *Ann.* 870.

[34] PRO, Exch. KR Deps by Commn 15 Jas Mich. 31 mm. 2(1)r., 7r.

[35] PRO, SPD Eliz. Add. 11/113 (cf. Eliz. 250/47); BL, Lans. 27 no. 66 fos. 148–9.

[36] Sup. 91.

[37] E. Power, *Paycockes of Coggeshall*, 1920, pp. 33, 41, 43; cf. 39; Ess. RO, Arch. Ct Colc. Reg. Wills 6 fo. 16.

[38] Inf. 98, 104.

[39] Stats 1 R.3 c.8; 14 & 15 H.8 c.1; cf. Ess. RO, Arch. Ct Colc. Reg. Wills 6 fo. 80; Emmison, *Home, Wk & Ld*, 76–7.

[40] *D.N.B.*

[41] Redstone, 'Engld', 176.

[42] De Smedt ii, 341 sqq., 350–1; Strieder 167, 169, 198, 201–2, 206, 362–3; Smit ii, 497, 562.

[43] De Sagher iii, 263–4, 288, 292 sqq., 308–9, 312–13, 317–20, 323, 328 sqq.; Coornaert, *Hondschoote*, 105; De Smedt ii, 386, 417; cf. Espinas & Pirenne i, 326, 331; De Poerck i, 245–6.

[44] Coornaert, *Hondschoote*, 26; Demey 229; Van Der Wee ii, 137; L. Roker, 'Fl. & Du. Commun. in Colc. in 16th & 17th cents.', ts. thes. MA Lond. Univ. 1963, p. 177.

[45] Kent RO, Sandwich Recs. L. Bl. Bk fos. 192, 204v.; & v. Kirk ii, 91.

[46] De Sagher i, pp. xviii, 196–7, 200, 371, 501, 505; iii, 7, 56–8, 98, 190–1, 197–8, 263, 288, 323, 327–8; Coornaert, *Hondschoote*, 26.

[47] A. Dietz ii, 269.

[48] Eggen 170–1; Posthumus, *Bronnen*, ii, 609, 613, 615–16, 632, 649–50, 694, 696; iii, 3, 4, 6, 8, 16, 20, 26, 35, 64; *Geschiedenis*, i, 96; ii, 22, 24–5, 33, 44–5, 53–6, 79, 98–9, 102.

[49] Maugis 76–7.

[50] Nfk RO, Cty Recs. Strangers Bk fos. 17, 19.

[51] H. Q. Janssen, 'De Hervormde Vlugtelingen van Yperen in Engeland', *Bijdragen tot de Oudheidkunde en Geschiedenis*, 1857 ii, 224, 231, 235–6, 246: 'Ende ic en twyfele niet God die zal ons helpen ende nemmermeer verlaeten. Wy zullen oock de costh wel winnen ghy sult u beste doen met spinnen baey ende ic in mijn ampt, zoo dat wy met Godes hulpe gheen ghebreck hebben zullen.' – 'Ic

zal zien om een huus alzo haest als ic mach, om ons in die neringe te behelpen, want daermede den cost wel te winnen es. Ic gaen doen maken een baey ghewant teghen uwe comste. . . . U zuster laet u weten dat Lein niet encomme om zijn ambacht te doene, want men daer niet en doet dan baeywerken.' – 'Franssen mijn broeder besteet es met eenen Willem Van Den Schoore ende strijct baeyen ende wynt voor het jaer ij £ grooten ende den goeden kost.' – 'Wij beiden leeren baai spinnen.'

[52] Ibid. 231, 246, 251; Cant. Cath. Lib. Wall. Recs. Misc. Docs. portf. 1 no. 7.

[53] G. H. Overend, 'Strangers at Dover', *Proc. H.S.L.*, 1892 iii, 159–62.

[54] Moens, *Colc.*, i–iii, 95 sqq.; W. Smith, *Part. Descron Engld, 1588*, 1879, p. 7; Ess. RO, Arch. Ct Mx (Ess. & Herts. Div.) Reg. Wills 3 fo. 340; Bp Lond's Commy Ct f. Ess. & Herts. O.W. 9/259; Arch. Ct Colc. O.W. 2/82; 5/119.

[55] Somner 175–6; Cross 18, 19; Cant. Cath. Lib. Cty Recs Burghmote Bk 1542–78 fo. 286; Chamb's Accts 1568–77 fos. 339–40, 384–5; Wall. Recs. Misc. Docs portf. 1 no. 2.

[56] Inf.

[57] Hessels, *Archivum*, iii, 573; Thetford, King's Ho. Boro. Recs vol. 1: 1st Min. Bk Corpn aft. Char. pp. 33, 110 (fos. 17v., 56); Nfk RO, Cty Recs. Strangers Bk fo. 91; cf. BL, Lans. 31 no. 29 fo. 78(71).

[58] Inf. 101.

[59] Posthumus, *Geschiedenis*, ii, 12, 58–9; *Bronnen*, iii, 75–6, 503.

[60] Hessels, *Archivum*, iii, 877–8.

[61] J. Opdedrinck, *Poperinghe en Omstreken tijdens de Godsdienstberoerten der XVIe eeuw of Den Geuzentijd*, Bruges 1898, pp. 52, 76, 79, 90, 102–4, 135 sqq., 153 sqq.

[62] Ibid. 161–2; *Cal. SP For.*, 1578–9 p. 43; De Sagher iii, 264, 344 sqq., 350, 353, 356–8, 361–2, 375–8, 381–2, 385 sqq.

[63] Ibid. 98–9, 189 sqq., 212 sqq., 220–1, 225; Coornaert, *Hondschoote*, 26.

[64] De Sagher i, 100, 435 sqq., 450–3, 465–6, 468–9, 475–7, 503 sqq.; ii, 95–6, 234, 570, 624; iii, 7, 61–4, 69 sqq.

[65] Ibid. ii, 560–1.

[66] Maugis 78–9; Deyon 153, 158, 173 sqq.

[67] Defoe, *Tour* i, 17, 88; Thornton 123, 192, 202–3, 230–1; Kirby 264; M. G. Davies 129; Blome 212; Fuller, *Worthes*, i, 494; Postlethwayt ii, 765; Emmison, *Home, Wk & Ld*, 196; *Eliz. Life: Disorder*, Chelmsford 1970, p. 298; *APC*, 1629–30, pp. 11, 114; Stat. 7 Jas c.7; BL, Lans. 27 no. 66 fos. 148–9; E. Sfk RO, Sess. Ord. Bk 1639–51 fo. 112; W. Sfk RO, Ep. Commy Ct Bury invs. 1660/21; 1662/115; 1665/97; 1666/81; 1667/1, 13, 170; 1670/39, 1680/202; 1711/49; Ess. RO, Bp Lond's Commy Ct f. Ess. & Herts. O.W. 6/179; 17/43; 35/262; 52/264; 55/298; 57/210; Regs Wills 8 fo. 467; 10 fo. 455; 17 fo. 320; Arch. Ct Colc. O.W. 17/201; Regs Wills 9 fo. 82; 11 fo. 115; PRO, SPD Eliz. 114/47; 157/3; Chas 147/43; 344/19; 345/84; 355/10, 67, 144.

[68] Ibid. Jas 131/15; 133/6, 8, 9, 37; W. de G. Birch 259; Shrewsbury Lib. MS 4274 Ords etc. Weavers' Co. agrt 9 Nov. 1600; Chester RO, Cty Recs. Ass. Bk 1539–1624 fo. 168(165)v.; cf. Woodward, *Trade Eliz. Chester*, 13.

[69] J. R. Chanter, *Collectanea*, s.l. n.d. 100; Bpl. N. Devon Athenaeum, Bpl. Boro. Recs. vol. 2 no. 3972 Recr's Accts 1389–1643 m. 124; D. W. Jones, '"Hallage" Recpts Lond. Cl. Mkts 1562–c.1720', *Econ. Hist. Rev.*, 2nd ser. 1972 xxv, 572.

[70] Ibid.; *VCH Dors.*, ii, 361–2; *Soms.* ii, 411; Mann, *Cl. Ind.*, 28; HMC, *13th Rep.*, App. pt ii, 275; PRO, PCC parch. invs p. 1660 no. 9326; cf. no. 7657.

[71] PRO, SPD Eliz. 253/5.

[72] Tupling 169, 180; Aikin 248; Wadsworth & Mann 13, 15, 30, 46, 280–1; T. Newbigging, *Hist. For. Rossendale*, 1868, pp. 209, 211–13; M. Gray, *Hist. Bury. Lancs. fr. 1660 to 1876*, Bury 1970, pp. 17, 181–2; Pococke i, 205; Willan, *Inld Trade*, 109; W. Bennett, *1400–1650*, 86; *1650–1850*, 78; *Pal. Notebk*, i, 126–7; D. R. Hainsworth, *Comm. Papers Sir Chris. Lowther 1611–44*, Surtees S. 1977 clxxxix, 197–8, 203; Lancs. RO, Cons. Ct Cestr. Supra invs Jn Bordeman 1628 Bolton; Jn Gregory 1675 Rochdale; cf. G. Jackson, *Hull in 18th cent.*, 1972, pp. 54, 337.

[73] Latimer, *Ann. Brist. 17th cent.*, 40–1; Brist. RO, Cons. Ct inv. Th. Cornock 1641 Temple par.; cf. G. D. Ramsay, *Engl. O'sea Trade during Cents Emer.*, 1957, pp. 139–40.

[74] D. W. Jones 572; Mann, *Cl. IND.*, ¾: Ramsay, *Wilts.*, 111; PRO, SPD Jas 131/15; 133/6, 8, 9.

[75] Ibid. 133/6, 8, 9; Cash 44; Alexander & Hooper 168.

[76] Kent RO, Cons. Ct Cant. Inv. Paper 7/80.

[77] Soms. RO, Arch. Taunton inv. 1667/78; *Cal. SPD*, 1611–18, p. 206.

[78] Heaton 268–9; HMC, *14th Rep.*, App. pt vi, 42.

[79] Rijpma 96, 110; Van Dillen, *Bronnen*, ii, 181–2; Schmoller 228, 541.

[80] BL, Lans. 71 no. 51 fo. 108(107)v.

[81] De Sagher iii, 56–8, 191, 193, 195–6, 202, 204, 213 sqq., 288, 293–5, 305, 309, 312, 317, 331, 340, 358, 375, 386, 388, 390–1, 393.

[82] Kent RO, Sandwich Recs. N. Red Bk fo. 41v.

[83] J. Nichols, *Progs & Pub. Procs Q. Eliz.*, 2 vols. 1788 i, [548](56); PRO, SPD Jas 129/70.

[84] N. W. Posthumus & W. L. J. De Nie, 'Een Handschrift over de Textielververij in de Republiek uit de eerste helft der 17e eeuw', *Economisch-Historisch Jaarboek*, 1936 xx, 252; Kent RO, Cons. Ct Cant. Inv. Papers 6/13; 9/81; 12/31; Inv. Regs 14. fo. 138; 16 fo. 443.

[85] Ibid. Arch. Ct Cant. Inv. Reg. 14 fo. 169; BL, Harl. 1878 fos. 99(84), 101(85); Lans. 114 no. 24 fo. 93; PRO, SPD Eliz. 250/47; Eliz. Add. 11/113.

[86] Hessels, *Archivum*, iii, 510–11; HMC, *Salisbury MSS*, iv, 573–4.

[87] Moens, *Colc.*, pp. ii–iv; *APC*, viii, 306; PRO, SPD Eliz. 78/9.

[88] Smith, *Mems Wl*, i, 176; PRO, SPD Jas 129/70; Chas 206/58.

[89] Ibid. 206/58–9; 378/40; Jas 15/17; 129/70.

[90] Fiennes 142.

[91] BL, Harl. 1878 fos. 99(84), 101(85); Lans. 26 no. 64 fo. 187; 27 no. 66 fos. 148–9; no. 60 fos. 177–8; 71 no. 51 fo. 107(108); 114 no. 24 fo. 93; PRO, Exch. KR Deps by Commn 15 Jas Mich. 31 mm. 3(2)r., 4(3)r.; SPD Eliz. 250/47; Eliz. Add. 11/113; Jas 26/1; 129/70; Stat. 12 Chas 2 c.22.

[92] Denucé 58–60; Posthumus & De Nie 252.

[93] Morant, *Colc.*, 74; Evelyn iii, 177; E. Misselden, *Free Trade, or the Meanes to make Trade Florish*, 1622, p. 128; Benham 250, 253–6; Ramsay, 'Rep.', 491; Stat. 12 Chas 2 c.22; PRO, SPD Jas 15/17; 120/95 (quot.); 129/70; Chas 206/58; 293/86; *APC*, 1630–1, p. 200.

[94] Ibid.

[95] A. F. J. Brown, 'Colc. in 18th cent.' in L. M. Munby, *E. A. Studs*, Cam. 1968, p. 148; Burley, thes. 401–2.

[96] PRO, Exch. KR Deps by Commn 15 Jas Mich. 31 mm. 2(1), 3(2)r.; De Sagher iii, 56–8.

[97] Hessels, *Archivum*, iii, 68.

[98] *APC*, 1630–1, p. 200; Posthumus & De Nie 252; PRO, PCC parch. invs p. 1660 no. 11398; SPD Jas 15/17; 129/70; Chas 378/40; Exch. KR Deps by Commn 15 Jas Mich. 31 mm. 2(1), 3(2)r., 4(3), 5(4)r., 7, 8d.

[99] Ibid. mm. 2(1), 3(2)r.; *APC*, 1616–17 p. 90.

[100] PRO, Exch. KR Deps by Commn 15 Jas Mich. 31 m.2(1)r.

[101] Lichfield Jt RO, Cons. Ct O.W. Th. Smyth 1603 Cov.; BL, Lans. 71 no. 51 fo. 107(108)v.

[102] Moens, *Norwich*, 20; Janssen, op. cit. pass.; Smit ii, 946, 953, 957.

[103] Nfk RO, Cty Recs. Strangers Bk fos. 22–3; Bk Mayor's Ct 12 p. 315.

[104] Ibid. Ords con. Wl fo. 10v.; Keure fo. 10v.

[105] Ibid. Strangers Bk fo. 51v.

[106] Ibid. fo. 49v.; Ords con. Wl fo. 2v.; Keure fo. 1v.: 'Quade Wulle. . . . zullen nyet moghen laten passeren ëenighe lams wolle, jeunenette ende ander corte wolle maer zullen die wysen uut der stede te doene oft emmer binnen xiiij daghen naer het waranderen to brenghen goede certificatie waer sy met de selve wulle bevaren syn oft wien zy de selve ghevaert sullen hebben dan wochtans.'

[107] Ibid. Strangers Bk fo. 49v.; Ords con. Wl fo. 2; Keure fo. 1: 'Nyemant wie hy zy coopman oft drapier open doe noch ende ontpacke eenighe plotwulle oft ander corte wulle . . .'.

[108] Ibid. Ords con. Wl fo. 19v.; Keure fo. 20v.: 'dat men gheen achtertreck ende sal moghen maecken noch wulle minghelen met cammelinghen om te doen spinnen.'

[109] Ibid. Ords con. Wl fo. 28v. ('of' = 'woof'); Keure fo. 32: 'nyemant wy hy sy tsy duytsch oft wale hem ende vervordere te coopene alhier binnen desen stede oft in de voorbochten van dier eenighen vetten inslach gaerne van uuten ghebrocht ten ware dat alvoren de wolle daer het selve gaerne af ghesponne waer alhier by den gouverneurs ghewarandeert gheweest hadde.'

[110] Ibid. Strangers Bk fo. 91.

[111] Ibid. fo. 91v.

[112] Ibid. fos. 86–7, 90, 100; Duties fos. 83–5; Cons. Ct inv. 1589/200.

[113] Ibid. Cty Recs. Strangers Bk fos. 52, 55, 78; Ords con. Wl fo. 23v.; Keure fo. 25v.: 'Smouten met olie: Item dat men gheen inslach wulle smouten ende smal met olie oft ander quaet smout maer alleene met buter.' Et v. Stat. 3 Geo. 3 c.20.

[114] Nfk RO, Cty Recs. Ords con. Wl fo. 25v.; Keure fo. 28: 'dat gheen vulders ende sullen vermoghen ter plancke te commene naect anders dan met een schortcleet oft bale van gortrieme neerwarts op de boete van vj pence telcher reyse tot profyte van bayllyus ende staen bovendien ter corectie van mannen.'

[115] Ibid. Strangers Bk fos. 49v. sqq.; Ords con. Wl fos. 2v., 3 (quot.), 4v., 5, 9, 11, 13, 19, 26v., 28v.–9 & pass.; Keure fos. 1v., 2 ('men de bayen scheren zal met xiiij pypen in 46 ganghe ende de 60 bayen in 51 ganghen ende half ende de 68 bayen in 58 ganghen'), 3v., 4, 9, 11, 14, 20, 29, 32 & pass.; N. Drapery in Norwich; PRO, SPD Eliz. 250/47; Eliz. Add. 11/113; BL, Lans. 26 no. 62 fo. 181(163); no. 64 fo. 187; 27 no. 66 fos. 148–9; cf. Hudson & Tingey ii, 99; Coornaert, *Hondschoote*, 200; De Poerck i, 72.

[116] *Rates Marchandizes*; Nfk RO, Cty Recs. Strangers Bk fos. 34v., 38.

[117] Ibid. Ords. con. Wl. fo. 5; Keure fo. 4; Bks Mayor's Ct 8 p. 565; 9 p. 679.

[118] Ibid. 1576 agrt of Guy de Lewaulle.

[119] Ibid. Strangers Bk fo. 25.

[120] Ibid. fo. 108; Ass. Bk 5 fos. 3(12)v., 4(13).

[121] Kent RO, Maidstone Recs. Burghmote Bks I fos. 43v.–4; 3 fo. 5 (p. 9); Chamb's Accts (Paper Bks) nos. 6 sqq.; *CPR*, Eliz. iv, 39, 40; PRO, SPD Eliz. 43/19, 21; 250/47; Eliz. Add. 11/113.

[122] *APC*, xxix, 646; Cant. Cath. Lib. Wall. Recs. Misc. Docs. portf. 1 nos. 2–5; Cty Recs. Burghmote Bk 1542–78 fo. 286.

[123] Ibid.; Chamb's Accts 1568–77 fos. 339–40, 384; 1577–87 fos. 23v.–4, 71, 112–13, 159–60, 205, 258, 307v., 357, 405, 454; 1587–92 fos. 25, 64, 104v.–5, 150v., 151v., 199; 1592–1602 fos. 25(26)v., 91(26)v., 147v.–8, 191v., 232, 276, 321v.–2, 374v., 423, 473; 1602–10 fos. 17v., 18, 68, 110, 151, 190v., 282, 330; & succ. accts; Wall. Recs. Misc. Docs. portf. 1 no. 8; Cowper, *Cant. Mar. Lics*, col. 96; *APC*, viii, 345; cf. 306, 336; xxix, 646; xxxiii, 8; Kent RO, Cons. Ct Cant. Reg. Accts & Invs 13 fo. 488.

[124] *APC*, ix, 161–2; xviii, 276–7, 413; xix, 127–8; xxii, 444; PRO, SPD Eliz. 108/54; 120/22; 146/63 (quot.); Emmison, *Home, Wk & Ld*, 307–8; Ess. RO, Arch. Ct Mx (Ess. & Herts. Div.) Reg. Wills 3 fo. 340; Hessels, *Archivum*, iii, 494–5, 566–7, 783, 867–8, 871–2, 875–8, 906–7.

[125] Ibid. 573–4: 'over een baije die hij teghens de kuere heeft in de vaerwe ghedaen tegens de sententie der loijers, waer over hij in de boete ghecondamneirt es'; *Archives*, 221.

[126] Thetford, King's Ho. Boro. Recs vol. 1 p. 110 (fo. 56); Nfk RO, Cty Recs. Strangers Bk fo. 91.

[127] Hessels, *Archives*, 1.

[128] Hessels, *Archivum*, iii, 366.

[129] Lichfield Jt RO, Cons. Ct O.W. Jn Showell 1599, Th. Smyth 1603; PRO, SPD Eliz. 253/5.

[130] Posthumus, *Bronnen*, iii, 564, 576, 578, 594, 615, 634–5, 637–8, 640, 661, 663; iv, 284; v, 457–60; *Geschiedenis*, ii, 332.

[131] *APC* xxiii, 349–50; xxix, 646–7, 737; BL, Lans. 26 no. 56 fo. 147; inf. 144.

[132] Hessels, *Archivum*, iii, 777: 'Onse baaij ende saij neeringhe, als in ander Duutsche Kerken, is een Gouvernement over der selver Draperie.'

[133] Ibid. 510–11, 573–4, 607–8.

[134] Ibid.607–8, retranslated fr. 'die wij nochtan als papisten voor eenen gruwel hebben'.

[135] *APC* xxxiii, 239–40; 1615–16 pp. 381–2, 420–3; 1630–1 p. 200; PRO, SPD Jas 129/70; Chas 161/81; 206/58; Nfk RO, Cty Recs. Strangers Bk fo. 25; Stat 12 Chas 2 c.22.

[136] PRO, Exch. KR Deps by Commn 15 Jas Mich. 31 mm. 2–3(1–2).

[137] Hessels, *Archivum*, iii, 867–8, 871–2, 875.

[138] *APC* xix, 127; xxii, 444; xxiii, 76–7; PRO, SPD Eliz. 146/63; Emmison, *Home, Wk & Ld*, 77, 196, 307–8.

[139] BL, Lans. 71 no. 51 fo. 107 (108)v.

[140] A. F. J. Brown 149. Fr. of later Colc. baize may be seen in Hollytrees Mus. there.

[141] D. W. Jones 572; Dunsford 31–2, 171–2; BL, Harl. 5827 fo. 9(7)v.

[142] HMC, *Downshire MSS*, ii, 336; Chanter 100; Chanter & Wainwright ii, 56, 79, 259; Gribble 542–3; Slee 214–16; Cash 44, 64–5, 88; Stephens, *Exeter*, 3, 10, 28–30, 67, 104, 125; 'Ply.', 128, 131; 'Trade Pt Bpl. at end Civ. War', *Devon & Corn. N. & Q.*, 1970 xxxi, 167, 170; Alexander & Hooper 168; Bourhis i, 97; E. B. Schumpeter 70; S. R. Gardiner, *Parl. Debates in 1610*, Camd. S. 1862 lxxxi, 159; McGrath, *Merchs*, 267–8; Westcote 61; Willan, *Coasting Trade*, 94–5; BL, Lans. 71 no. 51 fo. 107(108)v.; Bpl. N. Devon Athenaeum, Bpl. Boro. Recs vol. 2 no. 3972 Recr's Accts 1389–1643 m. 124.

[143] Shrewsbury Lib. MS 4274 Ords etc. Weavers' Co. agrt 9 Nov. 1600.

[144] Soms. RO, Arch. Taunton inv. 1667/78; *Cal. SPD*, 1611–18, p. 206.

[145] Latimer, *Ann. Brist. 17th cent.*, 40–1; Brist. RO, Cons. Ct inv. Th. Cornock 1641 Temple par.; cf. Ramsay, *O'sea Trade*, 139–40.

[146] Tupling 169, 185; Wadsworth & Mann 13, 46; Lancs. RO, Cons. Ct Cestr. inv. Supra 1675 Jn Gregory/Rochdale; PRO, Exch. KR Deps by Commn 26 Chas 2 East. 15 mm. 2, 6; 33 Chas 2 Mich. 33 mm. 2 sqq.; Willan, *Inld Trade*, 109.

[147] PRO, SPD Eliz. 106/47; 250/47; Eliz. Add. 11/113.

[148] Ibid.Eliz. 106/47; BL, Lans. 27 no. 66 fos. 148–9; 71 no. 51 fo. 107(108)v.; cf. Thornton 151–2; Sudbury, Tn Recs. Bk Proc. Boro. Ct 6 (1640–72), 1648 entry.

[149] BL, Lans. 71 no. 51 fo. 107 (108)v.; Plot, *Oxon.*, 278–9; PRO, SPD Eliz. 146/63; Jas 26/1; Nfk RO, Cty Recs. Strangers Bk fo. 91; W.Sfk RO, Ep. Commy Ct Bury inv. 1686/92.

[150] Hessels, *Archivum*, iii, 608; *Clothiers Complt*, 1692, pp. 2, 17–19; *Rsns Decay Clo. Trade*, 1691, pp. 2, 3.

[151] Espinas & Pirenne i, 331, 333; PRO, SPD Chas 355/10.

[152] PRO, SPD Eliz. Add. 33/71; BL, Lans. 114 no. 24 fo. 92v.

[153] PRO, SPD Chas 355/10; Posthumus & De Nie 212 sqq.

[154] Nfk RO, Cty Recs. Strangers Bk fo. 108.

[155] Edwards 29.

[156] Nfk RO, Con. Ct inv. 1629/134; W. Sfk RO, Ep. Commy Ct Bury inv. 1662/115.

[157] Ibid.210.

[158] Ibid. 1665/97.

[159] E. Sfk RO, Arch. inv. 3/45.

[160] W. Sfk RO, Ep. Commy Ct Bury inv. 1667/1.

[161] Ibid. 1666/81.

[162] Ibid. 1667/13.

[163] Ibid. 1686/15.

[164] PRO, PCC parch. invs p. 1660 no. 8752.

[165] Ibid. no. 7906.

[166] Ess. RO, Pec. Ct Bocking inv. no. 223.

[167] Ibid. no no.

[168] Ess. RO, Notebks Jos. Bufton of Coggeshall 1663–1710 no. 14: Rider's *Brit. Merlin*, f. 1668, used by Sam. Sparhawke f. rough accts.

[169] BL, Lans. 26 no. 62 fo. 182(164)v.; no. 64 fo. 187; 71 no. 51 fo. 107(108)v.; PRO, SPD Chas 355/10, 144.

[170] Tupling 181; Wadsworth & Mann 282; Newbigging 211–12.

[171] Posthumus, *Bronnen*, v, 12, 13.

[172] *C.J.*, xviii, 705. I thank Miss J. de L. Mann f. this ref.

[1173] Warner 400; E. Sfk RO, Arch. inv. 16/71; Nfk RO, Cons. Ct inv. 1634/195.

[174] *VCH Dors.*, ii, 361–2; Defoe, *Compl. Engl. Tradesman*, 79; Mann, *Cl. Ind.*, 125; Hants. RO, unclass. invs D/2/A: 2/178; PRO, PCC invs 1718–82 bdl. 35 no. 75; Munn 5; cf. Gribble 544; Suppa s.v. tessute flannella molto fine.

[175] W. Sfk RO, Ep. Commy Ct Bury inv. 1707/81.

[176] E. Sfk RO, Arch. inv. 16–71; Munn 5; Cty Lond. RO, Ct Orphs invs box 4, Edm. Fabian 1668.

[177] Postlethwayt i, 224; Fiennes 236; Hessels, *Archivum*, iii, 2518; *APC*, 1625–6 p. 402; J. Crofts, *Packhorse, Waggon & Post*, 1967, pp. 73, 130, 142; Piccope liv, p. 2; H. Verney, *L. P. Verney Fam. down to end yr 1639*, Camd. S. 1853 lvi, 273; Brist. RO, Cons Ct inv. 1662/31; Nfk RO, Cons. Ct inv. 1592/100; Guildhall Lib. Commy Ct Lond. (Lond. Div.) inv. box 2 Th. Soper 1665 St And's, Holborn; PRO, SPD Eliz. Add. 37/60.

[178] Ibid. Jas 15/15.

[179] Fiennes 142–3.

[180] A. F. J. Brown 148.

[181] Fiennes 142; W. Sfk RO, Ep. Commy Ct Bury inv. 1686/92.

[182] Slee 214.

[183] Kent RO, Sandwich Recs L. Bl. Bk fo. 192; Ld & W. Treas's Draft Accts 1574–5 pp. 4–6; 1585–6 pp. 7 sqq.

[184] Cant. Cath. Lib. Cty Recs. Chamb's Accts 1568–77 fos. 339–40, 384; 1577–87 fos. 23v.–4, 71, 112–13, 205, 258, 307v., 357, 405, 454; 1587–92 fos. 25, 64, 104v.–5, 150v., 151v., 199; 1592–1602 fos. 25(26)v., 91(26)v., 147v.–8, 191v., 232, 276, 321v.–2, 374v., 423, 473; 1602–10 fos. 17v., 18, 68, 110, 151, 190v., 282, 330.

[185] Nfk RO, Cty Recs. Duties fos. 1 sqq., 63–4, 65v., 66v., 67v., 68v., 69v., 70v.; Alnage Accts 1580–1610 (fr. 22 July 1580 to 22 July 1586); N. J. Williams, '2 Docs con. N. Draperies', *Econ. Hist. Rev.*, 2nd ser. 1952 iv, 355–6 has but a few minor errors.

[186] PRO, SPD Eliz. 146/63.

[187] Burley, thes. 114, 114a, 314, 317; Willan, *Coasting Trade*, 93–4.

[188] Notestein et al. iii, 373; v, 506, 514, 526; Stephens, *Exeter*, 29, 67; 'Ply.', 131; Bpl. N. Devon Athenaeum, Bpl. Boro. Recs. vol. 10 no. 3980 Sess. Ct Recs. 1661–7, 8 Jan. 17 Chas 2; BL, Lans. 71 no. 51 fo. 107(108)v.; cf. Gribble 543.

[189] Woodward, *Trade Eliz. Chester*, 13; Stephens, 'Chester', 25; PRO, SPD Eliz. 253/5.

[190] Nfk RO, Cty Recs. Duties fos. 1 sqq., 63–4, 65v., 66v., 67v., 68v., 69v., 70v.; PRO, Exch. KR Accts Var. bdl. 347 no. 19; cf. D. W. Jones 568, 575–6.

[191] PRO, SPD Eliz. 253/122.

[192] Pilgrim, thes. 203–4, 205a, b, d, 206–7.

[193] Smith, *Mems Wl*, ii, 153–4.

[194] BL, Lans. 846 fo. 284(254).

[195] Posthumus, *Geschiedenis*, iii, 1188–91.

[196] Flint. RO, Soughton Hall MS 1169: pattern sample flannel ellbroads 1680; cf. Stat. 4 Jas c.2.

[197] G. L. Fairs, *Hist. Hay*, Lond. & Chich. 1972, p. 69; *Winthrop Papers*, iii, 161; Nichols, *Unton Invs*, 11; Pococke ii, 15; Evelyn iv, 141; Defoe, *Compl. Engl. Tradesman*, 79; J. H. Matthews, *Cardiff Recs*, 6 vols. Cardiff 1898–1911, iii, 415.

[198] Nichols, *Invs Wardrobe*, 94; Du Cange, *Glossarium Mediae et Infimae Latinitatis*, s.v. flamineum; cf. Wilhelmsen 46; Jenkins, *W. Woollen Ind.*, 112.

[199] PRO, SPD Eliz. 250/76; Boys 742; E. Hasted, *Hist. & Topog. Svy Co. Kent*, 4 vols. Cant. 1778–1799, iv, 252; Coleman, thes. 188.

[200] Kent RO, Cons. Ct Cant. Reg. Accts & Invs 6 fo. 372v.; E. A. Lewis 40; Hakluyt, *Prin. Navs.*, iii, 269; Stats 23 Eliz. c.9; 4 Jas c.2; Tawney & Power iii, 200.

[201] Ibid.; Mann, *Cl. Ind.*, 43; *VCH Wilts.*, iv, 159; *Lancs.*, ii, 378; Mendenhall 223; Newbigging 209; Tupling 181, 183; W. de G. Birch 251; Gribble 542, 544; Eden iii, 752; R. Hine, *Hist. Beaminster*, Taunton 1914, p. 306; E. R. Horsfall-Turner, *Mun. Hist. Llanidloes*, Llanidloes 1908, p. 221; Skeel, 'W. Woollen Ind. 16th & 17th cents.', 226–7; BL, Add. 26774 fo. 50; Sloane 2902 fo. 137(135)v.; G. Williams, *Glam. Co. Hist.*, vol. iv Cardiff 1974 iv, 339; Soms. RO, Arch. Taunton inv. Ric. Spreat 1697 Taunton St Mary Magd.; Hants. RO, Arch. Ct O.W. & Invs Stephen Sibley 1691 Romsey; Wilts. RO, Arch. Ct Sarum. Jas Stantiall 1718 Melksham, Jos. Chub 1725 Downton; Aikin 248.

[202] Inf. 123.

[203] J. Child, *Br. Obs. con. Trade & Int. Money*, 1668, p. 7; Suppa s.v. tessuto flannella; Gribble 542, 544; Slee 215; Soms. RO, Arch. Taunton inv. Ric. Spreat 1697 Taunton St Mary Magd.; Munn 5.

[204] R. Benson & H. Hatcher, *O. & N. Sarum* (being vol. iv of R. C. Hoare, *Hist. Mod. Wilts.*, 6 vols. 1822–44), pp. 342, 579; Defoe, *Compl. Engl. Tradesman*, 77, 79; *Tour*, i, 189; *VCH Wilts.*, iv, 159; Slack 67–9; Pococke ii, 135; Haskins 94–5, 382; N. J. Williams, *Tradesmen in Early Stuart Wilts.*, Wilts. Rec. S., 1959 xv, 43; Suppa s.v. Salisbury white; PRO, PCC invs. 1718–82 bdl. 35 no. 75; Wilts. RO, Arch Ct Sub-dean Sarum. O.W. etc. 1713/19; 1714/6; Bodl. Aubrey 2 fos. 64, 142a; Postlethwayt ii, 836.

[205] Ibid. i, 633; ii, 289, 292; E. A. Lewis 40; Fairs 215, 296–7; Mendenhall 28, 214, 225; Defoe, *Compl. Engl. Tradesman*, 77–9; *Tour*, ii, 75; Tawney & Power iii, 200; Pococke ii, 20, 29, 210; C. A. J. Skeel, 'W. Woollen Ind. in 18th & 19th cents.', *Arch. Camb.* 1924 lxxix, 14; Clark *Mon.* i, 140; Horsfall-Turner 221, 244–5; Jenkins, *Wl Text. Ind.*, 286, 288–90: 'Woollen Ind. Montgoms.', 52, 54, 58–9; D. J. Evans, 'Drapers Shrewsbury & Welshpool Flannel Trade in 17th cent.', *Montgoms. Colls*, 1951–2 lii, 23 sqq.; E. P. Williams, 'Early Victorian Denbigh', *Denbighs. Hist. S. Trs*, 1973 xxii, 248; W. Davies 392–3; W. J. Smith, *Herbert Corr.*, Cardiff 1963, p. 226; HMC, *14th Rep.*, App. pt. vi, 42; Armour 37, 187, 260; PRO, SPD Eliz. 250/34; Aberystwyth, Ep. Cons. Ct St Asaph, O. W., Admons & Invs Th. Price 1661 Wrexham; Lodovick Lloyd gent. 1668 Gwested in Llanllwchaiarn; Ric. Paine 1668 Oswestry; Th. Price 1710 Broughton; cf. Gough 38, 47–8, 64, 78, 104, 143, 147, 149–50, 154.

[206] E. A. Lewis pp. ix, 164, 177, 182, 209; R. B. Westerfield, *Middlemen in Engl. Bus. 1660–1760*, Trs Conn. Acad. Arts & Sci., New Haven 1915 xix, p. 257; Woodward, *Trade Eliz. Chester*, 7; Bodl. Rawlinson A.478 fo. 7v.; Aberystwyth, Ep. Cons. Ct St Asaph, O.W., Admons & Invs Foulke Foulkes 1660 Denbigh; *Cal. Wynne Papers*, 190; Vanes, *Docs*, 9; inf. 147.

[207] W. Davies 394, 405; Horsfall-Turner 244; Fairs 213, 223; Jenkins, *W. Woollen Ind.*, 5, 6, 8; W. Marshall, Redhead & Laing, *Obs. on Diff. Breeds Sheep*, Edin. 1792, pp. 14, 15.

[208] PRO, SPD Jas 80/13; BL, Lans. 152 fos. 227–8 (238–9); cf. Skeel, '16th & 17th cents.', 236, 257.

[209] *A Short View of the Busines betweene the Clothier and Merchant of the Staple of Engld*, 1647, pp. 3, 4.

[210] Shak. *M.W.W.*, act v, sc. 5.

[211] Inf. 123.

[212] PRO, Exch. KR Deps by Commn 15 Jas Mich. 31 mm. 2(1)r., 3(2)r., 4(3)r., 7.

[213] De Sagher i, 194–7, 200, 205–6, 221–3, 332–5, 435 sqq., 443, 449 sqq., 465–7, 469, 474, 476 sqq.; ii, 314, 319 sqq., 327, 332, 334–6, 560, 606, 617, 619, 655–6; iii, 66, 69, 98–9, 216–18, 263, 312, 373, 398, 416, 418, 421, 604; Posthumus, *Bronnen*, iii, 517, 537, 608; iv, 335; v, 540; *Geschiedenis*, ii, 318; Vanhaeck ii, 142, 144; Coornaert, *Hondschoote*, 26; Van Dillen, *Bronnen*, ii, 181–2.

[214] Goris 252; Doren i, 97, 506 sqq.; Davidsohn vol. iv, pt ii, 69.

[215] Nfk RO, Cons. Ct inv. 1591/154; W. Sfk RO, Ep. Commy Ct Bury inv. 1682/156; PRO, PCC parch. invs p. 1660 no. 580; Exch. KR, Deps by Commn 15 Jas Mich. 31 m. 7r.

[216] Ibid. m. 4(3)r.

[217] Ibid. 44 & 45 Eliz. Mich. 1 mm. 1, 3r.; SPD, Eliz. 77/58; Nfk RO, Cty Recs. Bk Mayor's Ct 8

pp. 546, 548; 15 fo. 488; 16 fo. 463v.; Strangers Bk fos. 19, 25–7, 33, 34v., 36v.–8; Orders con. Wl
fos. 10v., 16v., 17v., 18v., 28; Keure fos. 10v., 17v., 18, 19, 31; Duties fos. 1, 3, 46v.; Cons. Ct inv.
1591/154; Moens, *Norwich*, 265; Hessels, *Archivum*, iii, 41–2; *CPR*, Eliz. iii, 209–10; BL, Add.
12504 no. 63; Lans. 26 no. 57 fo. 161(149).

[218] PRO, Exch. KR Deps by Commn 15 Jas Mich. 31 mm. 2(1)r., 3(2), 4(3)r., 7, 14r.

[219] Ibid. m. 3(2)r.; SPD Eliz. 43/19, 20; PCC parch. invs p. 1660 no. 4625; Cant. Cath. Lib.
Cty Recs. Chamb's Accts 1602–10 fo. 68; F. J. C. & D. M. Hearnshaw, *Ct Leet Recs*, 4 pts Soton
Rec. S. 1905–8 i, pt i, 106; HMC, *11th Rep.*, App. pt iii, 95; Smit ii, 856; Posthumus, *Bronnen*, v,
37.

[220] Ibid. iii, 133, 514, 517, 532, 537, 602–3; iv, 335, 449, 465–6; v, 18, 540; *Geschiedenis*, ii,
318; Cole ii, 577, 579; Smith, *Mems Wl*, ii, 436 sqq., 444, 452; Coornaert, *Hondschoote*, 191.

[221] B. Dietz 106; inf. 133.

[222] PRO, Exch. KR Deps by Commn 15 Jas Mich. 31 m. 3(2)r.; BL, Lans. 26 no. 58 fo.
164(151); no. 59 fos. 175v.–6(158v.–9); no. 60 fo. 178(160); no. 62 fo. 181(163)v.; no. 64 fo. 187.

[223] De Sagher i, 205–6; ii, 327; Smith, *Mems Wl*, ii, 412, 422, 425, 435–7, 439, 450, 454;
Posthumus, *Bronnen*, vi, 3, 5–8, 328–9, 388, 508, 516–7; *Geschiedenis*, ii, 320; Cole ii, 377–8, 577–9;
Deyon 174; Monceau, *Art de Friser*, 5.

[224] Burton 180.

[225] BL, Harl. 1878 fo. 101(85); Lans. 26 no. 58 fo. 164(151); no. 59 fos. 175v.–6(158v.–9); no.
60 fo. 178(160); no. 62, fo. 181(163)v.; no. 64 fo. 187; Nfk RO, Cty Recs. N. Drapery in Norwich;
PRO, SPD Eliz. 249/20; 250/76; Req. 157/134 fo. 83(9).

[226] Goris 252; Botero 56; Dallington 34; M. Battistini, *La Confrérie de Ste-Barbe des Flamands
à Florence*, Brux. 1931, pp. 87, 94, 101 sqq., et pass.; De Roover, *Bus.*, 95–8, 101, 113; G. Coniglio,
'Agricoltura ed Artigianato Mantovano nel secolo XVI' in *Studi in Onore di A. Fanfani*, 343, 353; F.
Edler, *Gloss. Med. Terms Bus.*, It. ser. 1200–1600 Cam. Mass. 1934, pp. 238, 280, 413 sqq.

[227] Ibid. 238; Munn 5; Coornaert, *Hondschoote*, 14; Bahr 150; De Sagher ii, 90; Guicciardini
120; Posthumus, *Geschiedenis*, ii, 318; Hants. RO, Cons. Ct O.W. & Invs Sam. Hoopper 1630
Soton; PRO, Exch. KR Deps by Commn 15 Jas Mich. 31 m. 7r.; SPD Eliz. 250/47.

[228] Ibid.; Exch. KR Accts Var. bdl. 347 no. 19; Guicciardini 120; Lamb 57; Hants. RO, Cons.
Ct O.W. & Invs Pet. Symens 1628 (1617) Soton.

[229] Ibid. Sam. Hoopper 1630 Soton; Arch. Ct O.W. & Invs Stephen Sibley 1691 Romsey; Jn
Dawkins sr 1720 Romsey Infra; Bodl. Arch. Ct Berks O.W. etc. 192/159; PRO, PCC parch. invs p.
1660 no. 4625; BL, Add. 26774 fo. 49v.

[230] BL, Add. 12504 no. 63; PRO, Exch. KR Accts Var. bdl. 347 no. 19; Req. 157/134 fo.
83(9); Nfk RO, Cty Recs. Strangers Bk fos. 17, 19.

[231] Cant. Cath. Lib. Cty Recs. Chamb's Accts 1592–3 fo. 26(27); Cowper, *Cant. Mar. Lics*,
cols 123, 336, 441.

[232] Friis 452; Hovenden 752; PRO, SPD Jas 15/17; Chas 378/40.

[233] Ibid. Jas 104/53, 97; Chas 189/40; Bacon 468; Fuller, *Worthies*, i, 494; Blome 211–12;
D. H. Allen, *Ess. Q. Sess. Ord. Bk 1652–61*, Chelmsford 1974, p. 3; Thornton 192, 202, 204;
A. G. H. Hollingsworth, *Hist. Stowmarket*, Ips. & Lond. 1844, p. 98; Nfk RO, Con. Ct invs 1626/
119; 1666/77; Ess. RO, Bp Lond's Commy Ct f. Ess. & Herts. Regs Wills 12 fo. 111; 13 fos. 71, 480;
14 fo. 75; Arch. Ct Colc. Regs Wills 9 fo. 212; 10 fo. 127; 11 fo. 43; 12 fos. 45, 128; Arch. Ct Mx
(Ess. & Herts. Div.) Reg. Wills 12 fo. 45; W. Sfk RO, Acc. 960 no. 73; MS 530/16; Ep. Commy Ct
Bury invs. 1647–8/41; 1650/80; 1662/115, 182, 210; 1665/22, 97; 1667/136; 1668/35, 78; 1670/174;
1675/105; 1677/87; 1682/14, 31, 156; 1686/100; 1692/9, 18; 1700/42; 1701/16, 87; 1705/92.

[234] Ibid. 1661/1.

[235] Ibid. 1660/170.

[236] Ibid. 189.

[237] Ibid. 1652/80; 1662/115; 1665/97; 1666/109; 1667/23, 38, 136; 1668/173; 1676/60; 1677/
145; 1682/156; 1686/79; 1688/7; 1696/91; cf. 1666/50.

[238] Ibid. 1660/189; 1661/115; 1666/50; 1667/136; 1677/145.

[239] Fiennes 231; Worcs. RO, Cons. Ct O.W. etc. 1712 Obad. Spencer; 1716 Stephen Lea er; 1717 Ed. Parrins; 1718 Wm Fereday; 1720 Abr. Jevons, Jn Williams.

[240] PRO, PCC parch. invs p. 1660 no. 3431.

[241] Pilgrim, thes. 204, 206; PRO, SPD Chas 189/40; W. Sfk RO, Ep. Commy Ct Bury invs 1660/170; 1661/1; 1664/34; 1665/22; 1667/38, 136; 1668/35; 1677/145; 1686/79; Acc. 960 no. 73.

[242] Kirby 264, 267; Postlethwayt ii, 765; Defoe, *Tour*, i, 48; Posthumus, *Bronnen*, v, 40, 159; *Geschiedenis*, ii, 260, 322; PRO, Chanc. Jud. Proc. (Eq. side) Chanc. Mrs' Docs. Exhibs. Mr Tinney nos. 17–19 bks 1, 6, 12, 15, 16, 18, 21, 25, 28, 31.

[243] *N. & Q.*, 4th ser. 1871 viii, 259; a little may also have been made in Rye – J. S. Cockburn, *Cal. Assize Recs: Kent Indictments Eliz.*, 1979, p. 238.

[244] Somner 175; *APC*, xxxiii, 8.

[245] Kent RO, Cons. Ct Cant. Reg. Accts & Invs 7 fos. 227, 270v.; Cant. Cath. Lib. Cty Recs. Burghmote Bk 1542–78 fo. 286; Chamb's Accts 1592–1602 fos. 191v., 232, 276, 321v., 374v., 423; 1602–10 fos. 17v., 18.

[246] Hants. RO, Cons. Ct O.W. & Invs 1623 Jn Pawlmer; 1626 Robt Parker; 1628 Pet. Symens; 1630 Sam.' Hoopper; 1642 Wr Barling – all of Soton; 1628 Ric. Hollis gent. Newport; Arch. Ct O.W. & Invs 1647 Robt Zanies/Soton; 1691 Stephen Sibley/Romsey; PRO, PCC parch. invs p. 1660 no. 4625; SPD Eliz. 127/80; *N. & Q.*, 4th ser. 1871 viii, 259; Moens, *Norwich*, 265; *VCH Hants.*, v, 424; HMC, *11th Rep.*, App. pt iii, 27, 95; *APC*, xxxii, 347–8; Wiggs 76, 85; Hearnshaw ii, 278; J. Rutherford, *Misc. Papers Capt. Th. Stockwell 1590–1611*, 2 vols. Soton Rec. S. 1932–3, i, 12, 33–4, 116; A. B. W. Chapman, *Bl. Bk Soton*, vol. iii idem 1915 pp. xv, xviii; J. W. Horrocks, *Ass. Bks Soton*, 4 vols. idem 1917–25, i, 15, 61, 64, 85, 95; ii, pp. xv, 11, 12, 18, 20, 31, 37, 42, 48, 50, 69, 94; iii, 10, 16, 36, 40–1, 46, 77, 82, 92; iv, 2, 19, 40–1, 47; G. H. Hamilton, *Bks Exams & Deps 1570–94*, idem 1914, pp. 115, 117, 147; R. C. Anderson, *Bk Exams 1601–2*, idem 1926, p. 19; *Bk Exams & Deps 1622–44*, i, 17, 26, 58, 62; ii, 15, 61, 69, 117.

[247] Ibid. i, 48; *APC*, xxvii 9, 10; *Rates Marchandizes*, s.v. rashes vocat. cloth-rashes; *Rates Merchandizes*, 86; Bodl. Rawlinson A.478 fo. 100v. (p. 195); Notestein et al. vii, 252; PRO, PCC parch. invs p. 1660 no. 4625; Coke, *2 Inst.*, 62; *Disc. f. Enl. & Freedome of Trade*, 29; Lamb 57, 224 sqq., 230–2, 234, 236 sqq., 243–6, 248, 252–3, 255 sqq., 261–2, 266–8, 270 sqq., 278, 373, 376, 381–2.

[248] A. J. Patterson, *Hist. Soton 1700–1914*, vol. i Soton 1966, p. 5.

[249] R. G. H. Whitly, *Ct Taunton in 16th & 17th cents.*, Taunton 1934, p. 80; Glouc. Lib. Smyth of Nibley MSS S.Z.23.2 no. 4; inf. 119.

[250] Soms. RO, Arch. Taunton invs. 1642/41; 1670/25; 1675 Robt Quears (Kewers) Creech; 1678/69.

[251] Ibid. 1638/24.

[252] Ibid. 1640/83.

[253] Ibid. 1644/70, 70a.

[254] Ibid. 1647–9/8.

[255] Ibid. 1667/46; 1670/25, 70; 1671 no no.; 1675 no no.; 1678/69; 1697 no nos.; 1730–1 no no.; PRO, PCC parch. invs p. 1660 nos. 8300, 10452 respectively.

[256] Soms. RO, Arch. Taunton inv. 1681/90.

[257] Ibid. 1690 no no.

[258] Ibid. 1691 no no.

[259] Ibid. 1699 fr., no no.

[260] PRO, PCC parch. invs p. 1660 no. 8661.

[261] Et. v. ibid. no. 6912; A. H. Powell 266; Soms. RO, Cons. Ct Bath & Well. bd & inv. Th. Barber 1676 W. Buckland; Arch. Taunton invs. 17th cent. fr. Taunton St Mary Magd.; 1642/41; 1647–9/49; 1666 Robt Band/N. Petherton; 1667/7; 1668/59; 1669/99; 1675 David Tuxwell sr Cannington; 1688 Lewes Pollard/ Holford; 1690 Jos. Lewis/Staplegrove; 1691 Jn Glasse/

Charlinch; 1695 Th. Waterman/Bridgwater; 1697 Hy Turner/id.; 1714–15 Robt Ducke/Fiddington; 1725/19 Mary Winter wid. Stogursey; DD/ TW9/1; Fuller, *Worthies*, iii, 88; Blome 199; *N. & Q. Soms. & Dors*, 1911 xii, 352; W. G. Hoskins, *Ind., Trade & People in Exeter 1688–1800*, Man. 1935, p. 38.

[262] J. H. Fox, *Woollen Manuf. at Well.*, 1914, f. p. 4; Stephens, *Exeter*, 134; J. James 231; Defoe, *Compl. Engl. Tradesman*, 78–9; *Cal. SPD*, 1655–6 pp. 260–1; T. Fuller, *Church-Hist. Brit.*, 1655, p. 112; Lancs. RO, Cavendish of Holker Coll. 1/46 pp. 48, 51, 54; PRO, SPD Interreg. 39/65; PCC parch. invs p. 1660 nos. 6886, 6912, 8300, 8662; Mx RO, Arch. Ct Mx inv. Jn Hoptkins 1673 St Clem. Danes; Soms. RO, Arch. Taunton invs 17th cent. fr. Taunton St Mary Magd.; 1644/70, 70a; 1667/7, 46; 1668/59; 1669/99; 1670/25, 29; 1671 Th. Hessom/Taunton St Jas; 1678/69; 1681/90; 1690 Agnes Pollard/Holford, Jos. Lewis/Staplegrove; 1697 Jane Bond/ Taunton St Mary Magd.; 1726–7/2 Wm Bowden/Minehead; 1730–1 Nic. Gooding/Monksilver.

[263] Ibid. 1681/90; 1695 Sam. Satchell/Taunton St Jas; 1725/19 Mary Winter wid. Stogursey; Haynes, *Clo. Trade*, 13: Fox, f. p. 4.

[264] Ibid.; Postlethwayt ii, 743; Collinson iii, 13, 226; J. James 265; A. L. Humphreys, *Mtls f. Hist. Tn & Par. Well.*, 4 pts 1908–14, pp. 66, 74, 82, 86, 101–3, 112, 116, 121, 338, 346, 623 sqq.

[265] *C.J.*, xxvii, 732; Tann 202; *VCH Glos.*, x, 296; Glos. RO, Marcham Coll. F26; Glouc. Lib. Smyth of Nibley MSS S.Z.23.2 nos. 4, 5; Smyth of Nibley Papers vol. viii, pp. 28, 30, 42.

[266] *APC*, xxxii, 347–8; Bourhis i, 97; A. H. A. Hamilton, *Q. Sess. fr. Q. Eliz. to Q. Anne*, 1878, p. 27; *VCH Soms.*, iv, 235; Stephens, *Exeter*, 135; Devon RO, Huntsham MS PZ1.

[267] Westcote 60–1; & v. 121.

[268] Ibid. 61; Devon RO, Huntsham MS PZ1; cf. Pococke i, 141.

[269] Wilts. RO, Pec. Ct Dean Sarum. Hy Bryant 1698, Jn Hutchings 1755 (sergeweavers), Ed. Skinner 1731, Th. Marsh 1773 (sergemakers), Jn Starke clothier 1682; Preb. Ct Uffculme bdl. 4 no. 19; ex Dioc. Reg. Sarum. Jn Gay jr clothier 1685.

[270] Stephens, *Exeter*, 49.

[271] Defoe, *Tour*, i, 221, 223, 233; Chapman, *Devon Cl. Ind.*, pass.; Cash 45–6, 126–7, 138–9, 143–6, 155–7; Blome 81–3; Alexander & Hooper 179; Slee 215; Gribble 542, 544; Postlethwayt i, 571; G. W. Hilton, *Tr. Syst.*, Cam. 1960, p. 75; *C.J.*, xii, 79; xvi, 72–4, 92, 99, 117, 120, 554, 595; J. Cock, *Recs Antient Boro. S. Molton*, S. Molton 1893, p. 133; Fuller, *Worthies*, i, 396; Hoskins, *Exeter*, 29; Dunsford 226, 242; PRO, Exch. KR Deps by Commn 12 Chas East. 41; Soms. RO, DD/X/HRG Misc. deeds 1/4; DD/TW11/11, TW12/3; Arch. Taunton inv. Jn Thomas 1697 Brompton Regis.

[272] Stephens, *Exeter*, 4; Cash 44–6, 90, 143–6, 155–6; *APC*, xxxiii, 365; Westcote 61; Youings 72; Wilts. RO, Pec. Ct Dean Sarum, Jn Starke 1682 Uffculme; Preb. Ct Uffculme bdl. 4 no. 19; ex Dioc. Reg. Sarum. inv. Jn Gay jr 1685 Uffculme.

[273] Cash 156–7; Dunsford 55, 209.

[274] Ibid. 208; Cash 155–6; Devon RO, Huntsham MS PZ1; Wilts. RO, Pec. Ct Dean Sarum. Jn Starke 1682 Uffculme.

[275] Notestein et al. vii, 252.

[276] *VCH Hants.*, v, 424.

[277] Ramsay, *Wilts.*, 110–11; Mann, *Cl. Ind.*, 6, 33; *VCH Wilts.*, x, 256; C. Dale 26, 115, 148; Nevill xxviii, 54, 56; xxx, 126; xxxiii, 120, 122, 203; xxxvii, 217; Pococke ii, 49, 55, 130, 158; Williams, *Tradesmen*, 43; Postlethwayt i, 939; Haskins 95, 382; PRO, PCC parch. invs p. 1660 nos. 2719, 8548; invs 1718–82 bdl. 18 no. 187; 35 no. 30; Bodl. Arch. Ct Berks. 121/142; 214/94; Wilts. RO, Cons. Ct Sarum. Robt Scott 1660, Wm Sheppard 1665, Robt Willis 1685, Jn Slade 1687, Ric. Farmer & Hy Painter 1692, Robt Scott 1699, Jas Lewis 1701, Hy Galloway 1704, Jacob Lawrance 1708, Th. Slade 1722, all Devizes; Ed. Powell 1693 Marlborough; Pec. Ct Dean Sarum. Ric. Laurence 1703 Wokingham; Arch. Ct Sarum. Roger Marks 1682 L. Cheverell, Jos. Chubb 1725 Downton; Hants. RO, Cons. Ct O.W. & Invs, Elias Morringe 1635 Andover; Isaac Cooper 1642 id.; Jasper Co(a)tman 1646 N. Alresford; Jn Hicks 1671 Andover; Th. Eastman 1672 Alton; Arch. Ct

O.W. & Invs, Hy Watridge 1650 Alton; unclass. invs D/2/A:2/181; 3/240; Lancs. RO, Cavendish of Holker Coll. 1/46 fo. IV.

[278] Lisle 427.

[279] Mann, *Cl. Ind.*, 40; *VCH Wilts.*, iv, 159; Munn 5; Wilts. RO, Cons. Ct Sarum. Ric. Farmer & Hy Painter 1692 Devizes.

[280] Ibid. Arch. Ct Sarum. Jos. Chubb 1725 Downton; PRO, PCC invs 1718–82 bdl. 35 no. 30.

[281] Wilts. RO, Arch. Ct Wilts. Jn Reade 1698 Chippenham Langley.

[282] Ibid. Jn Beere 1684 Lacock; Wm Webb 1684 Hawkstreet in Bromham; Th. Gengell 1722 Malmesbury; Zeph. Fry yr 1717 Chippenham; Cons. Ct Sarum. Wm Fuller 1662 Marston in Potterne; Wm Robins 1683 Hedington; Wm Millard 1692 Holt in Brad.; Hy Tucker 1714 Bromham; Arch. Ct Sarum. Jn Markes 1678 Brad.; Wm Coombs 1709 Warminster; Hy Gowen 1712 Broughton Gifford; Jn Hodges 1716 Ashley in Brad.; Jas Stantiall 1718 Melksham; Robt Boyd 1730 Steeple Ashton; Pec. Ct Prec. & Chantor bdl. 16 no. 66; Pec. Ct Treas. box 3 nos. 22, 38; 4 nos. 20, 65; 7 no. 40; Pec. Ct Dean Sarum. Jn Neate er 1710 Calne; C. Dale 18, 146; Ramsay, *Wilts.* 110–11; Nevill xxxiii, 123, 203; *C.J.*, xvi, 595; *VCH Wilts.*, iv, 159; Mann, 'Wilts. Fam.', 245; *Cl. Ind.*, 6, 33.

[283] Ibid. 28, 33; Collinson i, 2nd pt, 18; Blome 198; Stephens, *Exeter*, 51; *VCH Dors.*, ii, 361–2; *Soms.* iv, 20, 65, 97, 153; Hine 306; Postlethwayt ii, 743; Skeel, '16th & 17th cents.', 227; Matthews ii, 174; iii, 415, 425; PRO, PCC parch. invs p. 1660 no. 6341 (cf. 7657); Wilts. RO, Preb. Ct Netherbury in Ecclesia bdl. 4 no. 26; 5 no. 19; 7 no. 21; 8 no. 32; 9 no. 36; Pec. Ct Dean Sarum, Roger Meade 1670 Yetminster; Wm Lacke er 1692, Jn Hearne 1695, Jn Hearne 1716, Benj. Nossiter 1737 – all Beaminster; cf. Ed. May 1615 Sherborne; G. Williams iv, 339; Soms. RO, DD/X/SND nos. 5, 7.

[284] Tann 202.

[285] Ibid.; *Glos. N. & Q.*, 1887 iii, 406; Mann, *Cl. Ind.*, 8; Blome 103–4; W. A. Shaw, *Ltrs Denization & Acts Naturalization f. Aliens in Engld & Ire. 1603–1700*, Pubs H.S.L. 1911 xviii, 344; Wilts. RO, Cons. Ct Sarum. Jn Andrewes 1673, Ric. Farmer 1692, both Devizes; Glos. RO, Cons. Ct invs 1663/249; 1667/74; 1684/255, 257; 1686/248; 1687/41; 1690/185; 1695/180; 1697/138; 1701/65; 1705/36; 1715/71; 1721/54; 1726/28; 1730/106A; 1731/73; 1735/59; 1751/37.

[286] Ibid. 1663/196, 249; 1682/11, 115; 1684/165; 1691/116; 1696/51; 1709/40.

[287] Ibid. 1663/249; 1682/54, 81; 1684/256; 1686/248; 1694/56; 1701/65; 1705/36; 1721/54.

[288] Ibid. 1695/152.

[289] *APC*, xxxii, 347–8; Hants. RO, Arch. Ct O.W. & Invs Robt Zaines (Zanies) 1647 Soton; PRO, PCC parch. invs p. 1660 no. 4625.

[290] Fuller, *Worthies*, i 494; Thornton 204; W.Sfk RO, Ep. Commy Ct Bury invs 1662/115; 1665/97; 1666/109; 1667/23, 38; 1668/173; 1675/21; 1676/49, 60; 1677/145; 1682/156.

[291] Postlethwayt ii, 765.

[292] H. of L. RO, H. of L. Papers 27 Jan. 1596–7 to 1 June 1607, fo. 135; Soms. RO, Arch. Taunton invs 1638/24; 1670/29; 1681/90; W. Sfk RO, Ep. Commy Ct Bury invs 1668/32; 1670/77; Hants. RO, Cons. Ct O.W. & Invs, Sam. Hoopper 1630 Soton; PRO, PCC parch. invs. p. 1660 no. 4625.

[293] Wilts. RO, Arch. Ct Wilts. Jn Beere 1684 Lacock.

[294] Dunsford 36.

[295] PRO, SPD Jas 128/74; Roberts, *Marchants Mapp*, 2nd pt, 189, 193 erron. 181.

[296] Hants. RO, Arch. Ct O.W. & Invs, Hy Watridge 1650 Alton.

[297] Ibid. Cons. Ct O.W. & Invs, Sam. Hoopper 1630 Soton; PRO, PCC parch. invs p. 1660 no. 4625.

[298] Wilts. RO, Pec. Ct Dean Sarum, Wm Lacke er 1692 Beaminster.

[299] Ibid. Arch. Ct Wilts. Jn Beere 1684 Lacock.

[300] Cash 126–7, 155–6.

[301] Soms. RO, Arch. Taunton invs 1638/24; 1670/29; 1681/90.

[302] W. Sfk RO, Ep. Commy Ct Bury invs 1668/32; 1670/77.

[303] Heaton 267 sqq.

[304] Devon RO, Huntsham MS PZ1.

[305] Westcote 60–1, 121; Dunsford 36, 201; Stephens, *Exeter*, 48–9.

[306] Ibid. 134; *C.J.*, xii, 37, 79; Smith, *Mems Wl*, i, 303–4; ii, 12, 18, 19, 22, 25; H. Horwitz, *Parl. Diary Narcissus Luttrell 1691–3*, Oxf. 1972, p. 116; *N. & Q. Soms. & Dors.*, 1911 xii, 352; Cullen, *Econ. Hist. Ire.*, 23, 32; Shaw, *1603–1700*, 338, 344, 348 sqq.; *APC*, 1615–16 p. 637; *Ltr fr. Gent. in Ire. to his bro. in Engld*, 1677, p. 11; *H. of L. MSS*, n.s. 1905 iii, 388; BL, Sloane 2902 fos. 136–7, 139(134–5, 137); Add. 4761 fo. 79; PRO, SPD Chas 2, 176/130; 373/249.

[307] Ibid. Chas 149/55; 285/28; 320/4; Soms. RO, Arch. Taunton invs 1668/59; 1670/70; 1671 Th. Hessom/Taunton St Jas; 1697 Jane Bond/Taunton St Mary Magd.; *APC*, xxxiii, 364–6; Stephens, *Exeter*, 10, 28–30, 66–7, 103–4, 108–11, 117–18, 120–1; 'Chester', 25; 'Ply.', 131; Bourhis i, 97; *Rates Marchandizes*, s.v. perpetuanoes; Roberts, *Marchants Mapp*, 2nd pt, 68, 76, 92, 207; McGrath, *Merchs*, 282; K. G. Davies, *R. Af. Co.*, 1957, pp. 176–7, 234, 352; Hinton 34–5, 114, 195; *Cal. SP Ven.*, xx, 355; Vanhaeck i, 228–9; ii, 141–3, 146; E. B. Schumpeter 35, 70; cf. Bang iiA, 322, 330–1, 344–6, 348, 350, 372, 379, 394, 403 sqq., 410, 437, 449, 460–2, 472–3, 483–4, 486, 488, 490, 493, 495, 497, 522, 532–3, 542–4, 552–3, 560, 562–3, 567, 594, 600, 606.

[308] Guildhall Lib. Commy Ct Lond. (Lond. Div.) invs 1 Reba Conye wid. 1669 Long La. St Sepulchre's; Mx RO, Arch. Ct Mx inv. Jn Hoptkins 1673 St Clem. Danes; Lichfield Jt RO, Cons. Ct O.W. Jn Foxley 1635 St Mich's, Cov.; Kent RO, Cons. Ct Cant. Inv. Paper 11/114.

[309] *Disc. f. Enl. & Freedome of Trade*, 28; May, *Decl. Este Clo.*, 32; W.S. *Golden Fleece*, 37; Misselden, *Free Trade*, 41, 101; Child, *Br. Obs.*, 7; Defoe, *Wks*, 541; Notestein et al. ii, 286, 290, 325–6, 393; iii, 46, 106, 326; iv, 175, 216; v, 73; vi, 72; vii, 156, 234; PRO, SPD Jas 121/34.

[310] Ibid. Chas 126/52; *APC*, xxxiii, 364–5; Westcote 60–1.

[311] Fiennes 246–7; Defoe, *Tour*, i, 222; Chapman, *Devon Cl. Ind.*, 62 sqq., 78 sqq., 86 sqq.; Stephens, *Exeter*, 78, 125, 135–7; Vanhaeck i, 228–9; ii, 141; PRO, SPD Chas 285/28; PCC paper invs 1661–1725 no. 3416.

[312] Westcote 60, 121; Hoskins, *Exeter*, 40.

[313] Posthumus, *Bronnen*, iv, 112–15, 120, 131, 135–7, 139, 142–5, 147, 155 (cf. 116–17, 122–4, 134; v, 41); Notestein et al. vii, 549–52; Campbell 201; Guildhall Lib. Commy Ct Lond. (Lond. Div.) invs box 2 Wm Owen (St Sepulchre's) & Jn Bird cit. & clwkr 1665.

[314] Glouc. Lib. Smyth of Nibley MSS S.Z.23.2 no. 4; & v. PRO, SPD Jas 98/81.

[315] *APC*, xxxiii, 364–5.

[316] B. Jons. *Cynthia's Revels*, act iii, sc. 2; Emmison, *Disorder*, 314.

[317] *Disc. f. Enl. & Freedome of Trade*, 28; Soms. RO, Arch. Taunton inv. Jos. Lewis 1690 Staplegrove; cf. APC, xxxiii, 364–5.

[318] May, *Decl. Este Clo.*, 32; W.S., *Golden Fleece*, 37.

[319] Misselden, *Free Trade*, 101; PRO, SPD Jas 120/95.

[320] Ibid. Chas 126/52.

[321] Ibid. Jas 96/40.

[322] Ibid. 121/34–5; 155/17; Notestein et al. ii, 286; iv, 216; v, 73; vii, 156, 234–5, 549–52; J. F. Larkin & P. L. Hughes, *Stuart R. Procls*, i Oxf. 1973, pp. 470–1.

[323] HMC, *Exeter Recs*, 166; Stephens, *Exeter*, 53–4.

[324] *APC*, xxxiii, 364–6.

[325] *APC*, xxxii, 347–8.

[326] Hants. RO, Arch. Ct O.W. & Invs Robt Zaines (Zanies) 1647 Soton; PRO, PCC parch. invs p. 1660 no. 4625; Lamb 57, 224, 227–8, 230–2, 234, 236–8, 242 sqq., 252–4, 256–9, 261, 265, 267–8, 271–2, 274–5, 279; Anderson, *Bk Exams & Deps*, i, 46, 48; Notestein et al. vii, 549–40.

[327] Glouc. Lib. Smyth of Nibley MSS S.Z.23.2 no. 5.

[328] HMC, *14th Rep.*, App. pt vi, 42; *Var. Colls*, viii, 590; Burley, thes. 314; Pilgrim, thes. 39; *Magna Brit. & Hib.*, i, 722; Stat. 13 Anne c.20 para. 19; *H. of L. MSS*, iii, 389; Defoe, *Tour*, i, 48;

Postlethwayt ii, 765; J. Child, *New Disc. Trade*, 1693, p. 133; Martin ii, 57; PRO, SPD Interreg. 182/
48; PCC parch. invs p. 1660 nos. 7906, 8752; cf. Coleman, *Banks*, 27.

[329] Kent RO, Cons. Ct Cant. Inv. Paper 12/31; Inv. Reg. 8 fo. 78; Cant. Cath. Lib. Wall. Recs.
Misc. Docs portf. 1 no. 41; W.S., *Golden Fleece*, 38; May, *Decl. Este Clo.*, 32.

[330] Glos. RO, Cons. Ct inv. 1663/196; Aberystwyth, Ep. Cons. Ct St Asaph, O.W., Admons &
Invs, Th. Platt jr 1667 Wrexham; H. F. Kearney, *Strafford in Ire.*, Man. 1959, p. 136; Ramsay, *O'sea
Trade*, 145; Bang iiA, 410, 436–7, 448, 460–2, 472–3, 483–4, 486, 488, 490, 493, 495; *Sels fr. Hsehld
Bks Ld Wm Howard of Naworth Cas.*, Surtees S. 1878 lxviii, 295; Chester RO, Tn Clk's Recs.
Protested Bills etc. fo. 20.

[331] C. Dale 16, 39, 84, 92, 96, 146, 169, 173; Defoe, *Tour*, i, 82, 271; *Plan*, 86–7; *VCH Wilts.*, x,
256; C. Wilson, *Anglo-Du. Comm. & Fin. in 18th cent.*, Cam. 1941, pp. 37–8; Fowle 27; Smith, *Mems
Wl*, ii, 205; Dunsford 55, 57, 209, 242; J. James 265; Mann, *Cl. Ind.*, 33, 40; 'Wilts. Fam.', 245, 247;
Cash 144–6, 155–6; Collinson i, 2nd pt, 18; iii, 13, 294; Pococke i, 141; Fox, f. p. 4; Postlethwayt ii,
743; PRO, PCC paper invs 1661–1725 no. 3416; parch. invs p. 1660 no. 8300; invs 1718–82 bdl. 24 no.
99; 27 no. 60; 35 no. 30; SPD Chas 2, 379/127; Soms. RO, DD/X/WES nos. 1, 3; Arch. Taunton inv.
1714–15 Th. Hellyer/Taunton St Jas; Wilts. RO, Pec. Ct Dean Sarum. Wm Pike 1731 Lyme Regis;
Wm Halle 1755 Calne; Pec. Ct Treas. box 3 no. 12; 6 nos. 33, 38; Preb. Ct Uffculme bdl. 4 no. 19; ex
Dioc. Reg. Sarum. inv. Jn Gay jr 1685 Uffculme; Arch. Ct Wilts. Zeph. Fry yr 1717 Chippenham;
Arch. Ct Sarum. Jas Stantiall 1718 Melksham; Jas Poole 1732 Brad.; Nat. Harris 1739 N. Bradley;
David Jefferies 1739 Wheatley in Melksham; Robt Rogers 1748 Atford in Brad.; Cons. Ct Sarum. Jn
Barnes 1723 Rowde in N. Bradley.

[332] Ibid. Hy Galloway 1704, Woolstan Edwards 1719, Th. Read 1724, Geo. Phillips 1725, Ric.
Phillips 1729, Jas Phillips 1733, Sam. Leach 1736, all Devizes; Hants. RO, unclass. invs D/2/A: 2/
181; PRO, PCC parch. invs p. 1660 no. 8548; invs 1718–82 bdl. 18 no. 187; 24 no. 180; 25 no. 84; 35
no. 30; Nfk RO, Cons. Ct invs 1694–6/43; 1703/110; J. James 229, 231; C. Dale 5, 23, 50–1, 60, 110,
113; Pococke i, 83; ii, 55, 130, 135; Martin i, 91, 117; Defoe, *Tour*, i, 142, 180–1, 280–1; *Compl. Engl.
Tradesman*, 11, 77–8; *Wks*, 544; Curtis 123; Postlethwayt i, 245, 939; ii, 836; *Reply Cardmakers*; *VCH
Hants.*, v, 487–8.

[333] Rath 141; Brist. RO, Cons. Ct inv. Th. Avery 1720 stuffmaker; Glos. RO, Cons. Ct inv.
1698/132.

[334] Ibid.; PRO, PCC parch. invs p. 1660 no. 8300; invs 1718–82 bdl. 18 no. 187; 24 no. 99; 35 no.
30; Hants. RO, unclass. invs D/2/A: 2/181; Soms. RO, Arch. Taunton inv. 1714–15 Th. Hellyer/
Taunton St Jas; Wilts. RO, Preb. Ct Uffculme bdl. 4 no. 19; Pec. Ct Dean Sarum. Wm Pike 1731
Lyme Regis; Cons. Ct Sarum. Jer. Braxton 1733 Devizes; Hy Galloway 1704 id.; Arch. Ct Sarum. Jas
Stantiall 1718 Melksham; Robt Rogers 1748 Atford in Brad.; Arch. Ct Wilts. Zeph. Fry yr 1717
Chippenham; Defoe, *Tour*, i, 281; *Compl. Engl. Tradesman*, 11, 78; Mann, 'Wilts. Fam.', 245, 247,
250; *VCH Wilts.*, iv, 159; Lisle 427; Cash 144–6, 155–6; Haynes, *G.B.'s Glory*, 6; *Clo. Trade*, 13;
Munn 5.

[335] Ibid.; Curtis 123.

[336] Defoe, *Compl. Engl. Tradesman*, 78; Ches. RO, Cons. Ct Cestr. Supra inv. Robt Taylor 1711
Chester; E. Sfk RO, Arch. inv. 23/40.

## Chapter 8

[1] Nfk RO, F. C. Recs. Wall. Ch. 5, 6.

[2] Ibid. Cty Recs. Bk Mayor's Ct 8 pp. 516–17; Cons. Ct inv. 1590/130; Hooper 199–202; Kirk ii,
114, 275–6, 339; Gill 12; J. D. Alsop, 'Immigrant Weaver's Inv. f. 1573', *Text Hist.*, 1983 xiv, 78–9;
Kent RO, Cons. Ct Cant. Inv. Regs 16 fo. 388; 20 fo. 567; Maidstone Recs. Burghmote Bk 3 fo. 5v. (p.
10); & v. Bk 4 fos. 14, 28, 51, 116v., 120v., 165v., 173, 179, 189v., 193, 220v., 233v.; Bk 5 fos. 6v., 8.

[3] Hants. RO, Cons. Ct O.W. & Invs Jn Pawlmer 1623 Soton; Mann, *Docs*, pp. xx, xxi, 152; *VCH
Soms.*, ii, 414.

[4] PRO, SPD Eliz. 250/76; Eliz. Add. 34/23.

[5] R. Davies 152; *VCH Durh.*, ii, 315; Harte 102; Pococke i, 57.

[6] Ibid. 9; J. James 202; Defoe, *Tour*, ii, 259–60; Woodward, *Trade Eliz. Chester*, 16; Aikin 158, 302; Wadsworth & Mann 14, 28; Postlethwayt i, 655; Harte 103; Worcs. RO, Cons. Ct O.W. etc. Hannah Griffiths 1720 Kidderminster; Nfk RO, Cons. Ct inv. 1674/33.

[7] Ibid.; Harte 103; Aikin 158; Montgomery 217; Yarranton 145; *VCH Soms.*, ii, 414, 424; iv, 20, 46, 167, 186; HMC, *7th Rep.*, pt i App. pp. 693–4; C. Dale 149; Cunnington, *Recs Co. Wilts.*, 23; Nevill xxvii, 44; xxxi, 179; R. Machin, *Prob. Invs & Man. Excerpts Chetnole, Leigh & Yetminster*, Brist. 1976, nos. 91, 111; Defoe, *Compl. Engl. Tradesman*, 79; Gerard 171–2; Mann, *Docs*, pp. xvi, xx, xxi, 152; PRO, PCC parch. invs p. 1660 nos. 11072, 11331; Wilts. RO, Pec. Ct Dean Sarum. Ric. Bowell 1641, Ed. Fisher 1645, Th. Ford 1661, Jn Pitman 1679, Jn Bealinge (Woodland) & Jn Fisher 1685, Chris. Alford 1690, Robt Sheppard er & Nic. Fleet 1701, Jn Mead 1712, Jn Foreward 1729, all Mere; Th. Harcourt 1677 Wolverton; R. Pec. Ct Gillingham bdl. A: Th. Lane er 1679; B: Jer. Gatehouse 1684 Motcombe, Hugh Brady 1686 Milton, Ric. Peircy 1687 Bourton, Ric. Green 1689, Th. Bottwell 1700; C: Th. Lane 1705, Jn Green sr 1707; D: Hy Bryant & Wm Stafford 1710 Bourton (all Gillingham or dist.); ex Dioc. Reg. Sarum. Ed. Gildon 1598 (Woodland), Th. Pytman 1620, Tim. Meade 1634, all of Mere.

[8] Nfk RO, Cons. Ct invs 1633/295; 1703–8/300; Arch. Ct Norvic. inv. 1718–19/35; *VCH Hants.*, v, 488.

[9] Harte 74 sqq.; T. Birch i, 199, 200.

[10] Reed 71–2; Weiss i, 328 sqq.; ii, 423; *E.A. or N, & Q.*, n.s. 1907–8 xii, 21–2; Defoe, *Tour*, i, 45; Scoville 326; Papillon 117–19; Hands & Scouloudi 28, 31–2, 168, 174 et pass.; Yarranton 49; V. B. Redstone, 'Du. & Hug. Sets at Ips.', *Proc. H.S.L.*, 1924 xii, 188–91, 197, 199; W. D. Cooper, *Hist. Winchelsea*, 1850, p. 121; *Savile Corr.*, Camd. S. 1858 lxxi, 210–11, 236; Burn 96–7; W. R. Scott, *Const. & Fin. Engl., Sc. & Ir. Jt-Stk Cos to 1720*, 3 vols. Cam. 1910–12, iii, 90.

[11] Ibid. 98, 101–2; W. Knowler, *E. of Strafforde's Ltrs & Dispatches*, 2 vols. 1739, ii, 19, 20; Wilston, *Anglo-Du. Comm.*, 56 sqq.; Gill 6 sqq., 16–19, 21, 31–4; *H. of L. MSS*, n.s. 1921 vii, 233; Cullen, *Anglo-Ir. Trade*, 59–62; *Econ. Hist. Ire.*, 24, 48 sqq., 59 sqq.; Scoville 219, 336–8; McGrath, *Merchs*, 289; Firth & Rait ii, 1215; K. L. Carroll, 'Quaker Weavers at Newport, Ire. 1720–40', *Jnl Frds' Hist. S.*, 1976 liv, 15, 16.

[12] Nfk RO, Cty Recs. Strangers Bk fos. 24v., 33, 38; BL, Lans. 26 no. 57 fo. 161(149); no. 59 fos. 175v.–6(158v.–9); PRO, SPD Eliz. 77/58.

[13] Ibid. Jas 129/69; W. Sfk RO, Ep. Commy Ct Bury inv. 1670/77; Bristol RO, Cons. Ct inv. 1660/21; Kent RO, Cons. Ct Cant. Inv. Paper 12/31; Coleman, thes. 187–9; Pococke ii, 2; Eden iii, 752; Bouch & Jones 263; Fiennes 191; Marshall, 'Kendal', 196, 213–15; cf. Ferguson 24, 36, 79, 118, 196, 199.

[14] T. G. Barnes, *Soms. 1625–40*, n.d., p. 6; Fiennes 243; Soms. RO, Arch. Taunton inv. Marmaduke Corum 1664 Taunton.

[15] Guilding ii, 240, 252, 266; Pococke ii, 135, 146; Hants. RO, Arch. Ct O.W. & Invs, Jn Dawkins sr 1720 Romsey Infra; Bodl. Arch. Ct Berks. 192/59; PRO, PCC parch. invs p. 1660 no. 7998; Wilts. RO, Arch. Ct Sarum. Jos. Chubb 1725 Downton.

[16] Ibid. Jas Stantiall 1718 Melsham; Arch. Ct Wilts. Zeph. Fry yr 1717 Chippenham; Pec. Ct D. & C. Sarum. roll M no. 54; PRO, PCC invs 1718–82 bdl. 24 no. 99; Ramsay, *Wilts.*, 102; Mann, 'Wilts. Fam.', 245, 247; *VCH Wilts.*, iv, 159; cf. F. H. Goldney, *Recs Chippenham*, s.l. 1889, p. 237.

[17] F. G. Emmison, *Jac. Hsehld Invs*, Beds. Hist. Rec. S. 1938 xx, 58, 60, 63–5, 67–8, 73 sqq., 88–9, 94, 102–5, 108–9, 113–15, 119–21, 126–8, 132–3, 135 sqq.; C. E. Freeman, 'Eliz. Invs' in *Harrold Priory etc.*, idem 1952 xxxii, 103–4, 107; *Beds. N. & Q.*, 1893 iii, 252–4; Leics. RO, Arch. invs 1626/108; 1638/279; Commy Ct Man. Evington inv. Th. Platts 1632; W. H. B. Court, *Rise Midld Inds*, 1953, pp. 24–5, 36; V. Skipp, *Crisis & Devpt*, Cam. 1978, pp. 57–9.

[18] Hants. RO, Arch. Ct O.W. & Invs, Stephen Sibley 1691 Romsey; Wilts. RO, Arch. Ct

Sarum. Jas Stantiall 1718 Melksham; Jos. Chubb 1725 Downton; Arch. Ct Sub-dean Sarum. 1714/16; C. Gulvin, *Tweedmakers*, Newton Abbot 1973, pp. 27, 192; Hoskins, *Exeter*, 38; Wilson, *Anglo-Du. Comm.*, 38; Cash 155–6; Kent RO, Cons. Ct Cant. Inv. Paper 6/13.

[19] Ibid. 11/114; Wilts. RO, Arch. Ct Wilts. Jn Read 1698 Chippenham Langley; Jn Shipway 1704 Langley in Kington St Mich.; Pec. Ct D. & C. Sarum. roll M no. 54; Wilson, *Anglo-Du. Comm.*, 38–9; Cash 155–6; Hine 306–7; Stats 6 Geo. c.13; 10 Geo. c.18; Hoskins, *Exeter*, 38; Fleming 8; J. James 170, 204, 221; Smith, *Mems Wl*, i, 370.

[20] Ibid. ii, 425, 430–1, 436, 440, 443, 446–7, 450–3; *Engld's Int. Asserted in Improvemt of its Native Commodities*, 1669, p.5; Sion 168–70; Cole ii, 385, 574, 577; *Cal. SP Ven.*, xxxviii, 314; Hands & Scouloudi 141 (& v. 43, 50, 55, 95, 115, 128, 133, 183); Hants. RO, unclass. invs D/2/A: 2/181.

[21] Nfk RO, Cons. Ct inv. 1703–8/300; Postlethwayt ii, 836; Blome 235; Fleming 8; Ogilby 75.

[22] Kent RO, Sandwich Recs. N. Red. Bk fo. 41v.; Arch. Ct Cant. Inv. Reg. 11 fo. 219; PRO, SPD Jas 131/15; Hants. RO, Cons. Ct O.W. & Invs, Jn Pawlmer 1623 Soton; Kirk ii, 74; cf. Willan, *Ru. Co.*, 53.

[23] *APC*, ii, 109; Bacon 366, Add. p. iii; Verney 90–3; T. F. Ordish, 'E. E. Invs', *Antiquary*, 1885 xii, 4; Reed 30.

[24] Ibid.; *APC*, xxvii, 186; Sellers 65, 170; Blome 208, 213; *Rates Marchandizes*, s.v. linen, canvas; Nfk RO, Cons. Ct invs 1602/251; 1610/77; 1615/81; 1661/11; J. Webb, *Poor Relief in Eliz. Ips.*, Sfk Recs S. 1966 ix, 122; Serjeant 75, 77, 271, 334, 409, 527, 550.

[25] *Winthrop Papers*, iii, 49; Stats 1 Jas c.24; 9 Geo. 2 c.37; BL, Lans. 108 no. 78 fo. 141(151).

[26] Scoville 326; Weiss i, 328–30; Cooper, *Savile Corr.*, 210–11, 236; Redstone, 'Du. & Hug. Sets', 188–9.

[27] Doughty 100; my *Ag. Rev.*, 79, 85; BL, Lans. 108 no. 78 fo. 141(151)v.

[28] Bodl. Aubrey 2 fo. 66; & sup. 23.

[29] PRO, SPD Eliz. 15/67; Smith, *Mems Wl*, ii, 452; Posthumus, *Geschiedenis*, ii, 318; Leuridan, *Roubaix*, 95–6; 'Lannoy', 343; Suppa s.v. mollettone; BL, Lans. 26 no. 63 fo. 184(166); Bodl. Rawlinson A.478 fo. 100v. (p. 195).

[30] Sup. 88.

[31] Brist. RO, Cons. Ct invs 1628/59; 1642/7; 1643/40; McGrath, *Merchs*, 87, 271–4; J. Evans, *Chron. Outline Hist. Brist.*, Brist. 1824, pp. 223, 227; Lichfield Jt RO, Cons. Ct O.W. Ric. Kilbee 1630 Cov.; PRO, Exch. KR Deps by Commn 44 & 45 Eliz. Mich. 1; cf. De Sagher iii, 443, 592; Posthumus, *Bronnen*, iv, 3; *Rates Marchandizes*, s.v. carpets; Willan, *Tu. Bk Rates*, 14; B. Dietz 8, 21, 23, 50, 56, 68, 71, 83, 105, 115, 129.

[32] Nfk RO, F. C. Recs. Wall. Ch. 5, 6; Williams, thes. 140; Plummer, *Lond. Weavers' Co.*, 9, 10; *Rates Marchandizes*, s.v. fustians Engl. making; BL, Lans. 80 no. 8 fo. 23; PRO, SPD Chas 529/91; Interreg. 101/6; PCC parch. invs p. 1660 no. 7254.

[33] Ibid. nos. 694, 2890; SPD Eliz. 250/76; Blome 211; Thornton 231; HMC, *13th Rep.*, App. pt ii, 284; M. G. Davies 129, 227; Bacon 468; Emmison, *Wills at Chelmsford*, i, 260, 279; Reed 64; W. Sfk RO, Ep. Commy Ct Bury invs 1664/161; 1665/151; 1667/127; Nfk RO, Cons. Ct inv. 1606/39.

[34] M. & A. Grass, *Stockings f. Q.*, 1967, pp. 140, 145.

[35] *VCH Wilts.*, iv, 179; *Soms.*, iv, 20, 57; J. Smyth, *Names*, 2 sqq., 134–5, 186–8; Worcs. RO, Cons. Ct O.W. etc. 1606/12; Kent RO, Maidstone Recs. Burghmote Bks 2, rev. fo. 7; 3 fo. 5v. (p. 10); cf. Stephens, *Exeter*, 10; 'Ply.', 131.

[36] Guilding ii, 144.

[37] Fuller, *Worthies*, i, 362; Ogilby 76.

[38] *VCH Wilts.*, iv, 179; Nevill xxxiii, 126; Pococke ii, 248.

[39] Ibid. i, 11; ii, 9; Warner 399, 400; Fuller, *Worthies*, ii, 190; J. James 202; T. D. Hibbert, 'Ltrs rel. to Lancs. & Ches.', *Proc. & Papers*, Hist. S. Lancs. & Ches. sess. iv, 1852, pp. 189–90; F. R. Raines & C. W. Sutton, *Life Humph. Chetham*, Chetham S. n.s. xlix, l 1903, i, 10, 13, 14;

Roberts, *Treas.*, 33, 35, 41; *Marchants Mapp*, 2nd pt, 231 recte, 211 erron.; *Pal. Notebk*, i, 126–7; Boyson 1; Bennett, *1650–1850*, 77; *Rates Marchandizes*, s.v. fustians Engl. making; *Rates Merchandizes*, 68; Haynes, *G.B.'s Glory*, 16; Defoe, *Compl. Engl. Tradesman*, 77; Aikin 158–9; Miller 328; PRO, SPD Chas 364/122–3; Interreg. 69/7; PCR 1636 p. 188; Lancs. RO, Hopwood Coll. 39/24; Cons. Ct Cestr. Supra invs 1628 Jas Warde/L. Bolton; Jn Bordeman/Bolton; 1637 Laurence Molineux/ Bolton; Wm Isherwood/Bolton; 1661 Jn Bolton (1657) Blackburn; 1664 Th. Couper/id.; 1665 Jas Ogden/Blackley; 1667 Roger Nicholson/Bolton; 1670 Hy Yeats/Lindsay in Blackburn; 1674 Hy Heawood/Bury; 1678 Th. Cooke/Livesey; Wadsworth & Mann 15, 16, 21, 29 sqq., 79, 83 sqq., 90, 237, 328–9; cf. Defoe, *Tour*, i, 82; W. de G. Birch 259; Bang iiA, 372, 543–4.

[40] Pococke i, 205; Aikin 158, 163; Wadsworth & Mann 114, 174, 201, 266.

[41] Ibid. 76, 113 sqq., 401; Haynes, *G.B.'s Glory*, 16; Wood 75; Warner 399, 400; HMC, *13th Rep.*, App. pt ii, 284; Defoe, *Compl. Engl. Tradesman*, 77; W. de G. Birch 259; Roberts, *Treas.*, 33; Montgomery 219; Lichfield Jt RO, Cons. Ct, Sam. Smith 1722 Cov.

[42] Wadsworth & Mann 115–16, 127, 140, 151, 153, 328; Miller 328; Montgomery 216, 218; Bowman 427; BL, Add. 36666 fo. 9v.

[43] PRO, PCC parch. invs p. 1660 no. 7254.

[44] Wadsworth & Mann 84, 111–13, 172, 175–6, 275.

[45] Ibid. 125, 135; *C.J.*, xix, 295, 418.

[46] Guildhall Lib. Commy Ct Lond. (Lond. Div.) inv. box 4 Th. Aspinall 1726 St Dunstan's, Stepney; Wadsworth & Mann 122–3.

[47] Ibid. 125, 129 sqq.; F. Lewis 13, 15 sqq.

## Chapter 9

[1] E. Sabbe, *Anvers: métropole de l'occident*, Brux. 1952, pp. 70, 72; Denucé 97; Brulez, *Della Faille*, 152; Eggen 173–4; Thijs 13, 14; *Ca. Commonalty Corp. Weavers*; *Breviate Weavers Bus.*, n.d., p. 3.

[2] Rothstein 14, 28.

[3] Kent RO, Cons. Ct Cant. Inv. Paper 11/114; Inv. Reg. 9 fo. 117; Cross 196; Cant. Cath. Lib. Wall. Recs. Misc. Docs portf. 4 no. 65; BL, Harl. 1878 fo. 81v.; PRO, SPD Chas 529/91.

[4] Ibid. 302/41; HMC, *Salisbury MSS*, xiv, 190; Kirk ii, 218, 286v., 329; Stow, *Ann.* 869.

[5] Kent RO, Cons. Ct Cant. Inv. Reg. 11 fo. 652; cf. Reg. Accts & Invs 8 fo. 85; Nfk RO, F.C. Recs. Wall. Ch. 4–6.

[6] Nfk RO, Cons. Ct inv. 1603/117; Kent RO, Cons. Ct. Cant. Inv. Reg. 9 fo. 117.

[7] Ibid.

[8] Ibid. Reg. Accts & Invs 14 fo. 389; Notestein et al. vii, 156; Kirk iii, 209; PRO, SPD Eliz. 253/122.

[9] Ibid. Jas 121/155; 131/15; Chas 529/91; Hessels, *Archivum*, iii, 2128; Plummer, *Lond. Weavers' Co.*, 41.

[10] Kent RO, Cons. Ct Cant. Inv. Reg. 11 fo. 652.

[11] B. Dietz 133; *Rates Marchandizes*, s.v. taffeties; Kirk iii, 188; & sup. 76.

[12] Hessels, *Archivum*, iii, 1056, 1058; HMC, *Salisbury MSS*, iv, 574–5; xiv, 190, Stow, *Ann.*, 869; Waller 4, 5, 7; Kirk iii, 188, 193, 195–6, 216–7, 219–20, 228; PRO, SPD Jas 99/43–4; 102; Chas 302/41; 529/91.

[13] Ibid. 257/15; 427/89; PCR 1639 pp. 615–6 (fo. 303); Plummer, *Lond. Weavers' Co.*, 10.

[14] Warner 627; Kent RO, Cons. Ct Cant. Inv. Reg. 11 fo. 652; Cowper, *Cant. Mar. Lics*, col. 390.

[15] Kent RO, Cons. Ct Cant. Inv. Paper 11/114; Inv. Regs 7 fos. 5, 456; 11 fo. 652; Thijs 55; PRO, SPD Chas 412/23.

[16] Ibid. 302/41; Kirk iii, 191, 223–6.

[17] Kent RO, Cons. Ct Cant. Inv. Paper 7/92; Inv. Reg. 12 fo. 247v.; PRO, SPD Jas 131/15.

[18] Cant. Cath. Lib. Wall. Recs. Misc. Docs portf. 4 no. 63.

[19] Hessels, *Archivum*, iii, 2128; Hands & Scouloudi 58, 60, 73, 78, 80: PRO, SPD Jas 121/ 155; 131/15 (cf. Chas 529/91); Lancs. RO, Cavendish of Holker Coll. 1/45 fo. 3.

[20] Kent RO, Cons. Ct Cant. Inv. Reg. 14 fo. 245; Inv. Papers 26/120; 27/116.

[21] Hessels, *Archivum*, iii, 2128; PRO, PCC paper invs 1661–1725 no. 2518.

[22] D. G. Vaisey, *Prob. Invs Lichfield & Dist. 1568–1680*, Colls Hist. Staffs. 4th ser. 1969 v, 232–3; Stat. 12 Chas 2 c.4.

[23] HMC, *Salisbury MSS*, xiv, 190.

[24] Kent RO, Cons. Ct Cant. Inv. Paper 7/92; Inv. Reg. 9 fo. 117.

[25] Guildhall Lib. Weavers' Co. Ord. & Rec. Bk 1577–1641 p. 354; Stow, *Ann.*, 869.

[26] Roberts, *Marchants Mapp*, 2nd pt, 57, 76, 87, 95; cf. *Rsns f. Restraining Wearing Wrought Silks*; pace E. Hasted, *Kent*, iv, 421; *Hist. Antient & Metropolitical Cty Cant.*, 2 vols. Cant. 1801, i, 94.

[27] H. Stewart, *Hist. Wpfl Co. Gold & Silver Wyre-drawers*, 1891, pp. 13–15, 17, 19, 20, 41, 107–8; E. Glover, *Gold & Silver Wyre-drawers*, Lond. & Chich. 1979, p. 1; E. M. Veale, *Engl. Fur Trade in later M.A.*, Oxf. 1966, pp. 11, 136, 143–4; Goris 252, 319; Guicciardini 119–20; Nichols, 'Invs Wardrobe', 27, 30; Stats 9 W.3 c.39; 1 Anne c.11; 15 Geo. 2 c.20; Kirk i, 138.

[28] Plummer, *Lond. Weavers' Co.*, 41–2; Campbell 147, 149–51; McGrath, *Merchs*, 283.

[29] PRO, SPD Jas 88/113; 102; Ordish 117; Botero 56; Glover 6, 7; W. D. Cooper, *Lists For. Prots & Aliens res. in Engld 1618–88*, Camd. S. 1862 lxxxii, p. vi; S. R. Gardiner, *Nn. Debates in H. of L. 1621*, id. 1870 ciii, 24, 31, 43, 133; Stewart 18, 26, 29; Prestwich 278; & v. Larkin & Hughes i, 578–9; PRO, PCR 1635–6 p. 439 (fo. 209); P. Massinger, *The Bondman*, act ii, sc. 3.

[30] Stewart 26; Guildhall Lib. Weavers' Co. Ord. & Rec. Bk 1577–1641 p. 481; PRO, SPD Chas 529/91; Stow, *Ann.*, 869.

[31] Ibid.

[32] Guildhall Lib. Weavers' Co. Ord. & Rec. Bk 1577–1641 pp. 354, 480–3; PRO, SPD Chas 180/70 (prob. 1637–8); 458/89; PCR 1638 p. 267 (fo. 132); 1639 pp. 615–6 (fo. 303); Steele i, 216; W. H. Overall, *Anal. Ind. to . . . Remembrancia Cty Lond.*, 1878, p. 103.

[33] Leuridan, *Roubaix*, 53; Montgomery 219; Kent RO, Cons. Ct Ct Cant. Inv. Paper 16/32.

[34] Ibid. 26/120.

[35] Warner 399–401; PRO, SPD Chas 2, 315/158; *Cal. SPD*, Chas 2, 1672, p. 654.

[36] PRO, PCC paper invs 1661–1725 no. 2518; Cty Lond. RO, Ct Orphs invs box 1, Th. Marriott textor 1664.

[37] Colyer-Fergusson iii, 175 sqq.; Shaw, *1603–1700*, 68–9; W. & S. Minet, *Regs Ch Le Carré & Berwick St 1690–1788*, Pubs H.S.L. 1921 xxv, 31; Smith, *Mems Wl*, ii, 41; Kent RO, Cons. Ct Cant. Inv. Regs 9 fo. 333; 12 fo. 373; 14 fo. 405; 15 fo. 392; 20 fo. 183; Inv. Papers 13/111; 15/47; 20/53; 22/9; 26/157; Guildhall Lib. Commy Ct Lond. (Lond. Div.) invs box 4 Th. Short 1724; 8 Pet. Willemot 1716 St Dunstan's; Pet. Parr 1703 Spitalfields – all Stepney; 9 Th. Fowler 1699 St Botolph's W/o Jn Oldham 1701 Stepney; Th. Crette 1702 St Dunstan's, Stepney.

[38] Ibid. Dan. Nipp 1701 Bridewell Precinct; Roberts, *Marchants Mapp*, 2nd pt, 27, 29, 76; Minet, *Threadneedle St*, pp. xlix, l; Hands & Scouloudi 81; Colyer-Fergusson iii, 268, 352.

[39] Evelyn i, 94; ii, 146; iii, 65.

[40] Rothstein 141.

[41] Ibid. 141, 173, 273, 276; Guildhall Lib. Commy Ct Lond. (Lond. Div.) invs box 8 Abr. Lenningni 1714 Stepney; PRO, PCC paper invs 1661–1725 no. 2518; Hasted, *Kent*, iv, 421; Cty Lond. RO, Ct Orphs invs box 1, Th. Marriott textor 1664.

[42] PRO, SPD Chas 305/104.

[43] *Cal. SPD*, 1638–9 p. 623.

[44] PRO, PCC paper invs 1661–1725 no. 2518; Kent RO, Cons. Ct Cant. Inv. Paper 26/120; Van Nierop xlvi, 31; *Weavers Ans. to Objns made by Lustrings Co.*, n.d.; *Consids Humbly Offered by*

*Weavers f. bringing fine It. thrown silk overland*, n.d.; *Ca. Weavers who are petnrs to be relieved agst cl. in Coale Act*, 1695; Colyer-Fergusson iii, 349; cf. Rothstein 141, 299.

[45] *VCH Mx*, ii, 132–3; Hasted, *Kent*, iv, 421; Cole ii, 192; S. Ciriacono, 'Silk Manufg in Fr. & It. in 17th cent.', *Jnl Eur. Econ. Hist.*, 1981 x, 180–1.

[46] Ibid. 191–2; Cole ii, 137, 140, 192; W. A. Shaw, *Ltrs Denization & Acts Naturalization f. Aliens in Engld & Ire. 1701–1800*, Pubs H.S.L. 1923 xxvii, 25–6, 54, 64; *1603–1700*, 217, 223, 240–1, 252–4, 304; W. J. C. Moens, *Regs Fr. Ch. Threadneedle St*, idem ix, xiii, 1896–9, i, 22, 26; ii, 50, 56 sqq., 62, 65, 67–8; Warner 37, 41; Cunningham 234–5; Colyer-Fergusson iii, 5, 6, 20, 33, 38, 349; Minet, *Threadneedle St*, pp. xiv–vii, xxii–iii, xlix, l; *Livre des Conversions*, p. xxxi; Minet & Waller pp. xiv, xxi, 43; Waller 20, 25, 28, 31, 33–5, 37, 39, 45–7, 49, 51–2, 55, 58, 68; S. Fortrey, *Engld's Int. & Improvemt*, Cam. 1663, p. 23; Scoville 141, 176–7, 180–2, 211–14, 216–18, 324–6; *VCH Mx*, ii, 132–3; Bang & Korst ii pt i, 176–7, 427, 581–2.

[47] Ibid. 317, 504–5; Plummer, *Lond. Weavers' Co.*, 18, 55; Postlethwayt i, 381; Van Nierop xlvi, 124; Hasted, *Kent*, iv, 421; Warner 42–3, 51; Campbell 259; *VCH Mx*, ii, 133; Waller pp. xiii–iv, 52; *Abs. such pts sev. stats rel. to Silks called Alamodes & Lustrings*, 1699; PRO SPD Jas 2, vol. 337 p. 400; Kent RO, Cons. Ct Cant. Inv. Paper 26/120.

[48] Ibid.; Postlethwayt i, 35; Rothstein 123–4; Guildhall Lib. Commy Ct Lond. (Lond. Div.) inv. box 9 Isaac Delaneuvemaison 1701 Spitalfields, Stepney; *Weavers Ans. to Objns*; *Consids . . . f. bringing It. thrown silk overland*; *Ca. Weavers petnrs . . . agst cl. in Coale Act*.

[49] Ibid.; Waller xiii–iv, 50, 52.

[50] PRO, SPD Jas 2, vol. 337 p. 400; Reed 72; Hands & Scouloudi 76, 95, 136 & pass.; Redstone, 'Du. & Hug. Sets', 199, 202–4; *C.J.*, xii, 224–5; Scott iii, 73–5, 78.

[51] Campbell 255; Guildhall Lib. Commy Ct Lond. (Lond. Div.) invs box 8 Isaac Burgess 1714 St Dunstan's, Stepney; Abr. Lennigni 1714 Stepney.

[52] Warner 285, 290, 658E & I; Edwards 58; Kent RO, Cons. Ct Cant. Inv. Paper 16/32; Bridewell Mus. bk 'F. Tuthill & Fils'.

[53] Warner 642–3; Guildhall Lib. Commy Ct Lond. (Lond. Div.) invs box 4 Chas Grinnoneau 1725–6 Stepney; 8 Abr. Lennigni 1714, Jn Dollond 1715, both of Stepney; Nfk RO, Cons. Ct inv. 1688–9/59B; Hill ii, 195; Gras 128, 560, 575; Willan, *Tu. Bk Rates*, 51–2; *Rates Marchandizes*, s.v. sarcenets; Ramsay, *Isham*, 31, 160; Wheeler 23; B. Dietz 3, 7–9, 12, 27, 44, 61, 67–8, 72–5, 84, 92–3, 99, 101–2, 105–6, 112, 118, 126, 130, 154; Millard i, App. p. 35; ii, iii; Kent RO, Cons. Ct Cant. Reg. Accts & Invs 6 fo. 371.

[54] Ibid. Inv. Papers 26/120; 27/116; Nfk RO, Cons. Ct invs 1702/10; 1716–17/169; cf. 1718–21/282; Guildhall Lib. Commy Ct Lond. (Lond. Div.) invs box 4 Nic. You 1725 St Dunstan's; 8 Abr. Lennigni 1714 both of Stepney.

[55] Ibid. 4 Nic. You 1725 St Dunstan's; Chas Grinnoneau 1725–6; 8 Jn Dollond 1715 – all of Stepney; Warner 658C.

[56] Ibid. 51; *VCH Mx*, ii, 133; Cross 15, 204, 214; Rothstein 565; Defoe, *Compl. Engl. Tradesman*, 79; Guildhall Lib. Commy Ct Lond. (Lond. Div.) invs box 4 Josh. Maria 1705–6 St Dunstan's; 8 Abr. Lennigni 1714 both of Stepney.

[57] Cov. RO, Cty Recs. Leet Bk 30 Eliz.–1834, pp. 123, 260; 1950/7 Fellshp Silk & Worsted Weavers Ords Bk fos. 9, 24; Warner 324, 326–7, 330–1; Child, *New Disc. Trade*, 39; Alexander & Hooper 179; Colyer-Fergusson iii, 249; PRO, SPD Chas 2, 174/55.

[58] J. H. E. Bennett 223, 276, 321, 331, 335, 339, 365; Bodl. Hearne's Diaries 158 pp. 67, 104; Aubrey 2 fo. 65v.

[59] Cross 205–6; Cant. Cath. Lib. Wall. Recs. Misc. Docs portf. 4 no. 71; Warner 315; Hasted, *Cant.*, i, 95, 97.

[60] Edwards 398 sqq.

[61] Warner 318.

[62] D. C. Coleman, *Courtaulds*, vol. i Oxf. 1969, pp. 21, 36–8, 48, 63; Warner 88, 97, 150–1, 170, 298–300, 307, 318–19, 321–2, 333, 339–41; Poole 359–60; Grimwood & Kay 92–3; K. W. Glass

31; Courtauld 151; Curtis 123; Burton 181; Collinson i, 2nd pt, 213; iii, 226, 300; Burn 132; Eden ii, 177, 229; Plummer, *Lond. Weavers' Co.*, 369–70; Patterson i, 5; M. F. Davies 45; C. J. Palmer, *Hist. Gt Yarmouth*, Gt Yarmouth 1856, p. 108; J. Toulmin, *Hist. Taunton*, 1822, pp. 380–2; Wilts. RO, Pec. Ct Dean Sarum. Dan. Lester 1742 Sherborne; *VCH Wilts.*, x, 257; *Northants.*, ii, 334; *Hants.*, v, 487–8; *Glos.*, xi, 29; *Berks.*, i, 396.

## Chapter 10

[1] Grass 53–4; M. Hartley & J. Ingilby, *Yks. Vil.*, 1953, p. 68, 102–3; Stats 3 H.8 c.15; 8 Eliz. c.11; 13 Eliz. c.19. 4-needle knitting was found on the 'Mary Rose'.

[2] Grass 62; Webb, *Poor Relief*, 126, 134–5; Slack 74–5; E. M. Leonard, *Early Hist. Engl. Poor Relief*, Cam. 1900, p. 332; Hudson & Tingey ii, p. ciii; Nfk RO, Cty Recs. Bk Mayor's Ct 16 fo. 306v.; *VCH Yks.* iii, 468–9.

[3] Stat. 5 & 6 E.6 c.7.

[4] P. Stubbes, *Anatomie of Abuses*, 1583; & v. Hakluyt, *Orig. Writings*, 192; Soms. RO, Arch. Taunton inv. Robt Olford 1664 Crewkerne.

[5] S. D. Chapman, 'Gen. Brit. Hosiery Ind.', *Text. Hist.*, 1972 iii, 11; Lancs. RO, Cons. Ct Cestr. Supra inv. Jn Ogden 1676 (1675) Castleton; Tupling 184–5; Wilts. RO, Pec. Ct Dean Sarum. Jn Coward 1683 Mere.

[6] Northants. RO, Arch. Ct Northampton Admons & Invs 1723/34; Nfk RO, Arch. Ct Norvic. invs 1707–8/78; 1708–9/46; 1712–13/29; 1722–3/11; W. Sfk RO, Ep. Commy Ct Bury inv. 1686/79; Devizes Mus. Wm Gaby His Booke rev. pp. 64–5.

[7] PRO, SPD Eliz. 252/2; Exch. KR Deps by Commn 2 Chas Mich. 38; 29 Chas 2 Mich. 32; 30 Chas 2 Mich. 19; Postlethwayt ii, 836, 849; Bouch & Jones 263; Ogilby 75; Marshall, 'Kendal', 196, 200, 208 sqq.; H. Thwaite, *Abs. Abbotside Wills 1552–1688*, Yks. Archaeol. S. Rec. Ser. 1968 cxxx, 65–6; M. Hartley & J. Ingilby, *O. Handknitters Dales*, Clapham via Lanc. 1951, pp. 7, 11, 27–8; *Yks. Vil.*, 28, 68, 102–3, 231–2; Heaton 265, 267, 285–6; E. Hughes, *N. Country Life in 18th cent.*, 2 vols. 1952–65, ii, 4; *VCH Durh.*, ii, 315; Defoe, *Tour*, ii, 222, 224; *Compl. Engl. Tradesman*, 78–9; Eden iii, 752; Pococke i, 46; ii, 2.

[8] Ibid. i, 235; ii, 23; Westcote 61; Aubrey, *Sy*, iii, 347; Jenkins, *W. Woollen Ind.*, 210, 212–13; W. Davies 403–4; G. Kay, *Gen. View Ag. N.W.*, Edin. 1794, p. 39.

[9] PRO, PCC parch. invs p. 1660 no. 7779; Nfk RO, Cty Recs. Ass. Bk 5 fos. 8(17), 331(342)v.; Arch. Ct Norvic. invs 1682–3/197; 1707–8/78; 1708–9/46; 1712–13/29; 1722–3/11; Cons. Ct invs 1595/60; 1662/12.

[10] Ibid. 1680/58; W. Sfk RO, Ep. Commy Ct Bury inv. 1686/79.

[11] Stow, *Ann.*, 869; *Rates Marchandizes*, s.v. hose of cruell called Mantua hose; PRO, SPD Eliz. 231/11.

[12] Ibid.127/81; 231/11; Exch. KR Accts Var. bdl. 347 no. 19; Deps by Commn 2 Chas Mich. 38; 35 & 36 Chas 2 Hil. 19; BL, Add. 12504 no. 65 fo. 86v.(p. 2); Lans. 26 no. 58 fos. 166–7(153–4); no. 59 fos. 175v.–6(158v.–9); no. 63 fo. 184; Nfk RO, Cty Recs. Alnage Accts; Bks Mayor's Ct 13 p. 142; 16 fos. 306v., 326; Arch. Ct Norvic. inv. 1707–8/78; Cons. Ct inv. 1662/12; Bernard, op. cit.; *APC*, xxxiii, 358–9; 1621–3 p. 329; Blome 168, 172–3; Defoe, *Wks*, 544; T. Wilson, 'State Engld A.D. 1600' in *Camd. Misc. xvi*, Camd. 3rd ser. 1936 lii, 20–1; Pound, *Cs Poor*, 30, 42, 51, 62–3; Allison 590, 648; Hudson & Tingey ii, 77–8, 340–1; HMC, *13th Rep.*, App. pt ii, 270; Hakluyt, *Orig. Writings*, 183, 192; Fiennes 146.

[13] Ibid.; Webb, *Poor Relief*, 122 sqq.; W. Sfk RO, Ep. Commy Ct Bury inv. 1686/79; E. Sfk RO, Arch. invs 15/82; 18/65; 23/54.

[14] Northants. RO, Arch. Ct Northampton Admons & Invs 1723/34; Leics. RO, Arch. inv. 1690/108; *Wills & Admons fr. Knaresboro. Ct R.*, ii, 220, sqq.; Morton 23–4; Dyer, *Cty Worc.*, 119; Defoe, *Compl. Engl. Tradesman*, 79; Pococke ii, 280; Fiennes 161; Blome 253; *VCH Derbys*, ii, 321, 367, 371; *Northants.*, ii, 334; *Notts.*, ii, 285, 293; Postlethwayt ii, 352.

[15] Ibid. 848; R. Davies 116; Defoe, *Tour*, ii, 181; Blome 257; Evelyn iii, 127; HMC, *13th Rep.*, App. pt ii, 310; Nfk RO, Arch. Ct Norvic. invs 1682–3/197; 1722–3/11; PRO, SPD Eliz. 252/2; Exch. KR. Deps by Commn 2 Chas Mich. 38.

[16] Lichfield Jt RO, Cons. Ct O.W. etc. Hugh Atkyns 1547, Ric. Bromych 1551, Jn Armebrode 1560, all Cov. cappers; Stats 22 E.4 c.5; 7 E.6 c.8; 8 Eliz. c.11; 13 Eliz. c.19; *Disc. Com. Weal*, p. xvi; Harris, *Cov. Leet Bk*, 640, 645, 659, 663, 670–3, 693, 699, 701–2, 704, 707–8, 726, 729, 773–4, 791; Gras 647, 660; W. Camden, *Brit.*, 1594, p. 433; Stow, *Ann.*, 870; Phythian-Adams 44, 210; Hakluyt, *Prin. Navs*, iii, 269–70.

[17] Ibid. 269; *Worcs. Co. Recs: Div. I. Docs rel. to Q. Sess.*, *Cal. Q. Sess. Papers*, 2 vols. Worc. 1899, 1900, pp. xxxvi, 61, 624; C. E. Long, *Diary Marches R. Army during Gt Civ. War kept by R. Symonds*, Camd. S. 1859 lxxiv, 14; Martin ii, 152; Yarranton 111, 168, 174–5; Postlethwayt ii, 846; Blome 247; Stat. 13 Eliz. c.19; Shak. *Hy V*, act iv sc. 7.

[18] *C.J.*, ii, 578; Morton 23; Fuller, *Worthies*, ii, 498; *VCH Northants.*, ii, 334; Cox 289–90; PRO, Exch. KR Deps by Commn 2 Chas Mich. 38.

[19] *VCH Leics.*, iv, 90–2.

[20] Ibid. 91–2, 168 sqq.; Pococke i, 167; Chapman, 'Gen.', 33, 35–6, 41; Defoe, *Compl. Engl. Tradesman*, 79; Grass 79; A. P. Usher, *Hist. Mech. Invs*, Cam. Mass. 1954, pp. 278–81; C. Holme, *Hist. Midld Cos*, Rugby 1891, p. 22; W. G. Hoskins, *Midld Peasant*, 1957, p. 228.

[21] Fienes 73; Stukeley i, 52; Notts. RO, Man. Ct Mansfield O.W. etc. portf. 26 no. 2.

[22] Ibid. portf. 16, no. 13; 23 no. 28; 26 no. 2; 54 no. 14; 59 nos. 3, 19; 75 no. 7; 82 nos. 24, 35; 84 no. 33; A. Rogers, 'Rural Inds & Soc. Structure', *Text. Hist.*, 1981 xii, 16, 17; G. Henson, *Hist. Framewk Knitters*, Newton Abbot 1970, pp. 99, 106, 237; Chapman, 'Gen.', 25, 44; K. J. Smith 22; Holme 22–4; HMC, *Middleton MSS*, 499; Defoe, *Tour*, ii, 88–9, 145; Hoskins, *Midld Peasant*, 211–12, 228; E. W. Pasold, 'In Search of Wm Lee', *Text. Hist.*, 1975 vi, 12–15; M. Bloxsom, *Hist. Par. Gilmorton*, Lincoln 1918, p. 57; *VCH Derbys.*, ii, 285, 293, 358; *Ruts.*, i, 237; Northants. RO, Arch Ct Northampton Admons & Invs Jn Smith 1743 Towcester; Th. Henshaw 1747 Middleton Cheney; Jos. Emery 1755 Slapton; Wm Buckingham 1767 Middleton Cheney; Leics. RO, Arch. invs 1668/62; 1704/150; 1709/112; Sam. Harris 1738 Belgrave; Th. Kirbe 1731 Glenfield; Th. Glover 1729 Cas. Donington; Ric. Marshall 1728 Barkstone; Jn Wale 1727 Whetstone.

[23] Ibid. 1690/108; Hartley & Ingilby, *O. Handknitters*, 17, 95; *Yks. Vil.*, 232; Defoe, *Compl. Engl. Tradesman*, 79; Chapman, 'Gen.', 9, 10, 36, 41; Henson 43–4, 257 sqq.

[24] T. Wilson 20; Nfk RO, Cty Recs. Alnage Accts; N. Drapery in Norwich; Ass. Bk 4 fo. 7; Cons. Ct invs 1606–7/20; 1662/12; 1703–8/192; Arch. Ct Norvic. invs 1674–5/168; 1682–3/197; 1708–9/46; 1711–12/62; 1712–13/29; 1722–3/11; BL, Lans. 26 no. 57 fo. 161(149); no. 58 fos. 166–7(153–4); no. 59 fos. 175v.–6 (158v.–9); no. 62 fo. 181(163)v.; no. 64 fo. 187; PRO, PCC parch. invs p. 1660 no. 7779.

[25] Worcs. RO, Cons. Ct O.W. etc. 1690/142; Blome 246; Plot, *Oxon.* 278–9; Rath 140–1; Pococke ii, 277; *VCH Glos.*, viii, 144; HMC, *13th Rep.*, App. pt. ii, 303; G. May, *Hist. Evesham*, Evesham & Lond. 1834, p. 159; Postlethwayt ii, 846.

[26] Ibid. 743; Plot, loc. cit.; Collinson i, 2nd pt, 213; Defoe, *Tour*, i, 217, 271; G. Williams iv, 340–2; Matthews iii, 418, 425; Soms. RO, Arch. Taunton inv. Robt Olford 1664 Crewkerne; DD/X/SND nos. 5, 7, 8; PRO, PCC parch. invs p. 1660 nos. 2453, 4719; paper invs 1661–1725 no. 3279; Wilts. RO, Pec. Ct Dean Sarum. Wm Pike 1731 Lyme Regis.

[27] Smyth, *Names*, 182–3; Leics. RO, Arch. inv. 1690/108; Brist. RO, Cons. Ct inv. 1623/73.

[28] Marshall, 'Kendal', 200, 208, 210; Blome 235; Fleming 8; Pococke ii, 2.

[29] Ibid. i, 6; J. H. E. Bennett 163–4, 257, 290, 295, 305–6, 313, 319, 321, 329–31, 335, 339, 341, 350, 364–6, 368, 373, 378, 403; Chester RO, Cty Recs. Ass. Bks 1539–1624 fo. 171; 1624–84 fo. 182v.; Mayor's Recs, R. Freemen 1658–79, entry 1674.

[30] Fiennes 146; W. Sfk RO, Ep. Commy Ct Bury invs 1686/64, 79; 1701/52.

[31] Ibid. 1705/84; E. Sfk RO, Arch. invs 19/62; 23/5; Nfk RO, Cons. Ct invs 1680/58; 1703–8/301; Fiennes 146; Blome 215.

[32] Westcote 61; Plot, *Oxon.*, 278–9.

[33] T. F. Priaulx & R. de Sausmarez, 'Guernsey Stocking Exp. Trade in 17th cent.', *Trs Sté Guernesiaise*, 1960–5 xvii, 210 sqq., 217, 219–20; J. Poingdestre, *Caesarea*, Pubs Sté Jersiaise 1889 x, pp. v, 4; Smith, *Mems Wl*, i, 321; Lamb 65; B. Palliser, *Hist. Lace*, 1902, p. 372; PRO, SPD Chas 2, 152/62 (quot.), 153/115; Horrocks i, 97.

[34] Ibid.; Pococke i, 83; ii, 130; Postlethwayt i, 939; Defoe, *Tour*, i, 208; Clegg 180; *VCH Dors.*, ii, 328; *Hants.*, v, 488; Hasted, *Kent*, i, 270; Kent RO, Cons. Ct Cant. Inv. Paper 12/45; Dors. RO, MS Hist. Coll. Ch. Wimb. Minster by Ric. Russell, bet. marg. nos 3 & 4.

[35] Slack 65 sqq., 71–2, 74, 89; Bodl. Aubrey 2 fo. 117.

[36] Henson 60, 106, 182, 195; Hants. RO, unclass. invs D/2/A: 3/240.

[37] Stow, *Ann.*, 867; J. W. Burgon, *Life & Times Sir Th. Gresham*, 2 vols n.d. i, 103; B. Dietz 41.

[38] Millard i, App. pp. 12, 13; ii, iii; Brulez, *Della Faille*, 43, 57, 83–5, 109, 291, 302, 304, 517.

[39] Ibid. 304; Blome 215; Kirk i, 429, 443; iii, 413; cf. Beaumont & Fletcher, *Knt of the Burning Pestle*, act iv, sc. 3.

[40] Stubbes, op. cit.; cf. Shak. *Hy 4 pt 2*, act iii, sc. 2.

[41] K. G. Ponting, 'In Search of Wm Lee', *Text. Hist.*, 1978 ix, 174; Henson 47, 51–4, 105; Grass 54, 125, 129 sqq., 137, 141–4, 149–50, 155–6, 165–8; Warner 646; Plummer, *Lond. Weavers' Co.*, 169–70; Colyer-Fergusson iii, 249; Child, *N. Disc. Trade*, 39; PRO, SPD Jas 65/9; Guildhall Lib. Commy Ct Lond. (Lond. Div.) invs box 4 Wm Marshall 1706 St Dunstan's, Stepney; box 9 Jn Loill 1679 Stepney; Chapman, 'Gen.', 7, 8, 11 sqq., 17, 21.

[42] Ibid. 11, 16, 17, 22, 24, 26, 37; Notts. RO, Man. Ct Mansfield O.W. etc. portf. 26 no. 2; Henson 106; Fiennes 73; *VCH Leics.*, iv, 91.

[43] Ibid. 91–2; *Berks.*, i, 395; *Hants.*, v, 488; *Suss.*, ii, 258; Warner 323–4; Pococke ii, 164; Henson 106; Alexander & Hooper 179; J. H. E. Bennett 223, 276; Nevill xxx, 127; xxxiii, 200; Smyth, *Names*, 2 sqq.; Bigland 424; BL, Add. 10407; Shak. Bpl. Leigh Coll. Ct R. Cross Grange & Leek Wootton 18 Apr. 8 Jas; Wilts. RO, Pec. Ct Dean Sarum. Hy Ticknoll 1616 Wokingham; Kent RO, Maidstone Recs. Burghmote Bks 2, rev. fos. 3v., 5v.; 4 fo. 146v.

[44] H. Kamen, *Sp. in later 17th cent.*, 1980, p. 119.

[45] Henson 106, 237; Rath 141 sqq.; Blome 246; Fiennes 234; Defoe, *Tour*, ii, 42; *Compl. Engl. Tradesman*, 79; Postlethwayt i, 901; *VCH Glos.*, viii, 111.

[46] Wadsworth & Mann 171; *VCH Dors.*, ii, 328.

[47] J. D. Chambers, 'Wpfl Co. Frwk Knitters (1657–1778)', *Economica*, 1929 ix, 314; Henson 106, 237.

[48] Rath 142–5; Defoe, *Compl. Engl. Tradesman*, 79; Wadsworth & Mann 171.

[49] Henson 105–6.

[50] E. B. Schumpeter 35, 70; H. E. S. Fisher 128; Smith, *Mems Wl*, ii, 153–4; Plummer, *Lond. Weavers' Co.*, 171; *Rates Marchandizes*.

[51] Stow, *Ann.*, 869; Grass 129.

[52] Henson 54.

[53] Chapman, 'Gen.', 24; Scoville 183, 239–40; Ciriacono 169, 181, 195; M. Sonenscher, 'Hosiery Ind. Nîmes & Lwr Languedoc in 18th cent.', *Text. Hist.*, 1979 x, 142–3; PRO, SPD Interreg. 220/53.

[54] Sion 170.

[55] Munn 25–7.

[56] Posthumus, *Bronnen*, vi, 620–2, 632; Faber i, 238–9.

[57] Kirk i, 343, 404, 408, 413–14, 478; ii, 114, 267, 274, 291–2, 299, 328, 330, 332–3, 335, 355; Ramsay, *Wilts.*, 102; *APC*, 1629–30 p. 113; Brist. RO, Cons. Ct inv. 1662/17; PRO, SPD Jas 88/113; Chas 408/166; Unwin, *Ind. Org.*, 131 sqq.

[58] Ibid. 131, 215; Larkin & Hughes i, 299; Strieder 114; Kirk i, 1, 203 sqq., 212, 214, 273–4, 277, 279–80, 286, 288–91, 319–20, 343 sqq., 391, 427–8, 432, 449–50, 455, 458, 463, 468 sqq., 478;

Smith, *Mems Wl*, i, 169; *APC*, 1619–21 p. 18; Stat. 8 Eliz. c. 11; Wyatt, Apps A & C; Worcs. RO, Cons. Ct O.W. etc. 1622/152; Brist. RO, Cons. Ct inv. 1662/17; Hudson & Tingey ii, p. lxxii.

[59] Ibid. lxxiv–v; Stow, *Ann.*, 870; Willan, *Tu. Bk Rates*, 32; Redstone, 'Engld', 176; *Rates Marchandizes*; Stats 33 H.8 c.16; 1 E.6 c.6; 5 & 6 E.6 c.24; 8 Eliz. c.11; Nfk RO, Cty Recs. Misc. Docs con. Trade & Comm., Hatters Bk 1543; Ass. Bk 3 fo. 131v.; Allison 442–4, 760–1.

[60] Ibid. 442 sqq.; Pound, thes. 80; Scoville 228–9; Stow, loc. cit.; 'Aliens at K's Lynn', *Proc. H.S.L.*, 1898 v, 190; Hudson & Tingey ii, pp. lxxiii–v, 76; Millican, *Reg.*, 62, 84; Nfk RO, Cty Recs. Ass. Bk 3 fos. 25v., 147, 221v.; Bks Mayor's Ct 3 p. 9; 5 pp. 13, 14; 10 pp. 101, 165, 301, 325; 11 fo. 221; 12 pp. 206, 209, 354; Hatters Bk 1543 ut sup.; Cons. Ct invs 1590/188; 1621/126; 1626/130; 1631/223.

[61] J. S. Moore, *Gds & Chattels our Forefathers*, Lond. & Chich. 1976, pp. 16, 111, 114–15, 127, 135–6, 141–2, 144, 151, 153, 165–6, 182, 185, 188, 218, 220, 229–30, 234–6, 240, 246–7, 249–50, 253–4, 257, 265–6, 271.

[62] Watkin 333; Brears 77–9; E. A. Lewis 129, 178; C. Dale 31, 48, 54, 60, 65, 70, 113–14, 117–18, 121, 146, 172, 176; HMC, *13th Rep.* App. pt ii, 285–6; Ferguson 59–61, 67, 77, 79, 178, 184, 266–9, 271; Ogilby 75; Thornton 231; Nevill xxvii, 235; xxix, 42; xxx, 125, 182, 186, 239; xxxiii, 206; xxxvii, 101, 215; Ramsay, *Wilts.*, 102; Alexander & Hooper 179; Fleming 8; *VCH Soms.*, iv, 20; *Staffs.*, viii, 51; *Wilts.*, x, 255–6; Postlethwayt ii, 836; Charles 8, 31–2, 46–8, 211; W. Sfk RO, Ep. Commy Ct Bury inv. 1670/218; Worcs. RO, Cons. Ct O.W. etc. 1622/152; Aberystwyth, Ep. Cons. Ct St Asaph O.W. Admons & Invs 1667 Evan Lewis/Denbigh; Kent RO, Maidstone Recs. Burghmote Bk 4 fos. 116, 182; Denbighs. RO, Denbigh Boro. Recs A/51; Bodl. Arch. Ct Berks. 83/79; 113/74; 178/72; 192/150; 222/62; Aubrey 2 fo. 65; Lancs. RO, Cons. Ct Cestr. Supra inv. Ric. Isherwood 1664 Blackburn; R. Plot, *Nat. Hist. Staffs.*, Oxf. 1686, p. 257; Stukeley i, 72.

[63] Ibid.; Plot, *Staffs.*, 257–8; J. A. Van Houtte, 'Production et Circulation de la Laine comme Matière Première du XIIIe au XVII s.' in Spallanzani, *La Lana*, 394; L. S. Sutherland, *Lond. Merch. 1695–1774*, 1962, p. 29; Millard i, 53, App. p. 23; ii, iii; Charles 32; Pococke ii, 178; McGrath, *Merchs*, 229–31; Unwin, *Ind. Org.*, 132; Klein 34–5; Allison 442–3, 760–1; Strieder 114; Gras 325, 363–4, 367, 369–72; E. A. Lewis 178, 281, 287; Williams, thes. 207; Schanz, *Handelspolitik*, ii, 346; B. Dietz 8, 9, 25–6, 28, 32–3, 37, 42, 48–50, 56, 58, 60, 73, 75, 79, 80, 86, 88, 93, 97–8, 105, 113, 117, 129, 155; *Rates Marchandizes*, s.v. wool; Willan, *Tu. Bk Rates*, 24; *APC*, 1626 p. 39; PRO, SPD Eliz. 8/31; W.3 vol. 13 fo. 163; BL, Harl. 70 fo. 13 bis (p. 16); Lans. 9 no. 63 fo. 209; no. 24; no. 26 fo. 59(56); Brist. RO, Cons. Ct inv. 1662/17; Lancs. RO, Cons. Ct Cestr. Supra inv. Ric. Isherwood 1664 Blackburn; Worcs. RO, Cons. Ct O.W. etc. 1622/152; Nfk RO, Cty Recs. Bk Mayor's Ct 10, p. 101; Misc. Docs con. Trade & Comm. Hatters Bk 1543; Leics. RO, Arch. inv. Jn Stringer 1670 Leic.

[64] Ibid.; J. F. Crean, 'Hats & Fur Trade', *Can. Jnl Econ. & Pol. Sci.*, 1962 xxviii, 374, 379–80; Unwin, *Ind. Org.*, 145–6, 256; H. E. S. Fisher 128; *Rates Marchandizes*, s.v. wool, hair, beaver hair or wool; Moore 142; Millard ii, iii; PRO, PCR 1639 pp. 28, 623, 656–7 (fos. 10v., 307, 323v.–4); SPD Chas 408/166; Cty Lond. RO, Ct Orphs invs box 4, Jn Dixon 1665.

[65] Scoville 228–30, 329; Weiss i, 333–4; ii, 424; Burn 117–18; W. Marshall, *Rural Econ. Yks.*, 2 vols. 1788 ii, 265, 268; HMC, *13th Rep.*, App. pt ii, 276.

[66] Ibid. 274; *Gent's Mag.*, 1764 xxxiv, 58; Postlethwayt i, 230; Aspley Heath Sch. Hist. S., *Hist. our Dist.*, Aspley Guise 1931, p. 43; J. G. Dony, *Hist. Straw Hat Ind.*, Luton 1942, pp. 18–20.

[67] Purchas 262; Stow, *Ann.*, 870; Camden (ed. Gibson) 506; Clark, Smith & Tyacke 170–1.

[68] Kirk i, 428–9, 463, 479; ii, 67, 265, 268; Defoe, *Plan*, 288; Fiennes 271; PRO, SPD Jas 88/113; 99/43; 102; T. Wright, *Romance Lace Pillow*, 2 vols. Olney 1924, i, 29, 30, 33, 35, 37; B. Palliser 286, 320, 399, 400, 403, 503.

[69] Ibid. 371, 396 sqq., 403, 406, 414; T. Wright i, 35–6; Blome 79; Fuller, *Worthies*, i, 194, 396; Fiennes 271; McGrath, *Merchs*, 283; Pococke ii, 150; Roberts, *Lyme R.*, 156–7; Westcote 61; G. F. Nuttall, *Ltrs Jn Pinney 1679–99*, 1939, pp. xii, 37; G. F. R. Spenceley, 'Origs Engl. Pillow

Lace Ind.', *Agric. Hist. Rev.*, 1973 xxi, 87–8; J. S. Cockburn, *West. Assize Circ. Ords 1629–48*, Camd. 4th ser. 1976 xvii, 149; *VCH Soms.*, iv, 20.

[70] Defoe, *Plan*, 288; Collinson iii, 300; B. Palliser 371, 396–7, 399–401.

[71] Ibid. 371, 395; C. Dale 27, 67; Cunnington, *Recs Co. Wilts.*, 117; *VCH Wilts.*, iv, 180; Slack 66 sqq., 89, 104; Pococke ii, 135; *C.J.*, xiii, 269–70; Bodl. Aubrey 2 fo. 117; Postlethwayt ii, 836.

[72] Ibid. 765; Blome 213; Webb, *Poor Relief*, 122 sqq.

[73] *VCH Notts.*, ii, 285; Thoresby, *Ducatus Leodiensis*, 211; Pound, *Cs Poor*, 31, 33; Smyth, *Names*, 33–5; Bigland 424; C. Dale 86; Stocks, *Recs Leic.*, 101, 326.

[74] Fuller, *Worthies*, i, 194; Defoe, *Plan*, 288; *Tour*, i, 298; *Compl. Engl. Tradesman*, 79; Pococke i, 160; Fiennes 119, 332; Morton 26; W. Marshall, *Rev. Reps to Bd Agric. fr. Midld Dept Engld*, 1815, p. 202; *Gent's Mag.*, 1764 xxxiv, 58; Postlethwayt i, 230, 387; ii, 352; Spenceley 85–6; Eden ii, 536, 544, 548; F. E. Hyde & S. F. Markham, *Hist. Stony Stratford*, Wolverton & Lond. 1948, pp. 45–6, 90; PRO, SPD Jas 142/44; PCC invs 1718–82 bdl. 32 no. 167; Northants. RO, Arch. Ct Northampton Admons & Invs 1712/43; 1713/133; 1716/117; 1717/93; 1720/146; 1724/65; *C.J.*, xiii, 270; B. Palliser 371, 377 sqq.; T. Wright i, 30–2, 44–5, 69.

[75] Ibid. 37, 42, 44, 69, 74.

[76] Ibid. 40, 61; B. Palliser 312, 315–18.

[77] T. Wright ii, 213–16.

[78] Webb, *Poor Relief*, 122 sqq.; Stukeley ii, 28; Bulkeley-Owen, *Hist. Selattyn Par.*, Oswestry n.d., p. 322; HMC, *Portland MSS*, vi, 191; Pococke ii, 150; Mayo 402; Warner 128–9,138, 146; Defoe, *Compl. Engl. Tradesman*, 78; Haynes, *G.B.'s Glory*, 10; C. S. Davies 43, 122, f. 124; *Ca. Silkmen, Throwsters, Dyers, Twisters & Winders in & ab. Lond.*, n.d.; *Rsns Humbly Offered by Taylors, Button Sellers, Button Makers, Throwsters, Twisters, Dyers, Spinners & Winders etc. . . .* n.d., p. 1; *C.J.*, xiv, 504; xvi, 118; Stats 4 W. & M. c.10; 10 W.3 c.2; 8 Anne c.11; 4 Geo. c.7; 7 Geo. st. 1 c.12; PRO, SPD Jas 88/113; Chas 305/11, 104; PCC parch. invs p. 1660 no. 5509; Cant. Cath. Lib. Wall. Recs. Misc. Docs portf. 1 nos. 2–5; Kent RO, Cons. Ct Cant. Inv. Reg. 19 fo. 472; Ches. RO, Q. Sess. Recs, Q. Sess. Bk 13a (Nantwich 10 July 29 Chas 2).

[79] Ibid. Cons. Ct Cestr. Supra inv. Ric. Blacklache (erron. Blackhurst) 1635 Macclesfield; Nfk RO, Cons. Ct inv. 1634/195; Aikin 436/7.

[80] C. S. Davies 123; *Rates Marchandizes*, s.v. buttons of hair.

[81] Kirk i, 277, 406, 428, 431, 453; ii, 263, 265, 287, 292, 294, 297–8, 319, 321–2, 339, 372; iii, 138–41, 155, 167, 170, 177, 179, 191, 193–4, 197, 199, 210, 224; Ruytinck et al. 299; *APC*, 1617–19 p. 173; Moens, *Norwich*, 224, 308; PRO, SPD Jas 88/113; 99/43; 102; Chas 302/29; 305/11, 12, 104; 414/96.

[82] Kent RO, Maidstone Recs. Burghmote Bk 3 fo. 121v. (p. 243).

[83] Ibid. fos. 8v., 54v., 82v., 133 (pp. 16, 109, 165, 266); 4 fos. 7, 9, 11, 31v., 58v., 91, 116–17, 143, 153, 163v.–5, 168v., 171, 175, 180, 182v., 186v., 191v., 193, 200, 201v., 208v., 209v., 211v.–12, 213v., 214v.–15, 216v., 220v., 221v.–2, 227v., 231v., 234, 236v., 239, 241v., 250, 262v., 276; 5 fos. 6v., 10, 12v., 14, 208v., 215v., 216v.; 1 fos. 37v., 82v.; Cons. Ct Cant. Inv. Regs 7 fos. 16v., 17; 11 fo. 649; 12 fo. 133; 15 fos. 288–9, 436–7; 17 fos. 458–61; 18 Gabr. Knight yr 1636; Wm Usher 1636, Jn Callant sr 1635; 19 fo. 472; Reg. Accts & Invs 5 fos. 77–8; Inv. Papers 6/76; 8/3; PRO, PCC parch. invs p. 1660 no. 9946; SPD Jas 129/45; Chas 2, 97/51; HMC, *13th Rep.*, App. pt ii, 281; Fuller, *Worthies*, ii, 115; Hasted, *Kent*, ii, 109; R. C. Temple, *Travs Pet. Mundy in Eur. & As. 1608–67*, 5 vols. Hak. S. 2nd ser. xvii, xxxv, xlv–vi, lv, lxxviii, 1907–36, iv, 40; Pococke ii, 77.

[84] Ibid. 9; Unwin, *Ind. Org.*, 99.

[85] Defoe, *Tour*, i, 115; Fiennes 16, 17; Postlethwayt i, 1009; Westcote 61; S. C. Powell 50; J. Harris, *Hist. Kent*, vol. i 1719, p. 191; PRO, SPD Chas 2, 97/51.

[86] Leics. RO, Arch. invs 1626/215; 1632/53; Havinden 201–2; Nevill xxxi, 60, 121; C. Dale 21, 66, 126, 133; Millican, *Reg.* 112.

[87] M. G. Davies 152; Yarranton 144–5; Doughty 100; PRO, SPD Eliz. 78/10, 13; Kent RO, Maidstone Recs. Burghmote Bk 4 fo. 14; Webb, *Poor Relief*, 139.

[88] Ibid.; Fuller, *Worthies*, i, 452–3; W. Folkingham, *Feudigraphia*, 1610, p. 42; Coker 23; my *Ag. Rev.*, 119; Pococke i, 96; Camden 146; *VCH Soms.*, iv, 57; HMC, *6th Rep.*, pt i, App. pp. 491–2; Stat. 21 H.8 c.12; Wilts. RO, ex Dioc. Reg. Sarum. inv. Wm Coxe 19 Feb. 36 Eliz., Portland in Halstock; PRO, PCC parch. invs p. 1660 no. 9014.

## Chapter 11

[1] My *Ag. Rev.*, 85, 119, 130, 132, 137, 143, 145, 148, 152, 194, 196–7, 209, 213–15, 275, 309.

[2] Kent RO, Cons. Ct Cant. Inv. Paper 6/76; Inv. Regs 15 fos. 288–9; 17 fos. 458–61; 18 Jn Callant sr 1635, Gabr. Knight & Wm Usher 1636, all Maidstone; 19 fos. 472, 727; Maidstone Recs. Burghmote Bks 3 fo. 37v.; 4 fo. 152; Hessels, *Archivum*, iii, 1514–15; Harland 53, 61, 66, 77–8, 100, 104; Lowe 44–5; Wadsworth & Mann 28; Willan, *Eliz. Man.*, 60; Stat. 33 H.8 c.15.

[3] B. Dietz 4, 5, 26, 38, 44, 46, 51, 90, 95–6, 101, 104, 117, 126, 130–2, 153; Millard i, 34, 40, bet. 149–50, bet. 155–6, 169, 181, bet. 223–4, App. p. 12; ii, iii; BL, Lans. 8 fo. 75; Åström 25, 37 sqq., 202, 205–7, 230–1.

[4] Kent RO, Cons. Ct Cant. Inv. Paper 6/13; Inv. Reg. 17 fo. 460; sup. 87, 122.

[5] My *Ag. Rev.*, 79, 85, 119, 130, 132, 143, 145, 148, 176, 196–7, 209, 213, 270, 295, 298; Harland 40, 46, 60–1, 77–8, 100, 104.

[6] Åström 25, 37 sqq., 202, 206–7; sup. 24.

[7] Wood 73–5, 159; Horwitz 384; Smith, *Mems Wl*, i, 179; Roberts, *Treas.*, 33; Wadsworth & Mann 31, 33, 35; Millard i, 59, bet. 155–6, 221, bet, 223–4, 282–3, 287, 308–9, App. pp. 8, 14, 24, 30, 35; ii, iii; BL, Cott. Nero B. xl 11 fos. 304–5; PRO, SPD Eliz. 8/31; Sella, *Commerci e Industrie*, 5, 28, 49.

[8] Wood 72–3, 209; Haynes, *G.B.'s Glory*, 10.

[9] Ibid. 10, 11; K. N. Chaudhuri, *Trading Wld As. & Engl. E. I. C. 1660–1760*, Cam. 1978, pp. 345, 348–51; Rothstein 122, 124, 237, 582 sqq.; Horwitz 220, 239, 361; Steele i, 241; H. Koenigsberger, 'Engl. Merchs in Nap. & Sic. in 17th cent.', *Engl. Hist. Rev.*, 1947 lxii, 307, 311, 315, 317; Roberts, *Marchants Mapp*, 2nd pt, 57, 187; Wood 64, 72–3, 76, 103, 116; Denucé 165–7, 188 sqq.; Postlethwayt i, 101; D. Digges, *Defence of Trade*, 1615, pp. 41, 43; Firth & Rait i, 211–12; ii, 1218; *Rates Marchandizes*; HMC, *Salisbury MSS*, iv, 574; *APC*, 1629–30 pp. 252, 355; *Consids f. bringing It. thrown silk overland*; Millard i, 45, 49, 56, 97, bet. 149–50, bet. 155–6, 221, bet. 223–4, 282–3, 287, 300, App. pp. 8, 30, 31, 35, 37; ii, iii; BL, Harl. 1878 fos. 81v.–2; Lans. 8 fo. 75; PRO, SPD Eliz. 8/31; PCC paper invs 1661–1725 no. 2518; parch. invs p. 1660 no. 3602; Kent RO, Cons. Ct Cant. Inv. Papers 23/42; 27/116; Nfk RO, Arch. Ct Norvic. inv. 1674–5/216; Cons. Ct invs 1628–68/117; 1687/156; Cant. Cath. Lib. Wall. Recs. Misc. Docs portf. 4 nos. 63, 65; Guildhall Lib. Commy Ct Lond. (Lond. Div.) invs box 4 Nic. You 1725 St Dunstan's, Stepney; Jn George 1725 St Botolph's W/o; 8 Isaac Burgess 1714 St Dunstan's; Abr. Lennigni 1714 Stepney; Brist. RO, Cons. Ct inv. 1663/10; Sella, *Commerci e Industrie*, 7–9, 27, 41, 49.

[10] Brulez, *Della Faille*, 299.

[11] Ibid. 291; Kirk ii, 18, 19; Warner 390–2; PRO, SPD Jas 88/113; Interreg. 184/74.

[12] Pound, thes. 325; Kirk i, 278, 437; ii, 350, 393; iii, 411; Strutt ii, 4; *Rates Marchandizes*, s.v. silk; Page 193; Millican, *Reg.*, 121; Nfk RO, Cty Recs. Ass. Bk 4 rev. fos. 3, 75.

[13] Kirk i, 470, 475; iii, 167 sqq., 175, 177–80, 187, 198–201, 209–11; T. Mun, *Engld's Treas. by For. Trade*, Oxf. 1928, p. 11; Colyer-Fergusson iii, 232; Campbell 260; *Ca. Silkmen, Throwsters, Dyers, Twisters & Winders*; *APC*, 1629–30 p. 252; PRO, SPD Jas 88/113; 102; Chas 118/7; 294/11; 302/38, 41; 305/11, 12, 104; Stats 14 Chas 2 c.15; 19 & 20 Chas 2 c.11; Guildhall Lib. Commy Ct Lond. (Lond. Div.) invs box 2 Jn Profitt 1665; 9 Sam. Pantin 1700; Geo. Thackery 1701 St Dunstan's – all of Stepney; Cty Lond. RO, Ct Orphs invs box 1, Ant. Holliman 1665; Hessels, *Archivum*, iii, 920.

[14] Ibid. 164; R. De Roover, *Rise & Decline Medici Bk 1397–1494*, Cam. Mass. 1968, pp. 186–7; Kirk i, 428–30, 433, 440, 449, 453, 474, 479; ii, 20, 25, 32, 58, 80-1, 84, 123, 136, 262, 264 sqq.,

282, 285–7, 292, 296, 298, 305, 315, 317–19, 326–7, 329–30, 332, 335, 339, 368, 372, 392; iii, 138–40, 142, 156, 175, 336, 350, 374, 389–90, 405; Moens, *Norwich*, 308; Ruytinck et al. 299; *APC*, 1629–30 p. 252; *Rates Marchandizes*; PRO, SPD Chas 305/12.

[15] C. S. Davies 124; Brist. RO, Cons. Ct inv. 1663/10.

[16] Smith, *Mems Wl*, ii, 41; *Ca. Silkmen, Throwsters, Dyers, Twisters & Winders*; Guildhall Lib. Commy Ct Lond. (Lond. Div.) invs box 8 Ann Hue 1703 Stepney; 9 Gaspard & Eliz. Pilot 1701 & 1702 Wheeler St, Spitalfields, Stepney.

[17] Plot, *Staffs.*, 258; Dyer, *Cty Worc.*, 95–6; 'Prob. Invs', 14, 15; P. J. Bowden, *Wl Trade in Tu. & Stuart Engld*, 1962, p. 58; *APC*, 1616–17 p. 35; PRO, SPD Jas 80/13; PCC parch. invs p. 1660 no. 2130; sup. 20–1.

[18] M. E. Finch, *Wealth 5 Northants. Fams*, Northants. Rec. S. 1956 xix, 75; Smyth, *Berkeley*, 26; my *Ag. Rev.*, 96, 119; HMC, *Buccleuch MSS*, iii, 12; Ramsay, *Wilts.*, 6, 7; Westerfield 257–60; *VCH Wilts.*, iv, 144–5; Plot, *Staffs.*, 258; J. Luccock, *Essay on Wl*, 1809, pp. 275–6; Huntington Lib. ST. 48 Sir Th. Temple's Acct Bk Wl Sales, accts 1610, 1611; Wm Salt Lib. Paget of Beaudesert MSS D1734/4/1/9 fo. 5v.; Northants. RO, I(L) Coll. 2845 fo. 73; 3943 fos. 16, 21; PRO, SPD Eliz. 114/40; Jas 80/13; Exch. KR Deps by Commn 6 Jas East. 30; Req. 3/100; 16/21; 25/163; 45/100; 171/24; 202/2; 203/2; 206/29; Chanc. Early Chanc. Proc. file 790 no. 17; 1186 no. 2.

[19] Ramsay, *Wilts.*, 6; P. J. Bowden 63; Coker 4; Guilding iii, 211; BL, Lans. 152 fos. 225–6(237–8); PRO, Chanc. Early Chanc. Proc. bdl. 290 no. 3; Exch. KR Deps by Commn 14 Chas Mich. 21 m. 2d.; SPD Eliz. 250/47; Jas 80/13.

[20] Ibid.; Eliz. 46/8, 41; Gulley 205.

[21] D. Dymond & A. Betterton, *Lavenham*, Woodbridge 1982, p. 12; Allison pp. lxviii, 246, 254 sqq., 268, 285, 338, 454–5; Burley, thes. 298; Defoe, *Tour*, ii, 96; J. Thirsk, *Engl. Peasant Fmg*, 1957, p. 175; Lamb 338–9; Norden, *Ess.*, 9; BL, Add. 12504 no. 65 p. 3; Lans. 152 fos. 227–8(238–9); Lincs. RO, Massingberd-Mundy Dep. VI/5/18; Heneage of Hainton Coll. 3/2, acct 1620; Huntington Lib. ST. 48, accts 1615, 1616, 1621, 1622, 1624; Ess. RO, D/DBm Z no. 14; E. Sfk RO, Arch. inv. 12/8; W. Sfk RO, Ep. Commy Ct Bury inv. 1666/50; PRO, SPD Eliz. 46/8, 41; 114/40; 157/3; 250/47; Eliz. Add. 11/113; PCC will 24 Dyngeley; Exch. KR Deps by Commn 15 Jas Mich. 31 m. 2(1)r.; 14 Chas Mich. 21 m. 2d.; Chanc. Early Chanc. Proc. bdl. 390 no. 30; 449 no. 6.

[22] Ibid. file 1117 no. 33; Westcote 60; Leighton 136; G. L. Apperson, *Gleanings aft. Time*, 1907, pp. 167–8; BL, Harl. 5827 fo. 10(8); sup. 18, 19.

[23] Marshall, 'Kendal', 211–12, 214–15; *Rural Econ. in Yks in 1641*, Surtees S. 1857 xxxiii, 26, 30; Lowe 15, 106 sqq.; Longfield 220–3; P. J. Bowden 68–71; Plot, *Staffs.*, 258; Smith, *Mems Wl*, ii, 463–4; Blome 259; Willan, *Coasting Trade*, 89, 120–1; *Inld Trade*, 114–15; Morton 16; Crump & Ghorbal 33–4; Bowman 556–7; W. F. Rea, 'Rental & Accts Sir Ric. Shireburn 1571–77', *Trs Hist. S. Lancs. & Ches.*, 1959 cx, 51; HMC, *14th Rep.*, App. pt iv, 573; H. Stocks, *Recs Boro. Leicester 1603–88*, Cam. 1923, pp. 170–1; *APC*, 1617–19 pp. 136–7; my *Ag. Rev.*, 315; Stat. 2 & 3 P.&M. c. 13; Northants. RO, I(L) 2845 fo. 75; PRO, SPD Jas 80/113; 130/8; Exch. KR Deps by Commn 14 Chas Mich. 21 m. 2d.

[24] Sup. 8; inf. 145.

[25] McGrath, *Merchs*, 142; Westcote 60; Owen i, 56–7, 148; E. A. Lewis pp. xxxiii–iv, 30–2, 43, 86 sqq., 156–9; Stephens, *Exeter*, 49; *APC*, 1621–3 pp. 72–3; BL, Hargrave 321 p. 106(fo. 53); PRO, SPD Jas 123/54; Willan, *Coasting Trade*, 90.

[26] Ibid.; Dunsford 36; Westcote 60; BL, Harl. 5827 fo. 10(8); PRO, SPD Eliz. 157/3; Exch. KR Deps by Commn 6 Jas East. 30.

[27] Ibid.; Westcote 60; Pococke ii, 143; Stephens, *Exeter*, 49.

[28] Willan, *Coasting Trade*, 87–9, 120–1; *Inld Trade*, 114–15; HMC, *14th Rep.*, App. pt iv, 573; *Rural Econ. in Yks in 1641*, pp. 26–7, 30; P. J. Bowden 68–70; Blome 259; B. A. Holderness, 'Agric. Act. Massingberds S. Ormsby 1638–c.1750', *Midld Hist.*, 1972 i, 20; M. W. Barley, *Lincs. & Fens*, 1952, p. 81; Lincs. RO, Massingberd-Mundy Dep. VI/5/2, 19; Heneage of Hainton Coll. 3/2; PRO, PCR 1639–40, p. 656(fo. 323v.); BL, Lans. 152 fos. 227–8(238–9).

[29] Tann 209; Mann, 'Wilts. Fam.', 242–4, 250–1; PRO, SPD Jas 80/13; PCC invs 1718–82 bdl. 24 no. 100; Glouc. Lib. Smyth of Nibley MSS S.Z. 23.2 no. 5; Devizes Mus. Wm Gaby His Booke pp. 65, rev. 86, 94.

[30] My *Ag. Rev.*, 321–2; Steele i, 254; Bodl. Aubrey 2 fo. 153.

[31] PRO, SPD Eliz. 114/29, 31, 33, 37–40; Req. 169/12.

[32] Posthumus, *Bronnen*, v, 457–8; Rich 68.

[33] PRO, SPD Eliz. 39/43; 250/47; Eliz. Add. 11/113.

[34] BL, Lans. 26 no. 56 fo. 147; HMC, *3rd Rep.*, App. p. 7; PRO, Req. 45/100; 169/12.

[35] Morton 16; *APC*, ix, 223–4, 281, 366, 386; x, 24–5; PRO, SPD Eliz. 114/31, 40–1.

[36] Ibid. 114/25 sqq., 33 (quot.) sqq.; Eliz. Add. 11/133; *APC*, ix, 366; xxiii, 349–50; & v. prev. n. but one.

[37] Sup. 92.

[38] BL, Lans. 152 fo. 229(240); my *Ag. Rev.*, 313–14.

[39] Ibid. 322; Munn 4.

[40] *Sh. View Bus. bet. Clothier & Merch Staple*, 5; Thirsk 152; Westcote 60; Stephens, *Exeter*, 49, 123, 134; Willan, *Coasting Trade*, 90; J. H. Andrews, 'Trade Pt Faversham 1650–1750' in Roake & Whyman 131; G. Williams iv, 340; Kent RO, Sackvile & Knole MSS A418/5 fo. 7v.; 6 fo. 5; 8; A.424.

[41] Sup. 109–10.

[42] Nfk RO, Arch. Ct Norvic. invs 1692–3/128; 1706–7/85; Deene Ho. Bru. B. ii. 76; PRO, Exch. KR Deps by Commn 44 & 45 Eliz. Mich. 1 mm. 3d., 5r.; SPD Eliz. 157/3; BL, Add. 12504 no. 64 p. 3; *APC*, x, 24–5; 1621–3 pp. 295, 329, 455, 486; Stats 7 E.4 c.1; 6 H.8 c.12; 33 H.8 c.16; 1 E.6 c.6; *These Things following are so much concerning this Common Wealth & State*, s.l. 1647, p. 27; HMC, *13th Rep.*, App. pt ii, 272–3; *Var. Colls*, iii, 96; J. James 247; Allison 268, 338, 454, 689, map 15; Edwards 8, 24, 63, 66; Defoe, *Tour*, i, 82, 84; ii, 96; Smith, *Mems Wl*, i, 84, 314; Morton 16; Thirsk 194; S. D. White, *Sir Ed. Coke & Grievances Com. Wealth*, Man. 1979, p. 110; Willan, *Coasting Trade*, 87–8.

[43] Ibid. 87–9; Morton 16; HMC, *Var. Colls*, iii, 96; *5th Rep.*, pt i App. p. 391; Smith, *Mems Wl*, i, 176; P. J. Bowden 64; A. F. J. Brown 146; Andrews, 'Faversham', 131; Thirsk 152, 194; Pilgrim, thes. 128; Burley, thes. 298 sqq.; Defoe, *Tour*, ii, 96; *C.J.*, xiii, 720, 784; Barley 81, 143; *APC*, x, 24–5; Norden, *Ess.*, 9; Long 27–8; Stat. 6 H.8 c.12; W. Sfk RO, Ep. Commy Ct Bury inv. 1666/50; Huntington Lib. ST 48 accts 1615, 1616, 1621, 1624; PRO, SPD Eliz. 46/41; 157/3; Jas 80/13; Northants. RO, I(L)1491 acct 1582; Holderness 20.

[44] Ibid.; *VCH Ruts.*, i, 237; Tann 209; Plot, *Staffs.*, 258; Defoe, *Tour*, i, 84, 282; Allison 363–5, 444–5; Morton 16; Westerfield 257, 259–60, 269; Thirsk 152, 194; HMC, *Var. Colls*, iii, 96; Wadsworth & Mann 46; *C.J.*, xiii, 720, 784; xv, 477; W. Sfk RO, Ep. Commy Ct Bury inv. 1666/50; Kent RO, Sackvile & Knole MSS A.424; Huntington Lib. ST 48; Northants. RO, I(L) 1491 accts 1582, 1586; PRO, Req. 169/12; SPD Jas 80/13.

[45] Ibid.; BL, Add. 34258 fos. 5v., 6; Willan, *Coasting Trade*, 151–3; Andrews, 'Faversham', 131–2; Coleman, thes. 194; *APC*, 1615–16 pp. 642–3, 669–71; Long 27–8.

[46] Lowe 106 sqq.; Cullen, *Anglo-Ir. Trade*, 44; Kearney 135; Longfield 220–3; Stat. 33 H.8 c.15; sup. 15, 20.

[47] BL, Add. 34324 fo. 23; Sloane 2902 fos. 136(134), 137(135)v.; Bodl. Top. Kent a.I fo. 26; PRO, SPD Interreg. 11/62; Chas 2, 176/130; 335/35; *Cal. SP Ire.*, 1615–25 no. 548; 1669–70 p. 104; *Treatise Wl & Manuf. of it*, 1685, pp. 8–10; Armour 220, 265 sqq., 274, 321–2, 330 sqq., 340–1, 344; Cullen, *Anglo-Ir. Trade*, 30 sqq., 41–2; *Econ. Hist. Ire.*, 14, 15, 18, 33; Longfield 77–80; Smith, *Mems Wl*, i, 153, 217–18, 285, 296–7, 301–3, 345–8; ii, 3–5, 12, 214, 260–1; Lowe 15; P. J. Bowden 216–17; Millard i, App. p. 24; ii; *APC*, 1615–16 pp. 243, 639–40; 1616–17 p. 211; 1619–21 pp. 115–16, 265; Gribble 542; Defoe, *Plan*, 156, 284; HMC, *Ormonde MSS*, n.s. iv, 665 sqq.; *Int. Engld as it stands w. Rel. to Trade Ire. consid.*, 1698, p. 9; G. O'Brien, 'Ir. Staple Org. in reign Jas I', *Econ. Hist.*, 1926–9 i, 46–9, 52; *Rsns f. Ltd Exp. Wooll*, 14, 15; Wadsworth & Mann 13, 46.

[48] Ibid. 13, 46; Dunsford 209; Collinson ii, 28–9; Defoe, *Tour*, i, 262; Aikin 162; Kearney 143; Postlethwayt i, 639; Stephens, *Exeter*, 36, 49, 123, 134, 170; PRO, Exch. KR Deps by Commn 26 Chas 2 East. 15; Fox 9; Cullen, *Anglo-Ir. Trade*, 44, 58.

[49] Ibid. 44, 58; *C.J.*, xvi, 72–4, 92, 99, 119, 127, 554, 595; xxvii, 732; Defoe, *Tour*, i, 282–3; Yarranton 111; J. James 243; Wilts. RO, Arch. Ct Sub-dean Sarum, 1714/6; PRO, Exch. KR Deps by Commn 3 & 4 Chas Hil. 23; sup. 63, 66, 106, 109.

[50] PRO, Chanc. Jud. Proc. (Eq. side) Chanc. Mrs' Docs, Exhibs, Mr Unkn 114 no. 176; *Cal. SP Ire.*, 1615–25 no. 659; Wilts. RO, Arch. Ct Sub-dean Sarum. 1714/6; Nfk RO, Cons. Ct inv. 1650/60; Glos. RO, Cons. Ct invs 1682/81; 1695/152; 1701/65; 1709/40; W. Sfk RO, Ep. Commy Ct Bury invs 1666/109; 1676/49; 1686/79; 1701/52; 1709/48; E. Sfk RO, Arch. inv. 23/48; Worcs. RO, Cons. Ct O.W. etc. 1718 And. Walker, 1726 Th. Hill, 1727 Jos. Nicholls – all of Kidderminster; Northants. RO, Arch. Ct Northampton Admons & Invs 1716/99; Dunsford 208–9, 230; *C.J.*, xviii, 705; J. James 242; Steele ii, 39, 111; Cullen, *Anglo-Ir. Trade*, 14.

[51] Ibid. 56; Defoe, *Tour*, i, 262; J. James 242–3; *Substance Arguments f. & agst Bill f. Prohibiting Exp. Woollen Manufs fr. Ire. to Forreign Pts*, 1698, pp. 3, 14; R. Coke 11; *C.J.*, xii, 37; xv, 477; xvi, 111, 117–18.

[52] Dunsford 208–9, 230–1, 236; *C.J.*, xvi, 72–4, 92, 99, 120, 554.

[53] *APC*, 1616–17 p. 211; Stats 1 W.&M. c.32; 4 W.&M. c.24; 7 & 8 W.3 c.28; 10 W.3 c.16; 25 Geo. 2 cc.14, 19; 26 Geo. 2 cc.8, 11; Steele ii, 39; *Rsns . . . agst making Exeter . . . staple pt f. imp. wl fr. Ire.*, n.d.; *H. of L. MSS*, n.s. ii, 195; xii, 529–30.

[54] Ibid. v, 334; vii, 233; BL, Stowe 354 fo. 158; Stephens, *Exeter*, 36, 123, 170; 'Bpl.', 167–9; Postlethwayt i, 639; Wadsworth & Mann 13, 46; Vanes, *Docs*, 9; Cullen, *Anglo-Ir. Trade*, 44, 56.

[55] Ibid. 56–8; Willan, *Coasting Trade*, 93–4; Smith, *Mens Wl*, ii, 261; Defoe, *Plan*, 284; *Tour*, i, 282–3; Burley, thes. 155; W. H. Bidwell, *Ann. E. A. Bk*, Norwich 1900, pp. 23–4; D. Gurney, *Rec. Ho. Gournay*, 1848, p. 514; Nfk RO, Gurney of Bawdeswell Coll. RQG 484–6.

[56] Finch 19, 75; Plot, *Oxon.*, 278–80; M. James 167; Vaisey 115–18; *APC*, 1616–17 pp. 180–1; W. Sfk RO, Ep. Commy Ct Bury invs 1676/49; 1686/92; Brist. RO, Cons. Ct. inv. 1637 Th. Bibbie (1633) St Pet.'s; Hants. RO, Cons. Ct O.W. & Invs Jasper Cotman (Coatman) 1646 N. Alresford; Th. Eastman 1672 Alton; *VCH Leics.*, iv, 86; Chester RO, Cty Recs. Ass. File 1671–2 no. 43; Devizes Mus. Wm Gaby His Booke p. 23; Lichfield Jt RO, Cons. Ct O.W., Abr. Clarke 1675 Cov.; Denbighs. RO, Denbigh Boro. Recs A/52; PRO, Req. 16/21; 45/100; 169/12; SPD Eliz. 114/29, 31, 34; 146/77; Interreg. 14/87; 15/75, 86; 25/48–9; 35/116; PCC parch. invs p. 1660 no. 7931; Bodl. Cons. & Arch. Cts Oxf. 84/4/34; 172/1/52; 297/5/10.

[57] *Sh. View Bus. bet. Clothier & Merch Staple*, 4, 8, 9; my *Ag. Rev.*, 111, 113, 116, 119, 125, 127, 131, 133, 135, 138, 143–4, 146, 174; BL, Add. 34258 fos. 5v., 6; Huntington Lib. ST 48 acct 1623.

[58] *APC*, 1615–16 pp. 625, 642–3, 669–71; 1616–17 pp. 28–9, 180; Cant. Cath. Lib. Wall. Recs. Misc. Docs portf. 1 no. 8; PRO, SPD Eliz. 114/33; Jas 121/169.

[59] B. Winchester, *Tu. Fam. Port.*, 1955, p. 178; Hants. RO, Cons. Ct O.W. & Invs Sam. Hoopper 1630 Soton; Th. Eastman 1672 Alton; Leics. RO, Arch. inv. 1697/9 Th. Parnell sr Frolesworth. Cleft wool: fr. hindqrs.

[60] Plot, *Oxon.*, 278–80; Bodl. Cons. & Arch. Cts Oxf. 84/4/34; 297/5/10; PRO, PCC parch. invs p. 1660 no. 7931.

[61] PRO, SPD Eliz. Add. 33/71.

[62] Hants. RO, Cons. Ct. O.W. & Invs Sam. Hoopper 1630 Soton; Leics. RO, Arch. inv. 1614/2; Wilts. RO, ex Dioc. Reg. Sarum. inv. Aug. Pearson 1610 Stapleford.

[63] Lisle 427; Devizes Mus. Wm Gaby His Booke pp. 69, 71, rev. 10, 77, 91, 107, 112.

[64] PRO, SPD Jas 80/13.

[65] Willan, *Tu. Bk Rates*, 65: *Studs*, 76; Millard ii; *C.J.*, xvii, 397; Ess. RO, Pec. Ct Bocking inv. Ric. Chaplain 1739; Kent RO, Sandwich Recs N. Red Bk fo. 41v.; Worcs. RO, Cons. Ct O.W. etc. Wm Fereday 1718 Kidderminster; *Rates Marchandizes*, s.v. yarn.

[66] Ibid. s.v. wool; Defoe, *Plan*, 284; PRO, SPD Jas 127/19; Smith, *Mems Wl*, i, 193; ii, 63, 73, 213.

[67] Ibid. 137, 153–4; J. James 206; Stephens, *Exeter*, 36, 170, 177; 'Bpl.', 169; Millard i, 45, 53; ii, iii; P. McGrath, *Recs rel. to Soc. Merch Venturers Cty Brist. in 17th cent.*, Brist. Rec. S. 1952 xvii, 165; *Merchs*, 229–30; J. Webb, *Mems Civ. War bet. K. Chas I & Parl. Engld as it affected Herefs. & adj. cos.*, 2 vols. 1879, ii, 338; *Treatise Wl & Manuf.*, 9; Willan, *Inld Trade*, 37; H. Lapeyre, 'Les Exportations de Laine de Castille sous la règne de Philippe II' in Spallanzani, *La Lana*, 237; Kamen 71; PRO, SPD Interreg. 11/62; BL, Harl. 70 fos. 6v., 13 bis (pp. 1, 16); Lans. 9 no. 63 fo. 209; 29 no. 24; no. 26 fo. 59(56); 48 no. 64 fo. 152; Bpl. N. Devon Athenaeum, Bpl. Boro. Recs vol. 14 no. 3984 Sess. Ct Recs 1677–1716 fd loose bet. pp. 156–7.

[68] Stat. 1 Mary stat. 3 c.7; Dyer, 'Fleece' ii, 94; Hakluyt, *Orig. Writings*, 186.

[69] Heaton 206.

[70] Notestein et al. v, 488; Mann, *Cl. Ind.*, p. xvi; Tupling 172; P. J. Bowden 79–82; HMC, *14th Rep.*, App. pt iv, 595; *APC*, xix, 370–1; 1615–16 pp. 625, 642–3; 1616–17 p. 179; 1619–21 p. 65; *Sh. View Bus. bet. Clothir & Merch Staple*, 4, 7, 8; Stats 1 E.6 c.6; 2 & 3 P.&M. c.13; PRO, SPD Eliz. 117/38; Jas 80/13, 14, 16; Chas 319/42; Interreg. 11/62; 15/93; BL, Add. 34324 fo. 14.

[71] Ibid.; Lans. 28 no. 26 fo. 61(54); PRO, SPD Eliz. 114/31, 33–4; 115/14, 39, 40, 46; Eliz. Add. 9/56; 24/100; Req. 16/21; P. J. Bowden 84–5; Ramsay, *Wilts.*, 10, 13, 14; Larkin & Hughes i, 344; Westerfield 266–8; H. W. Saunders, *Off. Papers Sir Nat. Bacon of Stiffkey, Nfk, as J.P. 1580–1620*, Camd. 3rd ser. 1915 xxvi, 160; *APC*, ix, 386; x, 24–5; xix, 168–9, 370–1; xx, 302; xxiii, 349–50; xxiv, 371; 1615–16 pp. 624–5.

[72] *APC*, xxiii, 349–50.

[73] Ibid.; 1615–16 pp. 624–5; 1616–17 pp. 178–80; 1619–21 p. 207; Rich 69, 70; Bowden 161 sqq.; Mann, 'Wilts. Fam.', 250; M. James 166 sqq.; Smith, *Mems Wl*, ii, 465–7; C. Dale 19; Westerfield 268; Fowle 26; PRO, Req. 202/2; 203/2; SPD Eliz. 114/25–8, 31–2, 47; Jas 80/14; Huntington Lib. ST 48; BL, Lans. 26 no. 56 fo. 147; 28 no. 26 fo. 61(54); 152 fos. 227–8(238–9); *Rsns Decay Clo. Trade*, 5; *These Things fol.*, 27; *C.J.*, xii, 150.

[74] Ibid.; BL, Harl. 6846 fo. 128v.; PRO, SPD Interreg. 11/62; 15/93.

[75] Ibid. Eliz. 146/77; BL, Harl. 6846 fo. 128v.; Lans. 152 fo. 223(234).

[76] *Sh. View Bus. bet Clothier & Merch Staple*, 1–4.

[77] Ibid. 5, 6; Dunsford 36; *Rsns Decay Clo. Trade*, 7; Westcote 60; *C.J.*, xiii, 570, 720; Stat. 13 Anne c.20 para. 19; Soms. RO, Arch. Taunton invs Chris. Trot 1691 Taunton St Mary Magd.; fr. Jn Arnold 1699.

[78] B. H. Cunnington, *Some Ann. Boro. Devizes*, 2 vols. Devizes 1925–6, (1555–1791) pp. 130, 168–9, 199; *Recs Co. Wilts.*, 94, 101–2; Stocks 170–2; *APC*, 1616–17, pp. 180–1; PRO, SPD Jas 92/28.

[79] Stat. 13 Anne c.20 para. 19; Mann, 'Wilts. Fam.', 250; Willan, *Coasting Trade*, 87–90; Stephens, *Exeter*, 49; Defoe, *Wks*, 545; BL, Lans. 26 no. 56 fo. 147; Hants. RO, unclass. invs D/2/A: 4/U.9; E. Sfk RO, Arch. inv. 12/81(83); PRO, Req. 32/14; SPD Eliz. 114/47; Jas 80/13.

[80] Ibid.

[81] Rich 69, 70, 82.

[82] *Rsns Decay Clo. Trade*, 6, 7; *Clothiers Complt*, 5; *Blackwell Hall Factors Ca. agst provisoe to Bill f. better improving Woollen Manuf.*, n.d.; Mann, 'Wilts. Fam.', 248–9; *C.J.*, xii, 277.

[83] Mann, *Cl. Ind.*, 17; S. D. White 113–14; Notestein et al. ii, 214; iv, 150; J. Dyer, 'The Fleece' bk ii, in *Poems*, 1770, pp. 97–8.

[84] S. Webber, *Sh. Acct State our Woollen Manufs fr. Peace Ryswick to this Time*, 1739, pp. iv, v, 7, 9; Munn 21 sqq., 30–2, 46; Philanglus 39.

[85] *APC*, 1623–5 p. 44; Burn 67; Nfk RO, Cty Recs. Bk Mayor's Ct 5 pp. 13, 14; Stats. 6 H.8 c.12; 33 H.8 c.16; Smith, *Mems Wl*, ii, 48.

[86] Ibid. i, 330; W.C., op. cit. 4; M. James 165; PRO, PCR 1636–7 p. 30 (fo. 10v.); SPD Eliz. Add. 24/100; Interreg. 25/48–50; Chas 2, 95/20.

[87] Ibid. Jas 130/8; *APC*, 1617–19 pp. 136–7, 444–5, 461; M. James 169; Smith, *Mems Wl*, i, pp. iv–vi.

[88] Ibid. 170–3; Larkin & Hughes i, 317–19, 324–6; 545–6; ii, 258–61, 362 sqq. Steele i, 188, 196, 219, 371, 391; *APC*, 1623–5 pp. 285, 366; *Rsns f. Ltd Exp. Wooll*, 6, 8.

[89] PRO, PCR 1631–2 p. 153 (fo. 73); *Cal. SP Ire.*, 1615–25 nos. 154, 548, 659; 1669–70 p. 104.

[90] W. Notestein, *Jnl Sir Simonds D'Ewes fr. beg. Long Parl. to opg Trial E. of Strafford*, New Haven 1923, p. 317; *C.J.*, iii, 311, 411; vii, 119; T. Birch vii, 847–8; Firth & Rait i, 1059–61; *Rsns f. Ltd Exp. Wooll*, 6; Smith, *Mems Wl*, i, 255–8.

[91] Ibid. 153–4, 170 sqq., 270, 294, 296, 368–9; ii, 27–8, 31; Rich 85; *C.J.*, ix, 329; Stats 12 Chas 2 c.32; 14 Chas 2 c.18; 1 W.&M. cc.32, 34; 4 W.&M. c.24; 7 & 8 W.3 c.28; 9 W.3 c.40; 10 W.3 c.16; 11 W.3 c.13; *APC*, 1615–16 p. 243; 1616–17 pp. 195–6; Bodl. Rawlinson A.478 fos. 99, 100 (pp. 192–5).

[92] Smith, *Mems Wl*, ii, 73; Gulvin 15, 16, 19, 27, 36.

[93] N. J. Williams, *Contbd Cargoes*, 1959, pp. 1, 2, 6, 10–13, 17, 21–2, 27, 47–8; *APC*, xxiii, 349–50; 1616–17 pp. 28–9, 61; PRO, SPD Eliz. 115/16; 157/3.

[94] Ibid. Jas 111/86; Chas 2, 95/34, 57; 96/72; 109/133; *Cal. SP Ven.*, xxxvi, 163; Defoe, *Tour*, i, 112; Williams, *Contbd*, 73–6, 79–81, 87–9, 94–5; Long 13; Smith, *Mems Wl*, i, 231–3, 320–1; ii, 161 sqq., 206, 209, 320, 420; *Engld's Int. Asserted*, 17.

[95] Ibid. 18; Notestein et al. v, 505; Steele i, 391; Lamb 63; Stats 12 Chas 2 c.32; 1 W.&M. c.32; PRO, SPD Jas Add. 43/67; Chas 2, 152/62; 153/115.

[96] Ibid. 67/43–4; Williams, *Contbd*, 139–40; Haynes, *G.B.'s Glory*, 17; Cullen, *Antlo-Ir. Trade*, 140–3; Kearney 139–40, 143–4; *APC*, 1615–16 pp. 639–40; 1616–17 p. 347; 1617–19 p. 17; 1619–21 p. 115; Smith, *Mems Wl*, i, 345–6; ii, 171–3, 209, 421.

[97] Ibid. 163, 168; Long 2.

[98] Harper 101.

[99] Williams, *Contbd*, 75, 80, 87; R. Coke 9, 10; PRO, SPD Chas 2, 95/57; BL, Add. 2985 fos. 67, 75, 77, 79, 81; Sup. 85, 98, 130.

[100] Smith, *Mems Wl*, ii, 166 sqq., 419–20; Child, *N. Disc. Trade*, 128.

[101] *APC*, 1621–3 pp. 295, 455; Stats 6 H.8 c.12; 33 H.8 c.16; 1 E.6 c.6; sup. 8.

[102] Nfk RO, Cty Recs. Ass. Bk 2 fos. 147v.–50 (167v.–70); my *Ag. Rev.*, 140.

[103] Stat. 7 E.4 c.1; Smith, *Mems Wl*, i, 84; *APC*, 1621–3 p. 295; PRO, SPD Jas 137/16; 140/82; Chas 153/53; 530/116; Chas 2, 75/163; Exch. KR Deps by Commn 44 & 45 Eliz. Mich. 1 mm. 3d., 5r.; Allison 454.

[104] Ibid. map 16; Edwards 62; Nfk RO, Cty Recs. Bk Mayor's Ct 7 pp. 359–60; 16 fos. 41v., 43, 53, 58v.

[105] Ibid. Ass. Bk 2 fos. 147v., 149v.–50 (167v., 169v.–70).

[106] Ibid. Bk Mayor's Ct 16 fo. 306v.; Duties: 'Sale Hall f. Nyles & Flox'; Arch. Ct Norvic. inv. 1700–2/65; Cons. Ct invs. 1588/110; 1589/200; PRO, SPD Jas 131/103; Moens, *Norwich*, 152 sqq., 207 sqq.; Allison 742–3; Pound, thes. 94, 325, 337; *Cs Poor*, 58, 97; 'Soc. & Trade', 65 sqq.

[107] Millican, *Reg.*, 90, 151–2; Nfk RO, Cty Recs. Bk Mayor's Ct 13 p. 379; 16 fo. 306v.; Cons. Ct invs 1709–10/25; 1723/84; Arch. Ct Norvic. invs 1674–5/168; 1700–2/65, 280; 1708–9/46; 1712–13/29; 1715–17/67, 71; 1725–6/32.

[108] Ibid. 1707–8/78.

[109] Ibid. 29; Cons. Ct inv. 1703–8/169; Cty Recs. Bk Mayor's Ct 16 fo. 433; *Cal. Freemen Lynn*, 180, 183, 185.

[110] Nfk RO, Q. Sess. Bk 1583–6 (12 Jan. 27 Eliz.); Cty Recs. Bk Mayor's Ct 16 fo. 480v.; Arch. Ct Norvic. invs 1682–3/46; 1692–3/128; 1706–7/85; 1712–13/12; 1722–3/11; Cons. Ct invs 1681/59; 1684/102.

[111] Glos. RO, Cons. Ct invs 1682/11; 1686/248.

[112] Postlethwayt ii, 350; Defoe, *Tour*, i, 61; Smith, *Mems Wl*, ii, 261; Pococke i, 200; Corfield, 'Prov. Cap.', 284, 307; Clapham, 'Transf.', 207; Allison 742–4.

[113] Ibid. pp. lxviii, 363, 553–4, 741, 743–4, map 15; Blome 172; Randall 350; Nfk RO, Cons. Ct invs 1590/82, 186; 1634/92; 1637/76; 1638/75; 1640/39; 1642/171; 1729/13; Arch. Ct Norvic. invs 1674–5/18, 114; 1682–3/40; 1692/113; 1712–13/76; 1732–3/35; 1743–54 Jn Bacon 1749 Saham Toney; Cty Recs. Bk Mayor's Ct 16 fo. 480v.

[114] Ibid. 20 fos. 9v., 10; Cons. Ct inv. 1584/8.

[115] Thetford, King's Ho., Boro. Recs. 1st Min. Bk Corp. aft. Char. (1578–86) fos. 17v., 56 (pp. 33, 110); 2nd Min. Bk Corp. (Hall Bk 13–43 Eliz.) p. 59; HMC, *Var. Colls*, vii, 146; Allison, map 16; Nfk RO, Cty Recs. Strangers Bk fo. 91; Bk Mayor's Ct 16 fo. 41v.

[116] Ibid. 41v., 48; PRO, SPD Chas 147/50; 159/27; 530/116; W. Sfk RO, Ep. Commy Ct Bury inv. 1663/96.

[117] Ibid. 123; *APC*, 1621–3 p. 487; Nfk RO, Cty Recs. Bk Mayor's Ct 16 fos. 41v., 43, 48; 20 fos. 50v., 56v.; invs Cons. Ct 1650/60; 1676/62; Arch. Ct Norvic. 1682–3/120.

[118] Tymms 168–9; PRO, PCC parch. invs p. 1660 no. 4158; W. Sfk RO, Ep. Commy Ct Bury invs 1665/97; 1676/18; 1692/33, 65; 1701/46; 1709/24; 1711/36; 1729–30/2.

[119] Ibid. 1663/96.

[120] PRO, PCC parch. invs p. 1660 no. 4158.

[121] W. Sfk RO, Ep. Commy Ct Bury inv. 1729–30/2.

[122] Blome 208.

[123] *APC*, 1629–30 p. 156; *C.J.*, viii, 497; xi, 22; M. W. Hervey, *Ann. Sfk Vil.*, 1930, p. 80; Allison, map. 16; PRO, SPD Chas 530/116; PCC paper invs 1661–1725 no. 3440; Nfk RO, Cty Recs. Bk Mayor's Ct 16 fos. 41v., 43, 48, 58v.; Arch. Ct Norvic. inv. 1700–2/112; W. Sfk RO, Ep. Commy Ct Bury invs 1661/115; 1668/195; 1677/89; 1678/38; 1688/7; 1692/44; 1703/28; 1704/32, 74; 1712/35; 1731–6/22.

[124] Ibid. 1660/189; 1662/92, 102; 1696/83; 1774–85/84.

[125] Ibid. 1662/214; 1663/125; PRO, SPD Chas 530/116; Thornton 230; Allison, map 16.

[126] Nfk RO, Cty Recs. Bk Mayor's Ct 16 fos. 41v., 48; W. Sfk RO, Ep. Commy Ct Bury invs 1668/32; 1670/77; 1700/3.

[127] Stats 23 H.6 c.3; 7 E.4 c.1; 6 H.8 c.12; *C.J.*, xi, 22, 95.

[128] PRO, SPD Jas 80/16; E. Sfk RO, Arch. inv. 15/82; W. Sfk RO, Ep. Commy Ct Bury invs 1652/80; 1661/115; 1662/214; 1663/96, 123; 1666/50; 1668/32; 1670/77; 1680/208; 1686/79; 1688/7; 1701/52.

[129] Ibid. 1660/189.

[130] Ibid. 1660/170; 1661/1; 1666/109; 1667/1, 23, 136; 1676/60; Ess. RO, Pec. Ct Bocking inv. Ric. Chaplain 1739; Allen 189; HMC, *Var. Colls*, viii, 581, 588, 591.

[131] PRO, PCC parch. invs p. 1660 no. 4460; W. Sfk RO, Ep. Commy Ct Bury invs 1650/100; 1670/132; 1696/103; 1707/49; 1716/7; 1735–9/10.

[132] Ibid. 1662/39; 1663/221; 1668/174; 1669/26; 1680/23; 1706/7; 1712/35; E. Sfk RO, Arch. inv. 17/66; PRO, PCC parch. invs. p. 1660 no. 4160; Allen 189; Emmison, *Wills at Chelmsford*, i, 242, 319, 384.

[133] Nfk RO, Cons. Ct inv. 1637–68/118; W. Sfk RO, Ep. Commy Ct Bury invs 1667/30; 1677/88; 1686/79; 1703/28; 1705/84; 1707/1; 1711/42.

[134] Ibid. 1686/79; 1701/52; 1705/84; *APC*, 1621–3 pp. 295, 455.

[135] Nfk RO, Cty Recs. Bk Mayor's Ct 16 fos. 41v., 43, 48; PRO, SPD Jas 130/65.

[136] Ibid.; Ess. RO, Pec. Ct Bocking inv. Wm Deeks 1740 Hadleigh; Martin ii, 56; Postlethwayt ii, 765; *Magna Brit. et Hib.*, i, 722.

[137] Defoe, *Wks*, 544–5.

[138] PRO, Chanc. Jud. Proc. (Eq. side) Chanc. Mrs' Docs, Exhibs, Mr Unkn. no. 176; SPD Jas 129/70; Kent RO, Cons. Ct Cant. Inv. Paper 18/111; Long 27; *Magna Brit. et Hib.*, i, 722.

[139] Reyce 22–3.

[140] E. Sfk RO, Sess. Ord. Bk 1639–51 fo. 158v.; Arch. invs 6/145; 15/82; 23/5, 48; Nfk RO, invs Cons. Ct 1630/48; 1703–8/256, 301; 1723/28; Arch. Ct Nfk 1728–42/163; W. Sfk RO, Ep. Commy Ct Bury invs 1661/179; 1700/21, 59; Serjeant 211.

[141] C. Dale 39, 47, 55, 58, 105, 112, 119, 121, 152, 165; Slack 67–9, 83; Bodl. Arch. Ct Berks. 206/50; inf. 156–7.

[142] Horrocks i, 84, 95, 97; ii, pp. xv, 36–7; iii, 82; iv, 19, 40, 47; Patterson i, 5; G. H. Hamilton 63, 113, 153; Anderson i, 26–7; ii, 20, 29; iii, 20; Randall 350; HMC, *11th Rep.*, App. pt iii, 95; Hants. RO, unclass. invs D/2/A 2/61, 181.

[143] Boys 747; Kent RO, Cons. Ct Cant. Reg. Accts & Invs 15 fo. 295.

[144] Ibid. 7 fos. 270–1; Inv. Papers 12/45; 21/21; Inv. Regs 17 fo. 186; 20 fos. 392–3; Cowper, *Cant. Mar. Lics*, cols 25, 115, 127; *APC*, xxxiii, 8; Cant. Cath. Lib. Cty Recs. Burghmote Bks 1658–72 fo. 98v.; 1695–1744 pp. 1023, 1037, 1075; Wall. Recs. Misc. Docs portf. 1 nos. 8–11, 24; 2 nos. 84–5; 4 no. 17.

[145] Ibid. portf. 1 no. 24; BL, Egerton 2985 fo. 81; Kent RO, Cons. Ct Cant. Inv. Paper 12/45.

[146] Ibid. Arch. Ct Cant. Inv. Paper 17/87; Cant. Cath. Lib. Wall. Recs. Misc. Docs portf. 4 no. 17.

[147] BL, Add. 34258 fo. 5v.

[148] BL, Egerton 2985 fo. 81; Kent RO, Cons. Ct Cant. Inv. Paper 12/45; Cowper, *Cant. Mar. Lics.*, col 182.

[149] Lichfield Jt RO, Cons. Ct O.W. etc. Francis Allond (Alland) 1673 Cov.; K. J. Smith 11, 13, 21, 62, 68, 70, 87, 94, 133–4, 155.

[150] Randall 319–20, 350, 353; Pettit 182; PRO, PCC invs 1718–82 bdl. 21 no. 128; parch. invs p. 1660 no. 1917; Northants. RO, Arch. Ct Northampton Admons & Invs 1713/62, 70; 1714/47; 1723/34, 127; 1724/108; 1746 Th. Bolney/Gt Addington; 1748 Jn Askew/Cranford St And.

[151] Ibid. 1713/40; 1731 Th. Welch/Wellingborough; 1745 Ed. Brearley/Northampton; 1756 Jn Bunting/E. Haddon; 1764 Wm Rushall/Braunston; Bodl. Cons. & Arch. Cts Oxf. 83/4/13; Arch. Ct Berks. 139/59; Notts. RO, Man. Ct Mansfield O.W. etc. portf. 59 no. 3; Leics. RO, Arch. inv. 1668/62; 1690/63. *VCH Derbys.*, ii, 322; *Durh.*, ii, 316; *Leics.*, iv, 90–2; Cox 505; *C.J.*, xiii, 404; Bloxsom 57; Warner 174; J. A. S. L. Leighton-Boyce, *Smiths Bkrs 1658–1958*, 1958, p. 8; Thurley 105, 114, 159, 198.

[152] Ibid. 50; Morton 24; W. Sfk RO, Ep. Commy Ct Bury invs 1704/74; 1705/62.

[153] *Glos N. & Q.*, 1887 iii, 406; Rath 141; Blome 103–4; Randall 350; Defoe, *Tour*, i, 282; ii, 33; Westerfield 272; Glos. RO, Cons. Ct invs 1724/152; 1735/59; 1739/23; Soms. RO, Cons. Ct Bath & Well. inv. Wm Short 1629 Midsomer Norton.

[154] Ramsay, *Wilts.*, 33; Leland i, 129; *APC*, x, 24; PRO, SPD Eliz. 114/40; Req. 16/21; 202/2; Chanc., Early Chanc. Proc file 1115 nos. 88–9.

[155] *C.J.*, xiii, 404; PRO, PCC parch. invs p. 1660 no. 2998; paper invs 1661–1725 no. 2716; Glos. RO, Cons. Ct invs 1663/198, 249; 1677/74; 1682/11, 54, 81, 115; 1684/255–7; 1686/248; 1687/41; 1690/185; 1691/116; 1695/152, 180; 1696/75; 1698/132; 1701/65; 1705/36; 1715/71; 1721/54; 1726/28; 1730/106A; 1751/37; R. Atkyns, *Anc. & Pres. State Glocestershire*, 1768, pp. 181, 374; *N. Hist. Glos.*, 345.

[156] Ibid. 728; Postlethwayt i, 901; HMC, *13th Rep.*, pt ii, 300; Shaw, *1603–1700*, 344; *Glos. N. & Q.*, 1887 iii, 406; Glos. RO, Cons. Ct invs 1663/196; 1694/56; 1696/51; 1697/138; 1709/40; 1731/73.

[157] Westerfield 257–60, 271; Defoe, *Tour*, i, 282; ii, 33; *C.J.*, xv, 477; xvi, 111.

[158] Atkyns, *N. Hist. Glos.*, 728; *C.J.*, xv, 477; Glos. RO, Cons. Ct invs 1663/249; 1682/11; 1686/248.

[159] *VCH, Wilts.*, x, 257; Nevill xxviii, 56; Cunnington, *Recs Co. Wilts.*, 94; Wilts. RO, Pec. Ct Treas. box 2 nos. 57, 59, 96; 7 no. 88; Arch. Ct Sarum. Th. Dowse 1667 Eastcott in Urchfont; Jn Giddings 1693 Urchfont; Chris Ford 1703 id.; Cons. Ct Sarum. Robt Scott 1660 Devizes; Wm Fuller 1662 Marston in Potterne; Wm Sheppard 1665 Devizes; Wm Cooper 1676 Urchfont; Jn Slade 1687 Devizes; Ed. Powell 1693 Marlborough.

[160] Ibid. Scott, Fuller & Slade ut sup.; Hy Painter 1692 Devizes; Hy Galloway 1704 id.; Arch. Ct Sarum. Jn Markes 1678 Bradford; Jn Read 1698 Chippenham Langley; Robt Rogers 1748 Atford in Bradford; Soms. RO, DD/X/WES 1, 3, 4.

[161] Ibid. DD/X/SND 5, 7, 8; PRO, PCC parch. invs p. 1660 no. 2453; paper invs 1661–1725 no. 3279; Wilts. RO, Preb. Ct Netherbury in Ecclesia bdl. 5 no. 19; Pec. Ct Dean Sarum. Wm Pike 1731 Lyme Regis; Matthews ii, 174; iii, 425; G. Williams iv, 340–2; C. Dale 137; *VCH Soms.*, iv, 36.

[162] Tann 202.

[163] Lart 17; *C.J.*, xv, 533, 544, 547; xvi, 111, 119, 127, 595.

[164] Lyte 301–2; Humphreys i, 53, 86, 122; Randall 350; Eden ii, 647; *Cal. SPD*, 1655–6 pp. 260–1; *N. & Q. Soms. & Dors.*, 1911 xii, 352; 1969 xxix, 89; Soms. RO, Arch. Taunton invs 1640/ 83; 1647–9/8; 1667/7; 1670/25, 70; 1675 Jn Rice/Monksilver, David Tuxwell sr/Cannington, Robt Quears (Kewers) Creech; 1678/69; 1683/43; 1691 Chris. Trot/Taunton St Mary, Jn Glasse/ Charlinch; 1695 Th. Waterman/Bridgwater; 1699 fr. Jn Arnold; 1714–15 Robt Ducke/Fiddington.

[165] Ibid. 1697 Jn Thomas/Brompton Regis; DD/TW 12/3; Dunsford 54, 205–6, 208–9, 228 sqq., 236, 239; Cash 44, 76–7, 90, 155–6, 169–72; Cock 50, 133; A. H. A. Hamilton 243; Stephens, *Exeter*, 6, 54–5, 131, 134; PRO, SPD Chas 348/20.

[166] J. H. E. Bennett 164, 257, 295, 306, 313, 319, 329–30, 341, 350, 364, 368, 373, 378, 403; Chester RO, Mayor's Recs, Rolls Freemen 1658–79, s.a. 1674; Cty Recs. Ass. Bk 1624–84 fos. 182v., 184a.; Ass. File 1671–2 no. 43.

[167] Tupling 169, 180, 185; Lowe 15; Newbigging 215; Baines i, 567; Wadsworth & Mann 88.

[168] Ibid.; Heaton 269, 297–8; Marshall, 'Kendal', 200, 208, 210.

[169] G. D. Ramsay, 'Recruitment & Fortunes some Lond. Freemen in Mid-16th cent.', *Econ. Hist. Rev.*, 2nd ser. 1978 xxi, 532; Kirk i, 430; ii, 21, 81, 263–4, 266; iii, 140, 225, 229; Colyer-Fergusson iii, 230, 247, 350; PRO, SPD Chas 302/38, 41; 305/12, 104; Page 36, 248.

[170] Cullen, *Anglo-Ir. Trade*, 100–1; *Econ. Hist. Ire.*, 65–6.

[171] H. Lemon, 'Evol. Combing' in Jenkins, *Wl Text. Ind.*, 86–9, pls 7/2–5; combshop in Deutsche Museum, Munich; E. Sfk RO, Arch. invs 6/145; 15/82; PRO, Exch. KR Deps by Commn 2 Chas East. 19; Glouc. Lib. Smyth of Nibley Papers vol. viii, pp. 53, 102; Smyth of Nibley MSS S.Z. 23.2 nos. 2, 3, 8, 10; Soms. RO, Arch. Taunton invs 1670/25; 1678/69; W. Sfk RO, Ep. Commy Ct Bury invs 1660/170; 1661/1; 1662/102; 1666/109; 1677/88; 1705/62.

[172] Ibid. 1774–85/84.

[173] Haynes, *Clo. Trade*, 13; *Clothiers Complt*, 17.

[174] Nfk RO, Cty Recs. Bk Mayor's Ct 15 fo. 418v.

[175] Smith, *Mems Wl*, ii, 392.

[176] Hakluyt, *Orig. Writings*, 186; Stat. 33 H.8 c.18; PRO, SPD Eliz. 106/48.

[177] Westcote 121; Hooper 12; PRO, Exch. KR Deps by Commn 6 Jas East. 30.

[178] Sup. 116–7.

[179] Stat. 27 Eliz. c.18.

[180] Thornton 164–5.

[181] Bodl. Aubrey 2 fos. 64, 122; cf. Postlethwayt ii, 836.

[182] PRO, SPD Eliz. Add. 33/71.

[183] Nfk RO, Cons. Ct inv. 1589/200; Hants. RO, Cons. Ct O.W. & Invs, Sam. Hoopper 1630 Soton.

[184] Fiennes 146; HMC, *13th Rep.*, pt ii, 266; Burn 67; Dyer, 'Fleece' bk iii, 128.

[185] Webb, *Poor Relief*, 125 sqq.

[186] Kent RO, Cons. Ct Cant. Inv. Papers 9/107; 21/21; PRO, PCR 1637–8 pp. 82, 578 (fos. 39v., 291v.).

[187] PRO, Chanc. Jud. Proc. (Eq. side) Chanc. Mrs' Docs, Exhibs, Mr Unkn no. 176; & v. W. Sfk RO, Ep. Commy Ct Bury invs 1662/214; 1663/96; 1668/173, 183; 1677/145; E. Sfk RO, Arch. inv. 23/48; Worcs. RO, Cons. Ct O.W. etc. Ric. Billingsley 1727 Kidderminster; Northants RO, Arch. Ct Northampton Admons & Invs 1713/70; Hants. RO, Arch. Ct O.W. & Invs, Robt Zaines (Zanies) 1647 Soton; PRO, PCC parch. invs p. 1660 nos. 3715–6; Glos. RO, Cons. Ct inv. 1695/152.

[188] Ibid. 1682/11, 54; 1684/255; 1721/54; Soms. RO, Arch. invs 1668/59; 1671 Th. Hessom/ Taunton St Jas; 1675 Robt Quears (Kewers) Creech.

[189] Gretton 655–6; Giles 55.

[190] Dyer, *Cty Worc.*, 96–7; Slack 85; PRO, PCC invs 1718–82 bdl. 24 no. 100; cf. bdl. 20 no. 267.

[191] Pococke ii, 143; J. James 292; T. Wedge, *Gen. View Ag. Co. Pal. Ches.*, 1794, p. 60.

[192] Kent RO, Arch. Ct Cant. Inv. Paper 54/185; Cons. Ct Cant. Reg. Accts & Invs 10 fo. 29; Inv. Reg. 9 fo. 456; Cant. Cath. Lib. Wall. Recs. Misc. Docs. portf. 1 nos. 8, 21–4, 26; 4 no. 17; PRO, PCR 1637–8 pp. 82, 578 (fos. 39v., 291v.).

[193] W. Sfk RO, Ep. Commy Ct Bury invs 1666/50; 1668/173; 1686/20; & v. Tymms 168–9.

[194] Nfk RO, Cons. Ct inv. 1680/58.

[195] PRO, Chanc. Jud. Proc. (Eq. side) Chanc. Mrs' Docs, Exhibs, Mr Tinney nos. 17, 18, 19 vols. 1, 6, 15, 31.

[196] Fiennes 142; Yarranton 49.

[197] Ibid.; *C.J.*, xiii, 570, 720; Defoe, *Tour*, i, 45; *H. of L. MSS*, n.s. iii, 389.

[198] Ramsay, *Wilts.*, 88–9; BL, Harl. 5827 fo. 9(7)v.

[199] Blome 208, 211; Wadsworth & Mann 47.

[200] PRO, SPD Chas 243/23.

[201] Ibid. 180/71; 215/56; 243/23; 248/1; 275/49; 408/15; Eliz. 244/126–30; PCR 1632–3 p. 336 (fo. 146v.); 1634–5 pp. 102–3 (fos. 43v.–4); Ramsay, *Wilts.*, 95 sqq.

[202] PRO, SPD Eliz. 244/126–9; Jas 80/13; Chas 14/15; 180/71.

[203] Ibid. 243/25; 248/1; PCR 1632–3 p. 336 (fo. 146v.); 1633–4 p. 78 (fo. 37); Devizes Mus. Wm Gaby His Booke pp. 7–9, 18, 19, 23, 35, 38, 64, 68–9, 71; rev. pp. 1, 4, 6, 10, 16, 18, 36–7, 48–9, 51, 54–5, 58, 60, 62, 64–5, 71–3, 76, 86–7, 92–5, 100, 106–7, 111–13; cat. no. 233 invs Jas Filkes 1637, Wm Filkes 1655, both Devizes; Wilts. RO, Pec. Ct D. & C. Sarum. roll G no. 54; H. no. 6; Cons. Ct Sarum. Robt Palmer 1666, Jn Andrewes 1673; Ric. Farmer 1692, all Devizes; Wm Diffield sr 1713 Whitley in Melksham; Arch. Ct Sarum. Jn Tanner 1688, Jn Cooper er 1695, Wm Lillman 1704, all Urchfont; Mann, *Cl. Ind.*, 91–2; Cunnington, *Recs Co. Wilts.*, 133; C. Dale 36, 97, 172; *VCH Wilts.*, x, 257; Ramsay, *Wilts.*, 95 sqq.

[204] Ibid. 127; Mann, *Cl. Ind.*, 92; PRO, PCC parch. invs p. 1660 no. 9963.

[205] Blome 172, 208, 211, 215; Webb, *Poor Relief*, 122 sqq.; Pound, *Cs Poor*, 99.

[206] Burton 177; Cash 35; Cov. RO, Cty Recs. Leet Bk 30 Eliz.–1834 pp. 7, 8; Kent RO, Cons. Ct Cant. Regs Accts & Invs 3 fo. 131v.; 4 fo. 8; 6 fos. 163v., 337, 547; 8 fo. 358; 10 fo. 184; 11 fo. 90v.; 12 fos. 33v., 47v.; Inv. Paper 6/76; Inv. Regs 1 fos. 9v., 116v., 117v.; 18 Wm Usher 1636 Maidstone.

[207] Fiennes 234; *VCH Dors.*, ii, 328; Pound, *Cs Poor*, 99; sup. 75, 78, 124–5, 137.

[208] Coker 23; sup. 14, 23, 123–4, 140.

[209] Webb, *Poor Relief*, 122 sqq.; Pound, *Cs Poor*, 29, 99; thes. 230; Blome 170; Hudson & Tingey ii, 339–42; Leonard 308–10.

[210] W. Sfk RO, Ep. Commy Ct Bury invs 1573–8/66, 79; 1662/40; Fiennes 142, 146; Blome 172, 208, 211–12; HMC, *13th Rep.*, pt ii, 266; Colc. Tn Hall, Boro. Recs. Ass. Bk 21 Jan. 1590.

[211] Fiennes 161; Morton 24; Eden ii, 379, 536; Dyer, *Cty Worc.*, 96–7; *VCH Leics.*, iv, 90–2; Cov. RO, Cty Recs. Leet Bk 30 Eliz.–1834, p. 39.

[212] Cash 5, 6, 10–12, 17, 18, 21–4, 28, 35–6, 38 sqq., 68–71, 91–2, 95, 104–5, 113, 124, 129; *C.J.*, xvi, 73–4, 92, 99; BL, Harl. 5827 fo. 7(5)v.

[213] Baigent & Millard 355; Slack 84; Horrocks ii, 69; T. Davis, *Gen. View Ag. Co. Wilts.*, 1794, pp. 157–8.

[214] Marshall, 'Kendal', 216–17.

### Chapter 12

[1] W. Sfk RO, Ep. Commy Ct Bury invs 1667/170; 1680/200; PRO, PCC parch. invs p. 1660 nos. 2887, 2890, 2913; SPD Chas 319/42; 322/51; sup. 17, 36.

[2] Melling iii, 110–12; Kent RO, Arch. Ct Cant. Inv. Reg. 61 fo. 12; Cons. Ct Cant. Regs Accts &

Invs 8 fos. 243v.–4; 10 fo. 216; Inv. Papers 7/80; 16/10; 34/69; Inv. Reg. 4 fo. 33; PRO, PCC invs 1718–82 bdl. 18 no. 221; SPD Chas 363/55–6; 470/110; sup.

[3] Hants. RO, Cons. Ct. O.W. & Invs 1628 Ric. Hollis gent. Newport; Jn Guy/Andwell in Basingstoke; Jn Warner/Basingstoke; 1637 Ric. Bowden/Carisbrooke; 1638 Jn Smyth/Basingstoke; 1647 Hy Parr/Havant; 1650/3 Geo. Bayley/id.; unclass. invs D/2/A: 2/181; Arch. Ct O.W. & Invs Th. West 1649 Basingstoke; Hy Watridge 1650 Alton; Wilts. RO, Cons. Ct Sarum. Wm Sheppard 1665, Hy Galloway 1704, both of Devizes; Stat. 3 & 4 E.6 c.2; PRO, PCC invs ser. i nos. 174, 411; invs 1718–82 bdl. 24 no. 180.

[4] Ibid. no. 99; parch. invs p. 1660 nos. 1162, 6341, 6912, 11603; Dunsford 181, 208, 236, 284; Cash 130–1; Wilts. RO, Pec. Ct Dean Sarum. Jn Starke 1682 Uffculme; Arch. Ct Sarum. Robt Rogers 1748 Atford in Bradford; Soms. RO, Arch. Taunton invs 1667/7, 46; 1670/25; 1671 Th. Hessom/Taunton St Jas; 1681/90; 1691 Christ Trot/Taunton St Mary Magd.; 1714–15 Th. Hellyer/ Taunton St Jas; 1726–7/2 Wm Bowden/Minehead.

[5] Ibid. 1675 Robt Quears (Kewers) Creech; PRO, PCC parch. invs p. 1660 no. 9963; Kent RO, Cons. Ct Cant. Reg. Accts & Invs 8 fos. 243v.–4; Inv. Regs 17 fos. 458–9; 18 Jn Callant sr 1635.

[6] Brist. RO, Cons. Ct inv. 1643/92; Brist. Chars, Wills & Invs collected & transcribed E. M. Thompson no. 115; Worcs. RO, Cons. Ct O.W. etc. 1710 Jn Jones; 1712 Ob. Spencer; 1716 Stephen Lea er; 1717 Ed. Porrins; 1719 Jn Williams; 1720 Abr. Jevons; 1727 Edm. Read; W. Sfk RO, Ep. Commy Ct Bury inv. 1670/51; Soms. RO, Arch. Taunton inv. Lewes Pollard 1688 Holford; PRO, PCC parch. inv. p. 1660 no. 7892.

[7] Ibid. nos. 361, 368, 3422, 9658; invs 1718–82 bdl. 24 no. 100; 25 no. 83; Glos. RO, Cons. Ct inv. 1684/48; Marcham Coll. F26; sup. 21, 40.

[8] Notts. RO, Man. Ct Mansfield O.W. etc. portf. 1 nos. 2, 13; 16 no. 13; 23 no. 28; Hants. RO, Winch. Recs. 3rd Bk Ords fo. 11v.; Kent RO, Maidstone Recs. Burghmote Bks 3 fo. 8v. (p. 16); 4 fos. 72v., 185; Arch. Ct Cant. Inv. Paper 33/172; Baigent & Millard 319; HMC, *11th Rep.*, App. pt vii, 224; Mann, *Docs*, 27; 'Wilts. Fam.', 246.

[9] Stephens, *Exeter*, 121; Cash 155–6; Wadsworth & Mann 48, 55; Lancs. RO, Cons. Ct Cestr. Supra inv. 1633 Th. Howse (1614) Rochdale; PRO, PCR 1636 p. 190 (fo. 93v.).

[10] Dyer, 'Prob. Invs', 18, 19; sup.

[11] *APC*, xxvii, 10; Hughes & Larkin iii, 140; Kent RO, Arch. Ct Cant. Inv. Reg. 10 fos. 364–6; Cons. Ct Cant. Regs Accts & Invs 12 fos. 479–80; 13 fos. 250–3; Inv. Reg. 17 fo. 347; PRO, SPD Jas 131/100.

[12] Ibid. 131/103; Moens, *Norwich*, 79, 154; Nfk RO, Cty Recs. Strangers Bk fos. 20v.–1, 56, 79; Ass. Bks 2 fo. 135 (155); 3 fos. 34–5, 227, 280v.–1, 306v.–7; 5 fos. 4(13)v., 125(135)v.; Bks Mayor's Ct 9 pp. 12, 24, 108, 114, 146, 198, 253, 359, 454, 517; 10 pp. 40, 86, 240, 419, 727 bis; 11 fos. 1, 13, 130v., 233, 274v.; 12 pp. 135, 304, 418, 509.

[13] W. Sfk RO, Ep. Commy Ct Bury inv. 1686/64; Notts. RO, Man. Ct Mansfield O.W. etc. portf. 1 no. 2; 16 no. 13; 23 no. 28.

[14] *Wills & Admons fr. Knaresboro. Ct R.*, ii, 220 sqq.; Benham 7, 8, 58, 72, 80, 83, 96, 117; Webb, *Tooley*, 137; Mendenhall 8; Fiennes 247; Stephens, *Exeter*, 125; Dunsford 208, 284; Serjeant 4, 148, 315, 321, 342, 423, 499.

[15] Moens, *Norwich*, 153 sqq., 189 sqq., 207 sqq.; Pound, thes. 295, 325, 337; 'Soc. & Trade', 65, 67; Nfk RO, Cty Recs. O. Free Bk & Memo fo. 132(118); Ass. Bks 2 fo. 135(155); 3 fos. 34–5, 227, 280v.–1, 306v.–7; 5 fos. 4(13)v., 125(135)v.; Bk Mayor's Ct 9 pp. 12, 24, 108, 114, 146, 198, 253, 359, 454, 517; 10 pp. 40, 86, 240, 419, 727 bis, 782; 11 fos. 1, 13, 130v., 233, 274v.; 12 pp. 135, 304, 418, 509; Strangers Bk fo. 107; Allison. 764.

[16] Poole 33, 358; Unwin, *Ind. Org.*, 75; M. D. Harris, *Hist. Drapers Co. Cov.*, s.l. n.d. 21–2; *Life in O. E. Tn*, 1898, p. 302; *Cov. Leet Bk*, 697–8; Cov. RO, Weavers & Clothiers Co. Recs. no. 20 Misc. Papers re dispute bet. clothiers & drapers; *APC*, 1621–3 p. 265; 1626 p. 383; 1627 p. 80; 1627–8 pp. 130–1, 152–3; 1628–9 pp. 80, 399; PRO, SPD Jas 131/80–1; Chas 66/3; 105/102; 225/87; 527/97; Interreg. 3/13.

[17] Stephens, *Exeter*, 121; Fiennes 247; Ramsay, *Wilts.*, 28; Kirk i, 99, 103, 111, 132, 259, 292–3, 295, 308, 314–15, 322, 325, 328, 331–3, 335, 340, 366; iii, 139–40, 144, 158, 166, 168, 172, 177, 212, 218, 224–7, 335, 370, 379.

[18] Unwin, *Ind. Org.*, 255; PRO, SPD Chas 2, 55/108; 61/109; Kirk ii, 115, 124, 137, 260, 267, 280, 285, 323; iii, 167, 206, 218, 225, 227, 353, 376, 430.

[19] Larkin & Hughes i, 282; Guildhall Lib. Commy Ct Lond. (Lond. Div.) invs box 9 Gaspard & Eliz. Pilot 1701 & 1702 Wheeler St, Spitalfields, Stepney.

[20] Hessels, *Archivum*, iii, 1071; W. Cholmeley, 'Request & Suite of a True-Hearted Englishman' in *Camd. Misc. ii*, Camd. S. 1853 lv, 3; Overall 118–9; Kirk i, 445, 449–50, 462; ii, pp. xi, 124, 137, 260, 284–5; iii, 139–40, 144, 158, 187, 198–201, 209 sqq.; Wyatt 103–4, App. A; PRO, SPD Jas 88/113; 102; 133/3 sqq.

[21] Kent RO, Arch. Ct Cant. Inv. Reg. 5 fo. 19; Cons. Ct Cant. Reg. Accts & Invs fos. 28v., 29v.

[22] Friis 250–1; Bodl. Aubrey 2 fo. 122.

[23] Worcs. RO, Cons. Ct O.W. etc. 1639/127; 1720 Jn Williams/Kidderminster; Hants. RO, Cons. Ct O.W. & Invs Jn Warner 1628 Basingstoke; Hy Parr 1647 Havant; Arch. Ct O.W. & Invs Th. West 1649 Basingstoke; W. Petty, 'App. to Hist. Com. Practices Dying' in T. Sprat, *Hist. R. S. L.*, 1667 p. 301; & v. W. Sfk RO, Ep. Commy Ct Bury invs 1670/51; 1686/64; PRO, PCC parch. invs p. 1660 nos. 2890, 9946; invs 1718–82 bdl. 24 nos. 100, 180; Nfk RO, Cons. Ct inv. 1637/148; Kent RO, Arch. Cant. Inv. Reg. 10 fo. 365.

[24] Ibid. fos. 364–6; Cons. Ct Cant. Reg. Accts & Invs 8 fos. 242–4; Soms. RO, Arch. Taunton inv. 1726–7/2 Wm Bowden/Minehead; Hants. RO, Cons. Ct O.W. & Invs 1628 Ric. Hollis gent. Newport & Jn Guy/Andwell in Basingstoke.

[25] Ibid. 1650/3; Petty, 'App.', 288, 304; Fiennes 247; Munn 14; *VCH Leics.*, iv, 87–8; W. Sfk RO, Ep. Commy Ct Bury invs 1670/51; 1686/64; E. Sfk RO, Arch. inv. 18/69; Worcs. RO, Cons. Ct O.W. etc. 1601/91; 1711 Wm Pebody, 1716 Stephen Lea er, 1727 Edm. Read, all Kidderminster; PRO, PCC parch. invs p. 1660 no. 9658; invs 1718–82 bdl. 24 nos. 100, 180; invs ser. i no. 411.

[26] Nfk RO, Cty Recs. Strangers Bk fo. 107; Ass. Bk 3 fos. 34–5, 306v.–7; sup. 68.

[27] Fiennes 247–8; R. Holinshed, *Chrons*, 1587 iii, 1008; J. H. Thomas, *Tn Govt in 16th cent.*, 1933, pp. 59 sqq.

[28] Petty, 'App.', 292–3; Cholmeley 3, 8; Lappenberg pt ii, 169; Hants. RO, unclass. invs D/2/A: 2/181; Munn 14; Guildhall Lib. Commy Ct Lond. (Lond. Div.) invs box 1 Francis Mottershed 1665 Paul's Wharf; Cty Lond. RO, Ct Orphs invs box 1 Th. Champney 1666; Worcs. RO, Cons. Ct O.W. etc. Jn Williams 1720 Kidderminster; Notts. RO, Man. Ct Mansfield O.W. etc. portf. 1 nos. 1, 13; 16 no. 13.

[29] Ibid. portf. 1 no. 2; 16 no. 13; Fiennes 247; PRO, PCC invs ser. i no. 411; Hants. RO, Cons. Ct O.W. & Invs 1638 Jn Smythe/Basingstoke; 1650/3; unclass. invs D/2/A: 2/181.

[30] Soms. RO, Arch. Taunton invs 1667/7, 46; 1670/25; 1681/90; 1714–15 Th. Hellyer/Taunton St Jas; Wilts. RO, Arch. Ct Sarum. Robt Rogers 1748 Atford in Brad.

[31] Fiennes 243; PRO, PCC invs ser. i no. 411; J. U. Nef, *Rise Brit. Coal Ind.*, 2 vols. 1931, i, f. p. 19.

[32] Ibid. f. p. 57; T. S. Willan, *R. Nav. in Engld 1600–1750*, 1964, pp. vi, 32, 68; Notts. RO, Man. Ct Mansfield O.W. etc. portf. 1 nos. 2, 13.

[33] Melling iii, 110–12; Gulley 51; HMC, *14th Rep.*, App. pt viii, 140; Kent RO, Cons. Ct Cant. Reg. Accts & Invs 8 fo. 244; Inv. Paper 7/80; BL, Cott. Titus B.v fo. 254(251)(244)v.; W.Sfk RO, Ep. Commy Ct Bury inv. 1680/200; E. Suss. RO, Arch. Lewes inv. Samson Brightridge 1714 Hellingly; PRO, PCC invs 1718–82 bdl. 18 no. 221; parch. invs. p. 1660 no. 2913; SPD Chas 363/55–6.

[34] Ibid.; Gulley 56–7; Nef, *Coal*, i, f. p. 19, p. 192.

[35] Ibid. 79, 80; PRO, SPD Chas 322/51.

[36] Ibid. 363/56; 371/23; cf. J. B. Hurry, *Woad Plant & its Dye*, 1930, p. 177.

[37] Cholmeley 16.

[38] PRO, SPD Eliz. 127/68; Chas 363/56; 371/23; Guildhall Lib. Commy Ct Lond. (Lond. Div.) invs box 1 Francis Mottershed 1665 Paul's Wharf; 9 Gaspard Pilot 1701 Wheeler St, Spitalfields, Stepney; Nef, *Coal*, i, 157, 214–15.

[39] Ibid. 214; Fiennes 247; Stephens, *Exeter*, 36–7, 125; Mann, 'Wilts. Fam.', 246; cf. HMC, *14th Rep.*, App. pt viii, 140.

[40] PRO, SPD Chas 470/110; Jas 38/13; Chanc. Proc. ser. ii, bdl. 266 no. 43; Petty, 'App.', 291, 301.

[41] S. Fairlie, 'Dyestuffs in 18th cent.', *Econ. Hist. Rev.*, 2nd ser. 1965 xvii, 488, 492; D. Dawe, *Skilbecks: drysalters 1650–1950*, 1950, pp. 4, 30; Munn 15; Melling iii, 110–12; *Wills & Admons fr. Knaresboro. Ct R.*, ii, 220–4; Soms. RO, Arch. Taunton inv. 1683/56; Petty, 'App.', 292, 300; Kent RO, Arch. Ct Cant. Inv. Paper 33/172; Worcs. RO, Cons. Ct O.W. etc. Wm Pebody 1711 Kidderminster; Lancs. RO, Cons. Ct Cestr. Supra inv. Wm Crompton 1631 Bolton; PRO, PCC invs ser. i no. 411; parch. invs p. 1660 no. 2913; BL, Cott. Titus B.v fo. 254(251)(244)v.

[42] Ibid.; *C.J.*, ii, 528; Stat. 2 & 3 E.6 c.26; Nef, *Coal*, i, 214; Fairlie 493; Posthumus, *Bronnen*, iv, 42; Higgins 9, 10; PRO, SPD Chas 319/42; 322/51; PCR 1636 pp. 160, 165 (fos. 78v., 81).

[43] Ibid. pp. 160, 165 (fos. 78v., 81); SPD Chas 322/51; W. Sfk RO, Ep. Commy Ct Bury, Reg. Bk Wills 13 fo. 263; E. Sfk RO, Arch. inv. 1/65; Serjeant 118, 187, 453; Bacon 243; HMC, *11th Rep.*, App. pt vii, 224; Fairlie 495; E. S. Godfrey, *Devpt Engl. Glassmaking 1560–1640*, Oxf. 1975, pp. 3, 5, 89, 141, 158, 196–7.

[44] Petty, 'App.', 288–91, 293, 295, 298; Hughes & Larkin i, 454; Willan, *Eliz. Man.*, 75; Dawe 30; Vaisey 282; Allison 765; *Wills & Admons fr. Knaresboro. Ct R.*, ii, 220–4; Mann, 'Wilts. Fam.', 246; Brears 137; Melling iii, 110–12; Fairlie 492; Burley, thes. 408; Stat. 23 Eliz. c.9; Dyer, *Cty Worc.*, 18, 103; 'Prob. Invs', 18, 19; Skeel, '18th & 19th', 33; *Misc.*, Thoresby S. iv, 163–6; Hants. RO, Cons. Ct O.W. & Invs Ric. Bowden 1637 Carisbrooke; Worcs. RO, Cons. Ct O.W. etc. Wm Pebody 1711 Kidderminster; Wilts. RO, Arch. Ct Sarum. Robt Rogers 1748 Atford in Brad.; Soms. RO, Arch. Taunton invs 1667/7; 1670/25; 1681/90; 1683/56; 1714/15 Th. Hellyer/Taunton St Jas; Kent RO, Cons. Ct Cant. Regs Accts & Invs 8 fos. 243v.–4; 12 fo. 479v.; 13 fo. 251; Inv. Papers 7/80; 16/10; Inv. Reg. 17 fo. 348; Arch. Ct Cant. Inv. Reg. 61 nos. 12, 127; Lancs. RO, Cons. Ct Cestr. Supra invs Wm Crompton 1631 Bolton; Th. Howse 1633 (1614) Rochdale; Glos. RO, Cons. Ct inv. 1684/48; Cant. Cath. Lib. Wall. Recs. Misc. Docs portf. 4 no. 63; PRO, SPD Eliz. 88/24; PCC invs 1718–82 bdl. 18 no. 221; 25 no. 83; invs ser. i no. 411; parch. invs p. 1660 nos. 3422, 9963; Nfk RO, Cty Recs. Strangers Bk fo. 54; Ords con. Wl fo. 19; Keure fo. 19; Notts. RO, Man. Ct Mansfield O.W. etc. portf. 1 no. 2.

[45] Ibid. nos. 2, 13; 16 no. 13; Hurry 62; Fairlie 491; J. May 30; Cholmeley 3, 9, 10; Nef, *Coal*, i, 214; Allison 765; *Wills & Admons fr. Knaresboro. Ct R.*, ii, 220–4; Dyer, 'Prob. Invs', 18, 19; Burley, thes. 408; Pilgrim, thes. 12, 13; Dyer, 'Fleece' bk iii, 134; PRO, PCC invs ser. i no. 174; parch. invs p. 1660 no. 572; Kent RO, Arch. Ct Cant. Inv. Reg. 5 fo. 53v.; Cons. Ct Cant. Regs Accts & Invs 8 fo. 244; 13 fo. 251; Inv. Papers 7/80; 33/172; Inv. Reg. 4 fo. 33v.; Lancs. RO, invs Howse & Crompton, & Worcs. RO, inv. Pebody, ut sup.; W. Sfk RO, Ep. Commy Ct Bury inv. 1667/170; Hants. RO, Arch. Ct O.W. & Invs Hy Watridge 1650 Alton; Cons. Ct O.W. & Invs Jn Warner 1628 Basingstoke; Brist. RO, Brist. Chars, Wills & Invs (Thompson) no. 115; Nfk RO, Cty Recs. Strangers Bk fos. 20v.–1; Bk Mayor's Ct 6 p. 114; 9 pp. 198, 454; 11 fo. 130v.; Ass. Bks 3 fos. 34–5, 280v.–1, 306v.–7; 5 fo. 125(135)v.

[46] Ibid.; 3 fos. 34–5, 307v.; Bk Mayor's Ct 6 p. 114; PRO, SPD Eliz. 88/24; BL, Cott. Titus B.v fo. 254(251](244); Stats 4 E.4 c.1; 1 R.3 c.8; 24 H.8 c.2; 3 & 4 E.6 c.2; 4 & 5; 4 & 5 P&M. c.5; 23 Eliz. c.9; J. May 30; Hurry 47–8; Hughes & Larkin i, 454; Mann, *Docs*, 17, 27.

[47] Petty 'App.', 303; Cholmeley 10; Hurry 47; Stats 1 R.3 c.8; 24 H.8 c.2; 3 & 4 E.6 c.2; Nfk RO, Cty Recs. Ass. Bk 3 fos. 280v.–1, 306v.–7.

[48] PRO, SPD Chas 470/110; Mann, *Docs*, 14; W. Blith, *Engl. Improver Improved*, 1652, p. 230; J. May 30; Dyer, 'Fleece' bk iii, 134; BL, Lans. 121 no. 21 fo. 166.

[49] Kent RO, Cons. Ct Cant. Inv. Paper 7/80; Nfk RO, Cty Recs. Bk Mayor's Ct 6 p. 114; E. Sfk RO, Blois Fam. Archives, Hy Blois's Acct Led. fo. 41; Hughes & Larkin i, 454; Stat. 3 & 4 E.6 c.2; W. Lewis, *Commercium Philosophico-Technicum*, 1763, pp. 403–4.

[50] BL, Lans. 24 no. 66 fo. 156(172); 101 no. 20 fo. 82(78); 114 no. 24 fos. 92v.–3; Hurry 62–4; *APC*, xi, 147; Hakluyt, *Orig. Writings*, 137–9, 182, 188–9.

[51] Ibid. 182, 188; C. Singer, *Earliest Chem. Ind.*, 1948, pp. 263, 266; Vaisey 282; Willan, *Inld Trade*, 128; *Wills & Admons fr. Knaresboro. Ct R.*, ii, 220–4; Fairlie 490–1; Stats 23 Eliz. c.9; 13 Geo. c.24; BL, Cott. Titus B.v fo. 254(251)(244); Cant. Cath. Lib. Wall. Recs. Misc. Docs portf. 4 no. 63; Nfk RO, Cty Recs. Ass. Bk 5 fo. 125(135)v.; Hants. RO, Cons. Ct O.W. & Invs Jn Warner 1628 Basingstoke; Ric. Bowden 1637 Carisbrooke; Worcs. RO, Cons. Ct O.W. etc. Wm Pebody 1711 Kidderminster; Lancs. RO, Cons. Ct Cestr. Supra inv. Wm Crompton 1631 Bolton; PRO, PCC parch. invs p. 1660 nos. 572, 2913; Kent RO, Arch. Ct Cant. Inv. Paper 33/172; Cons. Ct Cant. Inv. Reg. 4 fo. 33v.; Notts. RO, Man. Ct Mansfield O.W. etc. portf. 1 no. 2; Pilgrim, thes. 12, 13.

[52] Ibid. 153–4; Petty, 'App.', 288, 295, 301; Ordish 63; Dawe 5, 30; Hurry 47; Unwin, *Ind. Org.*, 255; Hakluyt, *Orig. Writings*, 139, 192; Fairlie 490; Tawney & Power iii, 207; J. May 30; Heaton 221; Notestein et al. vii, 156; *APC*, 1621–3 p. 261; Larkin & Hughes i, 467–9, 548; Willson 111–12; Stats 23 Eliz. c.9; 39 Eliz. c.11; 13 Geo. c.24; PRO, SPD Jas 112/109; 122/96; 127/144; 129/67; 131/65; PCR 1631–2 p. 268 (fo. 134v.); BL, Hargrave 321 p. 107 (fo. 53v.).

[53] Singer 264; Dawe 6; Steele i, 188; Fairlie 490–1; W. Lewis 407, 409–10, 428; Willan, *Eliz. Man.*, 52, 75; Vaisey 282; Brears 137; Mann, 'Wilts. Fam.', 246; Dyer, 'Fleece' bk iii, 133; *Wills & Admons fr. Knaresboro. Ct R.*, ii, 220–4; Moore 265–6; Petty, 'App.', 301; Devizes Mus. Wm Gaby His Booke p. 18; PRO, PCC invs 1718–82 bdl. 18 no. 221; 24 no. 99; parch. invs p. 1660 nos. 6341, 9963; Kent RO, Cons. Ct Cant. Inv. Paper 16/10; Reg. Accts & Invs 12 fo. 479v.; Arch. Ct Cant. Inv. Reg. 61 no. 195; Worcs. RO, Cons. Ct O.W. etc. 1710 Jn Jones, 1711 Wm Pebody, both Kidderminster; Lancs RO, Cons. Ct Cestr. Supra invs Wm Crompton 1631 Bolton; Th. Howse 1633 (1614) Rochdale; Soms. RO, Arch. Taunton invs 1670/25; 1681/90; 1683/56; Wilts. RO, Arch. Ct Sarum. Robt Rogers 1748 Atford in Brad.; Notts. RO, Man. Ct Mansfield O.W. etc. portf. 1 no. 2; Skeel, '18th & 19th', 34.

[54] Ibid. 33; Petty, 'App.', 293, 298; W. Lewis 406, 420–1; Melling iii, 110–12; Nef. *Coal*, i, 214; Singer 261, 264; Willan, *Eliz. Man.*, 54, 75; Vaisey 282; Allison 765; Cholmeley 3, 10; *Wills & Admons fr. Knaresboro. Ct R.*, ii, 220–4; Dyer, 'Prob. Invs', 18, 19; *Cty Worc.*, 103; Burley, thes. 408; Fuller, *Worthies*, ii, 114; Mann, 'Wilts. Fam.', 246; Hughes & Larkin i, 454; Fairlie 490–1; *Misc.*, Thoresby S. iv, 163–6; Stats 1 R.3 c.8; 3 & 4 E.6 c.2; 23 Eliz. c.9; 14 Chas 2 c.30; 13 Geo. c.24; Kent RO, Arch. Ct Cant. Inv. Reg. 10 fo. 265v.; PRO, SPD Eliz. 88/24; PCC parch. invs p. 1660 no. 3422; invs ser. i no. 411; invs 1718–82 bdl. 25 no. 83; W. Sfk RO, Ep. Commy Ct Bury inv. 1670/51; Glos. RO, Cons. Ct inv. 1684/48; Hants. RO, Cons. Ct O.W. & Invs, 1628 Ric. Hollis gent. Newport; 1637 Ric. Bowden/Carisbrooke; Soms. RO, Arch. Taunton invs 1688 Lewes Pollard/Holford; 1714–15 Th. Hellyer/Taunton St Jas; Worcs. RO, Cons. Ct O.W. etc. 1711 Wm Pebody, 1712 Ob. Spencer, both Kidderminster; Notts. RO, Man. Ct Mansfield O.W. etc. portf. 1 no. 2; Lancs. RO, Cons. Ct Cestr. Supra inv. Wm Crompton 1631 Bolton.

[55] Petty, 'App.', 295–6; Stats 4 H.7 c.8; H.8 c.2; *Rates Marchandizes*, s.v. drugs.

[56] Petty, 'App.', 289, 298; Fairlie 490; Singer 262–3, 265–6; Dyer, 'Fleece' bk iii, 133; Skeel, '18th & 19th', 34; Allison 765; Hakluyt, *Orig. Writings*, 119; *APC*, xxxiii, 164, 321; PRO, SPD Eliz. 88/24; PCC parch. invs p. 1660 no. 3422; invs 1718–82 bdl. 25 no. 83; Stat. 6 Anne c.60; BL, Harl. 70 fo. 22(21)v.; Guildhall Lib. Commy Ct Lond. (Lond. Div.) inv. box 9 Gaspard Pilot 1701 Wheeler St, Spitalfields, Stepney; Notts. RO, Man. Ct Mansfield O.W. etc. portf. 1 no. 2; Cant. Cath. Lib. Wall. Recs. Misc. Docs portf. 4 no. 63.

[57] Ibid.; Petty, 'App.', 294; Kent RO, Cons. Ct Cant. Inv. Reg. 17 fo. 348.

[58] Ibid.; Inv. Paper 16/10; Regs Accts & Invs 8 fo. 244; 13 fo. 251; Arch. Ct Cant. Inv. Regs 10 fo. 365v.; 61 nos. 12, 195; Petty, 'App.', 295–8; Singer 262; Fairlie 490–1; Willan, *Eliz. Man.*, 52,

54, 75; McGrath, *Recs*, 164; Skeel, '18th & 19th', 34; Vaisey 282; *Wills & Admons fr. Knaresboro. Ct. R.*, ii, 220–4; Brears 137; Firth & Rait ii, 1222; Mann, 'Wilts. Fam.', 246; Stats 24 H.8 c.2; 3 & 4 E.6 c.2; Devizes Mus. Wm Gaby His Booke p.19; Sudbury, Tn Recs, Boro. Ct Bk 1 fo. 43(40)v.; BL, Stowe 354 fo. 63(104); PRO, SPD Eliz. 88/24; PCC invs ser. i no. 411; invs 1718–82 bdl. 18 no. 221; 24 no. 99; Lancs. RO, Cons. Ct Cestr. Supra inv. 1633 Th. Howse (1614) Rochdale; Wm Crompton 1631 Bolton; Allison 765; Hants. RO, Cons. Ct O.W. & Invs Ric. Bowden 1637 Carisbrooke; Soms. RO, Arch. Taunton invs. 1667/7; 1683/56; 1714–15 Th. Hellyer/Taunton St Jas; Worcs. RO, Cons. Ct O.W. etc. 1710 Jn Jones, 1711 Wm Pebody, 1712 Ob. Spencer, all Kidderminster; Notts. RO, Man. Ct Mansfield O.W. etc. portf. 1 no. 2; Cant. Cath. Lib. Wall. Recs. Misc. Docs portf. 4 no. 63.

[59] Ibid.; Petty, 'App.', 298.

[60] Ibid. 292, 299; Fairlie 490; Singer 266; Fuller, *Worthies*, ii, 113–14; Allison 765; Worcs. RO, inv. Pebody ut sup.; Hants. RO, Cons. Ct O.W. & Invs Jn Guy 1628 Andwell in Basingstoke; Kent RO, Cons. Ct Cant. Inv. Reg. 17 fo. 348; Arch. Ct Cant. Inv. Reg. 61 no. 36; Dyer, 'Fleece' bk iii, 133.

[61] Ibid.; Petty, 'App.', 299, 300; Singer 263; Fairlie 490; Allison 765; Vaisey 282; Burley, thes. 408; *Wills & Admons fr. Knaresboro. Ct R.*, ii, 220–4; Mann, 'Wilts. Fam.', 246; Brears 137; Skeel, '18th & 19th', 33; Kent RO, Cons. Ct Cant. Inv. Paper 16/10; PRO, PCC invs 1718–82 bdl. 18 no. 221; 24 no. 99; parch. invs p. 1660 nos. 6912, 7892; Lancs. RO, Cons. Ct Cestr. Supra inv. Wm Crompton 1631 Bolton; Notts. RO, Man. Ct Mansfield O.W. etc. portf. 1 no. 2; 22 no. 4; Worcs. RO, Cons. Ct O.W. etc. 1710 Jn Jones, 1711 Wm Pebody, 1712 Ob. Spencer, all Kidderminster; Soms. RO, Arch. Taunton invs 1683/56; 1714–15 Th. Hellyer/Taunton St Jas.

[62] Ibid. Jos. Lewes 1690 Staplegrove; Fairlie 490; Nfk RO, Arch. Ct Norvic. inv. 1703–6/12; Bodl. Top. Ess. e.9/3 fo. 6v.

[63] Petty, 'App.', 288.

[64] Ibid. 295–6, 299; Hakluyt, *Orig. Writings*, 189; Worcs. RO, inv. Pebody ut sup.; Kent RO, Cons. Ct Cant. Inv. Paper 16/10; Arch. Ct Cant. Inv. Reg. 61 no. 12.

[65] *Wills & Admons. fr. Knaresboro. Ct R.*, ii, 220–4; Nfk RO, Cty Recs. Ass. Bk 5 fo. 125(135)v.

[66] Ibid. Strangers Bk fo. 107; Petty, 'App.', 303.

[67] Hughes & Larkin i, 454; Stats 4 E.4 c.1; 1 R.3 c.8; 24 H.8 c.2; 3 & 4 E.6 c.2; Fairlie 489, 492–4, 497; Millard vol. ii; Allison 765.

[68] Ibid.; Petty, 'App.', 287, 289, 295–6; Kent RO, Cons. Ct Cant. Regs Accts & Invs 8 fo. 244; 12 fo. 479v.; Inv. Paper 16/10; Arch. Ct Cant. Inv. Reg. 61 no. 127; Hants. RO, Cons. Ct O.W. & Invs Ric. Bowden 1637 Carisbrooke; Wilts. RO, Arch. Ct Sarum. Robt Rogers 1748 Atford in Brad.; Soms. RO, Arch. Taunton invs 1670/25; 1681/90; Lancs. RO, Cons. Ct Cestr. Supra invs Wm Crompton 1631 Bolton; Th. Howse 1633 (1614) Rochdale; Notts. RO, Man. Ct Mansfield O.W. etc. portf. 1 no. 2; W. Lewis 401–3, 409–10.

[69] Ibid. 425, 430; Steele i, 132, 191; Larkin & Hughes i, 282–3; Nfk RO, Cty Recs. Strangers Bk fo. 54; Ords con. Wl fo. 18; Keure fo. 19; PRO, PCR 1634–5 p. 299 (fo. 142); SPD Chas 180/70; Petty, 'App.', 296–8, 305–6.

[70] Ibid. 288–9, 291, 295, 298, 304; Fiennes 247; Mann, *Cl. Ind.*, 9.

[71] PRO, SPD Eliz. 88/24.

[72] Nfk RO, Cty Recs. Ass. Bk 5 fo. 125(135)v.

[73] Dawe 3, 4; Mann, 'Wilts. Fam.', 246; A. H. John, 'Miles Nightingale, drysalter', *Econ. Hist. Rev.*, 2nd ser. 1965 xviii, 152 sqq.; Soms. RO, Arch. Taunton inv. 1683/56; Fairlie 488.

[74] Ibid. 495; Singer 115, 182 sqq., 319; J. H. Bettey, 'Prod. Alum & Copperas in S. Engld', *Text. Hist.*, 1982 xiii, 92, 94; A. F. Upton, *Sir Art. Ingram c.1565–1642*, Oxf. 1961, pp. 27, 109, 112, 117, 123, 126, 132–5, 144–5; D. Colwall, 'On Engl. Alum Wks', *Phil. Trans.*, ii, 458–61; J. U. Nef, *Conq. Mtl Wld*, Chic. & Lond. 1964, pp. 124–5; *Coal*, i, 184–5, 209; A. & N. Clow, *Chem. Rev.*, 1952, pp. 235–6; R. B. Turton, *Alum Fm*, Whitby 1938, pp. 37, 40–1, 59 sqq., 194;

Guicciardini 120, 124; J. Delumeau, 'L'Alun de Rome' in *Studi in Onore A. Fanfani*, iv, 577; Bodl. Hearne's Diaries 158 fos. 75, 77; PRO, SPD Eliz. 8/31; Millard i, bet. 149–50, bet. 155–6; ii, iii.

[75] Ibid. i, 34, 40, 56, bet. 149–50, 172, bet. 223–4; ii, iii; PRO, SPD Eliz. 8/31; my *Ag. Rev.*, 119, 127, 132, 196–7, 204, 209–10, 212–14, 217–19, 309, 328, 345, 347; Petty, 'App.', 300; Hurry 63, 65; Lamb 2, 3, 339; Tawney & Power iii, 205, 207–8; Webb, *Tooley*, 9, 32, 43; Vanes, *Led.*, 100; G. Connell-Smith, *Forerunners Drake*, 1954, pp. 208–9, 211–12; B. Dietz 49, 67–8, 74, 92, 94, 101, 105.

[76] Ibid. 39, 43–5, 49, 51–2, 54, 56, 60, 63, 66–8, 72–4, 80, 82, 84, 86, 88, 93–4, 98, 102, 104–6, 108, 113–15, 118, 123, 126–9, 131, 153; *Rates Marchandizes*; my *Ag. Rev.*, 59, 176, 196, 268, 298; Petty, 'App.', 299; Fairlie 496–7; Firth & Rait ii, 1215; McGrath, *Recs*, 164; *Merchs*, 284–7; Burley, thes. 408; Stat. 14 Chas 2 c.30; PR, SPD Eliz. 8/31; Jas 127/17; PCR 1631–2 pp. 285, 295 (fos. 143, 148); Millard i, 34, bet. 149–50, bet. 155–6, bet. 223–4, 251, App. p. 18.

[77] Ibid. App. p. 8; Chalklin 179; Fiennes 10, 11; Melling iii, 147–50; Nef, *Coal*, i, 184–5; D. Colwall, 'Engl. Grn Copperas', *Phil. Trans.*, ii, 461–3; W. Brereton, *Travs in Holl., Utd Provs, Engld, Sc. & Ire.*, Chetham S. 1844 i, 2, 3; R. H. Goodsall, 'Whitstable Copperas Ind.', *Arch. Cant.*, 1956 lxx, 143 sqq.; Andrews, 'Faversham', 131–2; E. P. Dickin, 'Nn. on Coast, Shipping & Seaborne Trade Ess. fr. 1565 to 1577', *Ess. Archaeol. S. Trs*, n.s. 1926 xvii, 164; Temple iv, 57; Bettey 92–4; Fairlie 495–6.

[78] Ibid. 497–9; Haynes, *G.B.'s Glory*, 10, 14; Millard i, bet. 149–50, bet. 155–6, 221, bet. 223–4, 251, 282–3, 287, 300, 312, App. pp. 17, 23–4, 30–1, 34, 36–7; ii, iii; Connell-Smith 210–12; Chaudhuri 330 sqq., 523; B. Dietz 108; McGrath, *Merchs*, 229–30, 288; Firth & Rait ii, 1199, 1212, 1222; J. James 206; Smith, *Mems Wl*, ii, 153–4; Guicciardini 119–20, 124–5; Tawney & Power iii, 202, 207, 209; P. Croft, *Sp. Co.*, Lond. Rec. S. 1973, p. xxv; Shepherd & Walton 35, 45–6, 49, 98, 100; Cant. Cath. Lib. Wall. Recs. Misc. Docs portf. 4 no. 63; PRO, SPD Eliz. 8/31; PCR 1636–7 p. 456 (fo. 223v.); Stats 6 Anne c.60; 13 Geo. c.25; BL, Lans. 24 no. 66 fo. 172; H. & P. Chaunu, *Séville & l'Atlantique (1504–1650)*, 8 vols in 12 pts Paris 1955–60, viii pt i, 366, 451, 520, 562, 771, 840–1.

## Chapter 13

[1] Usher 268, 273; H. Catling, 'Evol. Spinning' in Jenkins, *Wl Text. Ind.*, 102–3; Horrocks ii, 69; Dyer, 'Fleece' bk iii, 128; PRO, SPD Eliz. Add. 33/71; Hants. RO, Cons. Ct O.W. & Invs Sam. Hoopper 1630 Soton; Bodl. Aubrey 2 fo. 64; Mann, *Cl. Ind.*, 287.

[2] Nfk RO, Cty Recs. Bk Mayor's Ct 20 fo. 422.

[3] PRO, SPD Interreg. 184/74.

[4] J. James 336; Wadsworth & Mann 413–14.

[5] Nfk RO, invs Arch. Ct Norvic. 1709–10/61; Cons. Ct 1709–10/214; 1710–14/23.

[6] T. S. Ashton, *Ind. Rev. 1760–1830*, 1948, p. 71.

[7] Mann, *Cl. Ind.*, 123, 125–8; Catling 106–7; Wadsworth & Mann 414–15.

[8] Dyer, 'Fleece' bk iii, 138–9.

[9] W. English, 'Tech. Assmt L. Paul's Spinning Mach.', *Text. Hist.*, 1973 iv, 68, 71–2, 81; Wadsworth & Mann 282, 419 sqq., 515–16; J. James 337–8; Thoresby, *Ducatus Leodiensis*, 83; Catling 103–4.

[10] Ibid. 107; Warner 174.

[11] Ibid. 199–201; Stat. 5 Geo. c.8; De Roover, *Medici Bk*, 187; S. D. Chapman, *Cotton Ind. in Ind. Rev.*, 1972, pp. 14, 15; V. Zonca, *Novo Teatro di Machine et Edificii*, Padua 1607, pp. 68 sqq.; Stukeley i, 53–4.

[12] Warner 297–8.

[13] Ibid. 147, 170, 257, 298, 321–2, 333; Stephens, *Congleton*, 138; C. S. Davies 125; Chapman, *Cotton Ind.*, 15; Toulmin 380–1; Grimwood & Kay 92; K. W. Glass 31.

[14] Hooper 252, 306; sup. 49, 50.

[15] Fiennes 123–4; Nfk RO, Cons. Ct invs 1602/239; 1606/66; 1646/50; Guildhall Lib. Commy Ct Lond. (Lond. Div.) inv. box 9 Th. Crette 1702 St Dunstan's, Stepney; sup. 48, 50, 121.

[16] Mann, *Cl. Ind.*, 154; Plummer & Early 49; Wadsworth & Mann 450 sqq.; Burley, thes. 390; *VCH Ess.*, ii, 399; Postlethwayt i, 737; cf. Lebrun 247.

[17] Usher 282–4; Steele i, 216, 438; Posthumus, *Bronnen*, iii, pp. x, 696–9, 704, 706; iv, pp. x, 513–15, 519 sqq.; Waller 4; Bowman 420; Stukeley i, 58; Plummer, *Lond. Weavers' Co.*, 162 sqq.; G. N. Clark, *17th Cent.*, 1960, pp. 64–5; *C.J.*, ix, 375; *Cal. SP Ven.*, xxxviii, 446–7; Guildhall Lib. Weavers' Co. Ord. & Rec. Bk 1577–1641 pp. 157, 302, 358–9, 485; Commy Ct Lond. (Lond. Div.) inv. box 9 Jas Woolfinden 1699 St Dunstan's, Stepney; PRO, SPD Jas 81/56; 88/112; Chas 529/91; Chas 2, 372/189; 376/143; Bodl. Aubrey 2 fo. 67; BL, Lans. 691 fo. 55(56) (p. 91); Wadsworth & Mann 101 sqq., 285.

[18] Ibid. 301, 456; Usher 284.

[19] Ramsay, *Wilts.*, 13, 24; 'Rep.', 486; Wadsworth & Mann 281; Plummer & Early 45–7; Giles 49; Burley, thes. 390; Stat. 5 & 6 E.6 c.22; PRO, SPD Chas 241/36; 243/73; 244/1; 248/78; 250/53; 252/21; 254/45; 257/1 sqq.; 266/73; 287/77; PCR 1633–4 pp. 107, 372–3 (fos. 50, 193v.–4).

[20] Guildhall Lib. Commy Ct Lond. (Lond. Div.) inv. box 2 Wm Owen 1665 St Sepulchre's; W. Sfk RO, Ep. Commy Ct Bury invs 1664/34; 1665/22; Brist. RO, Cons. Ct inv. 1624/72; Hants. RO, unclass. invs D/2/A: 2/181; Soms. RO, Arch. Taunton invs 1688 Lewes Pollard/Holford; 17th-cent. fr. Taunton St Mary Magd.; Nfk RO, Cons. Ct inv. 1682/12; Worcs. RO, Cons. Ct O.W. etc. Jn Williams 1720 Kidderminster; Cash 130–1, 138–9; *APC*, xxvii, 10; PRO, PCC parch. invs p. 1660 no. 1946; invs 1718–82 bdl. 25 no. 83.

[21] Nfk RO, Cty Recs. O. Free Bk & Memo. fo. 132(118); Clouzot 49, 50; *Ords Clwkrs' Co.*, 60; Stats 5 H.8 c.4; 25 H.8 c.5; Campbell 262; cf. Posthumus, *Geschiedenis*, ii, 269, 278; *Bronnen*, iv, 81, 98, 109, 111, 159, 166–7, 172–3; v, 255–6, 292.

[22] Ibid. iv, 120, 131, 135; *Geschiedenis*, ii, 268; Campbell 201; Fiennes 246–7; Hudson & Tingey ii, 259; Larkin & Hughes i, 470–1; Stats 3 & 4 E.6 c.2; 5 & 6 E.6 c.6; Notts. RO, Man. Ct Mansfield O.W. etc. portf. 1 no. 2; 16 no. 13; Bodl. Arch. Ct Berks O.W. etc. 223/136; Guildhall Lib. Commy Ct Lond. (Lond. Div.) invs box 2 Wm Owen 1665 St Sepulchre's; Northants. RO, Arch. Ct Northampton Admons & Invs 1717/1; Worcs. RO, Cons. Ct O.W. etc. Wm Radford jr 1716 Kidderminster; Hants. RO, unclass, invs D/2/A: 2/181; Brist. RO, Cons. Ct inv. 1624/72; Nfk RO, Cons. Ct invs 1666/27; 1681/85; PRO, SPD Jas 155/17; PCC invs 1718–82 bdl. 18 no. 187.

[23] Ibid.; SPD Chas 2, Entry Bks 71 p. 10; 335 p. 188; PCR 1639 p. 44 (fo. 18v.); Chanc. Petty Bag: Misc. Papers & Exhibs bdl. (box) 70, folder marked 'no. 49–144', nos. 61–72; Worcs. RO, inv. Radford ut sup.; Soms. RO, Arch. Taunton inv. 1720/4 Ric. Startt mercer Porlock; *Rates Marchandizes*, s.v. chamlets; *VCH War*, ii, 256; B. Dietz 48, 75, 83; Willan, *Tu. Bk Rates*, 16; Lancs. RO, Cavendish of Holker Coll. 1/46 p. 51; Munn 29, 30; Evelyn i, 94; ii, 146; Bridewell Mus. Ord. Bk 'Norwich 1791'; Nfk RO, Cons. Ct inv. 1640/143.

[24] Ibid. Cty Recs. Ass. Bk 3 fos. 306v.–7, 310v.; Pec. Ct D. & C. inv. 1727–37/21; Bridewell Mus. Patts Norwich Manufs 1794–7; PRO, PCC parch. invs p. 1660 no. 1946.

[25] Posthumus, *Bronnen*, vi, 319, 517; Wadsworth & Mann 281–2; M. J. Dickenson, 'Fulling in W. R. Woollen Ind. 1689–1770', *Text. Hist.*, 1979 x, 130; Monceau, *Art de Frise*, 2, 3 & end pls.

[26] R. T. D. Richards, 'Devpt Mod. Woollen Carding Mach.' in Jenkins, *Wl Text. Ind.*, 73–4; PRO, SPD Interreg. 184/74.

[27] Dunsford 209; Dyer, 'Fleece' bk iii, 130; Nfk RO, invs Cons. Ct 1584/62; 1588/117; Arch. Ct Norvic. 1692–3/114; Worcs. RO, Cons. Ct O.W. etc. Ed. Abrahams 1721 Kidderminster; Kent RO, Cons. Ct Cant. Reg. Accts & Invs 12 fo. 480; Inv. Paper 16/59; PRO, PCC invs 1718–82 bdl. 25 no. 83.

[28] Kirk i, 454.

[29] Leic. Mus. Hall Papers bk xiv no. 593.

[30] *VCH Leics.*, iv, 90, 96–7.

[31] Boys 747; 'Aliens at K's Lynn in 1571', *Proc. H. S. L.*, 1898 v, 189–91; Overend, 'Strangers at Dover', 159–62; Kent RO, Cons. Ct Cant. Inv. Paper 16/59; Cant. Cath. Lib. Wall. Recs. Misc. Docs portf. 1 nos. 2–5, 7; PRO, SPD Eliz. 78/9.

[32] Henson 61–4.

[33] Cty Lond. RO, Repertories vol. 50 fos. 30v.–1; S. R. H. Jones, 'Devpt Needle Manuf. in W. Midlds befe 1750', *Econ. Hist. Rev.*, 2nd ser. 1978 xxxi, 355.

[34] Ibid. 356; Unwin, *Ind. Org.*, 258; PRO, SPD Jas 158/38.

[35] Chapman, 'Gen.', 21–2, 24; Leics. RO, Arch. inv. Th. Glover 1729 Cas. Donington.

[36] Steele i, 416; PRO, SPD Interreg. 184/34; cf. 220/53.

[37] Nfk RO, Cons. Ct inv. 1584/62.

[38] Janssen 231: 'Ic gaen doen maken een baey ghewant teghen uwe comste'.

[39] Kent RO, Cons. Ct Cant. Reg. Accts & Invs 12 fos. 479–80; Inv. Paper 16/59; Cant. Cath. Lib. Wall. Recs. Misc. Docs portf. 1 nos. 2–5, 7.

[40] Chapman, 'Gen.', 21–2, 24.

[41] Ibid. 36; Burton 182.

[42] M. G. Davies 96; Kirk i, 454; Glouc. Lib. Smyth of Nibley MSS S.Z. 23.2 no. 4; PRO, SPD Jas 129/70; Nfk RO, Cons. Ct invs 1584/62; 1588/117; Cant. Cath. Lib. Wall. Recs. Misc. Docs portf. 1 nos. 2–5, 7; Pound, thes. 337.

[43] Chapman, 'Gen.', 22; Leics. RO, Arch. inv. Th. Glover 1729 Cas. Donington; Notts. RO, Man. Ct Mansfield O.W. etc. portf. 26 no. 2.

[44] *VCH Leics.*, iv, 90; *Ess.*, ii, 401; Pound, *Cs Poor*, 97; Postlethwayt ii, 350; Smyth, *Names*, 121 sqq.; Nfk RO, Arch. Ct Nfk inv. 1728–42/106.

[45] HMC, *11th Rep.*, App. pt vii, 224; Horrocks ii, 42; Kent RO, Cons. Ct Cant. Reg. Accts & Invs 12 fos. 479–80; Inv. Paper 16/59; Kirk ii, 264; iii, 139, 140.

[46] Kirk ii, 104; iii, 139, 417; Pound, thes. 296, 325, 337; *Cs Poor*, 97; Smyth, *Names*, 163–5; Millican, *Reg.*, 121–2; *Cons. Ct Norwich Wills 1550–1603*, Ind. Lib., B.R.S. 1950 lxxiii, 124; Hudson & Tingey ii, 161; Marshall, 'Kendal', 200, 208; M. Bateson, *Recs. Boro. Leic.*, 3 vols. 1899–1905, iii, 309; PRO, SPD Chas 305/11; Worcs. RO, Cons. Ct O.W. etc. Ed. Abrahams 1721 Kidderminster; Nfk RO, Cty Recs. Free Bk & Memo. fo. 139 (125)v.; Ass. Bk 2 fo. 235(253)v.

[47] Ibid. Bk Mayor's Ct 13 p. 47; Ess. RO, Arch. Ct Colc. O.W. 7/132; PRO, SPD Jas 131/103; Kirk ii, 295; Smith, *Mems Wl*, i, 237.

[48] Ibid. 115; Bacon 238; Pound, thes. 325; *VCH Wilts.*, x, 254–5, 257; Kirk ii, 3, 280, 295, 318, 332; Cockburn, *Kent*, 45; Marshall, 'Kendal', 200, 206, 208; Ferguson 23, 35, 69, 70, 111, 265; Tyacke, App. i, p. xxi; App. iii, p. vi; Boys 747; B. Dietz 38, 41; HMC, *12th Rep.*, App. pt ix, 427; Mann, *Cl. Ind.*, 286; Dyer, *Cty Worc.*, 119; McGrath, *Merchs*, 8; Heaton 237; Slack 67, 75, 89; *C.J.*, xvi, 471; xxxvi, 7; Smyth, *Names*, 2 sqq., 163–5, 239 sqq., 265–7, 292–5; Guilding ii, 478; Hilton 73; Mayo 403; Nevill xxvii, 238, 266; xxxvii, 104; Hughes & Larkin iii, 147–8; Kramer, *Engl. Craft Gilds: studs*, 22, 77–8; Harris, *Cov. Leet Bk*, 707–8, 713, 793; *Rsns f. Prohibiting Imp. Wh. Iron-Wire*, n.d.; *Rsns . . . by Cardmakers & Wierdrawers Froome Selwood . . .*, n.d.; *Dial. bet. Dick Brazenface & Tim. Meanwell*, 2; Glos. RO, Cons. Ct inv. 1663/226; Aberystwyth, Ep. Cons. Ct St Asaph O.W. etc. Wm Powell 1662 Oswestry; PRO, SPD Eliz. 78/9.

[49] *APC*, 1630–1 pp. 126, 200–1, 212; *C.J.*, xvi, 471; Benham 11, 69, 98, 148; Burley, thes. 330–1.

[50] B. Dietz 22, 38, 41, 54, 58–9, 64, 71, 81, 86, 89, 109, 113, 122, 124, 132–3; Gras 562; *Rates Marchandizes*, s.v. cards; Stats 39 Eliz. c.14; 14 Chas 2 c.19.

## Chapter 14

[1] *Ind. Org.*

[2] Heaton 90 sqq., 107–8, 113–14, 290–1, 293 sqq.; Lowe 26 sqq., 35–6, 41–2, 106 sqq.; Preston 13–15, 24–5, 27–8, 33–4, 37–40, 48–9, 51, 53–4, 79, 80, 103–5, 131, 140–2; Willan, *Eliz. Man.*,

51–2, 56, 63; Wadsworth & Mann 7, 27–8, 39; Bowman 417, 556–7; Fishwick, *Hist. Rochdale*, 53–4; Tupling 179, 189–90; M. Gray 16, 17; PRO, SPD Eliz. 117/38; Stat. 2 & 3 P.&M. c.11; Lancs. RO, Cons. Ct Cestr. invs Infra: 1666 Wm Whittacar/Falinge in Rochdale; 1677 Jas Turner/Hundersfield; 1682 Jas Shaw/Saddleworth, Jas Cheetham/Sykebank in Spotland; 1684 Gil. Holden/Holcombe in Bury; 1686 Jn Crompton/Radcliffe; 1696 Jn Crompton/Darcy Lever; 1700 Abr. Healey/Catley La. in Spotland; 1701 Is. Clegg/Rochdale; 1704 Jas Haslam/Shawfield in Spotland; 1720 Jas Butterworth/Woodhouse La. Rochdale; Supra: 1633 Jn Smethurst/ Lowerplace; 1640 Ric. Lort/ Hollingworth in Butterworth; 1641 Edm. Taylor/Quicke, Randle Healey/Spotland; 1646 Ad. Boordall/Todmorden; 1661 Jas Howorth/Risingbridge, Jas Milne/ Marland, Roger Hartley/ Baxenden; 1662 Geo. Ormerod/Crawshawbooth; 1663 Geo. Ormerod (1649) Gambleside, Ric. Pollard/Goodshaw; 1664 Edm. Leigh/Rochdale, Abr. Walker/Radcliffe; 1665 Zach. Fielden/ Knowle, Th. Fletcher/Stondelph in Whitfield; 1667 Ric. Holte/For. Rossendale; 1672 Robt Whitworth/Shawfield in Rochdale; 1673 Ed. Ashworth/Cowpe, Alice Shepheard/ Spotland; 1674 Hy Heawood/Bury; 1676 Jn Haworth/Musbury, Jas Clegg sr Shawfield; 1677 Jas Hoyle/Tonge in Rochdale; 1678 Jn Fielden/Haslingden, Jn Roades/Marland; 1679 Hy Romsbotham/Rawtenstall; 1680 Ed. Nuttall/Cowpe, Robt Whitworth/Lowerplace; & ut sup. p. 57 n. 54; cf. Defoe, *Tour*, ii, 195.

[3] Stat. 2 & 3 P.&M. c.13.

[4] Heaton 94–5, 203–4, 208, 298, 359 sqq., 381; Wadsworth & Mann 9, 30–3, 37, 39, 41, 43–4, 48, 55, 62, 79 sqq., 281–2, 328–9; Lowe 37 sqq., 83; Tupling 172, 186, 191; Willan, *Eliz. Man.*, 53 sqq., 63; *Inld Trade*, 108–9, 'Man. Clothiers', 177 sqq.; Bowman 415; *VCH Derbys.*, ii, 371–2; *Pal. Notebk*, i, 126–7; HMC, *14th Rep.*, App. pt iv, 593, 605–6; H. Fishwick, *Svy Man. Rochdale 1626*, Chetham S. n.s. 1913 lxxi, p. xv; Earwaker, *Lancs. & Ches. Wills & Invs 1572 to 1696*, 18, 19; Stat. 33 H.8 c.15; *APC*, xxiv, 371; PRO, PCR 1639–40 p. 656 (fo. 323v.); PCC parch. invs p. 1660 nos. 3941–2; Lancs. RO, Cons. Ct Cestr. Supra invs 1633 Th. Howse (1614), 1641 Randle Healey, 1675 Jn Gregory, all Rochdale.

[5] Shrewsbury Lib. MS 4274 Ords etc. Weavers' Co.; Mendenhall 8, 10–12, 32, 39, 42–3, 211–12; Gough 38, 47–8, 78, 143, 147, 149–50; Aberystwyth, Ep. Cons. Ct St Asaph O.W., Admons & Invs 1661 Th. Edwards/Oswestry; Stat. 4 & 5 P.&M. c.5; BL, Cott. Titus B.v fo. 252(242)(249); PRO, SPD Eliz. 157/5 (quot.).

[6] Ibid. 117/38; Wadsworth & Mann 5; Stat. 2 & 3 P. & M. c. 11.

[7] Ferguson 24 sqq., 55, 85–6, 110, 138, 145–6, 176–7, 271, 273; Marshall, 'Kendal', 206, 208, 229, 234; Raine 152–3, 156, 274.

[8] Brist. RO, Cons. Ct invs 1624/72; 1635 Hugh Davis/St Mary Pt; 1636 Jn Jones/Clifton; Vanes, *Docs*, 14.

[9] BL, Harl. 5827 fo. 9(7)v.

[10] Fiennes 245–6; Cash 3, 11, 12, 38, 44, 55–7, 64–5, 70–1, 75, 88, 94–5, 101, 103, 113, 129–31, 143, 153 sqq.; Worthy 31, 163; Stephens, *Exeter*, 51, 138–9; Youings 67–9; Westcote 61; Soms. RO, Arch. Taunton inv. Hugh Strong 1668 Wootton Courtenay.

[11] BL, Harl. 5827 fo. 9(7)v.; PRO, PCC paper invs 1661–1725 no. 3416; Devon RO, Huntsham MS PZ1; Dunsford 216; Cash 138–9, 143; Stephens, *Exeter*, 81, 135.

[12] Ibid. 137–8; Youings 70–3.

[13] *Misc.*, Thoresby S. iv, 163–6; Heaton 115, 295–6.

[14] Ibid. 268 sqq., 297–8, 300, 387–9; Wadsworth & Mann 39, 88 sqq., 277 sqq.; Lancs. RO, Cons. Ct Cestr. Supra inv. Jn Gregory 1675 Rochdale.

[15] Ibid. Jn Bordeman 1628, Laurence Molineux 1637, Wm Isherwood 1638, all Bolton; Jn Bolton 1661 (1657), Th. Couper 1664, both Blackburn; Jas Ogden 1666 Blackley: Roger Nicholson 1667 Bolton; Hy Yeats 1670 Lindsay in Blackburn; Hy Heawood 1674 Bury; Th. Cooke 1678 Livesey; Wadsworth & Mann 27–8, 36–9, 78 sqq.; Aikin 158; Willan, 'Man. Clothiers', 177 sqq.; Raines & Sutton i, 14; ii, 263 sqq.

[16] Mendenhall 28, 223; Jenkins, *Wl Text. Ind.*, 286; Aberystwyth, Ep. Cons. Ct St Asaph

O.W., Admons & Invs Th. Price 1661 Wrexham; Lodowick Lloyd 1668 Gwestid in Llanllwchaiarn; Ric. Jones 1690 Darowen; Th. Price 1710 Broughton.

[17] Shrewsbury Lib. MSS 3359 Orig. Recs Co. Weavers & Clothiers vol. i fos. 3, 5v.; 4274 Ords Weavers' Co. 13 H.6 & temp. Eliz., arts 1595, agrt 1600; Gough 64.

[18] Marshall, 'Kendal', 199, 206–8, 210, 212–14.

[19] PRO, PCC invs ser. i no. 97; Brist. RO, Cons. Ct invs 1633 Philip Towenston (erron. Townsend) Temple par.; 1643/92.

[20] Ibid. 1635 Jn Marchant weaver; 1641 Th. Cornock/Temple par.; 1660/21; 1720 Th. Avery stuffmaker; Soms. RO, Cons. Ct Bath & Well. invs N–O no. 18.

[21] Brist. RO, Cons. Ct invs 1628/59; 1643/40.

[22] Unwin, *Ind. Org.*, 54, 75, 78, 96–7; PRO, SPD Eliz. 46/52; Stat. 1 & 2 P.&M. c.4.

[23] Harris, *Cov. Leet Bk*, 688–9.

[24] Cov. RO, Weavers & Clothiers Co. Recs 2c Title p. etc. Ord. Bk.

[25] Harris, *Cov. Leet Bk*, 776–7; PRO, SPD Chas 527/97; PCC parch. invs p. 1660 nos. 2335, 2348, 3442, 11135; Lichfield Jt RO, Cons. Ct O.W., Jn Bond 1550; Harry Bowettre 1558; Th. Bowater 1559; Matt. Arnold 1578; Jas Brisbie 1585–6; Th. Bowche 1592; Wm Cooke yr 1603; Allan Rylye 1604; Marmaduke Chambers 1604–5; Robt Baylye 1606; Th. Farnes 1607; Francis Rodes 1611; Sam. Gilbert & Ric. Falkner 1633; Jn Becke & Jn Browne 1634; Geo. Mathew & Wm Hunt 1636; Ed. Berry & Steven Burrow 1637; Ed. Harres 1640; Geo. Bagott & Ed. Clifton 1641; Nat. Cheese 1647; Simon Awson 1674; Benj. Bedford 1680; Th. Bowater 1681; Jn Baskeby 1715.

[26] Ibid. Jn Showell 1599; Th. Smythe 1603.

[27] Harris, *Cov. Leet Bk*, 688–9.

[28] Ibid. 694, 697–8, 704, 714–15; *Hist. Drapers Co. Cov.*, s.l. n.d. pp. 4, 7; pace Unwin, *Ind. Org.*, 97.

[29] Sup. 21, 164.

[30] Lichfield Jt RO, Cons. Ct O.W., Jn Baskeby 1715; Jn Barbar 1720; Sam. Smith 1722; Jos. Smith 1729.

[31] Unwin, *Ind. Org.*, 91–2; Worcs. RO, Cons. Ct O.W. etc. 1601/143; 1604/9; 1605/30, 76b; 1606/12; 1610/3, 66; 1613/103; 1641/161; 1644/28, 34; Dyer, *Cty Worc.*, 97, 117–18.

[32] Ibid. 34–5, 82–3, 85, 95 sqq., 225; 'Prob. Invs', 12–15; PRO, PCC parch. invs p. 1660 nos. 2130; 2428, 3595, 3672, 3716; invs 1718–82 bdl. 18 no. 170; 27 no. 79; Stats 25 H.8 c.18; 5 & 6 E.6 c.8; 1 Mary stat. 3 c.7; Worcs. RO, Cons. Ct O.W. etc. 1560/76; 1601/91; 1605/46, 118a, 145; 1608/7, 104a; 1610/ 163b; 1612/10, 47; 1614/39, 45; 1616/114; 1617/13; 1624/67; 1626/121, 138; 1629/62, 134; 1636/115; 1638/1, 73; 1639/127, 192; 1640/32; 1643/114, 119; 1644/25, 41, 106; 1645/54; 1690/263; 1720 Jn Fearne.

[33] Ibid. 1609/12, 167d; 1614/41b, 169; 1622/66; Baxter 94.

[34] PRO, PCC parch. invs p. 1660 no. 7892; Worcs. RO, Cons. Ct O.W. etc. 1606/27; 1613/ 204d; 1614/169; 1622/66, 138; 1624/72; 1625/212; 1631/170; 1632/15; 1638/82; 1646/79; 1648/126; 1649/27; 1668/161a; 1670/372–3; 1671/6; 1690/112, 193; 1710 Jn Jones; 1711 Ric. Callow sr; 1712 Ob. Spencer; 1713 Marg. Bellamy; 1714 Ed. Woodward; 1718 And. Walker; 1720 Jn Williams (1719); 1727 Jos. Nicholls & Ric. Billingsley.

[35] Ibid. 1711 Wm Pebody.

[36] Ibid. 1710 Jn Jones.

[37] Ibid. 1648/126.

[38] Burton 179–80.

[39] Baxter 94.

[40] Worcs. RO, Cons. Ct O.W. etc. 1712 Ob. Spencer; 1716 Stephen Lea er & Wm Radford jr; 1717 Ed. Parrins (1715); 1718 Wm Dearne, Marg. Lea, Wm Fereday & And. Walker; 1719 Jn Williams; 1720 Abr. Jevons; 1721 Ric. Clarke & Nic. Penn; 1724 Jn Pillet; 1726 Jos. Crane & Th. Hill; 1727 Hy Pearsall, Edm. Read, Ric. Billingsley, Jos. Nicholls; 1731 Jos. Reynolds.

[41] HMC, 12th Rep., App. pt ix, 416–18; Unwin, *Ind. Org.*, 50, 52 sqq.; Glos. RO, Cons. Ct inv. 1648/40.

[42] Plot, *Oxon.*, 278; Plummer & Early 9, 10; PRO, PCC parch. invs p. 1660 no. 7931; Bodl. Cons. & Arch Cts Oxf. O.W. etc. 5/3/38; 5/5/21; 17/2/42; 25/2/25; 30/4/11; 31/4/40; 41/4/33; 45/1/1; 53/2/8; 57/1/37; 60/4/27; 66/1/5; 79/1/45; 79/4/28; 80/4/27; 83/2/27; 83/3/50; 83/4/64; 86/4/6; 87/1/8; 116/4/27; 120/3/20; 133/2/28; 133/2/30; 139/3/8; 156/2/40; 161/1/32; 166/2/25; 169/4/3; 170/1/7; 170/4/9; 176/4/11; 295/2/72; 297/3/25; 300/2/15; 300/3/55; 300/6/44.

[43] Rath 141.

[44] Brears 61–2; Bodl. Pec. Ct Banbury O.W. & Admons 32/1/47; 50/3/19; Worcs. RO, Cons. Ct O.W. etc. 1690/41.

[45] Ibid. 1560/88; 1609/124; 1690/6; Notts. RO, Man. Ct Mansfield O.W. etc. portf. 1 no. 1; 9 no. 10; 16 no. 2; 33 no. 5; 46 no. 16; PRO, PCC parch. invs p. 1660 no. 3431; *VCH Leics.*, iv, 87; Leics. RO, invs Commy Ct Man. Evington, Th. Platts 1632; Arch. 1614/23, 45, 205(61); 1625/88; 1626/49, 108; 1627/18, 21, 104; 1628/68; 1631/104; 1636/217; 1637/14, 242; 1638/209, 279, 307; 1639/142; 1643/89; 1652–60/58, 63, 67, 127; 1661 (Arch.) 271; (Cmmnr) 40, 87; 1662 (Vic.-Gen.) 20; 1666/111; 1667/48; 1668 (Arch.) 41; (Bp's Visitation) 181; 1690/20, 47; 1706–10 (box 54) 48, 70, 80; 1709 (box 1067) 9; box 1068 Hy Bull 1728 Asfordby & Ed. Hardey 1728 Kegworth.

[46] Boys 742; Kent RO, Arch. Ct Cant. Inv. Regs 9 fo. 294; 14 fos. 168v.–9; 16 fo. 339; Cons. Ct Cant. Reg. Accts & Invs 7 fo. 23; Inv. Papers 6/13; 9/81; 12/31; Inv. Regs 14 fo. 138; 16 fo. 443.

[47] Ibid. Reg. Accts & Invs 13 fo. 488.

[48] Ibid. Inv. Papers 12/45; 16/32; 21/21; Inv. Reg. 20 fo. 369.

[49] Ibid. fos. 392–3.

[50] Ibid. Inv. Papers 12/45; 17/85.

[51] Ibid. 6/114; 7/92; 8/109; 9/107; 13/111; 15/47; 16/59, 77; 18/111; 20/53, 78; 22/9; 23/42; 26/120, 157; 27/116; Regs Accts & Invs 7 fos. 227, 270–1; 8 fo. 85; 9 fo. 100; 12 fo. 497; 13 fo. 488; 14 fos. 312, 389; Inv. Regs 7 fos. 5, 6, 265, 456; 8 fo. 78; 9 fo. 333; 11 fo. 652; 12 fos. 247–8, 373; 14 fos. 245, 256, 405, 588; 15 fo. 392; 17 fo. 456; 19 fos. 69, 70; 20 fos. 183, 256, 691; Arch. Ct Cant. Inv. Paper 54/185.

[52] Cant. Cath. Lib. Cty Recs. Chamb's Accts 1577–87 fos. 205, 258, 307v., 357, 405, 454–5; 1587–92 fos. 24v.–5, 64, 104v.–5, 150, 151v., 199; 1592–1602 fos. 26(91)v.–27(92), 147v., 191v., 232, 276, 321v., 373v., 375, 423, 473–4; 1602–10 fos. 18, 67, 68v., 110, 150v., 190v., 227, 283, 330.

[53] Fiennes 123; Hasted, *Cant.*, i, 94; J. Brent, *Cant. in Olden Time*, Cant. & Lond. 1860, p. 91.

[54] Cant. Cath. Lib. Cty Recs. Burghmote Bk 1630–58 fo. 176v.

[55] Kent RO, Arch. Ct Cant. Inv. Paper 54/185; Cons. Ct Cant. Regs Accts & Invs 7 fos. 227, 270–1; 8 fo. 85; 9 fos. 100, 307; 12 fo. 497; 14 fos. 312, 389; Inv. Papers 6/114; 7/92; 8/109; 9/107; 12/45; 13/99, 111; 15/47; 16/32, 59, 77; 17/85; 18/111; 20/53, 78; 21/21; 22/9; 23/42; 26/120, 157; 27/116; Inv. Regs 7 fos. 5, 6, 265, 456; 8 fo. 78; 9 fos. 117–18, 333; 11 fo. 652; 12 fos. 247–8, 373; 14 fos. 245, 256, 405, 588; 15 fo. 392; 17 fo. 456; 19 fos. 69, 70; 20 fos. 183, 256, 369, 392–3, 567–8, 691.

[56] *C.J.*, xii, 224–5; Waller 54 (Marishall); Cross 188; Guildhall Lib. Weavers' Co. Ord. & Rec. Bk 1577–1641 p. 354; Commy Ct Lond. (Lond. Div.) invs box 4 Chas Grinnoneau 1725–6; Th. Short 1724; Josh. Maria 1705–6 (St Dunstan's); Nic. You 1725 (id.); 8 Th. Flower 1702; Pet. Parr 1703 (Spitalfields); Abr. Lennigni 1714; Jn Dollond 1715; Isaac Burgess 1714 (St Dunstan's); Pet. Willemot 1716 (id.); 9 Th. Fowler 1699 St Botolph's W/o; & Dan. Nipp/Bridewell precinct. Isaac Delaneuvemaison (Spitalfields), Jn Oldham, Geo. Thackery (St Dunstan's) 1701; & all (exc. Nipp & Fowler) of Stepney; PRO, PCC paper invs 1661–1725 no. 2518; parch. invs p. 1660 nos. 271, 11192; Plummer, *Lond. Weavers' Co.*, 59.

[57] Ibid. 302.

[58] Hooper 252; F. Lewis, *Jas Leman. Spitalfields Dsgn.*, Leigh-on-Sea 1954, pp. vii, viii.

[59] Guildhall Lib. Commy Ct Lond. (Lond. Div.) invs box 8 Ann Hue wid. 1703; 9 Gaspard & Eliz. Pilot 1701 & 1702 Wheeler St, Spitalfields.

[60] Ibid. box 4 Th. Aspinall 1726 St Dunstan's; PRO, PCC parch. invs p. 1660 no. 7254.

[61] Ibid. nos. 580, 1604, 1614, 1753, 1771, 1789, 1946, 2336, 3602, 4051, 5543; W. Sfk RO, Ep. Commy Ct Bury invs 1676/47; 1696/91; Nfk RO, Cty Recs. Bk Mayor's Ct 15 fo. 202v.; 19 fos. 101–2; 2nd Bk Worstedweavers fos. 28, 61; Cons. Ct invs 1584/88; 1592/62, 138; 1593/375; 1603/160; 1615–16/30, 144; 1617/7, 15, 51, 87, 115, 157; 1626/69; 1631/137; 1633/56; 1634/2, 74; 1635/163, 165; 1637/94; 1639/98, 211B, 247, 254; 1640/10, 136, 143; 1646/28, 109; 1647/189; 1650/17, 60; 1651/32; 1662/4, 148; 1628–68/117; 1637–68/19; 1664/14; 1665/52; 1666/10, 41, 77; 1669/84; 1671/47; 1674/58; 1676/62; 1677/53; 1680/52; 1681/41, 67; 1682/12; 1684/80; 1692–3/65(64), 115, 140; 1694–6/23, 43; 1697–8/62; 1702–8/71; 1709–10/214; 1710–14/15, 23, 141, 231, 391; 1716–17/169; Arch. Ct Norvic invs 1674–5/51, 162–3, 216; 1682–3/120; 1692–3/114; 1700–2/45, 134; 1703–6/1; 1706–7/20; 1709–10/61; 1715–17/90; 1720–1/2; 1727–8/61; 1729–31/6; Arch. Ct Nfk invs 1728–42/246, 259, 350, 361; 1743–53/40, 70; Pec. Ct D. & C. invs. 1681–6/12, 14, 19, 23, 49; 1687–94/22, 30; 1737–82/6.

[62] Hudson & Tingey ii, 191.–2; Nfk RO, Cty Recs. Liber Albus fos. 94v.–5; 2nd Bk Worstedweavers fo. 64; Bk Mayor's Ct 5 p. 326.

[63] Sup. 42.

[64] Nfk RO, invs Pec. Ct D. & C. 1681–6/14; 1687–94/22; 1737–82/6; Arch. Ct Norvic. 1674–5/51; 1692–3/114; 1700–2/45, 134; 1715–17/21; 1720–1/2; 1729–31/6; Cons. Ct 1590/99; 1591/131; 1593/35; 1595/90, 120; 1597/71; 1602/52; 1603/119, 121; 1606–7/151; 1611/152, 304; 1618/174; 1634/2; 1639/254; 1640/195; 1646/98; 1637/68 Inventaria introducta sed non exhibita 11; 1666/10; 1667/66, 81; 1668/83; 1671/10; 1673/16; 1677/68; 1682/39; 1692–3/92.

[65] Ibid. 1617/115; 1639/247; 1640/48; 1646/28; 1647/189; 1651/32; 1662/4; 1628–68/117; 1637–68/19; Arch. Ct Norvic. 1682–3/171; 1727–8/61; Cty Recs. Bk Mayor's Ct 19 fos. 101–2.

[66] Ibid. invs Arch. Ct Norvic. 1674–5/200; 1700–2/62; 1715–17/103; 1754–67/43, 59; Cons. Ct 1681/66; 1687/156; 1702/10; 1709–10/152; 1710–14/150, 396; 1703–8/390; 1718–21/169; cf. J. T. Evans, *17th-cent. Norwich, Pol., Rel. & Govt 1620–90*, Oxf. 1979, p. 23.

[67] Sup. 187.

[68] E. Sfk RO, Arch. inv. 15/27; W. Sfk RO, Ep. Commy Ct Bury inv. 1701/79; Nfk RO, Cons. Ct invs 1592/269; 1595/73, 151; 1601/96, 152; 1603/119; 1611/152; 1615/162; 1625/72, 198; 1626/232; 1630/172, 198; 1632/58; 1635/103, 160; 1637/118; 1638/53, 74; 1639/1; 1640/93; 1642/49, 115; 1647/28; 1662/82; 1670/37; 1677/79, 117, 119; 1685/144; 1694–6/23; 1697–8/11; 1699/11, 50; 1700–1/16, 33, 43; 1702/7; 1709–10/149, 189, 195; 1710–14/149, 170, 205; 1716–17/134; 1718–21/44, 62, 115, 125, 264; 1722/44; 1723/81; 1726/75; 1728/55, 59, 63; 1736/3; 1738/15, 24; Arch. Ct Nfk inv. 1743–53/70; Arch. Ct Norvic. invs 1674–5/206; 1682–3/43; 1692–3/155; 1700–2/48, 119; 1706–7/17, 23, 25, 38, 49; 1707–8/18, 21, 64; 1709–10/59; 1712–13/27; 1717–18/43; 1724–5/5; 1728–9/76; 1739–43/66; 1754–67/24.

[69] Ibid. 1674–5/161, 194, 206, 231; 1682–3/43; 1692–3/155, 167, 245 (recte 1674–5); 1700–2/133; 1706–7/49; 1708/1, 38, 41, 114; 1718–19/35; 1723–4/44, 48; 1729–31/44; 1732–3/55; Cons. Ct invs 1589/183; 1591/273; 1592/16; 1594/36; 1598/192; 1603/120; 1608/5; 1610/18; 1613/179A; 1631/6; 1632/98; 1628–68/104; 1642/15; 1703–8/362; 1716–17/199; 1732/118; 1735/35; Pec. Ct D. & C. inv. 1681–6/22; Cty Recs. Bk Mayor's Ct 6 fo. 10v.

[70] Edwards 39; my *Ag. Rev.* 87–8; sup. 187.

[71] Sup. 51, 72.

[72] Nfk RO, Cons. Ct invs 1592/62, 103, 138; 1593/375; 1595/90, 120; 1598/147; 1603/160, 249; 1615/30; 1617/87; 1637/94.

[73] Ibid. 1598/147; 1635/190; 1640/93; 1642/49; 1664/14; 1730/26; Arch. Ct Norvic. inv. 1707–8/17; Cty Recs. Bk Mayor's Ct 16 fo. 303v.

[74] Ibid. Cons. Ct invs 1608/56; 1610/135; 1613/172; 1614/68; 1621/104.

[75] Ibid. 1590/130; 1592/100; 1594/29.

[76] Ibid. 1610/97.

[77] Ibid. 1589/200; 1590/95; 1603/13, 111, 117, 157; 1605/47; 1614/148; 1619/137; 1621/104; 1625/296; 1634/58; 1636/149; 1642/92.

[78] Moens, *Norwich*, pp. iv, 152 sqq., 189 sqq., 207 sqq.; BL, Lans 7 no. 82 fos. 202v.–3; & v. Janssen 236.

[79] Nfk RO, Cons. Ct invs 1606/66; 1615/52; 1625/264; 1639/98; 1640/81, 107; 1646/50; 1674/33; 1683–5/57; 1703–8/300; (& v. 1637/194); Arch. Ct Norvic. inv. 1706–7/30; Pec. Ct D. & C. inv. 1687–94/46; Cty Recs. Ass. Bk 2 fo. 194v.; Bk Mayor's Ct 5 p. 326.

[80] Hudson & Tingey ii, 150.

[81] Nfk RO, Cons. Ct invs 1589/119; 1592/53; 1603/145A; 1606/150; 1629/123; 1723/18; 1724/68; Arch. Ct Norvic. inv. 1720–1/43.

[82] PRO, PCC parch. invs p. 1660 no. 3225.

[83] Ibid. no. 5543; invs 1718–82 bdl. 23 no. 159; Nfk RO, Arch. Ct Norvic. invs 1700–2/62; 1715–17/103; 1754–67/43, 59; Cons. Ct invs 1636/149; 1681/66; 1687/156; 1702/10; 1703–8/390; 1709–10/152; 1710–14/150, 396; 1718–21/169.

[84] Ibid. 1640/136 & Pec. Ct D. & C. inv. 1687–94/30 f. excs; Cons. Ct 1602/261 f. special. scourer.

[85] Stats 14 & 15 H.8 c.3; 21 H.8 c.21; 26 H.8 c.16.

[86] Nfk RO, Cons. Ct invs 1584/43; 1588/127; 1592/4, 114A; 1593/264; 1597/52; 1605/138; 1606–7/176; 1611/69, 216; 1613/180, 191, 276; 1614/56; 1618/70, 122, 244; 1619/111; 1621/18, 28, 69; 1625/218; 1626/83, 217; 1628/165; 1629/16; 1630/168, 174; 1647/60; 1663/105, 155; 1665/72, 76; 1677/162, 170; 1692–3/129; 1703–8/369; 1709–10/117; 1730/3; Arch. Ct Norvic. inv. 1717–18/27; Arch. Ct Nfk invs 1728–42/235; 1743–53/72; W. Sfk RO, Ep. Commy Ct Bury invs 1652/18; 1660/134, 150; 1661/253, 270, 293; 1662/96, 237; 1663/16, 27, 52; 1664/47, 111; E. Sfk RO, Arch. invs 2/47, 60, 126; 3/8, 49, 155; 6/10; 7/93; 8/64; 9/8; 10/86; 12/22, 71; 13/90; 14/70; 15/8; 26/39; 27/21, 49; 31/36.

[87] Nfk RO, Cons. Ct invs 1602/251; 1610/77; 1615/81; 1661/11; Bacon 366.

[88] Invs ut sup.

[89] Lowe 43–5, 48, 53–5, 58–9; Wadsworth & Mann 11, 28, 47, 294–6.

[90] Ibid. 306; Cullen, *Econ. Hist. Ire.*, 48, 60–2, 93, 111–12; Gill 19, 31, 33, 64–6.

[91] Lowe 45; Wadsworth & Mann 11, 28; Higgins 9 sqq., 26, 28.

[92] Northants. RO, Arch. Ct Northampton Admons & Invs 1713/70; 1714/10, 47; 1716/99; 1717/1; 1718/118; 1719/5, 23; 1721/49; 1723/34, 127; 1724/49, 108.

[93] Hants. RO, Arch. Ct O.W. & Invs Robt Burbridge 1645; Th. West 1649; Cons. Ct O.W. & Invs Jn Warner & Jn Guy (Andwell) 1638; Ric. Frith 1633; Jn Smythe 1638; unclass. invs D/2/A: 3/240.

[94] Ibid. Cons. Ct O.W. & Invs Jn Prior 1624 Bramley; Jn Woodman 1637 Fetcham.

[95] Ramsay, *Wilts.*, 12, 17 sqq.; Wilts. RO, Arch. Ct Sub-dean Sarum. 1612/15; 1615/4, 12, 20; 1617/5; 1618/12; 1621/9; 1622/1; 1627/16; 1629/3, 7; 1632/9, 16; 1637/14; 1680/17; 1688/10; 1731/18; PRO, PCC invs ser. i no. 174; parch. invs p. 1660 no. 7998.

[96] Dors. RO, Pec. Ct Wimb. Minster inv. no 67A & inv. Sam. Smithe 18 Dec. 30 Eliz.; ex-par. wills nos. 13, 51, 134, 141(1).

[97] *VCH Berks.*, i, 391; *N. & Q. Soms. & Dors.*, 1968 xxix, 33–5; PRO, PCC parch. invs p. 1660 nos. 4625, 11133; invs ser. i nos. 411, 419; Wilts. RO, Cons. Ct Sarum. Wm Crosse 1605, Wm White 1676, both Devizes; Jn Willmott 1698 Reading; Hants. RO, Cons. Ct O.W. & Invs 1628 Ric. Hollis gent. Newport; 1629 Maud Snelling wid. Christchurch; 1635 Ric. Whiellier/Newport; 1637 Ric. Bowden/Carisbrooke; 1647 Hy Parr/Havant; 1650/3; 1664 Robt Gover/Romsey; Arch. Ct O.W. & Invs 1641 Jn Mathew/Alton; 1650 Hy Watridge/Alton; unclass. invs D/2/A: 2/69; Bodl. Arch. Ct Berks. O.W. etc. nos. 80/122; 99/3; 121/103, 116; 138/154; 183/49; 215/168; 222/47.

[98] Ibid. 45/116; 66/31; 99/35; 137/85; 179/74; 190/163; 192/98; 197/120; 203/44; 205/8; 209/14, 106, 146; 214/101; 215/31; 218/51, 109; 222/49, 59, 70; 223/147; Hants. RO, Arch. Ct O.W. & Invs 1653 Jn Morton/Soton; Wilts. RO, Pec. Ct Dean Sarum. Th. Kate 1689 Bere Regis; ex Dioc. Reg. Sarum. invs Ric. Kendoll 1600 Mere; Hy Noble 1601 Edington; *Wilts. N. & Q.*, 1902 iii, 500–1.

[99] Sup. 15, 17.

[100] Wiggs 217; Hants. RO, Arch. Ct O.W. & Invs 1647 Robt Zaines (Zanies) Soton; 1691 Stephen Sibley/Romsey; 1720 Jn Dawkins/Romsey Infra; Cons. Ct O.W. & Invs 1623 Jn Pawlmer/ Soton; 1626 Robt Parker/id.; 1628 Pet. Symens (1617) id.; 1630 Sam. Hoopper/id.; 1642 Wm Barling/id.; 1670 Th. Brackley/Romsey; 1692 Th. Bryant/id.; unclass. invs D/2/A: 2/40, 61.

[101] Wilts. RO, Arch. Ct Sub-dean Sarum. 1713/19; 1714/6.

[102] Pococke ii, 48; sup. 88.

[103] PRO, PCC invs 1718–82 bdl. 24 no. 18; parch. invs p. 1660 no. 8548; Bodl. Arch. Ct Berks. O.W. etc. 48/175.

[104] Hants. RO, Winton prob., unclass. invs D/2/A: 2/181.

[105] Ibid. Cons. Ct O.W. & Invs 1635 Elias Morringe; 1642 Isaac Cooper; 1671 Jn Hicks; Arch. Ct O.W. & Invs 1648 Robt Sweetaple; PRO, PCC parch. invs p. 1660 no. 2719.

[106] Wilts. RO, Cons. Ct Sarum. Robt Scott 1660; Robt Willis 1685; Jn Slade 1687; Hy Painter 1692; Jn Stokes 1699; Jas Lewes 1701; Hy Galloway 1704; Ed. Errwood 1714; Th. Slade 1722; PRO, PCC invs 1718–82 bdl. 18 no. 187; 35 no. 30.

[107] Ibid. bdl. 25 no. 84; Bodl. Arch. Ct Berks. O.W. etc. 121/142; 192/159; S. D. Chapman, 'Ind. Cap. befe Ind. Rev.' in Harte & Ponting, p. 122.

[108] PRO, SPD Hy 8 vol. 47 fo. 89; vol. 151 fos. 128–31; Eliz. 106/48; PCC invs ser. i nos. 7, 524; parch. invs p. 1660 nos. 572, 2887, 2913, 3610, 7798; Tymms 168–9; *Winthrop Papers*, i, 302– 3; Emmison, *Wills Ess. Gentry & Merchs*, 286–8; Nfk RO, Cons. Ct inv. 1636/187; E. Sfk RO, Arch. inv. 3/23; W. Sfk RO, Ep. Commy Ct Bury invs 1573–8/31, 43, 60, 97; 1647–8/15, 56, 88; 1650/55, 134, 139; 1652/80; 1662/55; 1663/96; 1664/22, 147; 1665/97, 139; 1666/50; 1667/80, 170; 1668/21; 1670/39, 51; 1680/200; *APC*, 1621–3 p. 278; Ess. RO, Pec. Ct Bocking invs no. 233 & Ric. Chaplain 1739.

[109] Ibid., both invs; BL, Lans. 26 no. 56 fo. 147; W. Sfk RO, Ep. Commy Ct Bury invs 1660/ 21; 1662/115, 210; 1665/97; 1666/81; 1667/1, 13, 170; 1670/39; 1680/202; 1686/15; 1707/81.

[110] Ibid. 1652/58; 1664/34; 1669/101; E. Sfk RO, Arch. inv. 3/6; Nfk RO, Cons. Ct invs 1618/ 96, 206; PRO, PCC invs ser. i no. 212; Emmison, *Wills Ess. Gentry & Merchs*, 269 sqq.

[111] Ibid. 269, 277–9, 282, 307–8, 317–18, 320; E. Sfk RO, Arch. inv. 3/23; Nfk RO, Cons. Ct inv. 1672/39; PRO, PCC parch. invs p. 1660 nos. 572, 2913, 3610, 7798; W. Sfk RO, Ep. Commy Ct Bury invs 1573–8/60; 1647–8/88; 1650/139; 1666/50; 1668/21; 1680/200.

[112] Ibid. 1573–8/43, 60, 97; 1647–8/15, 88; 1650/134, 139; 1660/21; 1664/22, 147; 1666/50, 81; 1667/13, 80, 170; 1668/21; 1669/106; 1670/39, 51; 1680/33, 200, 202; 1686/15; 1707/81; E. Sfk RO, Arch. inv. 3/23; Nfk RO, Cons. Ct invs 1629/134; 1672/39; PRO, PCC invs ser. i no. 7; parch. invs p. 1660 nos. 572, 2887, 2913, 3610; Power 29, 41 sqq.; McClenaghan 34, 84, 86–8; Emmison, *Wills Ess. Gentry & Merchs*, 300–1; *Magna Brit. & Hib.*, i, 709; Ess. RO, Pec. Ct Bocking invs no. 223 & Ric. Chaplain 1739; Notebks Jos. Bufton of Coggeshall 1663–1710 no. 9 his 1672 diary, list funeral sermons preached at Coggeshall by Mr Jessop; Bp Lond's Commy Ct f. Ess. & Herts. O.W. 22/48; Arch. Ct Colc. Reg. Wills 4 fo. 80; HMC, *Var. Colls.*, viii, 588–91.

[113] T. Arnold, *Mems St Edm's Abb.*, Rolls ser. 3 vols. 1890–6 iii, 363; Webb, *Tooley*, 24; BL, Add. 32901; Ess. RO, Bp Lond's Commy Ct f. Ess. & Herts. O.W. 12/68; 34/216; 37/57; Arch. Ct Colc. Regs Wills 1 fos. 3, 33, 187; 2 fo. 258; 3 fos. 53, 72v., 144v.; 4 fo. 183; 5 fo. 129v.; 6 fo. 80; E. Sfk RO, Arch. invs 1/120; 2/161; 3/21; W. Sfk RO, Ep. Commy Ct Bury invs 1573–8/31; 1647–8/56; 1650/55; 1661/31; 1662/26, 206, 216; 1664/29, 247; 1665/26, 65, 139; 1666/32; 1668/120, 184; 1669/ 6; 1675/46, 103; 1686/10; 1692/17; Nfk RO, Cons. Ct invs 1596/86; 1602/330; 1628/99.

[114] Ibid. 1647/6; PRO, PCC invs ser. i no. 212; E. Sfk RO, Arch. inv. 3/6; A. F. Northcote, *Notes on Hist. Monks' Eleigh*, Ips. 1930, p. 25; W. Sfk RO, Ep. Commy Ct Bury invs 1573–8/56; 1652/58; 1662/55, 211; 1666/2; 1668/141, 167; 1680/76, 169.

[115] Ibid. 1650/80; 1661/1; 1666/109; 1677/87; 1682/14; 1702/16; 1705/43; 1707/93; 1711/49; Acc. 960 no. 73; E. Sfk RO, Arch. invs 3/45; 15/69; PRO, PCC parch. invs p. 1660 nos. 694, 2890; Thornton 204–6; Nfk RO, Cons. Ct inv. 1625/196.

[116] Ibid. 1625/197; 1626/119; W. Sfk RO, Ep. Commy Ct Bury invs 1647–8/41; 1662/6, 182;

1665/151; 1667/127; 1668/78; 1670/174; 1675/21, 105; 1682/31; 1686/100; 1692/18; 1700/42; 1701/ 87; 1705/92; Sudbury, Tn Recs. Bk Proc. Boro. Ct 6, 'Ords & Decrees conserning saymakers weavers etc.' 31 Oct. 1648.

[117] Ibid.; Nfk RO, Cons. Ct inv. 1678/47; Burley, thes. 122; PRO, PCC parch. invs p. 1660 nos. 7906, 8752; Chanc. Jud. Proc. (Eq. side) Chanc. Mrs' Docs, Exhibs, Mr Tinney nos. 17–19; W. Sfk RO, Ep. Commy Ct Bury invs 1660/170; 1662/115, 210; 1665/22; 1667/23, 38; 1670/132; 1676/60; 1677/145; 1680/236; 1682/156; 1692/9; 1696/91.

[118] Ibid. 1662/115, 210; 1665/97; 1667/28; 1668/173; Tymms 168–70.

[119] HMC, *Var. Colls*, viii, 588–91.

[120] Ess. RO, Arch. Ct Colc. Reg. Wills 2 fos. 200, 265v.

[121] Colc. Tn Hall, Mon. Cts 1571–6 & Assemblies etc. 1573–6: 'Vuew of Strangers' 26 Apr. 1573.

[122] Ess. RO, Arch. Ct Colc. Reg. Wills 6 fo. 72; O.W. 4/334.

[123] PRO, SPD Jas 129/70.

[124] *APC*, 1616–17 p. 304.

[125] PRO, SPD Chas 355/92–4, 162–4.

[126] Colc. Tn Hall, Ass. Bks: 15 July 1602, 1 Nov. 1608, 25 Jan. 1612.

[127] PRO, PCC parch. invs p. 1660 nos. 7809, 11398; N. Goose, 'Du. in Colc.', *Immigrants & Minorities*, 1982 i, 271.

[128] Colc. Tn Hall, Ass. Bk 1 Sept. 1590; A. F. J. Brown 151; HMC, *Var. Colls*, viii, 589.

[129] Ramsay, *Wilts.*, 6, 12 sqq., 31 sqq., 47, 127–9; Mann, *Cl. Ind.*, 89 sqq.; *VCH Wilts.*, iv, 143–6; Smyth, *Names*, 153 sqq., 184, 193–4, 232–4, 239 sqq., 276–8, 290 sqq., 297 sqq., 309–11, 313–14; Tann 198; Goldney 303, 327, 332, 342; Pococke ii, 270–1; Lindley 152–4; W. P. W. Phillimore & G. S. Fry, *Abs. Glos. Inquisitiones Post Mortem in Reign Chas I*, Ind. Lib., B.R.S. 3 pts 1893–9, ii, 186; iii, 53, 61, 144; PRO, PCC parch. invs p. 1660 nos. 361, 363, 368, 1688, 2723, 3422, 3892, 4502, 7657, 8410, 8428, 8687, 9055, 9236, 9326, 9658, 10931; paper invs 1661–1725 no. 28; invs 1718–82 bdl. 18 nos. 109, 237; 21 nos. 9, 38; 22 no. 140; 24 nos. 42, 100; 25 nos. 67, 83; 33 no. 125; Wilts. RO, Acc. 122 Svys Bromham, Bremhill, Bowden & Stanley 1612 (w. ct bk), Stanley ct 1618 will & inv. And. Wilcocks (Wilcox) Stanley; Chittoe ct 1616 inv. Wm Rashwood/Studley; Cons. Ct Sarum. Jn Barsdale 1606 Seendhead; Wm Chiver 1614 Bromham; Wm Withers 1711 Boreham in Warminster; Pec. Ct Prec. or Chantor, bdl. 1 no. 37; 4 nos. 1, 21; 14 no. 57; 15 no. 45; Arch. Ct Wilts., Robt Eire (Ayre) 1603 Bromham; Gabr. Goldney 1670 & Gabr. Goldney 1684, of Chippenham; Arch. Ct Sarum. Geo. Paradise 1682 Sandridge Mill, Melksham; Pec. Ct Treas. bdl. 6 Jn Francklin 1630 Calne; 11 Jn Laurence 1688 id.; Glos. RO, Marcham Coll. F.26; Cons. Ct invs 1662/3; 1663/149, 230, 279; 1684/48, 148.

[130] Ibid. 1636 Ric. Dyer/Olvestone; 1663/54, 73, 83, 86, 91, 98, 148, 158, 164, 167, 202; 1664/ 30, 40; 1677/108; 1684/40, 44, 82, 89, 99; Wilts. RO, ex Dioc. Reg. Sarum. invs Jn Eyre 1610 Seend; Th. Batten 1626 Blackland; Wr Townsend 1629 Stockley in Calne; Edm. Chapman 1632 Blackland; Mary Fowler 1635 Calne; Jn Bedford, Wr Bishop & Jn Palmer 1637 Calne; Mary Piddle 1666 Ryme; Soms. RO, Cons. Ct Bath & Well. inv. Jn Slape 1589 Combe St Nic.; Arch. Taunton invs 1668/1, 69; Smyth, *Names*, 146–7, 150–2, 155 sqq., 166 sqq., 171 sqq., 186 sqq., 193–5, 239 sqq., 274 sqq., 282, 290 sqq., 297 sqq., 309–11; Ramsay, *Wilts.*, 15–17; *VCH Glos.*, ii, 167; Mann, *Cl. Ind.*, 94, 97–8; 'Clothiers & Weavers', 83, 92.

[131] Ibid. 83; Ramsay, *Wilts.*, 31.

[132] Ibid. 15; PRO, PCR 1634–5 p. 184 (fo. 83v.); PCC invs 1718–82 bdl. 21 no. 38; 24 no. 100; Wilts. RO, Pec. Ct Prec. or Chantor bdl. 15 no. 45.

[133] Ramsay, *Wilts.*, 90–1, 95 sqq., 127; Mann, *Cl. Ind.*, 92.

[134] Smyth, *Names*, 150 sqq., 186 sqq., 197–8, 232–4, 274 sqq., 282, 286 sqq., 297 sqq.; Mann, *Cl. Ind.*, 93; Glos. RO, Cons. Ct inv. 1732/124.

[135] Leland i, 131–2; cf. Ramsay, *Wilts.*, 17, 32–3.

[136] Mann, *Cl. Ind.*, 115; M. F. Davies 44.

[137] Glos. RO, Cons. Ct invs 1663/196; 1691/116; 1698/132; 1709/40; PRO, PCC parch. invs p. 1660 nos. 6341, 9326; paper invs 1661–1725 no. 2716; invs 1718–82 bdl. 24 no. 99; Wilts. RO, Arch. Ct Wilts. Jn Beere 1684 Lacock; Jn Read 1698 Chippenham Langley; Zeph. Fry yr 1717 Chippenham; Jn Jefferies 1740 Avon; Pec. Ct D. & C. Sarum. roll M no. 54; Cons. Ct Sarum. Wm Robins 1683 Heddington; Pec. Ct Dean Sarum. Roger Meade 1670 Yetminster; Wm Lacke er 1692, Jn Hearne 1695, & Jn Hearne 1715, all of Beaminster; Wm Pike 1731 Lyme Regis; Arch. Ct Sarum. Jn Markes 1678 Bradford; Roger Marks 1682 L. Cheverell; Hy Gowen 1712 Broughton Gifford; Jos. Chubb 1725 Downton; Robt Rogers 1748 Atford in Bradford.

[138] Ibid. Wm Coombs 1709 Warminster; Cons. Ct Sarum. Wm Millard 1692 Holt in Bradford; Pec. Ct Treas., box 4 no. 20; Preb. Ct Netherbury in Ecclesia bdl. 7 no. 21; 9 no. 36; Arch. Ct Wilts., Jn Beere 1684 Lacock; Wm Webb 1684 Hawkstreet in Bromham; Jn Shipway 1704 Langley in Kington St Mich.; Ramsay, *Wilts.*, 111.

[139] Soms. RO, Cons. Ct Bath & Well. invs Barth. Weston 1639 Stogursey; Th. Barber 1676 W. Buckland (w. bd); Arch. Taunton invs 1638/24; 1640/83, 90, 111; 1642/41; 1644/70, 70A; 1647–9/8; 1664 Marmaduke Corum/Taunton; 1666 Robt Band/N. Petherton; 1667/7, 46, 78; 1668/17, 45, 59 & Ric. Preiddy/Milverton; 1669/99; 1670/25, 29, 70; 1671 Th. Hessom/Taunton St Jas; 1675 Robt Quears (Kewers) Creech, Jn Rice/Monksilver, David Tuxwell sr Cannington; 1678/69; 1681/90; 1683/43 & Ric. Meare/Bradford; 1688 Lewes Pollard/Holford; 1690 Agnes Pollard/id., Jos. Lewes/ Staplegrove; 1695 Th. Waterman/Bridgwater; 1697 Uriah Wright/N. Petherton, & Ric. Spreat, Jane Bond & Hy Turner, all Taunton St Mary Magd.; 1714–15 Th. Hellyer/Taunton St Jas; 1725/19; 1726–7/2 (Wm Bowden/Minehead); 1730–1 Nic. Gooding/Monksilver; 17th-cent. fr. Taunton St Mary Magd.; Fox, f. p. 4; PRO, PCC invs 1718–82 bdl. 21 no. 65; parch. invs p. 1660 nos. 3887, 6886, 6912, 8300, 8661–2, 10452.

[140] Ibid. 1112, 9963, 11603; Wilts. RO, Pec. Ct Dean Sarum, Jn Starke 1682 Uffculme; Preb. Ct Uffculme bdl. 1 no. 23A; 2 no. 21; 3 no. 14; 4 no. 19; 5 no. 15; ex Dioc. Reg. Sarum. inv. Jn Gay jr Uffculme 1685; *APC*, 1621–3 p. 314; Cash 130–1; Stephens, *Exeter*, 51–2.

[141] Melling iii, 107 sqq.; R. Furley, *Hist. Weald Kent*, Ashford & Lond. 2 vols. 1871–4, p. 570; BL, Add. R. 19167; Cott. Titus B.i fo. 193(189); PRO, PCC invs 1718–82 bdl. 18 no. 221; Kent RO, Cons. Ct Roffen. Paper Invs 7/4; 9/2; Arch. Ct Cant. Inv. Regs 3 fos. 195v.–6; 10 fos. 364–6, 389, 392–4; 61 nos. 12, 24, 36, 74, 127, 189, 195; Inv. Papers 17/74; 41/201; Cons. Ct Cant. Inv. Regs 4 fo. 33; 17 fo. 320; 18 Jn Giles 1627 Cranbrook; Inv. Papers 7/80; 16/10; 34/69; Regs Accts & Invs 2 fos. 225v.–6, 364; 3 fos. 34v.–6, 131v.; 8 fos. 242–4, 357–8; 9 fos. 238, 263; 10 fos. 215v.–6; 11 fo. 274; 12 fo. 33; 16 fos. 219, 391v.–2.

[142] A. Haynes 32–4, 8; PRO, PCC parch. invs p. 1660 no. 1071; sup. 80.

[143] Pococke ii, 48; Burton 182–3.

[144] Glos. RO, Cons. Ct invs 1663/4, 207; Wilts. RO, Pec. Ct Treas. box 4 no. 32; Pec. Ct Dean Sarum. Ed. May 1615 & Th. Tiszer 1626, both Sherborne; Leics. RO, Arch. inv. 1614/205(61); D. M. Palliser 162; Bodl. Arch. Ct Berks O.W. etc. 58/1; 98/146; 209/30; 219/115; Worcs. RO, Cons. Ct O.W. etc. 1609/124; PRO, PCC parch. invs p. 1660 nos. 329, 16139.

[145] M. K. Dale 324 sqq.; Cty RO, Ct Orphs invs ut sup. p. 262, n. 108; Guildhall Lib. Commy Ct Lond. (Lond. Div.) invs box 2 Wm Taylor 1667 Stepney; 4 Jn George 1725 St Botolph's W/o; 6 Wm Gass 1720, Wm Nepton 1722 (both St Dunstan's); 9 Hy Wheeler 1678, Th. Deering 1701, Th. Cretle 1702 (St Dunstan's), all Stepney; Th. Baxter 1700 St Botolph's W/o; Stephen Dubarle 1701 St Giles-in-the-Fields.

[146] Ibid. Weavers Co. Ord. & Rec. Bk 1577–1641 p. 302.

[147] Brist. RO, Cons. Ct invs 1640 Ric. Day; 1646 Jn Middleton/St Mary Redcliffe; 1663/10, 57; Ches. RO, Cons. Ct Cestr. Infra invs Ralph Nixson 1666 O. Knutsford; Robt Booth 1667 Chester; Bodl. Arch. Ct Berks. O.W. etc. 204/95; Leics. RO, Arch. inv. 1678/150; Wilts. RO, Cons. Ct Sarum. Ric. Blanford 1689 Devizes; Lionel Day 1695 Abingdon; Ed. Steevins 1729 Hilperton; sup. 79.

[148] Nfk RO, Cons. Ct invs 1598/147; 1603/249; 1630/89.

[149] Ibid. 1592/62, 138; 1593/375; 1603/160; 1615/30; 1617/87; 1637/94.

[150] Ibid. 1592/103; 1595/90, 120.

[151] Kent RO, Arch. Ct Cant. Inv. Regs 9 fo. 294; 10 fos. 344–5; 16 fo. 339; Cons. Ct Cant. Inv. Reg. 17 fos. 320, 442; Regs Accts & Invs 7 fo. 23; 8 fos. 357–8.

[152] Ibid. 6 fo. 367; 10 fos. 238–9; 12 fos. 479–80; 13 fos. 250–3; Inv. Regs 11 fo. 472; 12 fo. 377; Arch. Ct Cant. Inv. Reg. 12 fo. 17.

[153] Guildhall Lib. Commy Ct Lond. (Lond. Div.) inv. box 9 Jas Wolfenden 1699 St Dunstan's, Stepney; Plummer, *Lond. Weavers' Co.*, 165, 167; W. Bowden, *Ind. Soc. in Engld towards end 18th cent.*, N.Y. 1925, pp. 150–1; Wadsworth & Mann 103–5, 285–6, 326–7.

[154] Sup. 12, 13.

[155] Allison 765–6.

[156] Nfk RO, Cons. Ct inv. 1618/206; Bodl. Arch. Ct Berks. O.W. etc. 73/75; 203/59; 214/145; Cons. & Arch Cts Oxf. O.W. etc. 11/1/4; 299/5/9; Aberystwyth, Ep. Cons. Ct St Asaph O.W., Admons & Invs Th. Edwards gent. 1661 Oswestry; Soms. RO, Arch. Taunton invs 1668/17, 50; Dors. RO, Pec. Ct Wimb. Minster no. 67A; Worcs. RO, Cons. Ct O.W. etc. 1638/82; Wilts. RO, Arch. Ct Sub-dean Sarum. 1685/22; 1715/10; Cons. Ct Sarum. Humph. Atheath 1635 Warfield; Leics. RO, Arch. invs Ralph Randall 1579 Leicester; 1639/79; 1648/20; Havinden 150 sqq.; Mendenhall 42–3; Unwin, *Ind. Org.*, 44–5, 57–9, 112–13; PRO, SPD Jas 133/36.

[157] B. Palliser 371, 377–8, 384, 400–1, 403, 414; Hyde & Markham 45–6; Hilton 44; PRO, PCC invs 1718–82 bdl. 32 no. 167.

[158] Ibid. parch. invs p. 1660 no. 5509; Ches. RO, Cons. Ct Cestr. Supra inv. Ric. Blacklache (erron. Blackhurst) 1635 Macclesfield; C. S. Davies 122–3; *C.J.*, xiv, 504; Aikin 437.

[159] Kent RO, Cons. Ct Cant. Regs Accts & Invs. 10 fo. 184; 11 fo. 90; Inv. Papers 6/76; 8/3; Inv. Regs 7 fos. 16v., 17; 11 fo. 649; 12 fo. 133; 14 fo. 599; 15 fos. 288–9, 436–7; 17 fos. 458–61; 18 Jn Callant sr 1635; Gabr. Knight yr & Wm Usher 1636; 19 fo. 472; Lichfield Jt RO, Cons. Ct O.W., Jn Smith 1728 St Mich's, Cov.; PRO, PCC parch. invs p. 1660 no. 9946.

[160] Ibid. no. 9014.

[161] Lichfield Jt RO, Cons. Ct O.W., Hugh Atkyns 1547, Ric. Bromych 1551 & Jn Armebrode 1560, all Cov. cappers; Harris, *Cov. Leet Bk*, 672–3, 773–4, 792.

[162] Purchas 521; Unwin, *Ind. Org.*, 196–8; Cty Lond. RO, Ct Orphs invs box 4 Jn Dixon 1665.

[163] Moore 111, 114–5, 127, 135–6, 141–2, 144, 151, 153, 165–6, 182, 185, 188, 218, 220, 229–30, 234–6, 240, 246–7; 249–50, 253–4, 257, 265–6, 271; Brist. RO, Cons. Ct inv. 1662/17; Worcs. RO, Cons. Ct O.W. etc. 1622/152; Aberystwyth, Ep. Cons. Ct St Asaph O.W., Admons & Invs, Evan Lewis 1667 Henllan St, Denbigh; Nfk RO, Cty Recs. Bk Mayor's Ct 12 p. 354; Cons. Ct invs 1590/188; 1621/126; 1626/130; 1631/223; Bodl. Arch. Ct Berks. O.W. etc. 83/79; 178/72; 192/150; 222/62.

[164] Sup. 134.

[165] Leicester Mus., Hall Papers, bk xiv, no. 591; bk xvii no. 245; Nfk RO, Bk Mayor's Ct 16 fo. 326.

[166] Ibid. Cons. Ct invs 1595/60; 1606–7/20; 1662/12; 1680/58; 1703–8/192; Arch. Ct Norvic. invs 1682–3/197; 1707–8/78; 1712–13/29; Allison 762–3; W. Sfk RO, Ep. Commy Ct Bury invs 1669/143; 1686/64; 1705/84; E. Sfk RO, Arch. invs 19/62; 23/5; 24/5; PRO, PCC parch. invs. p. 1660 no. 7779.

[167] Ibid. nos. 2453, 4719; paper invs 1661–1725 no. 3279.

[168] *VCH Leics.*, iv, 90–2.

[169] Worcs. RO, Cons. Ct O.W. etc. 1690/142; Wilts. RO, Pec. Ct Dean Sarum. Jn Coward 1683 Mere; Rath 141.

[170] *VCH Leics.*, iv, 91, 168–70; Leics. RO, Arch. invs 1678/150; 1691/40; 1704/150; 1709/112; Jn Wale 1727 Whetstone; Ric. Marshall 1728 Barkstone; Th. Kirbie 1731 Glenfield; Sam. Harris 1738 Belgrave; Jn Willmot 1810 Shepshed; Notts. RO, Man. Ct Mansfield O.W. etc. portf. 26 no. 2; 54 no. 14; 59 no. 19; 75 no. 7; 82 nos. 24, 35; 84 no. 33; Chapman, 'Gen.', 26; Rogers 17.

[171] Guildhall Lib. Commy Ct Lond. (Lond. Div.) invs box 4 Wm Marshall 1706 St Dunstan's; 9 Jn Loill 1678–9.

[172] Ibid. Benj. Blisset 1702 St Stephen's Coleman; box 1 Francis Mottershed 1665 Paul's Wharf; Lichfield Jt RO, Cons. Ct O.W. etc. Oliver Catorn (Catterne) 1672 Cov.; Leics. RO, Arch. inv. 1670/237; Bodl. Arch. Ct Berks. O.W. etc. 46/97; 203/15; Worcs. RO, Cons. Ct O.W. etc. 1612/10; Wm Pebody 1711 Kidderminster; Notts. RO, Man. Ct Mansfield O.W. etc. portf. 1 nos. 2, 13; 16 no. 13; 23 no. 28; Lancs. RO, Cons. Ct Cestr. Supra invs Jn Bordeman 1628, Wm Crompton 1631, both Bolton; Th. Howse 1633 (1614) Rochdale; Kent RO, Cons. Ct Cant. Inv. Reg. 17 fos. 347–8; Arch. Ct Cant. Inv. Paper 33/172; W. Sfk RO, Ep. Commy Ct Bury inv. 1652/ 25; E. Sfk RO, Arch. inv. 18/69; E. Suss. RO, invs main ser. Samson Brightridge 1714 Hellingly; Edwards 205; Ramsay, *Wilts.*, 24, 130; Smyth, *Names*, 90–2, 278–80, 289 sqq., 297–9; *Wills & Admons fr. Knaresboro. Ct R.*, ii, 220 sqq.; S. D. Chapman & S. Chassagne, *Eur. Text. Printers in 18th cent.*, 1981, p. 14; Nfk RO, Cons. Ct inv. 1637/148; Cty Lond. RO, Ct Orphs invs box 1 Phil. Hudson 1665, Th. Champney 1666; 2 Geo. Jackson 1666; 7 Ralph Lawrence 1670; Allison 765.

[173] Ibid. 765–6; Millican, *Reg.*, 88; Gross ii, 349; Edwards 205; Guildhall Lib. Commy Ct Lond. (Lond. Div.) invs box 2 Jn Bird cit. & Wm Owen (St Sepulchre), both 1665; Bodl. Arch. Ct Berks. O.W. etc. 223/136; Nfk RO, Cons. Ct invs. 1666/27; 1681/85; Wilt. RO, Cons. Ct Sarum. Jer. Braxton 1723 Devizes; Northants. RO, Arch. Ct Northampton Admons & Invs 1717/1; Brist. RO, Cons. Ct inv. 1624/72.

[174] Cty Lond. RO, Ct Orphs invs box 1 Ant. Holliman 1665; Campbell 260; C. S. Davies 124; Stats 14 Chas 2 c.15; 19 & 20 Chas 2 c.11; PRO, PCC parch. invs p. 1660 nos. 3500, 4271; Guildhall Lib. Commy Ct Lond. (Lond. Div.) invs box 1 Ric. Fouler 1667 St Sepulchre's; 2 Jn Profitt 1665 Stepney; Jn Hucking 1665 St Anne's, Aldersgate; 8 Ann Hue wid. 1703 Stepney; 9 Sam. Pantin 1700 & Geo. Thackery 1701 (St Dunstan's) both Stepney; Rothstein 137–40; Cant. Cath. Lib. Wall. Recs. Misc. Docs portf. 4 no. 58.

[175] Ibid. portf. 1 nos. 8–11; W. A. J. Archbold, 'Assmt Wages f. 1630', *Engl. Hist. Rev.*, 1897 xii, 310; Allen 189; Dunsford 229–30, 238–9; Randall 319–20; Moens, *Norwich*, 189 sqq.; Cash 44, 155–6; Hughes & Larkin ii, 501; Kent RO, Cons. Ct Cant. Reg. Accts & Invs 7 fos. 270–1; Inv. Paper 21/21; Inv. Reg. 20 fos. 392–3; Glos. RO, Cons. Ct invs 1715/71; 1726/28; 1730/160A; 1731/ 73; 1735/59; Northants. RO, Arch. Ct Northampton Admons & Invs 1713/70; 1714/47; 1723/127; 1724/108; Soms. RO, Arch. Taunton invs 1640/83; 1667/7; 1670/25, 70; 1678/69; 1683/43; Nfk RO, Arch. Ct Norvic. inv. 1700–2/65; Cons. Ct invs 1663/196, 249; 1682/11, 81; 1684/256; 1688–9/17; Wilts. RO, Arch. Ct Sarum. Chris. Ford 1703 Urchfont; Robt Rogers 1748 Atford in Bradford; Ess. RO, Pec. Ct Bocking inv. Ric. Chaplain 1739; E. Sfk RO, Arch. invs 6/145; 15/82; 17/66; Hants. RO, unclass. invs D/2/A:2/61, 181; W. Sfk RO, Ep. Commy Ct Bury invs 1660/170; 1661/1; 1662/ 102, 214; 1663/221; 1665/97; 1666/109; 1667/1, 23; 1669/26; 1676/60; 1680/23; 1700/3; 1704/32; 1712/35; Leics. RO, Arch. invs 1661/52; 1668/133; 1669/37; 1690/63, 108.

[176] Inf. 207.

[177] Moens, *Norwich*, 189 sqq.; Nfk RO, Cons. Ct inv. 1588/110.

[178] HMC, *Var. Colls*, viii, 591.

[179] W. Sfk RO, Ep. Commy Ct Bury invs 1676/18; 1678/38; 1692/33, 44, 65; 1701/46; 1709/24; Nfk RO, Cons. Ct invs 1590/82; 1637/76; 1640/39; 1642/171; Glos. RO, Cons. Ct invs 1684/257; 1694/56; 1696/51; 1701/65; Wilts. RO, Arch. Ct Sarum. Th. Dowse 1667 & Jn Giddings 1693, both Urchfont; Cons. Ct Sarum. Wm Fuller 1662 Marston in Potterne; Wm Cooper 1676 Urchfont; Ed. Powell 1693 Marlborough; PRO, PCC parch. invs p. 1660 no. 2998.

[180] Ibid. no. 4160; W. Sfk RO, Ep. Commy Ct Bury invs 1662/39; 1663/221; 1668/174; 1669/ 26; 1680/23; 1706/7; 1712/35; E. Sfk RO, Arch. inv. 17/66; HMC, *Var. Colls*, viii, 588, 591; Archbold 310; Allen 189.

[181] Soms. RO, Arch. Taunton inv. Jn Thomas 1697 Brompton Regis; Leics. RO, Arch. inv. 1632/51; Wilts. RO, Cons. Ct Sarum. Wm Fuller 1662 Marston in Potterne; Wm Cooper 1676 Urchfont; Arch. Ct Sarum. Jn Giddings 1693 id.; Glos. RO, Cons. Ct inv. 1694/56; Nfk RO, invs

Cons. Ct 1642/171; 1684/102; 1703–8/256; Pec. Ct. D.&C. 1737–82/7; Arch. Ct Norvic. 1692–3/128; 1706–7/85.

[182] Ibid. 1692–3/113.

[183] Ibid. Cons. Ct 1589/200; 1703–8/301; Northants. RO, Arch. Ct Northampton Admons & Invs 1723/34; E. Sfk RO, Arch. invs 6/145; 18/65; W. Sfk RO, Ep. Commy Ct Bury inv. 1709/24.

[184] Ibid. 1650/100; 1677/88; 1692/33; 1700/59; 1701/46; 1705/62; 1707/1, 49; 1711/36; 1716/7; Bodl. Cons. & Arch. Cts Oxf. O.W. etc. 83/4/13; Arch. Ct Berks. O.W. etc. 139/59; 206/50; Cant. Cath. Lib. Wall. Recs. Misc. Docs portf. 1 no. 10; Stephens, *Exeter*, 54–5; Notts. RO, Man. Ct Mansfield O.W. etc. portf. 59 no. 3; Lichfield JT RO, Cons. Ct O.W. etc. Francis Allond (Alland) 1673–4 Cov.; Nfk RO, invs Cons. Ct 1589/200; 1642/171; 1679/17; Arch. Ct Norvic. 1674–5/168; 1682–3/40; 1700–2/65; 1706–7/85; Soms. RO, Arch. Taunton invs Jn Glasse 1691 Charlinch; Jn Thomas 1697 Brompton Regis; Glos. RO, Cons. Ct invs 1684/257; 1694/56; 1696/51; 1697/138; 1701/65; *VCH Leics.*, iv, 90–2; Wilts. RO, Arch. Ct Sarum. Jn Giddings 1693 Urchfont; Cons. Ct Sarum. Wm Fuller 1662 Marston in Potterne; Wm Cooper 1676 Urchfont; Ed. Powell 1693 Marlborough.

[185] Ibid. Wm Sheppard 1665 Devizes; Soms. RO, Arch. Taunton inv. Christ Trot 1691 Taunton St Mary Magd.

[186] Nfk RO, Cons. Ct inv. 1589/200; Glos. RO, Cons. Ct invs 1663/196; 1691/116; 1709/40; W. Sfk RO, Ep. Commy Ct Bury invs 1663/96; 1667/136; 1668/32; 1670/77, 132; 1711/42.

[187] Ibid. 1686/64; 1701/52; 1705/84; E. Sfk RO, Arch. invs 18/65; 23/5; *VCH Leics.*, iv, 90–2; Nfk RO, Arch. Ct Norvic. invs 1707–8/78; 1715–17/71; 1722–3/11.

[188] Ibid. 1700–2/280; 1715–17/67; 1725–6/32; 1731–2/35; 1743–54 Jn Bacon 1749 Saham Toney; Pec. Ct D.&C. 1687–94/43; 1737–82/7; Cons. Ct 1709–10/25; 1723/84; 1729/13; PRO, PCC parch. invs p. 1660 no. 4158 (Cutting); paper invs 1661–1725 no. 3440; W. Sfk RO, Ep. Commy Ct Bury invs 1660/189; 1662/92, 102, 214; 1663/74, 123; 1668/183, 195; 1677/89; 1688/7; 1696/83; 1700/3; 1703/28; 1704/32; 1731–6/22; 1774–85/84 (Owers); Thetford, King's Ho., Boro. Recs vol. 1 fos. 17v., 56 (pp. 33, 110); Reyce 22.

[189] W. Sfk RO, Ep. Commy Ct Bury invs 1667/30; 1686/79; 1696/103; Nfk RO, Cons. Ct inv. 1637–68/118; A. F. J. Brown 146.

[190] PRO, Chanc. Jud. Proc. (Eq. side) Chanc. Mrs' Docs, Exhibs, Mr Unkn no. 176.

[191] PRO, SPD Jas 129/70.

[192] E. Sfk RO, Arch. invs 6/145; 15/82; 23/48; W. Sfk RO, Ep. Commy Ct Bury inv. 1700/21; Nfk RO, Cons. Ct inv. 1703–8/256.

[193] Kent RO, Cons. Ct Cant Reg. Accts & Invs 15 fo. 295; Bodl. Arch. Ct Berks. O.W. etc. 113/74; Wilts. RO, Cons. Ct Sarum. Wm Sheppard 1665 Devizes; Soms. RO, Arch. Taunton invs Chris. Trot 1691 Taunton St Mary Magd.; Jn Arnold 1699 par. unkn; Robt Ducke 1714–15 Fiddington.

[194] Glos. RO, Cons. Ct invs 1663/249; 1677/74; 1682/11, 54, 81, 115; 1684/255–6; 1686/248; 1687/41; 1690/185; 1695/152, 180; 1696/75; 1697/138; 1705/36; 1709/40; 1721/54.

[195] W. Sfk RO, Ep. Commy Ct Bury invs 1662/214; 1663/96; 1668/195; 1677/89; 1700/3; E. Sfk RO, Arch. invs 6/145; 15/82; 23/48; Burley, thes. 118; Edwards 30.

[196] Ut sup. p. 321 n. 203.

[197] Pound, thes. 230–1; *VCH Notts.*, ii, 347; Webb, *Poor Relief*, 138 (& v. 125, 128, 130); Leonard 332; Eden ii, 410; HMC, *11th Rep.*, App. pt iii, 247; *15th Rep.*, App. pt x, 38; & v. Hudson & Tingey ii, 340; 342; Cant. Cath. Lib. Wall. Recs. Misc. Docs portf. 4 no. 58.

[198] Defoe, *Plan*, 267–8; HMC, *Var. Colls*, i, 132; Leics. RO, Arch. inv. 1664/9; E. Sfk RO, Arch. inv. 3/110.

[199] G. Eland, *Purefoy Ltrs 1735–53*, 2 vols. 1931 i, 147; Yarranton 46; J. Wedge, *Gen. View Agric. Co. Pal. Ches.*, 1794, p. 60.

[200] T. Davis, *Gen. View Agric. Co. Wilts.*, 1794, p. 158; PRO, PCR 1632–3 p. 336 (fo. 146v.); Wilts. RO, ex Dioc. Reg. Sarum. invs Hy Noble 1601 & Joan Harse 1610 Edington; Wr Kember

1585 & Agnes Thorne 1569 Marten in Gt Bedwyn; Jn Savage 1627 L. Bedwyn; Wm Caston 1598 Hungerford; Jn Eadney 1610 Amesbury; Edm. Halford c.1540 S. Newton; Jn Crouche 1586 W. Combe in Gt Bedwyn; Wm Farmer 1628 Collingbourne Ducis; Th. Pearse 1634 Axford in Ramsbury; Edith Jerret 1585 Yatesbury; Jn Pardew 1560 Orcheston St Mary; Marg. Harvist 1633 Combe Bisset; Jn Marshman 38 Eliz. Broad Chalke; Th. Whithorne 1584 Nether Woodford; Jn Harsford 1634 Heale in Woodford; Hugh Lawse 1575 Bulford; Anne Shergoll 1593 Wedhampton; Eliz. Goldiker 1593 Cholderton; Cons. Ct Sarum. Jn Earle 1615 Patney; Arch. Ct Sarum. Jn Follyat 1638 Broad Chalke; Savernake Archives, box 13 no. 99a Ct Bk Collingbourne Ducis invs Eliz. Hearne 1580, Jn Reves 1587, Joan Farmer 1590, Jn Rutter 1592.

[201] Havinden 177–8; Aspley Heath Sch. Hist. S., op. cit. 21–3; Herts. RO, Gorhambury Coll. II.o.12A; Westmill-Wakeley-Buntingford Coll. no. 155; PRO, Exch. Augm. Off. Parl Svy Herts no. 21 fo. 9.

[202] Allison map. 15; Doughty 169; Blome 208, 211; Nfk RO, Cons. Ct invs 1590/136, 187; 1591/51; 1611/84; 1633/308.

[203] Ibid. 1611/30, 157; 1614/79, 133; 1638/147; Dyer, 'Fleece' bk iii, 128; W. Sfk RO, Ep. Commy Ct Bury invs 1573–8/18, 106; Steer 71–2, 82–4, 99.

[204] PRO, SPD Eliz. 106/48.

[205] BL, Add. 39245 fo. 65.

[206] Emmison, *Jac. Hsehld Invs*, 58, 60, 63, 77, 94, 104–5, 120–1, 127–8, 133, 135–8; Beds. RO, F.685; Birm. Lib. MSS 350254–5, 350275; Leics. RO, Commy Ct Evington invs nos. 7, 29, 32; O.W., Admons etc. Robt Rowe 1611; Arch. invs 1556–83/4, 51; 1614/170; 1616/28, 84; 1621/42, 173; 1625/19, 120; 1626/141; 1627/56, 197; 1628/2, 7; 1631/124; 1632/27, 45, 183; 1633/31, 43, 155; 1636/23, 62, 73–4, 204, 224; 1637/92; 1638/279, 309; 1639/44, 61, 116, 120, 124, 141; 1640/36; 1641/54; 1658/221; 1659/165, 314; 1660/107; 1661/111; 1667/183; 1669/22; 1710 Ann Coulson/ Brascoate in Newbold Verdon; 1738 Robt Seamington/Birstall.

[207] Wilts. RO, Acc. 122 Svys Bromham, Bremhill, Bowden & Stanley 1612 (w. ct bk), Stanley ct 1615 inv. Robt Long/Closewood in Chippenham; Chittoe ct 1616 inv. Wm Rashwood/Studley in Bremhill; ex Diox. Reg. Sarum invs Jn Grant 1607 Holt in Bradford; Jn Parker 1625 Greenhill; Wr Townsend 1629 Stockley; Jane Patie als Clarke 1634 Calne; Jn Palmer 1637 id.; Jn Robbins/ Stockley & Jos. White/Calne, 1638; Cons. Ct Sarum, Ric. Cradocke 1633 Minety.

[208] Ibid. Th. Bourne 1625 Semley; ex Dioc. Reg. Sarum. invs Jn Turner 1564 Gt Knoyle; Wm Stantor 1585 Horningsham; Ed. Gildon 1598 Mere Woodland; Th. Pytman 1620 Mere; Thomazine Gwyer 1633 Mere Zeales; Tim. Meade 1634 Mere; Th. Graye 1642 Tisbury.

[209] Cash 5, 6, 18, 21–3, 28–9, 35–6, 38 sqq., 45–6, 52–3, 57–9, 68–71, 91–2, 94, 104–5, 124, 134, 144–6.

[210] W. Bowden 110, 148; Mann, *Cl. Ind.*, 131–2; *VCH Wilts.*, iv, 63; *C.J.*, xxxvi, 7.

[211] Worcs. RO, Cons. Ct O.W. etc. 1690/41; 1720 Jas Lacy sr Bromsgrove; Dyer, *Cty Worc.*, 117.

[212] PRO, SPD Jas 80/16.

[213] Mann, 'Clothiers & Weavers', 88.

[214] Unwin, *Ind. Org.*, 12, 13.

[215] Stat. 14 Chas 2 c.5; Nfk RO, Cty Recs. Liber Albus fo. 95; 2nd Bk Worstedweavers fos. 91, 95v., 121; Bk Mayor's Ct 12 pp. 315, 875; 13 p. 153; 14 fo. 222; 16 fo. 63v.; 20 fo. 432; Ass. Bk 3 fos. 64v., 74, 131v.

[216] Ibid. 5 fo. 83(93)v.; PRO, SPD Chas 206/64; PCR 1631–2 p. 269 (fo. 135).

[217] Nfk RO, Cty Recs. Bk Mayor's Ct 12 fo. 315; 15 fo. 85; 16 fo. 63v.; Hilton 43; A. F. J. Brown 148; K. H. Burley, 'N. on Lab. Dispute in early 18th cent. Colc.', *Bull. I.H.R.*, 1956 xxix, 226.

[218] Stat. 5 Eliz. c.4.

[219] Allen 105, 143, 151, 158; T. Fuller, *Holy State & Profane State*, ed. J. Nichols 1841, p. 17; R. K. Kelsall, *Wage Reg. under Stat. Artifs*, repro. in W. E. Minchinton, *Wage Reg. in Pre-Ind.*

*Engld*, Newton Abbot n.d. pp. 133–4; A. Kussmaul, *Servts in Husb. in Early Mod. Engld*, Cam. 1981, p. 32.

[220] Sudbury, Tn Recs, Bk Proc. Boro. Ct 6 (1640–72) 'Ords. & Decrs conserning saymakers weavers etc.' 31 Oct. 1648; Kussmaul 32–3.

[221] Stats 5 Eliz. c.4; 1 Jas c.6.

[222] Cant. Cath. Lib. Wall. Recs. Misc. Docst portf. 1 no. 11.

[223] Stephens, *Exeter*, 151; A. H. A. Hamilton 163–4; & v. Heaton 113–15.

[224] Allen 187–90; HMC *Var. Colls.*, i, 162 sqq.

[225] Hughes & Larkin ii, 215–18, 265 sqq.; iii, 36–8, 140.

[226] Heaton 113–16.

[227] *Cal. SP Ven.*, vi, 1671–2; & v. my *Ag. Rev.*, 332–4.

[228] Fuller, *Worthies*, i, 498; ii, 447.

[229] Blome 208; Bodl. Aubrey 2 fo. 122.

[230] Ibid.; Munn 21, 23, 26–8, 32; Defoe, *Compl. Engl. Tradesman*, 76–7; *Plan*, 101; P. Earle, *World of Defoe*, 1976, pp. 108 sqq., 121, 124.

[231] Randall 350; Munn, pref.

[232] Allen 189.

[233] Archbold 310.

[234] HMC, *Var. Colls*, i, 162 sqq.; viii, 590–1; *C.J.*, xxvii, 683, 730–3; Allen 189; Hilton 77; Stat. 29 Geo. 2 c.23; Shrewsbury Lib. Orig. Recs Co. Weavers & Clothiers vol. i fo. 5v.; Ords etc. Weavers' Co., agrt 9 Nov. 1600; cf. Warner 101–2.

[235] E. Hall, *Chron.*, 1809, p. 699.

[236] PRO, SPD Hy 8 vol. 47 fo. 89.

[237] *APC*, xiv, 93.

[238] PRO, SPD Jas 127/102; 128/20, 49; 130/73.

[239] Ibid. 115/20; 129/79; *APC*, 1619–21 pp. 205–6; Soms. RO, DD/BR/gr, bdl. 18 no. i, N. on 1615 Thornbury deed.

[240] PRO, SPD Jas 127/76; 128/67; 137/13.

[241] Ibid. Chas 141/1; 176/36; 177/52, 56; 182/38; 186/23; 188/92; *APC*, 1630–1 p. 136.

[242] PRO, PCR 1639 p. 266 (fo. 128v.).

[243] A. F. J. Brown 148; Mann, 'Clothiers & Weavers', 71–2, 95; Ess. RO, Q. Sess. bdl. 184, 4 Apr. 1749.

[244] *APC*, xxv, 44; HMC, *Var. Colls*, i, 94.

[245] Child, *N. Disc. Trade*, 18; W. Petty, *Econ. Writings*, Cam. 2 vols. 1899, i, 274–5; Mann, 'Clothiers & Weavers', 77.

[246] Clark, 'Ess. Woollen Manufs', 203–6; *APC*, 1629–30 pp. 114–15; 1630–1 pp. 230–1, 358–9; PRO, SPD Chas 147/43.

[247] Ibid. 189/40; 533/87; *APC*, xiv, 93, 272–4; 1621–3 pp. 132–3; 1629–30 pp. 114–15; 1630–1 pp. 230–1, 358–9.

[248] Pound, *Cs Poor*, 97, 99; Stephens, *Exeter*, 151–2.

[249] Defoe, *Wks*, 541.

[250] Hilton 42–5, 64 sqq., 77–9, 88–9; A. H. A. Hamilton 245–6; Mann, 'Clothiers & Weavers', 73–5, 88–9; J. S. Davies 272; A. F. J. Brown 148; Burley, 'Lab. Dispute', 223–5; thes. 146; Harris, *Cov. Leet Bk*, 658, 707; BL, Cott. Titus B.i fo. 193(189); PRO, SPD Chas 354/143; 355/92–3, 136, 162–5.

[251] Warner 87–8.

[252] Defoe, *Tour*, ii, 195; J. James 194, 202; T. Wilson 20; HMC, *Var. Colls*, i, 135.

[253] Ibid. i, 132; Cov. RO, Cty Recs. Leet Bk 30 Eliz.–1834 p. 8; Ches. RO, Q. Sess. Files 1581 file 2 no. 1; Defoe, *Plan*, 267–8; pace Unwin, *Studs*, 271.

[254] Guildford Muniment Rm, Loseley MSS 1966/2–4.

[255] Reyce 23; & v. inf. 238.

[256] PRO, SPD Chas 153/53.

[257] Ibid. 284/1; & v. 180/71; 408/15; Jas 140/82.

[258] Ibid. Eliz. 244/126-9; Chas 147/50; Stat. 3 H.8 c.6; Mann, *Cl. Ind.*, 287; Cunnington, *Ann. Devizes*, 1555–1791 pp. 168–9; Chanter & Wainwright ii, 173, 175; HMC, *Var. Colls*, i, 167–8; Sudbury, Tn Recs, Bk. Proc. Boro. Ct 6 (1640–72) Ords & Decrs May 1647; Wilts. RO, Cons. Ct Sarum. Robt Palmer 1666 & Jn Andrewes 1673, both Devizes; Hants. RO, Cons. Ct O.W. & Invs Sam. Hoopper 1630 Soton.

[259] Nfk RO, Cons. Ct inv. 1584/8; SPD Chas 147/50; 159/27.

[260] Cov. RO, Cty Recs. Leet Bk 30 Eliz.–1834 pp. 39, 70; Lichfield Jt RO, Cons. Ct O.W., Jn Showell 1599 Cov.

[261] PRO, SPD Chas 147/50; 153/53; 159/27; 180/57; PCR 1631–2 pp. 269–70, 440, 443 (fos. 135, 215v., 217); 1633–4 p. 445 (fo. 227); *APC*, 1616–17 p. 49; 1617–19 p. 316; 1629–30 pp. 125, 155–6, 221, 275–6; Stats 7 Jas c.7; 14 Chas 2 c.5; Firth & Rait ii, 453, 777; Rymer xx, 41; Nfk RO, Cty Recs. Bk Mayor's Ct 15 fos. 140, 488; 16 fos. 322v.–3; Leic. Mus. Cty Recs. Hall Papers bk xvii no. 245.

[262] Steele ii, 36; Stat. 22 & 23 Chas 2 c.8.

[263] *C.J.*, xi, 22.

[264] Steele i, 207; PRO, Eliz. 103/33; Chas 189/40.

[265] PRO, PCR 1631–2 p. 440 (fo. 215v.).

[266] PRO, Exch. KR Deps by Commn 6 Jas East. 30.

[267] HMC, *Var. Colls*, i, 162, 167–8; PRO, SPD Eliz. 244/129.

[268] Heaton 116.

[269] PRO, Exch. KR Deps by Commn 44 & 45 Eliz. Mich. 1 m. 4r.; PCR 1631–2 p. 269 (fo. 135); Bodl. Hearne's Diaries 158 p. 32; Wilts. RO, Cons. Ct Sarum. Robt Palmer 1666, Jn Andrewes 1673 & Ric. Farmer 1692, all Devizes; Acc. 122 Svys Bromham, Bremhill, Bowden & Stanley (w. ct bk), Stanley ct 1618 will & inv. And. Wilcocks (Wilcox) Stanley; Ess. RO, Pec. Ct Bocking inv. Ric. Chaplain 1739; Hants. RO, Cons. Ct O.W. & Invs Sam. Hoopper 1630 Soton; Soms. RO, Arch. Taunton invs Chris. Trot 1691 Taunton St Mary Magd.; Jn Arnold 1699 par. unkn; Colc. Tn Hall, Ass. Bk 21 Jan. 1590; Glos. RO, Cons. Ct invs 1677/74; 1682/81; 1695/152; 1697/138; E. Sfk RO, Arch. invs 12/81; 15/82; W. Sfk RO, Ep. Commy Ct Bury invs 1652/80; 1660/189; 1666/50; 1668/173; 1677/89; 1686/20, 64; 1696/91; 1701/52; 1774–85/84; Brist. RO, Cons. Ct inv. 1623/73.

[270] Heaton 116; Defoe, *Plan*, 267; Cant. Cath. Lib. Wall. Recs. Misc. Docs portf. 1 no. 21 (& v. nos. 22–3); cf. BL, Add. 2985 fo. 75.

[271] PRO, PCR 1637–8 pp. 82, 578 (fos. 39v., 291v.); Cant. Cath. Lib. Wall. Recs. Misc. Docs portf. 1 no. 24; cf. Kent RO, Cons. Ct Cant. Inv. Paper 12/45.

[272] Guildhall Lib. Weavers' Co. Ord. & Rec. Bk 1577–1641 p. 660; PRO, SPD Jas 81/56; 129/70.

[273] Ibid. Interreg. 71/20; Kirk i, 390, 392–3; iii, 378–9, 416–17, 439; Stow, *Ann.*, 868; Cant. Cath. Lib. Cty Recs. Burghmote Bk 1578–1602 fo. 44v.

[274] Ibid. 1658–72 fos. 233–4; Stats 14 & 15 H.8 c.2; 21 H.8 c.16; Hessels, *Archivum*, iii, 270–3.

[275] Nfk RO, Cty Recs. Strangers Bk fos. 18v., 24v., 25, 27v., 29, 30, 33v.–4; Ass. Bk 5 fos. 14, 16, 17v., 52v., (23, 25, 26v., 62v.); Bks Mayor's Ct 8 p. 704; 11 fo. 403; Cant. Cath. Lib. Cty Recs. Burghmote Bk 1658–72 fos. 160; 233–4; Wall. Recs. Misc. Docs portf. 1 nos. 2–5.

[276] Cf. ibid. no. 10: 'Les maistres ne pourront donner conge a leurs ouvriers sans les avons paie et contente.'

[277] Ibid. nos. 2–5; portf. 2 no. 97; portf. 4 nos. 3, 15, 16, 19–21, 23, 25, 29, 30; portf. 5 no. 13; Cty Recs. Burghmote Bks 1578–1602 fo. 21v.; 1658–72 fo. 82; Chamb's Accts 1568–77 fos. 339 sqq.; 1587–92 fo. 199; 1592–1602 fos. 191, 473; 1602–10 fos. 67, 110, 190v.; Kent RO, Maidstone Recs. Chamb's Accts (Paper Bks) 6 & 7; Nfk RO, Cty Recs. Strangers Bk fos. 18v., 19,

26, 32–3; Colc. Tn Hall, Ass. Bk 20 Oct. 1605; PRO, SPD Eliz. 127/81; Jas 133/2, 4 sqq.; Morant, *Colc.* 74; Hessels, *Archivum*, iii, 612.

[278] Ibid. 928; PRO, SPD Eliz. 127/80; Jas 121/154–5, 164–5, 167; 133/2, 4, 5, 9; Chas 429/2; 431/22; 456/4.

[279] Cant. Cath. Lib. Wall. Recs. Misc. Docs portf. 1 nos. 21–3.

[280] Nfk RO, Cty Recs. Bks Mayor's Ct 10 fo. 298; 12 fo. 354.

[281] Scoville 321 sqq.; Hands & Scouloudi, pass.; Papillon 117–19; Moens, *Threadneedle St.*, i, p. iv; Hessels, *Archivum*, iii, 2699–700.

[282] Ibid. ii, 293, 397–400, 403 sqq., 412 sqq., 423–5, 437–8, 441, 445 sqq., 454–5, 471 sqq., 490 sqq., 513 sqq., 520–1, 542–3, 561 sqq., 567 sqq.; iii, 166, 168, 232, 284, 310, 434, 445–6, 466, 486–7, 580, 587, 591–2, 808–9, 853–4, 888–9, 1093–5, 1105–6, 1139–40, 1146–7, 1558–9, 1571, 1851–2, 1899, 2948 sqq.

[283] A. F. J. Brown 148; Hilton 43; Burley, 'Lab. Dispute', 226; Nfk RO, Cty Recs. Bks Mayor's Ct 12 fo. 315; 15 fo. 85; 16 fo. 63v.

[284] Mann, 'Clothiers & Weavers', 89; sup. 210.

[285] S. T. Bindoff, *Tu. Engld*, Harmondsworth 1950, p. 124.

[286] *Donations Pet. Blundell*, 7, 8, nn. on pp. iii, iv.

[287] Mann, 'Clothiers & Weavers', 83.


## Chapter 15

[1] BL, Lans. 28 no. 25 fo. 59; PRO, Exch. KR Deps by Commn 44 & 45 Eliz. Mich. 1 mm. 3, 4r., 5r.; SPD Chas 378/45; 380/80; Nfk RO, Cty Recs. Bks Mayor's Ct 5 p. 14; 16 fo. 13v.; Cons. Ct invs 1617/115; 1640/48; 1646/109; 1662/4; 1637–68/19; 1669/84; 1718–21/169; 1731/18; Allison 431, 767–8.

[2] Stephens, *Exeter*, 78, 131, 135 sqq.; Fiennes 245–6; Cash 138–9; Youings 72; Wilts. RO, Preb. Ct Uffculme bdl. 4 no. 19; Devon RO, Huntsham MS PZ1; PRO, PCC parch. invs p. 1660 no. 8300; Soms. RO, Arch. Taunton invs 1668/59; 1671 Th. Hessom/Taunton St Jas; 1690 Agnes Pollard/Holford; 1697 Jane Bond/Taunton St Mary Magd.

[3] Mendenhall 13, 21, 28–9, 32–4; *APC*, xxxiii, 9, 10; 1619–21 pp. 57–8; 1621–3 pp. 263–4; D. J. Evans 23 sqq.; Leighton iii, 136; Heylyn 490–1; PRO, SPD Eliz. 157/4.

[4] Ibid. Interreg. 127/20; Ferguson 24 sqq., 55, 85–6, 110, 138, 145–6, 176–7, 271, 273; Marshall, 'Kendal', 206, 208, 229, 234; Heaton 359 sqq.; Stat. 33 H.8 c.15; Wadsworth & Mann 7, 29 sqq., 37, 41, 43–4, 48, 55, 62, 79 sqq.; Willan, *Inld Trade*, 108 sqq.; *Eliz. Man.*, 53 sqq., 59 sqq.; 'Man. Clothiers', 177 sqq.; *Pal. Notebk*, i, 126–7; Tupling 170–1, 191; Earwaker, *Lancs. & Ches. Wills & Invs 1572 to 1596*, 18, 19; Lancs. RO, Cons. Ct Cestr. Supra inv. 1675 Jn Gregory/ Rochdale; Aikin 158; Raines & Sutton i, 14.

[5] Thornton 150–2, 160–1; Unwin, *Studs*, 274; Reed 12, 27; Kent RO, Maidstone Recs. Burghmote Bk 3 fos. 22v., 42v., 53 (pp. 45, 85, 106); W. Sfk RO, Ep. Commy Ct Bury inv. 1676/ 60; PRO, PCC parch. invs. p. 1660 no. 2890.

[6] Cash 130–1, 143; Stephens, *Exeter*, 117–18.

[7] Ramsay, *Wilts.*, 21, 23, 109, 142; Mann, *Cl. Ind.*, 64; Wiggs 45, 216; Smith, *Mems Wl*, ii, 124; PRO, PCC parch. invs p. 1660 no. 11133; Exch. KR Deps by Commn 6 Jas East. 30.

[8] Dyer, *Cty Worc.*, 105; Burton 180.

[9] PRO, PCC invs 1718–82 bdl. 18 no. 109.

[10] BL, Harl. 70 fos. 8(7)v., 10, 15(16), 27(26) (pp. 5, 10, 20).

[11] Kent RO, Maidstone Recs. Chamb's Accts (Paper Bks) no. 1 fo. 3; 2 fo. 3v.; 3 fo. 3; 5 fo. 3v.; nos. 6 sqq.

[12] Willan, *Inld Trade*, 33, 67; Williams, thes. 76; Edwards 62; Lowe 32; Defoe, *Tour*, i, 80–2; BL, Lans. 28 no. 25 fo. 59; E. Sfk RO, Blois Fam. Archives, Hy Blois's Acct Led. fo. 41; Bowman 418.

[13] PRO, SPD Chas 287/77.

[14] Willan, *Inld Trade*, 8; *Eliz. Man.*, 62; Wadsworth & Mann 8, 29, 46; Lowe 53, 58–9; *Compl. Engl. Tradesman*, 78; Wiggs 45; *Yks. Diaries & Autobiogs in 17th & 18th cents.*, Surtees S. 1886 lxxvii, 23; Bowman 418, 420, 556–7; *C.J.*, xiv, 504; G. W. Daniels, *E. E. Cotton Ind.*, Man. 1920, p. 61; *Trade of Engld Revived*, 1681; PRO, PCC parch. invs p. 1660 nos. 3941–2; Aikin 183–4.

[15] Kirk i, 390–1, 448, 475; ii, 34, 91, 372; Cross 189; Guildhall Lib. Weavers' Co. Ords & Rec. Bk 1577–1641 p. 355.

[16] *Rsns f. Presvg Publick Mkt Blackwell Hall*, s.l. n.d.; Thornton 161, 163, 207; Willan, *Coasting Trade*, 88; Burley, thes. 312–14; Melling iii, 112–13; Kent RO, Cons. Ct Cant. Inv. Reg. 4 fo. 33; Stat. 13 Anne c.20 para. 19; W. Sfk RO, Ep. Commy Ct Bury Reg. Bk Wills 27 (Wood) fo. A42; invs 1665/22; 1667/1, 13, 170; PRO, SPD Eliz. 146/63; Chas 251/27; PCC parch. invs p. 1660 nos. 572, 2887, 2913, 7798, 8752.

[17] Ibid. invs 1718–82 bdl. 18 no. 187; 24 no. 180; 25 no. 84; Wilts. RO, Cons. Ct Sarum. Jn Willmott 1698 Reading; Hants. RO, unclass. invs D/2/A: 2/69; Benson & Hatcher 580; Ramsay, *Wilts.*, 20–2.

[18] Ibid. 23 sqq.; *VCH Soms.*, iv, 57; *APC*, 1625–6 pp. 161–2, 211; Mann, 'Wilts. Fam.', 245, 248–50; Lindley 153; Tann 198; Wilts. RO, Arch. Ct Wilts. 1717 Zeph. Fry yr Chippenham; Devizes Mus., Wm Gaby His Booke pp. 5, 7, 46–7; Glouc. Lib. Smyth of Nibley MSS S.Z.23.2 no. 5; Glos. RO, Marcham Coll. F.26; PRO, PCC parch. invs p. 1660 nos. 363, 368, 1688, 3422, 8410, 8687, 9326, 9658, 11133; paper invs 1661–1725 no. 444; invs 1718–82 bdl. 22 no. 140; 24 nos. 42, 99; 25 no. 67; PCR 1639–40 pp. 373, 382–3 (fos. 182, 186v.–7).

[19] Ibid. 1639 p. 353 (fo. 172); Smith, *Mems Wl*, i, 327; Cros 200–1; Kent RO, Cons. Ct Cant. Regs Accts & Invs 9 fo. 307; 12 fo. 497; Inv. Papers 6/13; 16/32; 22/9; 26/120; Inv. Regs 7 fos. 5, 6, 456; 12 fos. 247–8; 14 fos. 245, 588; 15 fo. 392; 17 fo. 456; 20 fos. 567–8.

[20] Lowe 42, 59, 65; Wadsworth & Mann 8, 9, 30 sqq.; Willan, *Eliz. Man.*, 56–7, 76; Defoe, *Compl. Engl. Tradesman*, 78; Raine 107; Heaton 146–9; PRO, Exch. KR Deps by Commn 1656 Mich. 19 m.1.

[21] Plot, *Oxon.*, 279; Bodl. Cons. & Arch. Cts Oxf. O.W. etc. 83/2/27; 161/1/32; PRO, PCC parch. invs p. 1660 no. 7931.

[22] Ibid. no. 6192; Soms. RO, Arch. Taunton invs 1669/99; 1690 Jos. Lewes/Staplegrove; Defoe, loc. cit.; Cash 130–1; Stephens, *Exeter*, 132, 134.

[23] Ibid. 117–18, 121, 133; Cash 138–9; Willan, *Coasting Trade*, 94; Defoe, loc. cit.; Devon RO, Huntsham MS PZ1; PRO, PCC parch. invs p. 1660 no. 8300.

[24] Ibid. nos. 2130, 2428, 3442, 3672, 3715–6; Dyer, 'Prob. Invs', 14, 15; *Cty Worc.*, 99, 105; Worcs. RO, Cons. Ct O.W. etc. 1614/169; 1649/27; 1711 Ric. Callow sr Kidderminster; 1720 Jas Lacy sr Bromsgrove; Mendenhall 21, 32, 48; Defoe, loc. cit.

[25] C. Holmes, *E. Assoc. in Engl. Civ. War*, Cam. 1974, p. 1; Willan, *Coasting Trade*, 130; *Inld Trade*, 128; Edwards 62; Postlethwayt ii, 349; Allison 710 sqq.; Smith, *Mems Wl*, i, 327; T. Wilson 20; Hudson & Tingey ii, 145; BL, Lans. 28 no. 25 fo. 59; Nfk RO, Cons. Ct inv. 1718–21/169; Cty Recs. Ass. Bk 5 fos. 32(42)v., 265(275)v.; Bks Mayor's Ct 10 pp. 611–14; 11 fos. 260v., 291, 381; Strangers Bk fos. 20v.–1, 25, 36; PRO, SPD Chas 378/45; 380/80; PCC parch. invs p. 1660 nos. 1603–4, 2440, 3602.

[26] Ibid. paper invs 1661–1725 no. 3279; Fuller, *Worthies*, i, 396.

[27] PRO, Exch. KR Deps by Commn 1656 Mich. 19 m.1; Cty Lond. RO, Jnls Com. Cl vol. 11 fo. 366v.; H. of L. RO, H. of L. Papers 27 Jan. 1596–7 to 1 June 1607, fos, 129 sqq.

[28] Devon RO, Exeter Cty Lib. MS 1 Acct Bk Jn Newcombe 1599–1606 fos. 13, 24; PRO, SPD Chas 380/80; Kent RO, Cons. Ct Reg. Accts & Invs 12 fos. 1 sqq.; Nfk RO, Cons. Ct inv. 1703–8/110; W. Sfk RO, Ep. Commy Ct Bury inv. 1667/80; Burton 180; Williams, thes. 208; Stephens, *Exeter*, 118; Defoe, *Wks*, 544; *Compl. Engl. Tradesman*, 78.

[29] Ibid.; Stephens, *Exeter*, 118, 132–3; Williams, thes. 206–8; Pilgrim, thes. 203–5; Edwards 65; Stat. 13 Anne c.20 para.19; Smith, *Mems Wl*, ii, 204; Dyer, *Cty Worc.*, 105; Mendenhall 34, 36;

Willan, *Inld Trade*, 8–10, 122, 129; G. L. Turnbull, *Traffic & Trans.*, 1979, p. 12; PRO, SPD Chas. 380/80.

[30] *APC*, vi, 379–80.

[31] Ramsay, *Wilts.*, 25–6, 131; D. W. Jones 567 sqq.; W. de G. Birch 251 sqq.; Overall 72; Thornton 162; BL, Add. 34324 fo. 211; PRO, SPD Jas 128/73 sqq., 80, 95; PCR 1638 p. 59 (fo. 28).

[32] Ibid.; Stat. 14 & 15 H.8 c.1; Cty Lond. RO, Jnls Com. Cl vol. 11 fo. 366v.; & v. M. L. Zell, 'Exch. Lists Prov. Clothmakers fined in Lond. during 16th cent.', *Bull. I. H. R.*, 1981 liv, 130.

[33] Melling iii, 112–13.

[34] Ibid.; Hughes & Larkin iii, 54–6, 227–8; Thornton 163–5; Ramsay, *Wilts.*, 132; Unwin, *Ind. Org.*, 44–5, 233; PRO, Req. 171/25; SPD Eliz. 106/48; Jas 121/154; 127/19; 130/141; 133/36; Chas 278/104–6.

[35] Ibid. Jas 128/80; *APC*, 1615–16 pp. 122–3; Ramsay, *Wilts.*, 133; Williams, *Tradesmen*, 61, 63; Mann, *Cl. Ind.*, 64; D. W. Jones 573–4.

[36] Kirk i, 390–1, 448, 475; ii, 89; iii, 380–1; *Blackwell Hall Factors Ca.*; Lancs. RO, Cavendish of Holker Coll. 1/46 fo. 1, pp. 9–12, 20, 30–2, 53, 58; Nfk RO, Cty Recs. Ass. Bks 4 fo. 44v.; 5 fo. 331(342)v.; Bk Mayor's Ct 16 fo. 13v.; Misc. Docs. Controversy resp. Rts Cits. Norwich, Ans. Cits Norwich; Cons. Ct invs 1646/60; 1703–8/110; 1710–14/31; 1718–21/169; Yarmouth Lib. MSS, Pengelly Letters L13/2.1; 8; BL, Lans. 28 no. 25 fo. 59; PRO, Exch. KR Deps by Commn 44 & 45 Eliz. Mich. 1 mm. 3, 4r., 5r.; PCC parch. invs p. 1660 nos. 1603–4, 1789, 3602, 5543; PCR 1638 pp. 195, 214 (fos. 96, 105v.); SPD Chas 378/45; 380/80.

[37] Ibid. 1634–5 p. 424 (fo. 203v.); cf. Crofts 43.

[38] Lancs. RO, Hopwood Coll. 39/24; Cross 189; Kent RO, Cons. Ct Cant. Inv. Papers 16/32; 22/9; 26/120; Regs Accts & Invs 9 fo. 307; 12 fo. 497; Inv. Regs 12 fos. 247–8; 14 fos. 245, 588; 15 fo. 392; 17 fo. 456; 20 fos. 567–8; Guildhall Lib. Weavers' Co. Ord. & Rec. Bk 1577–1641 p. 355; Kirk i, 390–1, 448, 475; ii, 34, 89–91; iii, 380–1; *Blackwell Hall Factors Ca.*

[39] PRO, PCC paper invs 1661–1725 no. 3279.

[40] Ibid. nos. 444, 3127; parch. invs p. 1660 no. 2130; invs 1718–82 bdl. 18 no. 187; 22 no. 140; 25 no. 84; SPD Jas 128/80; PCR 1639 p. 353 (fo. 172); St. Ch. Jas bdl. 173 no. 9; Lancs. RO, Cavendish of Holker Coll. 1/46 fo. 1v., pp. 48, 51, 54; Kent RO, ut sup. last n. but one; Nfk RO, Cons. Ct inv. 1718–21/169; Soms. RO, Arch. Taunton inv. Jos. Lewes 1690 Staplegrove; Wilts. RO, Cons. Ct Sarum. Jn Willmott 1698 Reading; W. Sfk RO, Ep. Commy Ct Bury inv. 1667/1; Glouc. Lib. Smyth of Nibley MSS, S.Z. 23.2 no. 5; Glos. RO, Marcham Coll. F.26; Worcs. RO, Cons. Ct O.W. etc 1614/169; 1720 Jas Lacy sr Bromsgrove; Devizes Mus. Wm Gaby His Booke p. 5; Rymer xx, 221; Willan, *Inld Trade*, 108 sqq.; D. V. Glass, *Lond. Inhabs within Walls 1695*, Lond. Rec. Soc. 1966 ii, 33, 45, 119, 315; Defoe, *Compl. Engl. Tradesman*, 11, 81; Thornton 207; Ramsay, *Wilts.*, 133 sqq.; Cash 130–1; Smith, *Mems Wl*, i, 316; ii, 310; Mann, *Cl. Ind.*, 65; 'Wilts. Fam.', 248–50; 'Clothiers & Weavers', 81–2; Melling iii, 112–13; Mendenhall 50; A. F. J. Brown 147; *Blackwell Hall Factors Ca.*; *Engld's Int. Asserted*, 29; *Rsns Decay Clo. Trade*, 9; HMC, *Salisbury MSS*, xiii, 560; Stephens, *Exeter*, 132–3; Tann. 198; Yarranton 97–9; Wadsworth & Mann 43–4.

[41] Ibid. 30–3; Mendenhall 21, 39; *Pal. Notebk*, i, 126–7; Willan, *Eliz. Man.*, 56–7; Raines & Sutton i, 14.

[42] Fiennes 246; Kent RO, Maidstone Recs. Burghmote Bk 3 fos. 22v., 42v., 53 (pp. 45, 85, 106); Stephens, *Exeter*, 78, 80–1, 131.

[43] Ibid. 133.

[44] Kent RO, Cons. Ct Cant. Reg. Accts & Invs 9 fo. 307; Inv. Papers 12/31, 45; Hessels, *Archivum*, iii, 1989; Willan, *Studs*, 75–7.

[45] Ibid. 75; Evelyn iii, 177; PRO, SPD Chas 289/66; 290/11; Burley, thes. 317–18; Pilgrim, thes. 201, 206.

[46] Ibid. 199; Burley, thes. 323, 325; Hinton 24; *APC*, iv, 169; *Engld's Int. Asserted*, 26; *Rsns ... why Wagoners ought not to be obliged to any cert. Wt*, s.l. n.d.; W. Raleigh, *Obs. touching Trade & Comm. w. Hollander & other Nations*, 1653, p. 37; PRO, PCC parch. invs p. 1660 nos. 572, 2887; Willan, *Studs*, 46, 75.

[47] Ibid. 46; Postlethwayt ii, 349–50; Williams, thes. 82, 90, 140, 207, 345 sqq.

[48] Ramsay, *Wilts*, 21, 109, 142; Wiggs 45, 76, 85, 95, 98; Lamb 2, 3, 19, 54–5, 57–8, 76, 207–8, 218–19, 224 sqq., 230–2, 234, 236 sqq., 252 sqq., 261–2, 266–8, 270 sqq., 298, 301, 312, 314–15, 319–20, 322–3.

[49] PRO, PCC parch. invs p. 1660 no. 11133; Exch. KR Deps by Commn 6 Jas East. 30; Smith, *Mems Wl*, ii, 124; Weinstock 38.

[50] Hinton 17, 24, 34; Heaton 150–1; R. G. Wilson 12, 13; Aikin 248; *Rsns f. Presvg Publick Mkt Blackwell Hall*.

[51] Lowe 74; Mendenhall 73; Stephens, 'Chester', 25; Woodward, *Trade Eliz. Chester*, 42–3; 'O'seas Trade Chester 1600–50', *Trs Hist. S. Lancs. & Ches.*, 1971 cxxii, 31.

[52] Cash 126–7; Bourhis i, 97; Stephens, *Exeter*, 110–11, 120–1; E. Sfk RO, Blois Fam. Archives, Hy Blois's Acct Led. fos. 55v., 56v.

[53] Ibid. fo. 55v.; BL, Harl. 70 fo. 20(19)v.

[54] J. James 185–6; J. D. Gould, *Gt Debasemt*, Oxf. 1970, p. 125; Cole ii, 567–8.

[55] Ibid.; R. Davis, *Aleppo & Devons. Sq.*, 1967, pp. 96–8; Coleman, *Banks*, 26; Aubrey, *Sy*, iv, 4; Ramsay, *Wilts.*, 109; Heaton 150, 197–8; Lowe 65–6; Mendenhall 48, 58, 73, 76; Blome 209, 212; Willan, *Ru. Co.*, 53, 253, 260; Clark, 'Ess. Woollen Manufs', 206; De Smedt ii, 332 sqq., 350; Unwin, *Studs*, 277, 279, 288–9, 291; Friis 230; Goris 276, 298; Roberts, *Marchants Mapp*, 2nd pt, 28, 193; Hinton 24, 34–5, 85, 114; Reed 27; Connell-Smith 3, 207 sqq.; J. James 186; Edler, 'Van Der Molen', 104, 117, 119; Tawney & Power iii, 203; Burley, thes. 323, 325; Woodward, *Trade Eliz. Chester*, 42; McGrath, *Merchs*, 282; Stephens, *Exeter*, 30, 67; Prestwich 55, 57, 83; E. Sfk RO, Blois Fam. Archives, Hy Blois's Acct Led. fo. 77v.; BL, Cott. Titus B. v fo. 254; Bodl. Top. Kent a.I fo. 6; PRO, Exch. KR Deps by Commn 6 Jas East. 30; SPD Eliz. 15/67; 33/16; 209/102; Jas 72/70; Chas 2, 379/5; Jas 2 vol. 5 fos. 43–5, 51–4.

[56] Ibid. fos. 33 sqq.; Chaudhuri 216, 222–4; Davis, *Aleppo*, 98.

[57] Ibid.; Hinton 34; *Rsns f. Presvg Publick Mkt Blackwell Hall*; Mann, *Cl. Ind.*, 37.

[58] Ibid. 15, 16; *C.J.*, xvii, 366–7, 394, 398; Ramsay, *Wilts.*, 118, 142–3.

[59] Ibid. 118–20, 140 sqq.; Mann, *Cl. Ind.*, 15–18; Hinton 114; J. James 186; Cole ii, 567–8; Wood 44; H. E. S. Fisher 145; Sella, *Commerci e Industrie*, 61–2, 64; Stephens, *Exeter*, 28, 30, 67.

[60] Ibid. 28, 30, 67; Burley, thes. 323; McGrath, *Merchs*, 282; Raleigh, *Obs.*, 42–3; Denucé 58–60; Posthumus & De Nie 252; Roberts, *Marchants Mapp*, 2nd pt, 28, 33, 42, 52, 62, 68, 76, 92; Smith, *Mems Wl*, ii, 139; Ehrenberg 276, 280, 285, 287, 329–32, 355; Zins 161, 184, 186–7; J. James 186, 209; H. E. S. Fisher 7, 15, 41, 54, 56, 128, 135, 145; Van Dillen, *Bronnen*, iii, 730; Coornaert, *Hondschoote*, 65; Chanter & Wainwright ii, 56; Hinton 114; Evelyn iii, 177; Willan, *Studs*, 75, 77, 112; Haynes, *Clo. Trade*, 17; *VCH Ess.*, ii, 399; A. F. J. Brown 146, 148; Digges 46; Croft xxvii; Notestein et al. ii, 290; iv, 175; vi, 72; Braudel & Romano 66; Smit ii, 856, 953, 957, 1009, 1018, 1057, 1074, 1088, 1152, 1237–8, 1287; Brulez, *Della Faille*, 57, 107, 149–51, 423, 512; *Engld's Int. Asserted*, 12, 13; Alberti & Chapman 64–6; Coleman, *Banks*, 27; Kamen 117; Evelyn iii, 177; BL, Harl. 1878 fo. 99(84); E. Sfk RO, Blois Fam. Archives, Hy Blois's Acct Led. fo. 55v.; PRO, SPD Jas 15/15; Chas 317/67; 354/92; 355/144; Interreg. 25/52; Christensen 184; cf. Bang iiA, 60 et pass.; Bang & Korst, pass.; Sella, *Commerci e Industrie*, 79.

[61] J. James 185–6; Cole ii, 567; Craeybeckx 444; Wiggs 85; Lamb 76; Brulez, *Della Faille*, 151; Connell-Smith 18; Raleigh, *Obs.*, 42–3; Posthumus, *Bronnen*, v, 40, 159; Mendenhall 76; Evelyn iii, 177; Roberts, *Marchants Mapp*, 2nd pt, 52, 62, 68, 76, 92; Postlethwayt ii, 349–50; Kamen 119; Williams, thes. 90, 345 sqq.; Burley, thes. 317–18; Åström 75; Flint. RO, Soughton Hall MS 1169; Lancs. RO, Cavendish of Holker Coll. 1/46 p. 51; PRO, SPD Interreg. 22/139; BL, Add. 34324 fo. 211; H. E. S. Fisher 7, 15, 41, 53–4, 128 135, 145.

[62] Ibid. 15, 54, 145; Wood 119; Stephens, *Exeter*, 30, 67, 104–5, 111; J. James 186; Cole ii, 567–8; K. G. Davies 176–7, 234, 352; Chaudhuri 223; Dvis, *Aleppo*, 96–7; Coleman, *Banks*, 27; PRO, SPD Jas 2 vol. 5 fos. 36–7; Lev. Papers vol. 5 p. 230; Sella, *Commerci e Industrie*, 79.

[63] Dunsford 55–7; Smith, *Mems Wl*, ii, 139, 141, 226–8; Slee 216.

[64] Rothstein 431–4, 437, 590 sqq.

[65] Wiggs 45, 76, 85, 95, 98.

[66] Hinton 34–5, 114, 177, 195; Åström 31, 56, 69 sqq., 75.

[67] PRO, SPD Chas 2, 361/149 sqq.; 363/24; Child, *Essay on Wl*, 9; cf. Te Lintum 28, 53, 60, 81, 92, 117, 141, 233, 238.

[68] J. James 185–6; Cole ii, 567.

[69] H. C. Diferee, *De Geschiedenis van der Nederlandschen Handel tot den Val der Republiek*, Amst. 1908, pp. 296–7.

[70] E. B. Schumpeter 70.

[71] J. James 205–6; *C.J.*, xvii, 366–7; *H. of L. MSS*, n.s., v, 69, 70; W. G. Hoskins, 'Rise & Decline Serge Ind. in S.W. Engld', ts. thes. MSc Lond. Univ. 1929, Apps 1, B(ii).

[72] Child, *Essay on Wl*, 7, 9; Ramsay, *Wilts.*, 116–17; PRO, SPD W.3 vol. 13 fo. 149.

[73] BL, Lans. 846 no. 45 fo. 284(254); & v. Stephens, *Exeter*, 118; Mann, *Cl. Ind.*, 16.

[74] E. B. Schumpeter 29, 35; & v. S. D. White 101.

[75] Carus-Wilson & Coleman 138–9, 199, 200; cf. Gould 123–4.

[76] E. B. Schumpeter, op. cit.

[77] Craeybeckx 419, 422, 431, 433, 448, 451, 455; Faber i, 226; Eggen 222; Denucé 173–6; Goris 243, 277–8, 308–9, 311–12, 314–15; Guicciardini 121; Irsigler 289; Baasch 93–5; De Smedt ii, 379, 383, 385, 416–17; Schmoller 519; Brulez, *Della Faille*, 28, 249–50, 266, 588; Sabbe, *Vlasnijverheid*, i, 179, 221–3, 270 sqq., 285, 329 sqq.; Posthumus, *Bronnen*, iii, 675 sqq., iv, 507–10.

[78] Espinas & Pirenne iii, 272; De Smedt ii, 379, 417; De Sagher i, 191, 202, 361, 454; Bourhis i, 105–6; Deyon & Lottin 25.

[79] Posthumus, *Bronnen*, iii, 27, 35, 397, 399 sqq., 417, 428, 433, 436 sqq., 442–3, 451, 453; iv, 240; v, 174; vi, 127, 135; *Geschiedenis*, ii, 327–9; Schmoller 84, 219–20, 228, 240–1, 520, 571, 587; Eggen 171–3, 176; Brulez, *Della Faille*, 23, 28, 34; Craeybeckx 422, 425–6, 448, 451–2; Guicciardini 120; Davidsohn vol. iv pt ii, 77; Van Dillen, *Bronnen*, ii, 213–15, 218; Chapman & Chassagne 14.

[80] Cole ii, 192–3; Eggen 173–4; Posthumus, *Bronnen*, vi, 16; Goris 252, 262–3, 319; Van Dillen, *Bronnen*, i, 504, 645–6; ii, 363, 513; Maddalena 644 sqq.; Craeybeckx 425, 440, 451–2, 457; Baasch 27, 96, 98, 102–3; Van Nierop xlv, 24–5, 33–4, 37–8, 40, 156, 159, 161 sqq., 170; xlvi, 29, 31; Thijs 13 sqq., 23 sqq., 33 sqq., 51 sqq.; Denucé 97; Brulez, *Della Faille*, 43, 96, 152, 240, 283, 304; Davidsohn vol. iv pt ii, 71 sqq.; Botero 56; Ciriacono 167 sqq.; Benedict 155; Guicciardini 119–20, 124–5; Doehaerd & Kerremans 612–13; Mollwo 19; De Smedt ii, 416; Sabbe, *Anvers*, 70, 72; Vanhaeck i, 243; Sella, *Commerci i Industrie*, 125, 127, 129.

[81] B. Dietz 56, 67, 115, 133; *Rates Marchandizes*; Stat. 12 Chas 2 c.4.

[82] Craeybeckx 417, 445, 466.

[83] Ibid. 417, 451–2; Deyon 184; De Smedt ii, 379; De Sagher i, 397; Faber i, 239; Strieder 328; Van Dillen, *Bronnen*, i, p. xli; Eggen 173; Hessels, *Archives*, 18, 33; Posthumus, *Bronnen*, iii, pp. ix, 693 sqq., 707–8; iv, 511 sqq., 522–4; v, 701 sqq.; vi, 603 sqq.; *Geschiedenis*, ii, 330.

[84] Espinas & Pirenne i, 139, 223 sqq.; De Poerck i, 236–9; Schmoller 337–8; Thomson, *Hist. Tapestry*, 87 sqq., 105–6, 108 sqq., 126 sqq., 131 sqq., 189 sqq., 208 sqq., 223 sqq.; Eggen 175–8; Goris 303; Enno ii, 31, 33; Sabbe, *Anvers*, 22, 72; Craeybeckx 422, 441–3, 458, 460.

[85] Ibid. 422, 440; Brulez, *Della Faille*, 28, 46, 160, 305–6, 427.

[86] Sup. 100.

[87] Sup. 26–7, 29; & pp. 263–4 nn. 14–18.

[88] Sup. 29 sqq.

[89] Baasch 90; De Sagher iii, 376–7; Posthumus, *Geschiedenis*, ii, 319; *Bronnen*, iii, 16, 505, 614 sqq., 634–5, 638, 656; iv, 3; v, 18, 466–7.

[90] Ibid. iv, 448; Munn 19, 25, 44; Smith, *Mems Wl*, i, 215, 251; ii, 109, 410–12, 426–9, 438 sqq., 448–9; Cole ii, 383, 576–7; Scoville 140, 177–8, 226–7; Wood 141–2; Barkhausen 253; Thierry iv, 510; Kamen 71; E. Guitard, 'L'Industrie des Draps en Languedoc et ses protecteurs sous l'ancien régime' in J. Hayem, *Mémoires et Documents pour servir à l'Histoire du Commerce et de l'Industrie en France*, 1e serie Paris 1911, pp. 25, 31; Sella, 'Rise & Fall', 116; *Commerci e Industrie*, 65, 119–20; M. Bignon, 'Extrait du Mémoire de la Généralité d'Amiens ou de Picardie dressé par ordre de Monseigneur le Duc de Bourgogne' in Hayem i, 162.

[91] Ibid. 159–60; Munn 20, 32, 42, 45, 47; Postlethwayt i, 438; A. Dietz ii, 268; Davidsohn vol. iv pt ii, 69; Braudel & Romano 45; Brulez, *Della Faille*, 512, 522; Guiciardini 119; Deyon 173–4, 176, 184, 193, 531; Deyon & Lottin 25; Abrate, 'Industria Laniera Piemontese', 119; Craeybeckx 422, 429, 434, 438, 440; Cole ii, 177, 180–1, 577–8; Leuridan, *Roubaix*, 77, 81, 83, 96; 'Lannoy', 343; Vanhaeck i, 93–6, 144, 162, 243, 245, 247–8, 259, 285, 292, 294, 302, 317, 355; ii, 117–18, 237–8, 263 sqq.; Smith, *Mems Wl*, ii, 64, 211, 425, 434–6, 442, 446, 448, 458; Postlethwayt i, 221, 438; J. James 22–3, 209; Maugis 70–3; Sion 168; Denucé 47–8, 89–91; Van Dillen, *Bronnen*, ii, 562; P. Goubert, *Beauvais et le Beauvaisis de 1600 à 1730*, Paris 2 vols. 1960, p. 123; Posthumus, *Bronnen*, iii, 57; v, 8 sqq., 251 sqq.; vi, 6, 7, 211–12, 215–17, 278; *Geschiedenis*, ii, 324, 326.

[92] Ibid. 324; *Bronnen*, vi, 229, 237–9; De Poerck ii, 79; J. Hayem, 'Les Inspecteurs des Manufactures et le Mémoire de l'Inspecteur Tribert sur la Généralité d'Orléans' in Hayem, *Mémoires et Documents*, 2e série 1912, pp. 271–2; G. Hardy, 'La Localisation des Industries dans la Généralité d'Orléans au XVIIIe s. et au début du XIXe s.' ibid. 3e série 1913, p. 39; Pegoletti 425; Davidsohn vol. iv pt ii, 69; Cole i, 32; ii, 384, 576–8; Scoville 176–7; Ciriacono 180, 195; Bignon 159; Deyon 173–5, 184; Vanhaeck i, 93–4, 243–4, 246, 293, 305; ii, 118, 211–12; Smith, *Mems Wl*, ii, 434, 439, 442–3, 445–8, 452, 459, 462.

[93] Ibid. 434, 437, 439, 442–3, 450; Ciriacono 169, 171, 179, 189; Maugis 15, 51, 53, 62; Thierry iv, 359–61; Deyon 173–4, 184; Van Der Wee, *Antwerp Mkt*, ii, 187; Schanz, *Handelspolitik*, ii, 256; Vanhaeck i, 27, 47, 90–1, 95, 142, 240; ii, 44, 50–1, 90–1; Brulez, *Della Faille*, 5, 245, 267, 476, 478, 484, 490, 511; Leuridan, 'Lannoy', 339; Craybeckx 425–6; Eggen 173; Gras 572, 577–9, 703; De Smedt ii, 379, 386, 416; Cole ii, 379, 577–9; Goubert 282, 573; B. Dietz 74; Hessels, *Archives*, 8; *Archivum*, iii, 1158; Van Dillen, *Bronnen*, i, pp. xlviii–ix; ii, 547, 608; *Amst.*, p. xxxviii; Posthumus, *Bronnen*, iii, 53, 57, 469–70; iv, 206–7, 530.

[94] Ibid. iii, 16, 17, 21, 27, 35–6, 64, 133, 309, 393 sqq., 399–401, 403, 405, 416–17, 419, 428, 433–4, 436 sqq., 442–3, 445, 453, 469–70; iv, 3, 220–1; v, 18, 80; vi, 177–9, 185–8, 212–13, 218; *Geschiedenis*, ii, 280, 327–8; Rijpma 41, 96; Van Nierop xlv, 24; Thijs 54; Leuridan, *Roubaix*, 15, 16, 20–1, 27, 37–8, 54–6; 'Linselles', 214, 'Lannoy' 339–40, 343; Faber ii, 439; A. Dietz ii, 269–70; Vanhaeck i, 239, 241, 248, 259, 272–3, 317; ii, 58; Cole ii, 178–9, 577, 579; Brulez, *Della Faille*, 304, 522; De Sagher i, 194–5, iii, 416; Goris 279, 297; De Poerck ii, 211; Baasch 96; Craeybeckx 422, 438, 440; Gras 109, 572; De Smedt ii 378–9; Eggen 174, 176, 217 sqq.; Van Dillen, *Bronnen*, i, 573; ii, 294–5, 329; iii, 53–4; *Amst.*, p. xxxviii; Maugis 78, 98; Deyon 175; Bignon 162.

[95] Cole ii, 396; Posthumus, *Geschiedenis*, ii, 327; *Bronnen*, iii, 469–70, 546; v, 18; vi, 280–2; cf. Vanhaeck ii, 167.

[96] Ibid. 142, 144; Coornaert, *Hondschoote*, 26; De Sagher i, 194–7, 200, 205–6, 221–3, 332–5, 435 sqq., 443, 449 sqq., 465–7, 469, 474, 476 sqq.; ii, 314, 319 sqq. 327, 332, 334–6, 560, 606, 617, 619; iii, 66, 69, 98–9, 216–18, 263, 312, 373, 398, 416, 418, 421, 604; Goris 252; Davidsohn vol. iv pt ii, 69; Doren i, 97, 506 sqq.; Smith, *Mems Wl*, ii, 412, 422, 425, 435 sqq., 444, 450, 452, 454; Abrate, 'Memoriale', 14, 15; Craeybeckx 422, 429; Goubert 282, 588; Deyon 174; Cole ii, 377–8, 396, 577–9; Posthumus, *Geschiedenis*, ii, 318, 320; *Bronnen*, iii, 133, 514, 517, 532, 537, 602–3, 608; iv, 335, 449, 465–6; v, 540; vi, 3, 5–8, 328–9, 388, 508, 516–17.

[97] Ibid. v, 329, 346, 352, 356; vi, 218; Brulez, *Della Faille*, 266; Munn 26, 45; Guicciardini 119.

[98] Cole ii, 577; Van Dillen, *Bronnen*, iii, 134, 521; Baasch 96; Vanhaeck i, 300; Deyon 176–7; Eggen 173–4; Maddalena 635; Ciriacono 179; Bignon 159–60.

[99] Cole ii, 384, 577–8; Deyon 173; Posthumus, *Bronnen*, v, 79; Sella, *Commerci e Industrie*, 127.

[100] De Sagher ii, 587; Brulez, *Della Faille*, 245.

[101] Posthumus, *Bronnen*, iii, 16, 17, 133, 309; iv, 159; v, 297, 337, 428, 637; *Geschiedenis*, ii, 326, 330; cf. Van Dillen, *Bronnen*, ii, 295.

[102] Cole ii, 577, 579; Smith, *Mems Wl*, ii, 425, 434, 437; Millard i App. p. 24; G. Mathieu, 'Notes sur l'Industrie en Bas-Limousin dans la seconde moité du XVIIIe s.' in Hayem, *Mémoires et Documents*, 1e série pp. 54, 65.

[103] De Sagher iii, 443, 592; Posthumus, *Bronnen*, iv, 3; B. Dietz 8, 21, 23, 50, 56, 68, 71, 83, 105, 115, 129; Willan, *Tu. Bk Rates*, 14; *Rates Marchandizes*.

[104] Munn 25; Cole ii, 183; J. James 227.

[105] Bignon 159–60; Vanhaeck i, 228, 246; ii, 109; Sella, *Commerci e Industrie*, 127; Leuridan, 'Lannoy', 343; Goris 252; Edler, *Gloss.*, 238, 280, 413 sqq.; De Roover, *Bus.*, *Bkg & Econ. Thought*, 95–8, 101, 113; A. Dietz ii, 267; Coornaert, *Hondschoote*, 14; Coniglio 343, 353; Maddalena 635; Dallington 34; Van Dillen, *Bronnen*, ii, 181, 578; Deyon 173–4, 184; Eggen 170–1; Posthumus, *Geschiedenis*, ii, 128, 158, 271–2, 323; *Bronnen*, iii, 349 sqq.; v, 195 sqq.

[106] Ibid. 80; vi, 217–18; Munn 47; Maugis 98; Davidsohn vol. iv pt ii, 71 sqq.; Baasch 93; De Smedt ii, 379; Ciriacono 169, 172, 189, 194; Vanhaeck i, 243, 259, 273, 275–6, 314; ii, 106–7, 156–7; Smith, *Mems Wl*, ii, 458; Leuridan, *Roubaix*, 54–5, 100; Eggen 173; Van Dillen, *Bronnen*, ii, 363, 593; Sella, *Commerci e Industrie*, 127; Cole ii, 179.

[107] Ibid. 177, 385, 571, 574, 576–9; Munn 20–1, 25–6; PRO, SPD Chas 2, 379/127; Smith, *Mems Wl*, i, 219; ii, 206, 219–20, 315, 411, 425, 430–1, 436, 440, 443, 445–7, 449 sqq., 459; Hayem 273–4; G. Hardy 40; Bignon 160; Abrate, 'Industria Laniera Piemontese', 119; Sonenscher 151; Sion 168–70; Deyon 173–4; spec. at Plessis-les-Tours; Posthumus, *Bronnen*, v, 8, 11, 405, 407, 412, 416, 420, 428, 431, 433 sqq.; *Geschiedenis*, ii, 256, 320.

[108] Ibid. 158, 273, 275, 325; *Bronnen*, iii, pp. ix, 116, 299, 340–1, 479, 481–3; iv, p. ix; v, pp. ix, 8 sqq., 236; vi, 213 sqq.; Leuridan, *Roubaix*, 38; Brulez, *Della Faille*, 45, 251, 266, 326, 330, 511, 515, 589; Guicciardini 119; A. Dietz ii, 268; Ciriacono 170–1; De Sagher iii, 341, 349; Maugis 70; Eggen 23, 174; Barkhausen 270; Rijpma 95; Van Dillen, *Bronnen*, ii, 191, 236; Denucé 89–91, 97; Coornaert, *Hondschoote*, 25, 217, 219.

[109] Ibid. 218; Munn 23; Craeybeckx 417, 451; Rijpma 105; Faber i, 226–7, 229; Baasch 96, 100; A. Dietz ii, 267, 270; Maugis 78–9; De Sagher ii, 587; Vanhaeck i, 95; Van Dillen, *Bronnen*, i, pp. xli, xlviii, 573; ii, 213, 218, 281, 610, 777; iii, 99; Posthumus, *Bronnen*, iii, 40, 53, 57, 133, 395, 397, 416–17, 432–4, 443, 451, 469; iv, 3, 109, 197; v, 174; *Geschiedenis*, ii, 328–9.

[110] Ibid. 324; *Bronnen*, iii, 14, 38, 40, 53, 57, 133, 469; iv, 3; vi, 329; Van Dillen, *Bronnen*, i, pp. xli, xlviii, 645, 700; ii, 252; *Amst.*, p. xxxviii; Sonescher 150; Deyon & Lottin 25; Eggen 174; Vanhaeck i, 273, 314, 355; Leuridan, *Roubaix*, 37–40, 51–4, 88; 'Linselles', 214; Cole ii, 577, 579; Craeybeckx 422; Brulez, *Della Faille*, 152, 304; Smith, *Mems Wl*, ii, 455–6.

[111] Ibid. 425; Munn 26, 32; Mathieu 54; Craeybeckx 422; Leuridan, *Roubaix*, 61–2, 67, 69, 71, 88–9, 96–7, 100; 'Lannoy', 343; Faber i, 239; Postlethwayt i, 428; Vanhaeck i, 162, 246, 278–9, 355; ii, 238, 264; Posthumus, *Geschiedenis*, ii, 326; *Bronnen*, vi, 219.

[112] Ibid. v, 159, 423, 428; Bang iiA, 346; Deyon & Lottin 25; Bignon 162–3; Maddalena 619, 621, 628, 652; De Sagher ii, 587; *Rates Marchandizes*, s.v. misselanes; *Rates Merchandizes*, 41; Craeybeckx 429–30, 435, 438; Smith, *Mems Wl*, ii, 436, 451.

[113] Ibid. 434; Ciriacono 169, 180, 182; Munn 23, 47; Scoville 140; Vanhaeck i, 144, 226, 245–6; ii, 167, 172, 181, 238.

[114] Ibid. i, 239, 241; Ciriacono 187, 189, 195; Craeybeckx 452; Sella, *Commerci e Industrie*, 127; Cole ii, 578.

[115] Ibid.; De Poerck i, 225; Munn 47; Ciriacono 179, 195.

[116] Ibid. 195; Leuridan, *Roubaix*, 53; Haynes, *G.B.'s Glory*, 55; Vanhaeck i, 248, 277, 279.

[117] Ibid. i, 228–9, 238–41, 246; Deyon & Lottin 24, 29 sqq.; Abrate, 'Industria Laniera Piemontese', 119; Davidsohn vol. iv pt ii, 69; Munn 35, 43, 45; Maugis 53, 70, 98; De Sagher ii,

587; A. Dietz ii, 269; Craeybeckx 417, 422, 425–6, 429–30, 439, 446, 451; Maddalena 621, 628, 652; Schmoller 542; Brulez, *Della Faille*, 252, 312, 316, 330; Van Dillen, *Bronnen*, ii, 189, 191, 236, 578; Coornaert, *Hondschoote*, 36–8, 40–1, 219; Rijpma 93, 96; De Poerck i, 8, 217; Eggen 22–3, 170–1, 175; Denucé 62; Posthumus, *Bronnen*, iii, 6, 8, 16, 17, 20, 26–7, 35, 38, 40, 53, 57, 60, 64, 68, 99 sqq., 116–17, 121–2, 143–4, 147–8, 164 sqq., 172, 174–5, 194–6, 199, 216–17, 291 sqq.; iv, 64, 69, 73, 96–7, 109, 111–12; v, 109 sqq., 158, 169, 174, 188–9; vi, 3, 6, 8, 9; *Geschiedenis*, ii, 2, 3, 25, 80–1, 98–9, 128, 158, 259–60, 269, 321–3; R. Van Uytven, 'La Draperie Brabançonne et Malinoise du XIIe au XVIIe s.' in Spallanzani, *Panni di Lana*, 96.

[118] Ibid. 96–7; Posthumus, *Geschiedenis*, ii, 322–3; *Bronnen*, iii, 26; v, 428; vi, 219, 229, 422; Sonenscher 150; Bignon 159–62; Weiss i, 36; Hayem 270–1; De Sagher i, 194–5, 197–8; iii, 225, 465; Schmoller 542; A. Dietz ii, 269; Davidsohn vol. iv pt ii, 69; Munn 20–1, 23–5, 43; Smith, *Mems Wl*, ii, 430–2, 435 sqq., 450 sqq.; Haynes, *G.B.'s Glory*, 55; PRO, SPD Chas 2, 281/101A; *Rates Merchandizes*, 48; *Acct Fr. Usurpation upon Trade Engld*, 1679, p. 5; Fortrey 23; Sion 169–70; Scoville 176; Postlethwayt i, 815; Goubert 124, 127, 131–2, 159, 191, 247, 282, 573, 587; Coniglio 343–4, 353; Craeybeckx 426, 446, 448; Maddalena 621–3, 628, 652; Leuridan, *Roubaix*, 52–3, 100; 'Lannoy', 343; 'Linselles', 214; Deyon 174–5, 184, 194, 206–7, 512–13; Cole ii, 171 sqq., 175–6, 377–80, 383–4, 576–7; Vanhaeck i, 246, 277–9; ii, 141–3, 146; Goris 242–3, 292, 297; De Poerck i, 217, 224–5; Coornaert, *Bergues*, 58; *Hondschoote*, 24–7, 38.

[119] Ibid. 65–6; Van Uytven, 'Draperie', 96; Macek 587; Sonenscher 151; Kamen 71; Cole ii, 380, 396; Smith, *Mems Wl*, i, 361; ii, 129, 133, 433, 435, 455–6, 458; Postlethwayt i, 224; Stephens, *Exeter*, 111; Wadsworth & Mann 469; H. E. S. Fisher 48–9; A. D. Francis, 'Jn Methuen & Anglo-Port. Treaties 1703', *Hist. Jnl*, 1960 iii, 103–4; Haynes, *G.B.'s Glory*, 55; Maugis 76–7; Craeybeckx 429; Eggen 170–1; Faber i, 239; Smit ii, 1180–1; Schmoller 228, 541; Rijpma 96, 110; Van Dillen, *Bronnen*, ii, 181–2; Deyon 184; De Poerck i, 224–5; De Sagher i, 435 sqq., 451; ii, 587, 624–5; iii, 56–8, 191, 193, 195–6, 202, 204, 213 sqq., 288, 293–5, 305, 309, 312, 317, 331, 340, 343 sqq., 353,, 358, 375, 385–6, 388–91, 393; Posthumus, *Geschiedenis*, ii, 25, 33, 79, 98–9, 102, 254, 318–19, 332; *Bronnen*, ii, 609, 613, 615–17, 632, 649–50, 694, 696; iii, pp. ix, 3, 4, 6, 8, 16, 20, 26, 35, 60, 64, 66, 499, 540–1, 543–4, 564–5, 573–6, 578, 586 sqq., 594, 597–600, 615, 617, 627, 634–5, 638, 640, 644, 661, 663, 687; iv, 258, 271, 284, 314–15; v. 452, 457–60, 466; vi, 275, 280.

[120] Ibid. v, 443, 454; Van Dillen, *Bronnen*, ii, 181.

[121] Kent RO, Arch. Ct Cant. Inv. Reg. 1 fo. 4; Ess. RO, Arch. Ct Colc. Reg. Wills 3 fo. 136; Postlethwayt ii, 351; Sion 169; Cole ii, 384, 574, 576, 579; Smith, *Mems Wl*, ii, 450, 452; Somner 175–6; Bignon 162.

[122] Goris 252; Deyon 176; Leuridan, *Roubaix*, 53.

[123] Sonenscher 150–1; Stat. 12 Chas 2 c.4; *Rates Marchandizes*, s.v. caddas, cruell; Brist. RO, Cons. Ct inv. Jas Yevans 1636 St Phil's; Hants. RO, unclass. invs D/2/A: 2/181; Munn 5; Gras 573; De Smedt ii, 380; Smith, *Mems Wl*, ii, 434, 443, 448, 455–6; Coornaert, *Hondschoote*, 24; Cole ii, 396, 574, 579.

[124] Ibid. 177, 574; Faber i, 226; Vanhaeck i, 95; Posthumus, *Bronnen*, iii, 459; iv, 233; Denucé 86–7; Craeybeckx 422, 429, 434 sqq., 451–2, 460, 465; De Sagher ii, 12.

[125] G. de Malynes, *Treatise Canker Englds Com. Wealth*, 1601; App.; Vanes, *Docs*, 135, 148; J.B., *Merchs Avizo*, 25; *Rates Marchandizes*, s.v. calicoes; *Rates Merchandizes*, 37; Millard i, 300; ii, iii; Stat. 12 Chas 2 c.4; McGrath, *Merchs*, 73, 78, 85; Willan, *Inld Trade*, 65; Kent RO, Cons. Ct Cant. Reg. Accts & Invs 12 fo. 4; J. Irwin & K. B. Brett, *Origs Chintz*, 1970, pp. 3, 4, 24–7.

[126] Ibid. 4, 30; J.F., *Merchs Wareho.*, 22; Hughes & Larkin iii, 225–6; Firth & Rait i, 212; ii, 1216; *Petn & Remonstrance Govs & Co. Merchs Lond. trading to E.I.*, 1628, pp. 3, 15; Glos. RO, Cons. Ct inv. 1663/106; Leics. RO, Arch. inv. Jn Stringer 1670 Leic.; Hants. RO, Cons. Ct O.W. & Invs Humph. Bishopp 1666 Winch.

[127] Willan, *Inld Trade*, 98; Chaudhuri 281–2, 284; Smith, *Mems Wl*, i, 352–3; ii, 44; Plummer, *Lond. Weavers' Co.*, 292 sqq.; Irwin & Brett 4, 18, 25–7, 30–1; T. Mun. *Disc. Trade fr. Engld unto E.I.*, 1621, pp. 7, 8, 13, 23; *Rsns f. Restraining Wearing Wrought Silks etc.*; *5 Ques . . . rel. to Bill f.*

*Prohibiting Consumption E. I. Silks, Bengals & Pr. Callicoes*, n.d.; Cant. Cath. Lib. Wall. Recs. Misc. Docs portf. 4 nos. 59–62; A. W. Douglas, 'Cotton Texts in Engld', *Jnl Brit. Studs*, 1969 viii, 32–3; cf. Bodl. Aubrey 2 fo. 66.

[128] PRO, SPD Chas 431/22.

[129] *Anc. Trades Decayed, Repaired Again*, 1678, p. 16; Warner 629; Bodl. Aubrey 2 fo. 123; Smith, *Mems Wl*, i, 350–4, 404 sqq., 410, 413 sqq., 417 sqq.; ii, 46.

[130] Ibid. i, 351; Bodl. Aubrey 2 fo. 123; *5 Qus*, ut sup.

[131] Smith, *Mems Wl*, ii, 44–5.

[132] Ibid. 191–2, 195; Wadsworth & Mann 127, 130–3, 136–7; Colyer-Fergusson iii, 221, 229, 235, 237, 268; Irwin & Brett 2, 8, 18; Douglas 36–7; Chapman & Chassagne 6, 14. In resist dyeing parts were waxed to resist dyes.

[133] Cant. Cath. Lib. Wall. Recs. Misc. Docs portf. 4 no. 67.

[134] Ibid. nos. 59–62, 66, 71; Chapmen & Chassagne 10, 13, 25; Smith, *Mems Wl*, i, 351; ii, 198; Wadsworth & Mann 139; Stats 11 W.3 c.10; 7 Geo. stat. 1 c.7.

[135] Wood 141–3; Koenigsberger 323; Mann, *Cl. Ind.*, 18, 19, 41.

[136] Ibid. 19.

[137] T. Birch i, 200; Philanglus 59; M. Priestley, 'A.-Fr. Trade & "Unfavourable Balance" Controversy 1660–85', *Econ. Hist. Rev.*, 2nd ser. 1951 iv, 46–8; Wood 44; Posthumus, *Bronnen*, v, 12, 427–8; Sella, *Commerci e industrie*, 61–2, 117–18.

[138] HMC, *Var. Colls*, ii, 193–4, 200.

[139] Smith, *Mems Wl*, ii, 202–3, 223 sqq.; Defoe, *Plan*, 183–5.

[140] Ibid. 190.


**Chapter 16**

[1] Nfk RO, Cty Recs. Strangers Bk fo. 16.

[2] Scoville 116–17; sup. 22, 31–2.

[3] Cf. Dors. RO, MS Hist. Wimb. Minster Coll. Ch. by Russell, bet. marg. nos. 3 & 4.

[4] Cock 50; Randall 350; Cullen, *Econ. Hist. Ire.*, 23–5; *N. & Q. Soms & Dors.*, 1911 xii, 352; 1969 xxix, 89; Shaw, *1603–1700*, 344; Stephens, *Exeter*, 134.

[5] PRO, SPD Eliz. 27/19, 20.

[6] Ibid. vols. 82, 84; Stow, *Ann.*, 678–9; Kirk ii, 1 sqq., 113, 156.

[7] Ibid. 38, 57–8, 62, 70, 74, 92–3, 95, 124–6, 132.

[8] Ibid. 38, 59, 84, 156.

[9] Ibid. 41, 44, 53, 95.

[10] Ibid. 1, 2, 4, 10–12, 15–17, 24, 34, 37, 49, 50, 53, 59, 67–70, 72, 77–9, 81, 84–7, 89 sqq., 96, 99, 105, 111–12, 114, 116, 118, 120–1, 126–7, 138.

[11] Hessels, *Archives*, 2.

[12] Moens, *Colc.*, p. ii.

[13] Cant. Cath. Lib. Cty Recs. Burghmote Bk 1578–1602 fo. 44v.; 1630–58 fo. 164.

[14] Waller p. xv; & v. pp. xii, xiii, 14, 24, 26–9, 32–4, 45–7, 52; Plummer, *Lond. Weavers' Co.*, 147 sqq.; Bodl. Rawlinson A. 478 fo. 97 (p. 188).

[15] PRO, SPD Jas 81/56.

[16] Scoville 4.

[17] Ibid. 176–7, 181–2, 212–14, 217, 220.

[18] Ibid. 181, 366 sqq., 376 sqq., 389 sqq., 397 sqq., 415, 421 sqq.; Craeybeckx 458, 465.

[19] Scoville 177–9, 183, 222–3, 225–6, 228, 239–40, 375.

[20] Ibid. 5, 226.

[21] Ibid. 219–20.

[22] Redstone, 'Engld', 174 sqq.; sup. 8, 11, 24.

[23] Janssen 224, 228–31, 235–6, 238–9, 243–4: 'Wy zullen oock de costh wel winnen. . . . Wilt

oock niet besoorcht zijn on uwen cost te winnen. . . . sult met uwe kinderen wel den cost winnen. . . . den cost wel te winnen es. . . . mijn broeder . . . wynt . . . den goeden kost. . . . ick de cost wel winnen. . . . wy zijn hebben wy goeden tit ende win van alles.'

[24] G. N. Clark, *Wealth Engld*, 50.

[25] Janssen 229–30: 'men hier meer coopt om een stuiver dan soo ick hoore t'Yper om drie.'; & v. 238–9; Moens, *Norwich*, 71.

[26] HMC, *Salisbury MSS*, xiv, 190.

[27] Nfk RO, Cty Recs. Strangers Bk fo. 16; Stow, *Ann.*, 868; Nef, *Conq.*, 251 sqq.

[28] Hakluyt, *Orig. Writings*, 189.

[29] T. Birch i, 200.

[30] Child, *N. Disc. Trade*, pref.

[31] PRO, SPD Interreg. 69/7.

[32] Defoe, *Compl. Engl. Tradesman*, 77.

[33] CF. Earle, *Defoe*, 124.

[34] Munn 35; *H. of L MSS*, n.s. iii, 387; Nfk RO, Nfk Rec. S. MS 15950.

[35] De Smedt i, 46–7; Rich 13, 14.

[36] T. Birch i, 200; cf. De Sagher ii, 560–1.

[37] Posthumus, *Bronnen*, v, 12, 159, 427–8.

[38] PRO, SPD Chas 2, 281/101A.

[39] Priestley 46–8.

[40] Wood 44, 141–3; Mann, *Cl. Ind.*, 18, 19, 41; Koenigsberger 323; Sella, *Commerci e Industrie*, 61–2, 64; Smith, *Mems Wl*, ii, 97–8.

[41] Ibid. 228, 262–4.

[42] Chester RO, Mayor's Recs. R. Freemen 1658–79, entry 1674; Cty Recs. Ass. Bk 1624–84 fos. 182v., 184a.

[43] Ibid. Ass. Bk 1539–1624 fos. 166v., 168, 171 (163v., 165, 168).

[44] Redstone, 'Du. & Hug. Sets', 188–91, 197, 199, 202–4; Reed 71–2.

[45] Bateson iii, pp. xlviii–ix, 200, 204.

[46] Latimer, *17th cent.*, 40; Brist. RO, Cons. Ct inv. Th. Cornock 1641 Temple par.; Ramsay, *O'sea Trade*, 139–40.

[47] Wadsworth & Mann 88.

[48] PRO, SPD Jas 38/71–3.

[49] Ibid. 96/39, 40; 115/13; Chas 1/24.

[50] E. King, *O. Times Revisited in Boro. & Par. Lymington*, 1900, pp. 60–1.

[51] Kemp, *Bl. Bk Warwick*, 48.

[52] Chester RO, Cty Recs. Ass. Bk 1539–1624 fos. 168v.–70, 173 (165v.–7, 170).

[53] PRO, SPD Eliz. 157/4, 5; Mendenhall 133.

[54] Chester RO, Cty Recs. Ass. Bks 1539–1624 fos. 166v., 168v., 171 (163v., 165v., 168); 1624–84 fos. 182v., 184a.

[55] D. M. Palliser 275–7.

[56] Heaton 65–8; *VCH Yks.*, iii, 469.

[57] Gill 7–9; Knowler ii, 19, 20.

[58] Cf. Coornaert, *Bergues*, 96–7.

[59] Kemp, *Bl. Bk Warwick*, 48.

[60] *VCH Wilts.*, iv, 181.

[61] J. Humphreys 182–4.

[62] Hudston & Tingey ii, pp. lxxii sqq., 381, 408–11.

[63] Moens, *Norwich*, 152 sqq., 189 sqq., 207 sqq., 221–3; Janssen 236; BL, Lans. 7 no. 82 fos. 202v.–3; Nfk RO, Cty Recs. Strangers Bk fo. 17.

[64] PRO, SPD Eliz. 78/9; 129/70; Boys 742; Kent RO, Maidstone Recs. Misc. Doc. 51.

[65] PRO, Exch. KR Deps by Commn 15 Jas Mich. 31 m. 7r.

[66] Randall 315, 318; Dunsford 201.

[67] PRO, Exch. KR Deps by Commn 6 Jas East. 30; BL, Lans. 80 no. 8 fos. 22v.–3; Weinstock 35.

[68] Poole 358; Lichfield Jt RO, Cons. Ct O.W., Sam. Smith 1722.

[69] Moir 256 sqq.; Glouc. Lib. Smyth of Nibley MSS S.Z. 23.2 nos. 2–4; Bodl. Aubrey 2 fo. 144; PRO, SPD Jas 98/81.

[70] Sup. 37, 40.

[71] Burton 180; Glouc. Lib. Smyth of Nibley MSS S.A. 23.2 no. 4; Leese, 'N. Draperies at Cov.', 8, 9; Stat. 1 & 2 P.&M. c. 14; BL, Lans. 80 no. 8 fo. 23.

[72] Sup. 93–4.

[73] Moir 263; Glouc. Lib. Smyth of Nibley MSS S.Z. 23.2 nos. 2, 3.

[74] Bodl. Aubrey 2 fo. 144; & v. PRO, SPD Chas 475/64.

[75] Dunsford 201, 209.

[76] Nfk RO, Nfk Rec. S. MS 15950.

[77] Stats 20 H.5 c.10; 1 & 2 P.&M. c.14; Nfk RO, Cty Recs. Controversy resp. Rts Cits Norwich, Touching the Allegacion that the Queenes Majestie doth lose her custume; & v. Strangers Bk fo. 16.

[78] BL, Add. 12504 no. 64 fo. 83.

[79] J. A. Schumpeter, *Bus. Cycs*, N.Y. & Lond. 2 vols. 1939, i, 72 sqq., 130 sqq.

[80] Stat. 1 & 2 P.&M. c.14; Nfk RO, Cty Recs. Strangers Bk fo. 16; Hudston & Tingey ii, pp. lxxv–vii, 410.

[81] *Rsns ... Why Wagoners ought not to be obliged to any cert. Wt.*

[82] BL, Lans. 26 no. 56 fo. 147.

[83] Burton 180.

[84] Thornton 165, 192.

[85] Cant. Cath. Lib. Wall. Recs. Misc. Docs portf. 1 no. 26.

[86] Cross 186; sup. 53, 63.

[87] BL, Add. 12504 no. 65 fo. 86.

[88] Nfk RO, Cty Recs. Ass. Bk 3 fo. 131v.

[89] BL, Lans. 26 no. 56 fo. 147.

[90] PRO, SPD Eliz. 250/47 (cf. 39/43); Eliz. Add. 11/113.

[91] Ibid.; Eliz. 114/25 sqq., 33; *APC*, ix, 366.

[92] Reyce 23.

[93] PRO, Exch. KR Accts Var. bdl. 343 no. 15.

[94] PRO, SPD Chas 243/23.

[95] Ibid. 240/23.

[96] Ibid. 206/56–7; 215/56; 243/23; 248/1; 275/49; Eliz. 244/126 sqq.; Ramsay, *Wilts.*, 87 sqq.

[97] Warner 318; Collinson iii, 226.

[98] Hughes & Larkin iii, 54–6, 227–30; *APC*, 1630–1 pp. 329–30, 342; *H. of L. MSS*, n.s. xi, 42; PRO, SPD Eliz. 132/21–2; Jas 40/25.

[99] Ibid. 128/73, 80; & v. Chas 366/71.

[100] Dunsford 201.

[101] PRO, SPD Chas 240/23.

[102] Defoe, *Wks*, 542; Bodl. Top. Kent a.I fo. 26v.; sup. 25 sqq.

[103] PRO, SPD Jas 80/16.

[104] BL, Lans. 152 fo. 272.

[105] Notestein et al. ii, 393; vi, 6.

[106] BL, Add. 34324 fo. 211(180).

[107] Stephens, *Exeter*, 49.

[108] Blome 208; PRO, SPD Chas 533/86.

[109] *Disc. Com Weal*, 128.

[110] Nfk RO, Nfk Recs. S. MS 15950.

[111] Notestein et al. v, 27.

[112] Reyce 22; Child, *Essay on Wl*, 7; Haynes, *G.B.'s Glory*, 6, 8, 9, 11; W.S. op. cit. 6, 7; HMC, *14th Rep.*, App. pt iv, 572–3; PRO, SPD Eliz. 106/49; Jas 80/16.

[113] My *Ag. Rev.*, 211–12, 310 sqq., 321–3.

[114] Clark, 'Ess. Woollen Manufs', 203–5; Burley, thes. 101–3; Ess. RO, Q. Sess. bdl. 184, pet. Colc. baizeweavers 4 Apr. 1749; PRO, SPD Eliz. 106/49; Interreg. 69/7; Stat. 2 & 3 P.&M. c.13; Soms. SO, DD/BR/gr bdl. 18 no. 1 Thornbury deed 1615; & v. A. Murray, *Rsn & Soc. in M.A.*, Oxf. 1978, pp. 177, 179–80.

[115] Dunsford 181–2; Defoe, *Tour*, i, 61–3; Corfield, 'Prov. Cap.', 306.

[116] Soms. RO, Thornbury deed 1615, ut sup.; Mann, *Cl. Ind.*, 316.

[117] A. F. J. Brown 150–1; Burley, thes. 103; Brent 91; Hasted, *Cant.*, i, 94; Gibbons 44; Baxter 89, 94.

[118] HMC, *Buccleuch & Queensberry MSS*, vi, 40–1; *Rsns f. Ltd Exp. Wooll*, 6.

[119] Craeybeckx 411; cf. H. Van Der Wee, 'Str. Changes & Special. in Ind. S. Neth. 1100–1600', *Econ. Hist. Rev.*, 2nd ser. 1975 xxviii, 213, 216–17.

[120] Defoe, *Plan*, 267–8; Burley, thes. 390; cf. Bodl. Aubrey 2 fo. 122.

[121] PRO, SPD Eliz. 106/49.

[122] Bodl. Top. Kent a.I fo. 26v.; BL, Egerton 2985 fo. 75.

[123] My *Ag. Rev.*, 216–17, 246, 248.

[124] Nef, *Coal*, i, f. p. 19, p. 192; Gulley 56–7; PRO, SPD Chas 363/55–6; cf. Godfrey 47–50, 53, 57–9.

[125] Gulley 211; Postlethwayt i, 737; J. James 231; PRO, SPD Interreg. 69/7.

[126] Cullen, *Econ. Hist. Ire.*, 23–4, 34–5; *Ltr fr. Gent. in Ire. to his bro. in Engld*, 11; BL, Sloane 2902 fos. 136–7, 139(134–5, 137); Stat. 10 W.3 c.16; Stephens, *Exeter*, 134; *C.J.*, xii, 37, 79; Horwitz 116; *N. &. Q. Soms. & Dors.*, xii, 352; Shaw, *1603–1700*, 338, 344, 348 sqq.; *H. of L. MSS*, n.s. iii, 386–8; PRO, SPD Chas 2, 176/130; 373/249; Smith, *Mems Wl*, i, 303–4, ii, 12, 18, 19, 22, 25.

[127] Ibid. i, 215, 378; Munn 21, 23, 26–8, 32; Cole ii, 142–4, 149 sqq., 171 sqq.

[128] Posthumus, *Bronnen*, iii, 564; v, 12, 13, 458–60.

[129] Cole ii, 380; Haynes *G.B.'s Glory*, 54–5; Smith, *Mems Wl*, ii, 435.

[130] Ibid. i, 361; ii, 140; *Proc. H.S.L.*, iii, 341; H. E. S. Fisher 48–9.

[131] Craeybeckx 426; Abrate, 'Industria Lanier Piemontese', 119.

[132] Munn 20, 24–5; Smith, *Mems Wl*, ii, 432, 436 sqq., 450, 452–3; Weiss i, 36; Haynes, *G.B.'s Glory*, 54–5; Vanhaeck i, 246, 277; ii, 143, 146; Cole ii, 171 sqq., 383–4, 576, 578; Sion 170; Leuridan, *Roubaix*, 53; Goubert 124, 587; Bignon 160.

[133] Posthumus, *Bronnen*, v, 159, 427–8.

[134] Ibid. iv, 112–15, 120, 131, 135–7, 139, 142–5, 147, 155 (cf. 116–17, 121–4); *Geschiedenis*, ii, 322; Faber i, 226; Van Dillen, *Bronnen*, ii, 292, 305, 578; & v. Vanhaeck i, 277.

[135] H. E. S. Fisher 49; Wood 119; Denucé 196; De Sagher iii, 99, 225; Smith, *Mems Wl*, ii, 126, 133, 206, 425, 432–3.

[136] Ibid. 437, 439; J. James 190; Posthumus, *Geschiedenis*, ii, 325; *Bronnen*, vi, 219; Leuridan, *Roubaix*, 100.

[137] Ibid. 77; Munn 26; Vanhaeck i, 144; ii, 237, 267.

[138] Munn 20; Abrate, 'Industria Laniera Piemontese', 119.

[139] Goubert 282, 573; Smith, *Mems Wl*, ii, 434, 437; Cole ii, 578.

[140] Munn 47; Leuridan, *Roubaix*, 54, 100; Vanhaeck i, 259, 273, 275–6; ii, 106–7, 156–7; & v. Smith, *Mems Wl*, ii, 458.

[141] Munn 21, 24; Haynes, *G.B.'s Glory*, 54–5; cf. Smith, *Mems Wl*, ii, 440.

[142] Munn 26, 32; Postlethwayt i, 428; Leuridan, *Roubaix*, 61–2, 67, 69, 71, 88–9, 96–7, 100; 'Lannoy', 343; Craeybeckx 422; Faber i, 239; Vanhaeck i, 162, 246, 278–9; ii, 238, 264; Posthumus, *Geschiedenis*, ii, 326; Mathieu 54; Smith, *Mems Wl*, ii, 425, 459.

[143] Ibid. 434, 437; Cole ii, 577, 579; Deyon 184; Mathieu 35, 54, 65.

[144] Vanhaeck ii, 167, 181, 238; & v. Scoville 140.

[145] Munn 23; Smith, *Mems Wl*, ii, 434.

[146] Grass 140, 145.

[147] Leuridan, *Roubaix*, 53; Vanhaeck i, 248, 277, 279; Haynes, *G.B.'s Glory*, 54–5.

[148] Munn 20–1, 23; *Engld's Int. Asserted*, 5; Smith, *Mems Wl*, ii, 206, 425, 430–1, 440, 443; Abrate, 'Industria Laniera Piemontese', 119.

[149] Deyon 176–7; Cole ii, 577; Vanhaeck i, 300.

[150] Munn 26; Leuridan, *Roubaix*, 96–7, 100.

[151] A. F. J. Brown 150–1, 156–7, 159; Burley, thes. 147, 153–4; Ess. RO, Q. Sess. bdl. 184, pet. Colc. baizeweavers 1749; D/DO B1 Cash Bk 1810; Gribble 542–4; Kirby 264; Heaton 268 sqq.; Tupling 81; cf. Chanter & Wainwright ii, 259.

[152] Dunsford 235–6, 244–5, 257 (erron. 237).

[153] Aubrey, *Sy*, iii, 314, 346; Defoe, *Tour*, i, 118; Pococke ii, 135, 158, 163, 165; Postlethwayt i, 244.

# SELECT BIBLIOGRAPHY

**Printed and typescript books and journals**

(Place of publication of books, except in record society series, is London, unless otherwise stated.)

Anonymous or various:

*Abstract of such Parts of several Statutes relating to Silks called Alamodes and Lustrings, An,* Royal Lustrings Company, 1699.

*Account of the French Usurpation upon the Trade of England, An,* 1679.

*Acts of the Privy Council of England,* new series, edited by J. R. Dasent, 32 vols, 1890–1907.

*Acts of the Privy Council of England,* 14 vols, 1921–64.

*Algemene Geschiedenis der Nederlanden,* deel iv, Utrecht, Antwerp, Brussels, Ghent and Louvain, 1952.

'Aliens at Great Yarmouth in 1571', *Proceedings of the Huguenot Socity of London,* v, 1898 (1894–6).

'Aliens at King's Lynn in 1571', *Proceedings of the Huguenot Society of London,* v, 1898 (1894–6).

*Ancient Trades Decayed, Repaired Again, The,* by a Country Tradesman, 1678.

*Berisfords the Ribbon People: the story of a family business,* 2nd edition, London and York, 1966.

*Blackwell Hall Factors Case against a Provisoe to the Bill for the Better Improving the Woollen Manufacture, whereby the Factors will be prohibited from selling Wool to Clothiers as now they do, both English and Spanish* sine loco nec data.

*Breviate of the Weavers Business before the Committee of the House of Commons in Star Chamber* sine loco nec data.

*Calendar of the Freemen of Great Yarmouth 1429–1800, A,* Norfolk and Norwich Archaeological Society, 1910.

*Calendar of the Freemen of Lynn, 1292–1836, A,* Norfolk and Norwich Archaeological Society, 1913.

*Calendar of Letters and State Papers relating to English Affairs preserved principally in the Archives of Simancas,* edited by M. A. S. Hume, 4 vols, 1892–9.

*Calendar of the Patent Rolls preserved in the Public Record Office: Edward II,* 5 vols, 1894–1904; *Richard II,* 6 vols, 1895–1909; *Edward VI,* 6 vols, 1924–9; *Elizabeth,* several vols, 1939–, in progress.

*Calendar of State Papers, Domestic Series, of the Reigns of Edward VI* ... (and of successors).

*Calendar of State Papers, Foreign Series, of the Reign of Edward VI* ... (and of succesors).

*Calendar of the State Papers relating to Ireland, of the Reigns of Henry VIII* ... (and successors).

*Calendar of State Papers and Manuscripts relating to English Affairs, existing in the Archives and Collections of Venice, and in other Libraries of Northern Italy,* several vols, 1864–, in progress.

*Calendar of Wynn (of Gwydir) Papers 1515–1690,* London, Aberystwyth and Cardiff, 1926.

*Cambridge Economic History of Europe,* ii, ed. M. Postan and E. E. Rich, Cambridge, 1952.

*Case of the Commonalty of the Corporation of Weavers truly stated, The,* sine loco nec data.

*Case of the Manufacturers of Grograin Yarn, The,* no date.

*Case of the Silkmen, Throwsters, Dyers, Twisters and Winders in and about the City of London,* no date.

*Case of the Weavers who are Petitioners to be relieved against a Clause in the Coale Act, The,* sine loco 1695.

*Clothiers Answer to the Cardmakers Reply, The,* sine loco nec data.

*Clothiers Complaint, or Reasons for passing the Bill against the Blackwell Hall Factors, The,* 1692.

*Considerations humbly offered by the Weavers for the Bringing of fine Italian Thrown Silk over Land,* sine loco nec data.

*Consistory Court of Norwich Wills 1550–1603,* Index Library, British Record Society, lxxiii, 1950.

*Copies of the Charters and Grants of the Town of Ludlow,* Ludlow, no date. 'Description of Bedfordshire', *Gentleman's Magazine,* xxxiv, 1764.

*Dialogue between Dick Brazenface the Cardmaker and Timothy Meanwell the Clothier, A,* sine loco nec data.

*Discourse consisting of Motives for the Enlargement and Freedome of Trade, A,* 1645.

*Discourse of the Common Weal of this Realm of England, A,* edited by E. Lamond, Cambridge, 1929.

*Donations of Peter Blundell (Founder) and other Benefactors to the Free Grammar School at Tiverton,* Exeter, 1792.

*Ducatus Lancastriae,* 3 vols, 1823–34.

*England's Interest Asserted in the Improvement of its Native Commodities,* by a True Lover of His Majesty and Native Country, 1669.

*England's Interest in securing the Woollen Manufacture of the Realm,* 1689.

*Facsimile of the Ancient Book of the Weavers' Company, the original of which is in the possession of the Company,* no date.

*Five Queries humbly tendered relating to the Bill for Prohibiting the Consumption of East India Silks, Bengals and Printed Callicoes,* no date.

*Gloucestershire Notes and Queries,* vol. iii, 1887 (1885–7).

'History of the Bocking cloth industry', typescript, in Essex Record Office, reference no. T/Z 27.

*Index to Wills proved in the Consistory Court of Norwich 1370–1550,* Index Library, British Record society, vol. lxix, 1945.

*Interest of England as it stands with Relation to the Trade of Ireland considered, The,* 1698.

*Journals of the House of Commons.*

*Journals of the House of Lords.*

*Laws in Venice for Prohibition of Foreign Cloth, The,* sine loco nec data.

*Letter from a Gentleman in Ireland to his Brother in England relating to the Concerns of Ireland in Matter of Trade, A,* 1677.

*Letters and Papers, foreign and domestic, of the Reign of Henry VIII, preserved in the Public Record Office, the British Museum, and elsewhere in England,* 23 vols in 38 parts, 1862–1932.

*Linnen and Woollen Manufactory Discoursed, The,* 1691.

*Magna Britannia et Hibernia,* several vols, 1720–31.

*Manners and Household Expenses of England in the Thirteenth and Fifteenth Centuries,* Roxburgh Club, 1841.

*Manuscripts of the House of Lords, The,* see under House of Lords.

'Mercury' *Dictionary of Textile Terms, The,* Manchester, no date.

*Miscellanea,* Publications of the Thoresby Society, vol. iv, 1895.

*Notes and Queries,* 4th series, vol. viii, 1871.

*Notes and Queries for Somerset and Dorset,* vol. xii, 1911 (1910–11); vol. xix, 1929 (1927–9); vol. xxii, 1938 (1936–8); vol. xxiv, 1946 (1943–6); vol. xxvi, 1955 (1951–4); vol. xxix, 1969 (1968–9).

*Ordinances of the Clothworkers' Company,* 1881.

*Palatine Notebook, The,* vol. i, Manchester, 1881.

*Petition and Remonstrance of the Governors and Company of the Merchants of London trading to the East Indies, The,* 1628.

*Philosophical Transactions of the Royal Society of London,* 18 vols, 1809.

*Rates of Marchandizes . . . , The,* (1609?).

*Rates of Merchandizes . . . , The*, 1642.

*Reasons for a Limited Exportation of Wooll*, sine loco, 1677.

*Reasons for Preserving the Publick Market of Blackwell Hall and Restraining the Levant Company of Merchants from deferring their Shipping as long as they please*, sine loco nec data.

*Reasons for Prohibiting the Importation of White Iron-Wire and against putting old Wire into new Leather*, sine loco nec data.

*Reasons humbly offer'd against making Exeter, or any other Port in the British Channel, a Staple Port for Importation of Wool from Ireland*, sine loco nec data.

*Reasons humbly offer'd by the Cardmakers and Wierdrawers of Froome Selwood . . . shewing the Necessity for an Act for Preventing the Sale of Old Woollcards etc.*, sine loco nec data.

*Reasons humbly offered by the Taylors, Button Sellers, Button Makers, Throwsters, Twisters, Dyers, Spinners and Winders etc. for explaining and amending an Act made the Eighth of her late Majesty, Entituled An Act for Employing the Manufacturers by Encouraging the Consumption of Raw Silk and Mohair Yarn*, sine loco nec data.

*Reasons humbly offered for Restraining the Wearing of Wrought Silks, Bengals, and Dyed, Printed and Stained Callicoes, of the Product and Manufacture of Persia and the East Indies, in England and our Plantations*, no date.

*Reasons humbly offered to the Honourable House of Commons, Why the Wagoners ought not to be obliged to any certain Weight*, sine loco nec data.

*Reasons humbly offered to the House of Commons by the Clothiers of Essex, viz. Colchester, Coxhall, Bocking, Braintree, Witham and the Towns adjacent, against the intended Additional Duty to be laid upon Wines*, sine loco nec data.

*Reasons of the Decay of the Clothing Trade*, by a Well-Wisher to the Trade and the true English Interest, 1691.

*Reply of the Cardmakers and English-Wooll Clothiers to the Objections of the Spanish–Wooll Clothiers against the Bill in the House to prohibit the Importation of foreign Woollcards*, sine loco nec data.

*Rotuli Parliamentorum*, 6 vols, no date.

*Selections from the Household Books of the Lord William Howard of Naworth Castle*, Surtees Society, vol. lxviii, 1878.

*Short View of the Busines betweene the Clothier and Merchant of the Staple of England, A*, sine loco, 1647.

*Studi in Onore di Amintore Fanfani*, vol. iv, Evo Moderno, Milan, 1962.

*Substance of the Arguments for and against the Bill for Prohibiting the Exportation of Woollen Manufactures from Ireland to Forreign Parts, The*, 1698.

*These Things following are so much concerning this Common Wealth and State*, sine loco, 1647.

*Trade of England Revived, ad the Abuses thereof rectified The*, 1681.

*Treatise of Wool and the Manufacture of it, A*, 1685.

*Victoria History of the Counties of England, The*, several vols, 1901–, in progress.

*Weavers Answer to the Objections made by the Lustrings Company*, no date.

*Wills and Administrations from the Knaresborough Court Rolls*, Surtees Society, vols civ, cx, 1902–5.

*Wills and Inventories from the Registry at Durham*, parts ii and iv, Surtees Society, vols xxxviii, cxlii, 1860, 1929.

*Wiltshire Notes and Queries*, vol. ii, 1899 (1896–8); vol. iii, 1902 (1899–1901); vol. iv, 1905 (1902–4).

*Winthrop Papers*, Massachusetts Historical Society, 5 vols, 1925–47.

*Worcestershire County Records: Division I, Documents relating to Quarter Sessions: Calendar of the Quarter Sessions Papers 1591–1643*, Worcestershire Historical Society (and Worcestershire County Council, Records and Charities Committee), 2 vols, 1899, 1900.

*Yorkshire Diaries and Autobiographies in the Seventeenth and Eighteenth Centuries*, Surtees Society, lxxvii, 1886.

Abrate, M., 'Il Memoriale di Henry Pugnet' in *Studi in onore di Amintore Fanfani*, vol. iv, q.v.

—— 'Imprenditori e Tecnici Stranieri nell' Industria Laniera Piemontese agli Inizi del XVIII secolo' in Spallanzani, *Panni di Lana*, q.v.

Aikin, J., *A Description of the Country from Thirty to Forty Miles round Manchester*, 1795.

Alberti, L. de, and Chapman, A. B. W., *English Merchants and the Spanish Inquisition in the Canaries*, Royal Historical Society, Camden 3rd series, vol. xxiii, 1912.

Alexander, J. J., and Hooper, W. R., *The History of Great Torrington in the County of Devon*, Sutton, Surrey, 1948.

Allen, D. H., *Essex Quarter Sessions Order Book 1652–1661*, Chelmsford, 1974.

Allison, K. J., 'The wool supply and the worsted cloth industry in Norfolk in the sixteenth and seventeenth centuries', typescript PhD thesis, Leeds University, 1955.

Ammann, H., 'Deutschland und die Tuchindustrie Nordwesteuropas im Mittelalter', *Hansische Geschichtsblätter*, lxxii, 1954.

Anderson, R. C., *The Book of Examinations 1601–1602*, Southampton Record Society, 1926.

—— *The Book of Examinations and Depositions 1622–1644*, 4 vols, Southampton Record Society, 1929–36.

Andrews, J. H., 'The trade of the port of Faversham, 1650–1750' in Roake, M., and Whyman, J., *Essays in Kentish History*, 1973.

Apperson, G. L., *Gleanings after Time*, 1907.

Archbold, W. A. J., 'An assessment of wages for 1620', *English Historical Review*, vol. xii, 1897.

Armour, C., 'The trade of Chester and the state of the Dee navigation 1600–1800', typescript PhD thesis, London University, 1956.

Arnold, T., *Memorials of St Edmund's Abbey*, 3 vols, 1890–6.

Ashtor, E., 'Observations on Venetian trade in the Levant in the XIVth century', *Journal of European Economic History*, vol. v, 1976.

Aspley Heath School Historical Society, *A History of Our District*, Aspley Guise, 1931.

Åström, S.-E., *From Cloth to Iron: the Anglo-Baltic Trade in the late Seventeenth Century*, Societas Scientiarum Fennica, Commentationes Humanarum Litterarum, tomus xxxiii, no. i, Helsingfors (Helsinki) 1963.

Atkinson, T., *Elizabethan Winchester*, 1963.

Atkyns, R., *The Ancient and Present State of Glocestershire*, 1768.

—— *A New History of Gloucestershire*, ed. Rudder, Cirencester, 1779.

Aubrey, J., *The Natural History and Antiquities of Surrey*, 5 vols, 1719.

—— *The Natural History of Wiltshire*, ed. J. Britton, 1847.

B., J. (I.), *The Merchants Avizo*, 1607.

Baasch, E., *Holländische Wirtschaftsgeschichte*, Jena, 1927.

Bacon, N., *The Annalls of Ipswiche*, ed. W. H. Richardson, Ipswich, 1884.

Bahr, K., *Handel und Verkehr der Deutschen Hanse in Flanderen während des vierzehnten Jahrhunderts*, Leipzig, 1911.

Baigent, F. J., and Millard, J. E., *A History of the Ancient Town and Manor of Basingstoke*, 1889.

Bailey, C., *Transcripts from the Municipal Archives of Winchester*, Winchester, 1856.

Baines, E., *History, Directory and Gazeteer of the County Palatine of Lancaster*, 2 vols, Liverpool, 1824.

Bang, N. E. (and Korst, K.), *Tabeller over Skibsfart og Varetransport gennem Øresund 1497–1660*, 2 vols in 3 parts, Copenhagen and Leipzig, 1906–33.

Bang, N.E. and Korst, K., *Tabeller over Skibsfart og Varetransport gennem Øresund 1661–1783 og gennem Storebaelt 1701–1748*, 2 parts (vols), Copenhagen and Leipzig, 1939–53.

Barkhausen, M., 'Government control and free enterprise in West Germany and the Low Countries in the eighteenth century' in Earle, P., *Essays in European Economic History 1500–1800*, Oxford, 1974.

Barley, M. W., *Lincolnshire and the Fens*, 1952.

Barnard, E. A. B. and Wace, A. J. B., 'The Sheldon tapestry weavers and their work', *Archaeologia*, vol. lxxviii (2nd series, vol. xxviii), 1928.

Barnes, T. G., *Somerset 1625–1640: a county's government during the 'Personal Rule'*, no date.

Bateson, M., *Records of the Borough of Leicester*, 3 vols, Cambridge, 1899–1905.

Battistini, M., *La Confrérie de Sainte-Barbe des Flamands à Florence: documents relatifs aux tisserands et aux tapissiers*, Commission Royale d'Histoire, Brussels, 1931.

Baxter, R., *Reliquiae Baxterianae*, ed. M. Sylvester, 1696.

Beaumont, G. F., *A History of Coggeshall, in Essex*, Coggeshall and London, 1890.

Beck, S. W., *The Draper's Dictionary*, no date.

Benedict, P., *Rouen during the Wars of Religion*, Cambridge, 1981.

Benham, W. G., *The Oath Book or Red Parchment Book of Colchester*, Colchester, 1907.

Bennett, J. H. E., *The Rolls of Freemen of the City of Chester*, 2 parts, Record Society of Lancashire and Cheshire, vols li, lv, 1906–8.

Bennett, W., *The History of Burnley 1400 to 1650*, Burnley, 1947.

—— *The History of Burnley 1650 to 1850*, Burnley, 1948.

Benson, R. and Hatcher, H., *Old and New Sarum, or Salisbury* (vol. iv. of Hoare, R. C., *The History of Modern Wiltshire*, q.v.), 1843.

Bernard, Garter King of Arms, *The Joyfull Receyving of the Queenes most excellent Majestie into hir Highnesse Citie of Norwich*, no date.

(Best, H.), *Rural Economy in Yorkshire in 1641, being the farming and account books of Henry Best of Elmswell*, ed. C. B. Robinson (Norcliffe), Surtees Society, vol. xxxiii, 1857.

Bestall, J. M., and Fowkes, D V., *Chesterfield Wills and Inventories 1521–1603*, Derbyshire Record Society, vol. i. 1977.

Bettey, J. H., 'The production of alum and copperas in southern England', *Textile History*, vol. xiii, 1982.

Bidwell, W. H., *Annals of an East Anglian Bank*, Norwich 1900.

Bigland, R., *An Original History of the City of Gloucester*, ed. T. D. Fosbrooke, 1819.

Bignon, M., 'Extrait du mémoire de la généralité d'Amiens ou de Picardie dressé par ordre de Monseigneur le Duc de Bourgogne' in Hayem, *Mémoires et Documents*, 1e série, q.v.

Birch, T., *A Collection of the State Papers of John Thurloe*, 7 vols, 1742.

Birch, W. de G., *The Historical Charters and Constitutional Documents of the City of London*, 1887.

Bischoff, J., *A Comprehensive History of the Woollen and Worsted Manufactures*, 2 vols, 1842.

Blith, W., *The English Improver Improved*, 1652.

Blome, R., *Britannia, or a geographical description of the kingdoms of England, Scotland and Ireland*, 1673.

Bloxsom, M., *A History of the Parish of Gilmorton*, Lincoln, 1918.

Bonds, N., 'Some Industrial Price Movements in Medieval Genoa (1155–1255)' in Herlihy, Lopez and Slessarev, *Economy, Society and Government in Medieval Italy*, q.v.

Borlase, W., *The Natural History of Cornwall*, Oxford, 1758.

Botero, W., *A Treatise concerning the Causes of the Magnificencie and Greatnes of Cities*, 1606.

Bouch, C. M. L. and Jones, G.P., *A Short Economic and Social History of the Lake District 1500–1830*, Manchester, 1961.

Bourde, A. J., *The Influence of England on the French Agronomes, 1750–1789*, Cambridge, 1953.

Bourhis, J. J., 'Le trafic du port de Dartmouth 1599–1641', typescript thesis, Diplôme d'études supérieures de l'histoire moderne, Université de Bretagne Occidentale, Brest, 2 vols, 1972.

Bowden P. J., *The Wool Trade in Tudor and Stuart England*, 1962.

Bowden, W., *Industrial Society in England towards the End of the Eighteenth Century*, New York, 1925.

Bowman, W. M., *England in Ashton-under-Lyne*, Ashton-under-Lyne, 1960.

Boys, W., *Collections for a History of Sandwich*, 2 vols, Canterbury, 1842.

Boyson, R., *The Ashworth Cotton Enterprise*, Oxford, 1970.

Braudel, F. and Romano, R., *Navires et Marchandises à l'entrée du Port de Livourne (1547–1611)*, Paris, 1951.

Brears, P. C. D., *Yorkshire Probate Inventories 1542–1689*, Yorkshire Archaeological Society Record Series, cxxxiv, 1972.

Brent, J., *Canterbury in the Olden Time*, Canterbury and London, 1860.

Brereton, W., *Travels in Holland, the United Provinces, England, Scotland and Ireland*, Camden Society, vol. i, 1844.

Brown, A. F. J., 'Colchester in the eighteenth century', in Mumby, L. M., *East Anglian Studies*, q.v.

Brulez, W., *De Firma Della Faille en de Internationale Handel van Vlaamse Firma's in de Zestiende Eeuw*, Brussels, 1959.

—— 'Engels Laken in Vlaanderen in de 14e en 15e Eeuw', *Handelingen van de Genootschap voor Geschiedenis te Brugge* (Société d'Emulation), vol. cvii, 1972.

—— 'Les Routes commerciales d'Angleterre en Italie au XVIe siècle', in *Studi in onore di Amintore Fanfani*, vol. iv, q.v.

Bulkeley-Owen, (Mrs), *History of Selattyn Parish*, Oswestry, no date.

Burgon, J. W., *The Life and Times of Sir Thomas Gresham, Knt*, 2 vols, no date.

Burley, K. H., 'The economic development of Essex in the later seventeenth and early eighteenth centuries', typescript PhD thesis, London University, 1957.

—— 'An Essex clothier of the eighteenth century', *Economic History Review*, 2nd series, vol. xi, 1958.

—— 'A note on a labour dispute in early eighteenth century Colchester', *Bulletin of the Institute of Historical Research*, vol. xxix, 1956.

Burn, J. S., *The History of the French, Walloon, Dutch and other foreign Protestant Refugees settled in England from the Reign of Henry VIII to the Revocation of the Edict of Nantes*, 1846.

Burnham, D. K., *A Textile Terminology: warp and weft*, 1982.

Burton, J. R., *A History of Kidderminster*, 1890.

C., W., *England's Interest by Trade Asserted*, 1671

Camden, W., *Britannia*, 1594; also, ed. Gibson, 1695.

Campbell, R., *The London Tradesman*, 1747.

Carew, R., *The Survey of Cornwall* (1602), 1769.

Carroll, K. L., 'Quaker weavers at Newport, Ireland, 1720–1740', *Journal of the Friends' Historical Society*, vol. liv, 1976.

Carus-Wilson, E. M., 'Evidences of industrial growth in some fifteenth century manors', *Economic History Review*, 2nd series, vol. xii, 1959.

—— 'The Iceland trade' in Power, E. and Postan, M. M., *Studies in English Trade in the Fifteenth Century*, 1933.

—— 'An industrial revolution in the thirteenth century' in Carus-Wilson, E. M., *Essays in Economic History*, 1954.

—— 'The overseas trade of Bristol' in Power, E. and Postan, M. M., *Studie in English Trade in the Fifteenth Century*, 1933.

—— 'The woollen industry' in *Cambridge Economic History*, vol. ii, q.v.

Carus-Wilson, E. M. and Coleman, O., *England's Export Trade 1275–1547*, Oxford, 1963.

Cash, M., *Devon Inventories in the Sixteenth and Seventeenth Centuries*, Devon and Cornwall Record Society, new series, vol. xi, 1966.

Cate, J. L., and Anderson, E. N., *Medieval and Historiographical Essays in honor of James Westfall Thompson*, Chicago, 1938.

Cathrall, W., The History of Oswestry, Oswestry, no date.

Chalklin, C. W., *Seventeenth-Century Kent: a social and economic history*, 1965.

Chamberlayne, J., *Magna Britanniae Notitia*, 1710.

Chambers, J. D., 'The Worshipful Company of Framework Knitters (1657–1778)', *Economica*, vol. ix, 1929.

Chanter, J. R., *Collectanea: papers relating to Barnstaple and North Devon*, sine loco nec data.

Chanter, J. R. and Wainwright, T., *Reprint of the Barnstaple Records*, 2 vols, Barnstaple, 1900.

Chapman, A. B. W., *The Black Book of Southampton*, 3 vols, Southampton Record Society, 1912–15.

Chapman, S. D., *The Cotton Industry in the Industrial Revolution*, 1972.

—— *The Devon Cloth Industry in the Eighteenth Century*, Devon and Cornwall Record Society, new series, vol. xxiii, 1978.

—— 'The genesis of the British hosiery industry 1600–1750', *Textile History*, vol. iii, 1972.

—— 'Industrial capital before the Industrial Revolution: an analysis of the assets of a thousand textile entrepreneurs circa 1730–1750', in Harte, N. B. and Ponting, K. G., *Textile History and Economic History*, q.v.

Chapman, S. D. and Chassagne, S., *European Textile Printers in the Eighteenth Century*, 1981.

Charles, B. G., *Calendar of the Records of the Borough of Haverfordwest 1539–1660*, Cardiff, 1967.

Chaudhuri, K. N., *The Trading World of Asia and the English East India Company 1660–1760*, Cambridge, 1978.

Child, J. (C., J.), *Brief Observations concerning Trade and Interest of Money*, 1668.

—— *An Essay on Wool and Woollen Manufacture*, 1693.

—— *A New Discourse of Trade*, 1693.

—— *A Tract against Usurie presented to the High Court of Parliament*, 1668

Childrey, J., *Britannia Baconica*, 1660.

Cholmeley, W., 'The request and suite of a true-hearted Englishman', ed. W. J. Thoms, in *Camden Miscellany*, vol. ii, Camden Society, vol. lv, 1853.

Christensen, A. E., *Dutch Trade to the Baltic about 1600*, Copenhagen and The Hague, 1941.

Ciriacono, S., 'Silk manufacturing in France and Italy in the XVIIth century: two models compared', *Journal of European Economic History*, vol. x, 1981.

Clabburn, P., *Norwich Shawls*, Norwich, 1975.

Clapham, J. H., 'The transference of the worsted industry from Norfolk to the West Riding', *Economic Journal*, vol. xx, 1910.

Clarendon, Earl of (Hyde, E.), *The History of the Rebellion and Civil Wars in England begun in the Year 1641*, 6 vols, Oxford, 1878.

Clark, A., 'Essex woollen manufactures, 1629', *Essex Review*, vol. xvii, 1908.

Clark, A., *The Story of Monmouthshire*, i, Llandybie, Carmarthenshire, 1962.

Clark, G. N., *The Seventeenth Century*, 1960.

—— *The Wealth of England*, 1946.

Clark, P. and Slack, P., *Crisis and Order in English Towns 1500–1700*, 1972.

Clark, P., Smith, A. G. R. and Tyacke, N., *The English Commonwealth 1547–1640: essays in politics and society presented to Joel Hurstfield*, Leicester, 1979.

Clegg, A. L., *A History of Wimborne Minster and District*, Bournemouth, 1960.

Clouzot, H., *Le Métier de la Soie en France (1466–1815)*, Paris, no date.

Clow, A. and N., *The Chemical Revolution: a contribution to social technology*, 1952.

Cock, J., *Records of the Antient Borough of South Molton*, S. Molton, 1893.

Cockburn, J. S., *Calendar of Assize Records: Kent Indictments, Elizabeth I*, 1979.

—— *Western Assize Circuit Orders 1629–1648*, Royal Historical Society, Camden 4th series, vol. xvii, 1976.

Coke, E., *Institutes of the Laws of England*, parts ii–iv, 1642–4.

Coke, R., *England's Improvement*, 1675.

Coker, (J.), *A Survey of Dorsetshire*, 1732.

Cole, C. W., *Colbert and a Century of French Mercantilism*, 2 vols, 1964.

Coleman, D. C., *Courtulds: an economic and social history*, i, Oxford, 1969.

—— 'The economy of Kent under the later Stuarts', typescript PhD thesis, London University, 1951.

—— *Sir John Banks baronet and businessman: a study of business, politics and society in later Stuart England*, Oxford, 1963.

Coleman, D. C. and John, A. H., *Trade, Government and Economy in Pre-Industrial England: essays presented in F. J. Fisher*, 1976.

Collinson, J., *The History and Antiquities of the County of Somerset*, 3 vols Bath, 1791.

Colwall, D., 'On the English alum works', *Philosophical Transactions of the Royal Society of London* (q.v.), vol. ii.

—— 'The English green copperas', *Philosophical Transactions of the Royal Society of London* (q.v.), vol. ii.

Colyer-Fergusson, T. C., *Registers of the French Church, Threadneedle Street, London*, vols iii and iv, Publications of the Huguenot Society of London, vols xvi and xxiii, 1906 and 1916.

Coniglio, G., 'Agricoltura ed Artigianato Mantovano nel secolo XVI', in *Studi in Onore de Amintore Fanfani*, vol. iv, q.v.

Connell-Smith, G., *Forerunners of Drake*, 1954.

Consitt, F., *The London Weavers' Company*, vol. i, Oxford, 1933.

Conyers, A., *Wiltshire Extents for Debts, Edward I–Elizabeth I*, Wiltshire Record Society, vol. xxviii, 1973.

Cooper, J. P., 'Economic regulation and the cloth industry in the seventeenth century', *Transactions of the Royal Historical Society*, 5th series, vol. xx, 1970.

Cooper, W. D., *The History of Winchelsea, one of the ancient towns added to the Cinque Ports*, 1850.

—— *Lists of Foreign Protestants and Aliens resident in England 1618–1688, from returns in the State Paper Office*, Camden Society, vol. lxxxii, 1862.

—— *Savile Correspondence: letters to and from Henry Savile, Esq.*, Camden Society, vol. lxxi, 1858.

Coornaert, E., *Un Centre industriel d'autrefois: La Draperie-Sayetterie d'Hondschoote (XIVe–XVIIIe siècles)*, Paris, 1930.

—— *Une Industrie urbaine du XIVe au XVIIe siècle: L'Industrie de la Laine à Bergues-Saint-Winoc*, Paris, 1930.

—— *Les Français et le Commerce international à Anvers fin du XVe et XVIe siècle*, 2 vols, Paris, 1961.

Corfield, P., 'A provincial capital in the late seventeenth century', in Clark, P. and Slack, P., *Crisis and Order in English Towns 1500–1700*, 1972.

Court, W. H. B., *The Rise of the Midland Industries 1600–1838*, 1953.

Courtauld, S. A., 'East Anglia and the Huguenot textile industry', *Proceedings of the Huguenot Society of London*, vol. xiii, 1929.

Coward, E., 'William Gaby, His Booke 1656', *Wiltshire Archaeological and Natural History Magazine*, xlvi, 1932–4.

Cowper, J. M., *Canterbury Marriage Licences, first series, 1568–1618*, Canterbury, 1892.

Cox, J. C., *The Records of the Borough of Northampton*, vol. ii, Northampton, 1898.

Cozens-Hardy, B., 'The maritime trade of the port of Blakeney, which included Cley and Wiveton, 1587 to 1590', in Norfolk Record Society, vol. vii, 1936.

Craeybeckx, J., 'Les Industries d'exportation dans les villes flamandes au XVIIe siècle, particulièrement à Gand et à Bruges', in *Studi in onore di Amintore Fanfani*, vol. iv, q.v.

Crean, J. F., 'Hats and the fur trade', *Canadian Journal of Economics and Political Science*, vol. xxviii, 1962.

Croft, P., *The Spanish Company*, London Record Society, 1973.

Crofts, J., *Packhorse, Waggon and Post*, 1967.

Cross, F. W., *History of the Walloon and Huguenot Church at Canterbury*, Publications of the Huguenot Society of London, vol. xv, 1898.

Crump, W. B., and Ghorbal, G., *History of the Huddersfield Woollen Industry*, Huddersfield, 1935.

Cullen, L. M., *Anglo-Irish Trade 1660–1800*, Manchester, 1968.

—— *An Economic History of Ireland since 1660*, 1972.

Culpepper, T., *A Tract against Usurie*, 1621.

Cunningham, W., *Alien Immigrants to England*, 1897.

Cunnington, B. H., *Records of the County of Wiltshire*, Devizes, 1932.

—— *Some Annals of the Borough of Devizes 1555–1791*, Devizes, 1925–6.

Curtis, W., *A Short History and Description of the Town of Alton*, Winchester and London, 1896.

Dale, B., *The Annals of Coggeshall, otherwise Sunnedon, in the County of Essex*, Coggeshall and London, 1863.

Dale, C., *Wiltshire Apprentices and their Masters 1710–1760*, Wiltshire Record Society, vol. xvii, 1961.

Dale, M. K., 'The London silkwomen in the fifteenth century', *Economic History Review*, vol. iv, 1932–4.

Dallington, R., *A Survey of the Great Dukes State of Tuscany in the Year of Our Lord 1596*, 1605.

Daniels, G. W., *The Early English Cotton Industry*, Manchester, 1920.

Darby, H. C., *The Medieval Fenland*, Cambridge, 1940.

Davenport, F. G., *The Economic Development of a Norfolk Manor 1086–1565*, Cambridge, 1906.

Davidsohn, R., *Geschichte von Florenz*, vol. iv, pt ii, Berlin, 1925.

Davies, C. S., *A History of Macclesfield*, Manchester, 1961.

Davies, J. S., *A History of Southampton*, Southampton, 1883.

Davies, K. G., *The Royal African Company*, 1957.

Davies, M. F., *Life in an English Village: an economic and historical survey of the parish of Corsley in Wiltshire*, London and Leipzig, 1909.

Davies, M. G., *The Enforcement of English Apprenticeship: a study in applied mercantilism 1563–1642*, Cambridge, Mass., 1956.

Davies, R., *The Life of Marmaduke Rawdon of York*, Camden Society, vol. lxxxv, 1863.

Davies, W., *A General View of the Agriculture and Domestic Economy of North Wales*, 1810.

Davis, R., *Aleppo and Devonshire Square: English Traders in the Levant in the Eighteenth Century*, 1967.

—— 'The rise of Antwerp and its English connection 1406–1510', in Coleman, D. C. and John, A. H., *Trade, Government and Economy in Pre-Industrial England*, q.v.

Davis, T., *A General View of the Agriculture of the County of Wiltshire*, 1794.

Dawe, D., *Skilbecks: drysalters 1650–1950*, 1950.

Dechesne, L., *Industrie Drapière de la Vesdre avant 1800*, Paris and Liège, 1926.

Defoe, D., *The Complete English Tradesman*, Edinburgh, 1839.

—— *A Plan of the English Commerce*, 1728.

—— *A Tour through England and Wales*, 2 vols, 1928.

—— *The Works of Daniel Defoe*, ed. J. S. Keltie, Edinburgh, 1869.

Deloney, T., *The Pleasant History of John Winchcombe, in his younger yeares called Jacke of Newberie*, 1633.

Delumeau, J., 'L'alum de Rome – moyen de domination économique du Midi sur le Nord jusque vers 1620', in *Studi in Onore di Amintore Fanfani*, vol. iv, q.v.

Demey, J. 'De "Mislukte" Aanpassingen van de Nieuwe Draperie, de Saainijverheid en de Lichte Draperie te Ieper', *Tijdschrift voor Geschiedenis*, jaarg. lxxxiii, 1950.

Denucé, J., *Koopmansleerboeken van de XVIe en XVIIe Eeuwen in Handschrift*, Antwerp, Brussels, Ghent and Louvain, 1941.

De Pauw, N., *Ypre jeghen Poperinghe angaende den Verbonden*, Ghent, 1899.

De Poerck, G., *La Draperie Médiévale en Flandre et en Artois: technique et terminologie*, 3 vols, Bruges, 1951.

Derode, V., 'Quelques documents pour servir à l'histoire de l'industrie à Lille', *Mémoires de la Société Impériale des Sciences et de l'Agriculture et des Arts de Lille*, 3e série, tome iv, 1868 (1867).

De Roover, R., *Business, Banking and Economic Thought in late medieval and early modern Europe*, ed. J. Kirshner, Chicago and London, 1976.

—— *The Rise and Decline of the Medici Bank 1397–1494*, Cambridge, Mass., 1968.

De Sagher, H.-E., *Recueil de Documents relatifs à l'Histoire de l'Industrie drapière en Flandre. Deuxième Partie. Le Sud-Ouest de la Flandre depuis l'Époque Bourguignonne*, 3 vols, Brussels, 1951–66.

De Smedt, O., *De Engelse Natie te Antwerpen in de Zestiende Eeuw (1496–1582)*, 2 vols, Antwerp, 1950–4.

Derville, A., 'Les draperies flamandes et artésiennes vers 1250–1350', *Revue du Nord*, tome liv, 1972.

De Vries, J., *The Dutch Rural Economy in the Golden Age 1500–1700*, New Haven and London, 1974.

Deyon, P., *Amiens – capitale provinciale: étude sur la société urbaine au 17e siècle*, Paris and The Hague, 1967.

Deyon, P. and Lottin, A., 'Evolution de la production textile à Lille au XVIe et XVIIe siècles', *Revue du Nord*, tome xlix, 1967.

Dickenson, M. J., 'Fulling in the West Riding woollen cloth industry, 1689–1770', *Textile History*, vol. x, 1979.

Dickin, E. P., 'Notes on the coast, shipping and seaborne trade of Essex from 1565 to 1577', *Essex Archaeological Society's Transactions*, new series, vol. xvii, 1926.

Dietz, A., *Frankfurter Handelsgeschichte*, 2 vols, Frankfort on the Main, 1910–21.

Dietz, B., *The Port and Trade of early Elizabethan London*, London Record Society, 1972.

Diferee, H. C., *De Geschiedenis van der Nederlandschen Handel tot den Val der Republiek*, Amsterdam, 1908.

Digges, D., *The Defence of Trade*, 1615.

Doehaerd, R. and Kerremans, C., *Les Relations commerciales entre Gênes, la Belgique et l'Outremont d'après les Archives notariales Génoises 1400–1450*, Brussels and Rome, 1952.

Donaldson, P. S., 'George Rainsford's *Rittrato d'Inghilterra* (1556)' in *Camden Miscellany*, vol. xxvii, Royal Historical Society, Camden 4th series, vol. xxii, 1979.

Dony, J. G., *A History of the Straw Hat Industry*, Luton, 1942.

Doren, A., *Studien aus der Florentiner Wirtschaftsgeschichte*, 2 vols, Stuttgart, 1901–8.

Doughty, H. M., *Chronicles of Theberton: a Suffolk village*, 1910.

Douglas, A. W., 'Cotton textiles in England: the East India Company's attempt to exploit developments in fashion 1660–1721', *Journal of British Studies*, vol. viii, 1969.

Duby, G., 'La révolution agricole mediévale', *Revue de Géographie de Lyon*, tome xxix, 1954.

Dumon, R., *Types of Rural Economy*, 1957.

Dunning, R. W. and Tremlett, T. D., with Dilks, T. B., *Bridgwater Borough Archives*, vol. v, Somerset Record Society, vol. lxx, 1971.

Dunsford, M., *Historical Memoirs of the Town and Parish of Tiverton in the County of Devon*, Exeter, 1790.

Dyer, A. D., *The City of Worcester in the Sixteenth Century*, Leicester, 1973.

—— 'Probate inventories of Worcester tradesmen 1545–1614' in *Miscellany ii*, Worcestershire Historical Society, new series, vol. v, 1967.

Dyer, J., 'The Fleece' in *Poems*, 1770.

Dymond, D. and Betterton, A., *Lavenham: 700 Years of Textile Making*, Woodbridge, Suffolk, 1982.

Earle, P., *Essays in European Economic History 1500–1800*, Oxford, 1974.

—— *The World of Defoe*, 1976.

Earwaker, J. P., *Lancashire and Cheshire Wills and Inventories at Chester*, Chetham Society, new series, vol. iii, 1884.

—— *Lancashire and Cheshire Wills and Inventories, 1572 to 1696, now preserved at Chester*, Chetham Society, new series, vol. xxviii, 1893.

Eden, F. M., *The State of the Poor*, 3 vols, 1797.

Edler, F., *Glossary of Medieval Terms of Business, Italian series, 1200–1600*, Cambridge, Mass., 1934.

—— 'The Van Der Molen, commission merchants of Antwerp: trade with Italy 1538–1544' in Cate, J. L. and Anderson, E. N., *Medieval and Historiographical Essays in Honor of James Westfall Thompson*, q.v.

—— 'Winchcombe kerseys in Antwerp (1538–1544)', *Economic History Review*, vol. vii, 1937,

Edwards, J. K., 'The economic development of Norwich 1750–1850', typescript PhD thesis, Leeds University, 1963.

Eggen, J. L. M., *De Invloed door Zuid-Nederland op Noord-Nederland uitgeoefend op het Einde der XVIe en het Begin der XVIIe Eeuw*, Ghent, 1908.

Ehrenberg, R., *Hamburg und England im Zeitalter der Königin Elisabeth*, Jena, 1896.

Eland, G., *Purefoy Letters 1735–1753*, 2 vols, 1931.

Ellis, H., *Original Letters Illustrative of English History*, 3rd series, vol. i, 1846.

Emmison, F. G., *Elizabethan Life: Disorder*, Chelmsford, 1970; *Home*, Work and Land, Chelmsford, 1976; *Wills of Essex Gentry and Merchants proved in the Prerogative Court of Canterbury*, Chelmsford, 1978.

—— *Jacobean Household Inventories*, Bedfordshire Historical Record Society, vol. xx, 1938.

—— *Wills at Chelmsford (Essex and East Hertfordshire)*, 2 vols, Index Library, British Record Society, vols lxxviii–ix, 1958–61.

Endrei, W., 'English kersey in Eastern Europe, with special reference to Hungary', *Textile History*, vol. v, 1974.

—— *L'Évolution des Techniques du Filage et du Tissage du Moyen Âge à la Révolution Industrielle*, Paris and The Hague, 1968.

English, W., 'A technical assessment of Lewis Paul's spinning machine', *Textile History*, vol. iv, 1973.

—— *The Textile Industry: an account of the early inventions of spinning, weaving and knitting machines*, 1969.

Enno van Gelder, H. A., *Gegevens Betreffende Roerend en Onroerend Bezit in de Nederlanden in de 16e Eeuw*, 2 vols, The Hague, 1972–3.

Espinas, G., *La Vie Urbaine de Douai au Moyen Age*, 3 vols, Paris, 1913.

Espinas, G. and Pirenne, H., *Recueil de Documents relatifs à l'Histoire de l'Industrie drapière en Flandre. Première Partie. Des Origines à l'Époque Bourguignonne*, 4 vols, Brussels, 1906–24.

Evans, D. J., 'The drapers of Shrewsbury and the Welshpool flannel market in the seventeenth century', *Montgomeryshire Collections*, lii, 1951–2.

Evans, J., *A Chronological Outline of the History of Bristol and the Stranger's Guide through its Streets and Neighbourhood*, Bristol, 1824.

Evans, J. T., *Seventeenth-Century Norwich: politics, religion and government, 1620–1690*, Oxford, 1979.

Evans, N., 'The community of South Elmham, Suffolk, 1550–1640', typescript MPhil thesis, University of East Anglia, 1978.

Evelyn, J., *The Diary of John Evelyn*, ed. E. S. De Beer, 6 vols, Oxford, 1955.

Exelby, H. R., 'The Industrial Revolution in the textile industries of Wiltshire', typescript MA thesis, Bristol University, 1928.

F., J., *The Merchant's Warehouse laid open, or the plain dealing Linnen-Draper*, 1696.

Faber, J. A., *Drie Eeuwen Friesland: economische en sociale ontwikkelingen van 1500 tot 1800*, 2 vols, being *Afdeling Agrarische Geschiedenis Bijdragen*, xvii, 1972.

Fairlie, S., 'Dyestuffs in the eighteenth century', *Economic History Review*, 2nd series, vol. xvii, 1965.

Fairs, G. L., *A History of the Hay: the story of Hay-on-Wye*, London and Chichester, 1972.

Fedorowicz, J. K., *England's Baltic Trade in the Early Seventeenth Century: a study in Anglo-Polish commercial diplomacy*, Cambridge, 1980.

Ferguson, R. S., *A Boke off Recorde or Register containing all the Acts and Doings in or concerning the Corporation within the Town of Kirkbiekendall beginning … 1575*, Cumberland and Westmorland Antiquarian and Archaeological Society, extra series, vol. vii, 1892.

Fiennes, C., *The Journeys of Celia Fiennes*, ed. C. Morris, 1949.

Finch, M. E., *The Wealth of Five Northamptonshire Families 1540–1640*, Northamptonshire Record Society, vol. xix, 1956.

Firth, C. H. and Rait, R. S., *Acts and Ordinances of the Interregnum*, 3 vols, 1911.

Fisher, F. J., *Essays in the Economic and Social History of Tudor and Stuart England*, Cambridge, 1961.

Fisher, H. E. S., *The Portugal Trade: a study of Anglo-Portuguese Commerce 1700–1770*, 1971.

Fishwick, H., *The History of the Parish of Rochdale*, Rochdale and London, 1889.

—— *The Survey of the Manor of Rochdale 1626*, Chetham Society, new series, lxxi, 1913.

Fleming, D., *Description of the County of Westmoreland* (1671) ed. G. F. Duckett, Cumberland and Westmorland Antiquarian and Archaeological Society, tract series, vol. i, 1882.

Fortrey, S., *England's Interest and Improvement*, Cambridge, 1663.

Fowle, J. P. M., *Wiltshire Quarter Sessions and Assizes, 1736*, Wiltshire Record Society, vol. xi, 1955.

Fox, J. H., *The Woollen Manufacture in Wellington, Somerset*, 1914.

Francis, A. D., 'John Methuen and the Anglo-Portuguese treaties of 1703', *Historical Journal*, vol. iii, 1960.

Freeman, C. E., 'Elizabethan inventories', in *Harrold Priory: a twelfth-century dispute, and other articles*, Bedfordshire Historical Record Society, vol. xxxii, 1952.

Fréville, E. de, *Mémoire sur le Commerce Maritime de Rouen depuis les temps les plus reculés jusqu'à la fin du XVIe siècle*, 2 vols, Rouen and Paris, 1857.

Friis, A., *Alderman Coockayne's Project and the Cloth Trade: the commercial policy of England in its main aspects 1603–1625*, Copenhagen and London, 1927.

Fuller, T., *The Church-History of Britain from the Birth of Jesus Christ untill the year 1648*, 1655.

—— *The History of the Worthies of England*, ed. P. A. Nuttall, 3 vols, 1840.

—— *The Holy State and the Profane State*, ed. J. Nichols, 1841.

Furley, J. S., *City Government of Winchester from the Records of the XIV and XV Centuries*, Oxford, 1923.

Furley, R., *A History of the Weald of Kent*, 2 vols, Ashford and London, 1871–4.

Gardiner, D., *Historic Haven: the story of Sandwich*, Derby, 1954.

Gardiner, S. R., *Constitutional Documents of the Puritan Revolution 1625–1660*, Oxford, 1906.

—— *Notes of the Debates in the House of Lords officially taken by Henry Elsing, Clerk of the Parliaments, A.D. 1621*, Camden Society, vol. ciii, 1870.

—— *Parliamentary Debates in 1610*, Camden Society, lxxxi, 1862.

Gay, J., *Poetry and Prose*, ed. V. A. Dearing, 2 vols, Oxford, 1974.

Gelder, *see* Enno van Gelder.

Gerard, T., *The Particular Description of the County of Somerset*, ed. E. H. Bates, Somerset Record Society, vol. xv, 1900.

Gervers, V., *Studies in Textile History in Memory of Harold B. Burnham*, Royal Ontario Museum, Toronto, 1977.

(Gibbons, B.), *Notes and Suggestions for a History of Kidderminster*, Kidderminster, 1859.

Giles, (J. A.), *History of Witney*, 1852.

Gill, C., *The Rise of the Irish Linen Industry*, Oxford, 1925.

Gittins, L., 'Innovations in textile bleaching in Britain in the eighteenth century', *Business History Review*, liii, 1979.

Glass, D. V., *London Inhabitants within the Walls, 1695*, London Record Society, vol. ii, 1966.

Glass, K. W., *A Short History of Glemsford*, Glemsford, 1962.

Glover, E., *The Gold and Silver Wyre-Drawers*, London and Chichester, 1979.

Godfray, H. M., *Registre des Baptesmes, Mariages et Morts et Jeusnes de leglise Wallonne et des Isles de Jersey, Guernesey, Serq, Origny, etc. establie a Southampton par Patente du Roy Edouard Sixieme et de la Reine Elizabeth*, Publications of the Huguenot Society of London, vol. iv, 1890.

Godfrey, E. S., *The Development of English Glassmaking 1560–1640*, Oxford, 1975.

Goldney, F. H., *Records of Chippenham*, sine loco, 1889.

Goodsall, R. H., 'The Whitstable copperas industry', *Archaeologia Cantiana*, vol. lxx, 1956.

Goris, J. A., *Étude sur les Colonies Marchandes Méridionales (Portugais, Espagnols, Italiens) à Anvers de 1488 à 1567*, Louvain, 1925.

Goubert, P., *Beauvais et le Beauvaisis de 1600 à 1730*, 2 vols, Paris, 1960.

Gough, R., *The History of Myddle*, Sunninghill, Ascot, Berkshire, 1979.

Gould, J. D., *The Great Debasement: currency and the economy in Mid-Tudor England*, Oxford, 1970.

Gras, N. S. B., *The Early English Customs System*, Cambridge, Mass., 1918.

Grass, M. and A., *Stockings for a Queen: the life of the Reverend William Lee, the Elizabethan inventor*, 1967.

Gray, H. L., 'English foreign trade from 1446 to 1482' in Power, E. and Postan, M. M., *Studies in English Trade in the Fifteenth Century*, 1933.

—— 'Tables of enrolled customs and subsidy accounts, 1399 to 1482' in Power, E. and Postan, M. M., *Studies in English Trade in the Fifteenth Century*, 1933.

Gray, M., *The History of Bury, Lancashire, from 1660 to 1876*, Bury, 1970.

Green, E., 'On some Flemish weavers settled at Glastonbury A.D. 1551', *Somerset Archaeological and Natural History Society's Proceedings*, vol. xxvi, part ii, 1880.

Gretton, R. H., *The Burford Records*, Oxford, 1920.

Gribble, J. B., *Memorials of Barnstaple*, Barnstaple, 1830.

Grimwood, C. G. and Kay, S. A., *History of Sudbury, Suffolk*, Sudbury, 1952.

Gross, C., *The Gild Merchant*, 2 vols, Oxford, 1890.

Grubb, I., *Quakerism and Industry before 1800*, 1930.

Guicciardini, L., *Descrittione di Tutti Paesi Bassi*, Antwerp, 1567.

Guilding, J. M., *Reading Records: diary of the corporation*, 4 vols, 1892–6.

Guitard, E., 'L'Industrie des draps en Languedoc et ses protecteurs sous l'ancien régime' in Hayem, *Mémoires et Documents*, 1e serie, q.v.

Gulley, J. L. M., 'The Wealden landscape in the early seventeenth century and its antecedents', typescript PhD thesis, London University, 1960.

Gulvin, C., *The Tweedmakers: a history of the Scottish fancy woollen industry 1600–1914*, Newton Abbot, 1973.

Gurney, D., *The Record of the House of Gournay*, privately printed, 1848.

Hainsworth, D. R., *Commercial Papers of Sir Christopher Lowther 1611–1644*, Surtees Society, vol. clxxxxix, 1977.

Hakluyt, R., *The Original Writings and Correspondence of the two Richard Hakluyts*, ed. E. G. R. Taylor, Hakluyt Society, 2nd series, vols lxxvi–vii, 1935.

—— *The Principal Navigations, Voyages, Traffiques and Discoveries of the English Nation*, 12 vols, Glasgow, 1903–5.

Hall, H., *A History of the Custom-Revenue in England from the earliest times to the year 1827*, 2 vols, 1885.

Hall, O., 'A Dutch master weaver's home in 1609', *Essex Journal*, vol. iv, 1969.

Hamilton, A. H. A., *Quarter Sessions from Queen Elizabeth to Queen Anne*, 1878.

Hamilton, G. H., *Books of Examinations and Depositions 1570–1594*, Southampton Record Society, 1914.

Hamilton, J. and Beldiceanu, N., 'Recherches autours de Qars, nom dune étoffe de poil', *Bulletin of the School of Oriental and African Studies*, vol. xxxi, 1968.

Hands, A. P. and Scouloudi, I., *French Protestant Refugees relieved through the Threadneedle Street Church, London, 1681–1687*, Publications of the Huguenot Society of London, quarto series, vol. xlix, 1971.

Hardy, G., 'La localisation des industries dans la généralité d'Orléans au XVIIIe siècle et au debut du XIXe siècle' in Hayem, *Mémoires et Documents*, 3e serie, q.v.

Hardy, W. J., 'Foreign settlers at Colchester and Halstead', *Proceedings of the Huguenot Society of London*, vol. ii, 1889 (1887–8).

Harland, J., *The House and Farm Accounts of the Shuttleworths of Gawthorpe Hall*, Chetham Society, vols xxxv, xli, xliii, xlvi, 1856–8.

Harper, L. A., *The English Navigation Laws: a seventeenth-century experiment in social engineering*, New York, 1939.

Harris, J., *The History of Kent*, vol. i, 1719.

Harris, M. D., *The Coventry Leet Book A.D. 1420–1555*, Early English Text Society, vols cxxxiv, cxxxv, cxxxviii, cxlvi, 1907–13.

—— *The History of the Drapers Company of Coventry*, sine loco nec data.

—— *Life in an Old English Town: a history of Coventry from the earliest times, compiled from official records*, 1898.

Harrison, W., *The Description of England*, ed. G. Edelen, Ithaca, N.Y., 1968.

Harte, N. B., 'The rise of protection and the English linen trade, 1690–1790' in Harte, N. B. and Ponting, K. G., *Textile History and Economic History*, q.v.

Harte, N. B. and Ponting, K. G., *Textile History and Economic History: essays in honour of Miss Julia de Lacy Mann*, Manchester, 1973.

Hartley M. and Ingilby, J., *The Old Hand-knitters of the Dales*, Clapham via Lancaster, 1951.

—— *Yorkshire Village*, 1953.

Hartley, T. E., *Proceedings in the Parliaments of Elizabeth I*, vol. i, 1558–81, Leicester, 1981.

Haskins, C., *The Ancient Trade Guilds and Companies of Salisbury*, Salisbury, 1912.

Hasted, E., *The History of the Antient and Metropolitical City of Canterbury*, 2 vols, Canterbury, 1801.

—— *The History and Topographical Survey of the County of Kent*, 4 vols, Canterbury, 1778–99.

Havinden, M. A., *Household and Farm Inventories in Oxfordshire 1550–1590*, Oxford Record Society (Historical Manuscripts Commission, Joint Publication 10), 1965.

Hayem, J., *Mémoires et Documents pour servir a l'Histoire du Commerce et de l'Industrie en France*, Paris: 1e série, 1911; 2e série, 1912; 3e série, 1913.

—— 'Les inspecteurs des manufactures et le mémoire de l'Inspecteur Tribert sur la généralité d'Orléans' in Hayem, *Mémoires et Documents*, 2e série, q.v.

Haynes, A., 'The Mortlake tapestry factory, 1619–1703', *History Today*, xxxiv, 1974.

Haynes, J., *Great Britain's Glory*, 1715.

—— *A View of the Present State of the Clothing Trade in England*, 1706.

Head, R. and Kirkman, F., *The English Rogue described in the Life of Meriton Latroon*, 1928.

Hearnshaw, F. J. C and D. M., *Court Leet Records*, Southampton Record Society, 4 parts, 1905–8.

Heaton, H., *The Yorkshire Woollen and Worsted Industries*, Oxford, 1965.

Heers, J., *L'Occident aux XIVe et XVe siècles: aspects économiques et sociaux*, Paris, 1963.

Henson, G., *History of the Framework Knitters*, Newton Abbot, 1970.

Herlihy, D., Lopez, R. S. and Slessarev, V., *Economy, Society and Government in Medieval Italy*, Kent, Ohio, 1969.

Hervey, M. W., *Annals of a Suffolk Village, being historical notes on the parish of Horringer*, privately printed, 1930.

Hessels, J. H., *Archives of the London-Dutch Church*, London and Amsterdam, 1892.

—— *Ecclesiae Londino-Batavae Archivum*, 3 vols in 4 parts, Cambridge, 1887–97.

Hey, D. G., *An English Rural Community: Myddle under the Tudors and Stuarts*, Leicester, 1974.

Heylyn, P., *Microcosmus: a little description of the great world*, Oxford, 1636.

Hibbert, T. D., 'Letters relating to Lancashire and Cheshire: *tempore* James I, Charles I and Charles II', Historic Society of Lancashire and Cheshire, *Proceedings and Papers*, session iv, 1852(1851–2).

Higgins, S. H., *A History of Bleaching*, 1924.

Hill, G., *A History of English Dress*, ii, 1893.

Hilton, G. W., *The Truck System, including a history of the British Truck Acts, 1465–1960*, Cambridge, 1960.

Hine, R., *The History of Beaminster*, Taunton, 1914.

Hinton, R. W. K., *The Eastland Trade and the Common Weal in the Seventeenth Century*, Cambridge, 1959.

Historical Manuscripts Commission, *First Report*, 1870; *Third Report*, 1872; *Fifth Report*, part i, 1876; *Sixth Report*, part i, 1877; *Seventh Report*, part i, 1879; *Eleventh Report*, Appendix, part iii, 1887; part vii, 1888; *Twelfth Report*, Appendix, part ix, 1891; *Thirteenth Report*, Appendix, part i, 1891; part ii, 1893; part iv, 1892; part vi, 1901; *Fourteenth Report*, Appendix, part iv, 1894; part vi, 1894; part viii, 1895; *Fifteenth Report*, Appendix, part x 1899.

—— *Calendar of the Manuscripts of the Right Honourable Lord Sackville of Knole, Sevenoaks, Kent*, vol. ii, Cranfield Papers 1597–1612, ed. F. J. Fisher (HMC vol. lxxx) 1966.

—— *Calendar of the Manuscripts of the Marquess of Ormonde at Kilkenny Castle*, new series, vol. iv, 1906.

—— *Calendar of the Manuscripts of the Marquess of Salisbury at Hatfield House*, part iv, 1892; part xiii (addenda), 1915; part xiv (addenda), 1923; part xix, 1965; part xxii, 1971.

—— *Report on the Manuscripts of the Duke of Buccleuch and Queensberry at Montagu House*, vol. vi, The Montagu Paers, 2nd series, 1926.

—— *Report on the Manuscripts of Lord De L'Isle and Dudley at Penshurst Place*, 4 vols, 1925–42.

—— *Report on the Manuscripts of Lord Middleton at Wollaton Hall*, 1911.

—— *Report on the Manuscripts of the Marquess of Downshire at Easthampstead Park*, ii, 1926.

—— *Report on Manuscripts in Various Collections*, 8 vols, 1901–14.

—— *Report on the Records of the City of Exeter*, 1916.

Hoare, R. C., *The History of Modern Wiltshire*, 6 vols, 1822–44.

Hodgson, J. C., *Six North Country Diaries*, Surtees Society, vol. cxviii, 1910.

Hoffman, M., *The Warp-weighted Loom*, Universitetsforlaget (Norway), 1964.

Holderness, B. A., 'The agricultural activity of the Massingberds of South Ormsby, Lincolnshire, 1638–circa 1750', *Midland History*, vol. i, 1972.

Holinshed, R., *The last volume of the Chronicles of England*, 1577.

—— *Chronicles*, book (vol.) iii, augmented by J. Hooker alias Vowell, 1587.

Hollaender, A. E. J. and Kellaway, W., *Studies in London History: essays in honour of P. E. Jones*, 1969.

Hollingsworth, A. G. H., *The History of Stowmarket*, Ipswich and London, 1844.

Holloway, B., 'An account of the pits of fuller's earth in Bedfordshire', in *Philosophical Transactions of the Royal Society of London* (q.v.), vol. vi.

Holme, C., *A History of the Midland Counties*, Rugby, 1891.

Holmes, C., *The Eastern Association in the English Civil War*, Cambridge, 1974.

Hooper, L., *Hand-loom Weaving, plain and ornamental*, 1920.

Horman, W., *Vulgaria*, 1519.

Horrocks, J. W., *The Assembly Books of Southampton*, Southampton Record Society, 4 vols, 1917–25.

Horsfall-Turner, E. R., *A Municipal History of Llanidloes*, Llanidloes, 1908.

Horwitz, H., *The Parliamentary Diary of Narcissus Luttrell 1691–1693*, Oxford, 1972.

Hoskins, W. G., *Industry, Trade and People in Exeter 1688–1800*, Manchester, 1935.

—— *The Midland Peasant*, 1957.

—— 'The rise and decline of the serge industry in the south-west of England, with special reference to the eighteenth century', typescript MSc thesis, London University, 1929.

(House of Lords), *House of Lords Manuscripts*, new series, several vols, 1900–, in progress.

Hovenden, R., *The Registers of the Wallon or Strangers' Church in Canterbury*, Publications of the Huguenot Society of London, vol. v, in 3 parts, 1891–8.

Howells, B. E., *A Calendar of Letters relating to North Wales, 1533–circa 1700*, Cardiff, 1967.

Hudson, W., *Leet Jurisdiction in the City of Norwich during the XIIIth and XIVth centuries*, Selden Society, vol. v, 1892.

Hudson, W., and Tingey, J. C., *The Records of the City of Norwich*, 2 vols, Norwich and London, 1906–(1910).

Hughes, E., *North Country Life in the Eighteenth century*, 2 vols, 1952–65.
Hughes, P. L., and Larkin, J. F., *Tudor Royal Proclamations*, 3 vols, New Haven and London, 1964–9.
Humphreys, A. L., *Materials for the History of the Town and Parish of Wellington*, 4 parts, 1908–14.
Humphreys, J., 'Elizabethan Sheldon tapestries', *Archaeologia*, lxxiv (2nd series, xxiv), 1925 (1923–4).
Hurry, J. B., *The Woad Plant and its Dye*, 1930.
Hyde, F. E. and Markham, S. F., *A History of Stony Stratford*, Wolverton and London, 1948.
Irsigler, F., 'Industrial production, international trade, and public finances in Cologne (XIVth and XVth centuries)', *Journal of European Economic History*, vol. vi, 1977.
Irwin, J. and Brett, K. B., *Origins of Chintz*, 1970.
Jack, R. I., 'The cloth industry in medieval Ruthin', *Denbighshire Historical Society's Transactions*, vol. xii, 1963.
—— 'The cloth industry in medieval Wales', *Welsh History Review*, vol. x, 1981.
—— 'Fulling mills in Wales and the March before 1547', *Archaeologia Cambrensis*, vol. cxxx, 1982 (1981).
Jackson, G., *Hull in the Eighteenth Century*, 1972.
Jacquart, J., 'French agriculture in the seventeenth century', in Earle, P., *Essays in European Economic History 1500–1800*, q.v.
James, J., *History of the Worsted Manufacture in England*, 1857.
James, M., *Social Problems and Policy during the Puritan Revolution*, 1930.
Janssen, H. Q., 'De Hervormde Vlugtelingen van Yperen in Engeland', *Bijdragen tot de Oudheidkunde en Geschiedenis*, deel ii, 1857.
Jenkins, J. G., *The Welsh Woollen Industry*, Cardiff, 1969.
—— 'The woollen industry of Montgomeryshire', *Montgomeryshire Collections*, vol. lviii, 1963–4.
—— *The Wool Textile Industry in Great Britain*, London and Boston, 1972.
John, A. H., 'Miles Nightingale, drysalter', *Economic History Review*, 2nd series, vol. xviii, 1965.
Johnson, A. H., *The History of the Worshipful Company of the Drapers of London*, 5 vols, Oxford, 1914–22.
Johnson, R., *The Ancient Customs of the City of Hereford*, 1882.
Jones, D. and King, H. W., 'Edward Grey, the last feudal baron of Powys', *Montgomeryshire Collections*, xviii, 1885.
Jones, D. W., 'The "hallage" receipts of the London cloth markets, 1562–c.1720', *Economic History Review*, 2nd series, vol. xxv, 1972.
Jones, E. M., *Exchequer Proceedings (Equity) concerning Wales: Henry VIII–Elizabeth*, Cardiff, 1939.
Jones, W. H., *Bradford-on-Avon: a history and description*, Bradford-on-Avon, 1907.
Kamen, H., *Spain in the later Seventeenth Century, 1665–1700*, 1980.
Kay, G., *A General View of the Agriculture of North Wales*, Edinburgh, 1794.
Kearney, H. F., *Strafford in Ireland 1633–1641*, Manchester, 1959.
Keen, R., 'Messrs Best, Brewers of Chatham' in Roake, M. and Whyman, J., *Essays in Kentish History*, 1973.
Kellenbenz, H., 'Rural industries in the West from the end of the Middle Ages to the eighteenth century' in Earle, P., *Essays in European Economic History 1500–1800*, q.v.
Kelsall, R. K., *Wage Regulation under the Statute of Artificers*, 1938, reprinted in W. E. Minchinton, *Wage Regulation in Pre-Industrial England*, Newton Abbot, no date.
Kemp, T., *The Black Book of Warwick*, Warwick, no date.
—— *The Book of John Fisher*, Warwick, no date.
Kendrick A. F., *English Decorative Fabrics of the Sixteenth to Eighteenth Centuries*, Benfleet, Essex, 1934.
Kent, H. S. K., *War and Trade in Northern Seas: Anglo-Scandinavian economic relations in the mid-eighteenth century*, Cambridge, 1973.

Kerling, N. J. M., *Commercial Relations of Holland and Zealand with England from the late Thirteenth Century to the close of the Middle Ages*, Leiden, 1954.

Kerridge, E., *The Agricultural Revolution*, 1967.

—— 'Social and economic history of Leicester 1500–1660', in *Victoria History of Leicestershire*, vol. iv, 1958.

Ketton-Cremer, R. W., *Norfolk in the Civil War*, 1969.

Keutgen, F., *Urkunden zur Städtischen Verfassungsgeschichte*, Berlin, 1901.

King, E., *Old Times Re-visited in the Borough and Parish of Lymington, Hampshire*, 1900.

Kingsford, C. L., *The Stonor Letters and Papers 1290–1483*, Royal Historical Society, Camden 3rd series, vols. xxix, xxx, 1919.

Kirby, J., *The Suffolk Traveller*, 1764.

Kirk, R. E. G. and E. F., *Returns of Aliens dwelling in the City and Suburbs of London from the reign of Henry VIII to that of James I*, Publications of the Huguenot Society of London, x, in 4 parts, 1900–8.

Klein, J., *The Mesta: a study in Spanish economic history 1273–1836*, Cambridge, Mass., 1920.

Knowler, W., *The Earl of Strafforde's Letters and Dispatches*, 2 vols, 1739.

Koenigsberger, H., 'English merchants in Naples and Sicily in the seventeenth century', *English Historical Review*, vol. lxii, 1947.

Kramer, S., *The English Craft Gilds: studies in their progress and decline*, New York, 1927.

Kussmaul, A., *Servants in Husbandry in Early Modern England*, Cambridge, 1981.

Lamb, D. F., 'The seaborne trade of Southampton in the first half of the seventeenth century', typescript MPhil thesis, Southampton University, 2 vols, 1971.

Lambert, J. M., *Two Thousand Years of Gild Life*, Hull and London, 1891.

Lane F. C., *Andrea Barbarigo, merchant of Venice 1418–1449*, Baltimore, 1944.

—— *Venice and History*, Baltimore, 1966.

Lapeyre, H., 'Les exportations de la laine de Castile sous la règne de Philippe II' in Spallanzani, *La Lana come Materia Prima*, q.v.

Lappenberg, J. M., *Urkundliche Geschichte des Hansischen Stahlhofes zu London*, 2 parts, Hamburg, 1851.

Larkin, J. F., and Hughes, P. L., *Stuart Royal Proclamations*, 2 vols, Oxford, 1973-83.

Lart, C. E., *Registers of the French Churches of Bristol, Stonehouse and Plymouth*, Publications of the Huguenot Society of London, vol. xx, 1912.

Latimer, J., *The Annals of Bristol in the Seventeenth Century*, Bristol, 1900.

—— *The Annals of Bristol in the Eighteenth Century*, Bristol, 1893.

Laurent, H., *Un Grand Commerce d'Exportation au Moyen Âge: les draperies des Pays-Bas en France et dans les Pays méditerranéens*, Paris, 1935.

Leadam, I. S., *Select Cases in the Court of Requests A.D. 1497–1569*, Selden Society, xii, 1898.

Lebrun, P., *L'Industrie de la Laine à Verviers pendant le XVIIIe et le Début du XIXe siècle*, Liège, 1948.

Leconfield, Lord, *Petworth Manor in the Seventeenth Century*, 1954.

Leese, F. E., 'A calendar and analysis, with introduction, of two Elizabethan port books', typescript BLitt thesis, Oxford University, no date.

—— 'New draperies at Coventry', typescript in Coventry City Library.

Lefebvre, G., *Les Paysans du Nord pendant la Révolution Française*, Bari, 1959.

Leighton, S., 'The records of the corporation of Oswestry', *Transactions of the Shropshire Archaeological Society*, vol. iii, 1880.

Leighton-Boyce, J. A. S. L., *Smiths the Bankers 1658–1958*, 1958.

Leland, J., *The Itinerary*, ed. L. T. Smith, 5 vols, 1906–10.

Lemon, H., 'The evolution of combing' in Jenkins, J. G., *The Wool Textile Industry in Great Britain*, q.v.

Leonard, E. M., *The Early History of English Poor Relief*, Cambridge, 1900.

Leuridan, T., *Histoire de la Fabrique de Roubaix*, Roubaix, Paris and Lille, 1864 (4e partie de l'*Histoire de Roubaix*, 1863).

—— 'Histoire de Linselles', *Bulletin de la Commission Historique du Département du Nord*, tome xvi, 1883.

—— 'Précis de l'histoire de Lannoy', *Mémoires de la Société Impériale des Sciences, de l'Agriculture et des Arts de Lille*, 3e série, tome iv, 1868.

Lewis, E. A., *The Welsh Port Books (1550–1603)*, Cymmrodorion Record Series, Hon. Cymmrodorion Society, vol. xii, 1927.

Lewis, F., *English Chintz from the earliest times to the present day*, Benfleet, Essex, 1935.

—— *James Leman (working 1706–1718) Spitalfields Designer*, Leigh-on-Sea, 1954.

Lewis, W., *Commercium Philosophico-Technicum; or the Philosophical Commerce of Arts*, 1763.

Lindeboom, J., *Austin Friars: History of the Dutch Reformed Church in London 1550–1950*, The Hague, 1950.

Lindley, E. S., *Wotton under Edge*, 1962.

Lisle, E., *Observations in Husbandry*, 1757.

Long, C. E., *Diary of the Marches of the Royal Army during the Great Civil War kept by Richard Symonds*, Camden Society, vol. lxxiv, 1859.

Longfield, A. K., *Anglo-Irish Trade in the Sixteenth Century*, 1929.

Lowe, N., *The Lancashire Textile Industry in the Sixteenth Century*, Chetham Society, 3rd series, vol. xx, 1972.

Luccock, J., *An Essay on Wool*, 1809.

Lynes, A., *History of Coventry Textiles*, Coventry, 1952.

Lyte, H. C. M., *A History of Dunster and of the families of Mohun and Luttrell*, part i, 1909.

Macek, J., 'La posizione sociale dei tessitori nelle Città Cèche et Morave nei secoli XIV–XVI', in Spallanzani, M., *Produzione, Commercio e Consumo dei Panni di Lana nei secoli XII–XVIII*, q.v.

Machin, R., *Probate Inventories and Manorial Excerpts of Chetnole, Leigh and Yetminster*, Bristol, 1976.

Maddalena, A. de, 'L'industria tessile a Mantova nel '500 e all' inizio del '600', in *Studi in Onore di Amintore Fanfani*, vol. iv, q.v.

Malynes, G. de, *A Treatise of the Canker of Englands Common Wealth*, 1601.

Mann, J. de L., *The Cloth Industry in the West of England from 1640 to 1880*, Oxford, 1971.

—— 'Clothiers and weavers in Wiltshire during the eighteenth century', in Pressnell, L. S., *Studies in the Industrial Revolution*, q.v.

—— *Documents Illustrating the Wiltshire Textile Trades in the Eighteenth Century*, Wiltshire Record Society, xix, 1963.

—— 'Textile industries since 1550', in *Victoria History of Wiltshire*, vol. iv, 1959.

—— 'A Wiltshire family of clothiers: George and Hester Wansey, 1683–1714', *Economic History Review*, 2nd series, vol. ix, 1956.

Markham, G., *The English House-Wife*, 1631.

Marshall, J. D., 'Kendal in the late seventeenth and eighteenth centuries', *Transactions of the Cumberland and Westmorland Antiquarian and Archaeological Society*, new series, vol. lxxv, 1975.

Marshall, W., *A Review (and Complete Abstract) of the Reports to the Board of Agriculture from the Midland Department of England*, 1815.

—— *The Rural Economy of the West of England*, 2 vols, 1796.

—— *The Rural Economy of Yorkshire*, 2 vols, 1788.

Marshall, W., Redhead and Laing, *Observations on the Different Breeds of Sheep*, Edinburgh, 1792.

Martin, B., *The Natural History of England*, 2 vols, 1759–63.

Mascall, L., *Cattell*, 1587.

Mason, I. L., *Sheep Breeds in the Mediterranean*, sine loco, 1967.

Mathieu, G., 'Notes sur l'industrie en Bas-Limousin dans la seconde moité du XVIIIe siècle' in Hayem, *Mémoires et Documents*, 1e série, q.v.

Matthews, J. H., *Cardiff Records*, 6 vols, Cardiff, 1895–1911.

Maugis, E., 'La saieterie à Amiens, 1480–1587', *Vierteljahrschrift für Sozial-und-Wirtschaftsgeschichte*, Band v, 1907.

May, G., *The History of Evesham, its Benedictine monastery, conventual church, existing edifices, municipal institutions, parliamentary occurrences, civil and military events*, Evesham and London, 1834.

May, J., *A Declaration of the Estate of Clothing now used within this Realme of England*, 1613.

Mayo, C. H., *The Municipal Records of the Borough of Dorchester, Dorset*, Exeter, 1908.

Mazzaoui, M. F., *The Italian Cotton Industry in the later Middle Ages 1100–1600*, Cambridge, 1981.

McClenaghan, B., *The Springs of Lavenham and the Suffolk Cloth Trade in the XV and XVI centuries*, Ipswich, 1924.

McGrath, P., *Merchants and Merchandise in Seventeenth Century Bristol*, Bristol Record Society, vol. xix, 1955.

—— *Records relating to the Society of Merchant Venturers of the City of Bristol in the Seventeenth Century*, Bristol Record Society, vol. xvii, 1952.

McMurray, W., *The Records of Two City Parishes, SS. Anne and Agnes, Aldersgate, and St John Zachary, London, from the twelfth century*, 1925.

Melling, E., *Kentish Sources iii: aspects of agriculture and industry*, Maidstone, 1961.

—— *Kentish Sources vi: crime and punishment*, Maidstone, 1969.

Mendenhall, T. C., *The Shrewsbury Drapers and the Welsh Wool Trade in the XVI and XVII centuries*, 1953.

Merson, A. L., *The Third Book of Remembrance of Southampton 1514–1602*, vol. iii, Southampton, 1965.

Millard, A. M., 'The import trade of London 1600–1640', typescript PhD thesis, London University, 3 vols, 1956.

Miller, G. C., *Blackburn: the evolution of a cotton town*, Blackburn, 1951.

Millican, P., *A History of Horstead and Stanninghall*, Norwich, 1937.

—— *The Register of the Freemen of Norwich 1548–1713*, Norwich, 1934.

Minet, W. and S., *Livre des Conversions et des Reconnoissances faites à l'Eglise Francoise de la Savoye 1684–1702*, Publications of the Huguenot Society of London, vol. xxii, 1914.

—— *Livre des Tesmoignages de l'Eglise de Threadneedle Street 1669–1789*, Publications of the Huguenot Society of London, vol. xxi, 1909.

—— *Registers of the Church of Le Carré and Berwick Street 1690–1788*, Publications of the Huguenot Society of London, vol. xxv, 1921.

—— *Registres des Eglises de la Savoye, de Spring Gardens et des Grecs 1684–1900*, Publications of the Huguenot Society of London, vol. xxvi, 1922.

Minet, W. and Waller, W. C., *Registers of the Church known as La Patente in Spittlefields from 1689 to 1785*, Publications of the Huguenot Society of London, vol. xi, 1898.

Misselden, E., *Free Trade or the Meanes to make Trade Florish*, 1622.

Moens, W. J. C., *Register of Baptisms in the Dutch Church at Colchester from 1645 to 1728*, Publications of the Huguenot Society of London, vol. xii, 1905.

—— *The Registers of the French Church, Threadneedle Street, London,*, 2 vols, Publications of the Huguenot Society of London, vols ix, xiii, 1896–9.

—— *The Walloons and their Church at Norwich: their history and registers 1565–1832*, 2 parts, Publications of the Huguenot Society of London, vol. i, 1887–8.

Moir, E., 'Benedict Webb, clothier', *Economic History Review*, 2nd series, vol. x, 1957.

Mollow, C., *Das Handlungsbuch von Hermann und Johan Wittenborg*, Leipzig, 1901.

Monceau, Duhamel du, *Art de la Draperie, principalement ce qui regarde les draps fins*, sine loco, 1765.

—— *Art de Friser ou Ratiner les Étoffes de Laine*, sine loco, 1766.

Money, W., 'The Guild or Fellowship of the Clothworkers of Newbury', *Journal of the British Archaeological Association*, new series, vol. ii, 1896.

—— *The History of the Ancient Town and Borough of Newbury in the County of Berkshire*, Oxford and London, 1887.

Montgomery, F. M., 'John Holker's mid-eighteenth century *Livre d'Échantillons*' in Gervers, V., *Studies in Textile History*, q.v.

Moore, J. S., *The Goods and Chattels of our Forefathers: Frampton Cotterell and district probate inventories 1539–1804*, London and Chichester, 1976.

Morant, P., *The History and Antiquities of Colchester*, 1748.

Morton, J., *The Natural History of Northamptonshire*, 1712.

Mun, T., *A Discourse of Trade from England unto the East Indies*, 1621.

—— *England's Treasure by Foreign Trade*, Oxford, 1928.

Munby, L. M., *East Anglian Studies*, Cambridge, 1968.

(Munn, J.), *Observations on British Wool and the Manufacturing of it in this Kingdom*, by a Manufacturer of Northamptonshire, 1739.

Munro, J. H. A., *Wool, Cloth, and Gold: the struggle for bullion in Anglo-Burgundian trade 1340–1478*, Brussels and Toronto, 1972.

—— 'Wool-price schedules and the qualities of English wools in the later Middle Ages c. 1270–1499', *Textile History*, vol. ix, 1978.

Nahlik, A., 'The wool of the Middle Ages', in Spallanzani, M., *La Lana come Materia Prima*, q.v.

Nef, J. U., *The Conquest of the Material World*, Chicago and London, 1964.

—— *The Rise of the British Coal Industry*, 2 vols, 1932.

Nevill, E., 'Marriage licences of Salisbury', *Genealogist*, new series, vols xxvii–xxxi, 1911–15, vol. xxxiii, 1917, and (with R. Boucher) vol. xxxvii, 1921.

Newbigging, T., *History of the Forest of Rossendale*, 1868.

Nichols, J., *The Progresses and Public Processions of Queen Elizabeth*, 2 vols, 1788.

Nichols, J. G., 'Inventories of the wardrobes, plate, chapel stuff etc. of Henry Fitzroy, Duke of Richmond, and of the wardrobe stuff at Baynard's Castle of Katherine, Princess Dowager', in *Camden Miscellany*, vol. iii, Camden Society, vol. lxi, 1855.

—— *The Unton Inventories relating to Wadley and Faringdon, County Berkshire*, Berkshire Ashmolean Society, 1841.

Nicolas, N. H., *Privy Purse Expenses of Elizabeth of York: and Wardrobe Accounts of Edward the Fourth*, 1830.

Nirrnheim, H., *Das Handlungsbuch Vickos von Geldersen*, Hamburg and Leipzig, 1895.

Norden, J., *Speculi Britanniae Pars: An Historical and Chorographical Description of the County of Essex*, ed. H. Ellis, Camden Society, 1840.

Northcote, A. F., *Notes on the History of Monks' Eleigh*, Ipswich, 1930.

Notestein, W., *The Journal of Sir Simonds D'Ewes from the beginning of the Long Parliament to the opening of the trial of the Earl of Strafford*, New Haven, 1923.

Notestein, W., Relf, F. H. and Simpson, H., *Commons Debates 1621*, 7 vols, New Haven, 1935.

Noy, W., *Reports and Cases taken in the time of Queen Elizabeth, King James and King Charles*, 1669.

Nuttall, G. F., *Letters of John Pinney 1679–1699*, 1939.

O'Brien, G., 'The Irish Staple Organisation in the reign of James I', *Economic History*, vol. i, 1926–9 (supplement to *Economic Journal*).

Oelsner, G. H., *Die Deutsche Webschule: mechanisch Technologie der Weberei*, Altona, 1902.

Ogilby, J., *Britannia*, 1675.

Opdedrinck, J., *Poperinghe en Omstreken tijdens de Godsdienstberoerten der XVI Eeuw of Den Geuzentijd*, Bruges, 1898.

Ordish, T. F., 'Early English inventions', *The Antiquary*, vol. xii, 1885.

Origo, I., *The Merchant of Prato: Francesco di Marco Datini*, 1957.

(Overall, W. H.), *Analytical Index to the Series of Records known as the Remembrancia preserved among the Archives of the City of London A.D. 1579–1664*, 1878.

Overend, G. H., 'The strangers at Dover', *Proceedings of the Huguenot Society of London*, vol. iii, 1892 (1888–91).

Owen, G., *The Description of Penbrokshire*, ed. H. Owen, Cymmrodorion Record Series, Hon. Cymmrodorion Society, 2 vols in 4 parts, 1892–1936.

Page, W., *Letters of Denization and Acts of Naturalization for Aliens in England 1509–1603*, Publications of the Huguenot Society of London, vol. viii, 1893.

Palliser, B., *History of Lace*, edited by M. Jourdain and A. Dryden, 1902.

Palliser, D. M., *Tudor York*, Oxford, 1979.

Palmer, C. J., *The History of Great Yarmouth*, Great Yarmouth, 1856.

Papillon, A. F. W., *Memoirs of Thomas Papillon of London, merchant (1623–1702)*, Reading, 1887.

Parker, H., *Of a Free Trade*, 1648.

Pasold, E. W., 'In search of William Lee', *Textile History*, vol. vi, 1975.

Patten, J. H. C., 'The urban structure of East Anglia in the sixteenth and seventeenth centuries', typescript PhD thesis, Cambridge University, 1972.

Patterson, A. J., *A History of Southampton 1700–1914*, vol. i, Southampton, 1966.

Pegolotti, F. B., *La Pratica della Mercatura*, ed. A. Evans, Cambridge, Mass., 1936.

Pepys, S., *The Diary of Samuel Pepys*, ed. R. Latham and W. Matthews, 9 vols, 1970–6.

Perry, R., 'The Gloucestershire woollen industry 1100–1690', *Transactions of the Bristol and Gloucestershire Archaeological Society*, vol. lxvi (1945) 1947.

Pettit, P. A. J., *The Royal Forests of Northamptonshire: a study in their economy 1558–1714*, Northamptonshire Record Society, vol. xxiii, 1968.

Petty, W., 'An apparatus to the history of the common practices of dying', in Sprat, T., *The History of the Royal Society of London*, q.v.

—— *Economic Writings*, ed. C. H. Hull, 2 vols, Cambridge, 1899.

Philanglus (W. Petyt?), *Britannia Languens or a discourse of trade*, 1680.

Phillimore, W. P. W. and Fry, G. S., *Abstracts of Gloucestershire Inquisitiones Post Morten in the reign of King Charles I*, Index Library, 3 parts (vols), British Record Society, 1893–9.

Phillips, D. R., *The History of the Vale of Neath*, Swansea, 1925.

Phythian-Adams, C., *Desolation of a City: Coventry and the urban crisis of the late middle ages*, Cambridge, 1979.

Piccope, G. P., *Lancashire and Cheshire Wills and Inventories from the Ecclesiastical Court, Chester*, 3 portions, Chetham Society, vols xxxiii, li, liv, 1857–61.

Pilgrim, J. E., 'The cloth industry in Essex and Suffolk 1558–1640', typescript MA thesis, London University, 1939.

—— 'The rise of the "new draperies" in Essex', *University of Birmingham Historical Journal*, vii, 1959–60.

Playne, A., *A History of the Parishes of Minchinhampton and Avening*, Gloucester, 1915.

Plot, R., *The Natural History of Oxfordshire*, Oxford, 1677.

—— *The Natural History of Staffordshire*, Oxford, 1686.

Plummer, A., *The London Weavers' Company 1600–1970*, 1972.

—— *The Witney Blanket Industry: records of the Witney blanket weavers*, 1934.

Plummer, A. and Early, R. E., *The Blanket Makers 1669–1969: a history of Charles Early and Marriot (Witney) Ltd.*, 1969.

Pococke, R., *The Travels through England of Dr Richard Pococke, successively bishop of Meath and Ossory, during 1750, 1751, and later years*, 2 vols, Camden Society, new series, vols xlii and xliv, 1888–9.

Poingdestre, J., *Caesarea: or a discourse of the Isle of Jersey*, ed. W. Nicolle, La Société Jersiaise publication no. 10, 1889.

Ponting, K. G., *A History of the West of England Cloth Industry*, 1957.

—— 'In search of William Lee', *Textile History*, vol. ix, 1978.

Poole, B., *Coventry: its history and antiquities*, London and Coventry, 1870.

Postan, M .M., 'The economic and political relations of England and the Hanse from 1400 to 1475', in Power, E. and Postan, M. M., *Studies in English Trade in the Fifteenth Century*, 1933.

Posthumus, N. W., *Bronnen tot de Geschiedenis van de Leidsche Textielnijverheid*, 6 vols, The Hague, 1910–22.

—— *De Geschiedenis van de Leidsche Lakenindustrie*, 3 vols, The Hague, 1908–39.

—— *De Oosterse Handel te Amsterdam*, Leiden, 1953.

Posthumus, N. W. and De Nie, W. L. J., 'Een Handschrift over de Textielververij in de Republiek uit de eerste helft der zeventiende eeuw', *Economisch-Historische Jaarboek*, deel xx, 1936.

Postlethwayt, M., *The Universal Dictionary of Trade and Commerce, translated from the French of M. Savary, with large additions and improvements*, 2 vols, 1757.

Pound, J. F., 'Government and society in Tudor and Stuart Norwich 1525–1675', typescript PhD thesis, Leicester University, 1974.

—— *The Norwich Census of the Poor 1570*, Norfolk Record Society, vol. xl, 1971.

—— 'The social and trade structure of Norwich 1525–1575', *Past and Present*, no. xxxiv, 1966.

Powell, A. H., *The Ancient Borough of Bridgwater*, Bridgwater, 1907.

Powell, S. C., *Puritan Village*, Middletown, Conn., 1963.

Power, E., *The Paycockes of Coggeshall*, 1920.

Power, E. and Postan, M. M., *Studies in English Trade in the Fifteenth Century*, 1933.

Powicke, F. J., *A Life of the Reverend Richard Baxter 1615–1691*, 1924.

Pressnell, L. S., *Studies in the Industrial Revolution presented to T. S. Ashton*, 1960.

Prest, J., *The Industrial Revolution in Coventry*, 1960.

Preston, W. E., *Wills proved in the Court of the Manor of Crosley, Bingley, Cottingley and Pudsey, in County York, with inventories and abstracts of bonds*, Bradford Historical and Antiquarian Society, Local Record Series, vol. i, 1929 (1914–29).

Prestwich, M., *Cranfield: politics and profits under the early Stuarts*, Oxford, 1966.

Priaulx, T. F., and Sausmarez, R. de, 'Guernsey stocking export trade in the seventeenth century', *Transactions of La Société Guernesiaise*, vol. xvii, 1960–5

Priestley, M., 'Anglo-French trade and the "unfavourable balance" controversy, 1660–1685', *Economic History Review*, 2nd series, vol. iv, 1951.

Prigg, H., *Icklingham Papers*, Woodbridge, 1901.

Pullan, B., *Crisis and Change in the Venetian Economy in the Sixteenth and Seventeenth Centuries*, 1968.

Purchas, S., *Microcosmus, or the Historie of Man (Purchas his Pilgrim)*, 1619.

Racine, P., 'À propos d'une matière première de l'industrie placentine: la *Carzatura*', in Spallanzani, M., *La Lana come Materia Prima*, q.v.

Raine, J., *Wills and Inventories from the Register of the Archdeacon of Richmond*, Surtees Society, vol. xxvi, 1853.

Raines, F. R. and Sutton, C. W., *Life of Humphrey Chetham*, Chetham Society, new series, vols. xlix, l, 1903.

Raleigh, W., *Observations touching Trade and Commerce with the Hollander and other Nations, as it was presented to King James*, 1653.

Ramsay, G. D., *The City of London in International Politics at the accession of Elizabeth Tudor*, Manchester, 1975.

—— 'The distribution of the cloth industry in 1561–2', *English Historical Review*, vol. lvii, 1942.

—— *English Oversea Trade during the Centuries of Emergence*, 1957.

—— *John Isham, Mercer and Merchant Adventurer*, Northamptonshire Record Society, vol. xxi, 1962.

—— *The Politics of a Tudor Merchant Adventurer: a letter to the Earls of East Friesland*, Manchester, 1979.

—— 'Recruitment and fortunes of some London freemen in the mid-sixteenth century', *Economic History Review*, 2nd series, vol. xxi, 1978.

—— 'The report of the Royal Commission on the clothing industry', *English Historical Review*, vol. lvii, 1942.

—— *The Wiltshire Woollen Industry in the Sixteenth and Seventeenth Centuries*, 1965.

Randall, H. A., 'The Kettering worsted industry of the eighteenth century', *Northamptonshire Past and Present*, vol. iv, 1970–1.

Ratcliffe, S. C. and Johnson, H. C., *Warwick County Records*: vol. v, *Sessions Order Book 1665–1674*; vol. vi, *Quarter Sessions Indictment Book 1631–1674*; vol. vii, *Quarter Sessions Records 1674–1682*; vol. viii, *Quarter Sessions Records 1682–1690* – Warwick, 1939, 1941, 1946, 1953.

Rath, T., 'The Tewkesbury hosiery industry', *Textile History*, vol. vii, 1976.

Rea, W. F., 'The rental and accounts of Sir Richard Shireburn, 1571–77', *Transactions of the Historic Society of Lancashire and Cheshire*, vol. cx, 1959.

Reath, N. C. and Sachs, E. B., *Persian Textiles and their Technique from the Sixteenth to the Eighteenth Centuries*, New Haven, 1937.

Redstone, V. B., 'The Dutch and Huguenot settlements at Ipswich', *Proceedings of the Huguenot Society of London*, vol. xii, 1924 (1917–23).

—— 'England during the Wars of the Roses', *Transactions of the Royal Historical Society*, new series, vol. xvi, 1902.

Reed, M., 'Ipswich in the seventeenth century', typescript PhD thesis, Leicester University, 1973.

Rees, W., *A Survey of the Duchy of Lancaster Lordships in Wales, 1609–13*, Cardiff, 1953.

Rendall, G. H., *Dedham in History*, Colchester, 1937.

Reyce, R., *The Breviary of Suffolk: Suffolk in the XVIIth century (1618)*, edited by F. Hervey, 1902.

Rich, E. E., *The Ordinance Book of the Merchants of the Staple*, Cambridge, 1937.

Richards, R. T. D., 'The development of the modern wool-carding machine' in Jenkins, J. G., *The Wool Textile Industry in Great Britain*, q.v.

Rijpma, E., *De Ontwikkelingsgang van Kampen tot omstreeks 1600*, Groningen and The Hague, 1924.

Risdon, T., *The Chorographical Description or Survey of the County of Devon*, 1723.

Roake, M. and Whyman, J., *Essays in Kentish History*, 1973.

Roberts, G., *The History and Antiquities of the Borough of Lyme Regis and Charmouth*, 1834.

Roberts, L., *The Marchants Mapp of Commerce*, 1638.

—— *The Treasure of Traffike*, 1641.

Rogers, A., 'Rural industries and social structure: the framework knitting industry in South Nottinghamshire 1670–1840', *Textile History*, vol. xii, 1981.

Roger, L., 'The Flemish and Dutch community in Colchester in the sixteenth and seventeenth centuries', typescript MA thesis, London University, 1963.

Rothstein, N. K. A., 'The silk industry in London 1702–1766', typescript MA thesis, London University, 1961.

Rowlands, R., *The Post for Divers Partes of the World*, 1576.

Ruinen, J., *De Oudste Handelsbetrekkingen van Holland en Zeeland met Engeland tot in het laatste Kwartaal der XIVe Eeuw*, Amsterdam, 1919.

Russell, J. M., *The History of Maidstone*, 1881.

Rutherford, J., *The Miscellaneous Papers of Captain Thomas Stockwell 1590–1611*, Southampton Record Society, 2 vols, 1932–3.

Rutt, J. T., *Diary of Thomas Burton, Esquire*, 4 vols, 1828.

Ruytinck, S., Calandrinus, C., and Van Culenbergh, A., *Gheschiedenissen ende Handelingen die voornemelick aengan de Nederduytsche Natie ende Gemeynten wonende in Engelant ende mit bysonder tot Londen*, ed. J. J. Van Toorenbergen, Wereker der Marnix-Vereeniging, serie iii, deel i, Utrecht, 1873.

Ryder, M. L. and Stephenson, S. K., *Wool Growth*, London and New York, 1968.

Rymer, T., *Foedera*, 20 vols, 1735.

S., W., *The Golden Fleece*, 1656.

Sabbe, E., *Anvers: métropole de l'occident (1492–1566)*, Brussels, 1952.
—— *De Belgische Vlasnijverheid*, vol. i, Bruges, 1943.
Salzman, L. F., *English Industries of the Middle Ages*, Oxford, 1923.
Saunders, H. W., *The Official Papers of Sir Nathaniel Bacon of Stiffkey, Norfolk, as Justice of the Peace 1580–1620*, Royal Historical Society, Camden 3rd series, vol. xxvi, 1915.
Schanz, G., *Englische Handelspolitik gegen Ende des Mittelalters mit besonderer Berücksichtigung des Zeitalters der beiden ersten Tudors Heinrich VII und Heinrich VIII*, 2 vols, Leipzig, 1881.
Schmoller, G., *Die Strassburger Tucher-und Weberzunft: Urkunden und Darstellung*, Strasbourg, 1879.
Schumpeter, E. B., *English Overseas Trade Statistics 1697–1808*, Oxford, 1960.
Schumpeter, J. A., *Business Cycles: a theoretical, historical and statistical analysis of the capitalist process*, 2 vols, New York and London, 1939.
Scott, W. R., *The Constitution and Finance of English, Scottish and Irish Joint-Stock Companies to 1720*, 3 vols. Cambridge, 1910–12.
—— *The Records of a Scottish Cloth Manufactory at New Mills, Haddingtonshire 1681–1703*, Scottish Record Society, vol. xlvi, 1905.
Scoville, W. C., *The Persecution of Huguenots and French Economic Development 1680–1720*, Berkeley and Los Angeles, 1960.
Sella, D., *Commerci e Industrie a Venezia nel secolo XVII*, Venice and Rome, 1961.
—— 'The rise and fall of the Venetian woollen industry' in Pullan, B., *Crisis and Change in the Venetian Economy*, q.v.
Sellers, M., *The Acts and Ordinances of the Eastland Company*, Royal Historical Society, Camden 3rd series, vol. xi, 1906.
Serjeant, W. R. and R. K., *Index of the Probate Records of the Court of the Archdeacon of Suffolk 1444–1700*, Index Library, British Record Society, vols xc, xci, 1979–80.
Shaw, W. A., *Letters of Denization and Acts of Naturalization for Aliens in England and Ireland 1603–1700*, Publications of the Huguenot Society of London, vol. xviii, 1911.
—— *Letters of Denization and Acts of Naturalization for Aliens in England and Ireland 1701–1800*, Publications of the Huguenot Society of London, vol. xxvii, 1923.
Shepherd, J. F. and Walton, G. M., *Shipping, Maritime Trade and the Economic Development of Colonial North America*, Cambridge, 1972.
Singer, C., *The Earliest Chemical Industry: an essay in the historical relations of economics and technology illustrated from the Alum Trade*, 1948.
Sion, J., *Les Paysans de la Normandie Orientale*, Paris, 1909.
Skeel, C. A. J., 'The Welsh woollen industry in the eighteenth and seventeenth centuries', *Archaeologia Cambrensis*, vol. lxxvii (7th series, vol. ii). 1922.
—— 'The Welsh woollen industry in the eighteenth and nineteenth centuries', *Archaeologia Cambrensis*, vol. lxxix (7th series, vol. iv) 1924.
Skipp, V., *Crisis and Development: an ecological case study of the Forest of Arden 1570–1674*, Cambridge, 1978.
Slack, P., *Poverty in Early Stuart Salisbury*, Wiltshire Record Society, vol. xxxi, 1975.
Slack, W. J., *The Lordship Oswestry*, Shrewsbury, 1951.
Slee, A. H., 'Some dead industries of North Devon', *Report and Transactions of the Devonshire Association*, vol. lxx, 1938.
Smit, H. J., *Bronnen tot de Geschiedenis van den Handel met Engeland, Schotland en Ierland*, 2 vols in 4 parts, The Hague, 1928–50.
Smith, K. G., *Warwickshire Apprentices and their Masters 1710–1760*, Dugdale Society, vol. xxix, 1975.
Smith, J., *Chronicon Rusticum-Commerciale or Memoirs of Wool etc.*, 2 vols, 1747.
Smith, T., *English Gilds*, Early English Text Society, vol. xl, 1870.
Smith, W., *The Particular Description of England, 1588*, ed. H. B. Wheatley and E. W. Ashbee, 1879.
Smith, W. and Webb, W., *The Vale Royall of England*, 1656.
Smith, W. J., *Herbert Correspondence: the sixteenth and seventeenth century letters of the Herberts of*

*Chirbury, Powis Castle, and Dolgenog, formerly at Powis Castle in Montgomeryshire*, Cardiff and Dublin, 1963.

Smyth, J., *The Description of the Hundred of Berkeley* (Berkeley Manuscripts vol. iii), ed. J. Maclean, Gloucester, 1885.

—— *The Names and Surnames of all the Able and Sufficient Men in the Body fit for His Majesty's Service in the Wars, within the County of Gloucester . . . in the month of August 1608*, 1902.

Somner, W., *The Antiquities of Canterbury*, 1640.

—— *The Antiquities of Canterbury*, revised and enlarged by N. Battely, 1703.

Sonenscher, M., 'The hosiery industry of Nîmes and the Lower Languedoc in the eighteenth century', *Textile History*, vol. x, 1979.

Spallanzani, M., *La Lana come Materia Prima: i fenomeni della sua produzione e circolazione nei secoli XIII–XVII*, Florence, 1974.

—— *Produzione, Commercio e Consumo dei Panni di Lana nei secoli XII–XVIII*, Florence, 1976.

Spenceley, G. F. R., 'The origins of the English pillow lace industry', *Agricultural History Review*, vol. xxi, 1973.

Sprandel, R., 'Zur Geschichte der Wollproduktion in Nordwestdeutschland', in Spallanzani, M., *La Lana come Materia Prima*, q.v.

Sprat, T., *The History of the Royal Society of London for the improving of natural knowledge*, 1667.

Staley, E., *The Guilds of Florence*, 1906.

Steele, R., *A Bibliography of the Royal Proclamations of the Tudor and Stuart Sovereigns*, 2 vols, Oxford, 1910.

Steer, F. W., *Farm and Cottage Inventories of Mid-Essex, 1635–1739*, Chelmsford, 1950.

Stephens, W. B., 'The foreign trade of Plymouth and the Cornish ports in the early seventeenth century', *Report and Transactions of the Devonshire Association*, vol. ci, 1969.

—— *The History of Congleton*, Manchester, 1970.

—— 'The overseas trade of Chester in the early seventeenth century', *Transactions of the Historic Society of Lancashire and Cheshire*, vol. cxx, 1969.

—— *Seventeenth Century Exeter: a study of industrial and commercial development, 1625–1688*, Exeter, 1958.

—— 'The trade of the port of Barnstaple at the end of the Civil War', *Devon and Cornwall Notes and Queries*, vol. xxxi, 1970.

Stewart, H., *History of the Worshipful Company of Gold and Silver Wyre Drawers and of the origin and development of the industry which the company represents*, 1891.

Stocks, H., *Records of the Borough of Leicester 1603–1688*, Cambridge, 1923.

Stow, J., *The Annales or Generall Chronicle of England . . .*, continued and augmented by Edmond Howes, 1615.

Strieder, J., *Aus Antwerpener Notariatsarchiven*, Stuttgart, Berlin and Leipzig, 1930.

Strutt, J., *A Complete View of the Dress and Habits of the People of England*, ed. J. R. Planché, 2 vols, 1842.

Stubbes, P., *The Anatomie of Abuses*, 1583.

Stukeley, W., *Itinerarium Curiosum, or an Account of the Antiquities and Remarkable Curiosities in Nature or Art observed in Travels through Great Britain*, 2 vols, 1776.

Suppa, P. I. G., *Glossario Italiano Tessile*, Biella, no date.

Sutherland, L. S., *A London Merchant 1695–1774*, Oxford, 1933.

Symonds, W., *A New-Years-Gift to the Parliament or England's Golden Fleece preserv'd*, 1702.

Tann, J., 'Aspects of the development of the Gloucestershire woollen industry', typescript PhD thesis, Leicester University, 1964.

Tattersall, C. E. C., *A History of British Carpets*, Benfleet, Essex, 1934.

Tawney, R. H. and Power, E., *Tudor Economic Documents*, 3 vols, 1935–7.

Taylor, A. M., *Gilletts: bankers at Banbury and Oxford*, Oxford, 1964.

Taylor, J., *The Praise of Hemp-seed*, 1620.

Te Lintum, C., *De Merchant Adventurers in de Nederlanden*, The Hague, 1905.

Temple, R. C., *The Travels of Peter Mundy in Europe and Asia 1608–1667*, vol. iv: *Travels in Europe 1639–1647*, Hakluyt Society, series ii, vol. lv, 1925.

Thierry, A., *Recueil de Monuments Inédits de l'Histoire du Tiers État*, 1e série, Région du Nord, tome iv, Paris, 1870.

Thijs, A. K. L., *De Zijdenijverheid te Antwerpen in de Zeventiende Eeuw*, sine loco, 1969.

Thirsk, J., *English Peasant Farming: the agrarian history of Lincolnshire from Tudor to recent times*, 1957.

Thomas, J. H., *Town Government in the Sixteenth Century*, 1933.

Thomson, W. G., *A History of Tapestry from the earliest times until the present day*, 1930.

—— *Tapestry Weaving in England from the earliest times to the end of the XVIIIth century*, no date.

Thoresby, R., *Ducatus Leodiensis, or the topography of the ancient and populous town and parish of Leedes and parts adjacent*, 1715.

Thornton, G. A., *A History of Clare, Suffolk*, Cambridge, 1930.

Thrupp, S. L., 'Aliens in and around London in the fifteenth century', in Hollaender, A. E. J. and Kellaway, W., *Studies in London History*, q.v.

—— 'A survey of the alien population of England in 1440', *Speculum*, vol. xxxii, 1957.

Thurley, C. A. and D., *Index of the Probate Records of the Court of the Archdeacon of Ely 1513–1857*, Index Library, British Record Society, vol. lxxxviii, 1976.

Thwaite, H., *Abstracts of Abbotside Wills 1552–1688*, Yorkshire Archaeological Society Record Series, vol. cxxx, 1968 (1967).

Topsell, E., *The Historie of Foure-footed Beasts*, 1607.

Toulmin, J., *The History of Taunton*, ed. J. Savage, 1822.

Townsend, G. F., *The Town and Borough of Leominster*, Leominster, no date.

Tupling, G. H., *The Economic History of Rossendale*, Chetham Society, new series, vol. lxxxvi, 1927.

Turnbull, G. L., *Traffic and Transport: an economic history of Pickfords*, 1979.

Turton, R. B., *The Alum Farm*, Whitby, 1931.

Twiss, T., *The Black Book of the Admiralty*, 4 vols, 1871–6.

Tyacke, N. C. P., 'Migration from East Anglia to New England before 1660', typescript PhD thesis, London University, 1951.

Tymms, S., *Wills and Inventories from the Registers of the Commissary of Bury St Edmunds and the Archdeacon of Sudbury*, Camden Society, vol. xlix, 1850.

Unger, W. S., *Bronnen tot de Geschiedenis van Middelburg in den Landsheerlijken Tijd*, 3 vols, The Hague, 1923–31.

—— *De Tol van Iersekeroord*, The Hague, 1939.

Unwin, G., *Industrial Organisation in the Sixteenth and Seventeenth Centuries*, 1963.

—— *Studies in Economic History*, ed. R. H. Tawney, London and New York, 1958.

Usher, A. P., *A History of Mechanical Inventions*, Cambridge, Mass., 1954.

Vaisey, D. G., *Probate Inventories of Lichfield and District 1568–1680*, Collections for a History of Staffordshire, 4th series, vol. v, 1969.

Van Der Wee, H., *The Growth of the Antwerp Market and the European Economy*, 3 vols, The Hague, 1963.

—— 'Structural changes and specialization in the industry of the Southern Netherlands 1100–1600', *Economic History Review*, 2nd series, vol. xxviii, 1975.

Van Dillen, J. G., *Amsterdam in 1585*, Amsterdam, 1941.

—— *Bronnen tot de Geschiedenis van het Bedrijfsleven en het Gildewezen van Amsterdam*, 3 vols, The Hague, 1929–74.

Vanes, J., *Documents Illustrating the Overseas Trade of Bristol in the Sixteenth Century*, Bristol Record Society, vol. xxxi, 1979.

—— *The Ledger of John Smythe 1538–1550*, Bristol Record Society, vol. xx, 1975 (Historical Manuscripts Commission, Joint Publication 19, 1974).

Vanhaeck, M., *Histoire de la Sayetterie à Lille*, 2 vols, Société d'Études de la Province de Cambrai, Mémoires, tomes xvi, xvii, Lille, 1910.

Van Houtte, J. A., 'Production et circulation de la laine comme matière première du XIIIe au XVIIe siècle', in Spallanzani, M., *La Lana come Materia Prima*, q.v.

Van Nierop, L., 'De Zijdenijverheid van Amsterdam Historisch Geschetst', *Tijdschrift voor Geschiedenis*, jaarg. xlv, xlvi, 1930–1.

Van Uytven, R., 'La draperie Brabançonne et Malinoise du XIIe au XVIIe siècle: grandeur éphemère et décadence', in Spallanzani, M., *Panni di Lana*, q.v.

—— 'The fulling mill: dynamic of the revolution in industrial attitudes', *Acta Historiae Neerlandica*, deel v, 1971.

Van Waesberghe, W., 'De Invoering van de Belse Draperie te Brugge tijdens het Calvinistisch Bewind, en verdere Evolutie', *Handelingen der Genootschap voor Geschiedenis te Brugge* (Société d'Émulation), deel cix, 1972.

Van Werveke, H., *Brugge en Antwerpen: aacht eeuwen Vlaamsche handel*, Ghent, no date.

Veale, E. M., *The English Fur Trade in the later Middle Ages*, Oxford, 1966.

Verellen, J. R., 'Lakennijverheid en Lakenhandel van Herentals in de 14e, 15e en 16e eeuw', *Taxandria*, nieuwe reeks, deel xxvii, 1955.

Verhulst, A. E., 'La laine indigène dans les anciens Pays-Bas entre le XIIe et le XVIIe siècle', in Spallanzani, M., *La Lana come Materia Prima*, q.v.

Verlinden, C., 'Draps des Pays-Bas et du nord de la France en Espagne au 14e siècle', *Le Moyen Âge*, tome xlvii, 1937.

Verney, H., *Letters and Papers of the Verney Family down to the end of the year 1639*, Camden Society, vol. lvi, 1853.

Victoria History of the Counties of England, see under Anon. and Var.

Vives, J. V., *An Economic History of Spain*, Princeton, NJ, 1969.

Wadley, T. P., *Notes or Abstracts of the Wills contained in the Volume 'The Great Orphan Book and Book of Wills'*, Bristol, 1886.

Wadsworth, A. P. and Mann, J. de L., *The Cotton Trade and Industrial Lancashire 1600–1780*, Manchester, 1931.

Waller, W. C., *Extracts from the Court Books of the Weavers' Company of London 1600–1730*, Publications of the Huguenot Society of London, vol. xxxiii, 1931.

Warner, F., *The Silk Industry of the United Kingdom*, no date.

Watkin, I., *Oswestry*, London and Oswestry, 1920.

Watson, W., *Textile Design and Colour*, London, New York and Toronto, 1937.

—— *Advanced Textile Design*, 1947.

Watts, R., *The Young Mans Looking-Glass*, 1641.

Waylen, J., *A History Military and Municipal of the Town ... of Marlborough*, 1844.

Weaver, F. W., *Somerset Medieval Wills (Second Series 1501–1530)*, Somerset Record Society, vol. xix, 1903.

—— *Wells Wills*, 1890.

Webb, J. *Great Tooley of Ipswich*, Suffolk Records Society, 1962.

—— *Poor Relief in Elizabethan Ipswich*, Suffolk Records Society, vol. ix, 1966.

Webb, J., *Memorials of the Civil War between King Charles I and the Parliament of England as it affected Herefordshire and the adjacent counties*, 2 vols, 1879.

Webber, S., *A Short Account of the State of our Woollen Manufactures from the Peace of Ryswick to this Time*, 1739.

Weinstock, M., *Studies in Dorset History*, Dorchester, 1953.

Weiss, C., *Histoire des Réfugiés Protestants de France depuis la Révocation de l'Édit de Nantes*, 2 vols, Paris, 1853.

Westcote, T., *A View of Devonshire in 1630*, Exeter, 1845.

Westerfield, R. B., *Middlemen in English Business, 1660–1760*, Transactions of the Connecticut Academy of Arts and Sciences, vol. xix, New Haven, 1915.

Wheeler, J., *A Treatise of Commerce*, 1601.

White, K. D., *Roman Farming*, 1970.

White, L., *Medieval Technology and Social Change*, Oxford, 1964.

White, S. D., *Sir Edward Coke and the Grievances of the Common Wealth*, Manchester, 1979.

Whitly, R. G. H., *The Court of Taunton in the Sixteenth and Seventeenth Centuries*, Taunton, 1934.

Whittingham, W., *Troubles abowte the Booke of Common Prayer*, sine loco, 1574.

Wiggs, J. L., 'The seaborne trade of Southampton in the second half of the sixteenth century', typescript MA thesis, Southampton University, 1955.

Wild, J. P., 'Prehistoric and Roman textiles', in Jenkins, J. G., *The Wool Textile Industry in Great Britain*, q.v.

—— *Textile Manufacture in the Northern Roman Provinces*, Cambridge, 1970.

Wilhelmsen, L. J., *English Textile Nomenclature*, Bergen 1943.

Willan, T. S., *The Early History of the Russia Company*, Manchester, 1956.

—— *Elizabethan Manchester*, Chetham Society, 3rd series, xxvii, 1980.

—— *The English Coasting Trade*, Manchester, 1938.

—— *The Inland Trade*, Manchester, 1976.

—— 'Manchester clothiers in the early seventeenth century', *Textile History*, vol. x, 1979.

—— *River Navigation in England 1600–1750*, 1964.

—— *Studies in Elizabethan Foreign Trade*, Manchester, 1959.

—— *A Tudor Book of Rates*, Manchester, 1962.

Willemsen, G., 'La grève des foulons et des tisserands en 1524–1525 et le règlement général de la draperie Malinoise', *Bulletin du Cercle Archéologique de Malines*, tome xx, 1910.

—— 'La technique et l'organisation de la draperie à Bruges, à Gand et à Malines au milieu du XVIe siècle', *Annales de l'Académie Royale d'Archéologie de Belgique*, 6e serie, tomes viii, ix (lxviii, lxix), 1920–1.

Williams, E. P., 'Early Victorian Denbigh', *Denbighshire Historical Society Transactions*, vol. xxii, 1973.

Williams, G., *Glamorgan County History*, vol. iv, Cardiff, 1974.

Williams, N. (J.), *Contraband Cargoes: seven centuries of smuggling*, 1959.

—— 'The maritime trade of the East Anglian ports 1550–1590', typescript DPhil thesis, Oxford University, 1952.

—— *Tradesmen in Early Stuart Wiltshire*, Wiltshire Record Society, vol. xv, 1959.

—— 'Two documents concerning the new draperies', *Economic History Review*, 2nd series, vol. iv, 1952.

Willson, D. H., *The Parliamentary Diary of Robert Bowyer 1606–1607*, Minneapolis, 1931.

Wilson, C.(H.), *Anglo-Dutch Commerce and Finance in the Eighteenth Century*, Cambridge, 1941.

—— 'Cloth production and international competition in the seventeenth century', *Economic History Review*, 2nd series, vol. xiii, 1960.

Wilson, R. G., *Gentlemen Merchants: the merchant community in Leeds 1700–1830*, Manchester, 1971.

Wilson, T., 'The state of England A.D. 1600', edited by F. J. Fisher, *Camden Miscellany*, vol. xvi, Royal Historical Society, Camden 3rd series, vol. lii, 1936.

Winchester, B., *Tudor Family Portrait*, 1955.

Wood, A. C., *A History of the Levant Company*, Oxford, 1935.

Woodger, A., 'The eclipse of the Burel weaver: some technological developments in the thirteenth century', *Textile History*, vol. xii, 1981.

Woodward, B. B., *A History and Description of Winchester*, Winchester, no date.

Woodward, D. M., 'The overseas trade of Chester 1600–50', *Transactions of the Historic Society of Lancashire and Cheshire*, vol. cxxii, 1971.

—— *The Trade of Elizabethan Chester*, Hull, 1970.

Worthy, C., *Devonshire Wills*, 1896.

Wright, T., *The Romance of the Lace Pillow*, 2 vols, Olney, Bucks., 1924.

Wyatt, T. G., 'The part played by aliens in the social and economic life of England during the reign of Henry VIII', typescript MA, thesis, London University, 1951.

Yarranton, A., *England's Improvement by Sea and Land*, 1677.

Youings, J., *Tuckers Hall, Exeter*, Exeter, 1968.

Zell, M. L., 'The exchequer lists of provincial clothmakers fined in London during the sixteenth century', *Bulletin of the Institute of Historical Research*, vol. liv, 1981.

Zins, H., *England and the Baltic in the Elizabethan Era*, Manchester, 1972.

Zonca, V., *Novo Teatro di Machine et Edificii*, Padua, 1607.

# SUMMARY OF SELECT MANUSCRIPT SOURCES

*Public record office*
Colonial Office: Board of Trade Original Correspondence.
Court of Chancery: Early Chancery Proceedings
    Proceedings series ii
    Judicial Proceedings (Equity side): Chancery Masters' Documents: Exhibits
    Petty Bag: Miscellaneous Papers, Exhibits etc.
Court of Exchequer: Augmentation Office: Parliamentary Surveys
    Land Revenue: Miscellaneous Books
    King's Remembrancer: Accounts Various; Bills and Answers; Depositions by Commission;
       Entry Books of Decrees and Orders; Miscellaneous Books
Court of Requests: Proceedings
Court of Star Chamber: Proceedings
Court of Wards and Liveries: Feodaries' Surveys
Duchy of Lancaster: Miscellaneous Books; Rentals and Surveys
Prerogative Court of Canterbury: Inventories: series i; 1718–82; Paper 1660–*circa* 1725; Parchment
    post 1660
Privy Council Registers
Special Collections: Rentals and Surveys
State Papers: Domestic; Foreign; Levant

*British Library*
Additional Manuscripts, Charters and Rolls
Cottonian Manuscripts
Egerton Manuscripts
Hargrave Manuscripts
Harleian Manuscripts
Lansdowne Manuscripts
Sloane Manuscripts
Stowe Manuscripts

*Aberystwyth, National Library of Wales*
Episcopal Consistory Court of St Asaph: Original Wills, Administrations and Inventories

*Barnstaple, North Devon Athenaeum*
Barnstaple Borough Records: Receivers' Accounts; Sessions Court Records; Barum Farms Survey
    Book

*Birmingham Reference Library*
Bournville Village Trust Collection
General Collection

*Bodleian Library, Department of Western Manuscripts*
Archdeaconry Court of Berkshire: Original Wills etc.
Consistory and Archdeaconry Courts of Oxford: Original Wills etc.
Peculiar Court of Aylebury: Original Wills and Administrations etc.
Peculiar Court of Banbury: Original Wills and Administrations etc.
Aubrey Manuscripts
Rawlinson Manuscripts
Topographical Manuscripts

*Bridewell Museum, Norwich*
Patterns of Norwich Manufactures 1769; Patterns of Norwich Manufactures 1794–7; Order Book
    'Norwich 1789'; 'F. Tuthill & Fils Norwich'.

*Bristol Record Office*
Bristol Charters, Wills and Inventories transcribed by E. M. Thompson
Consistory Court of the Bishop of Bristol with the Deanery of Bristol: Inventories
Records of the Bristol and Frenchay Society of Friends: Administrative

*Bury and West Suffolk Record Office (Suffolk Record Office)*
Accession 634, Survey of Glemsford 1658; Accession 960
Bury Records
Episcopal Commissary Court for Bury St Edmunds with the Archdeaconry of Sudbury: Inventories;
    Register Books of Wills; Register Copy Wills
Miscellaneous Documents

*Canterbury Cathedral Library*
City (Burgh) Records: Burghmote Books; Chamberlain's Accounts Walloon Records: Actes du
    Consistoire de l'Église Francaise a Canterbury 1581–4; Le Livre des Actes du Consistoire de
    l'Eglise Wallone de Cantorbery: les choses resolues et arrestees du 5 du juillet 1576 au 24 de juin
    1578; Walloon Wills; Miscellaneous Documents

*Cheshire Record Office*
Court of the Vicar-General of the Chancellor of the Diocese in the Episcopal Consistory of Chester
    and the Rural Deaneries of the Archdeaconry: Original Wills and Administrations (with
    Inventories)
Quarter Sessions Records: Quarter Sessions Books

*Chester Record Office*
City Records: Assembly Books; Assembly Files
Guild Records: Weavers' Company Book 1697–1817
Mayor's Records: Rolls of Freemen
Town Clerk's Records: Protested Bills etc.

*City of London Records Office*
Court of Orphans: Inventories
Journals of the Common Council
Repertories

*Colchester Town Hall*
Colchester Borough Records: Assembly Books

*Coventry Record Office*
City Records: Leet Book 30 Elizabeth – 1834
Fellowship of the Silk and Worsted Weavers Records: Orders Book
Weavers and Clothiers Company Records: Miscellaneous Papers; Weavers' Account Books; Weavers' Minute Book of Orders 1659–1771; Title page etc. of Order Book

*Deene House*
Brudenell Manuscripts

*Denbighshire Record Office (Clwyd Record Office)*
Denbigh Borough Records

*Devizes Museum (Wiltshire Natural History and Archaeological Society)*
Inventories of James and William Filkes of Devizes, 1637 and 1655
William Gaby His Booke 1656

*Devon Record Office*
Bedford (Russell) Collection
Exeter City Library Manuscripts
Fortescue Collection
Huntsham Manuscripts
Marwood Collection

*Dorset Record Office*
History of the Collegiate Church of Wimborne Minster by Richard Russell
Peculiar Court of Wimborne Minster: Inventories; Ex-parish Wills etc.
Wimborne Minster Apprenticeship Indentures

*East Suffolk Record Office, see* Ipswich and East Suffolk Record Office

*East Sussex Record Office*
Consistory Court of the Bishop of Chichester for the Archdeaconry of Lewes: Inventories

*Essex Record Office*
Archbishopric of Canterbury: Peculiar Court of the Archbishop in the Peculiar Deanery of Bocking: Inventories; Original Wills
Bishopric of London: Archdeaconry of Colchester: Original Wills; Register Copy Wills
   Archdeaconry Court of Essex: Registered Wills Archdeaconry Court of Middlesex (Essex and Hertfordshire Division): Register Copy Wills
    Bishop of London's Commissary Court for Essex and Hertfordshire: Original Wills; Register Copy Wills

*Calendar of the Essex assize files*
D/DBm Z nos. 7–14: Notebooks of Joseph Bufton of Coggeshall 1663–1710 D/GGy T.6; D/DO B.1: Cash Book 1610; D/DO T.123
Quarter Sessions Records: Bundles; Great Rolls; Order Books

*Flintshire Record Office (Clwyd Record Office)*
Erddig Manuscripts
Plas Teg Manuscripts
Soughton Hall Manuscripts


*Friends' House, London (Society of Friends' Library)*
James Dix's Manuscripts
Manuscript Box D1/15/1,2


*Gloucester Library*
Smyth of Nibley Manuscripts
Smyth of Nibley Papers


*Gloucestershire Record Office*
Consistory Court of Gloucester: Inventories
Marcham Collection


*Greater London Record Office*
Episcopal Consistory Court of London: Original Wills


*Guildford Muniment Room*
Loseley Manuscripts


*Guildhall Library, London*
Commissary Court of London (London Division): Inventories
Weavers' Company Records: Ordinance and Record Book 1577–1641


*Hampshire Record Office*
Archdeaconry Court of Winchester: Original Wills and Inventories
Consistory Court of Winchester: Original Wills and Inventories
Consistory and Archdeaconry Courts of Winchester: Unclassified Inventories (D/2/A)
Peculiar Court of Meonstoke: Original Wills and Inventories
Peculiar Court of West Meon: Original Wills and Inventories


*Hertfordshire Record Office*
Gorhambury Collection
Westmill-Wakeley-Buntingford Collection


*House of Lords Record Office*
House of Lords Papers


*Huntington Library, San Marino, California*
Stowe Manuscripts

*Ipswich and East Suffolk Record Office (Suffolk Record Office)*
Archdeaconry of Suffolk: Inventories; Original Wills
Blois Family Archives
Sessions Order Books

*Kent Archives Office*
Archdeaconry Court of Canterbury: Inventory Papers; Inventory Registers
Consistory Court of Canterbury: Inventory Papers; Inventory Registers; Registers of Accounts and
    Inventories
Consistory Court of Rochester: Paper Inventories
Maidstone Borough Records: Burghmote Books; Chamberlain's Accounts (Paper Books); Miscel-
    laneous Documents
Quarter Sessions Records: Gaol Delivery Rolls
Sackville (Knole) Manuscripts
Sandwich Borough Records: Copy of Letter to Sir William Cecil, 1561
    Land and Water Treasurer's Accounts
    Land and Water Treasurer's Draft Accounts
    Letters Patent for Strangers, 3 Elizabeth
    Little Black Book (1552–67)
    New Red Book (1568–81)
    Return by Mayor to Lord Warden, 1565
    Treasurer's Volumes of Accounts
    Year Book A and B (1582–1608)
    Year Book C and D, alias New Black Book (1608–42)

*Lambeth Palace*
Peculiars of the Archbishop of Canterbury in the Peculiar Deaneries of the Arches, of Shoreham and
    of Croydon: Inventories

*Lancashire Record Office*
Cavendish of Holker Collection
Court of the Vicar-General of the Chancellor of the Diocese in the Episcopal Consistory of Chester
    and in the Rural Deaneries of the Archdeaconry: Original Wills and Administrations (with
    Inventories)
Hopwood Collection
Kenyon of Peel Collection
Towneley of Towneley Manuscripts

*Leicester Museum*
City Records: Hall Papers

*Leicestershire Record Office*
Commissary of the Bishop of Lincoln in the Archdeaconry of Leicester and the Court of the
    Archdeacon: Inventories; Wills and Administrations (with Inventories)
Commissary Court of the Manor of Evington: Inventories; Wills and Administrations (with
    Inventories)
Prebend of St Margaret in Leicester with the Chapelry of Knighton: Inventories; Wills and
    Administrations (with Inventories)

*Lichfield Joint Record Office*
(Staffordshire County Council and City of Lichfield Joint Record Office): Episcopal Consistory
    Court of Lichfield: Original Wills (with Inventories)

*Lincolnshire Archives Office*
Heneage of Hainton Collection
Massingberd-Mundy Deposit


*Longleat House*
Thynne Papers: General Papers


*Middlesex Record Office (Greater London Council)*
Archdeaconry Court of Middlesex (Middlesex Division): Inventories


*Norfolk Record Office*
Diocesan Records: Archdeaconry Court of Norfolk: Inventories
   Archdeaconry Court of Norwich: Inventories
   Episcopal Consistory Court of Norwich: Inventories
   Peculiar Court of the Dean and Chapter of Norwich: Inventories
City Records: Alnage Accounts 1580–1610
   Books of Minutes of Court of Assembly Proceedings
   Books of Minutes of the Mayor's Court
   Dutch and Walloon Strangers Book 1564–1643
   Duties on Articles Manufactured
   First Book of Worstedweavers
   Second Book of Worstedweavers
   Keure aengaende de Warandatie van Wulle (Book of Dutch Orders)
   Liber Albus
   New Drapery in Norwich
   Old Free Book and Memoranda 1317–1549
   Orders concerning Wool 1577
   Miscellaneous Documents: Account Roll 1420–1 (Account of the Alderman of the Gild of St
      George); Agreement of Guy de Lewaulle 1576; Ordinances of the Worstedweavers 1511; The
      Hatters Book 1543
   Miscellaneous Documents concerning Trade and Commerce: Controversy respecting the Rights
      of the Citizens of Norwich to sell their Wares and Merchandise free of Customs in the City of
      London, about 1575: Replies to Assertions by Citizens of London in support of their Design
      to abolish Norwich Sale Halls: Answer of the Citizens of Norwich – Touching the Allegacion
      that the Queenes Majestie doth lose her Custume
Free Church Records: Walloon Church in Norwich
Gurney of Bawdeswell Manuscripts
Norfolk County Records: Quarter Sessions Books
Norfolk Record Society Manuscripts
Yarmouth Library Manuscripts: Pengelly Letters


*Northamptonshire Record Office*
Archdeaconry Court of Northampton: Administrations and Inventories
Fitzwilliam (Milton) Collection
Isham (Lamport) Collection
Lambe and Holmes Collection
Y.Z. Collection


*Nottinghamshire Record Office*
Manorial Court of Mansfield: Original Wills etc.

*Plessis-les-Tours, le château*
Tours fabrics collection

*Shakespeare's Birthplace, Stratford-on-Avon*
Leigh Collection

*Shrewsbury Library*
Original Records of the Company of Weavers and Clothiers (MSS 3359–60)
Ordinances etc. of the Weavers Company (MS 4274)

*Somerset Record Office*
Consistorial Court of the Archdeaconry of Taunton: Inventories Episcopal Consistory Court of Bath
and Wells: Inventories and Bonds DD/BR/gr: bundle 18 no. i, Thornbury deed 1615; DD/HRG
no. 1/4; DD/SND nos. 5, 7, 8; DD/TW nos. 9/1; 11/11; 12/3; DD/WES nos. 1, 3, 4; DD/X/ GB:
Combe Survey Book 1704

*Sudbury Borough Offices*
Town Records: Book of Pleas in the Borough Court 1560–1608; Books of Proceedings of the
Borough Court nos. 1 (1562–82), 4 (1598–1619), 6 (1640–72)

*Thetford, King's House, Borough Offices*
Borough Records: Vol. 1, First Minute Book of the Corporation after Charter, from 1578 to 1586;
Vol. 2, Second Minute Book, from 1570 to 1622, alias Hall Book from 13 Elizabeth to 43; Vol. 4,
Assembly Book, from 1624 to 1639; Vol. 9, Sessions, Court of Record and Freemen's Register
Book, from 1610 to 1756

*Victoria and Albert Museum, Textile Department*
A Counterpart of Patterns sent to Spain and Lisbon by Mr J.K., 1763
Norwich Weaver's Pattern Book 1767
Study Room exhibits A.35, A.36

*West Suffolk Record Office, see* Bury and West Suffolk Record Office

*William Salt Library, Stafford*
Paget of Beaudesert Manuscripts

*Wiltshire Record Office*
Accession 122: Surveys of Bromham, Bremhill, Bowden and Stanley, with Court Book
Archdeaconry Court of Salisbury: Original Wills, Administrations and Inventories
Archdeaconry Court of the Sub-dean of Salisbury: Original Wills, Administrations and Inventories
Archdeaconry Court of Wiltshire: Original Wills, Administrations and Inventories
Episcopal Consistory Court of Salisbury: Original Wills, Administrations and Inventories
Ex Diocesan Registry of Salisbury: Unclassified Original Wills, Administrations and Inventories
Peculiar Court of the Dean and Chapter of Salisbury: Original Wills, Administrations and
Inventories
Peculiar Court of the Dean of Salisbury: Original Wills, Administrations and Inventories
Peculiar Court of the Precentor or Chantor of Salisbury: Original Wills, Administrations and
Inventories
Peculiar Court of the Treasurer of the Cathedral Church of Salisbury annexed to the Prebendal Stall
of Calne in the Prebend of Calne: Original Wills, Administrations and Inventories

Prebendal Court of Chardstock: Original Wills, Administrations and Inventories
Prebendal Court of Netherbury in Ecclesia: Original Wills, Administrations and Inventories
Prebendal Court of Uffculme: Original Wills, Administrations and Inventories
Royal Peculiar Court of Gillingham: Original Wills, Administrations and Inventories
Savernake Archives: Elizabethan Court Books of Collingbourne Ducis; Stitchcombe Court Book

*Worcestershire Record Office (Hertfordshire and Worcestershire Record Office)*
Episcopal Consistory Court of Worcester: Original Wills, Administrations and Inventories

# INDEX OF PERSONS

# INDEX OF PLACES

# GLOSSARIAL INDEX OF SUBJECTS

(asterisk indicates glossarial entry)

Shalloons
serge de Nimes, 61–2*
serge dimity, 61*
serge duroy, 62*, 65, 120
surplices, 64
tammy, 63–6, 83, 235–7
tammy say, 60–1
twiste(re)d say, 56*, 60–1
union drugget, 120, 237
unions, 60–1, 97 sqq., 131, 146–7, 151, 178,
  193, 219, 237–8, 241
union say, 60–1, 67, 111–13, 237
union serge, 67, 113 sqq.
wheels, 61, 159, 169
Jerseys, 6, 7, 36, 44, 56, 58 sqq., 69, 72, 75 sqq.,
  80–1, 83, 97 sqq., 110–11, 120, 131, 146,
  148, 151, 180, 185, 190–1, 193–4, 219,
  235 sqq., 241–2
Jobbers, 149
Joiners, 174–5
Jollyboys, 57, 67, 83
Jollymother, 57
Journeymen, 207–9; and see Servants
Juries, 48, 81–2
Justices of Peace, 115, 131, 205, 207, 211

Keighley white, 25–6
Kemp, 108
Kendal cloth, 3, 20*, 143, 177, 233
Kennet, 20*; and see Grey cloth
Kentish cloth, 17*, 31, 39, 142, 216, 218, 221,
  239
Kerchiefs, 126, 139
Kermes, 4, 167–8
Kersey (cloth), viii, 5*, 16 sqq., 25 sqq., 32, 65,
  86, 91, 93, 104–5, 110–11, 113, 115, 117,
  133, 143–4, 150, 153, 163–4, 167, 173,
  177, 179, 185, 191–2, 213–16, 218–21,
  232, 237–8, 242
Kersey (yarn), 5*, 18*, 23, 25–6, 83, 112, 148,
  153
Kersey baize, 104–7
  blanket, 33
  looms, 5, 117, 179
  reeds or sleys, 5
  say, 112–13
  stockings, 25
Kidderminster carpet, 88, 124
  linsey-woolsey, 87
  stuff, 65, 87*, 146, 148, 182–3, 214, 237
King's Lynn Dutch, 101
King's Lynn Flemings, 69, 101
Kirtles, 69
Knitters, 27, 130, 133 sqq., 156, 175, 199, 200
Knitting, 1, 8, 12, 27, 79, 133 sqq., 153–4, 199,
  201, 203, 209–10, 216, 228, 232–3, 239
Knitting frames, 130, 134–7, 174–5, 200
Knitwear, see Hosiery

Labour costs, 12, 32, 41, 146, 208, 230–1,
  241–2
Lac, 167–8; and see Lake
Lace, see Bonelace, Loomlace
Laced princilato, 58*

russell, 48
say, 56
Lace-looms, 22, 79, 80, 175, 185, 187–8, 198
Lacemen, 198–9
Laceweavers, 24, 72, 79, 130, 198
Lacing, 48, 56*, 61, 85
Lake, 224; and see Lac
Lambs' wool, 10, 27, 97–100, 104–6, 115, 120
Lancashire Plain, 23–4, 121–2, 124, 141, 161,
  190
Lancaster kersey, 26
Landowners, 12, 80, 138, 147, 190, 195, 232–4
Lank sheep & wool, 3, 25, 143
Large masters, 179 sqq.
Laths, 18
Lawn, 126
Lead calx, 168
Leadenhall, 216–17
Leashes, 51, 127
Leaving weaving, 75, 204–5, 213
Leeds cloth, 28, 178, 219
Legge (Legis) silk, 141
Lemon juice, 167
Leominster (Ryeland) wool, 2, 20, 34, 38, 40,
  91–2, 138, 142–4
Letters Patent, viii; and see Patents
Levantine camlet, 73
Licensed victuallers, 58
Lichen, 167
Liège wool, 32
Ligature, 223*
Lille camlet, 62
  grograin, 73
  lace, 138–9
Lime, 165, 167
Lincolnshire wool, 153
Linen (cloth), 6, 7, 14, 15, 23–4, 28, 51, 57,
  82, 121–3, 125, 127, 162, 167, 173, 185,
  201, 219, 221, 224, 235, 240
Linen-cotton camlet, 125
  dimity, 125, 235
  paragon, 125
  unions, 124–5, 221, 235
Linen damask, 51, 122, 185
  sackcloth, 122
  say, 6
  serge, 7, 116
  thread (yarn), 6, 7, 10, 11, 22–4, 42, 47, 49,
    51, 66 sqq., 108–9, 111, 116, 121 sqq., 133,
    138–41, 150, 159, 165, 169–70, 178, 190,
    199, 203, 211, 217, 224, 235
  tiffany, 127
  union beds, 10
  union drugget, 123
  union flannel, 108, 110, 123
  unions, 5, 7, 10, 11, 16, 18, 21–4, 32, 47, 49,
    63–5, 69, 76–7, 87, 89, 108, 110, 116,
    122–5, 128, 143, 146, 148, 154, 179, 182–
    3, 185, 190, 194, 214, 221–4, 231–2, 235,
    237
  union serge, 7, 116, 122
Linenweavers, 58, 121–3, 161, 185, 189–90,
  228, 232, 234, 241
Line, 122